Love is an Illusion!

1

Story & Art by
Fargo

Licensed by Lezhin Entertainment, LLC.
Published by Seven Seas Entertainment, LLC.

Seven Seas press and purchase enquiries can be sent to
Marketing Manager Lianne Sentar at press@gomanga.com.

Seven Seas and the Seven Seas logo are trademarks of
Seven Seas Entertainment. All rights reserved.
sevenseasentertainment.com
sevenseaswebtoons.com

Originally serialized as a webtoon on the Lezhin Comics platform:
lezhinus.com

Love is an Illusion! is rated MATURE for language and
sexual content. Reader discretion is advised.

WRITER/ARTIST: **Fargo**
PRODUCER: **Yuni Kim**
TRANSLATION: **Lezhin Entertainment, America Localization Team**
LETTERING: **Karis Page**
SENIOR EDITOR: **Kristiina Korpus**
PRODUCTION DESIGNER: **Ria Linn Johnson**
BRAND MANAGER: **Lissa Pattillo**
PREPRESS TECHNICIAN: **Melanie Ujimori**
PRINT MANAGER: **Rhiannon Rasmussen-Silverstein**
EDITOR-IN-CHIEF: **Julie Davis**
ASSOCIATE PUBLISHER: **Adam Arnold**
PUBLISHER: **Jason DeAngelis**

ISBN: 978-1-63858-565-7
Printed in Canada
First Printing: September 2022
10 9 8 7 6 5 4 3 2 1

CONTENTS

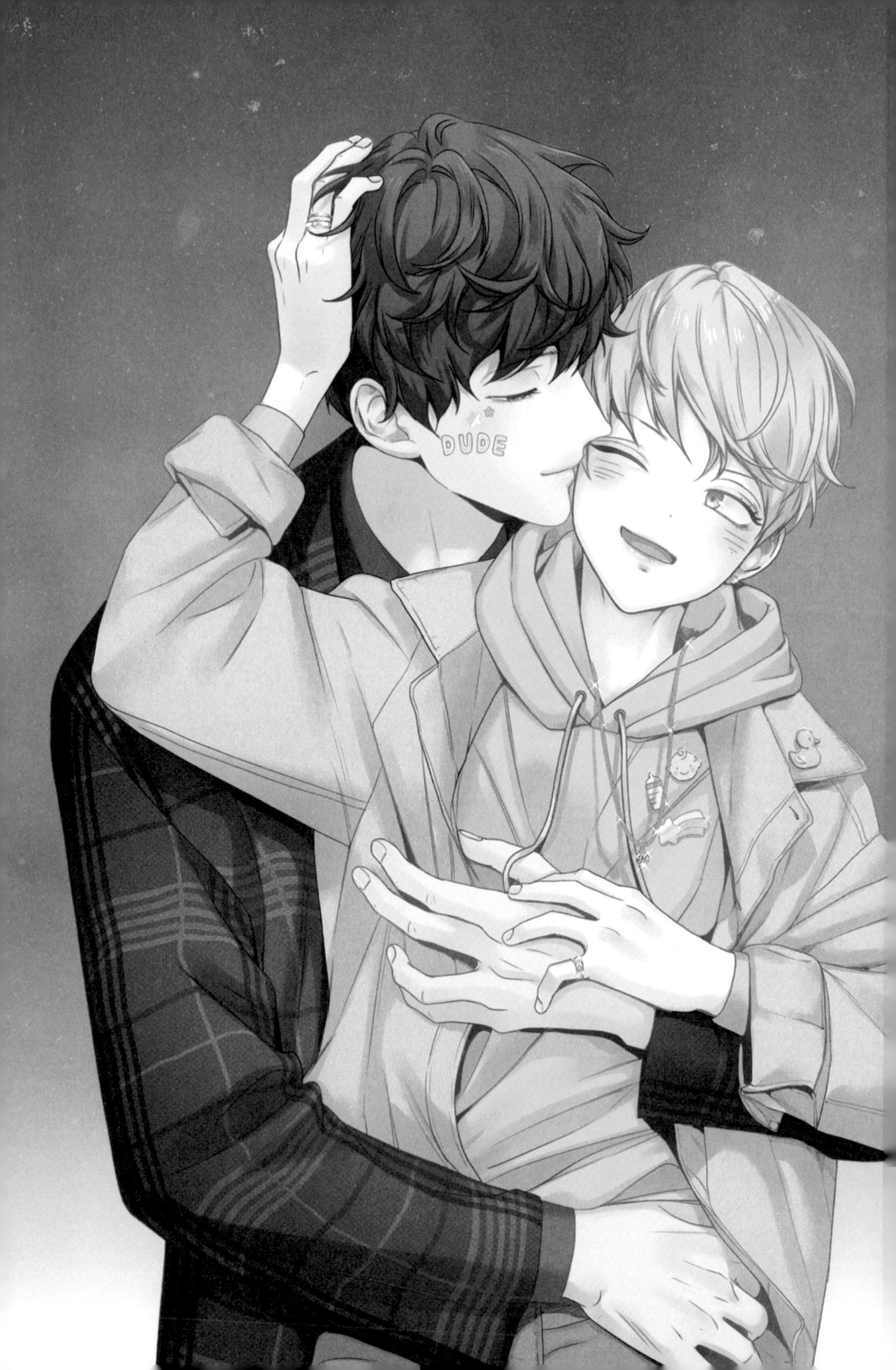
DUDE

OMEGAVERSE

A world where everyone has a secondary biological gender and males can become pregnant.

Omega
Can be impregnated by an alpha, regardless of base gender.

Alpha
Responds to omegas' pheromones and can impregnate an omega.

Beta
Neither an alpha nor an omega, but a regular human.

Pheromone: The unique odor emitted by alphas and omegas.

Heat Cycle: A period of a few days where an omega secretes pheromones stronger than usual to seduce an alpha. Omegas often take medications to control this.

Love is
an Illusion!

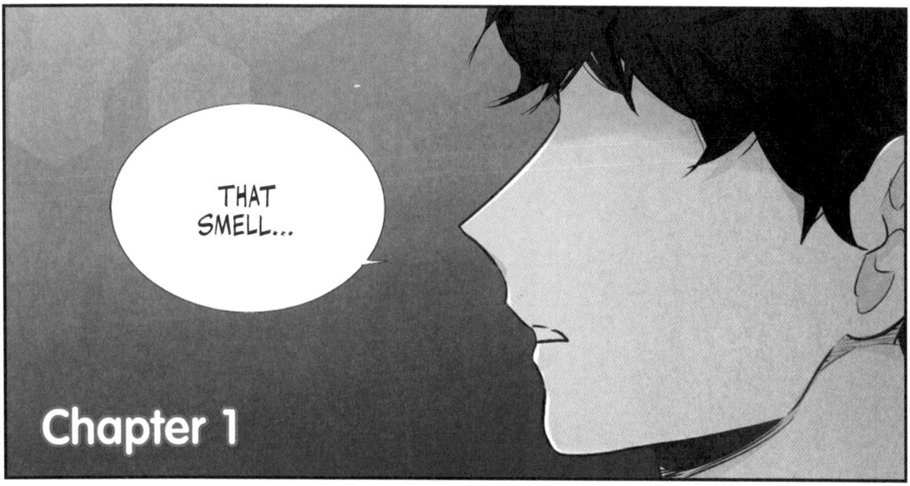
THAT SMELL...
Chapter 1

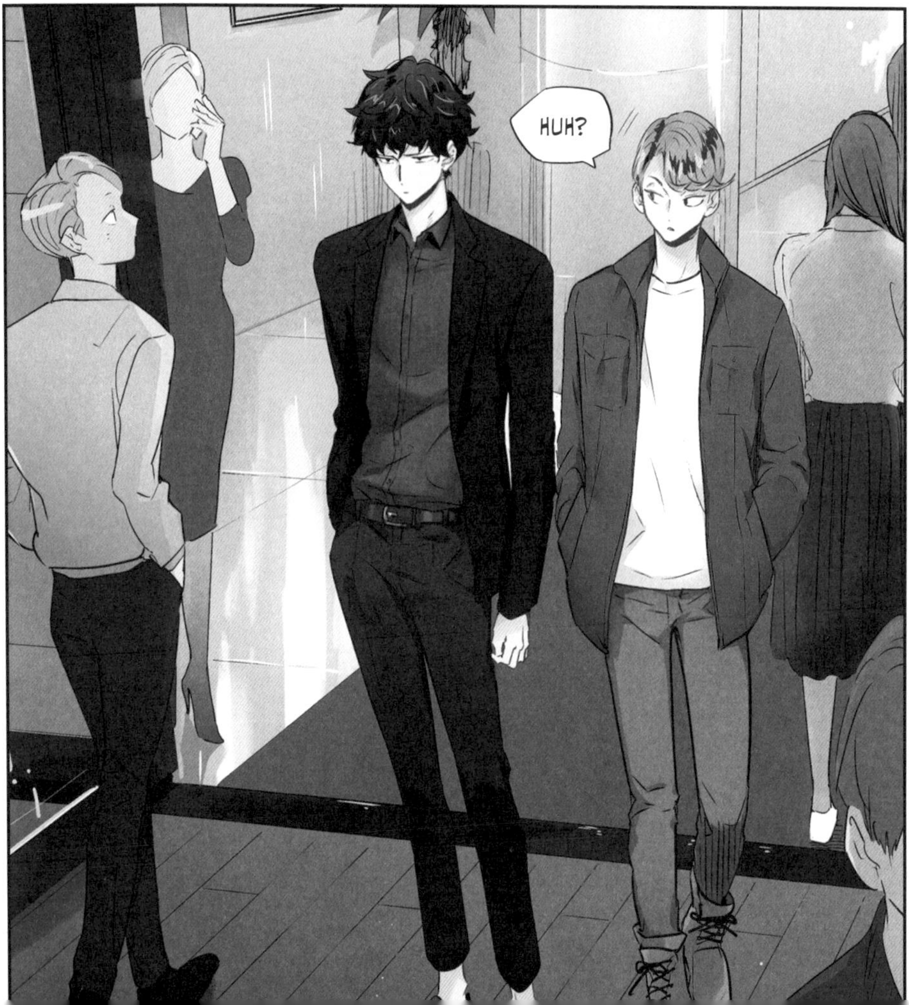
HUH?

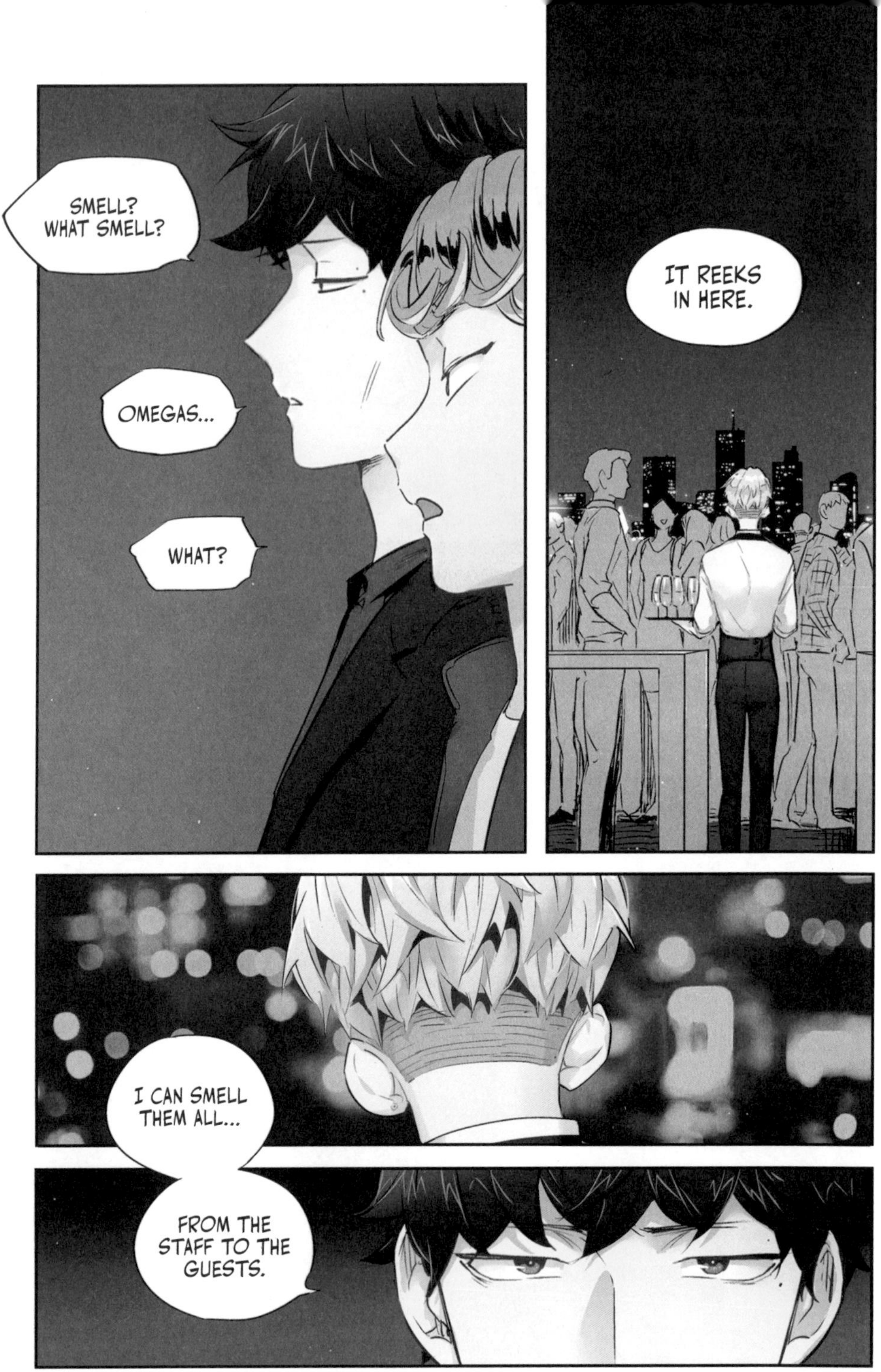
SMELL? WHAT SMELL?
OMEGAS...
WHAT?
IT REEKS IN HERE.
I CAN SMELL THEM ALL...
FROM THE STAFF TO THE GUESTS.

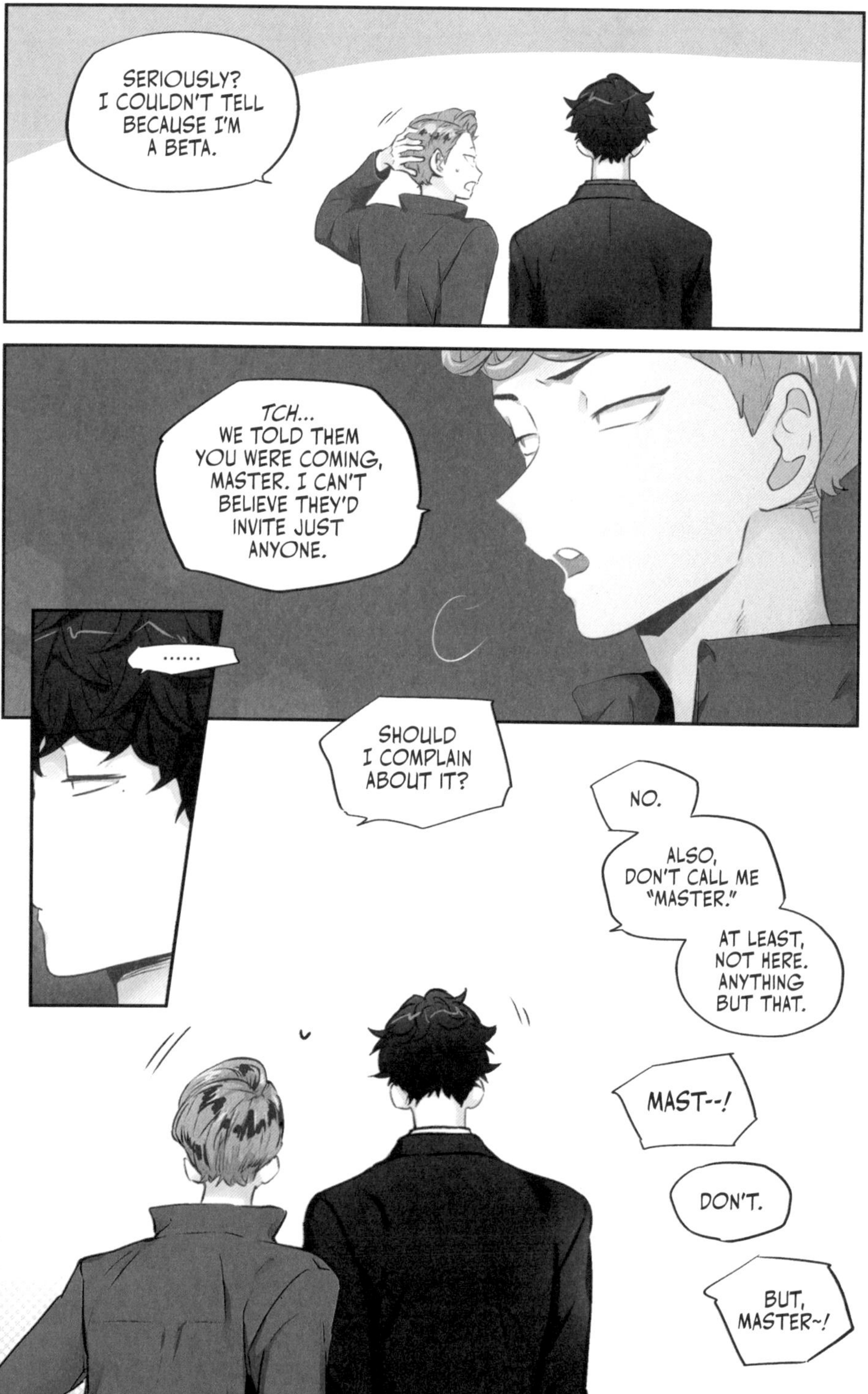
SERIOUSLY? I COULDN'T TELL BECAUSE I'M A BETA.
TCH... WE TOLD THEM YOU WERE COMING, MASTER. I CAN'T BELIEVE THEY'D INVITE JUST ANYONE.
......
SHOULD I COMPLAIN ABOUT IT?
NO.
ALSO, DON'T CALL ME "MASTER."
AT LEAST, NOT HERE. ANYTHING BUT THAT.
MAST--!
DON'T.
BUT, MASTER~!

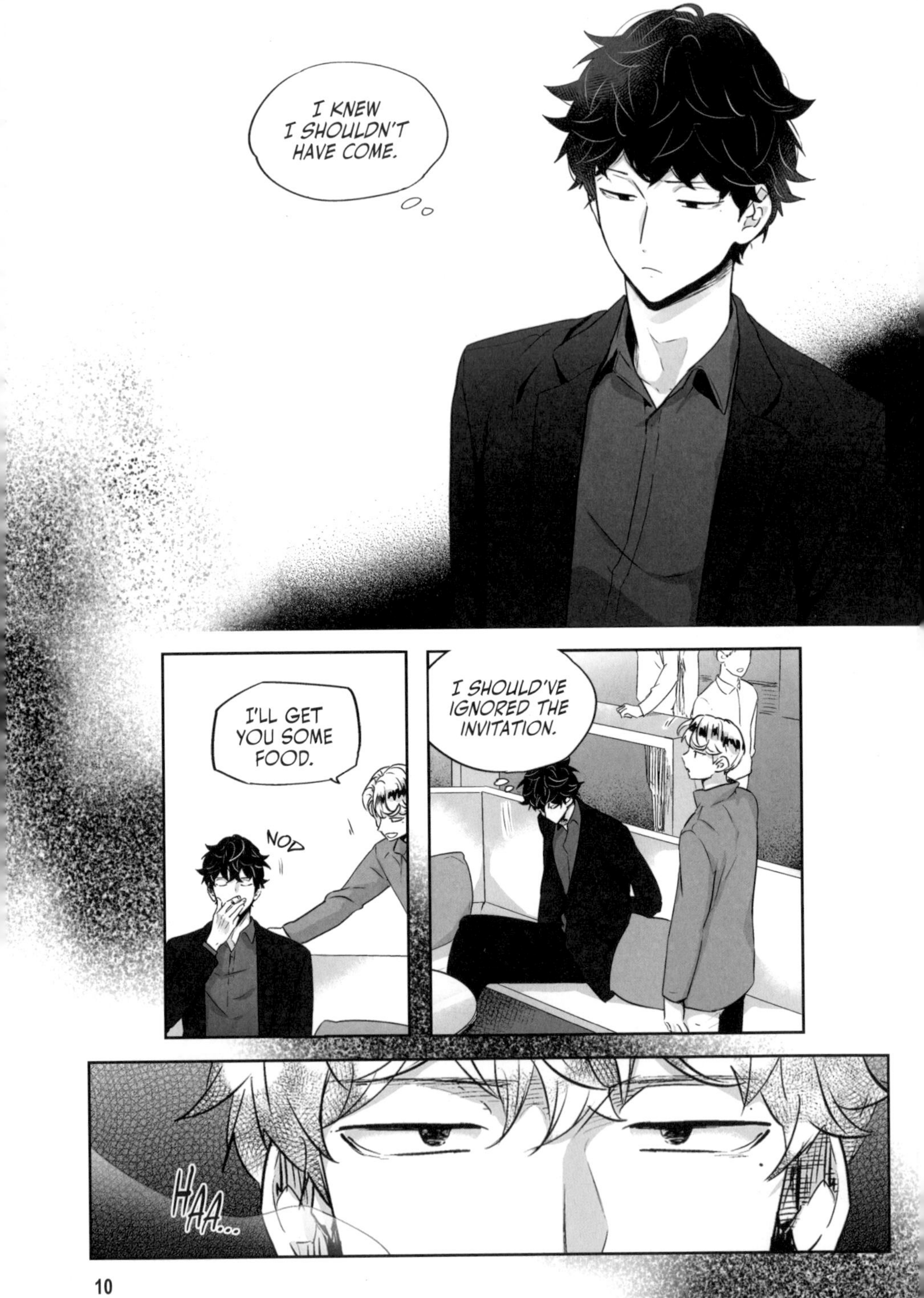
I KNEW I SHOULDN'T HAVE COME.
I'LL GET YOU SOME FOOD.
NOD
I SHOULD'VE IGNORED THE INVITATION.
HAA...

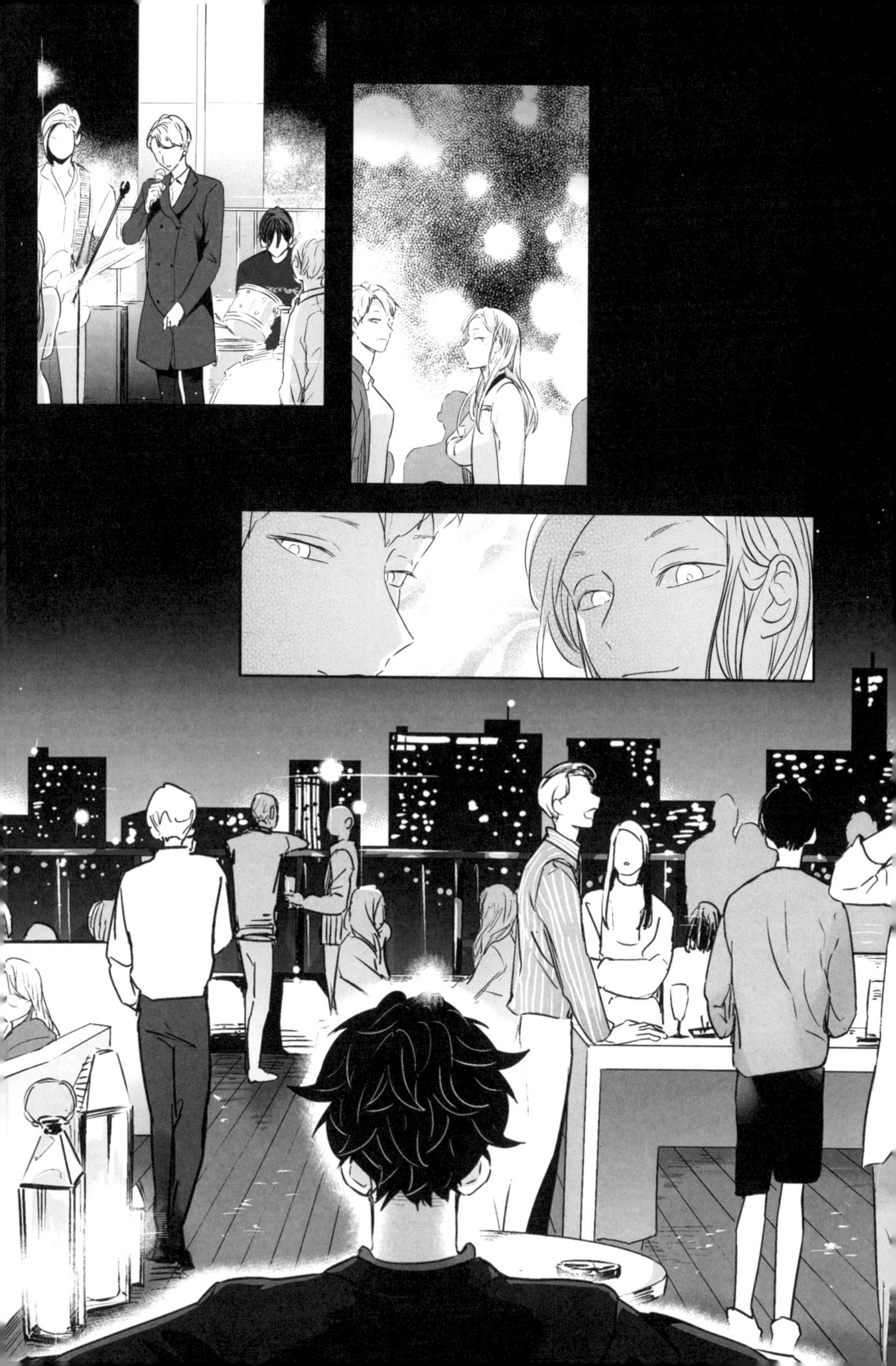

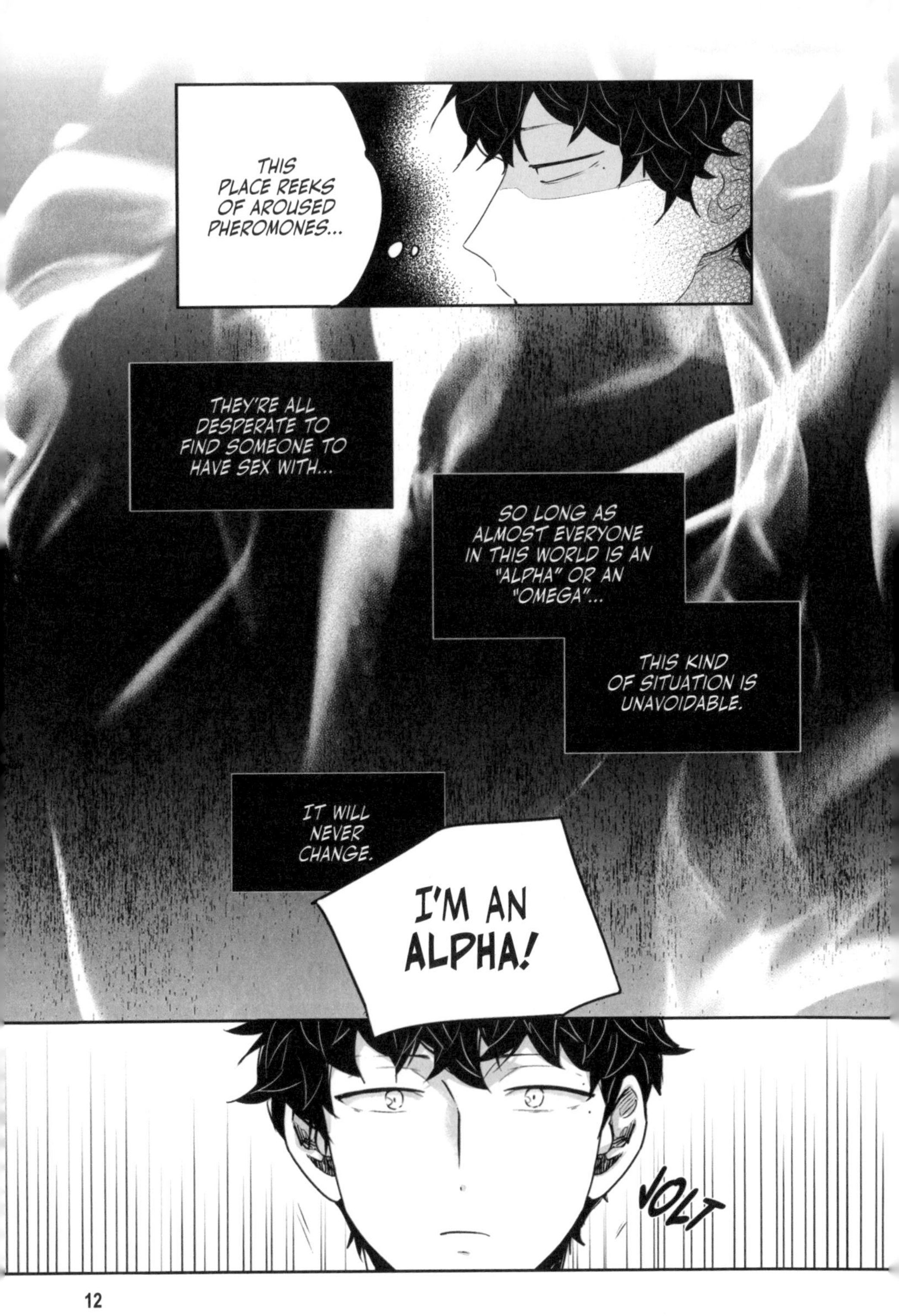

THIS PLACE REEKS OF AROUSED PHEROMONES...
THEY'RE ALL DESPERATE TO FIND SOMEONE TO HAVE SEX WITH...
SO LONG AS ALMOST EVERYONE IN THIS WORLD IS AN "ALPHA" OR AN "OMEGA"...
THIS KIND OF SITUATION IS UNAVOIDABLE.
IT WILL NEVER CHANGE.
I'M AN ALPHA!
JOLT

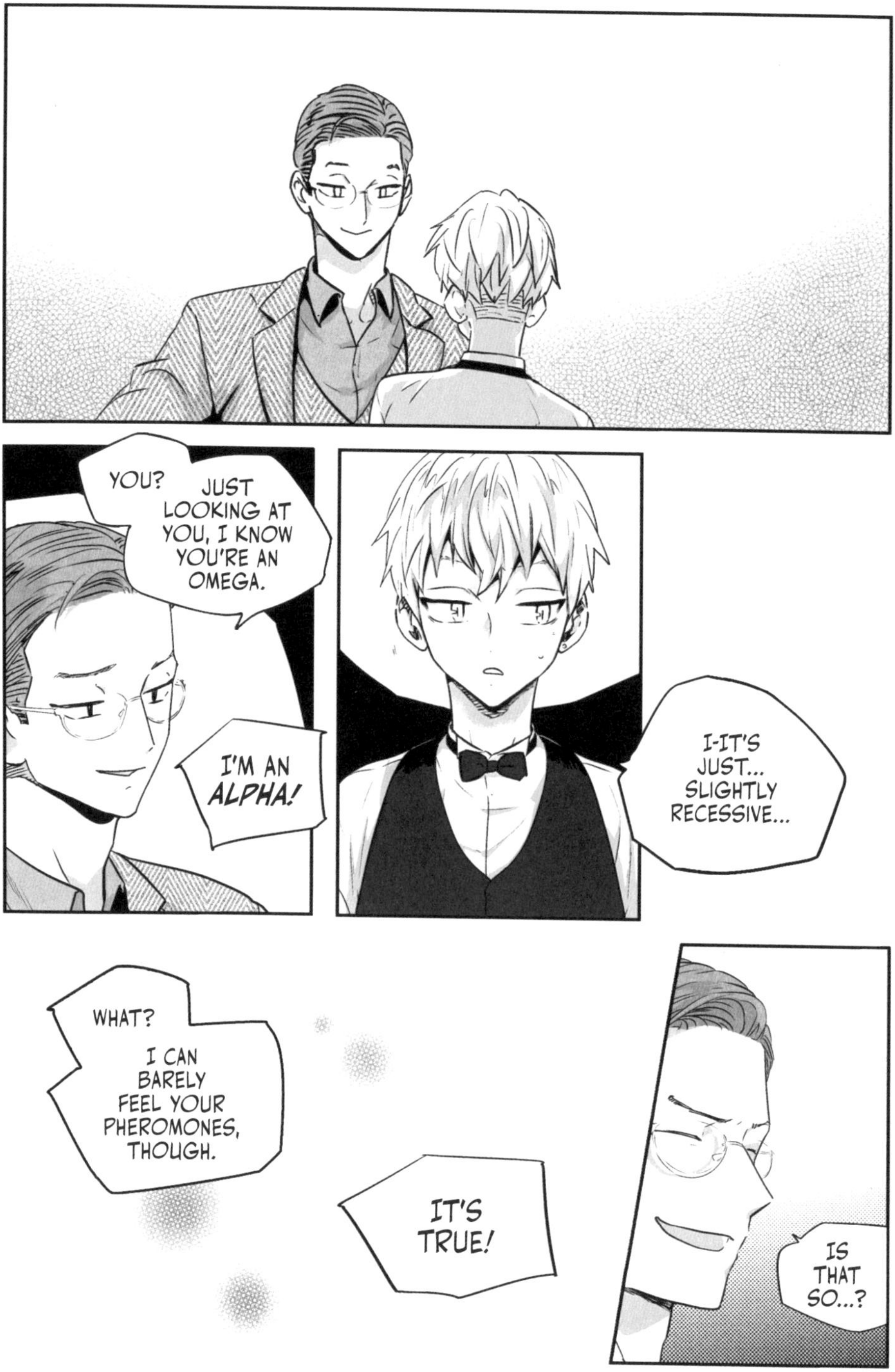
YOU? JUST LOOKING AT YOU, I KNOW YOU'RE AN OMEGA.
I'M AN *ALPHA!*
I-IT'S JUST... SLIGHTLY RECESSIVE...
WHAT? I CAN BARELY FEEL YOUR PHEROMONES, THOUGH.
IT'S TRUE!
IS THAT SO...?

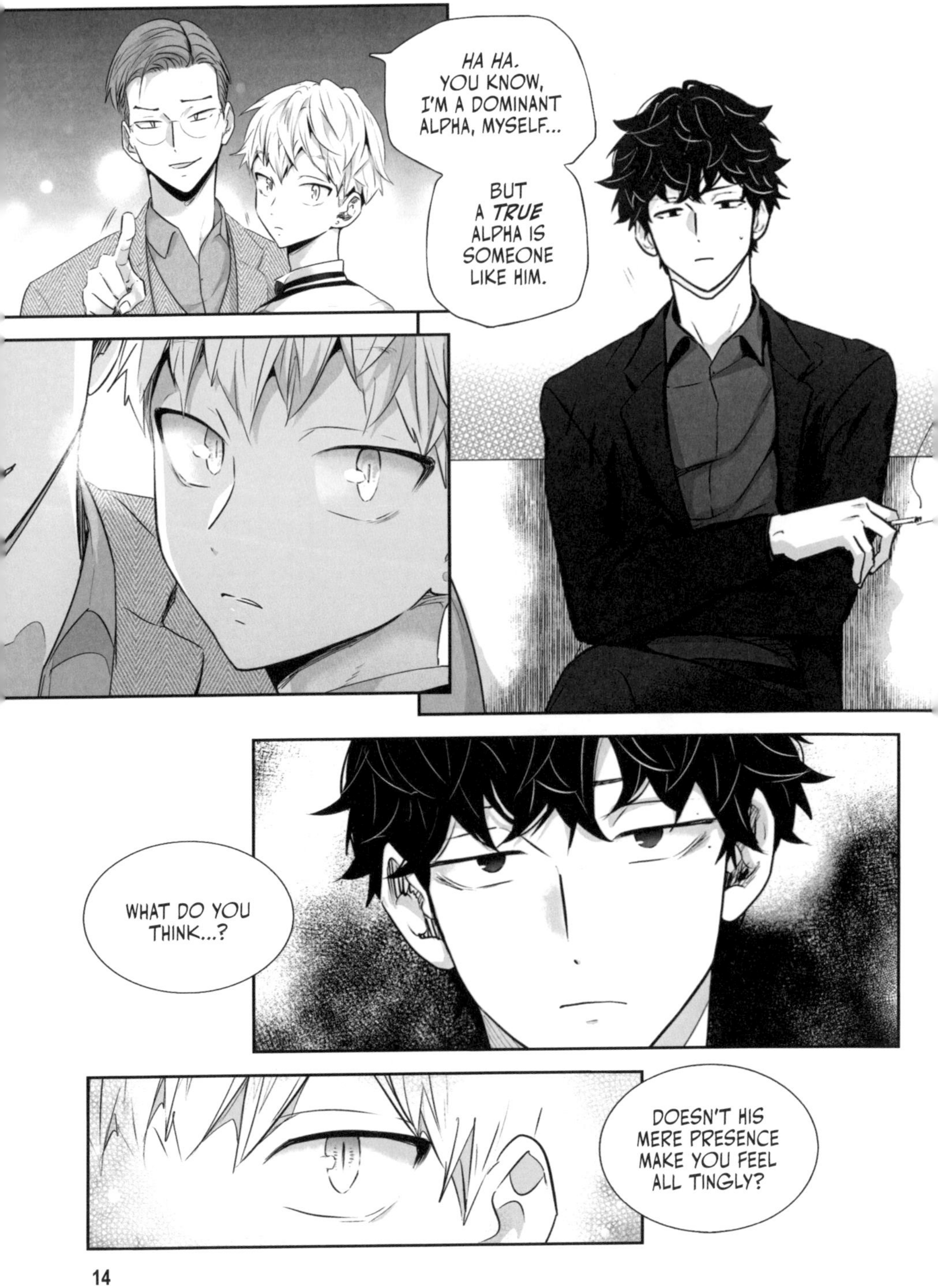
HA HA. YOU KNOW, I'M A DOMINANT ALPHA, MYSELF...
BUT A *TRUE* ALPHA IS SOMEONE LIKE HIM.
WHAT DO YOU THINK...?
DOESN'T HIS MERE PRESENCE MAKE YOU FEEL ALL TINGLY?

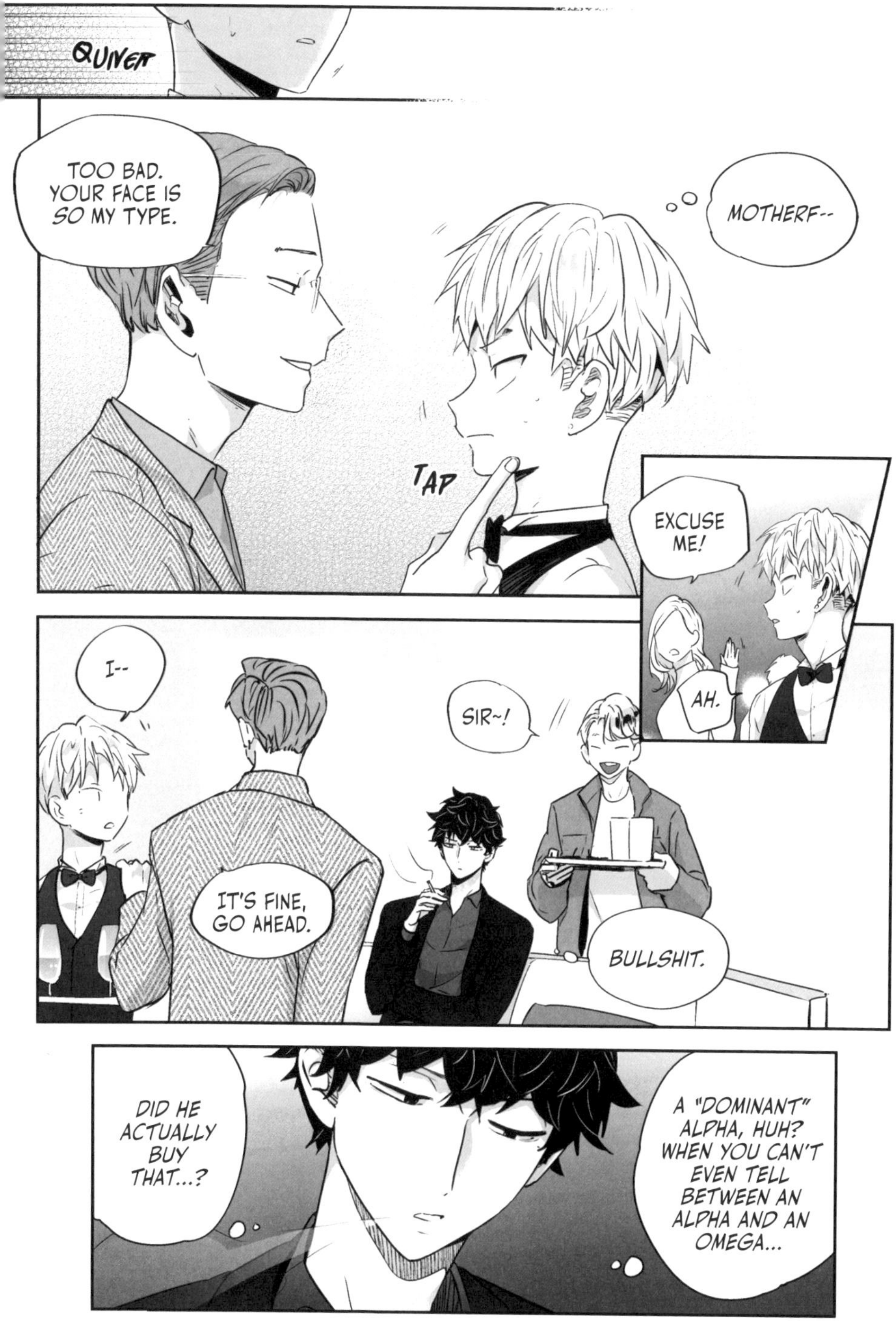
QUIVER
TOO BAD. YOUR FACE IS SO MY TYPE.
MOTHERF--
TAP
EXCUSE ME!
AH.
I--
IT'S FINE, GO AHEAD.
SIR~!
BULLSHIT.
DID HE ACTUALLY BUY THAT...?
A "DOMINANT" ALPHA, HUH? WHEN YOU CAN'T EVEN TELL BETWEEN AN ALPHA AND AN OMEGA...

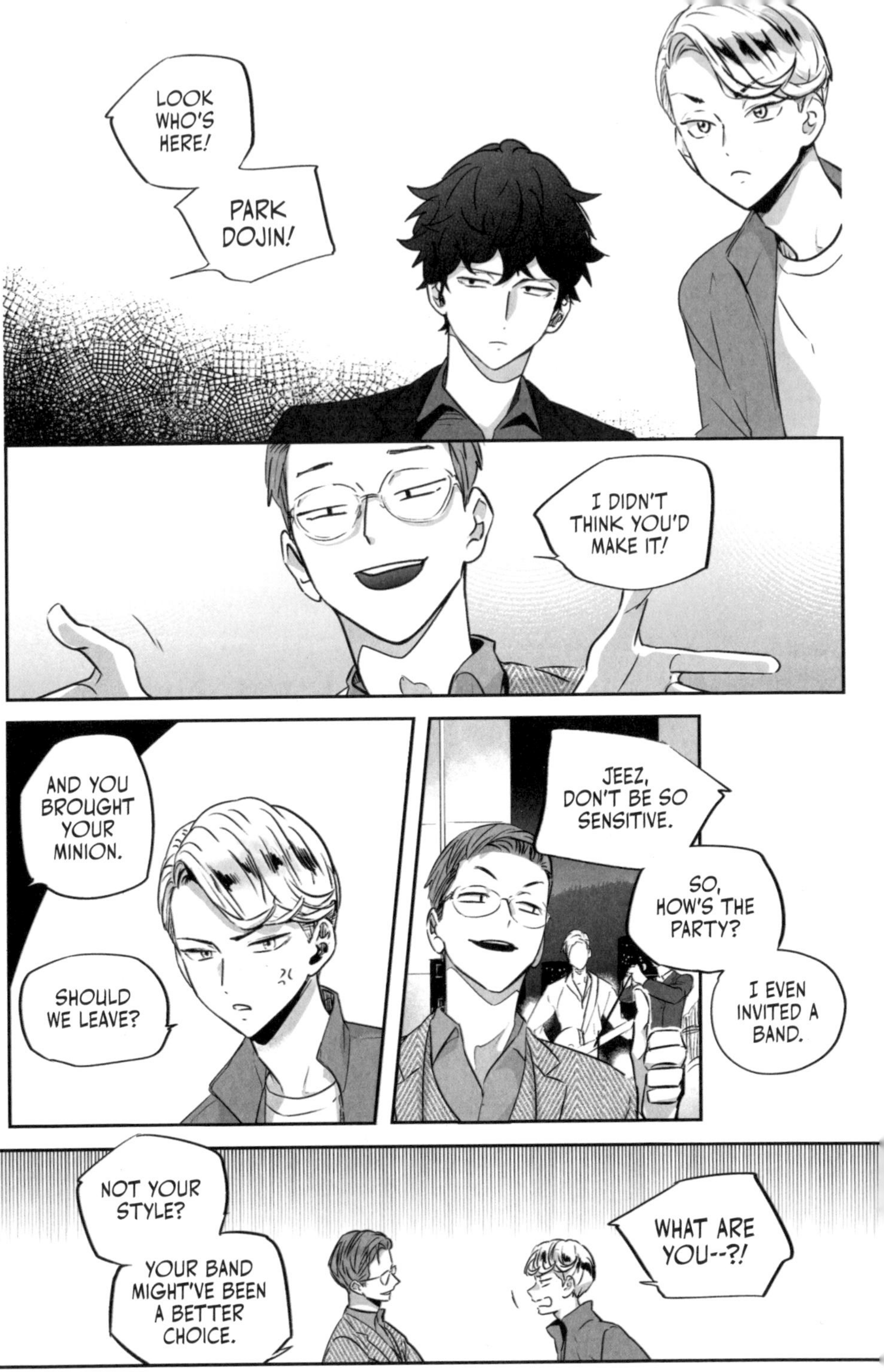
LOOK WHO'S HERE!
PARK DOJIN!
I DIDN'T THINK YOU'D MAKE IT!
AND YOU BROUGHT YOUR MINION.
SHOULD WE LEAVE?
JEEZ, DON'T BE SO SENSITIVE.
SO, HOW'S THE PARTY?
I EVEN INVITED A BAND.
NOT YOUR STYLE?
YOUR BAND MIGHT'VE BEEN A BETTER CHOICE.
WHAT ARE YOU--?!

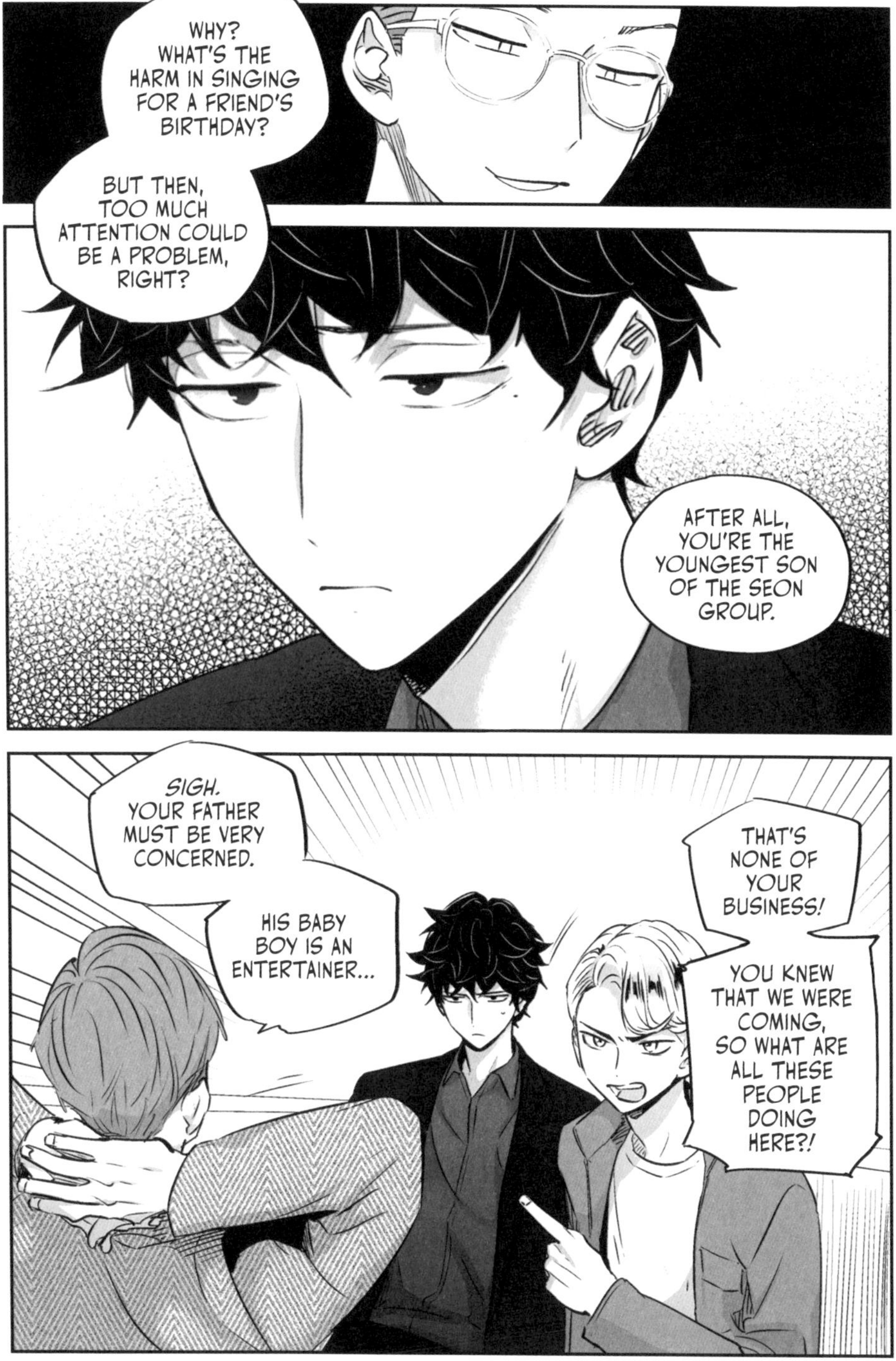
WHY? WHAT'S THE HARM IN SINGING FOR A FRIEND'S BIRTHDAY?
BUT THEN, TOO MUCH ATTENTION COULD BE A PROBLEM, RIGHT?
AFTER ALL, YOU'RE THE YOUNGEST SON OF THE SEON GROUP.
SIGH. YOUR FATHER MUST BE VERY CONCERNED.
HIS BABY BOY IS AN ENTERTAINER...
THAT'S NONE OF YOUR BUSINESS!
YOU KNEW THAT WE WERE COMING, SO WHAT ARE ALL THESE PEOPLE DOING HERE?!

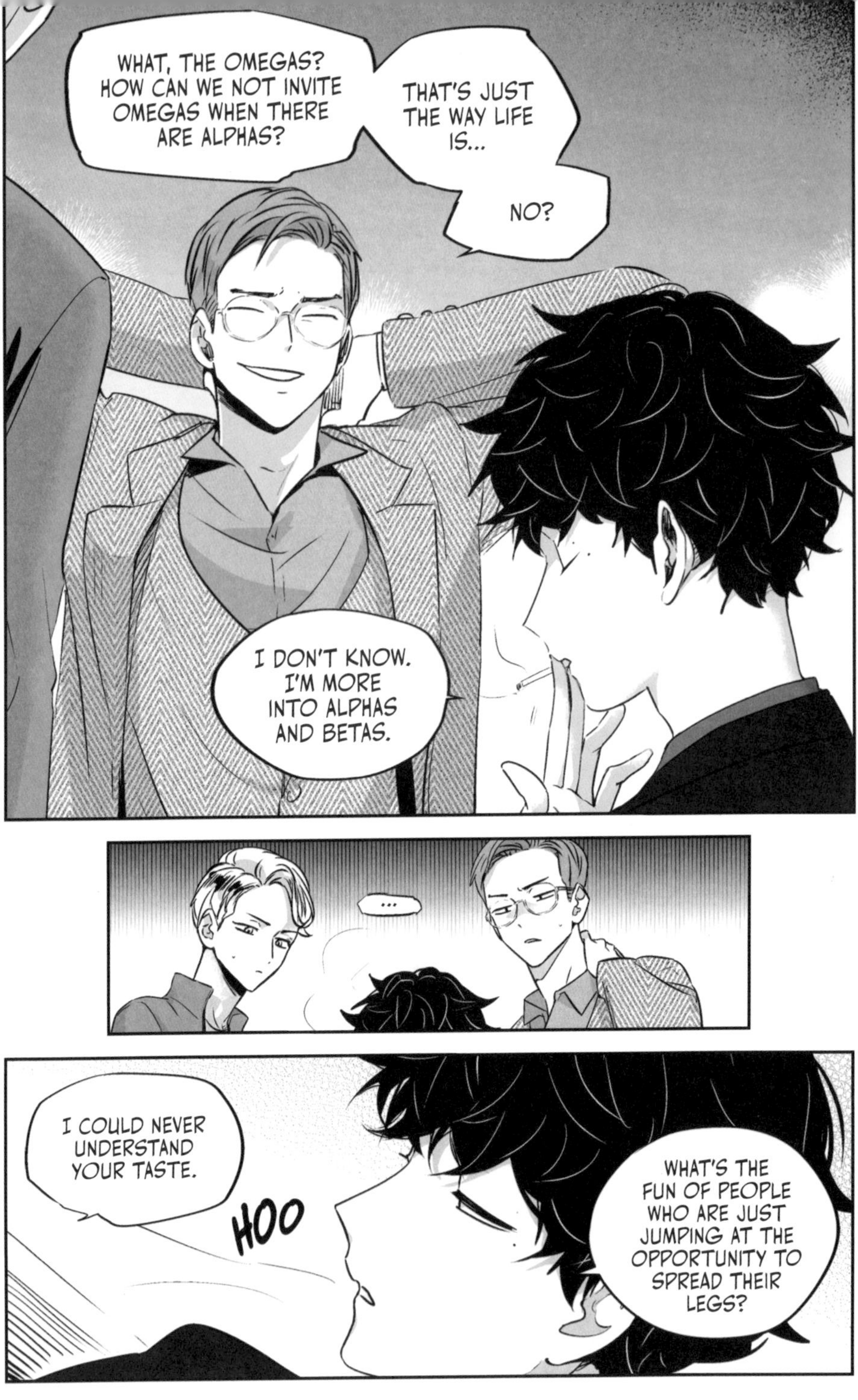
WHAT, THE OMEGAS? HOW CAN WE NOT INVITE OMEGAS WHEN THERE ARE ALPHAS?
THAT'S JUST THE WAY LIFE IS...
NO?
I DON'T KNOW. I'M MORE INTO ALPHAS AND BETAS.
...
I COULD NEVER UNDERSTAND YOUR TASTE.
HOO
WHAT'S THE FUN OF PEOPLE WHO ARE JUST JUMPING AT THE OPPORTUNITY TO SPREAD THEIR LEGS?

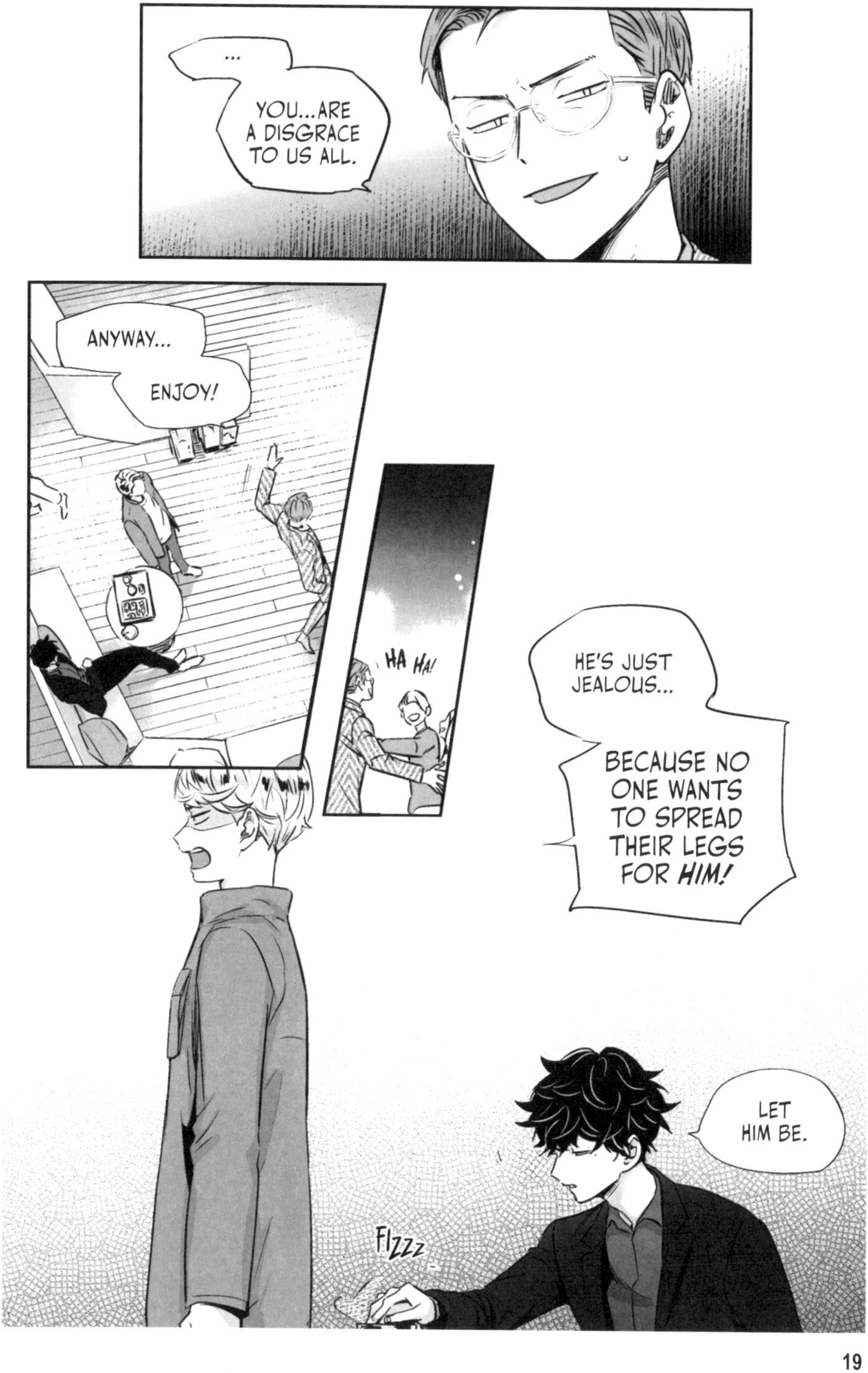
...
YOU...ARE A DISGRACE TO US ALL.
ANYWAY...
ENJOY!
HA HA!
HE'S JUST JEALOUS...
BECAUSE NO ONE WANTS TO SPREAD THEIR LEGS FOR ***HIM!***
LET HIM BE.
FIZZZ

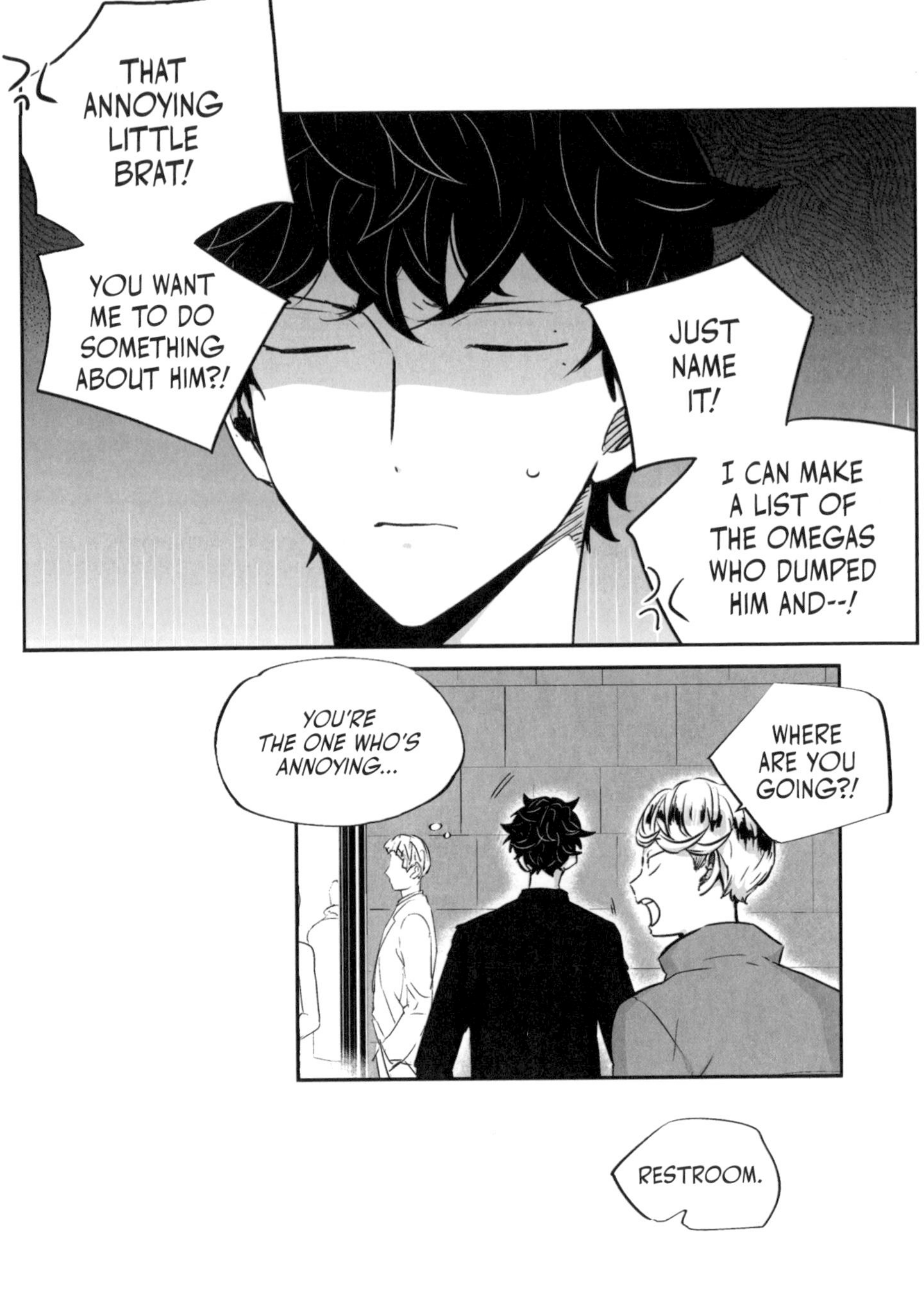
THAT ANNOYING LITTLE BRAT!
YOU WANT ME TO DO SOMETHING ABOUT HIM?!
JUST NAME IT!
I CAN MAKE A LIST OF THE OMEGAS WHO DUMPED HIM AND--!
YOU'RE THE ONE WHO'S ANNOYING...
WHERE ARE YOU GOING?!
RESTROOM.

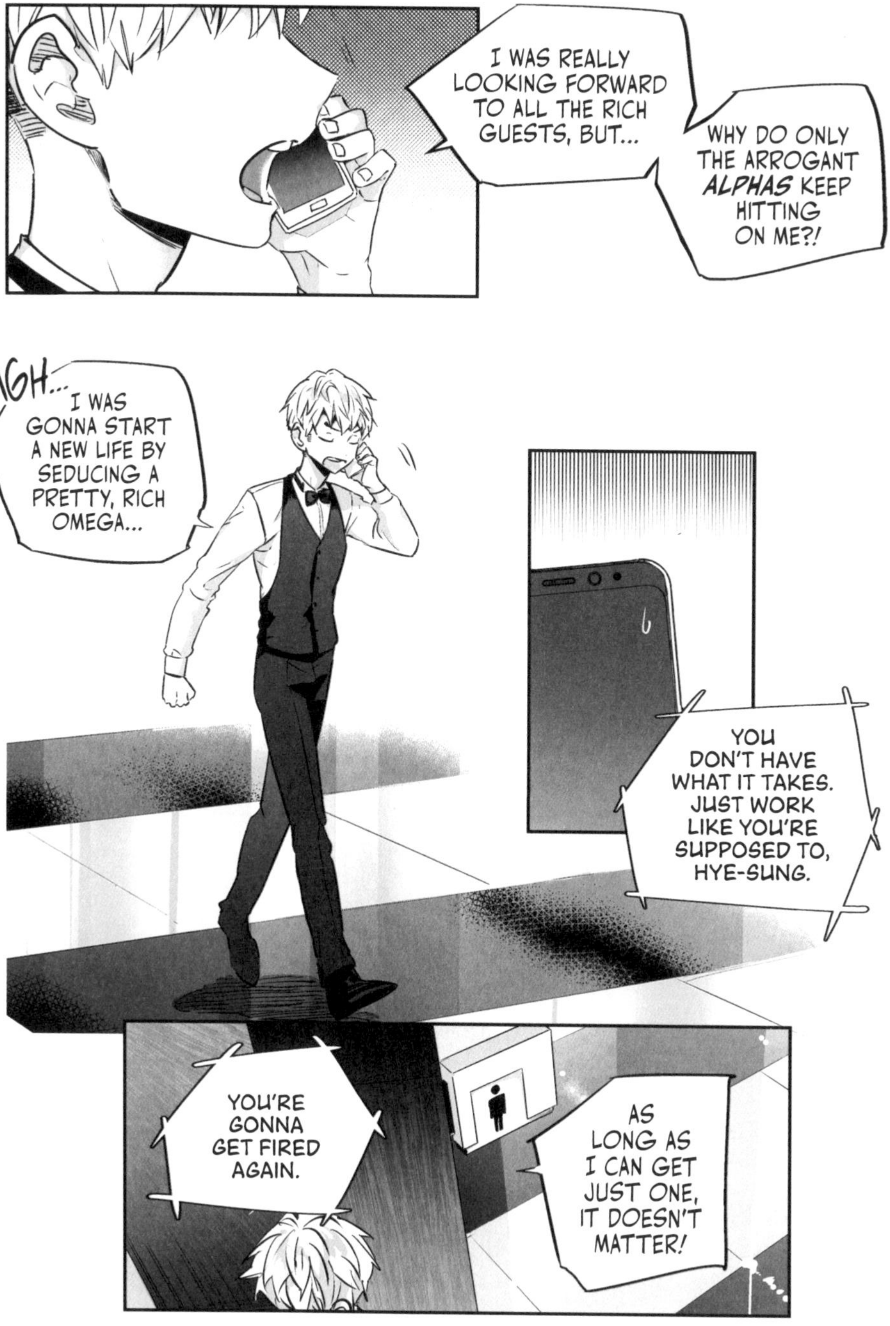
I WAS REALLY LOOKING FORWARD TO ALL THE RICH GUESTS, BUT...
WHY DO ONLY THE ARROGANT *ALPHAS* KEEP HITTING ON ME?!
SIGH...
I WAS GONNA START A NEW LIFE BY SEDUCING A PRETTY, RICH OMEGA...
YOU DON'T HAVE WHAT IT TAKES. JUST WORK LIKE YOU'RE SUPPOSED TO, HYE-SUNG.
YOU'RE GONNA GET FIRED AGAIN.
AS LONG AS I CAN GET JUST ONE, IT DOESN'T MATTER!

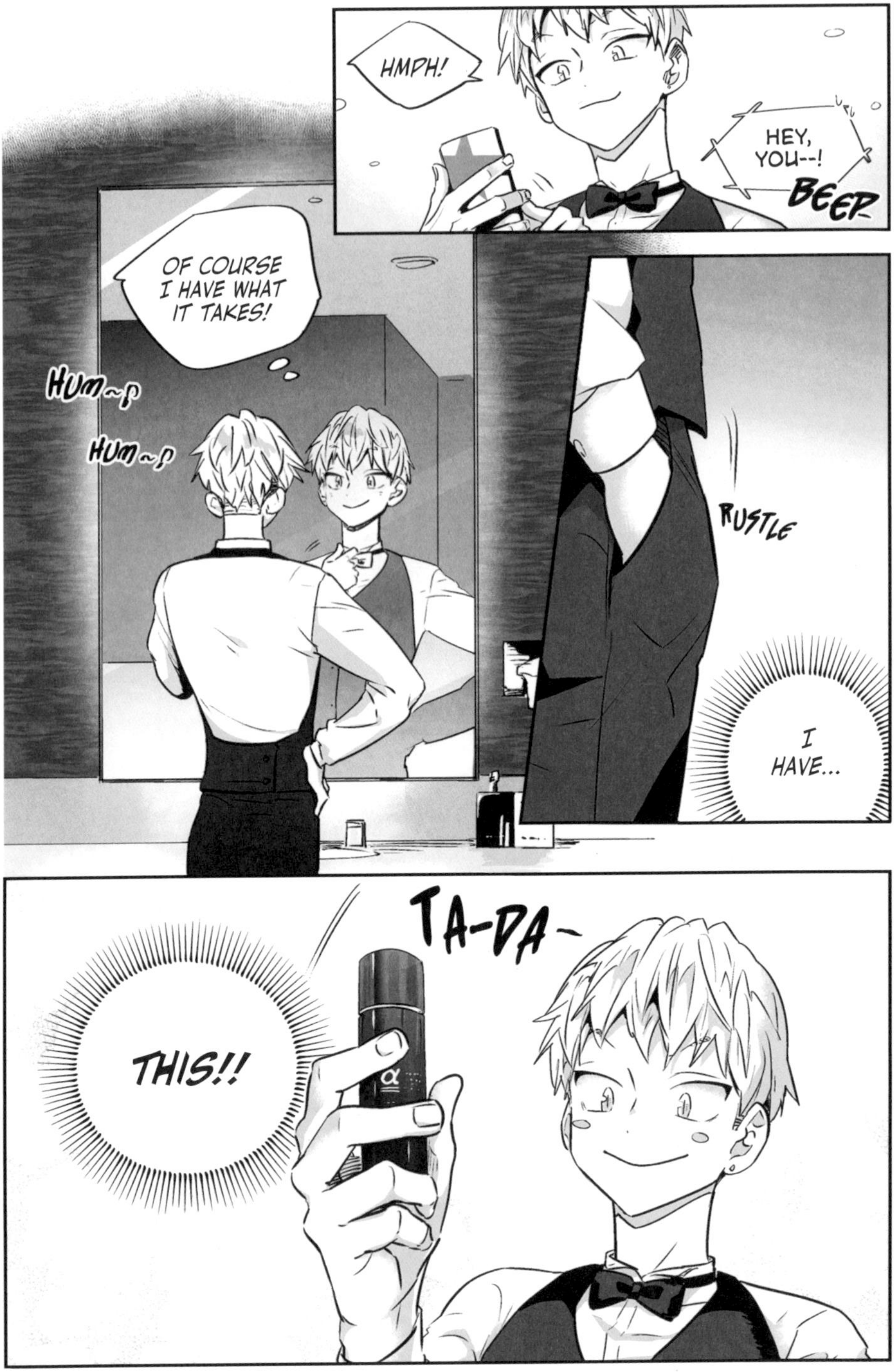
HMPH!
HEY, YOU--!
BEEP
OF COURSE I HAVE WHAT IT TAKES!
HUM~♪
HUM~♪
RUSTLE
I HAVE...
TA-DA~
THIS!!

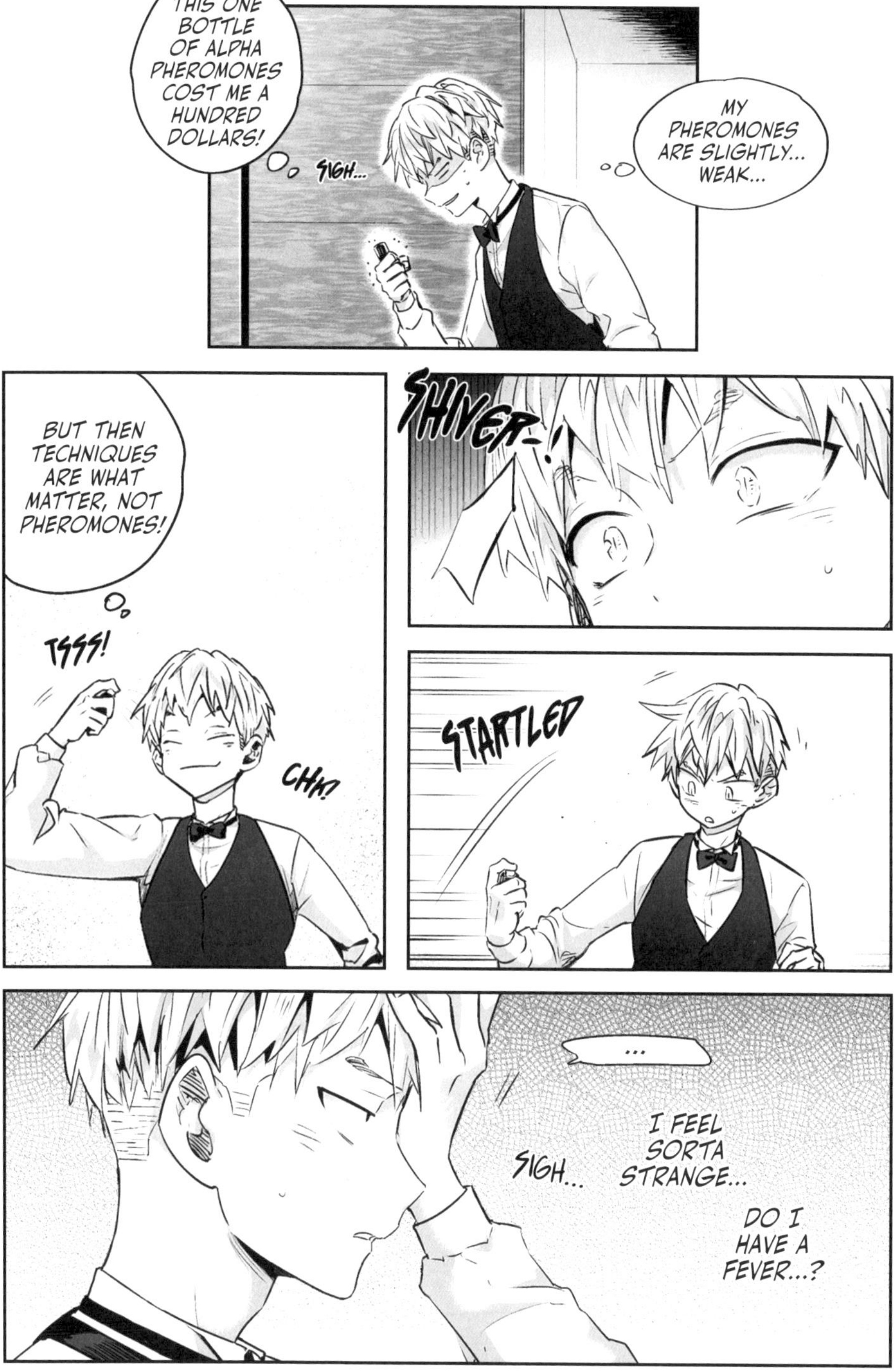
THIS ONE BOTTLE OF ALPHA PHEROMONES COST ME A HUNDRED DOLLARS!
SIGH...
MY PHEROMONES ARE SLIGHTLY... WEAK...
BUT THEN TECHNIQUES ARE WHAT MATTER, NOT PHEROMONES!
TSSS!
CHK!
SHIVER--!
STARTLED
...
SIGH...
I FEEL SORTA STRANGE...
DO I HAVE A FEVER...?

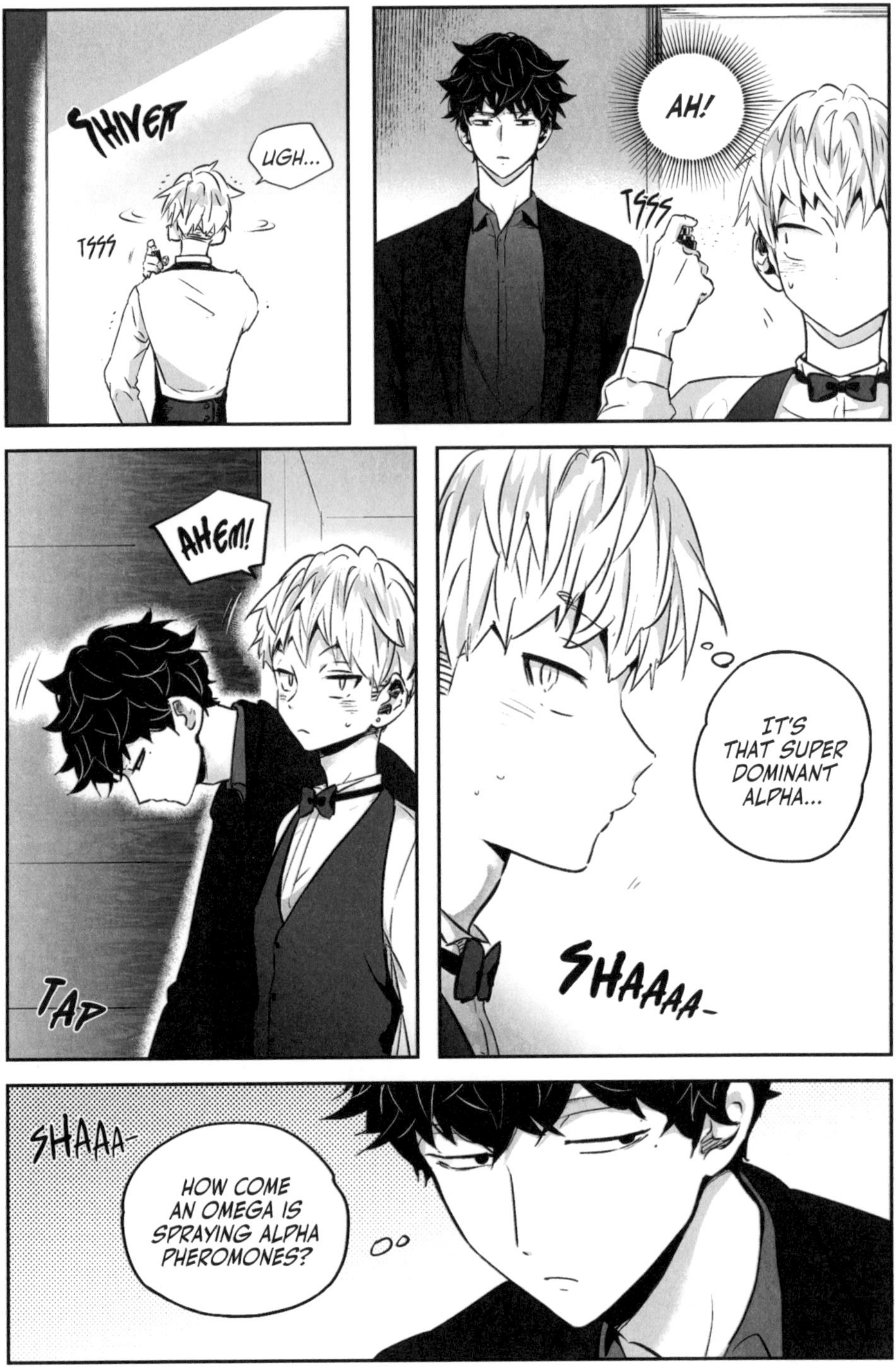
SHIVER
UGH...
TSSS
AH!
TSSS
AHEM!
TAP
IT'S THAT SUPER DOMINANT ALPHA...
SHAAAA-
SHAAA-
HOW COME AN OMEGA IS SPRAYING ALPHA PHEROMONES?

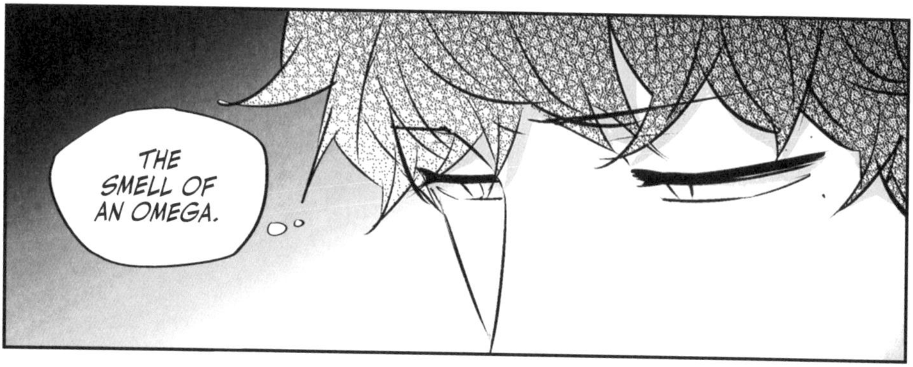
THE SMELL OF AN OMEGA.

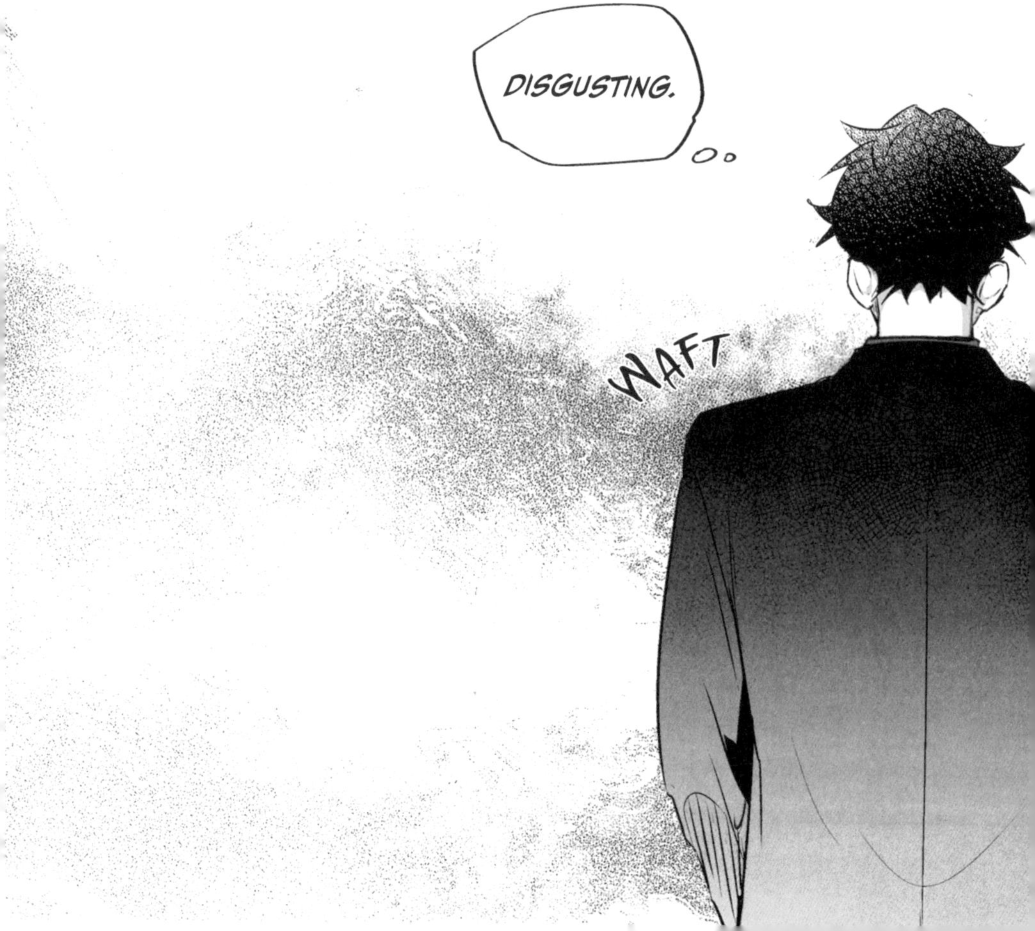
DISGUSTING.
WAFT

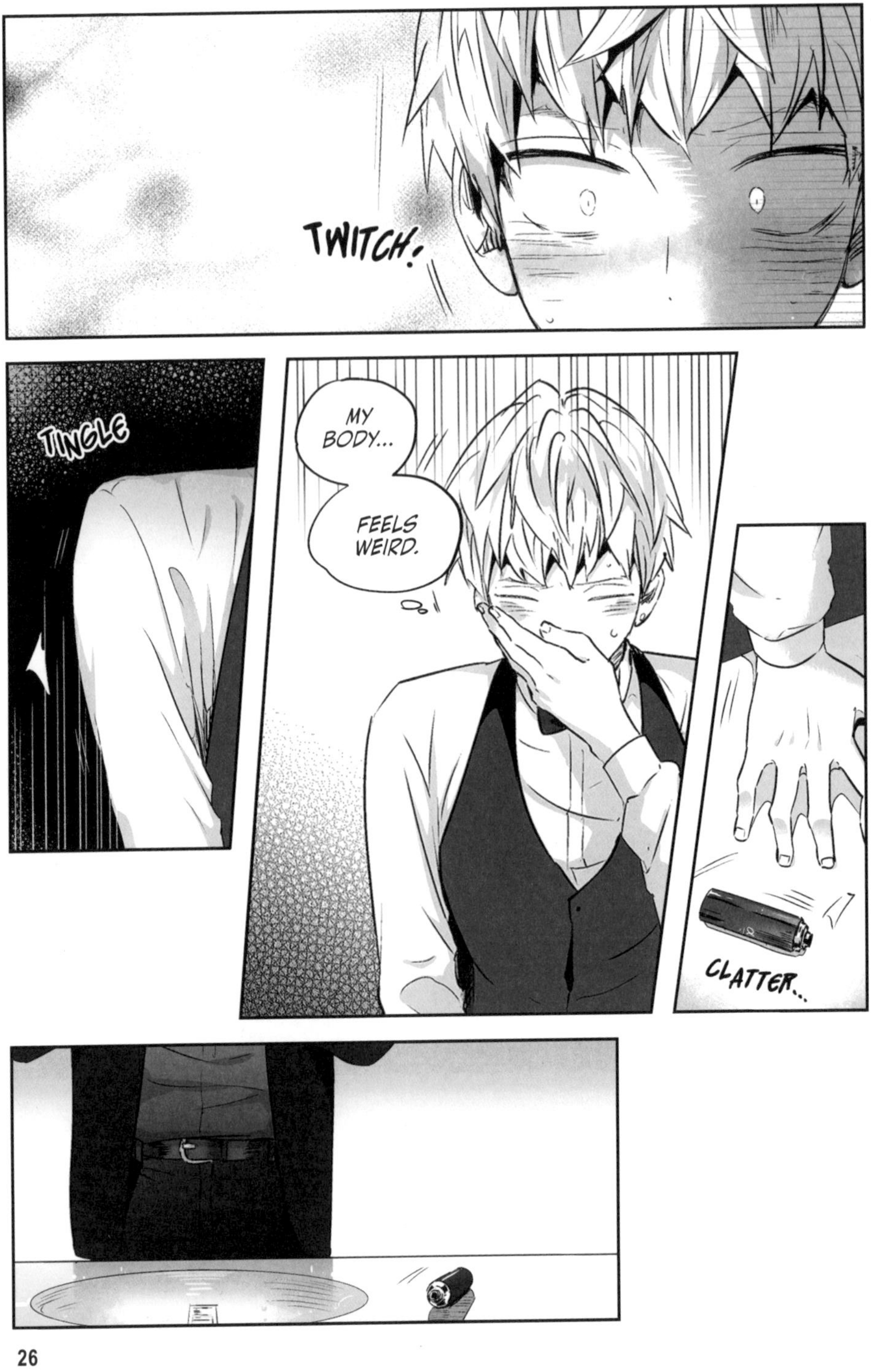
TWITCH!
TINGLE
MY BODY...
FEELS WEIRD.
CLATTER...

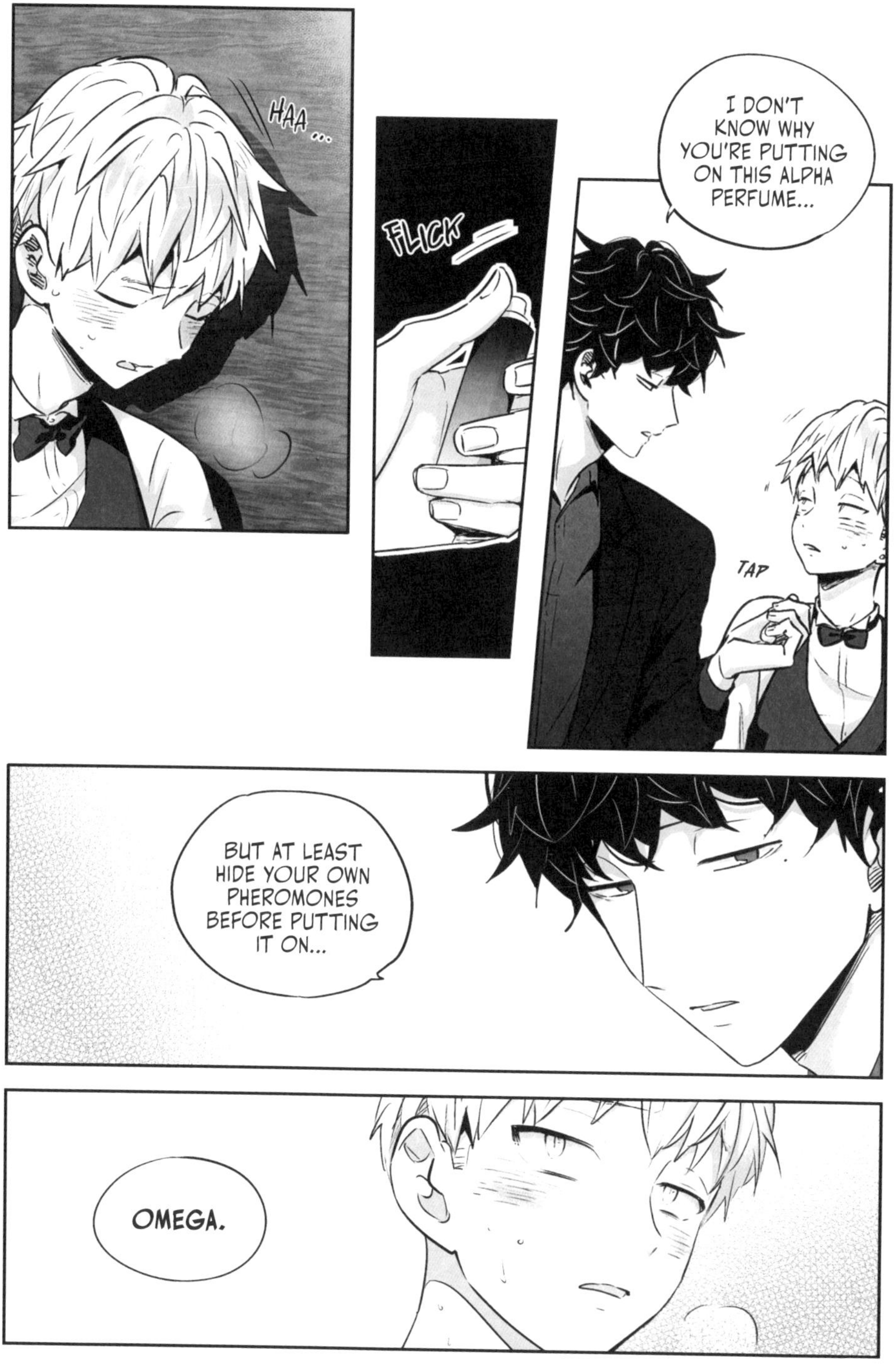
HAA...
FLICK
I DON'T KNOW WHY YOU'RE PUTTING ON THIS ALPHA PERFUME...
TAP
BUT AT LEAST HIDE YOUR OWN PHEROMONES BEFORE PUTTING IT ON...
OMEGA.

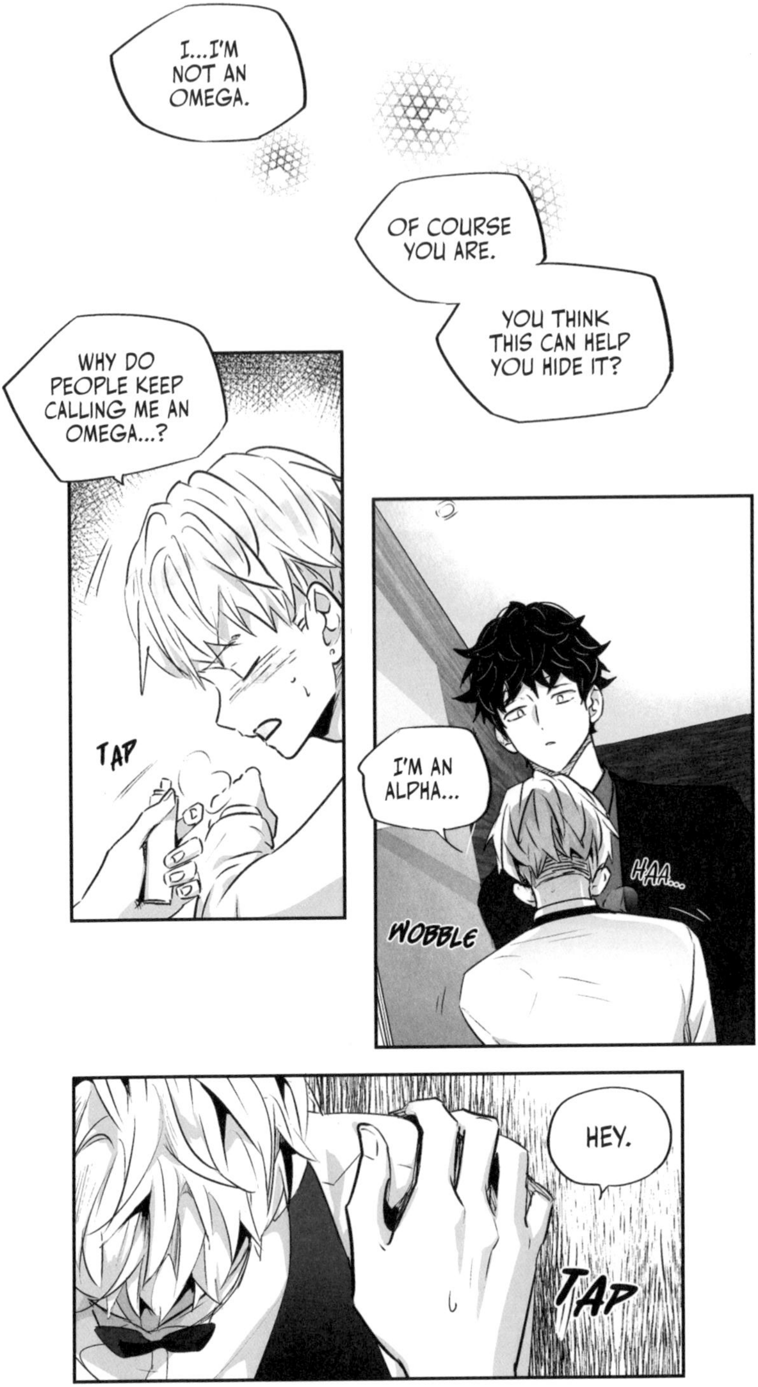

I...I'M NOT AN OMEGA.
OF COURSE YOU ARE.
YOU THINK THIS CAN HELP YOU HIDE IT?
WHY DO PEOPLE KEEP CALLING ME AN OMEGA...?
TAP
I'M AN ALPHA...
HAA...
WOBBLE
HEY.
TAP

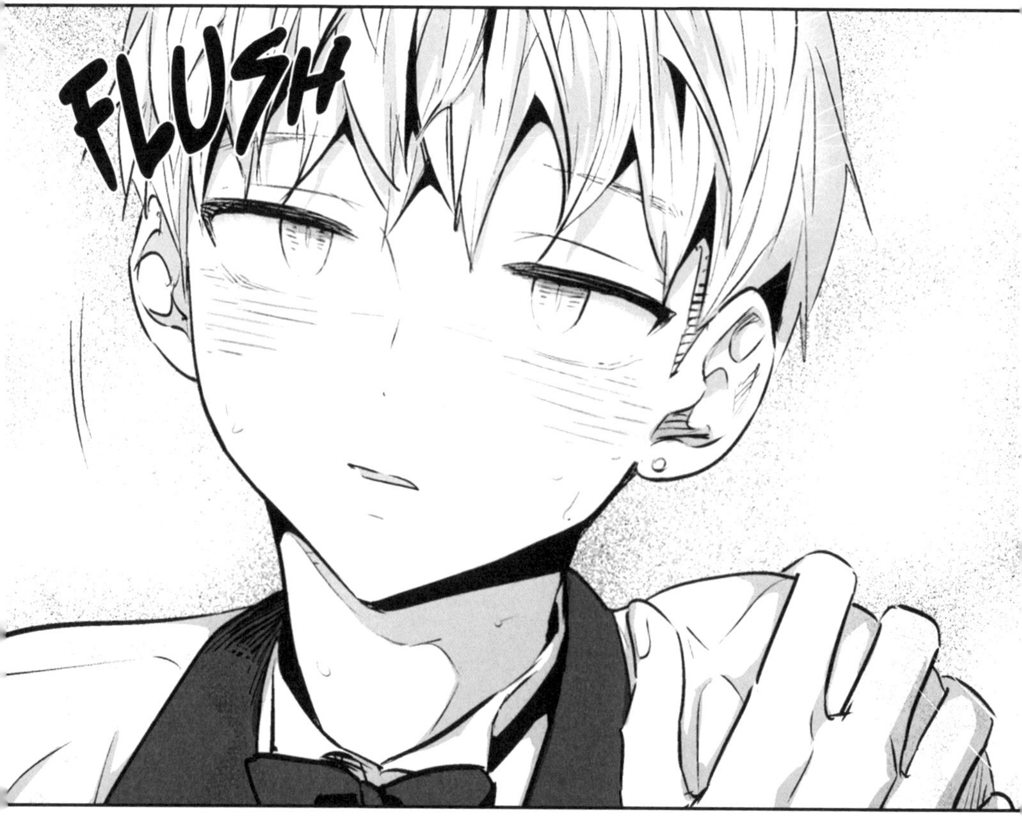
FLUSH

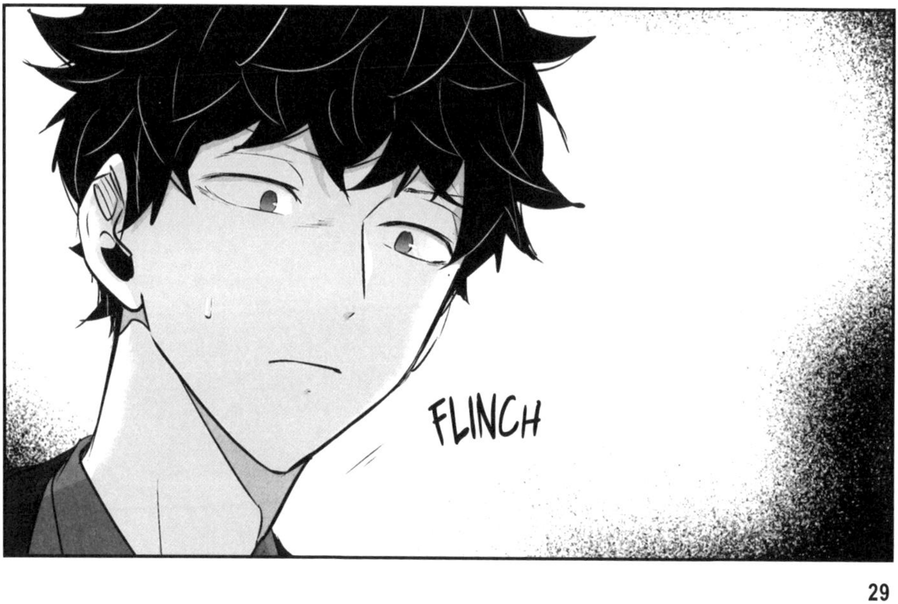
FLINCH

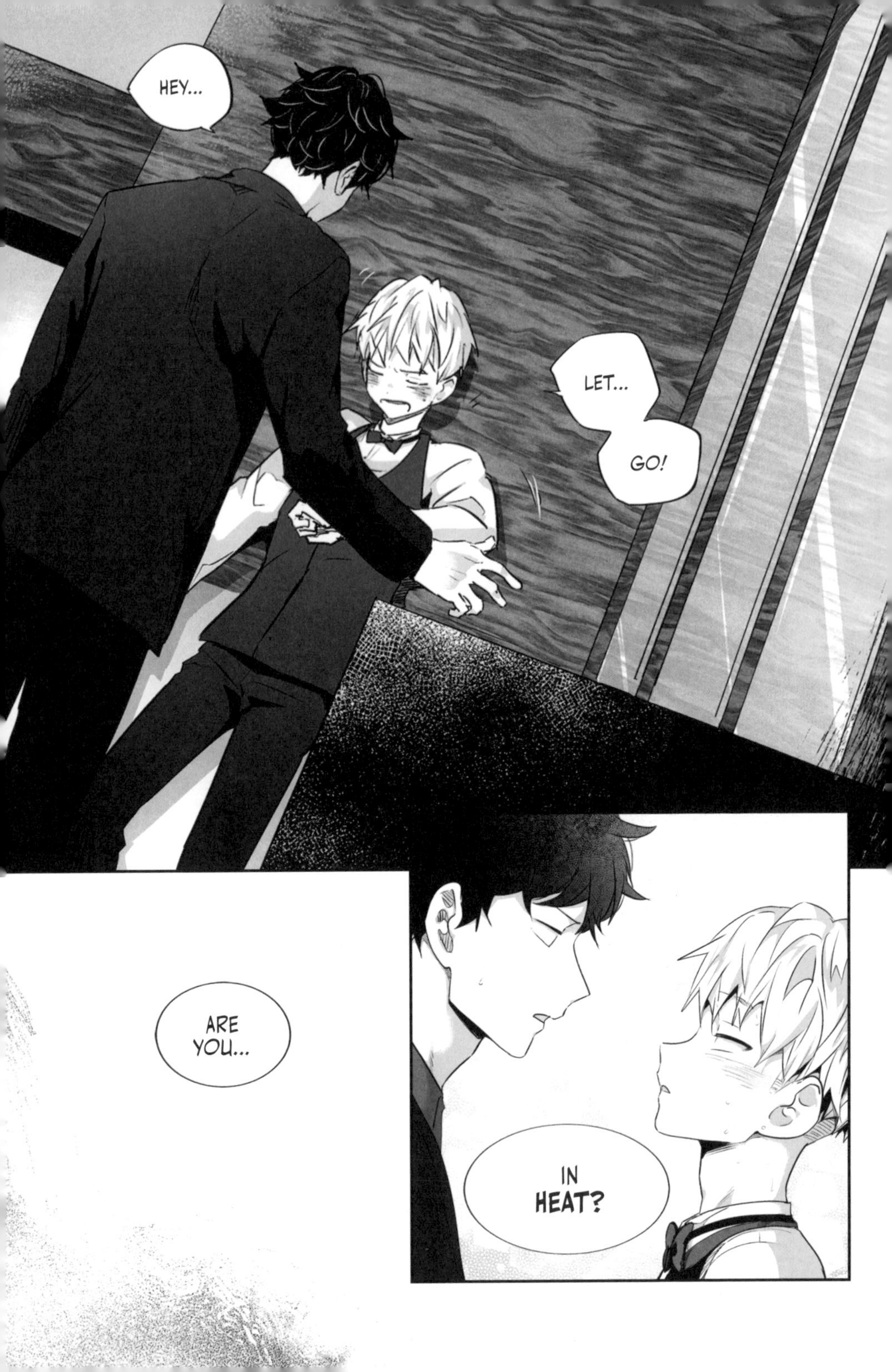
HEY...
LET...
GO!
ARE YOU...
IN HEAT?

Love is
an Illusion!

Love is
an Illusion!

Chapter 2

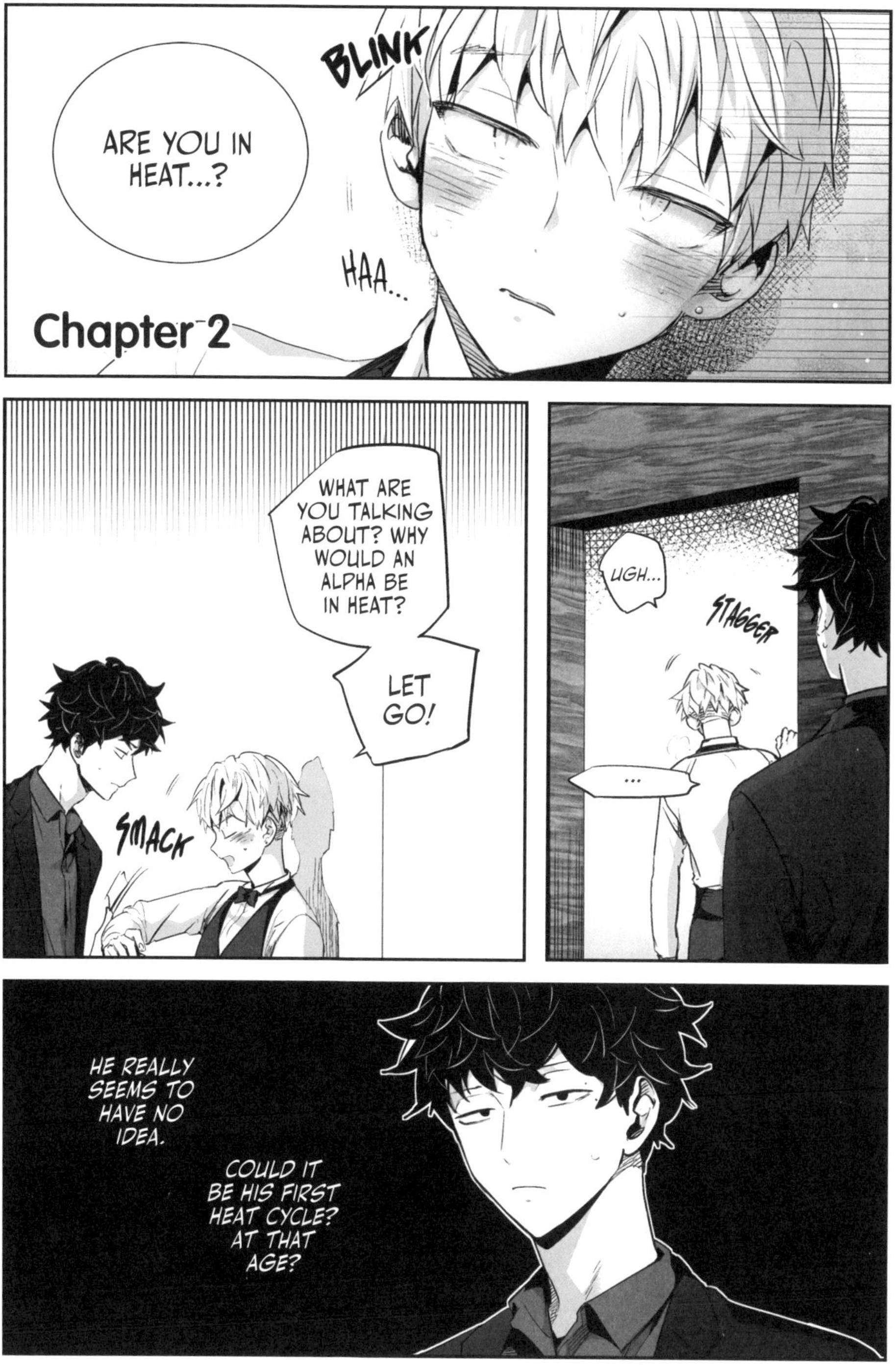

ARE YOU IN HEAT...?
BLINK
HAA...
WHAT ARE YOU TALKING ABOUT? WHY WOULD AN ALPHA BE IN HEAT?
LET GO!
SMACK
UGH...
STAGGER
...
HE REALLY SEEMS TO HAVE NO IDEA.
COULD IT BE HIS FIRST HEAT CYCLE? AT THAT AGE?

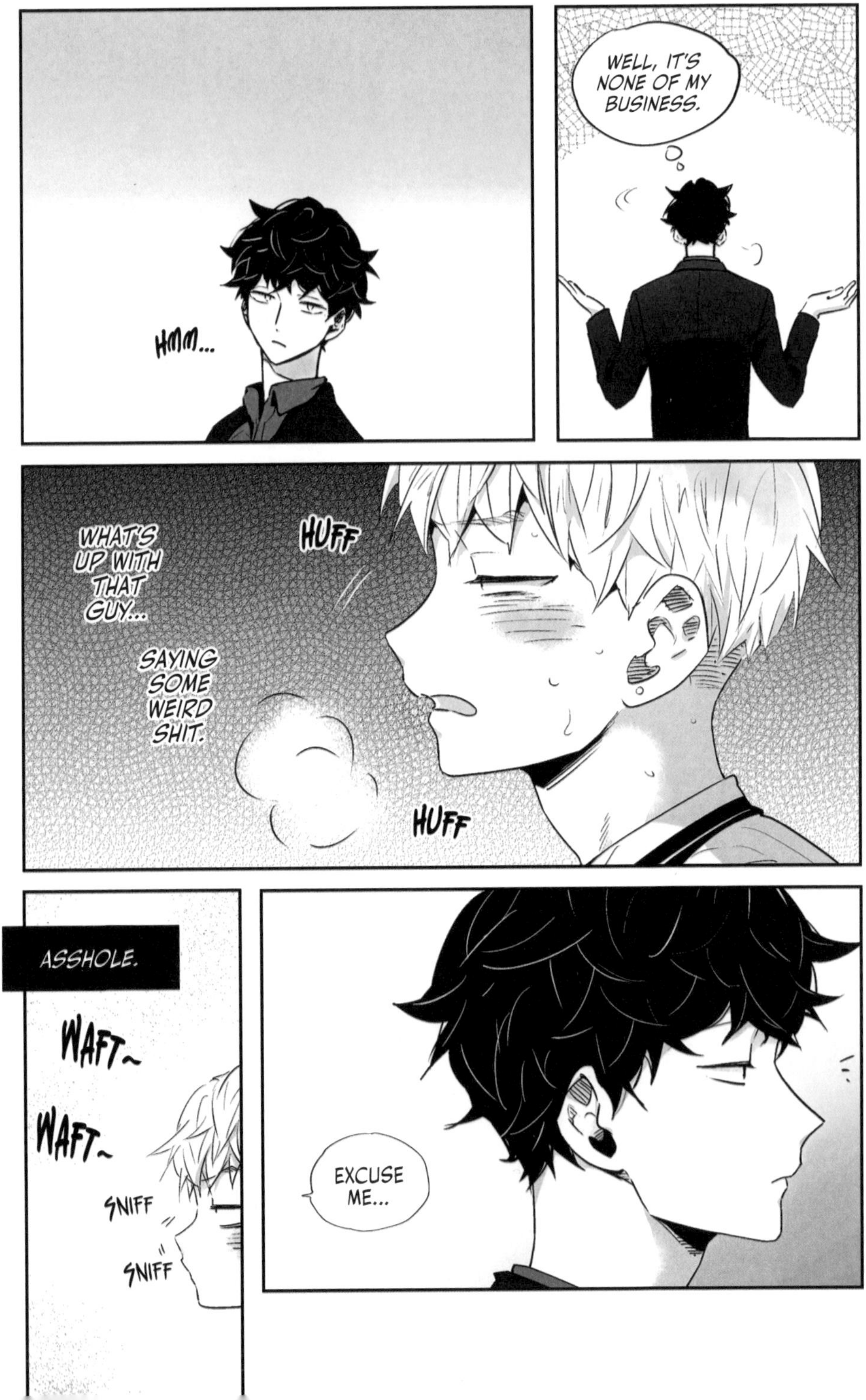
HMM...
WELL, IT'S NONE OF MY BUSINESS.
WHAT'S UP WITH THAT GUY...
HUFF
SAYING SOME WEIRD SHIT.
HUFF
ASSHOLE.
WAFT~
WAFT~
SNIFF
SNIFF
EXCUSE ME...

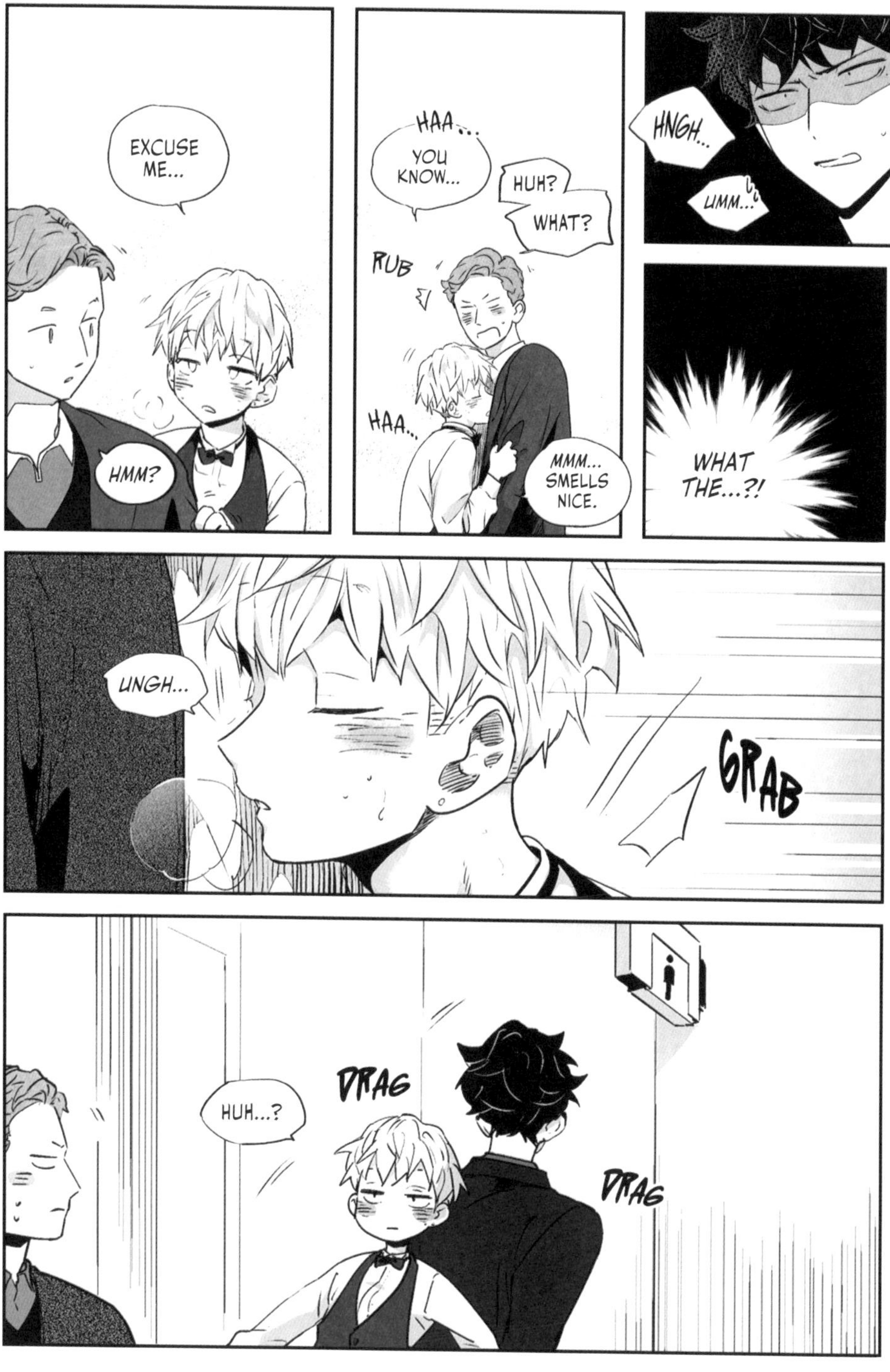
EXCUSE ME...
HMM?
HAA...
YOU KNOW...
HUH?
WHAT?
RUB
HAA...
MMM... SMELLS NICE.
HNGH...
UMM...
WHAT THE...?!
UNGH...
GRAB
DRAG
HUH...?
DRAG

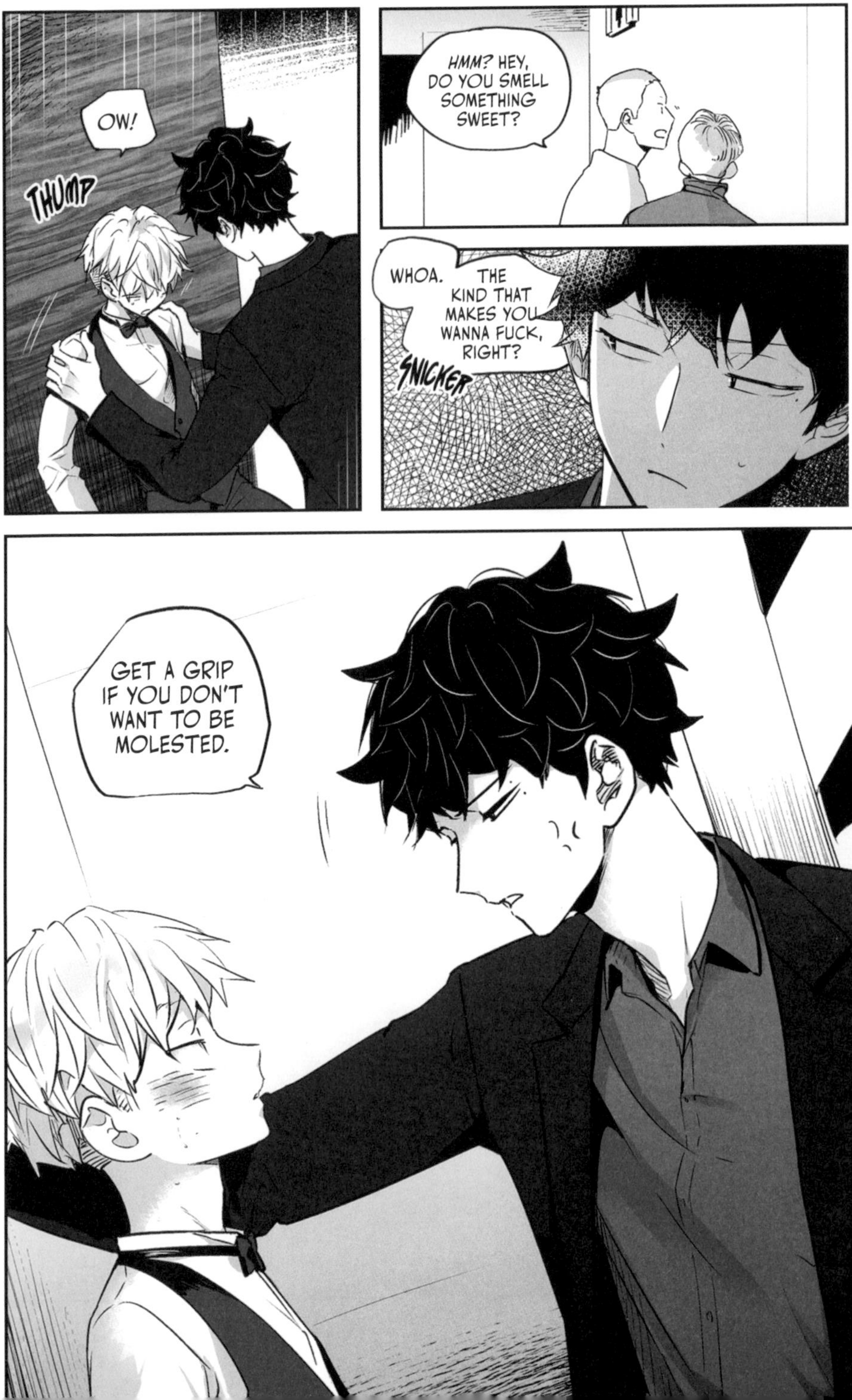
OW!
THUMP
HMM? HEY, DO YOU SMELL SOMETHING SWEET?
WHOA.
THE KIND THAT MAKES YOU WANNA FUCK, RIGHT?
SNICKER
GET A GRIP IF YOU DON'T WANT TO BE MOLESTED.

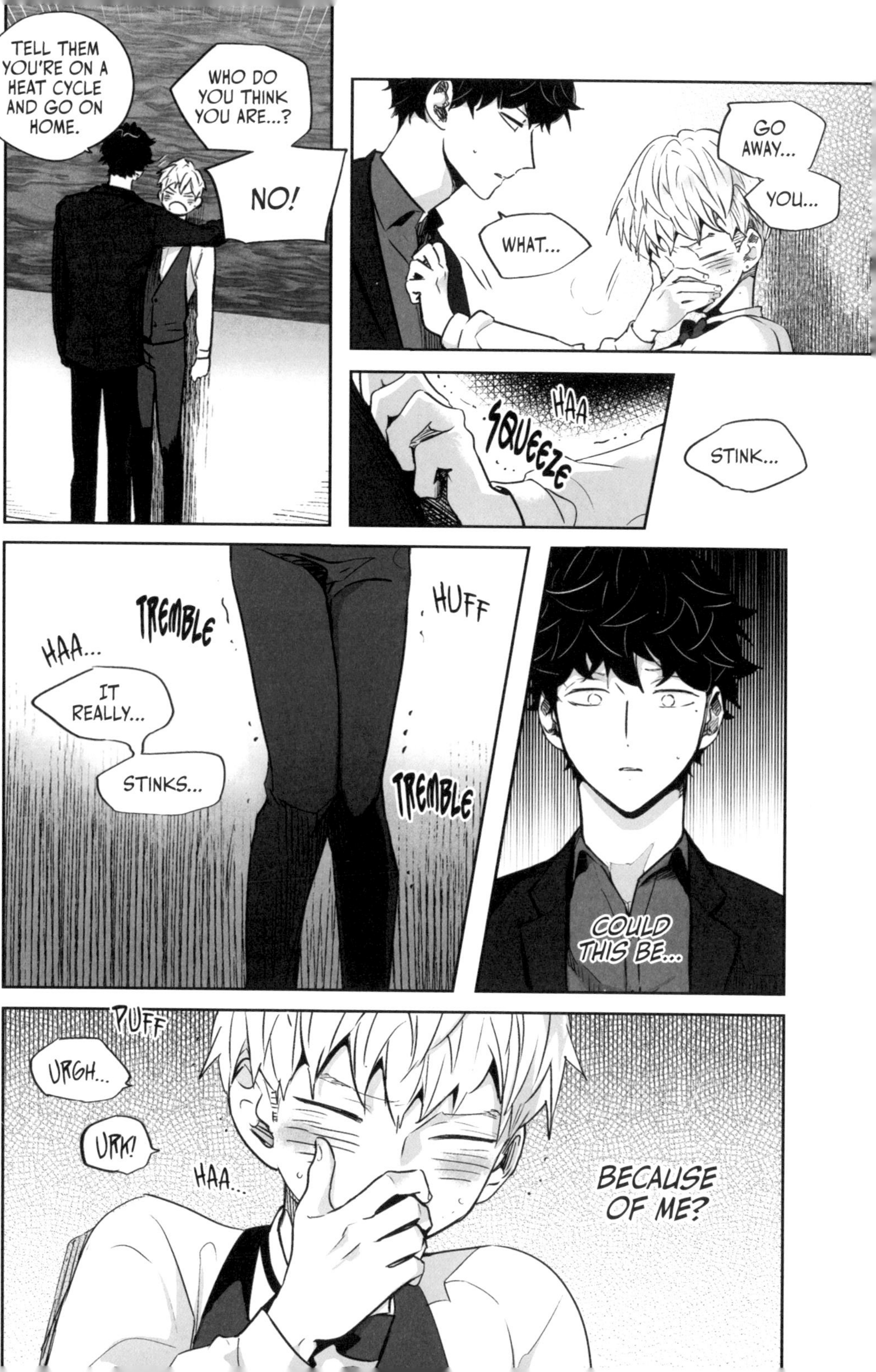
TELL THEM YOU'RE ON A HEAT CYCLE AND GO ON HOME.
WHO DO YOU THINK YOU ARE...?
NO!
GO AWAY...
YOU...
WHAT...
HAA
SQUEEZE
STINK...
HAA...
TREMBLE
IT REALLY...
STINKS...
HUFF
TREMBLE
COULD THIS BE...
PUFF
URGH...
URK!
HAA...
BECAUSE OF ME?

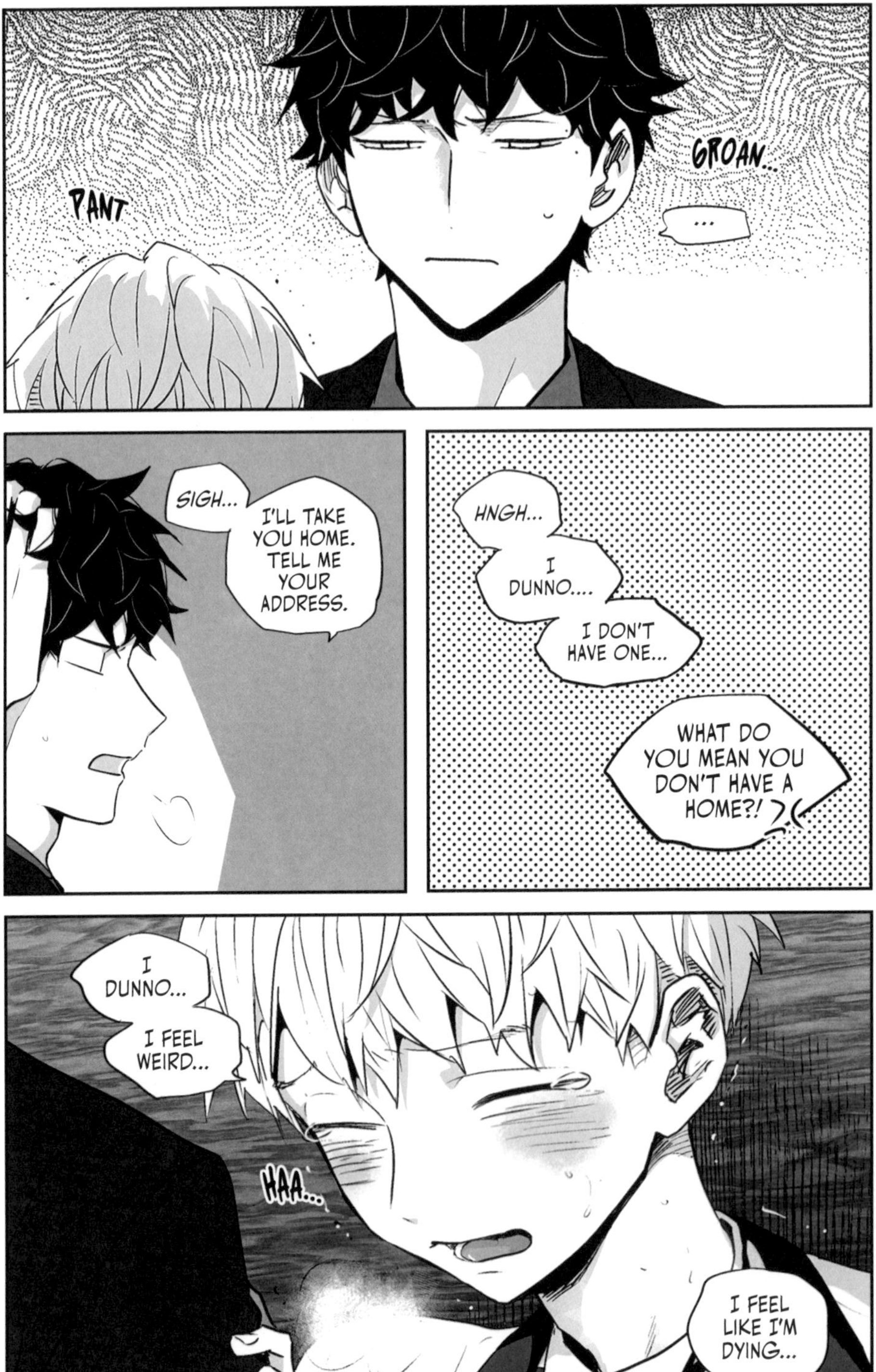
PANT
GROAN...
...
SIGH...
I'LL TAKE YOU HOME. TELL ME YOUR ADDRESS.
HNGH...
I DUNNO....
I DON'T HAVE ONE...
WHAT DO YOU MEAN YOU DON'T HAVE A HOME?!
I DUNNO...
I FEEL WEIRD...
HAA...
I FEEL LIKE I'M DYING...

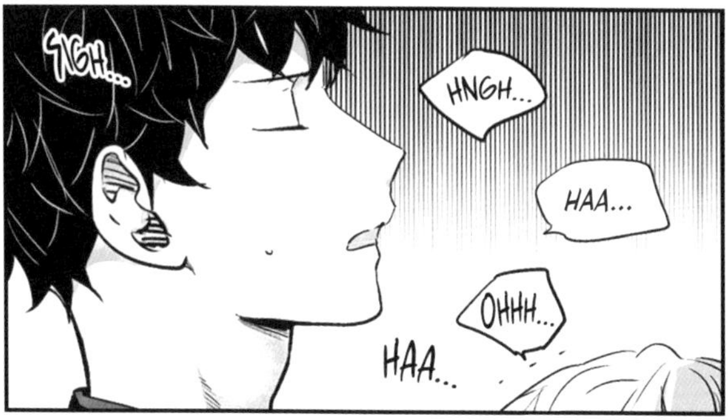
SIGH...
HNGH...
HAA...
OHHH...
HAA...

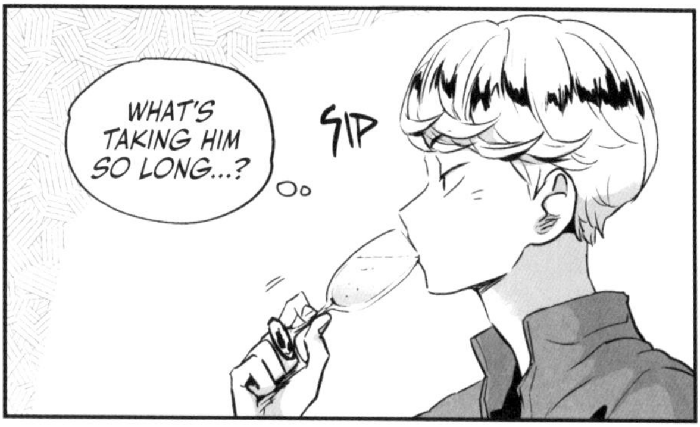
WHAT'S TAKING HIM SO LONG...?
SIP

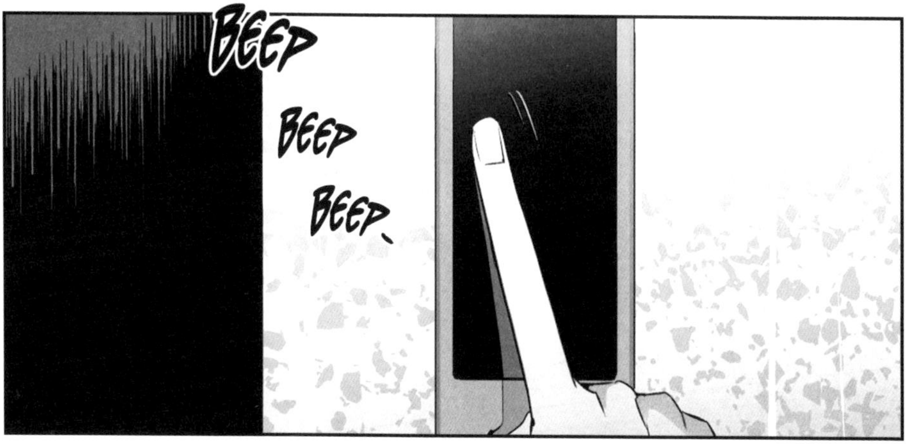
BEEP
BEEP
BEEP

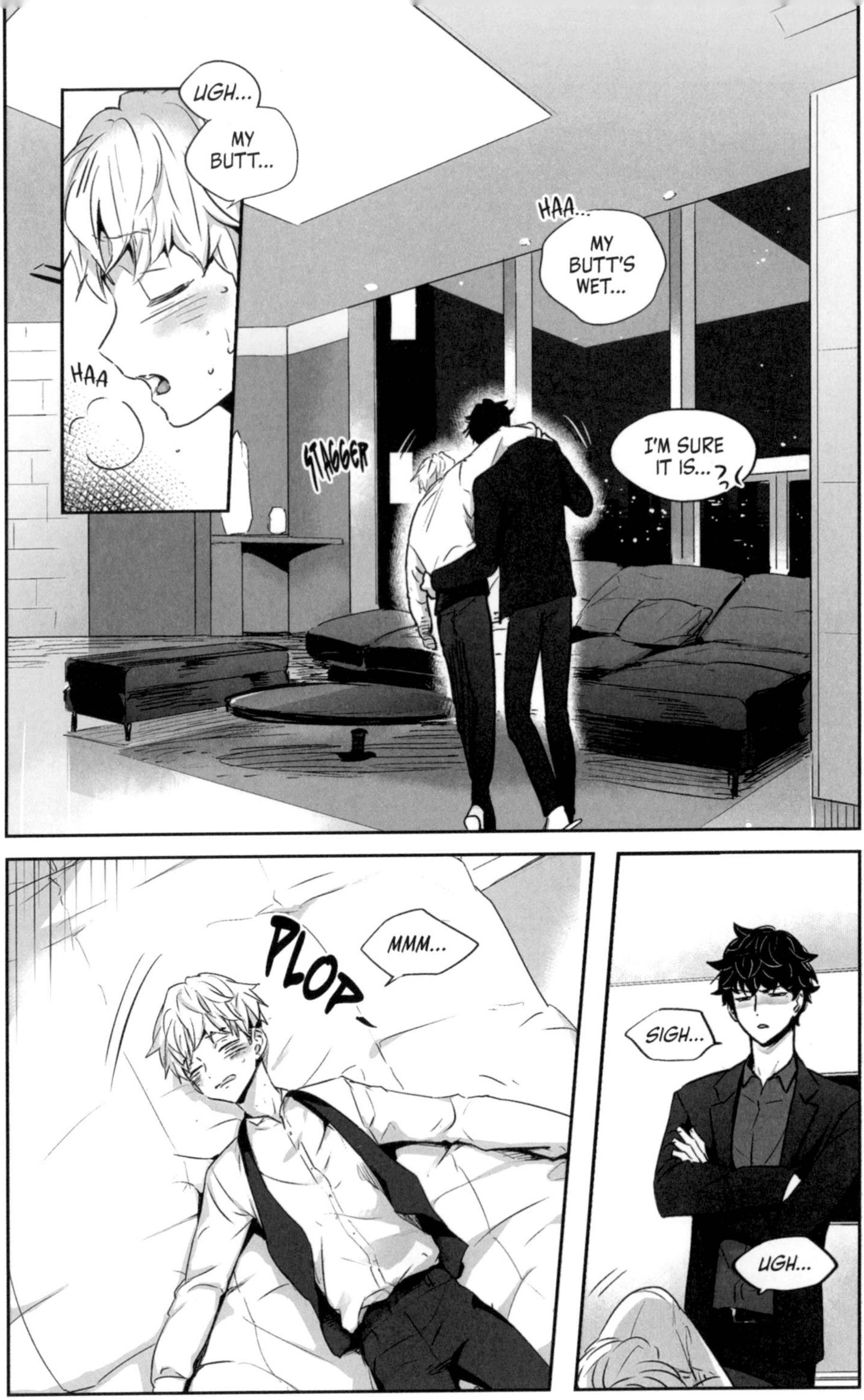
UGH...
MY BUTT...
HAA
STAGGER
HAA...
MY BUTT'S WET...
I'M SURE IT IS...
PLOP
MMM...
SIGH...
UGH...

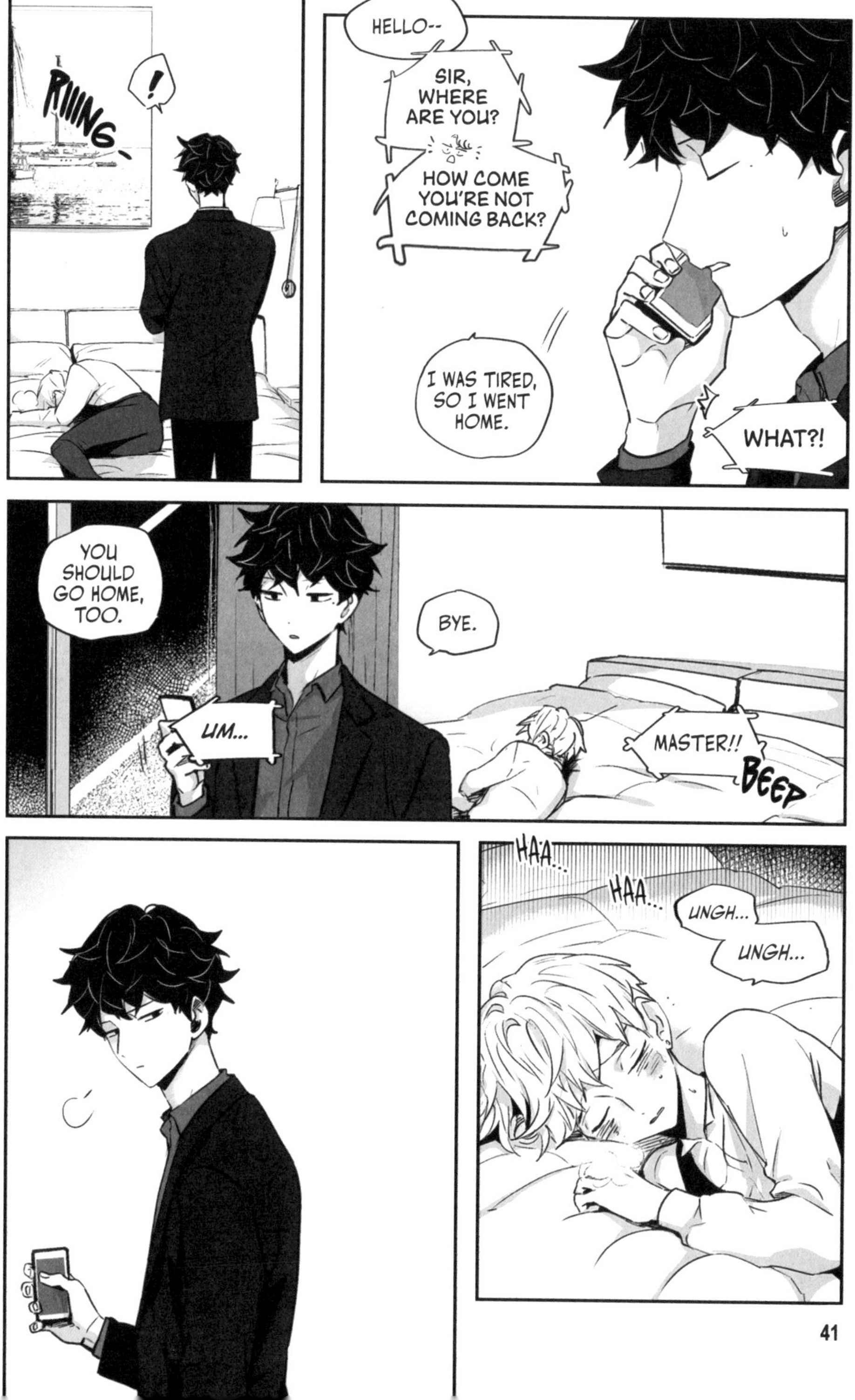
RIIING
!
HELLO--
SIR, WHERE ARE YOU?
HOW COME YOU'RE NOT COMING BACK?
I WAS TIRED, SO I WENT HOME.
WHAT?!
YOU SHOULD GO HOME, TOO.
UM...
BYE.
MASTER!!
BEEP
HAA...
HAA...
UNGH...
UNGH...

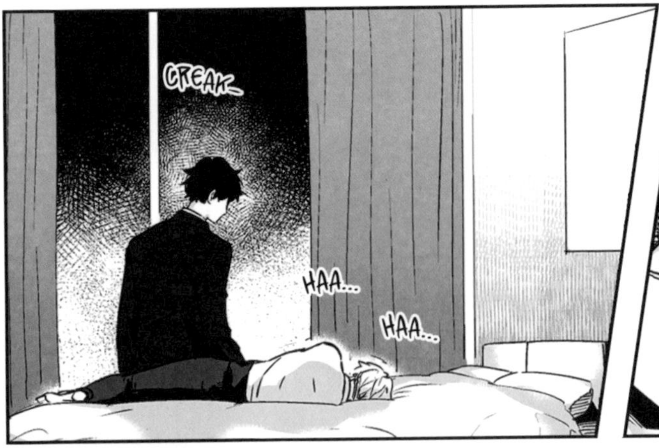
CREAK
HAA...
HAA...

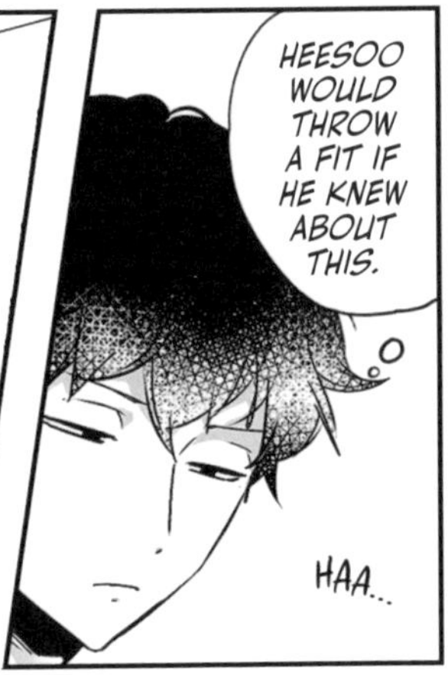
HEESOO WOULD THROW A FIT IF HE KNEW ABOUT THIS.
HAA...

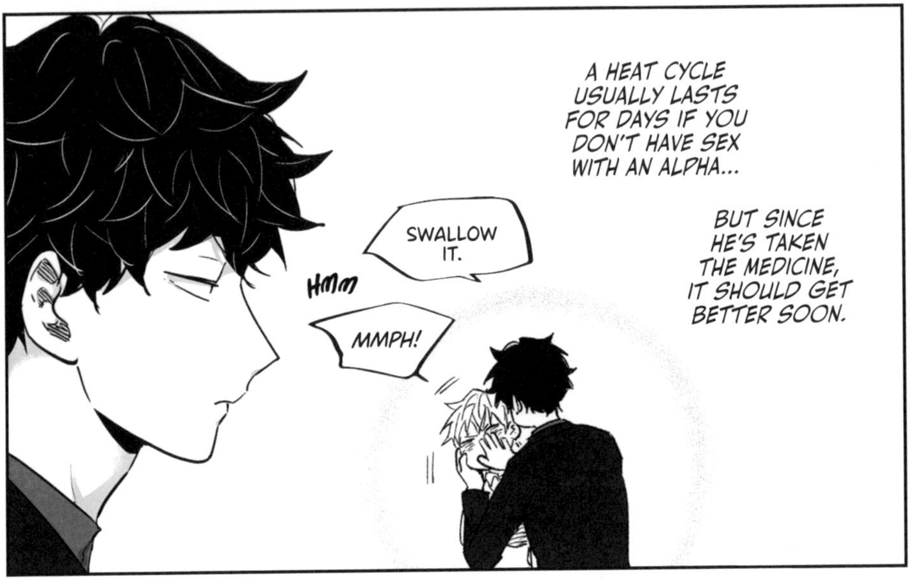
A HEAT CYCLE USUALLY LASTS FOR DAYS IF YOU DON'T HAVE SEX WITH AN ALPHA...
BUT SINCE HE'S TAKEN THE MEDICINE, IT SHOULD GET BETTER SOON.
SWALLOW IT.
HMM
MMPH!

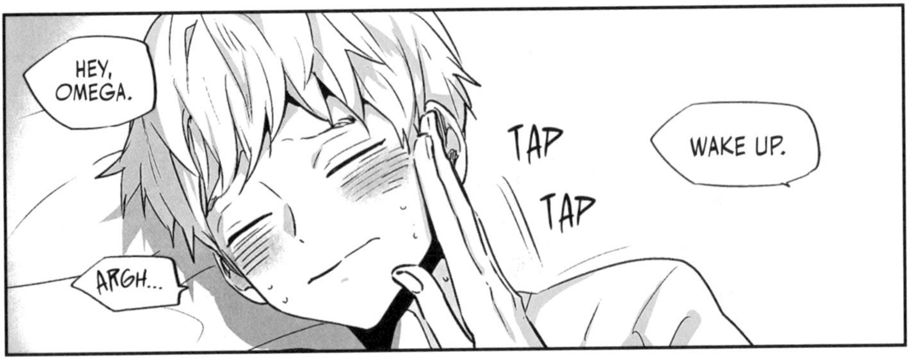
HEY, OMEGA.
TAP
TAP
WAKE UP.
ARGH...

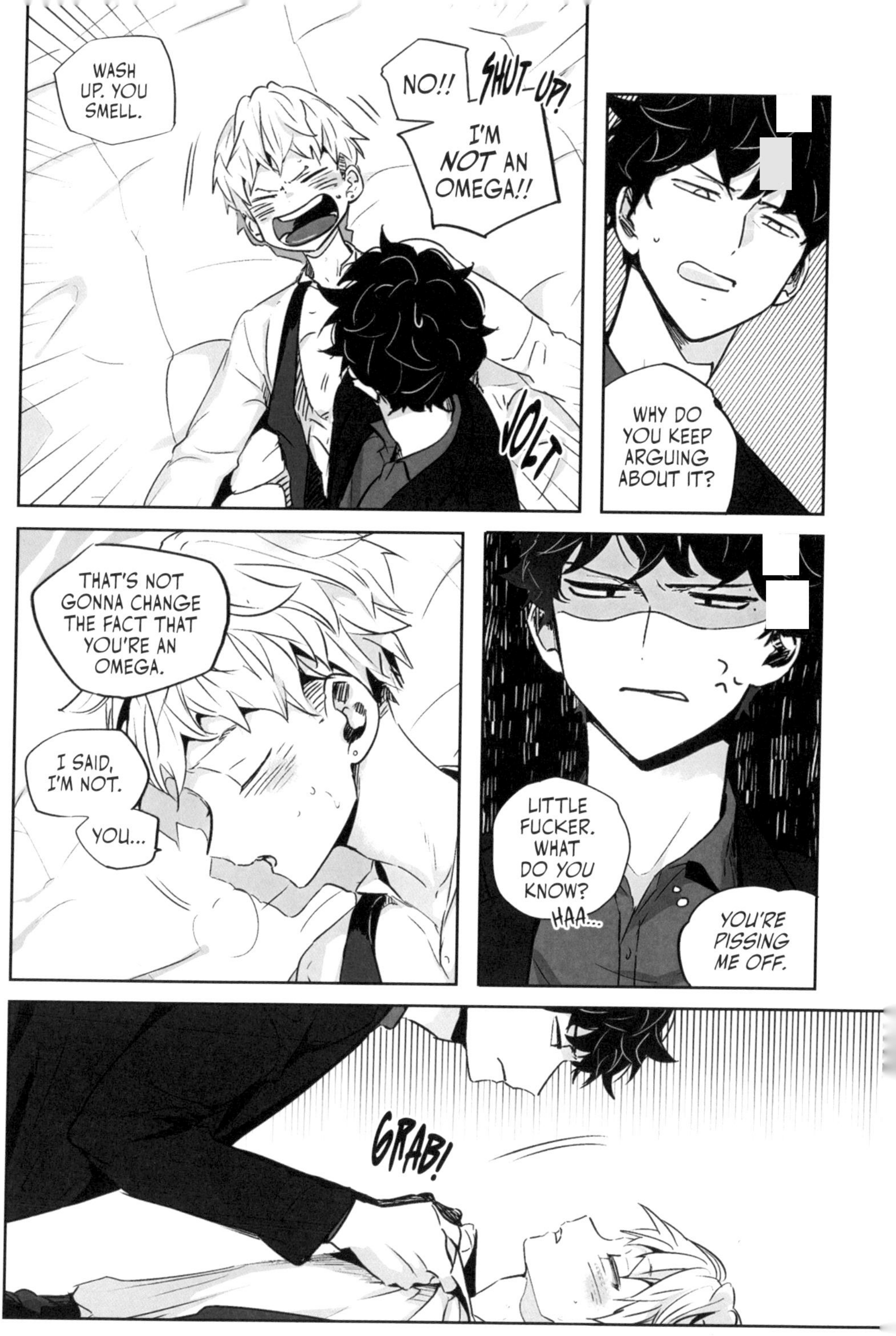
WASH UP. YOU SMELL.
NO!!
SHUT-UP!
I'M NOT AN OMEGA!!
JOLT
WHY DO YOU KEEP ARGUING ABOUT IT?
THAT'S NOT GONNA CHANGE THE FACT THAT YOU'RE AN OMEGA.
I SAID, I'M NOT.
YOU...
LITTLE FUCKER. WHAT DO YOU KNOW?
HAA...
YOU'RE PISSING ME OFF.
GRAB!

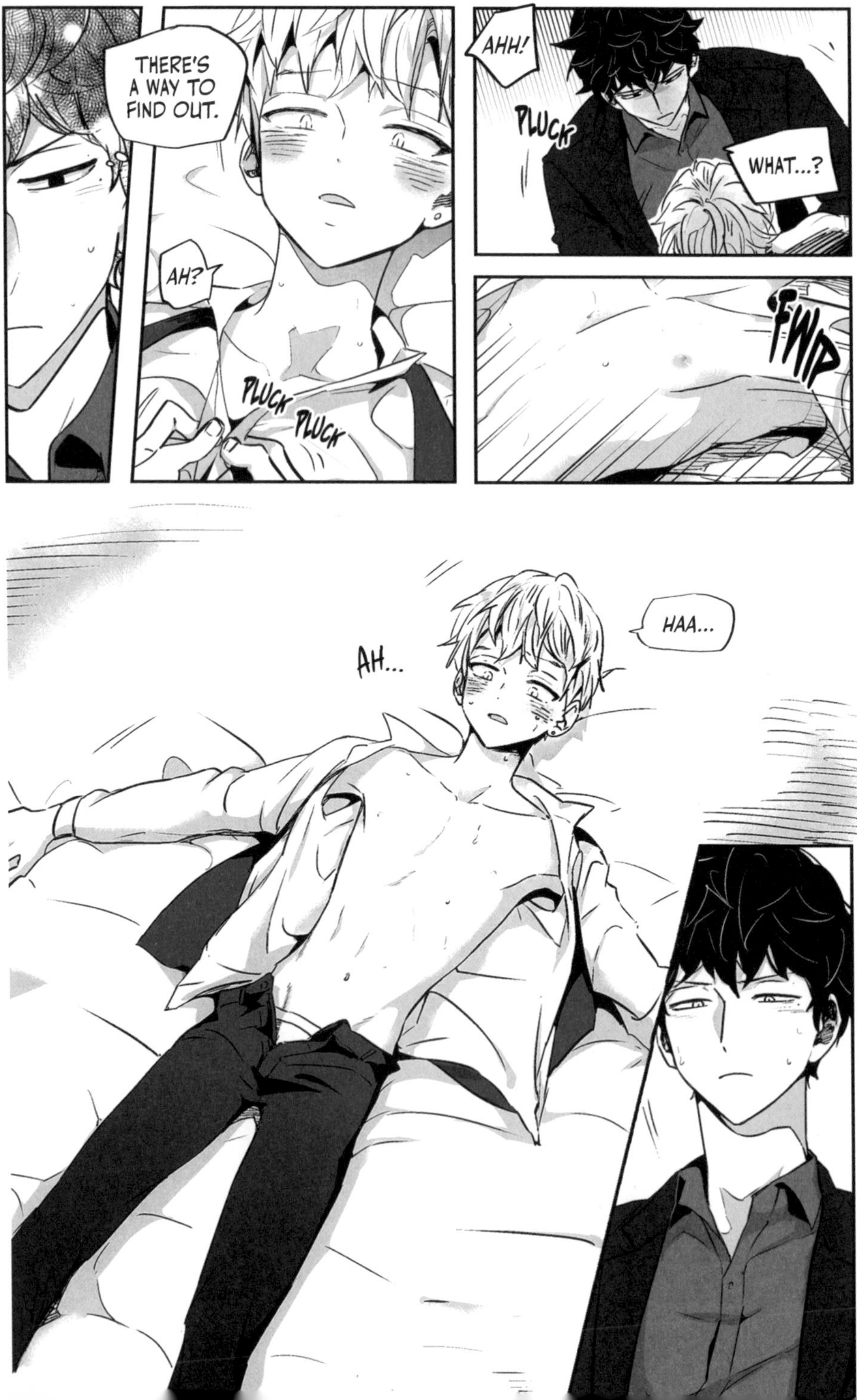
THERE'S A WAY TO FIND OUT.
AH?
PLUCK
PLUCK
AHH!
PLUCK
WHAT...?
FWIP
AH...
HAA...

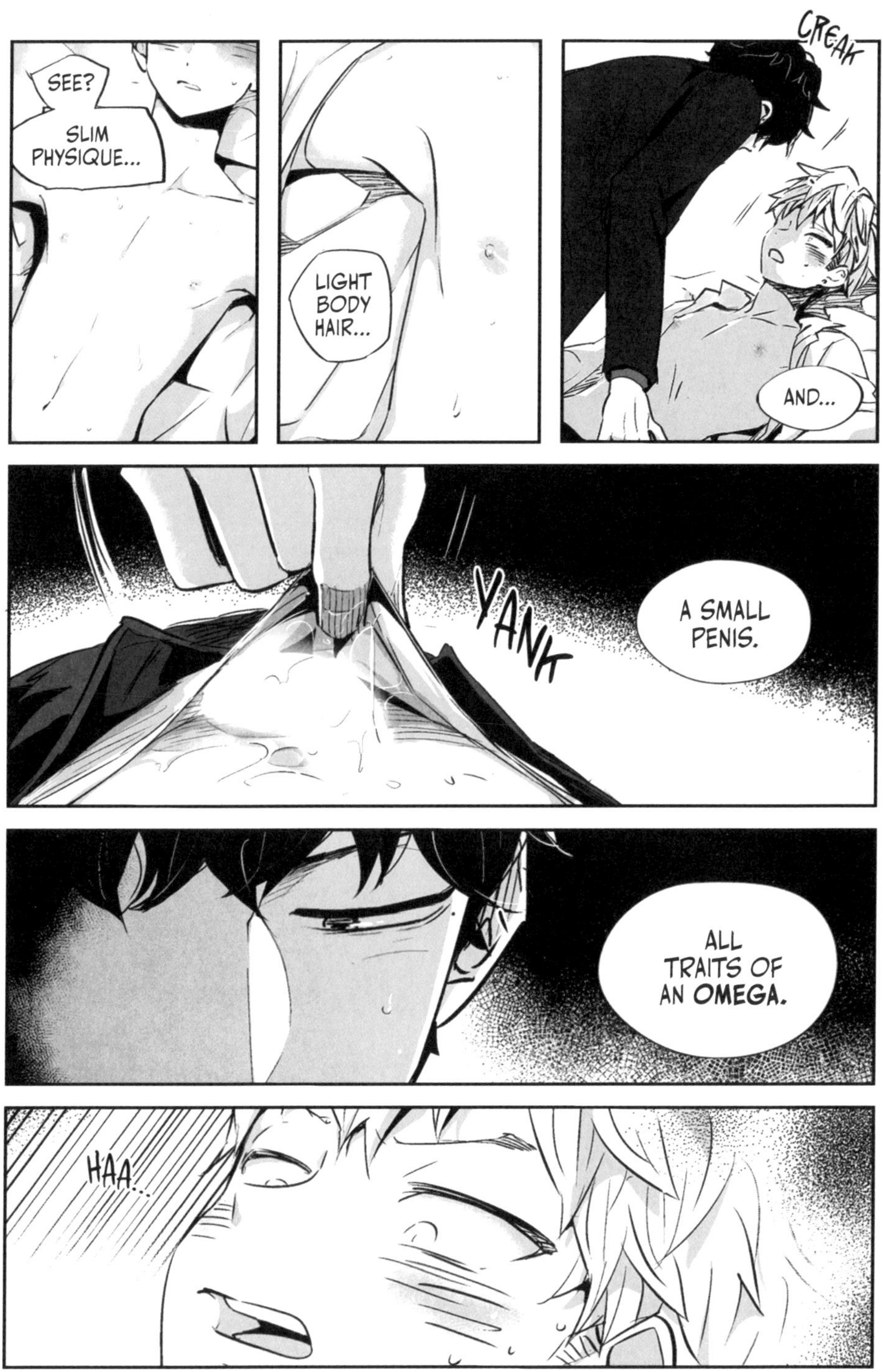
SEE?
SLIM PHYSIQUE...
LIGHT BODY HAIR...
CREAK
AND...
YANK
A SMALL PENIS.
ALL TRAITS OF AN OMEGA.
HAA...

WHAT ARE YOU DOING, YOU *PERV*?!

TH-THAT'S NOT ALWAYS THE CASE!

THE TEST SHOWED THAT I'M AN *ALPHA!*

THEN THE TEST RESULT WAS WRONG.

GRAB

YANK

AH!

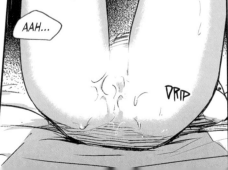

AAH...

DRIP

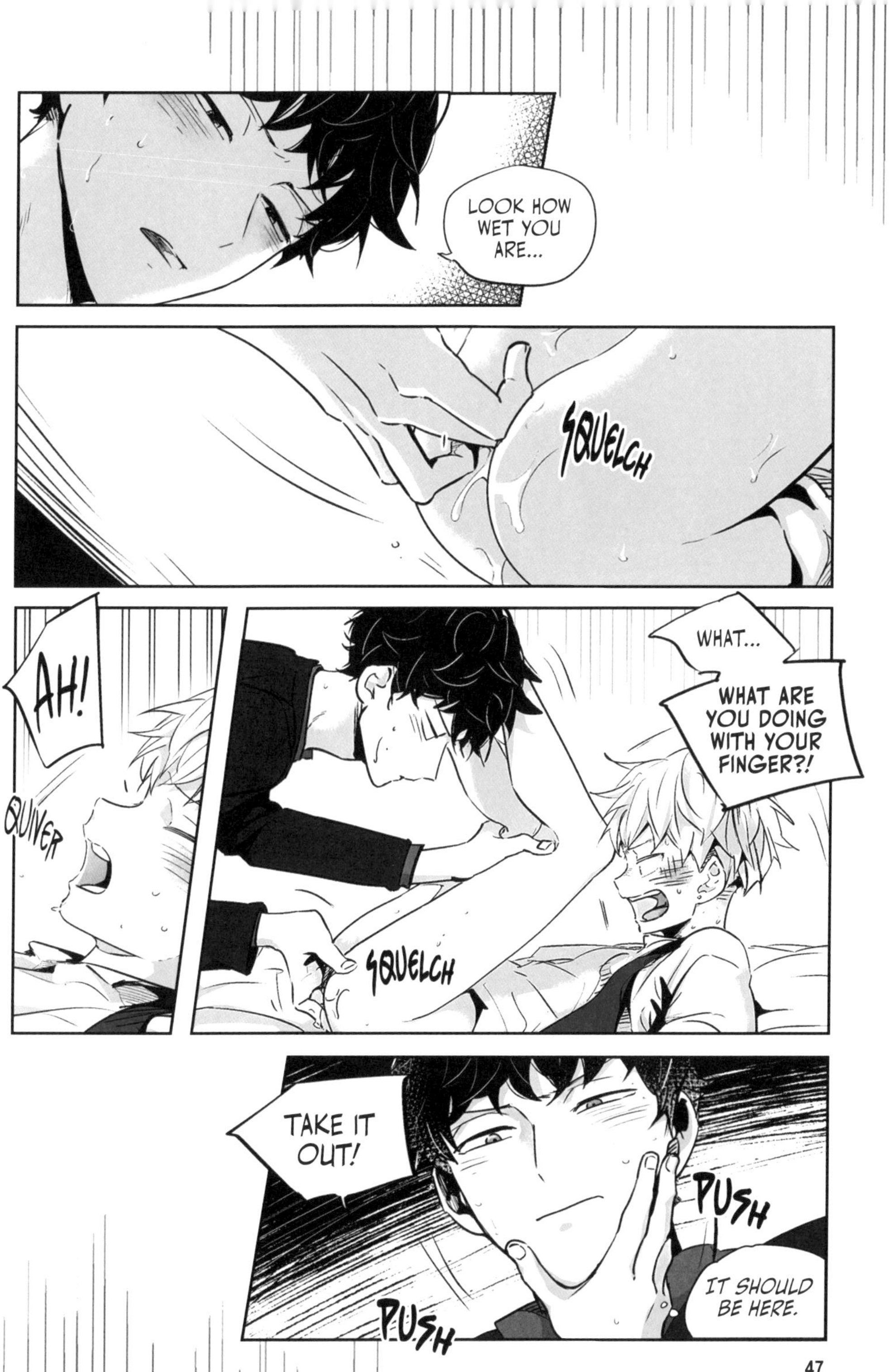
LOOK HOW WET YOU ARE...
SQUELCH
AH!
QUIVER
WHAT...
WHAT ARE YOU DOING WITH YOUR FINGER?!
SQUELCH
TAKE IT OUT!
PUSH
IT SHOULD BE HERE.
PUSH

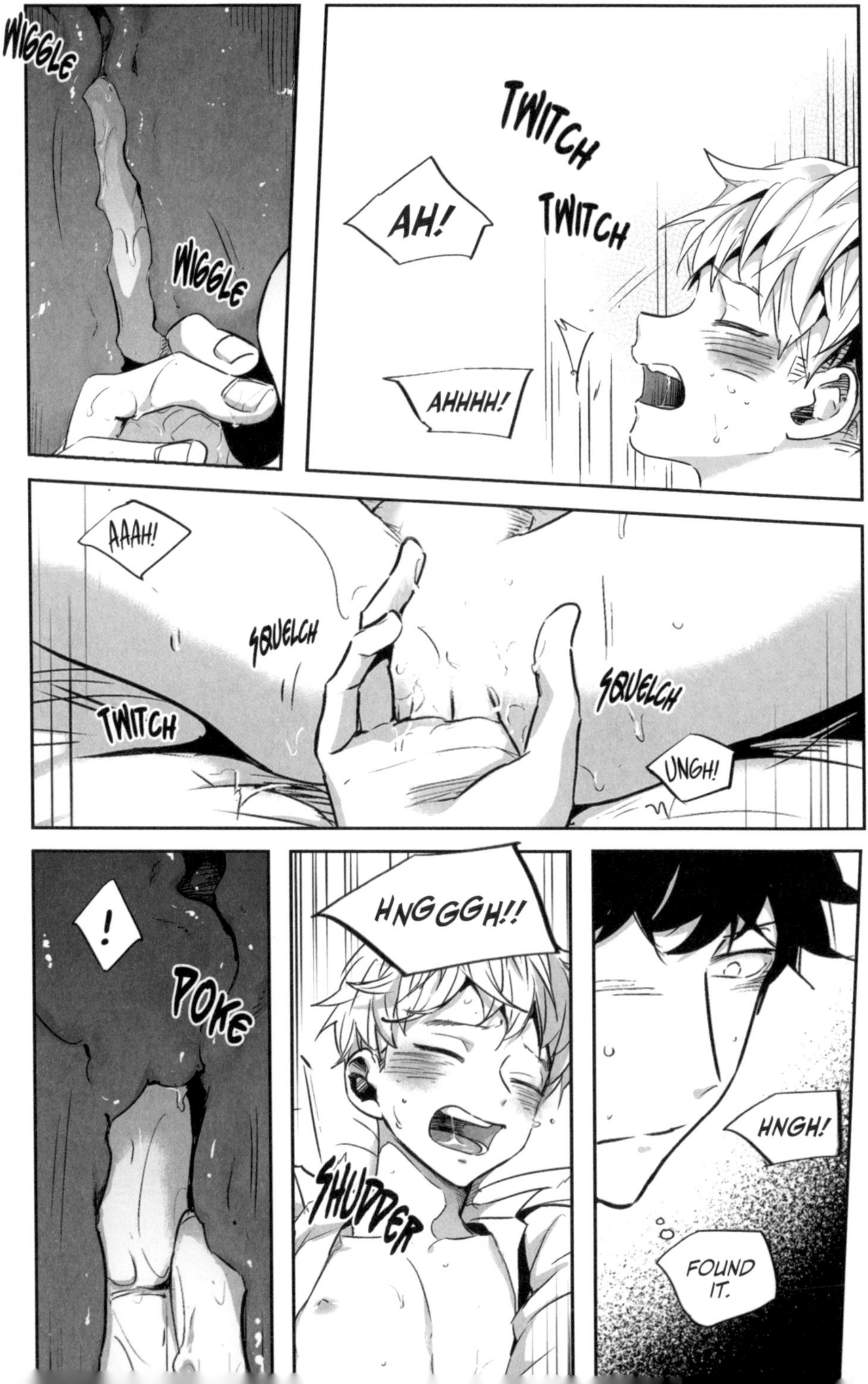
WIGGLE
WIGGLE
TWITCH
AH!
TWITCH
AHHHH!
AAAH!
SQUELCH
TWITCH
SQUELCH
UNGH!
!
POKE
HNGGGH!!
SHUDDER
HNGH!
FOUND IT.

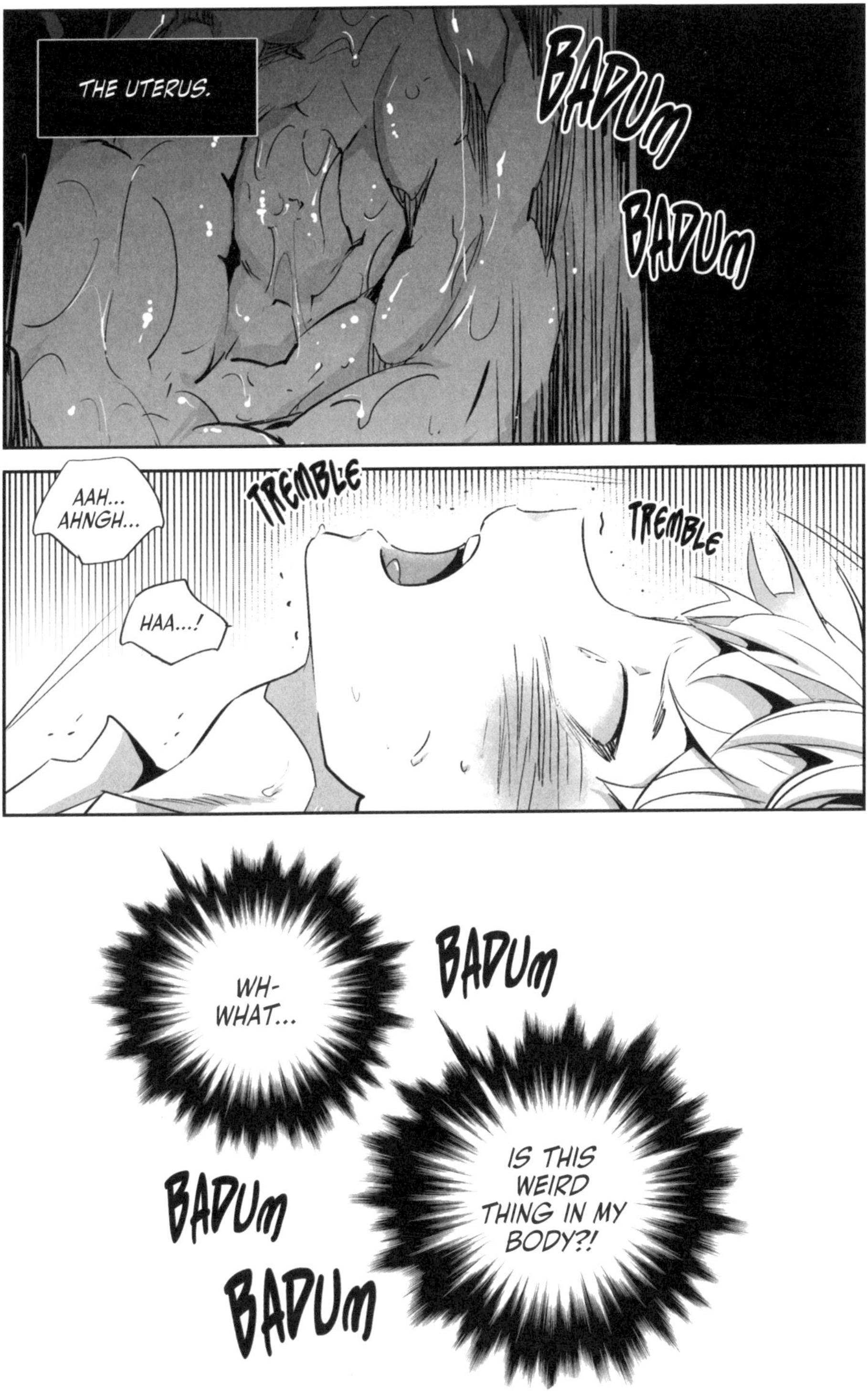
THE UTERUS.
BADUM
BADUM
AAH... AHNGH...
TREMBLE
HAA...!
TREMBLE
WH- WHAT...
BADUM
BADUM
BADUM
IS THIS WEIRD THING IN MY BODY?!

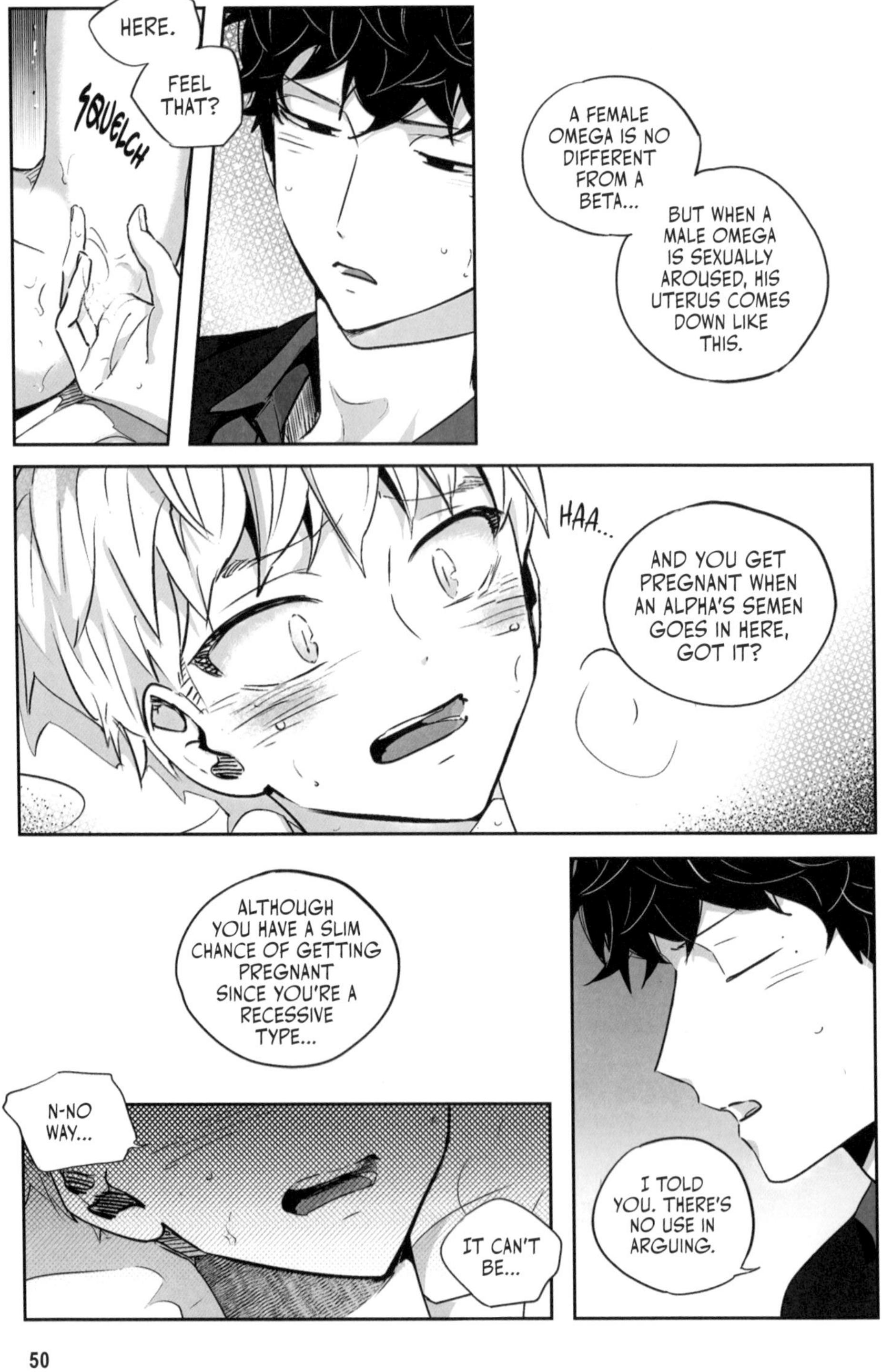
HERE.
FEEL THAT?
SQUELCH
A FEMALE OMEGA IS NO DIFFERENT FROM A BETA...
BUT WHEN A MALE OMEGA IS SEXUALLY AROUSED, HIS UTERUS COMES DOWN LIKE THIS.
HAA...
AND YOU GET PREGNANT WHEN AN ALPHA'S SEMEN GOES IN HERE, GOT IT?
ALTHOUGH YOU HAVE A SLIM CHANCE OF GETTING PREGNANT SINCE YOU'RE A RECESSIVE TYPE...
N-NO WAY...
IT CAN'T BE...
I TOLD YOU. THERE'S NO USE IN ARGUING.

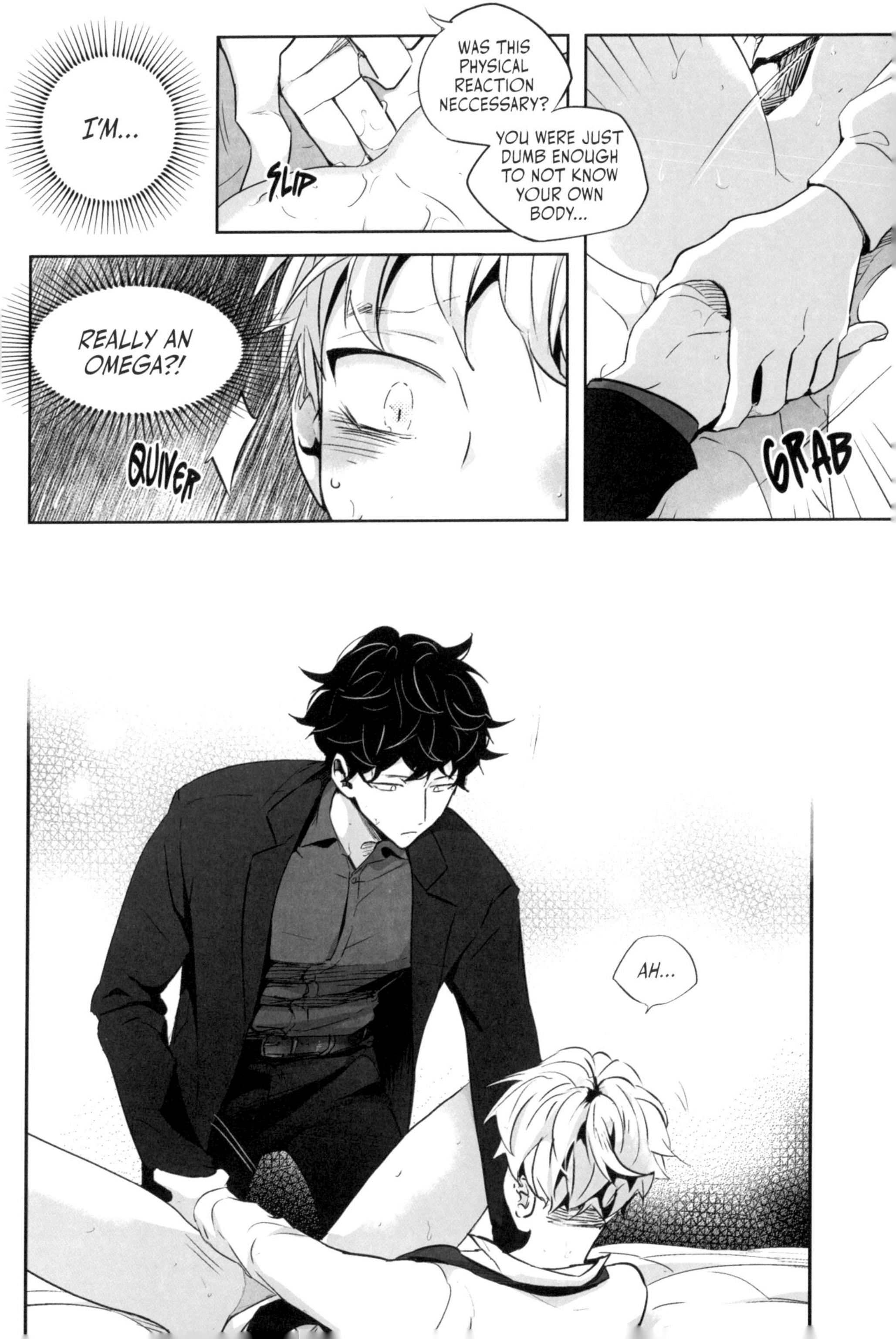
I'M...
WAS THIS PHYSICAL REACTION NECCESSARY?
YOU WERE JUST DUMB ENOUGH TO NOT KNOW YOUR OWN BODY...
SLIP
REALLY AN OMEGA?!
QUIVER
GRAB
AH...

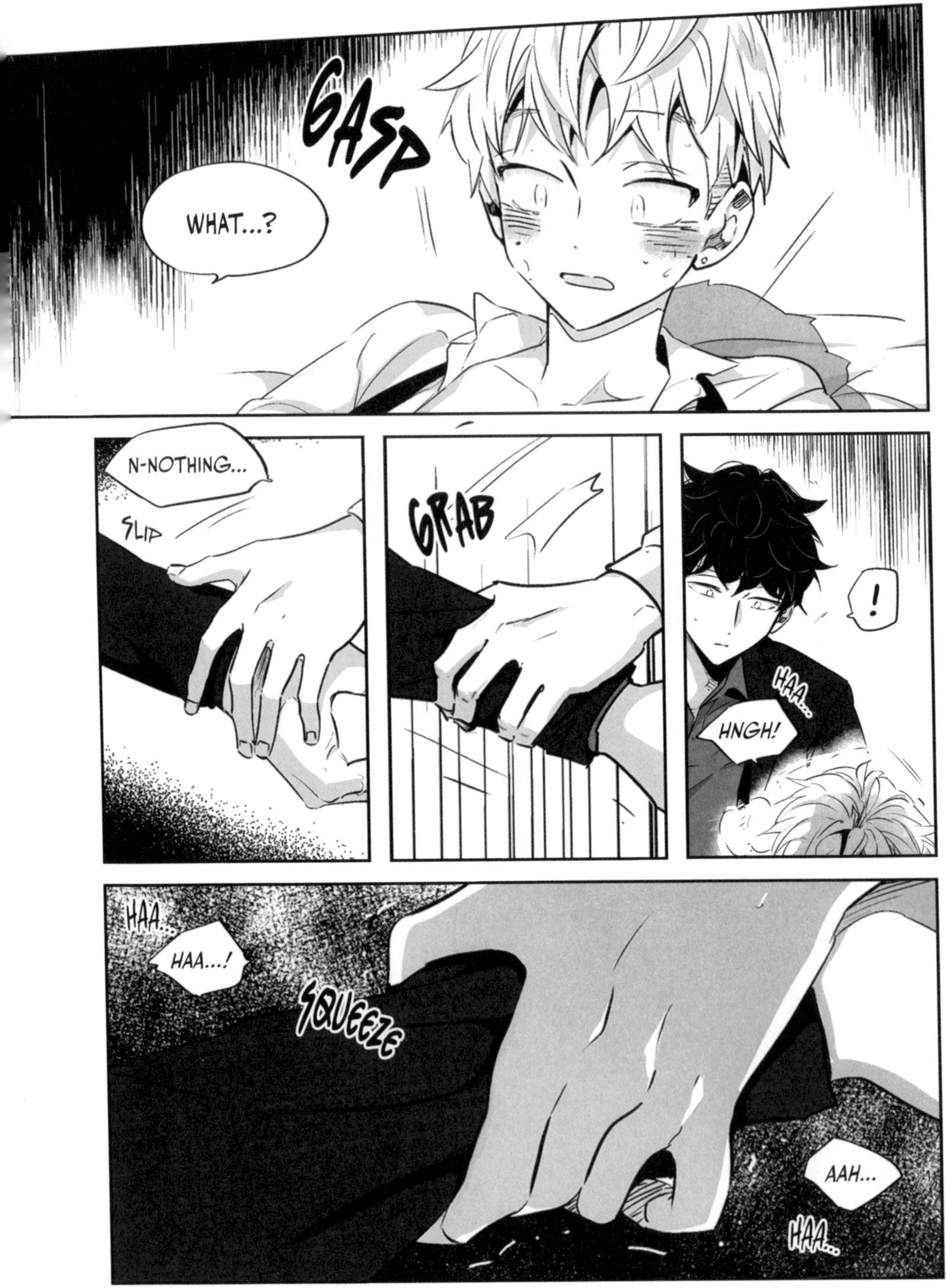
GASP
WHAT...?
N-NOTHING...
SLIP
GRAB
!
HAA...
HNGH!
HAA...
HAA...!
SQUEEZE
AAH...
HAA...

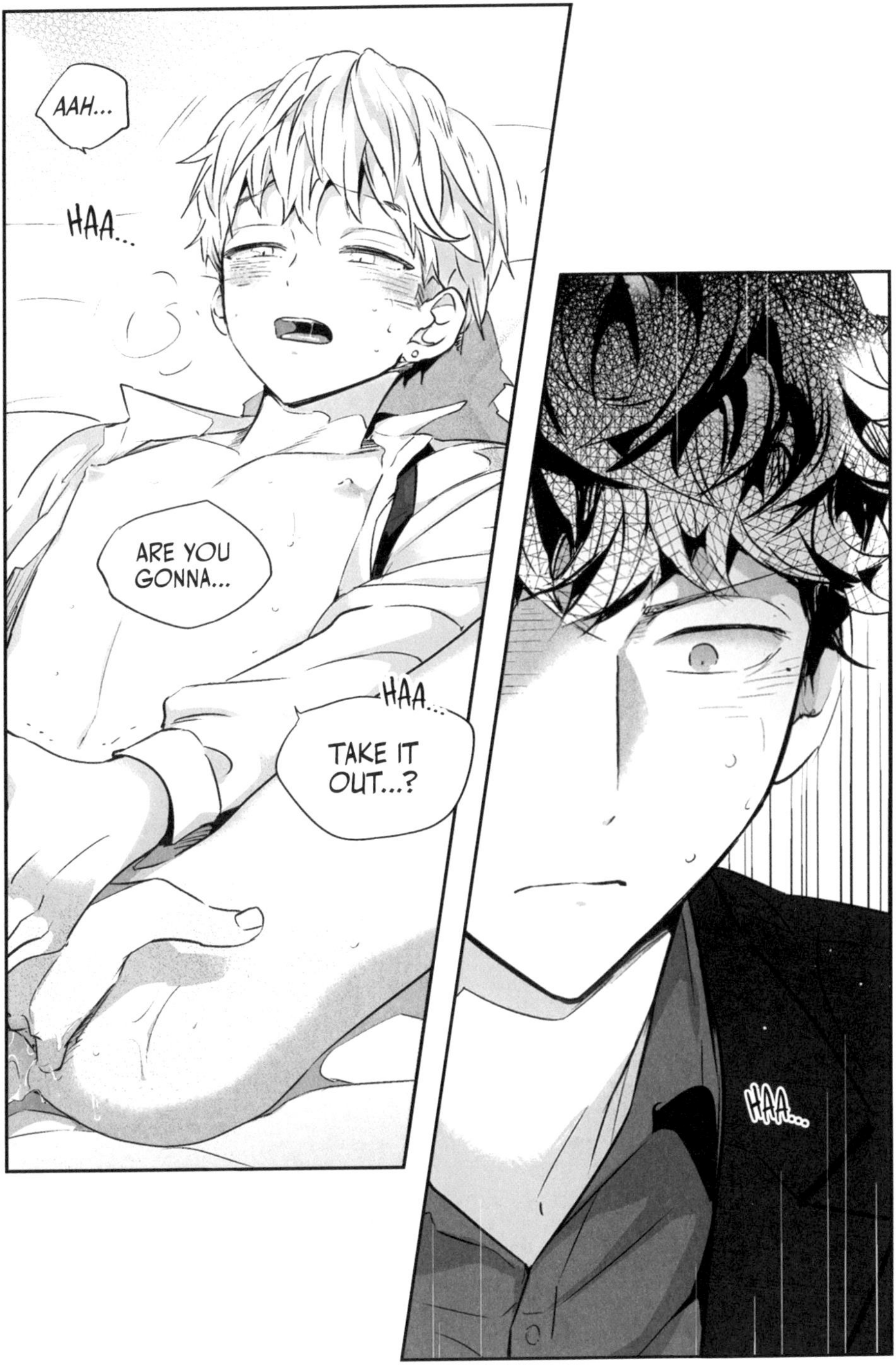
AAH...
HAA...
ARE YOU GONNA...
HAA...
TAKE IT OUT...?
HAA...

Love is
an Illusion!

Chapter 3

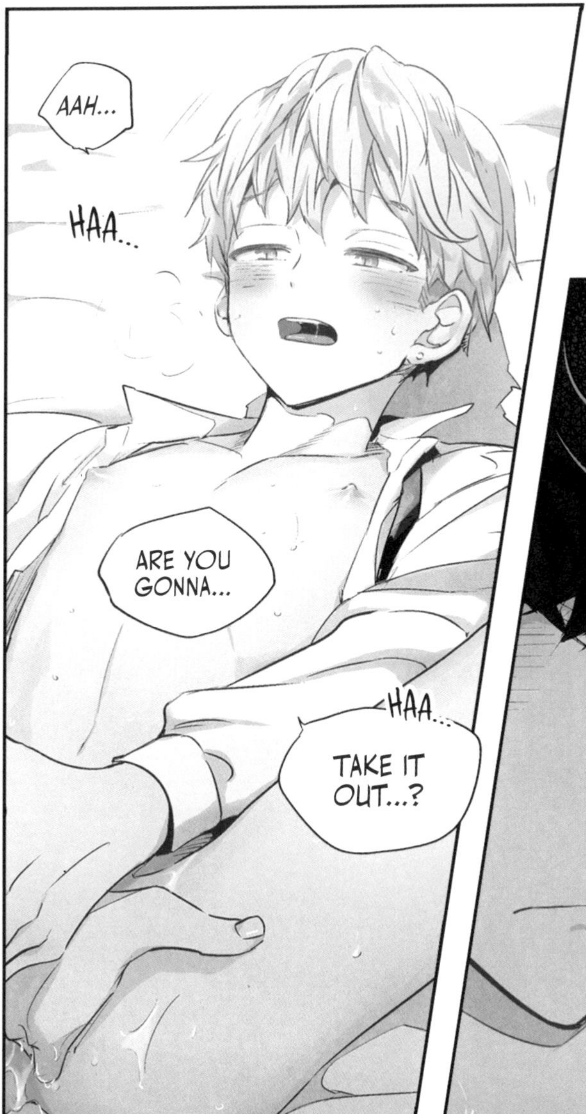
AAH...
HAA...
ARE YOU GONNA...
HAA...
TAKE IT OUT...?

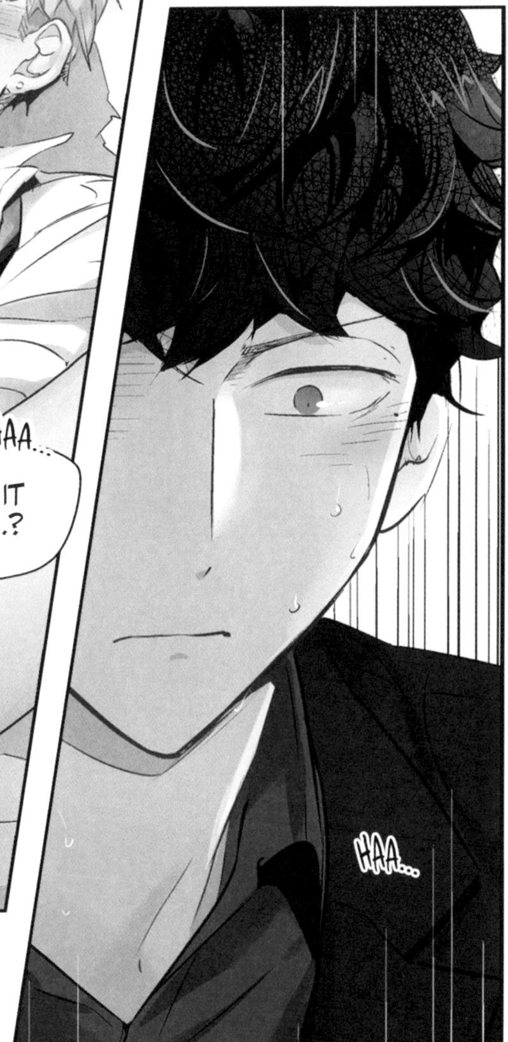
HAA...

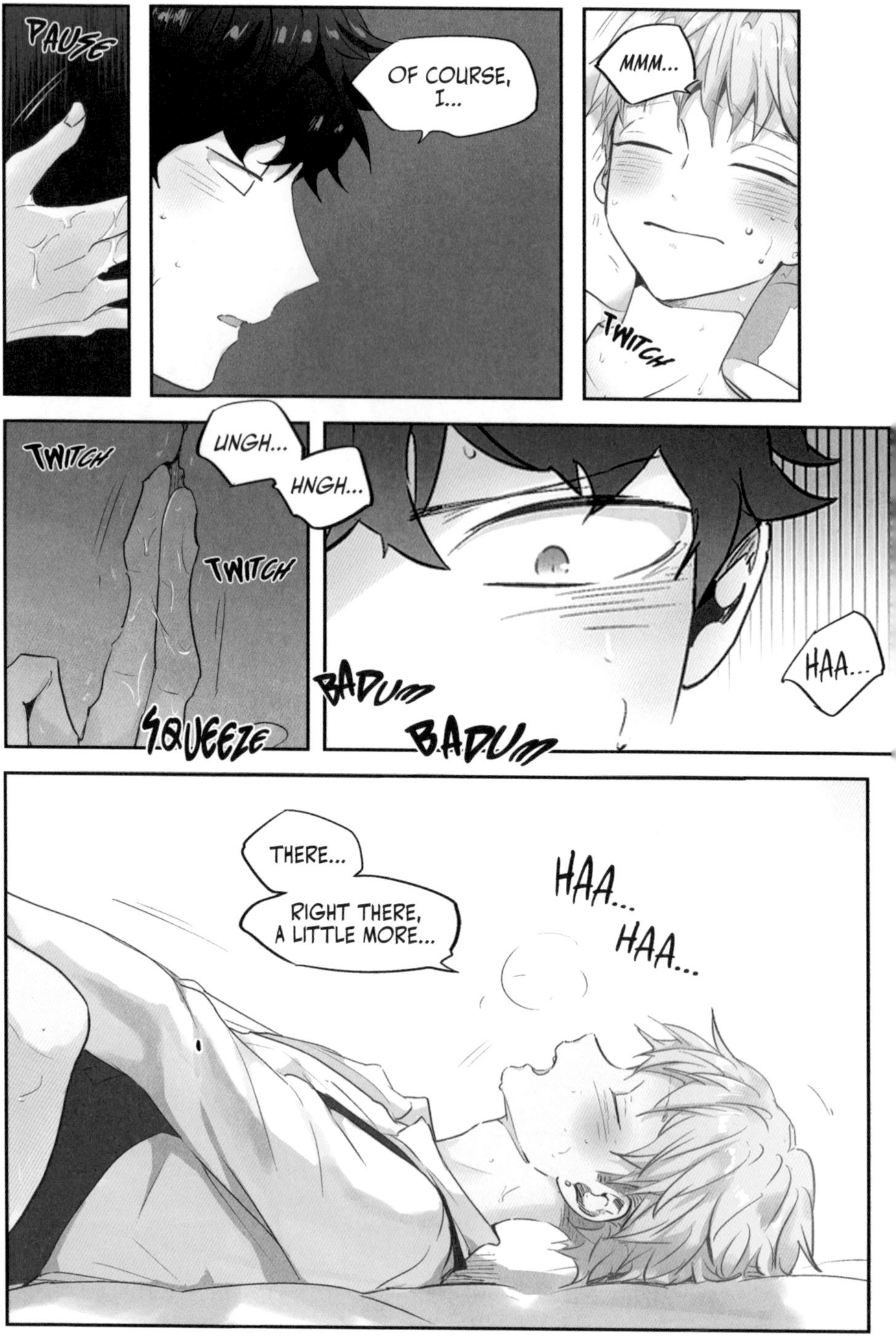
PAUSE
OF COURSE, I...
MMM...
TWITCH
TWITCH
UNGH...
HNGH...
TWITCH
SQUEEZE
BADUM
BADUM
HAA...
THERE...
RIGHT THERE, A LITTLE MORE...
HAA...
HAA...

HAA...

AH...

IS THE MEDICATION...

NOT WORKING FOR HIM?

HAA!

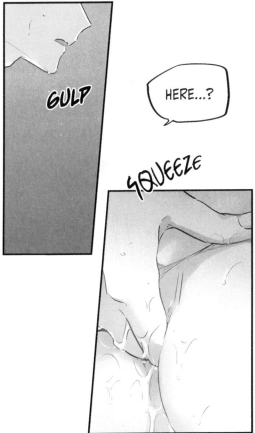

GULP

HERE...?

SQUEEZE

FLINCH

AHNGH!

SQUELCH

SQUELCH

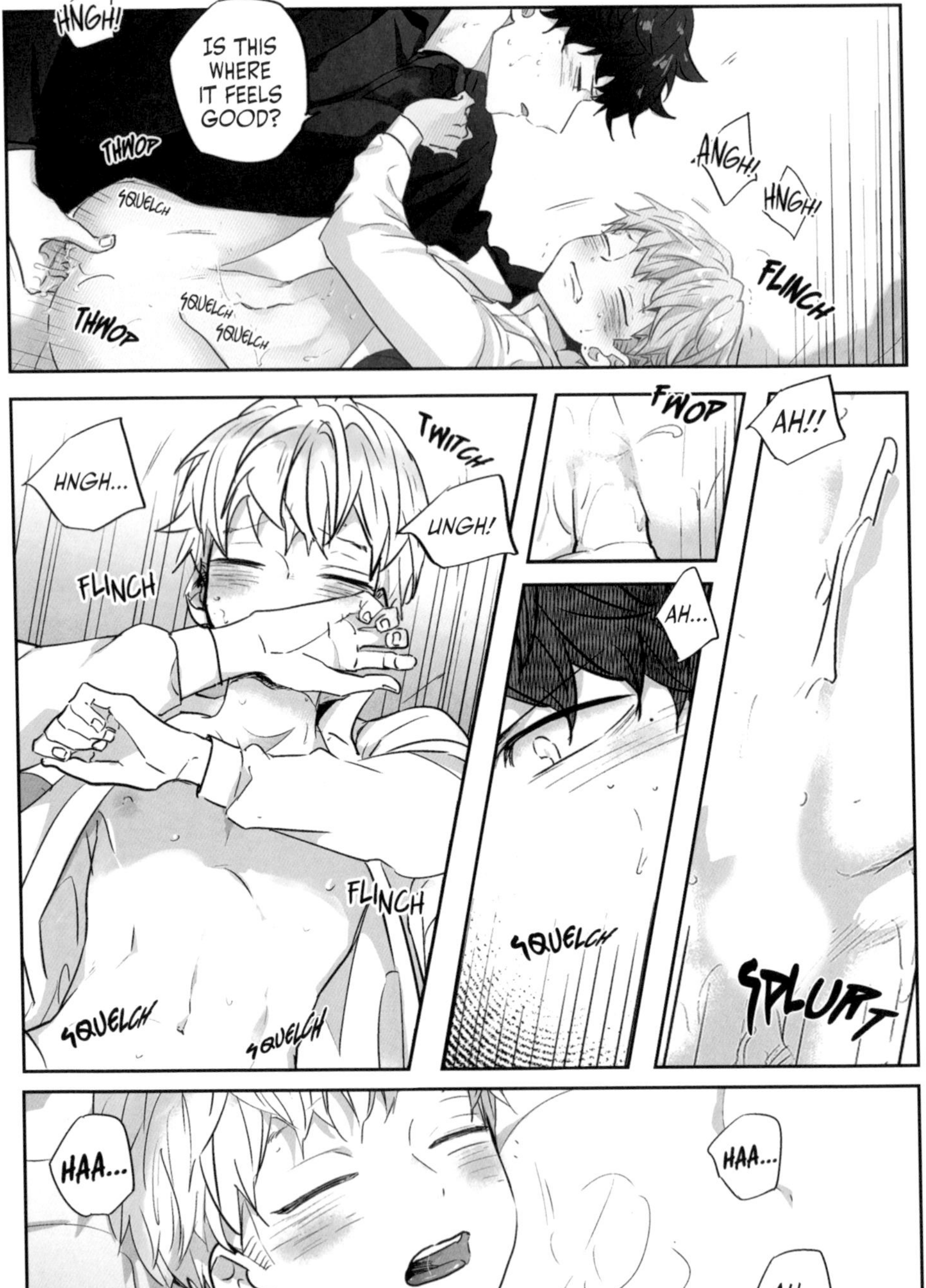
HNGH!
IS THIS WHERE IT FEELS GOOD?
THWOP
SQUELCH
THWOP
SQUELCH
SQUELCH
ANGH!
HNGH!
FLINCH
HNGH...
TWITCH
UNGH!
FLINCH
FLINCH
SQUELCH
SQUELCH
FWOP
AH...
SQUELCH
AH!!
SPLURT
HAA...
HAA...
AH...

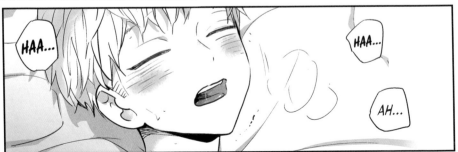

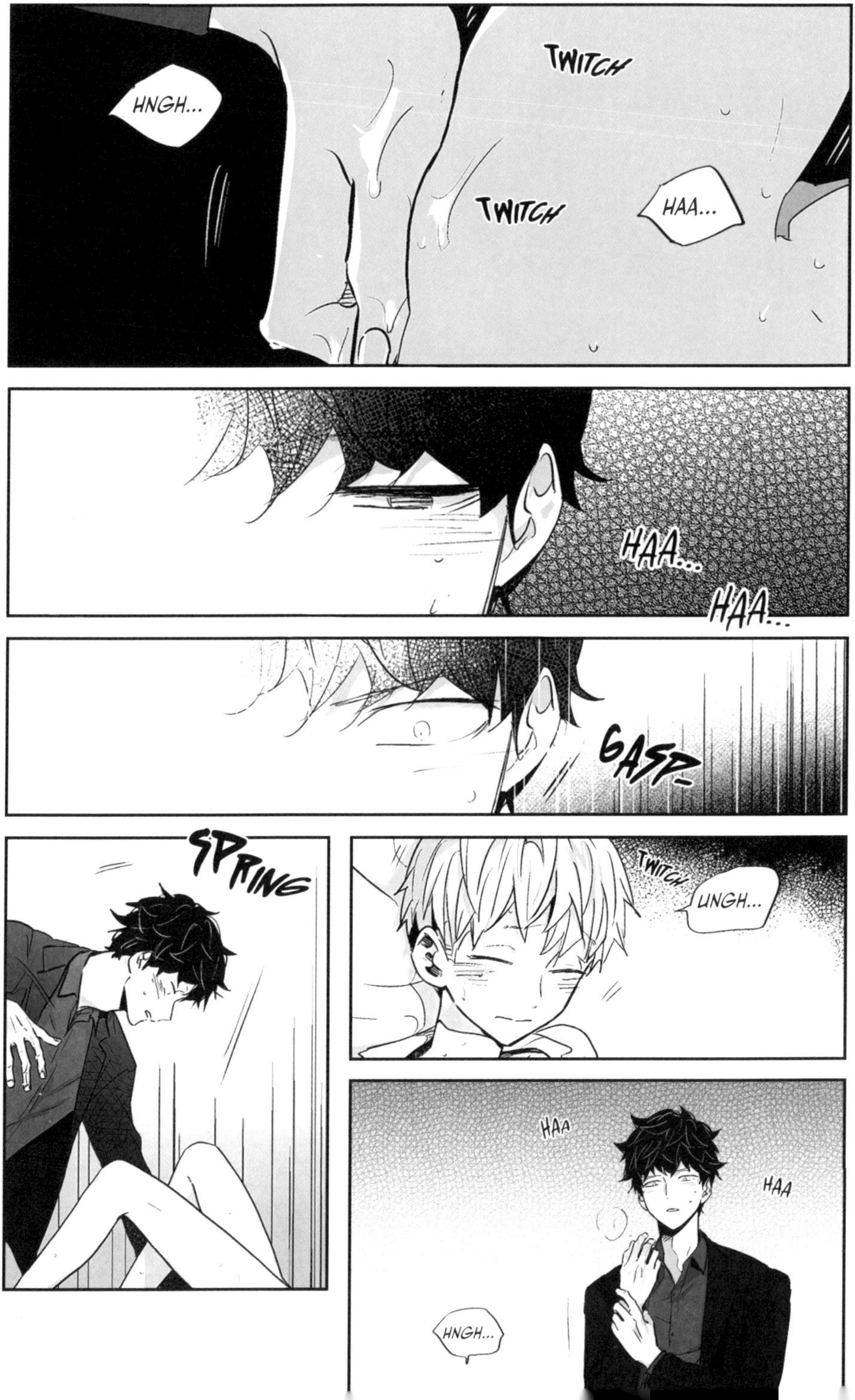
HNGH...
TWITCH
TWITCH
HAA...
HAA...
HAA...
GASP-
SPRING
TWITCH
UNGH...
HAA
HAA
HNGH...

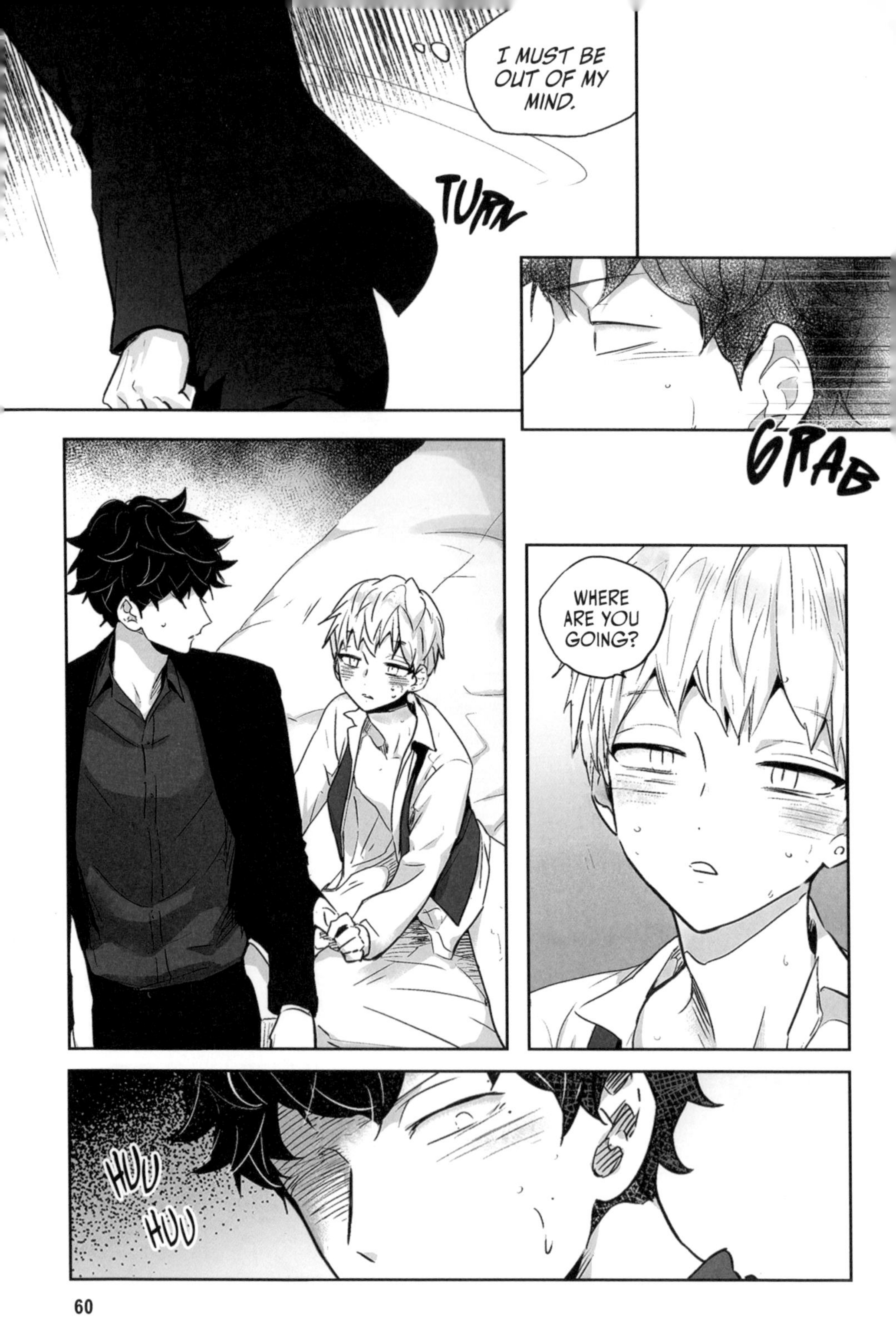
I MUST BE OUT OF MY MIND.
TURN
GRAB
WHERE ARE YOU GOING?
HUU HUU

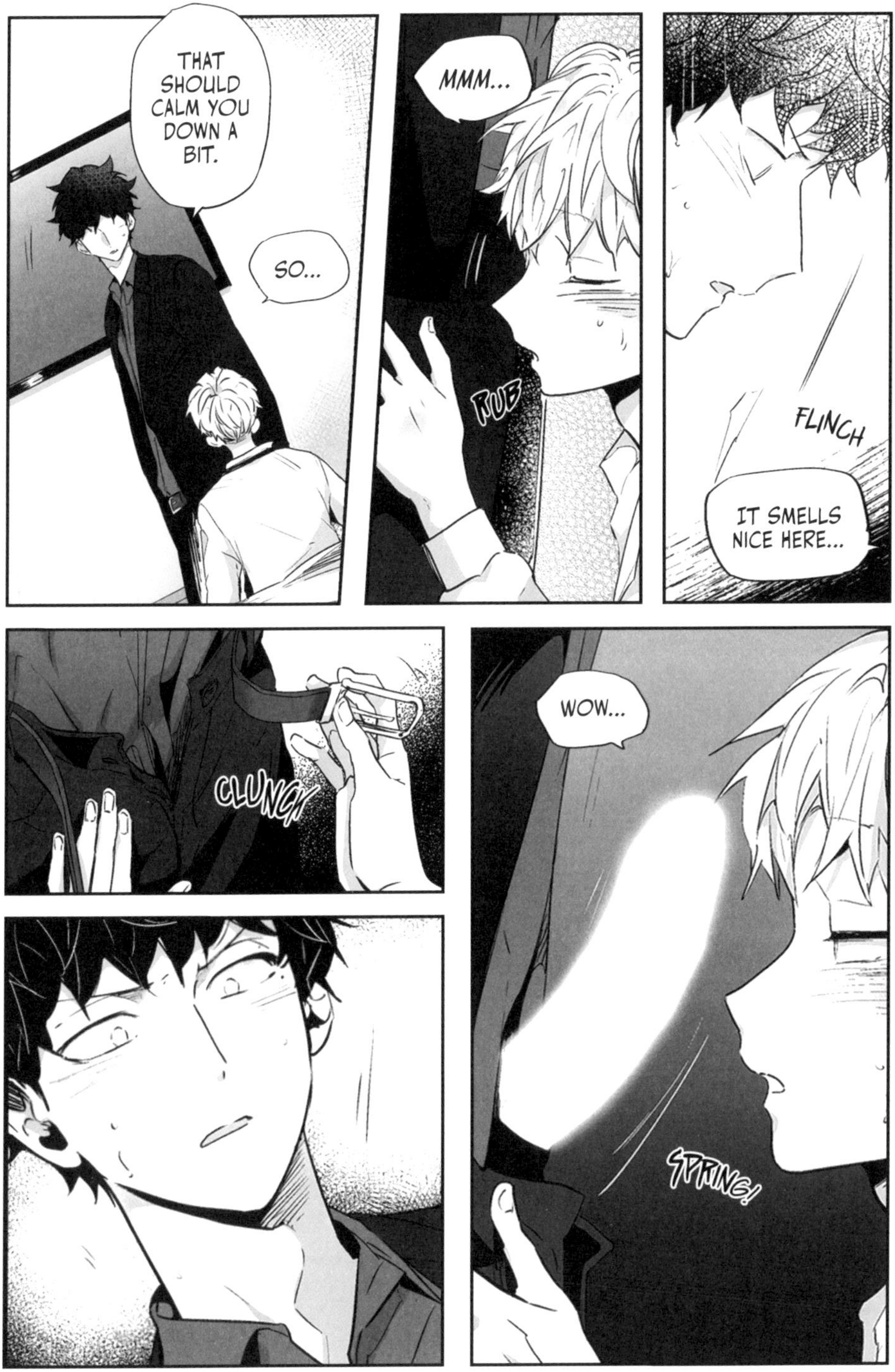
THAT SHOULD CALM YOU DOWN A BIT.
SO...
MMM...
RUB
FLINCH
IT SMELLS NICE HERE...
CLUNCK
WOW...
SPRING!

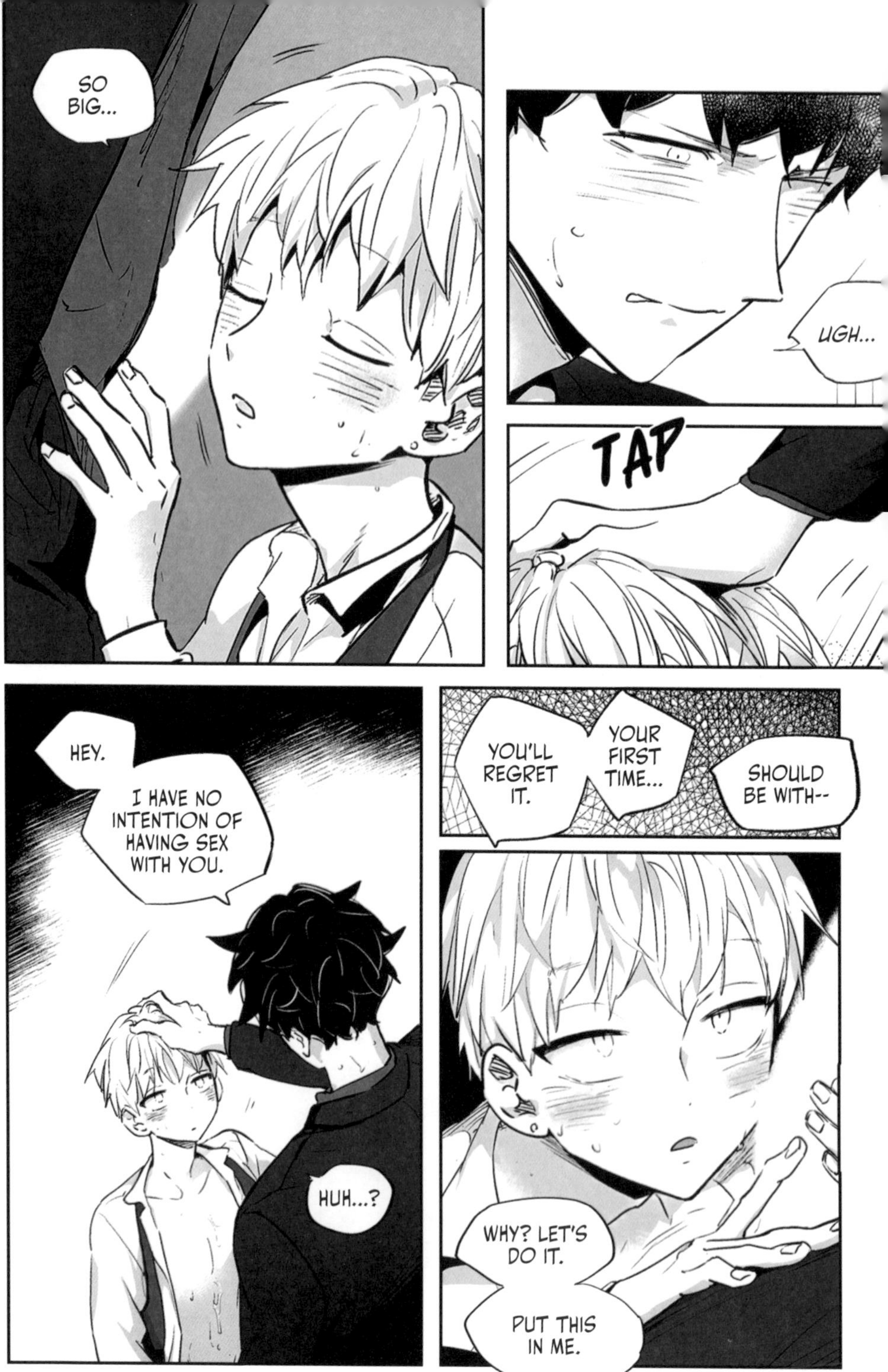
SO BIG...
UGH...
TAP
HEY.
I HAVE NO INTENTION OF HAVING SEX WITH YOU.
HUH...?
YOU'LL REGRET IT.
YOUR FIRST TIME...
SHOULD BE WITH--
WHY? LET'S DO IT.
PUT THIS IN ME.

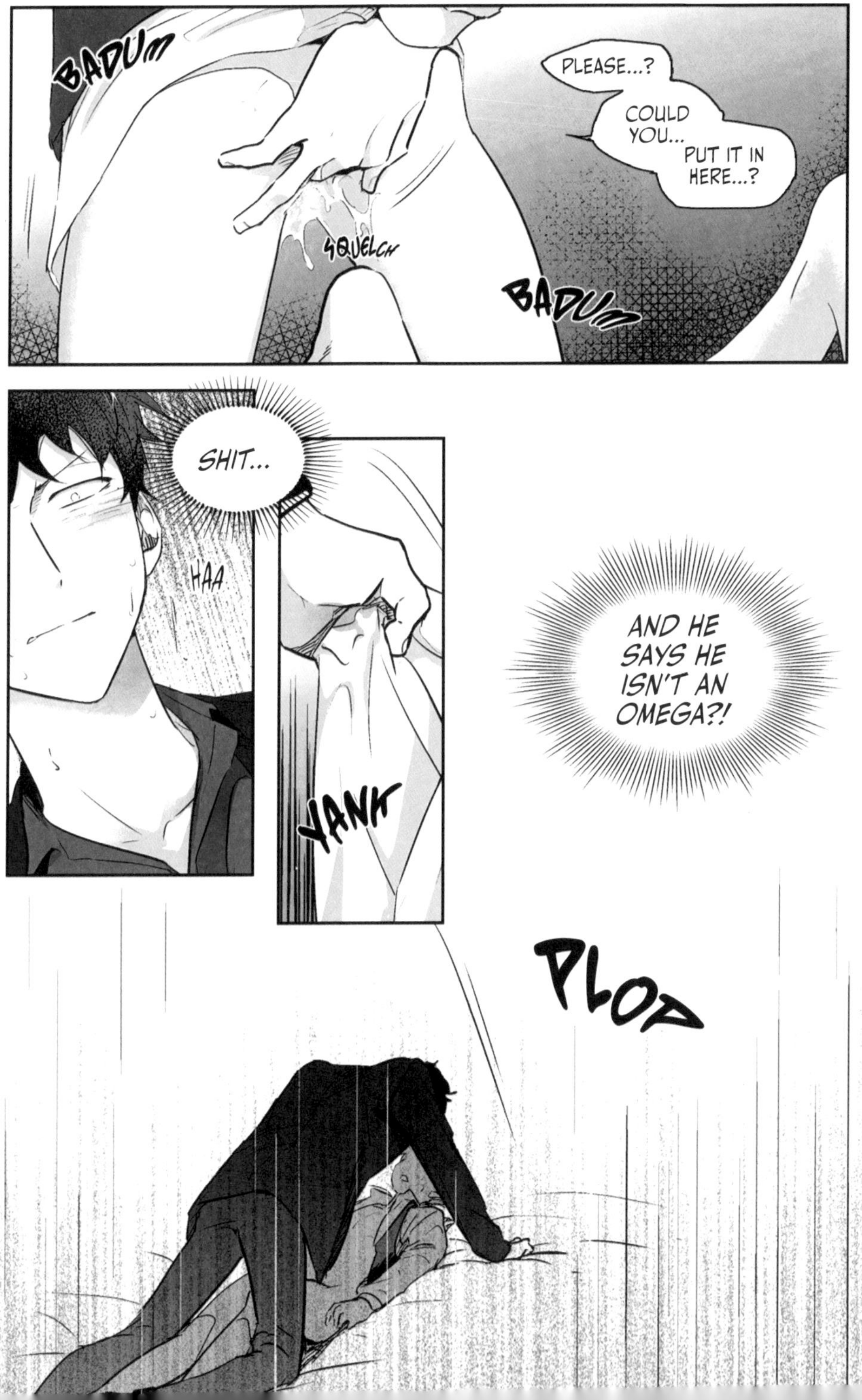
BADUM
PLEASE...?
COULD YOU... PUT IT IN HERE...?
SQUELCH
BADUM
SHIT...
HAA
YANK
AND HE SAYS HE ISN'T AN OMEGA?!
PLOP

PANT

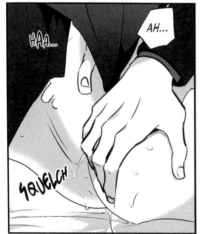

HAA...

AH...

SQUELCH

AAHH!

TWITCH

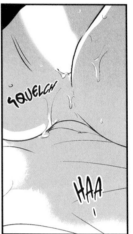

SQUELCH

HAA

AH!

SHIT....!

HUFF

HUFF

HNGH!

KRIK

FWIP

NO....!

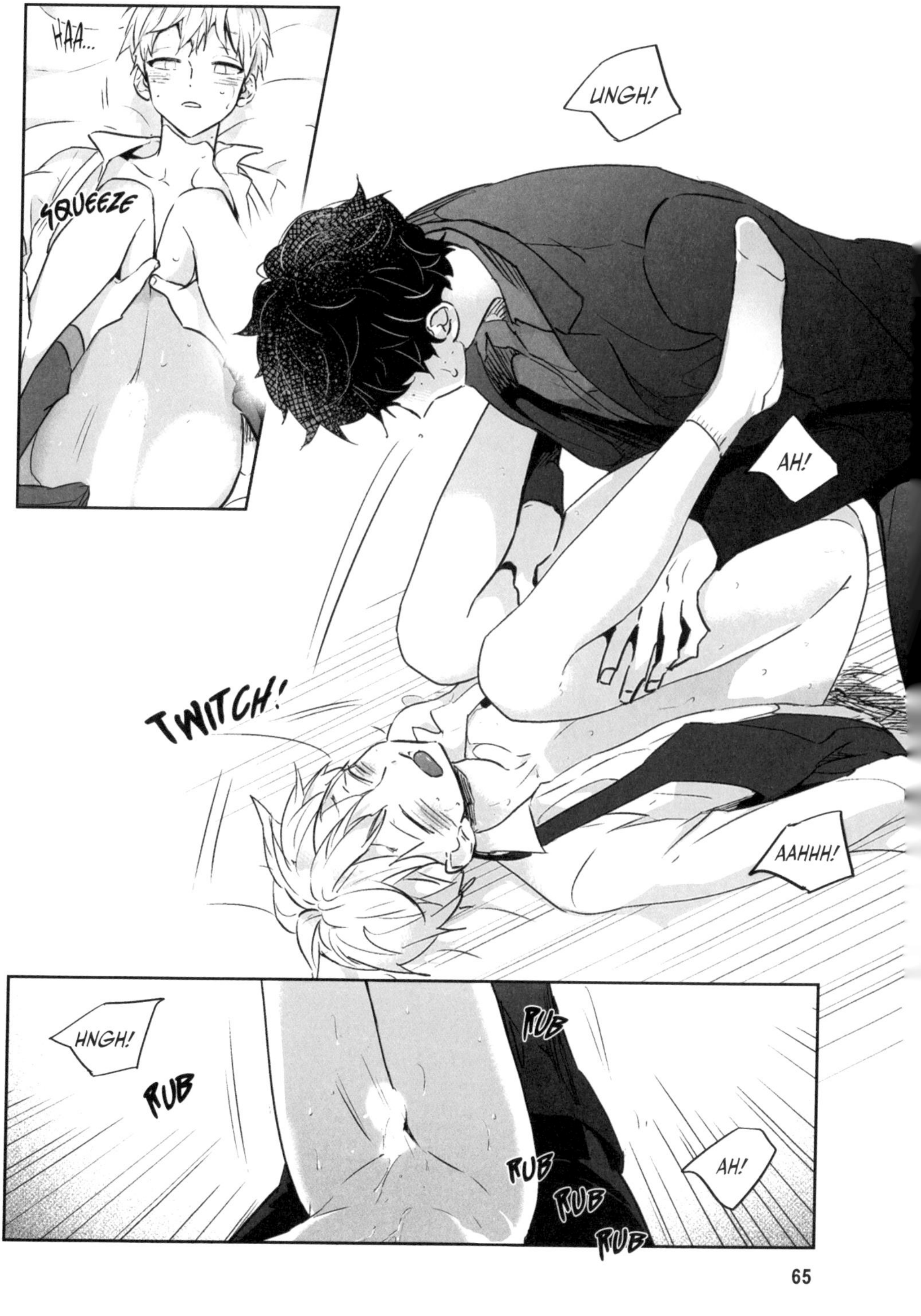
HAA...
SQUEEZE
UNGH!
AH!
TWITCH!
AAHHH!
HNGH!
RUB
RUB
RUB
AH!
RUB
RUB

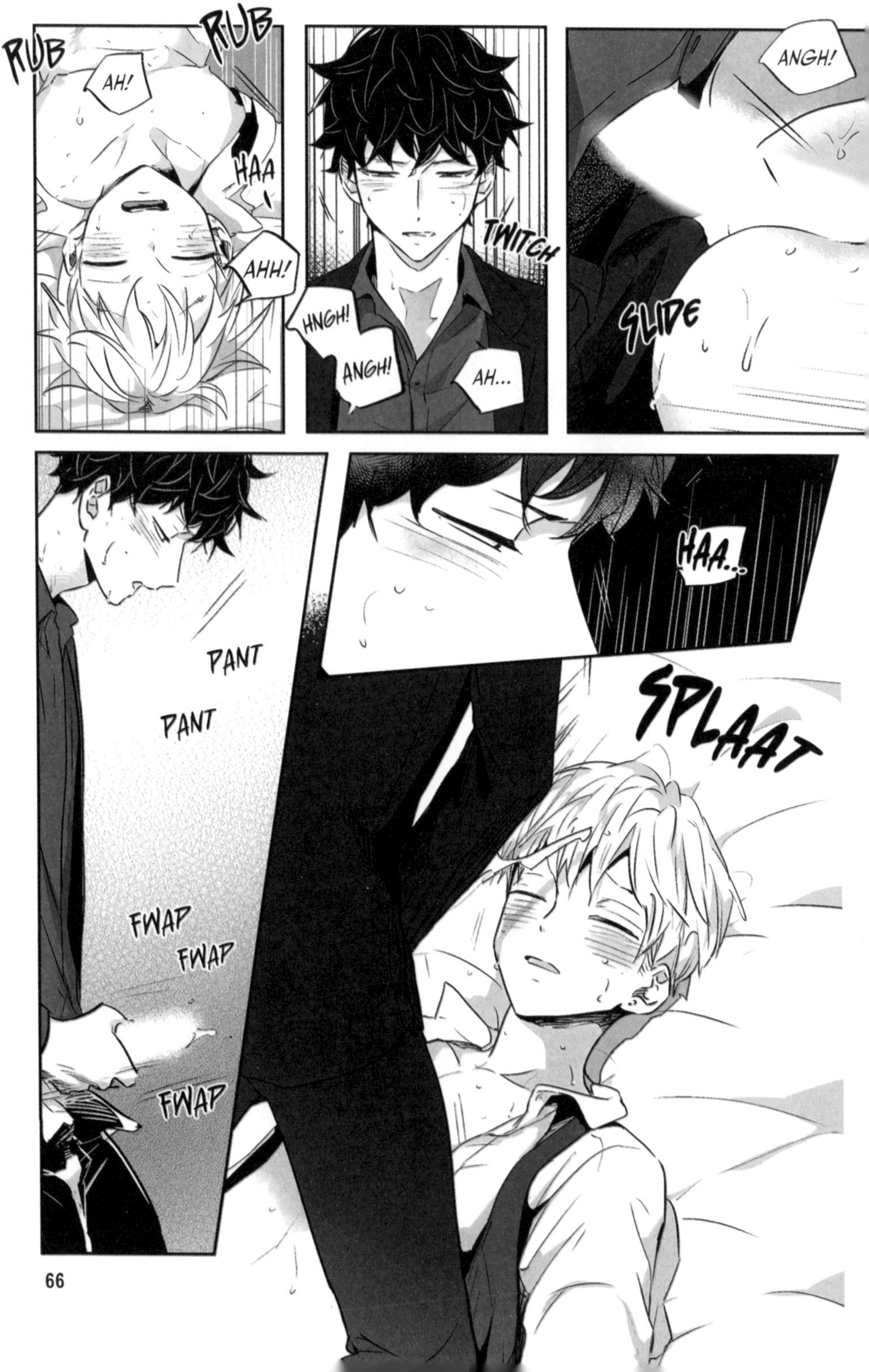
RUB
RUB
AH!
HAA
AHH!
TWITCH
HNGH!
ANGH!
AH...
ANGH!
SLIDE
PANT
PANT
FWAP
FWAP
FWAP
HAA...
SPLAAT

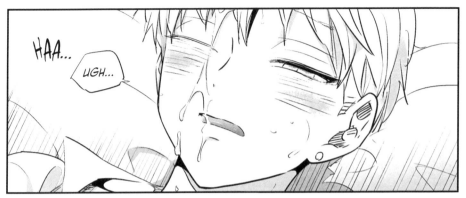

HAA...

UGH...

LICK

PANT

PANT

UNGH...

GASP

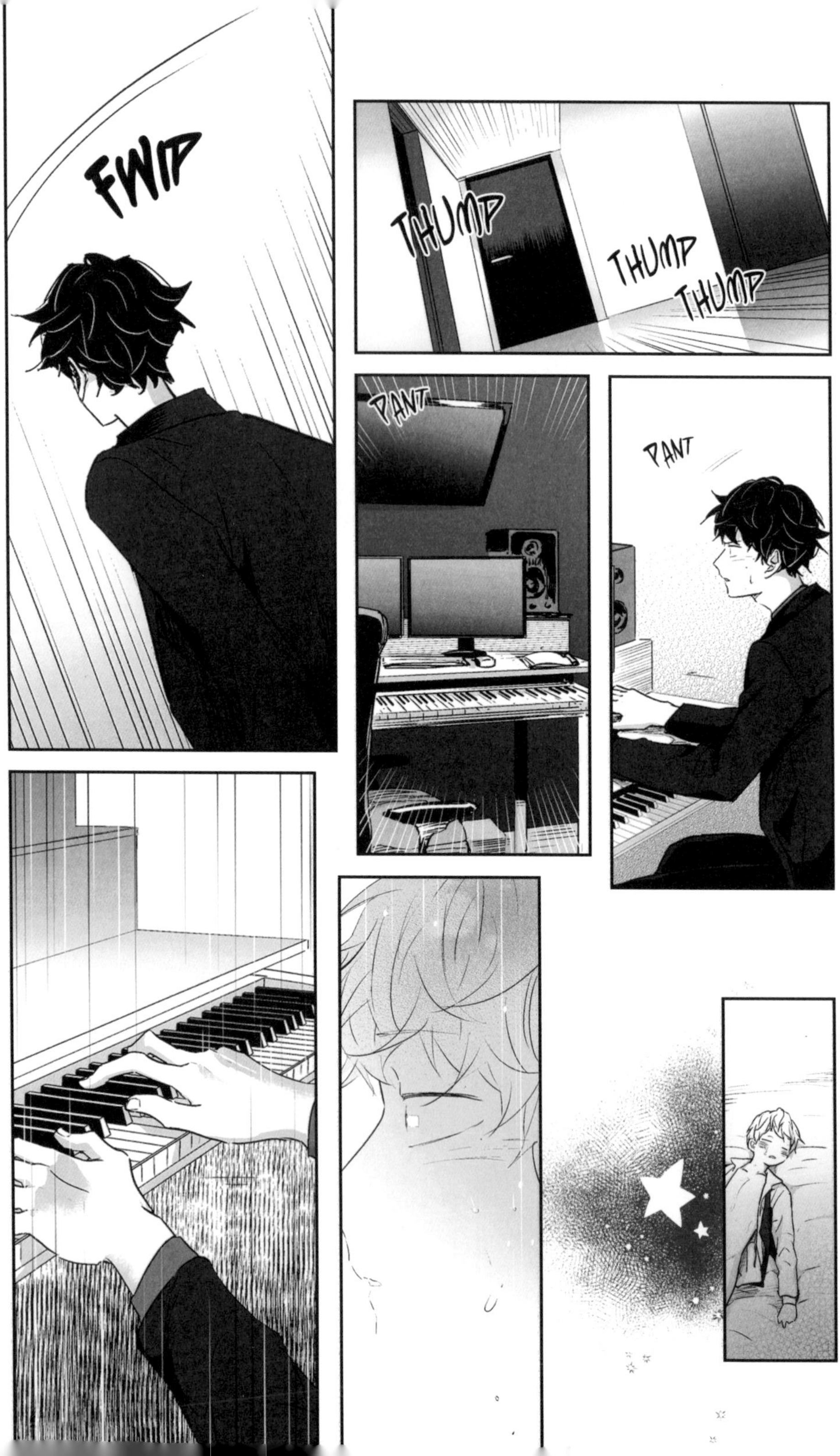
FWIP
THUMP
THUMP
THUMP
PANT
PANT

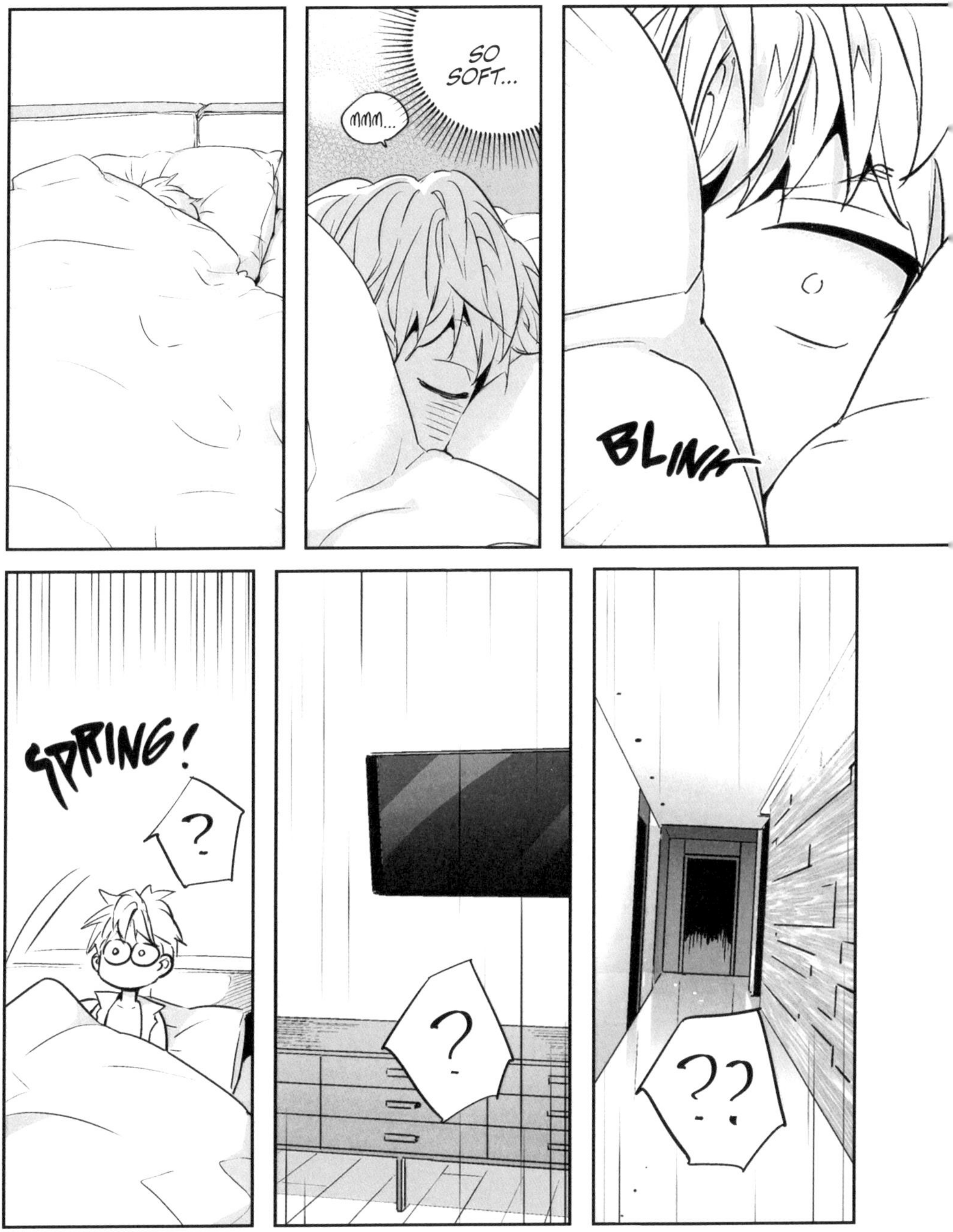
SO SOFT...
mmm...
BLINK
SPRING!
?
?
??

WHERE...

HUH?!

NAKED!

WH-WHAT THE...

FUMBLE

FUMBLE

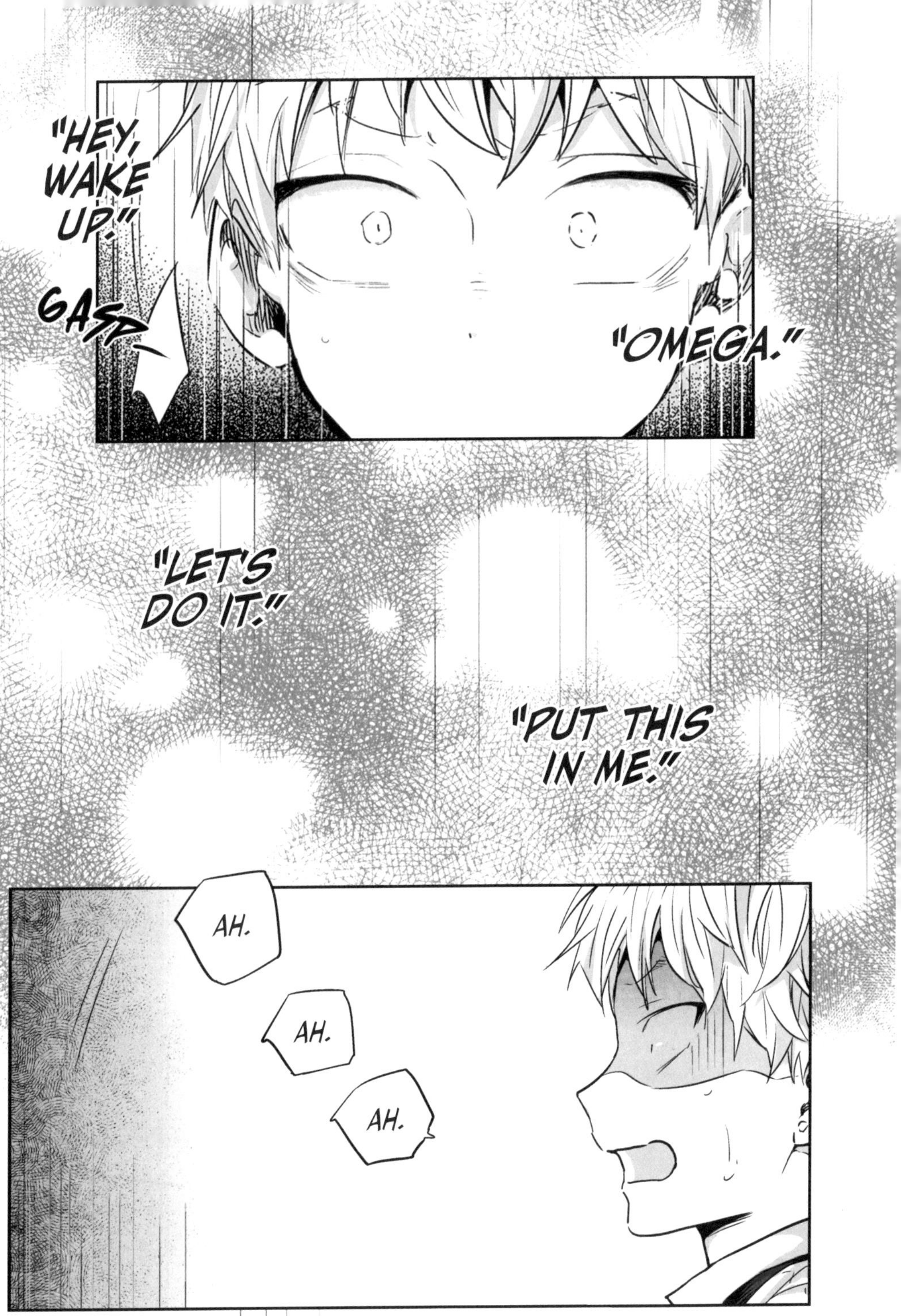
"HEY, WAKE UP."
GASP
"OMEGA."
"LET'S DO IT."
"PUT THIS IN ME."
AH.
AH.
AH.

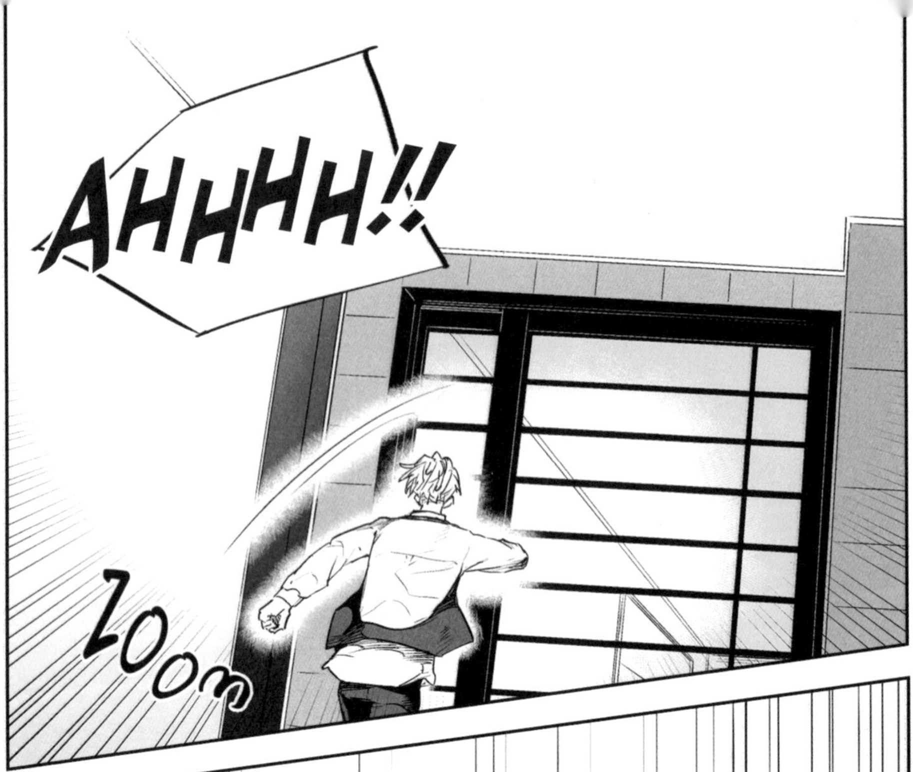
AHHHH!!
ZOOM
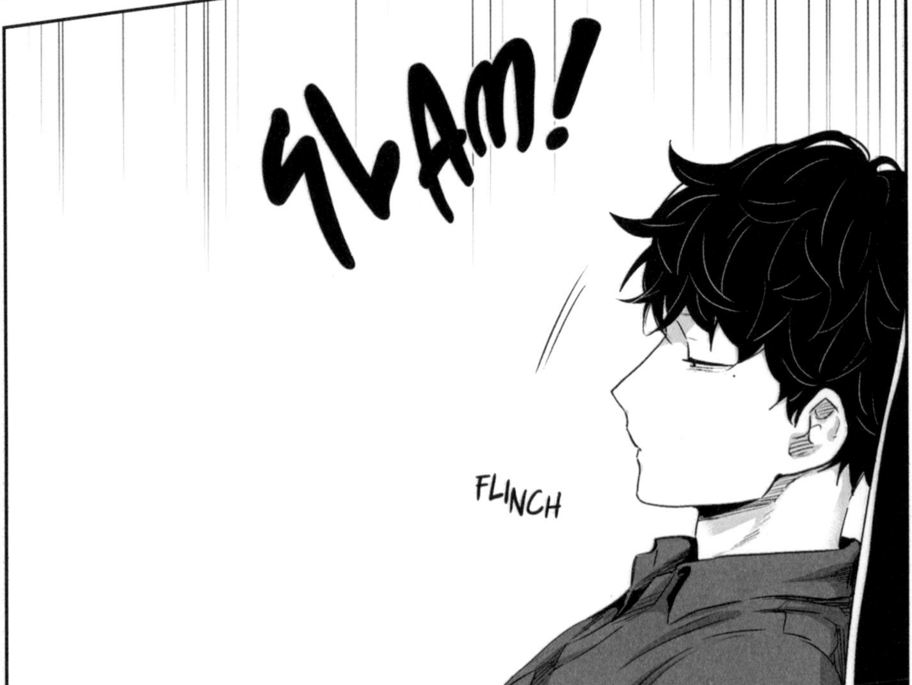
SLAM!
FLINCH

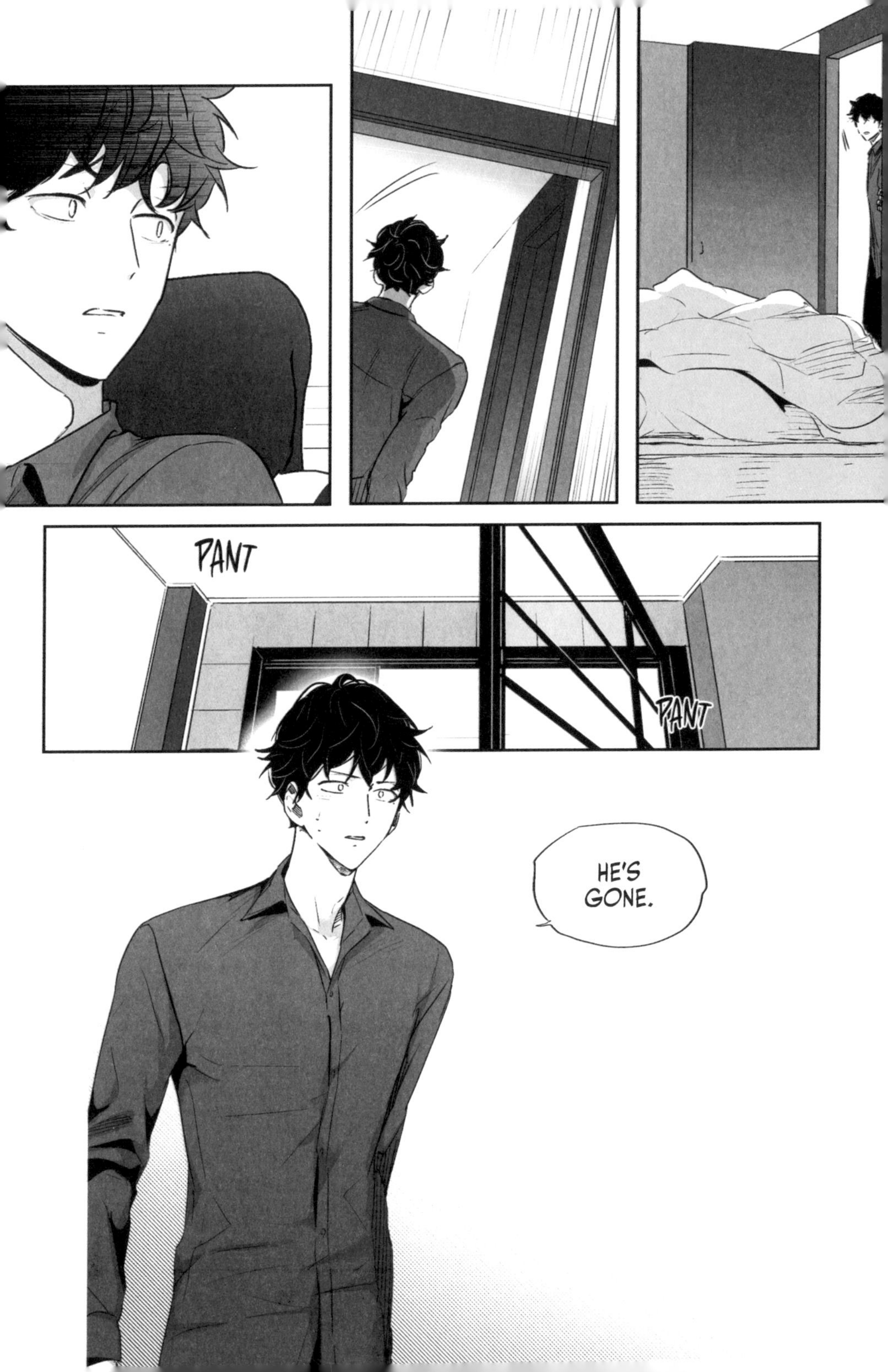
PANT
PANT
HE'S GONE.

Love is
an Illusion!

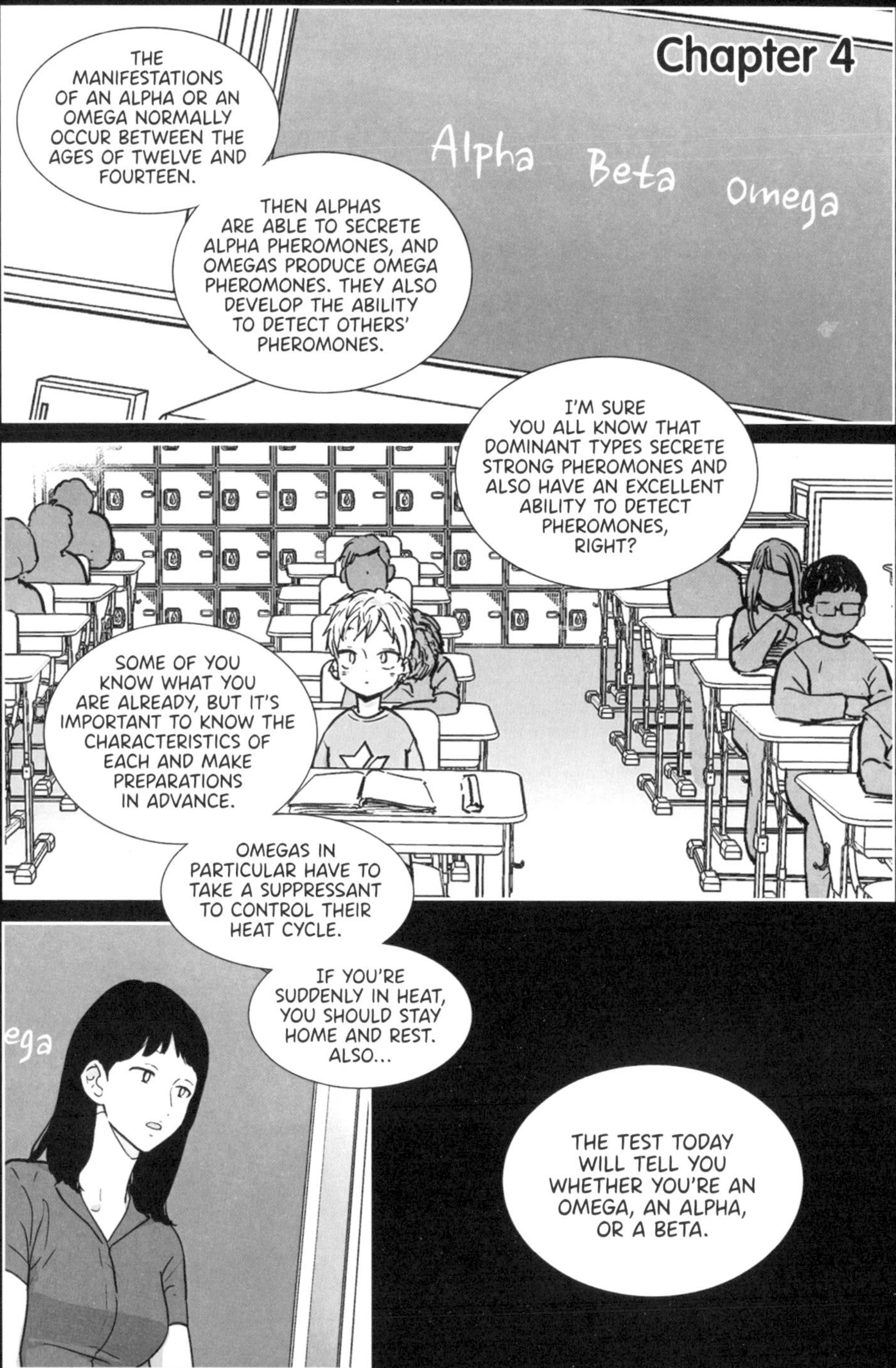
Chapter 4
THE MANIFESTATIONS OF AN ALPHA OR AN OMEGA NORMALLY OCCUR BETWEEN THE AGES OF TWELVE AND FOURTEEN.
Alpha Beta Omega
THEN ALPHAS ARE ABLE TO SECRETE ALPHA PHEROMONES, AND OMEGAS PRODUCE OMEGA PHEROMONES. THEY ALSO DEVELOP THE ABILITY TO DETECT OTHERS' PHEROMONES.
I'M SURE YOU ALL KNOW THAT DOMINANT TYPES SECRETE STRONG PHEROMONES AND ALSO HAVE AN EXCELLENT ABILITY TO DETECT PHEROMONES, RIGHT?
SOME OF YOU KNOW WHAT YOU ARE ALREADY, BUT IT'S IMPORTANT TO KNOW THE CHARACTERISTICS OF EACH AND MAKE PREPARATIONS IN ADVANCE.
OMEGAS IN PARTICULAR HAVE TO TAKE A SUPPRESSANT TO CONTROL THEIR HEAT CYCLE.
IF YOU'RE SUDDENLY IN HEAT, YOU SHOULD STAY HOME AND REST. ALSO...
THE TEST TODAY WILL TELL YOU WHETHER YOU'RE AN OMEGA, AN ALPHA, OR A BETA.

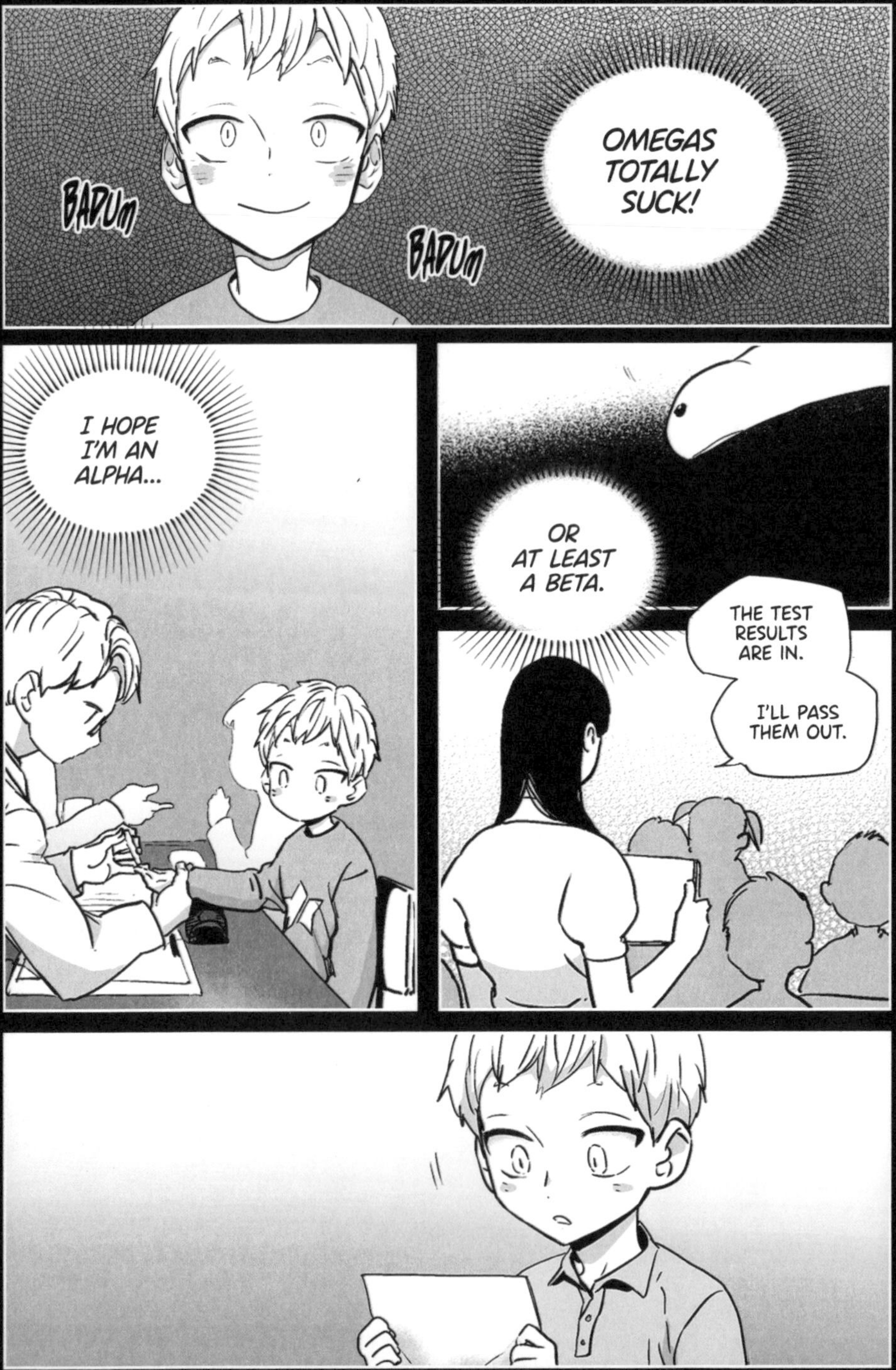
OMEGAS TOTALLY SUCK!
BADUM
BADUM
I HOPE I'M AN ALPHA...
OR AT LEAST A BETA.
THE TEST RESULTS ARE IN.
I'LL PASS THEM OUT.

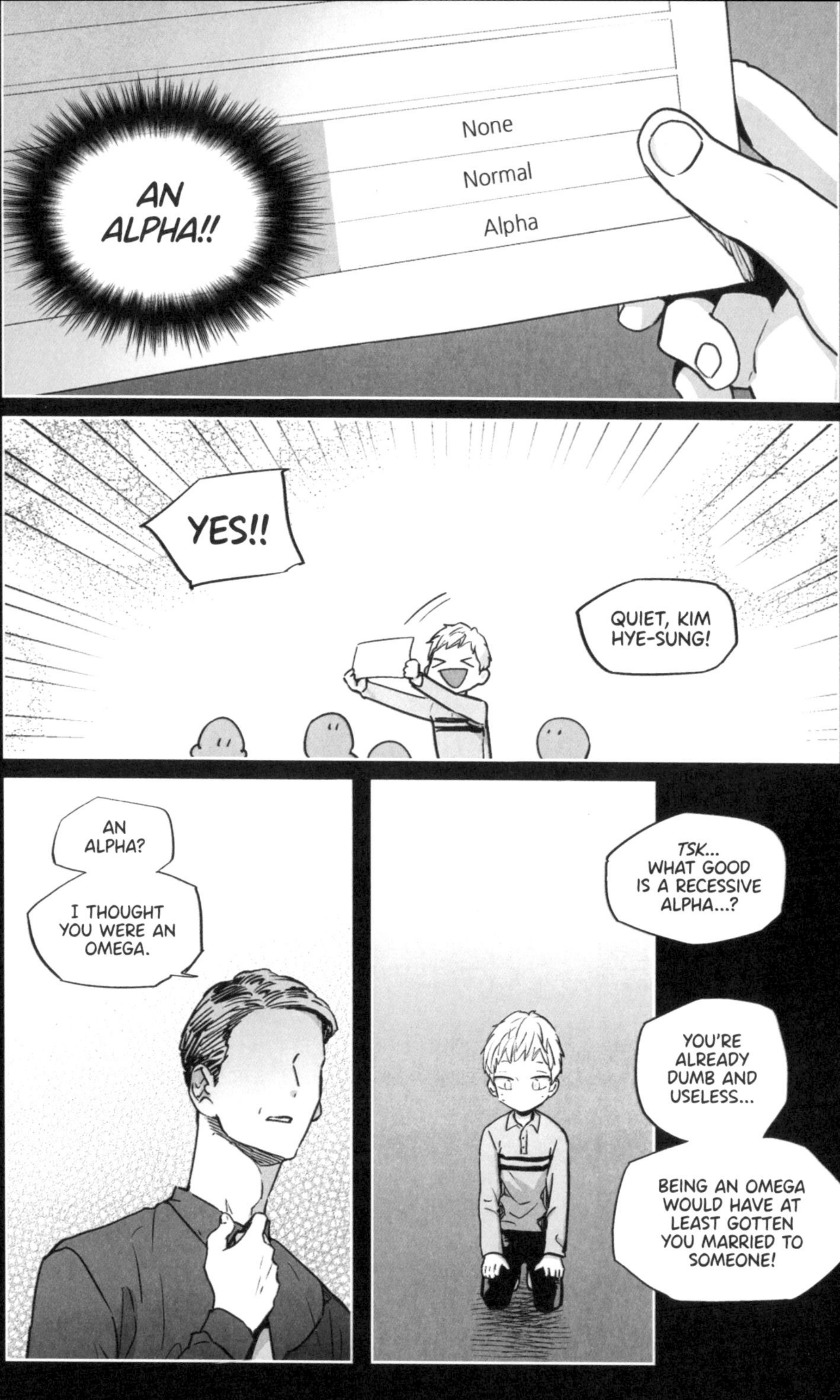
AN ALPHA!!
None
Normal
Alpha
YES!!
QUIET, KIM HYE-SUNG!
AN ALPHA?
I THOUGHT YOU WERE AN OMEGA.
TSK... WHAT GOOD IS A RECESSIVE ALPHA...?
YOU'RE ALREADY DUMB AND USELESS...
BEING AN OMEGA WOULD HAVE AT LEAST GOTTEN YOU MARRIED TO SOMEONE!

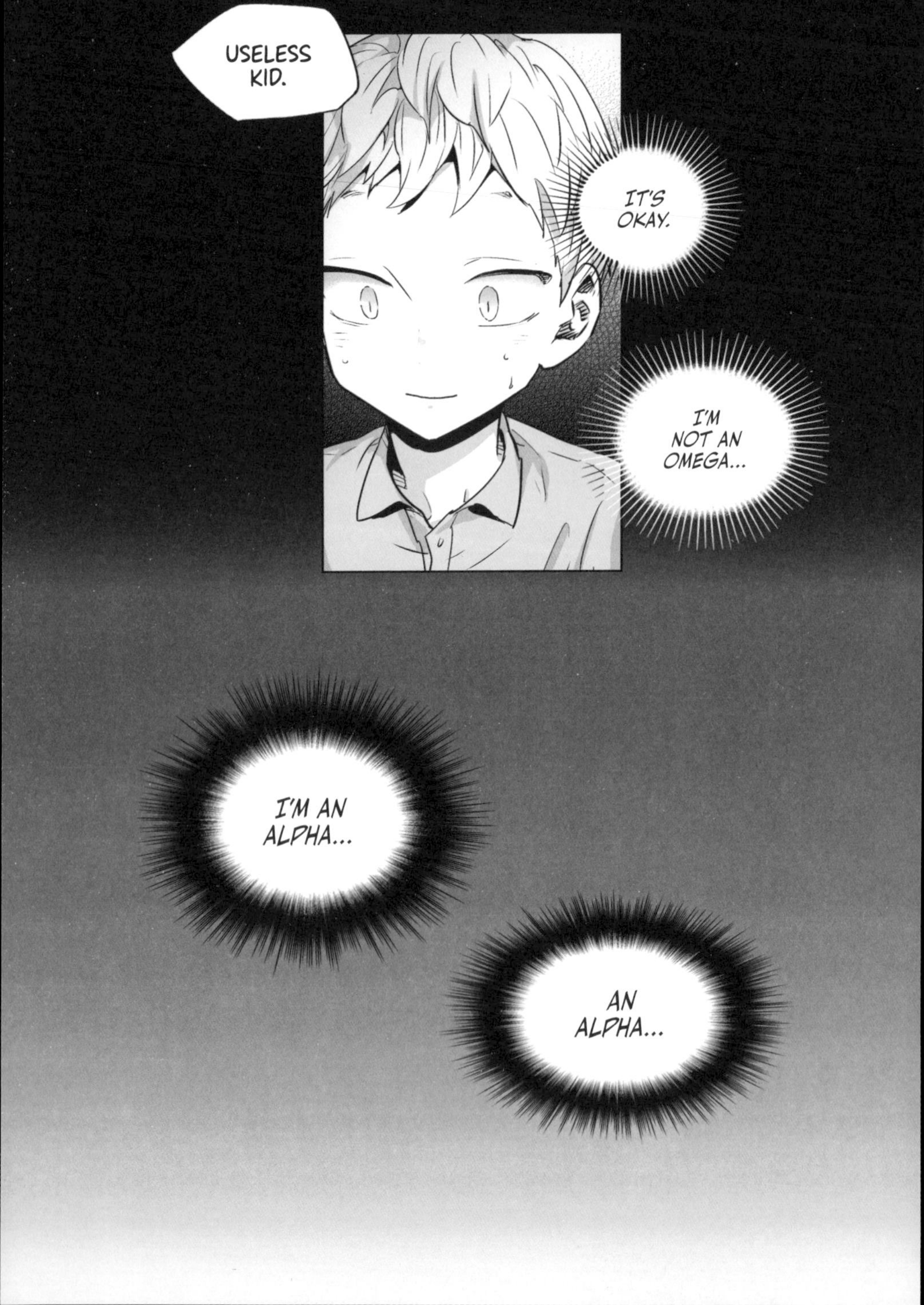
USELESS KID.
IT'S OKAY.
I'M NOT AN OMEGA...
I'M AN ALPHA...
AN ALPHA...

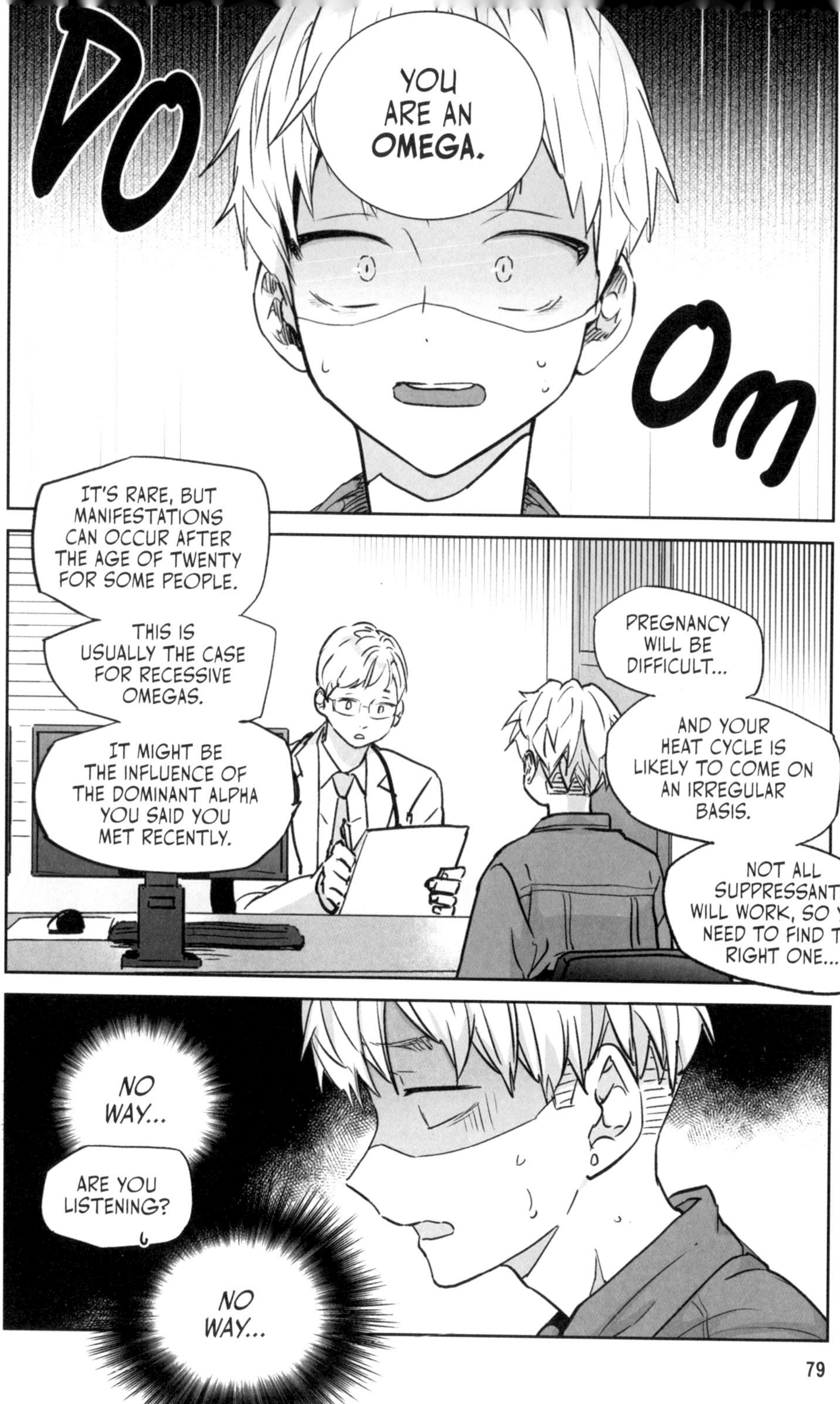
DO
YOU ARE AN OMEGA.
OM
IT'S RARE, BUT MANIFESTATIONS CAN OCCUR AFTER THE AGE OF TWENTY FOR SOME PEOPLE.
THIS IS USUALLY THE CASE FOR RECESSIVE OMEGAS.
IT MIGHT BE THE INFLUENCE OF THE DOMINANT ALPHA YOU SAID YOU MET RECENTLY.
PREGNANCY WILL BE DIFFICULT...
AND YOUR HEAT CYCLE IS LIKELY TO COME ON AN IRREGULAR BASIS.
NOT ALL SUPPRESSANTS WILL WORK, SO YOU NEED TO FIND THE RIGHT ONE...
NO WAY...
ARE YOU LISTENING?
NO WAY...

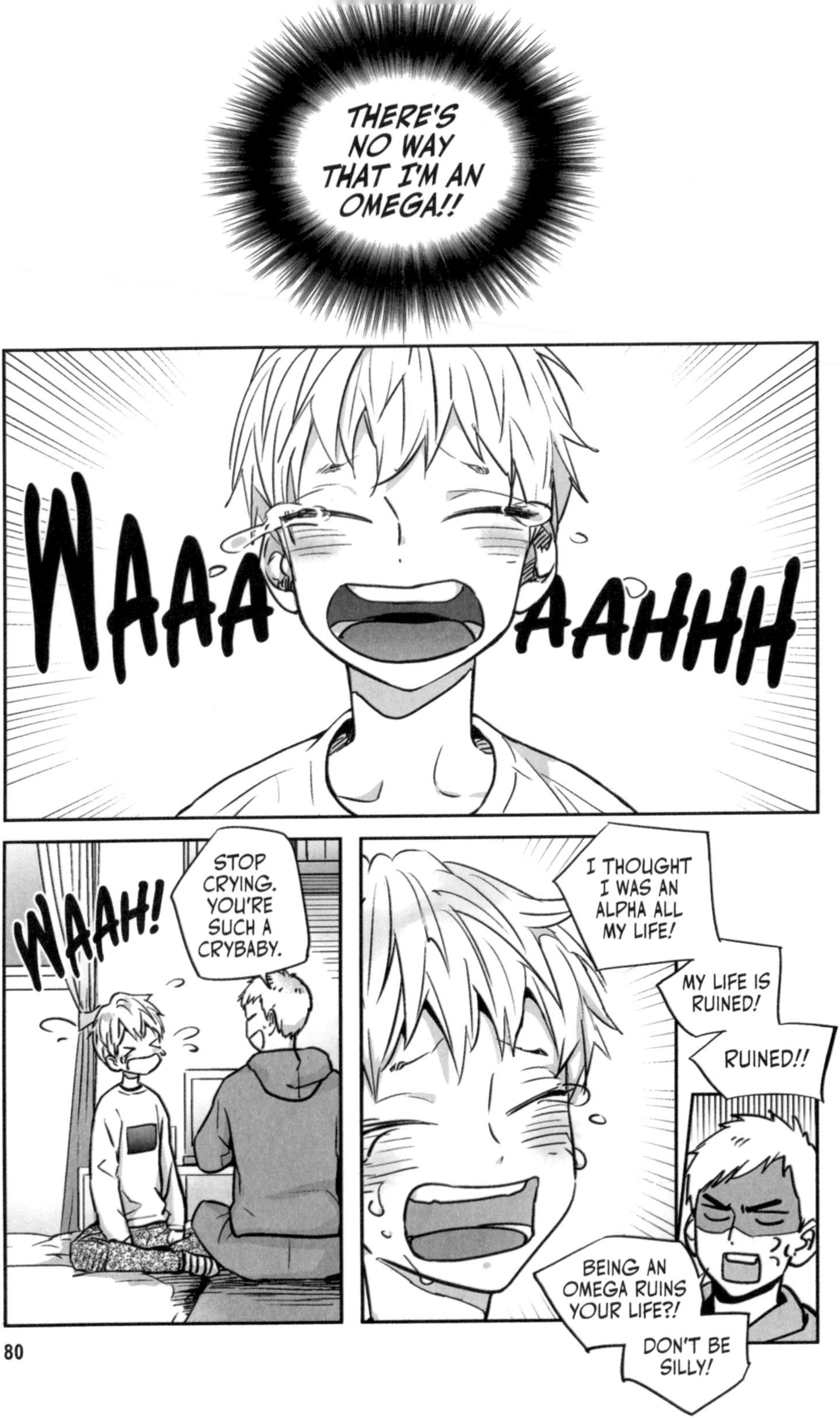
THERE'S NO WAY THAT I'M AN OMEGA!!
WAAAAAHHH
WAAH!
STOP CRYING. YOU'RE SUCH A CRYBABY.
I THOUGHT I WAS AN ALPHA ALL MY LIFE!
MY LIFE IS RUINED!
RUINED!!
BEING AN OMEGA RUINS YOUR LIFE?!
DON'T BE SILLY!

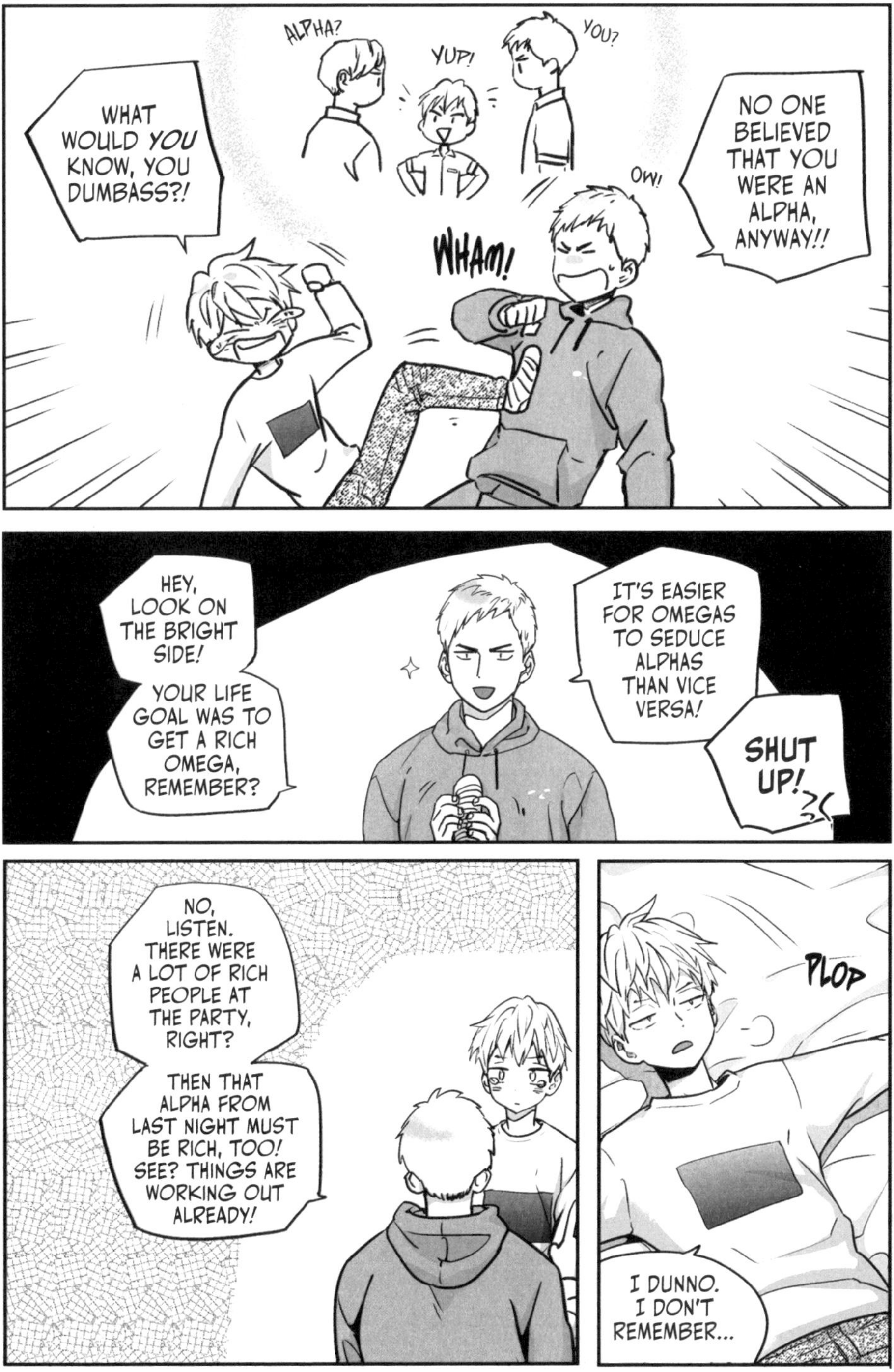

WHAT WOULD YOU KNOW, YOU DUMBASS?!
ALPHA?
YUP!
YOU?
NO ONE BELIEVED THAT YOU WERE AN ALPHA, ANYWAY!!
OW!
WHAM!
HEY, LOOK ON THE BRIGHT SIDE!
YOUR LIFE GOAL WAS TO GET A RICH OMEGA, REMEMBER?
IT'S EASIER FOR OMEGAS TO SEDUCE ALPHAS THAN VICE VERSA!
SHUT UP!
NO, LISTEN. THERE WERE A LOT OF RICH PEOPLE AT THE PARTY, RIGHT?
THEN THAT ALPHA FROM LAST NIGHT MUST BE RICH, TOO! SEE? THINGS ARE WORKING OUT ALREADY!
PLOP
I DUNNO. I DON'T REMEMBER...

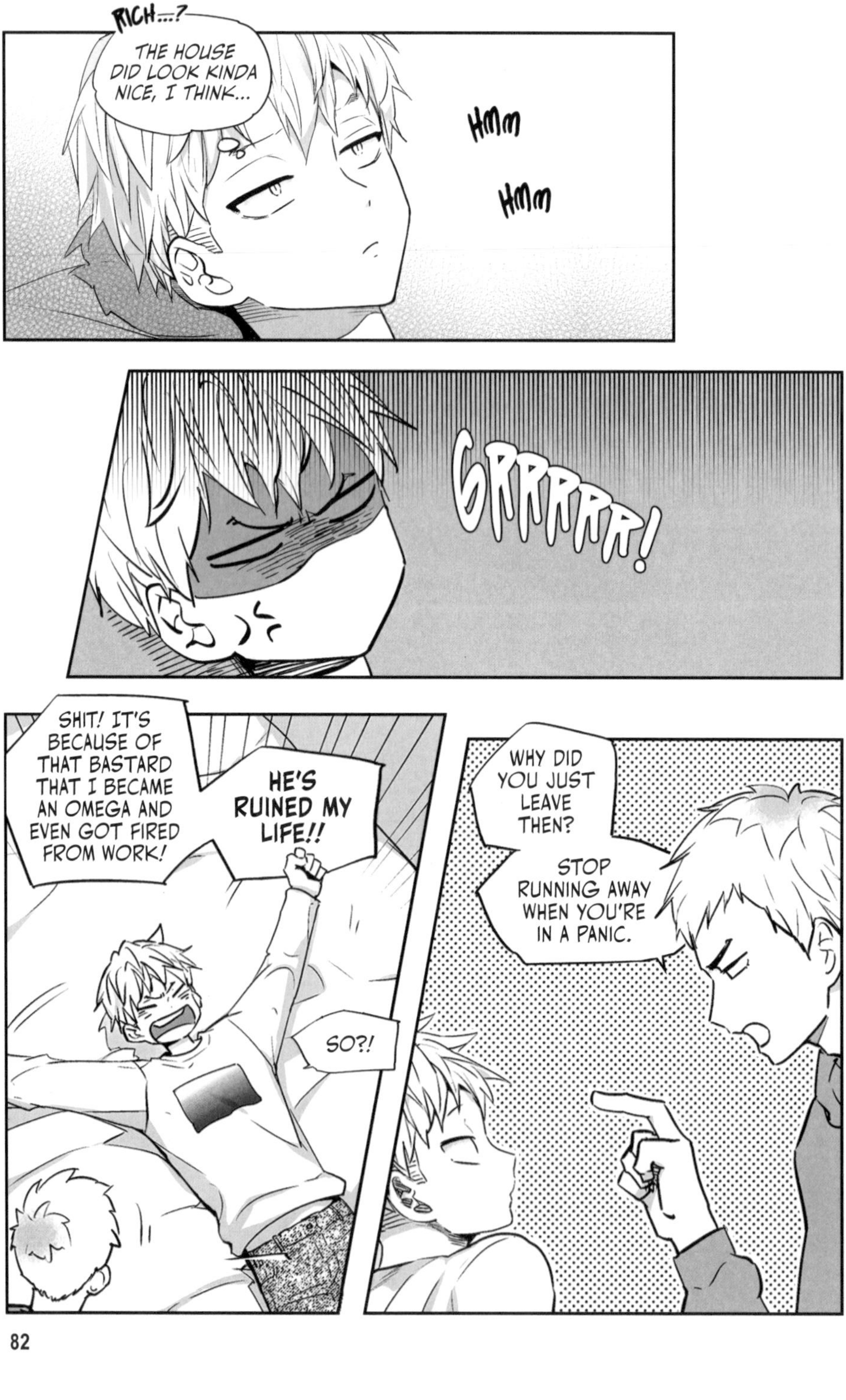
RICH...?
THE HOUSE DID LOOK KINDA NICE, I THINK...
HMM
HMM
GRRRRRR!
SHIT! IT'S BECAUSE OF THAT BASTARD THAT I BECAME AN OMEGA AND EVEN GOT FIRED FROM WORK!
HE'S RUINED MY LIFE!!
SO?!
WHY DID YOU JUST LEAVE THEN?
STOP RUNNING AWAY WHEN YOU'RE IN A PANIC.

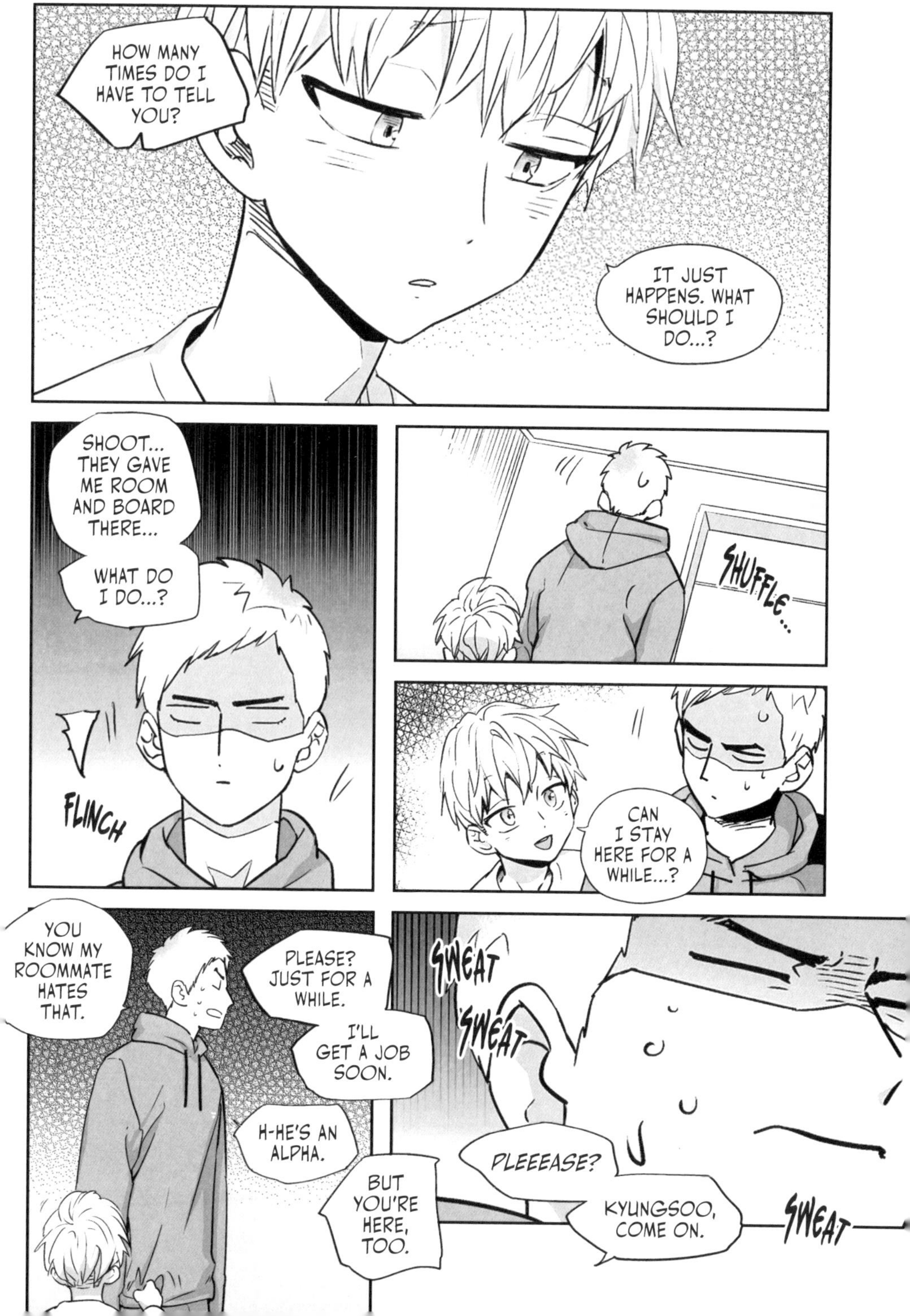
HOW MANY TIMES DO I HAVE TO TELL YOU?
IT JUST HAPPENS. WHAT SHOULD I DO...?
SHOOT... THEY GAVE ME ROOM AND BOARD THERE...
WHAT DO I DO...?
FLINCH
SHUFFLE...
CAN I STAY HERE FOR A WHILE...?
YOU KNOW MY ROOMMATE HATES THAT.
PLEASE? JUST FOR A WHILE.
I'LL GET A JOB SOON.
H-HE'S AN ALPHA.
BUT YOU'RE HERE, TOO.
SWEAT
SWEAT
PLEEEASE?
KYUNGSOO, COME ON.
SWEAT

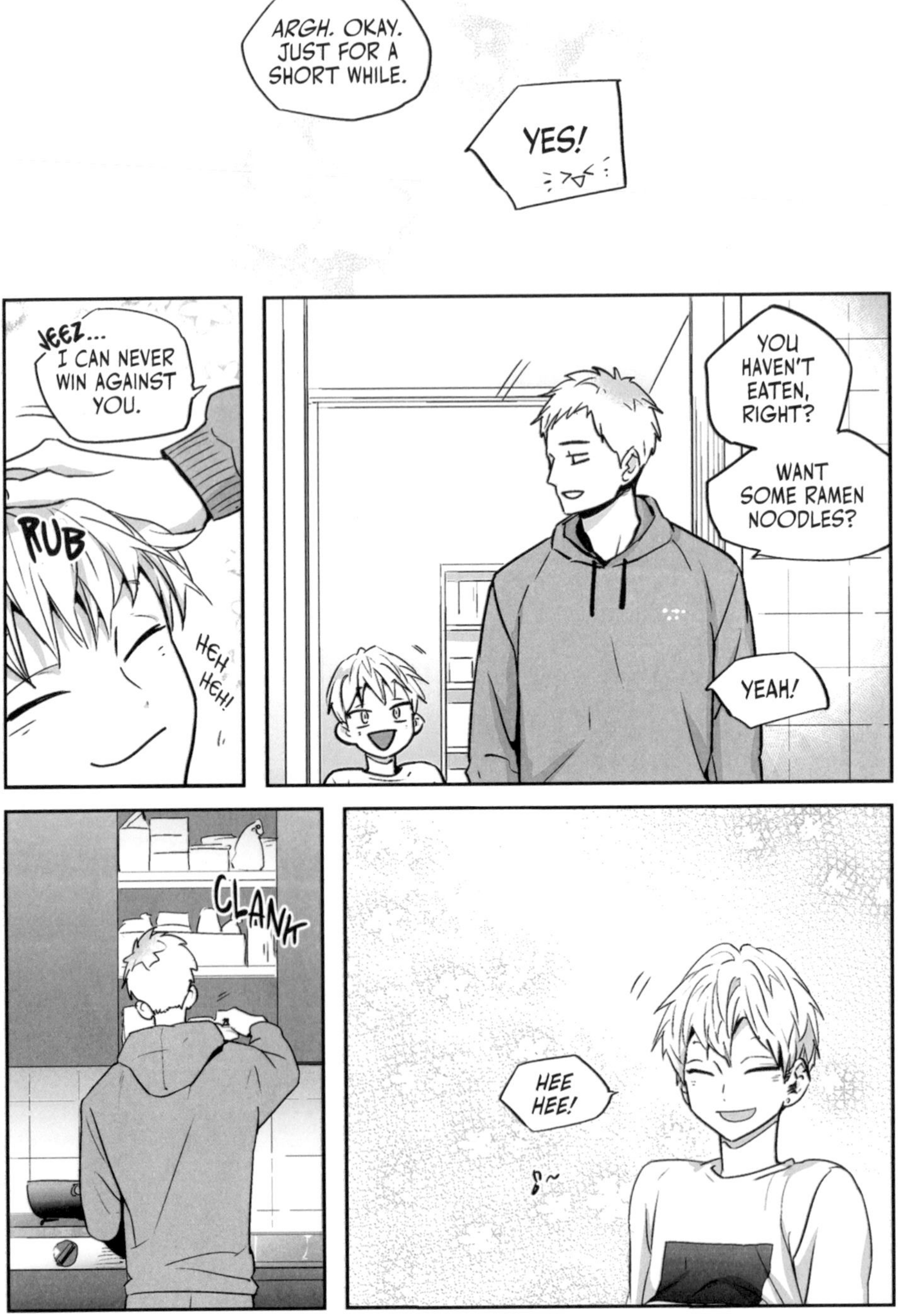
ARGH. OKAY. JUST FOR A SHORT WHILE.
YES!
JEEZ... I CAN NEVER WIN AGAINST YOU.
RUB
HEH HEH!
YOU HAVEN'T EATEN, RIGHT?
WANT SOME RAMEN NOODLES?
YEAH!
CLANK
HEE HEE!

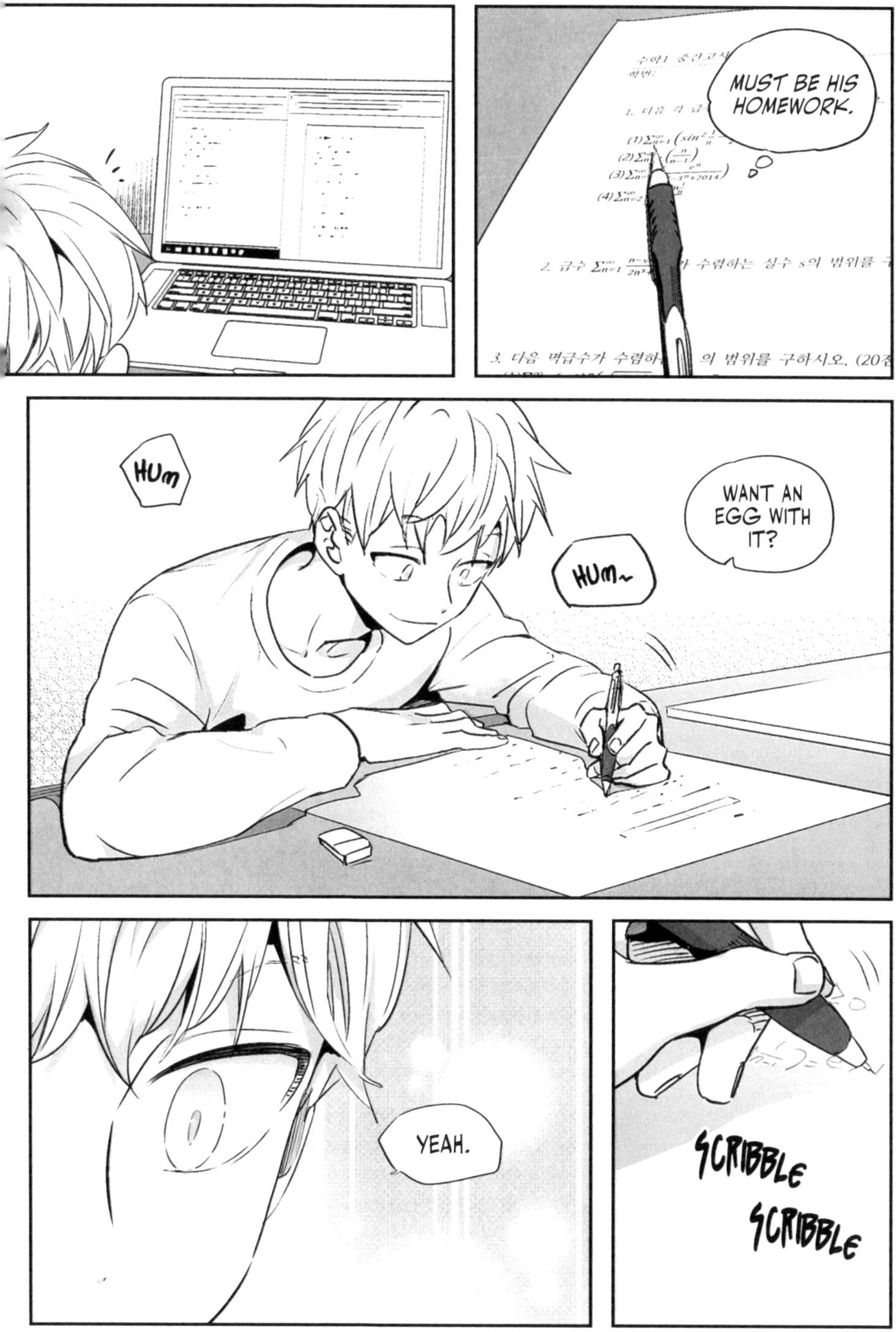
MUST BE HIS HOMEWORK.
HUM
WANT AN EGG WITH IT?
HUM~
YEAH.
SCRIBBLE
SCRIBBLE

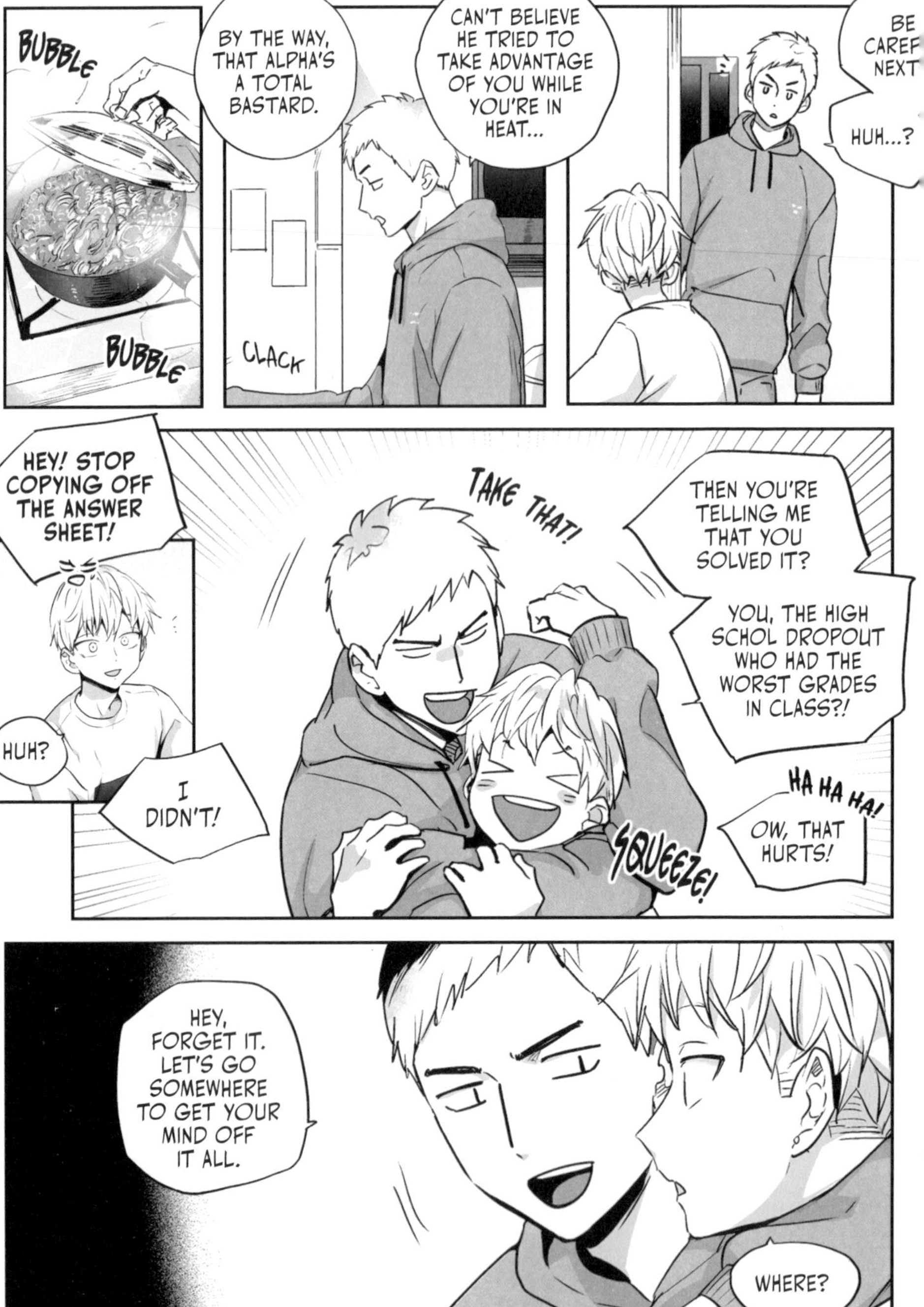

BUBBLE
BUBBLE
BY THE WAY, THAT ALPHA'S A TOTAL BASTARD.
CAN'T BELIEVE HE TRIED TO TAKE ADVANTAGE OF YOU WHILE YOU'RE IN HEAT...
CLACK
BE CAREF NEXT
HUH...?
HEY! STOP COPYING OFF THE ANSWER SHEET!
HUH?
I DIDN'T!
TAKE THAT!
THEN YOU'RE TELLING ME THAT YOU SOLVED IT?
YOU, THE HIGH SCHOL DROPOUT WHO HAD THE WORST GRADES IN CLASS?!
HA HA HA!
OW, THAT HURTS!
SQUEEZE!
HEY, FORGET IT. LET'S GO SOMEWHERE TO GET YOUR MIND OFF IT ALL.
WHERE?

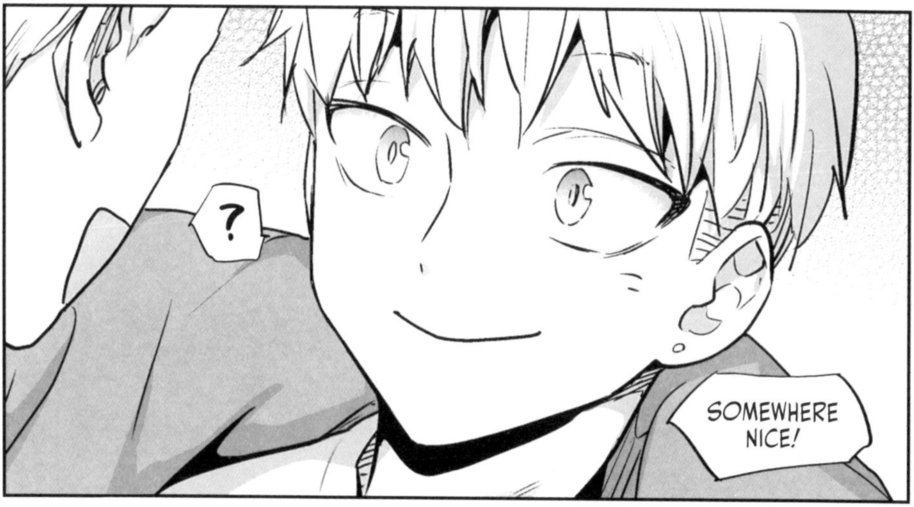
?
SOMEWHERE NICE!

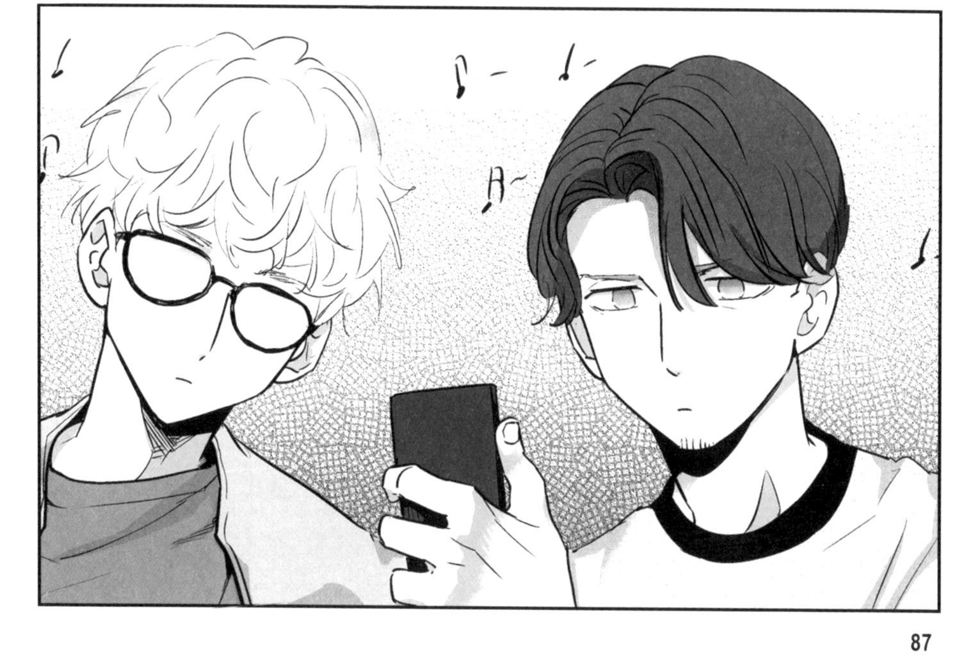

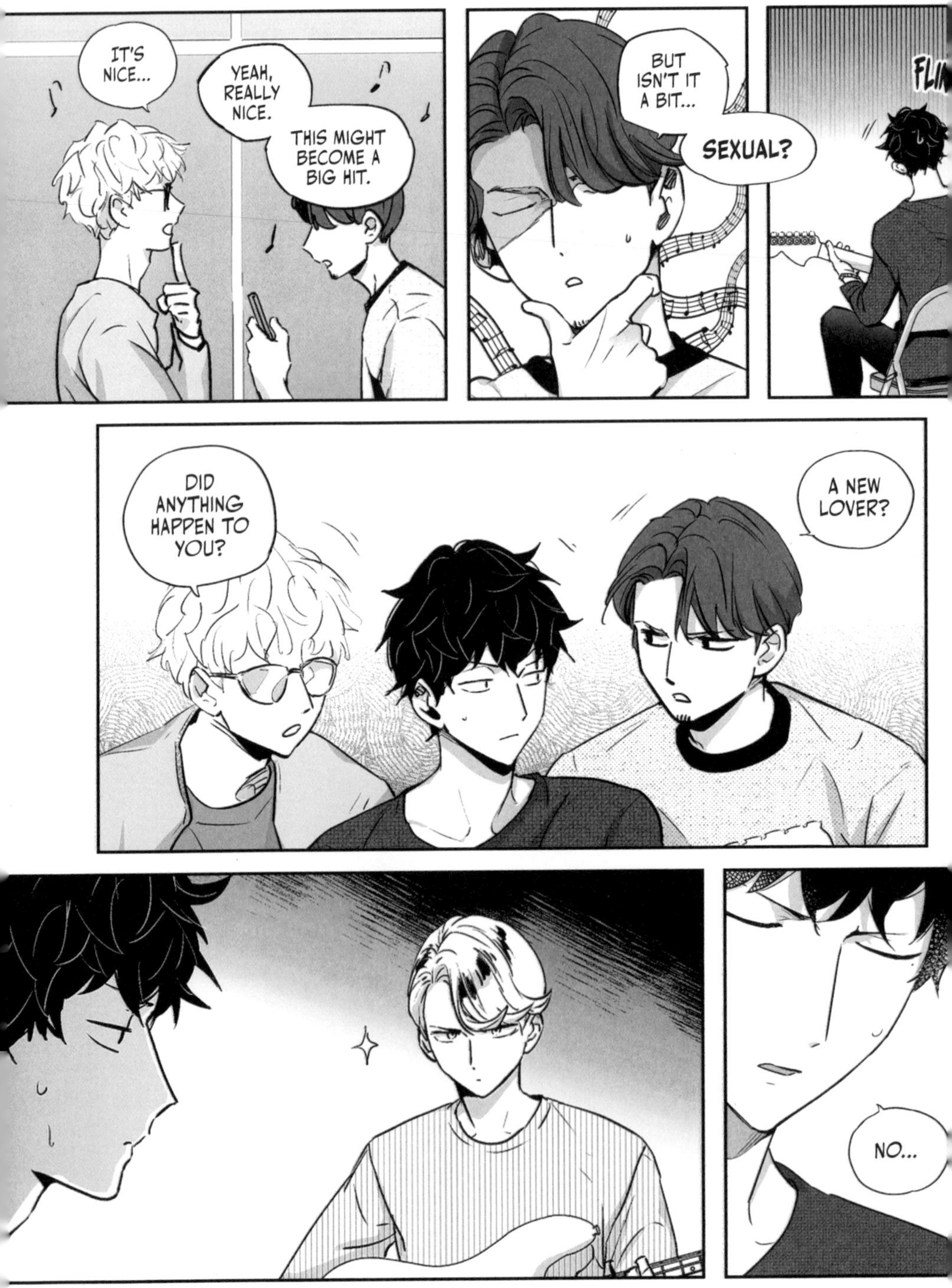

IT'S NICE...
YEAH, REALLY NICE.
THIS MIGHT BECOME A BIG HIT.
BUT ISN'T IT A BIT...
SEXUAL?
DID ANYTHING HAPPEN TO YOU?
A NEW LOVER?
NO...

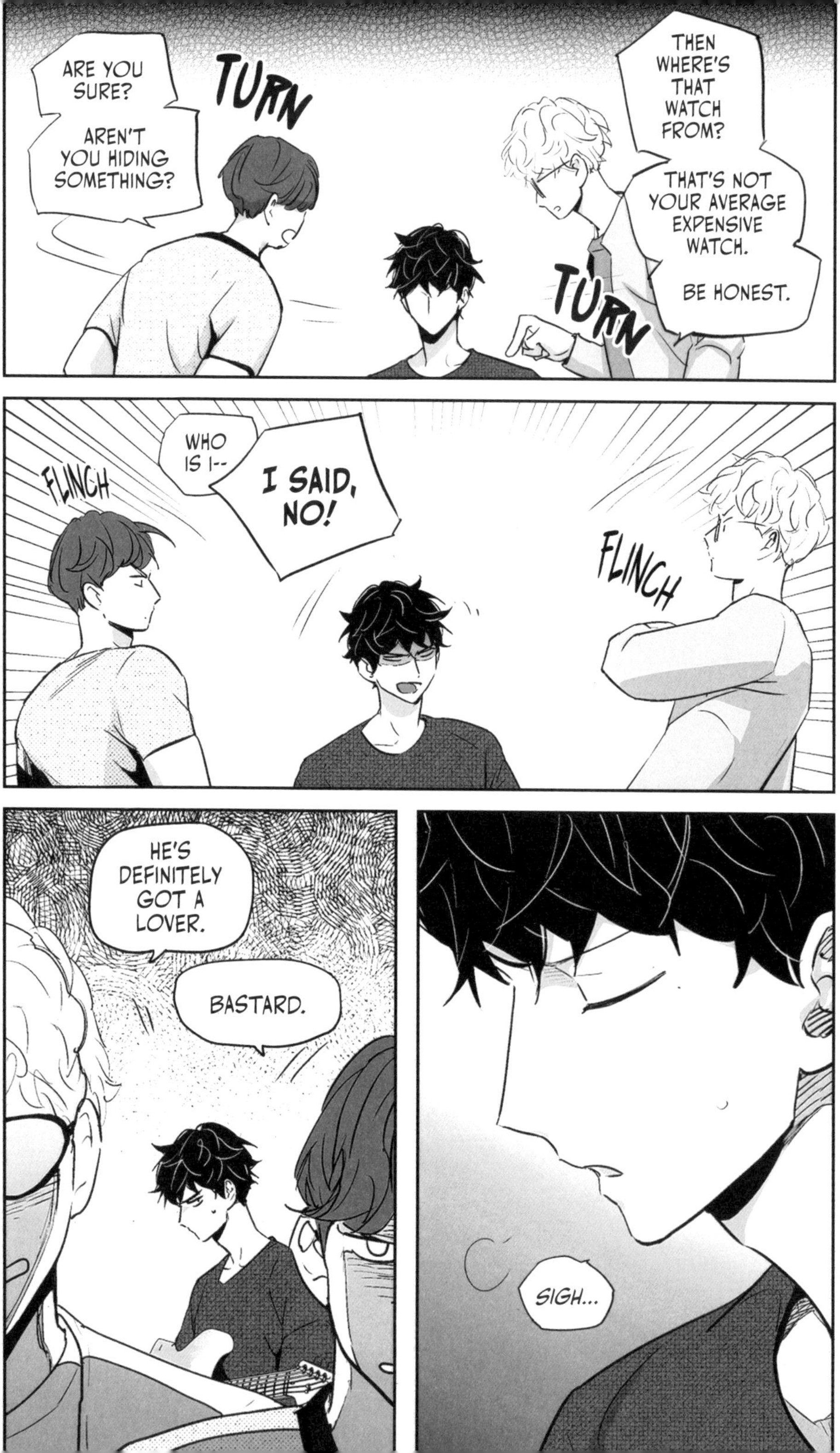
ARE YOU SURE?
AREN'T YOU HIDING SOMETHING?
TURN
THEN WHERE'S THAT WATCH FROM?
THAT'S NOT YOUR AVERAGE EXPENSIVE WATCH.
BE HONEST.
TURN
FLINCH
WHO IS I--
I SAID, NO!
FLINCH
HE'S DEFINITELY GOT A LOVER.
BASTARD.
SIGH...

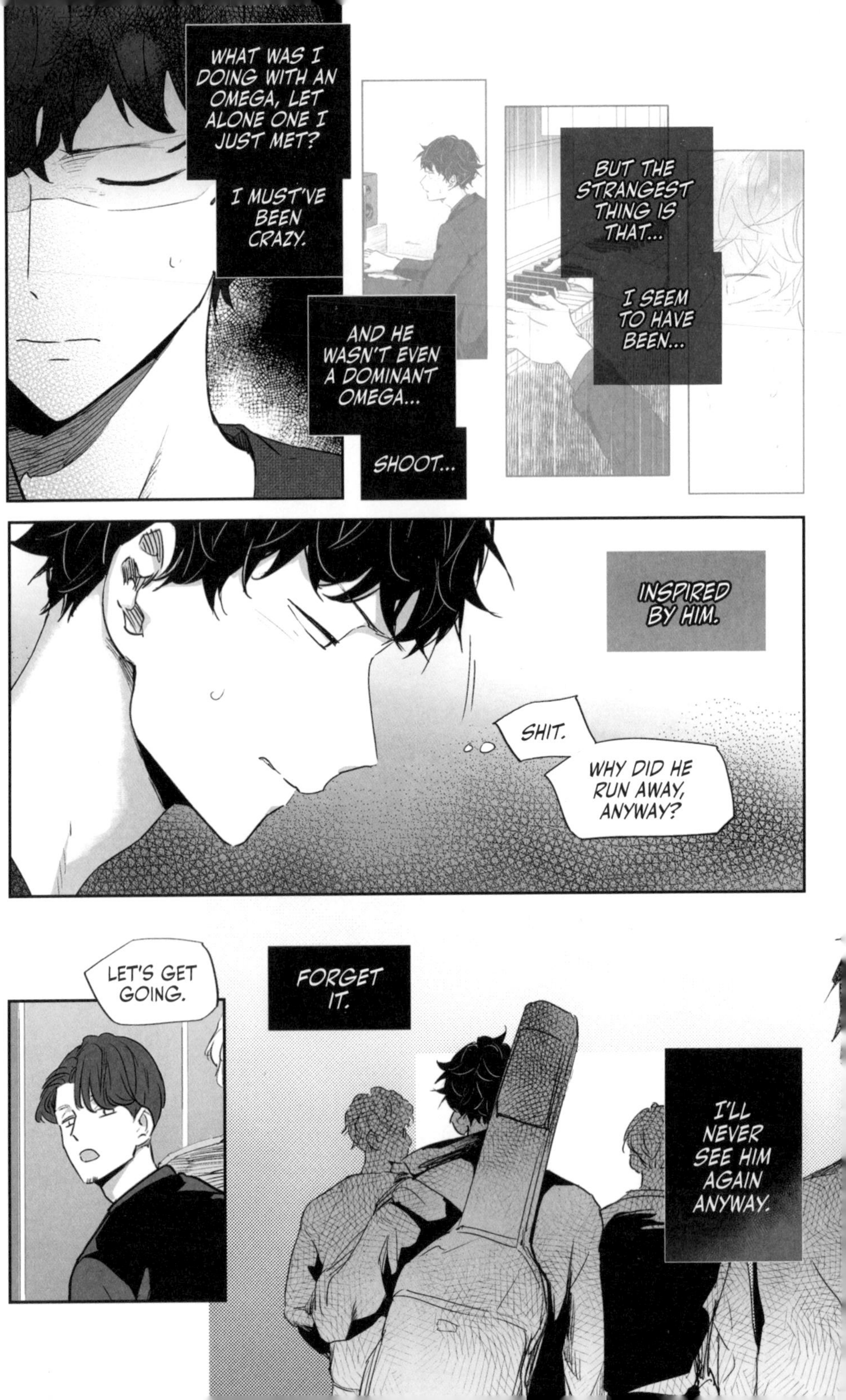
WHAT WAS I DOING WITH AN OMEGA, LET ALONE ONE I JUST MET?
I MUST'VE BEEN CRAZY.
AND HE WASN'T EVEN A DOMINANT OMEGA...
SHOOT...
BUT THE STRANGEST THING IS THAT...
I SEEM TO HAVE BEEN...
INSPIRED BY HIM.
SHIT.
WHY DID HE RUN AWAY, ANYWAY?
LET'S GET GOING.
FORGET IT.
I'LL NEVER SEE HIM AGAIN ANYWAY.

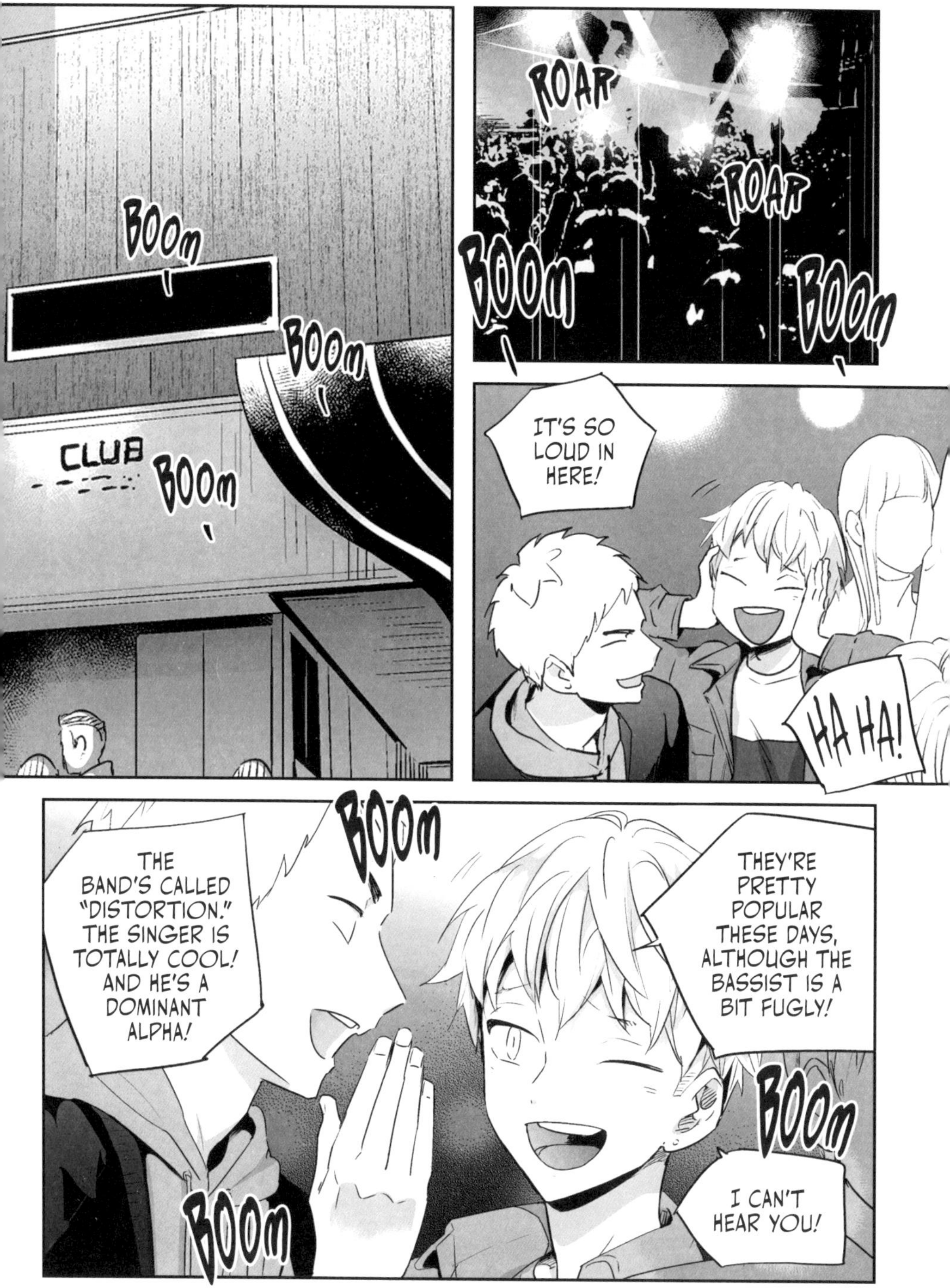
BOOm
BOOm
CLUB
BOOm
ROAR
ROAR
BOOM
BOOm
IT'S SO LOUD IN HERE!
HA HA!
THE BAND'S CALLED "DISTORTION." THE SINGER IS TOTALLY COOL! AND HE'S A DOMINANT ALPHA!
BOOm
THEY'RE PRETTY POPULAR THESE DAYS, ALTHOUGH THE BASSIST IS A BIT FUGLY!
BOOm
BOOm
I CAN'T HEAR YOU!

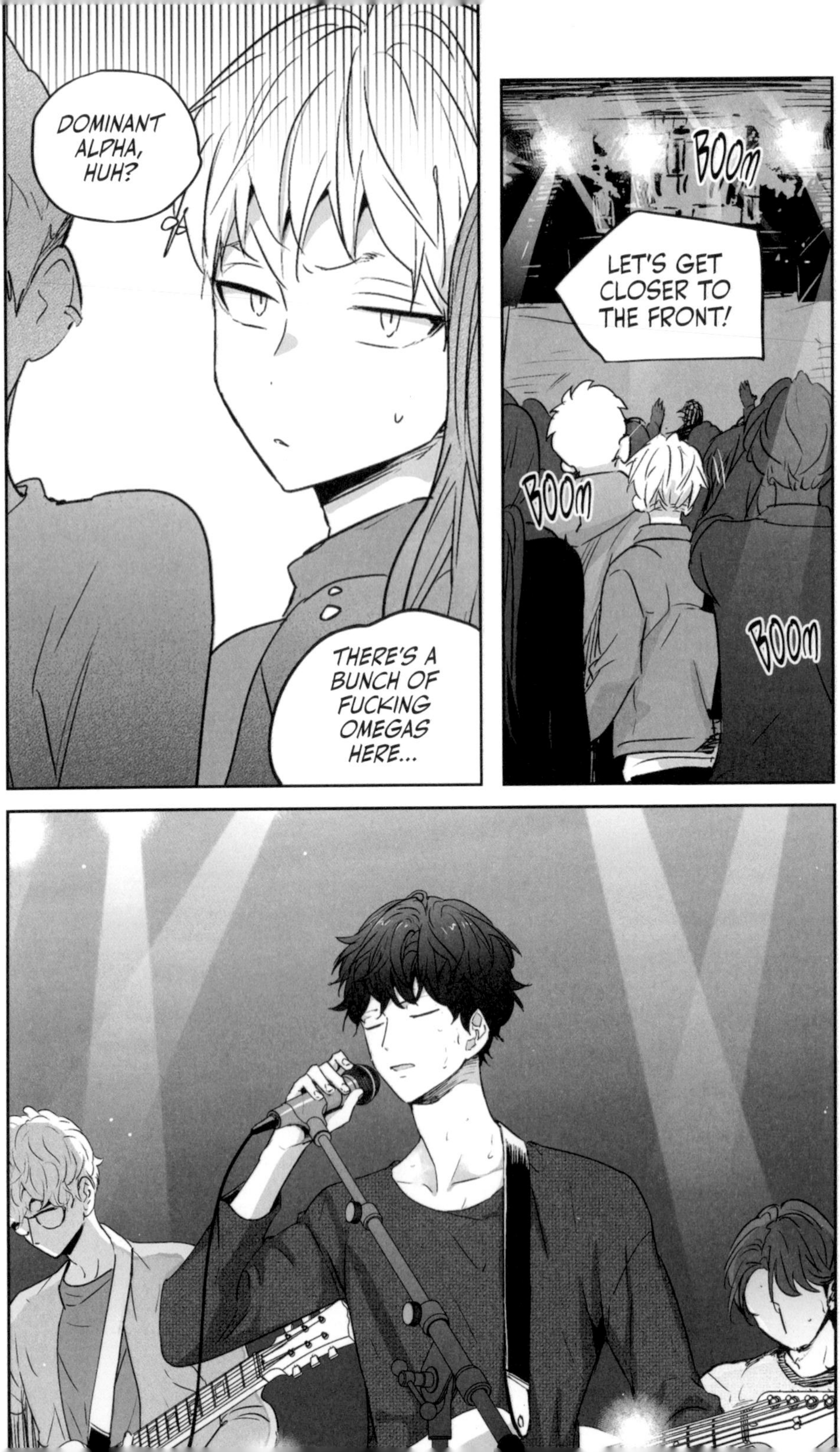
DOMINANT ALPHA, HUH?
THERE'S A BUNCH OF FUCKING OMEGAS HERE...
BOOM
LET'S GET CLOSER TO THE FRONT!
BOOM
BOOM

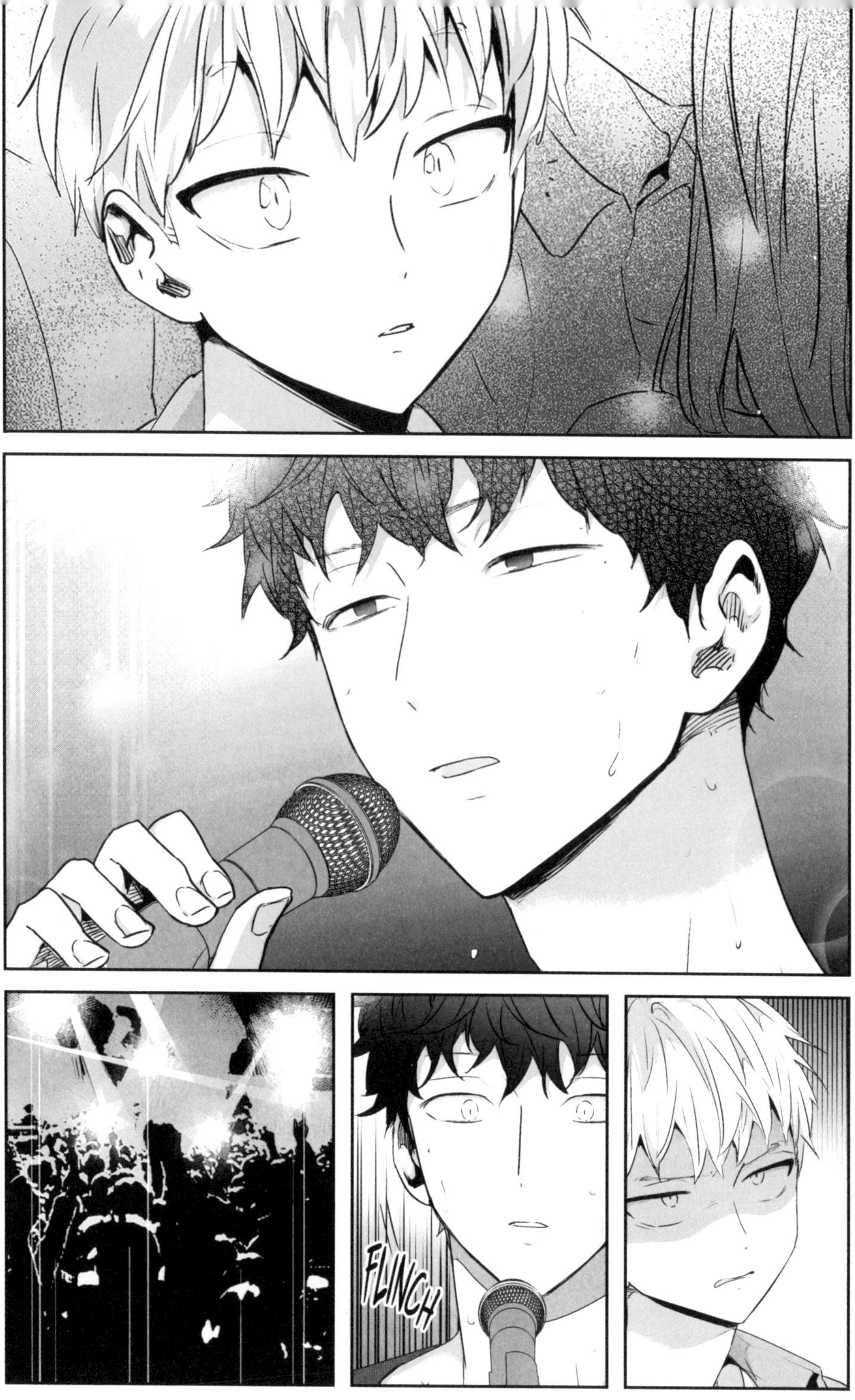
FLINCH

Love is
an Illusion!

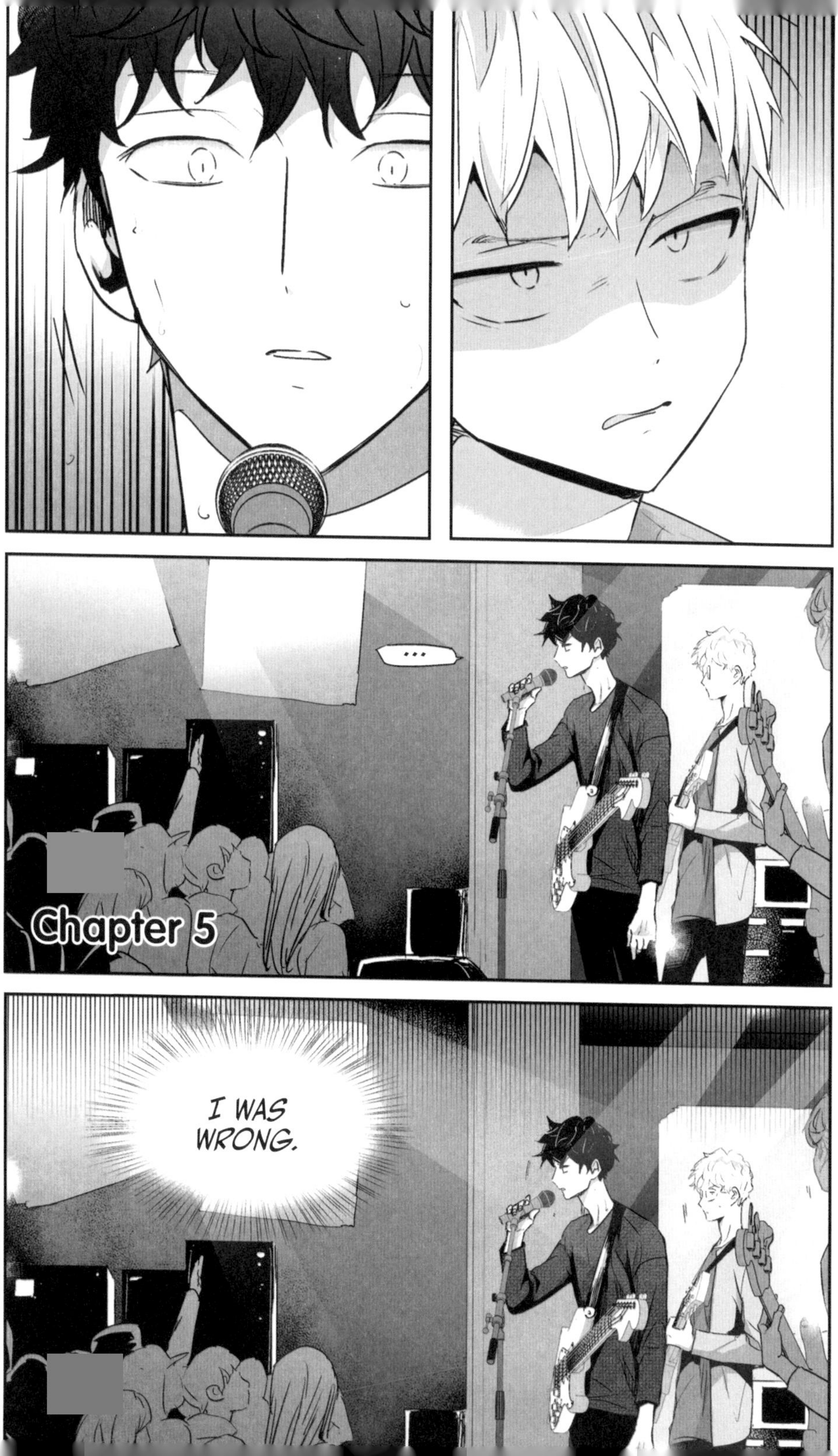
...
Chapter 5
I WAS WRONG.

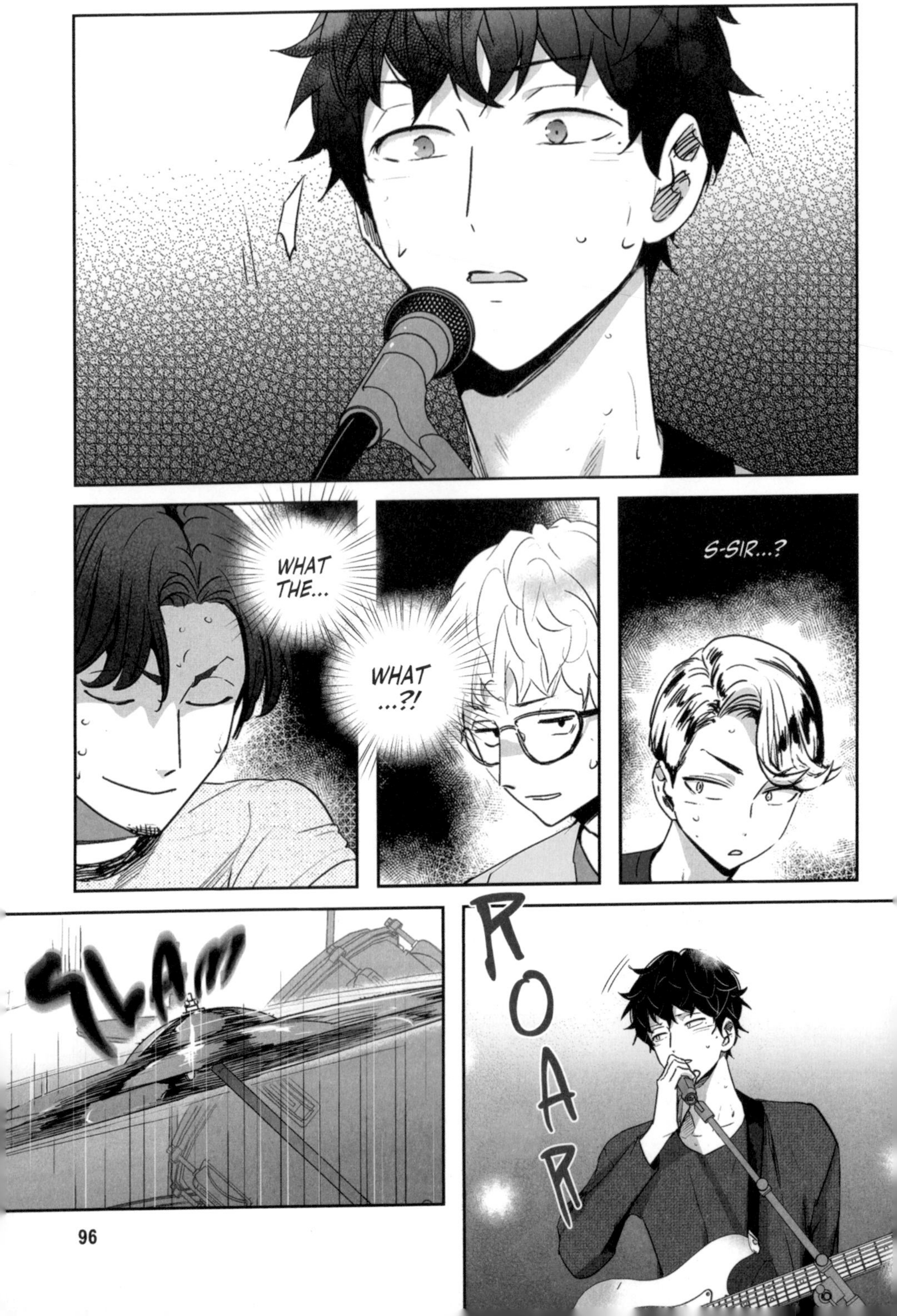
WHAT THE...
WHAT ...?!
S-SIR...?
SLAM
ROAR

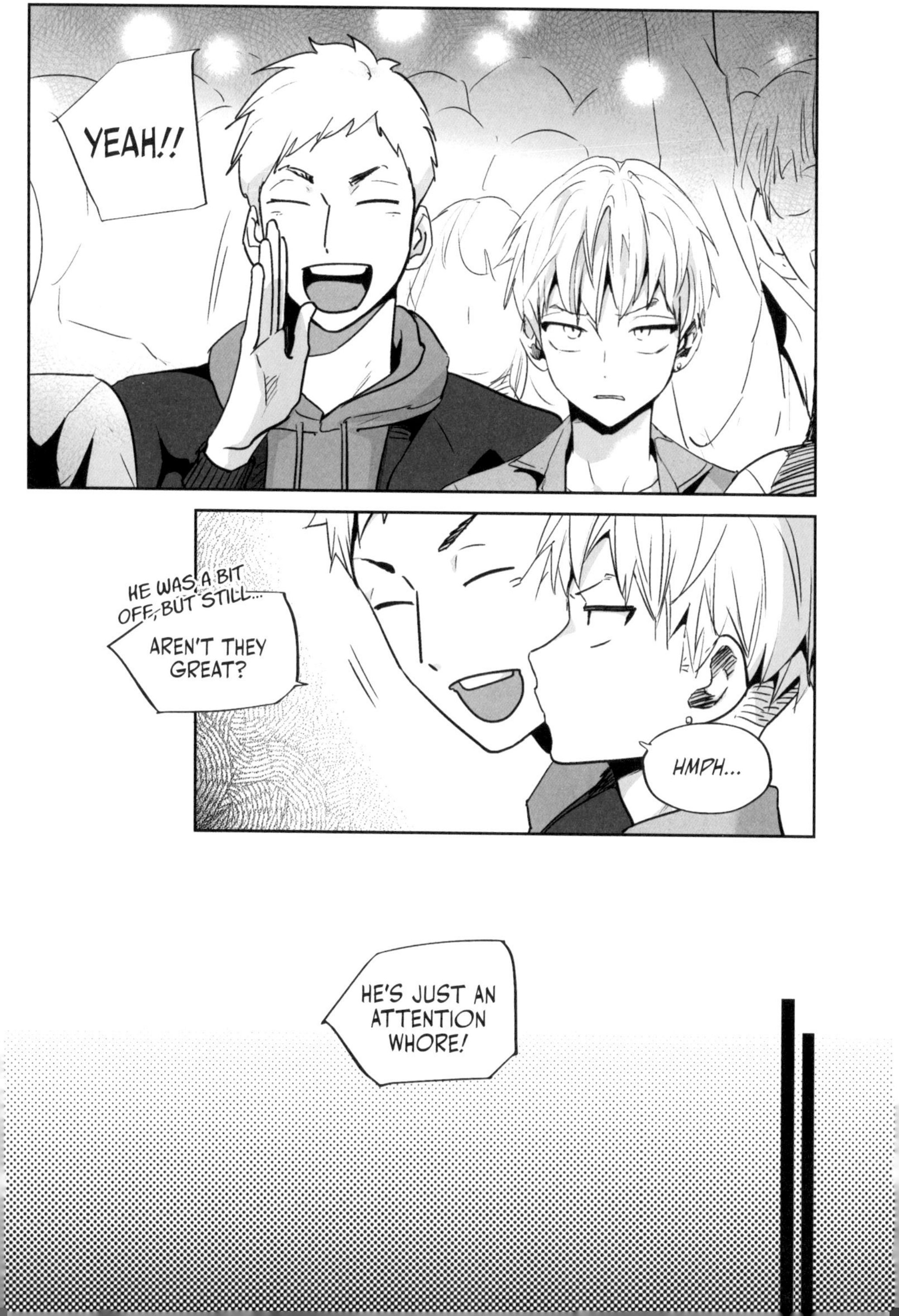
YEAH!!
HE WAS A BIT OFF, BUT STILL...
AREN'T THEY GREAT?
HMPH...
HE'S JUST AN ATTENTION WHORE!

COME ON, LET'S GO!

WAIT, I WANNA GET THEIR AUTOGRAPH.

WHY? THEY'RE NOT EVEN CELEBRITIES!

'CAUSE I'M A FAN!!

THE SINGER IS A TOTAL DOUCHEBAG, SO HE NEVER SIGNS AUTOGRAPHS... BUT T OTHE

UGH, JUS HURRY U ALREADY

HE HE! WAIT FOR ME!

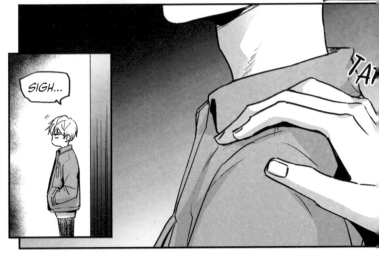

SIGH...

T.A

JOLT

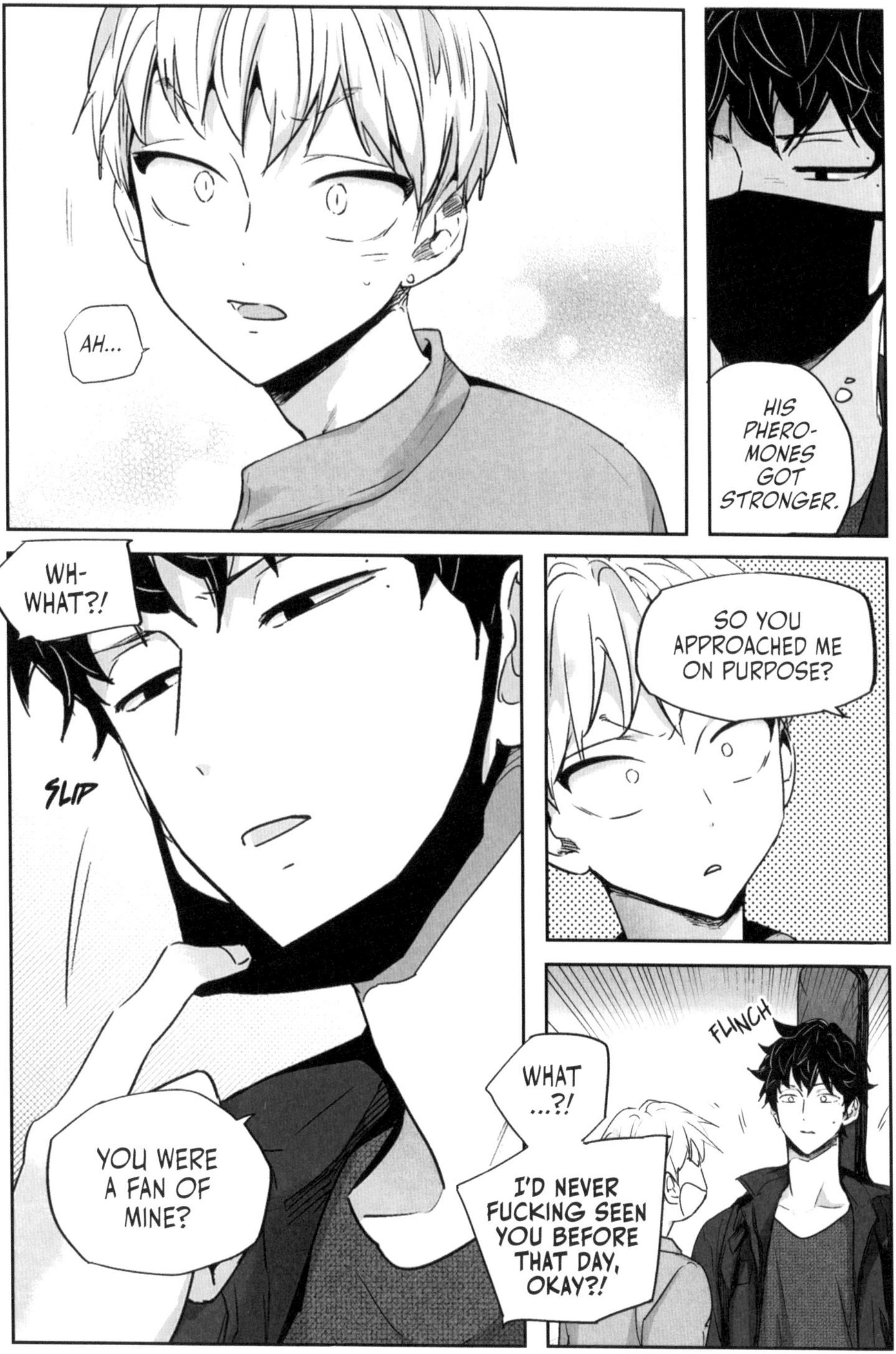
AH...
HIS PHERO-MONES GOT STRONGER.
WH-WHAT?!
SLIP
YOU WERE A FAN OF MINE?
SO YOU APPROACHED ME ON PURPOSE?
FLINCH
WHAT ...?!
I'D NEVER FUCKING SEEN YOU BEFORE THAT DAY, OKAY?!

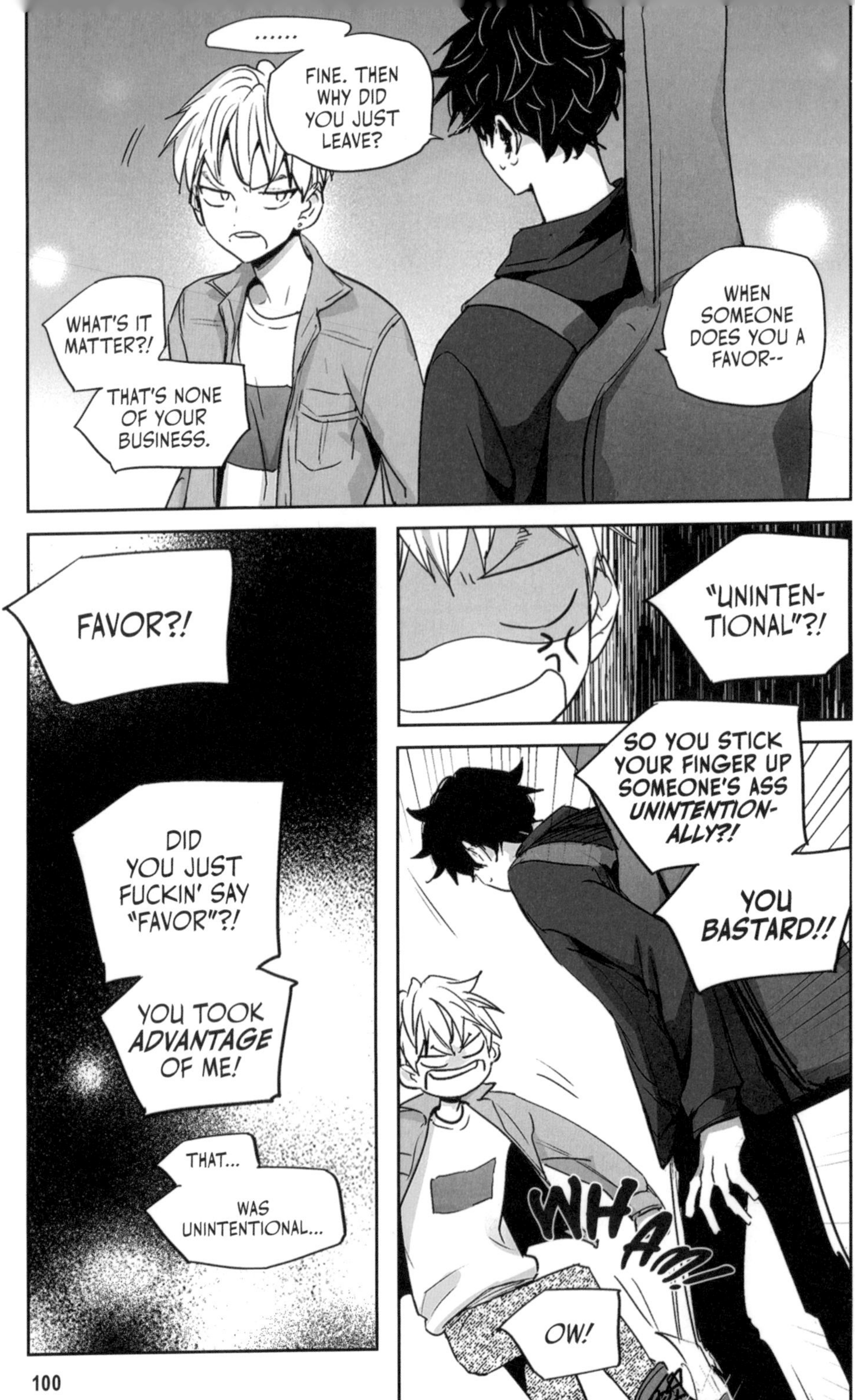
......
FINE. THEN WHY DID YOU JUST LEAVE?
WHAT'S IT MATTER?!
THAT'S NONE OF YOUR BUSINESS.
WHEN SOMEONE DOES YOU A FAVOR--
FAVOR?!
DID YOU JUST FUCKIN' SAY "FAVOR"?!
YOU TOOK *ADVANTAGE* OF ME!
THAT...
WAS UNINTENTIONAL...
"UNINTEN-TIONAL"?!
SO YOU STICK YOUR FINGER UP SOMEONE'S ASS *UNINTENTION-ALLY?!*
YOU BASTARD!!
WHAM!!
OW!

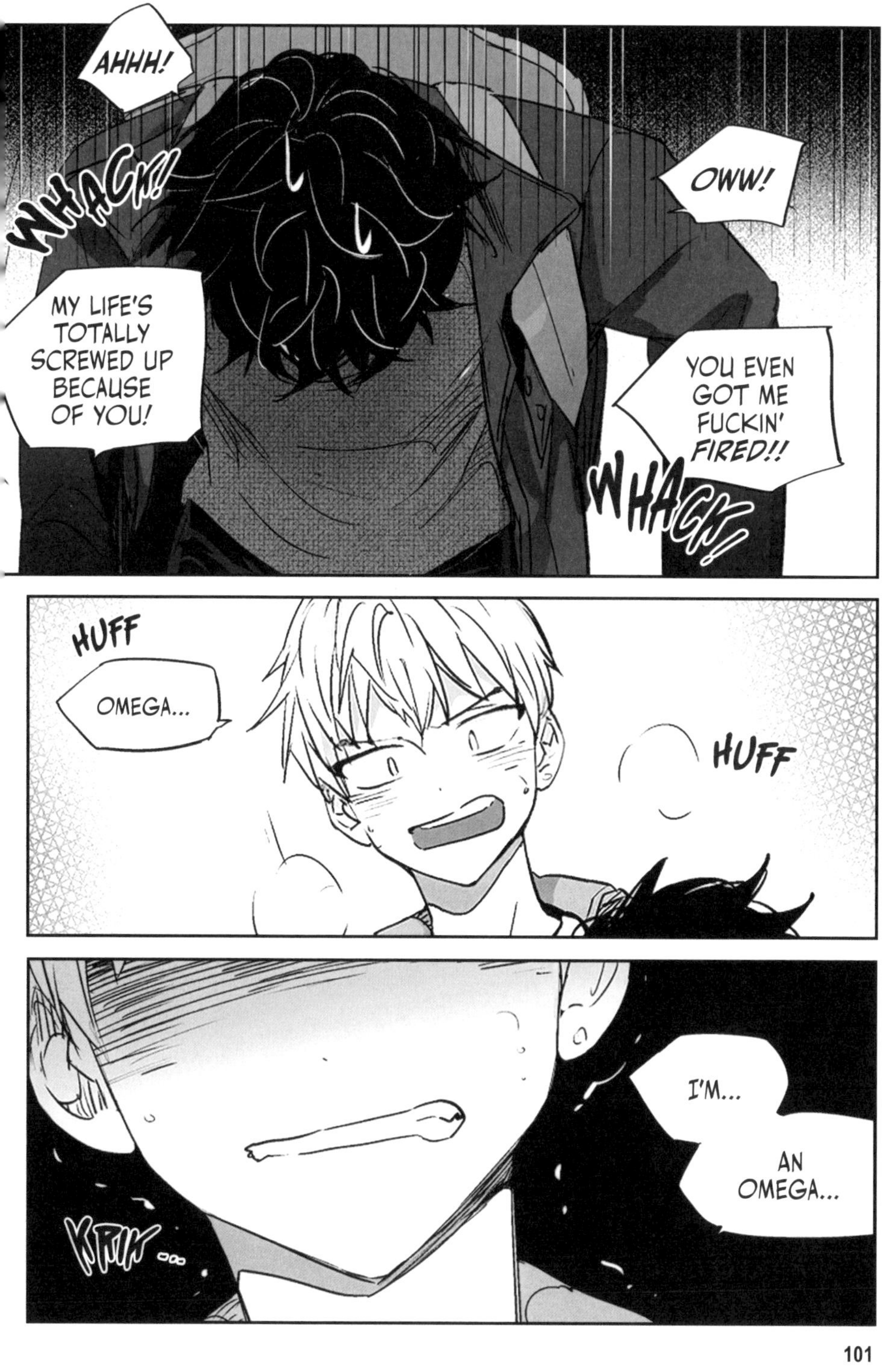
AHHH!
WHACK!
OWW!
MY LIFE'S TOTALLY SCREWED UP BECAUSE OF YOU!
YOU EVEN GOT ME FUCKIN' FIRED!!
WHACK!
HUFF
OMEGA...
HUFF
I'M...
AN OMEGA...
KRIK...

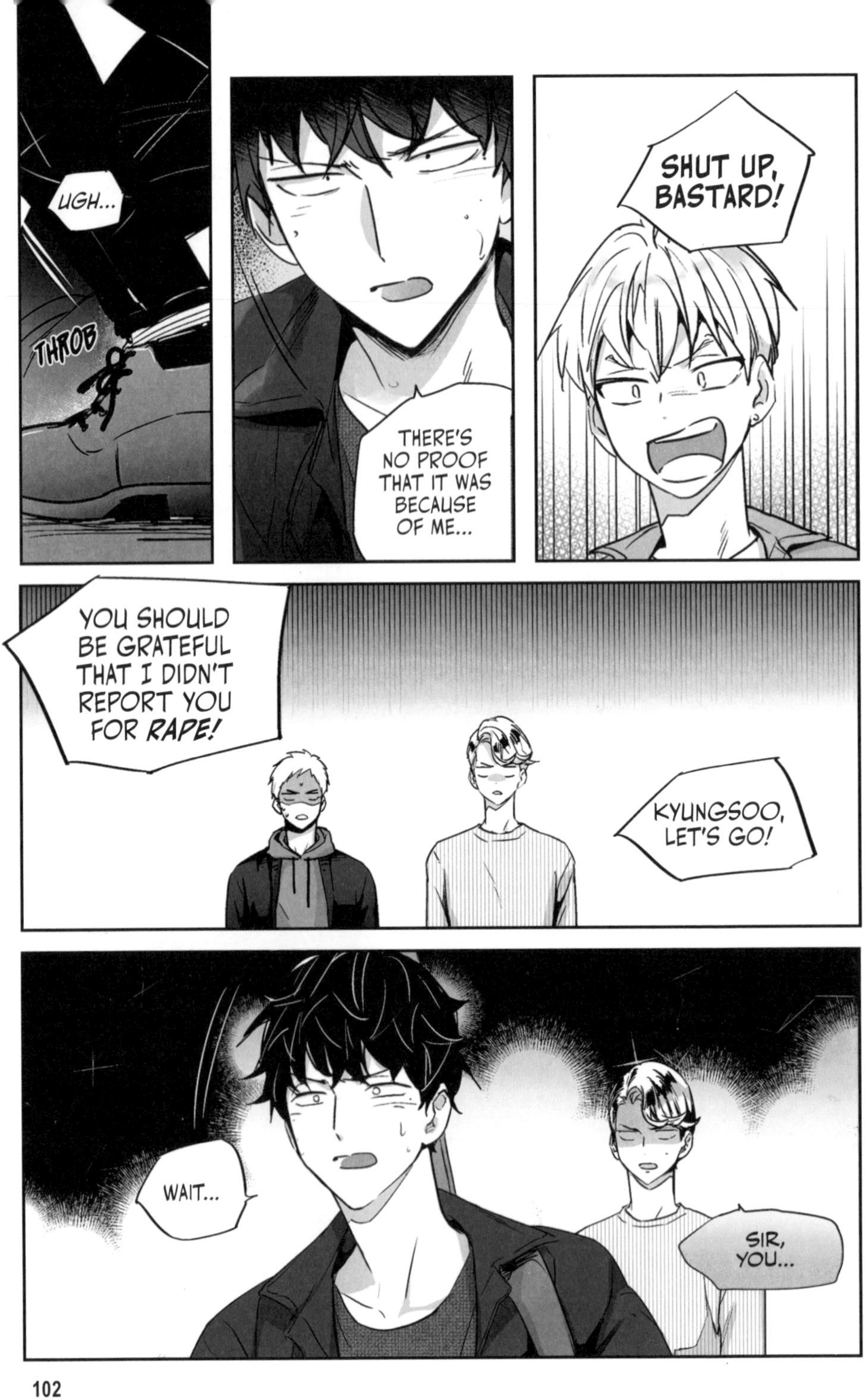
UGH...
THROB
THERE'S NO PROOF THAT IT WAS BECAUSE OF ME...
SHUT UP, BASTARD!
YOU SHOULD BE GRATEFUL THAT I DIDN'T REPORT YOU FOR *RAPE!*
KYUNGSOO, LET'S GO!
WAIT...
SIR, YOU...

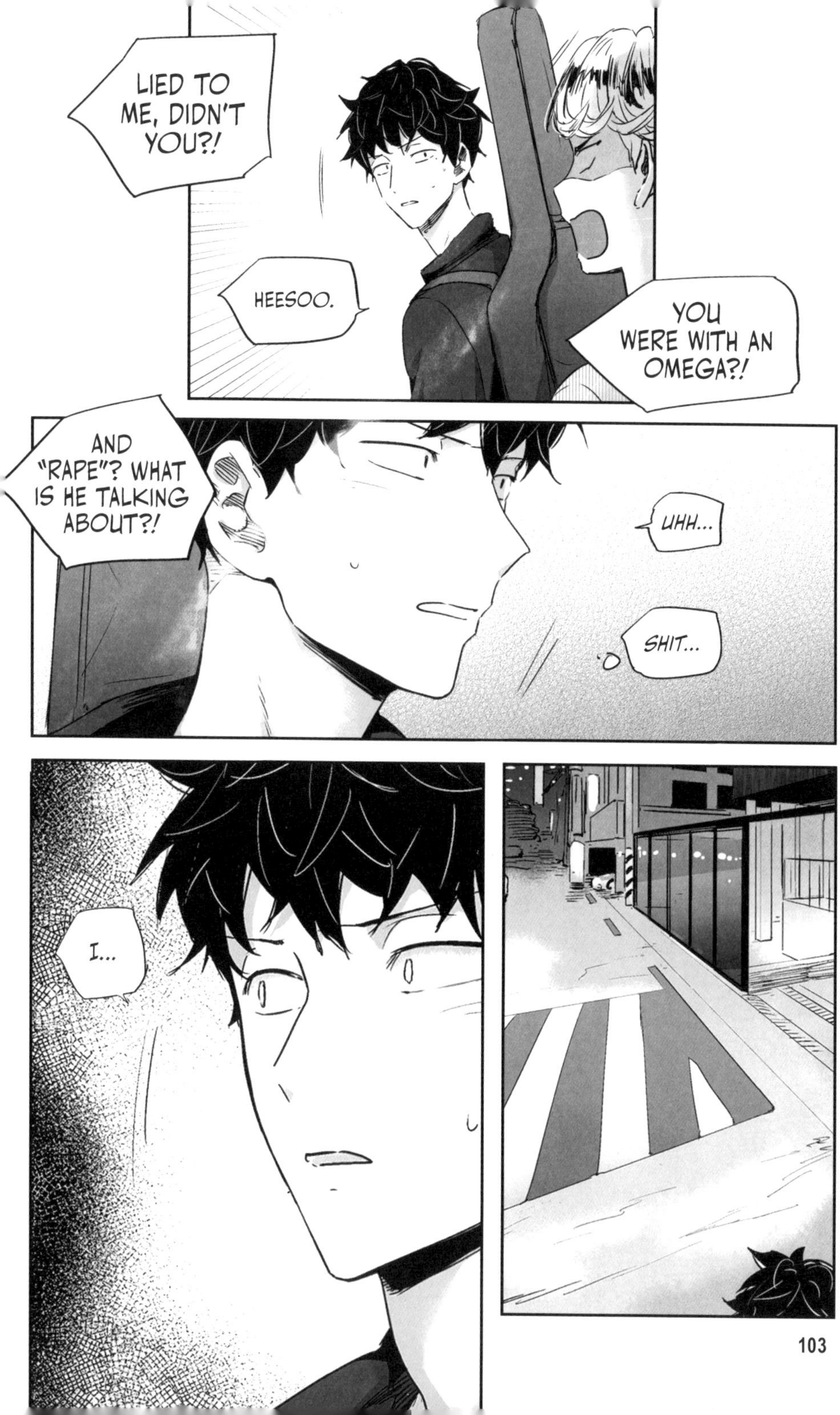
LIED TO ME, DIDN'T YOU?!
HEESOO.
YOU WERE WITH AN OMEGA?!
AND "RAPE"? WHAT IS HE TALKING ABOUT?!
UHH...
SHIT...
I...

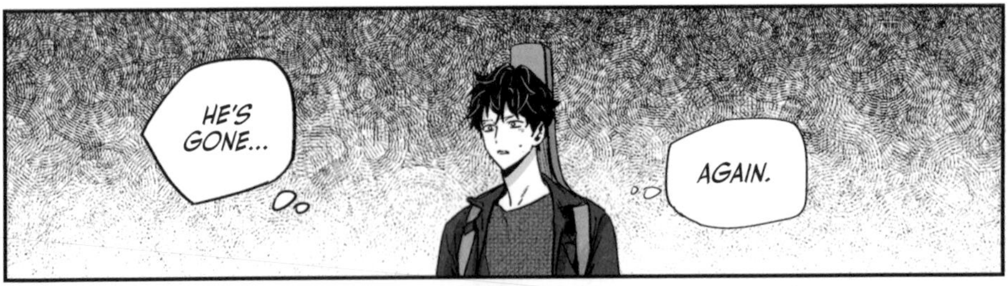
HE'S GONE...
AGAIN.
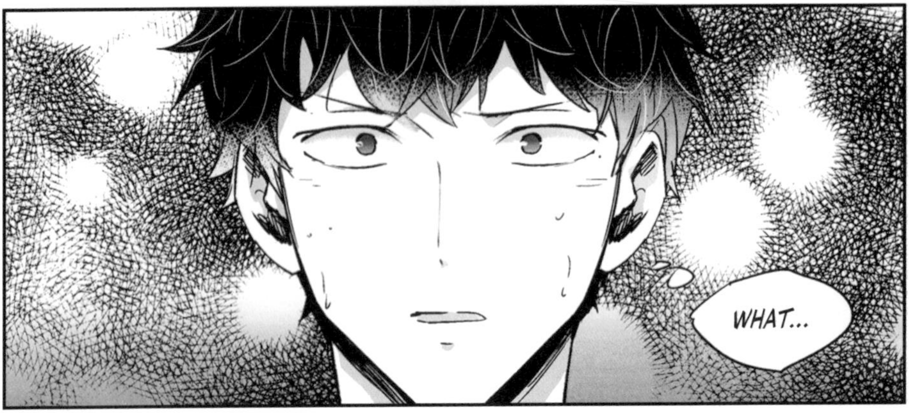
WHAT...

IS...

WITH THAT RUDE OMEGA...?

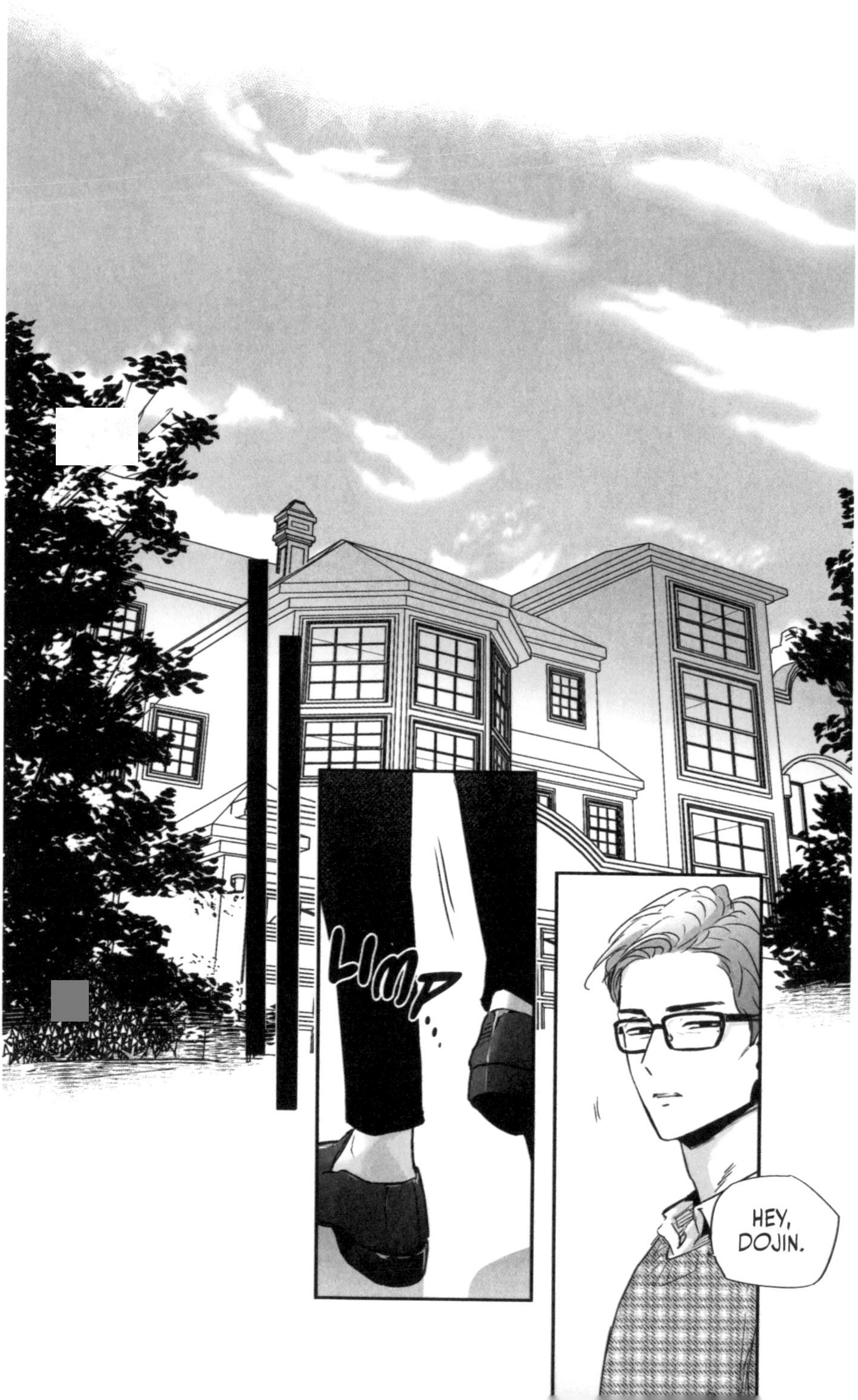
LIMP...
HEY, DOJIN.

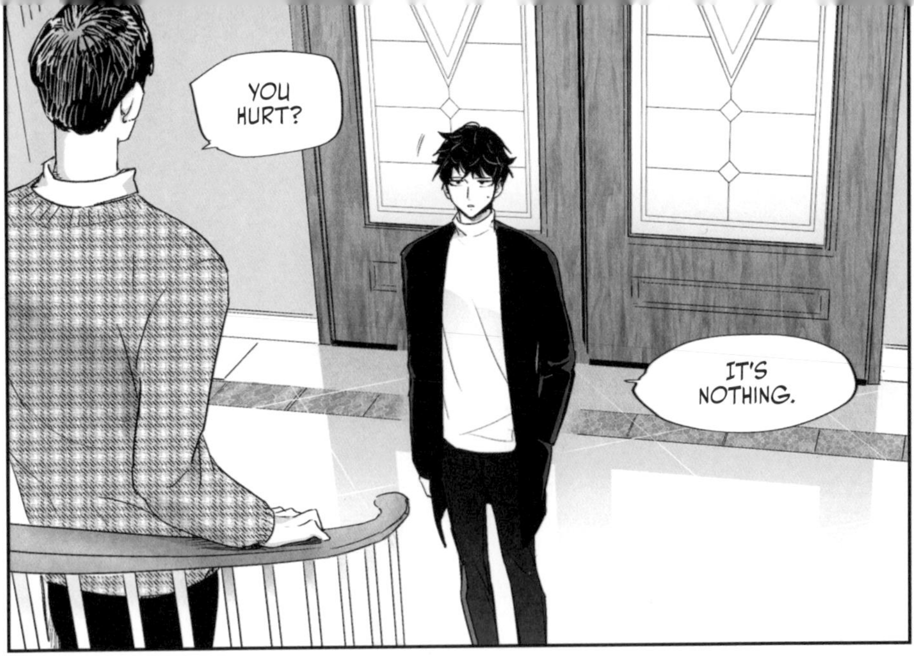
YOU HURT?
IT'S NOTHING.

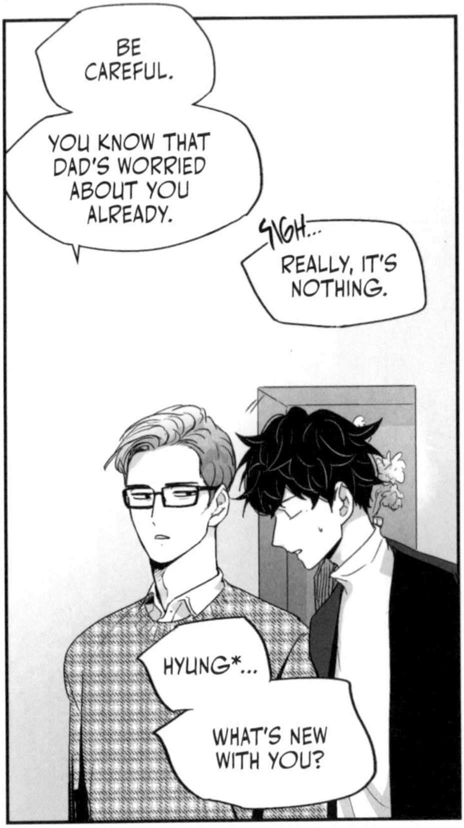
BE CAREFUL.
YOU KNOW THAT DAD'S WORRIED ABOUT YOU ALREADY.
SIGH...
REALLY, IT'S NOTHING.
HYUNG*...
WHAT'S NEW WITH YOU?

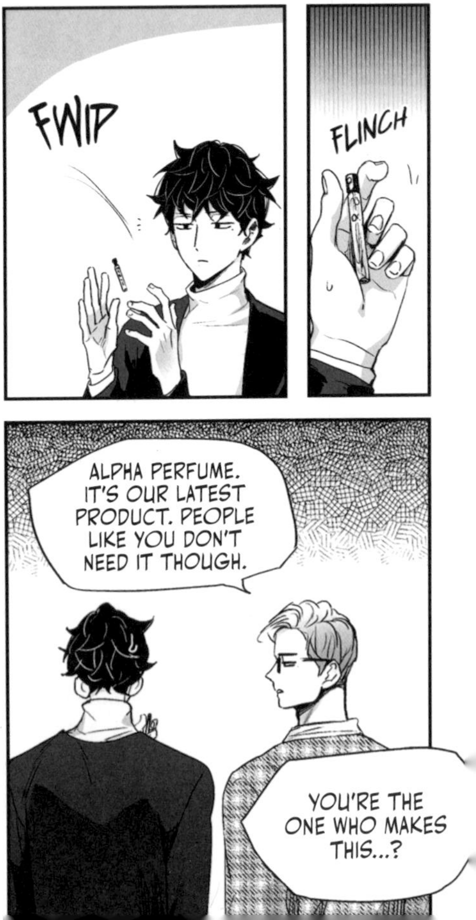
FWIP
FLINCH
ALPHA PERFUME. IT'S OUR LATEST PRODUCT. PEOPLE LIKE YOU DON'T NEED IT THOUGH.
YOU'RE THE ONE WHO MAKES THIS...?

*Hyung: Honorific title used by males to address elder brothers or other males older than themselves.

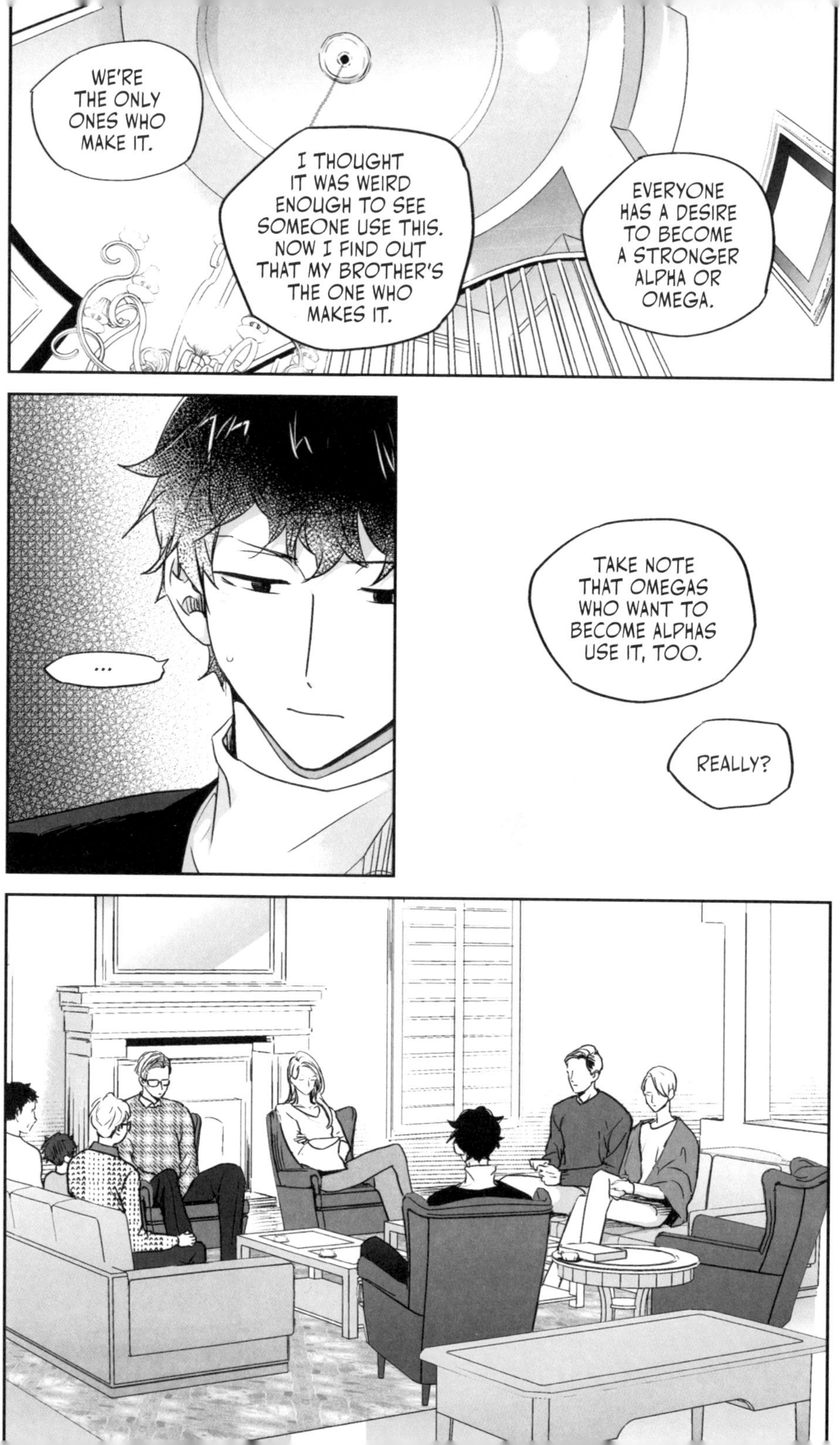
WE'RE THE ONLY ONES WHO MAKE IT.
I THOUGHT IT WAS WEIRD ENOUGH TO SEE SOMEONE USE THIS. NOW I FIND OUT THAT MY BROTHER'S THE ONE WHO MAKES IT.
EVERYONE HAS A DESIRE TO BECOME A STRONGER ALPHA OR OMEGA.
...
TAKE NOTE THAT OMEGAS WHO WANT TO BECOME ALPHAS USE IT, TOO.
REALLY?

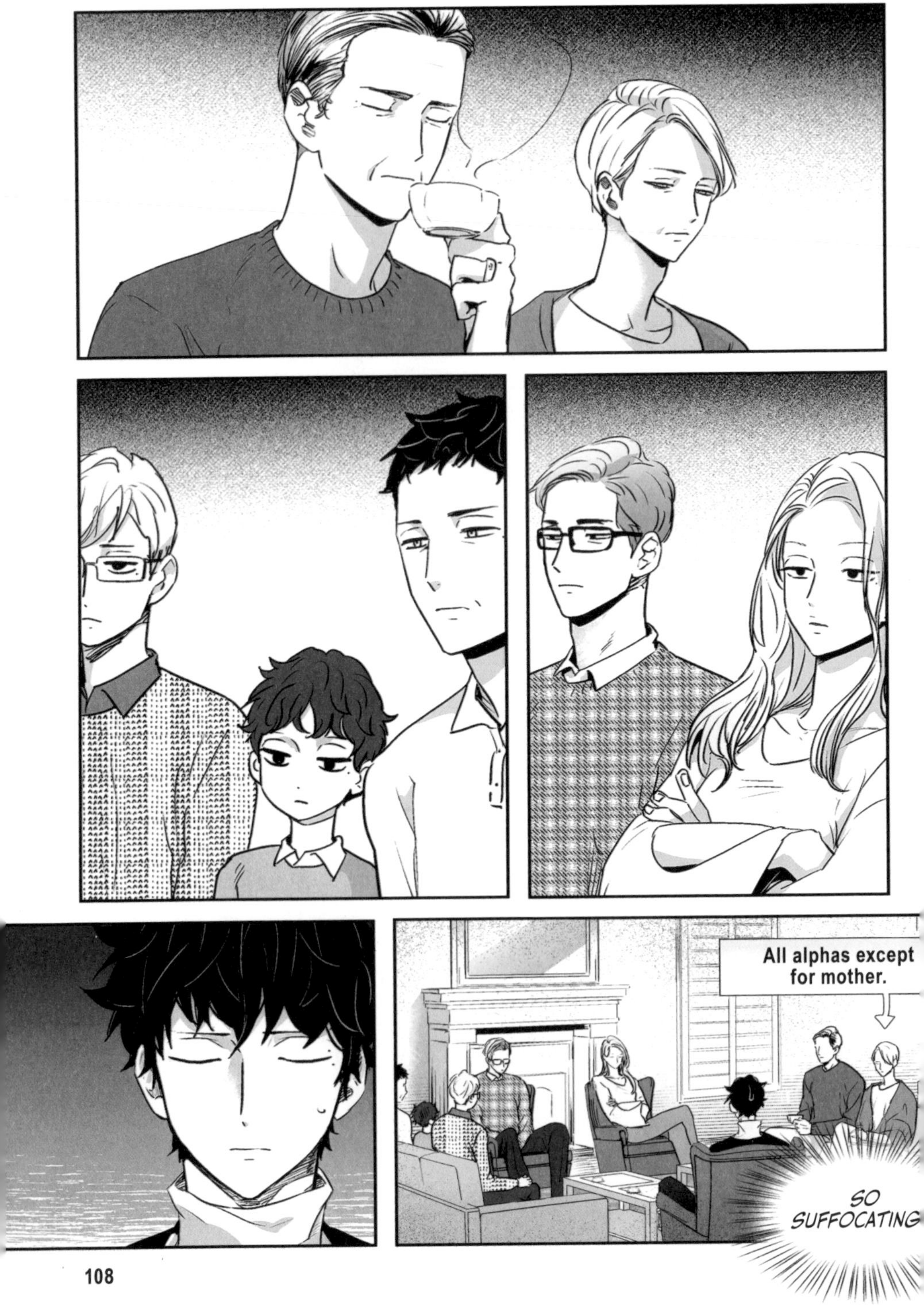
All alphas except for mother.
SO SUFFOCATING

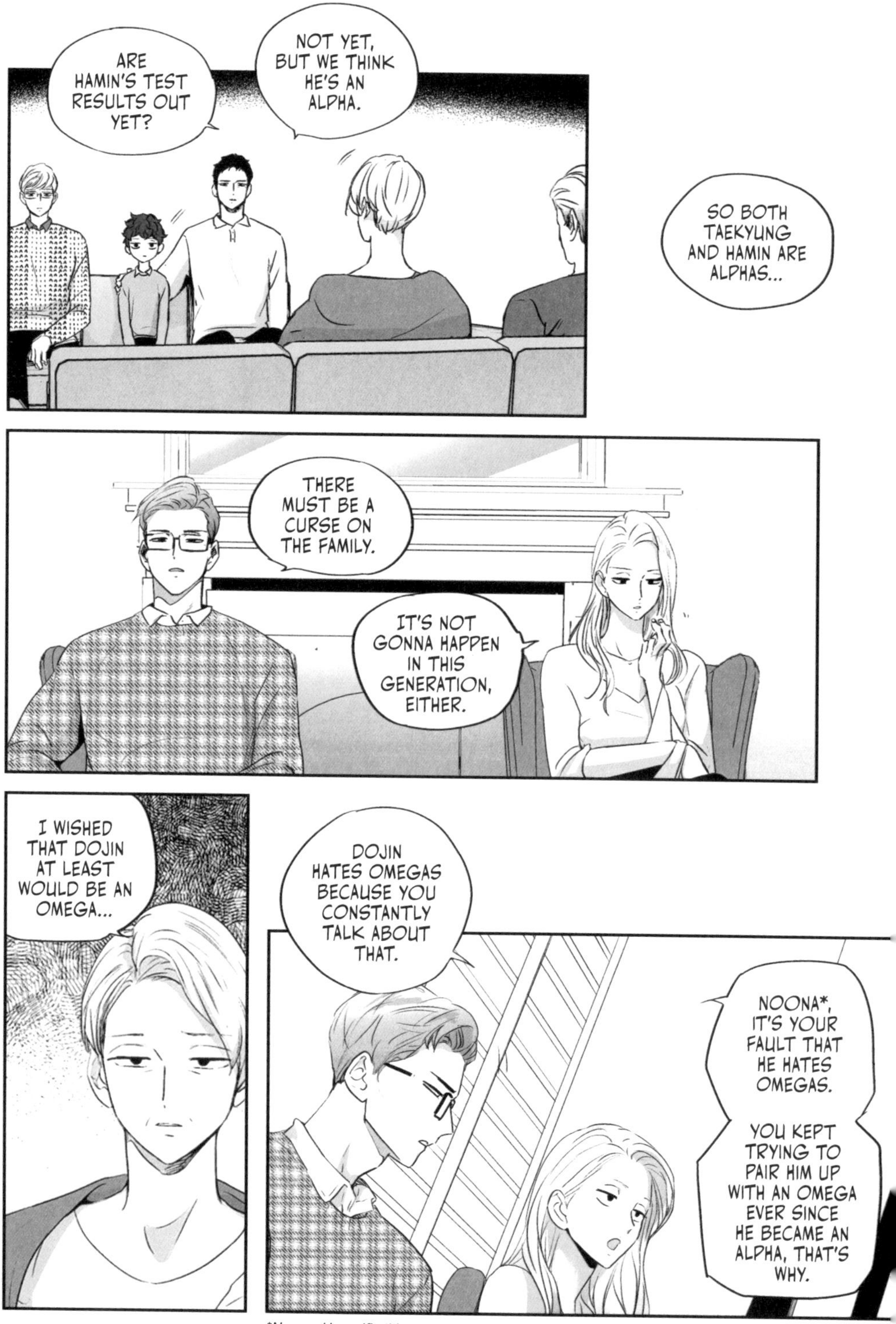
ARE HAMIN'S TEST RESULTS OUT YET?
NOT YET, BUT WE THINK HE'S AN ALPHA.
SO BOTH TAEKYUNG AND HAMIN ARE ALPHAS...
THERE MUST BE A CURSE ON THE FAMILY.
IT'S NOT GONNA HAPPEN IN THIS GENERATION, EITHER.
I WISHED THAT DOJIN AT LEAST WOULD BE AN OMEGA...
DOJIN HATES OMEGAS BECAUSE YOU CONSTANTLY TALK ABOUT THAT.
NOONA*, IT'S YOUR FAULT THAT HE HATES OMEGAS.
YOU KEPT TRYING TO PAIR HIM UP WITH AN OMEGA EVER SINCE HE BECAME AN ALPHA, THAT'S WHY.

*Noona: Honorific title used by males to address elder sisters or other females older than themselves.

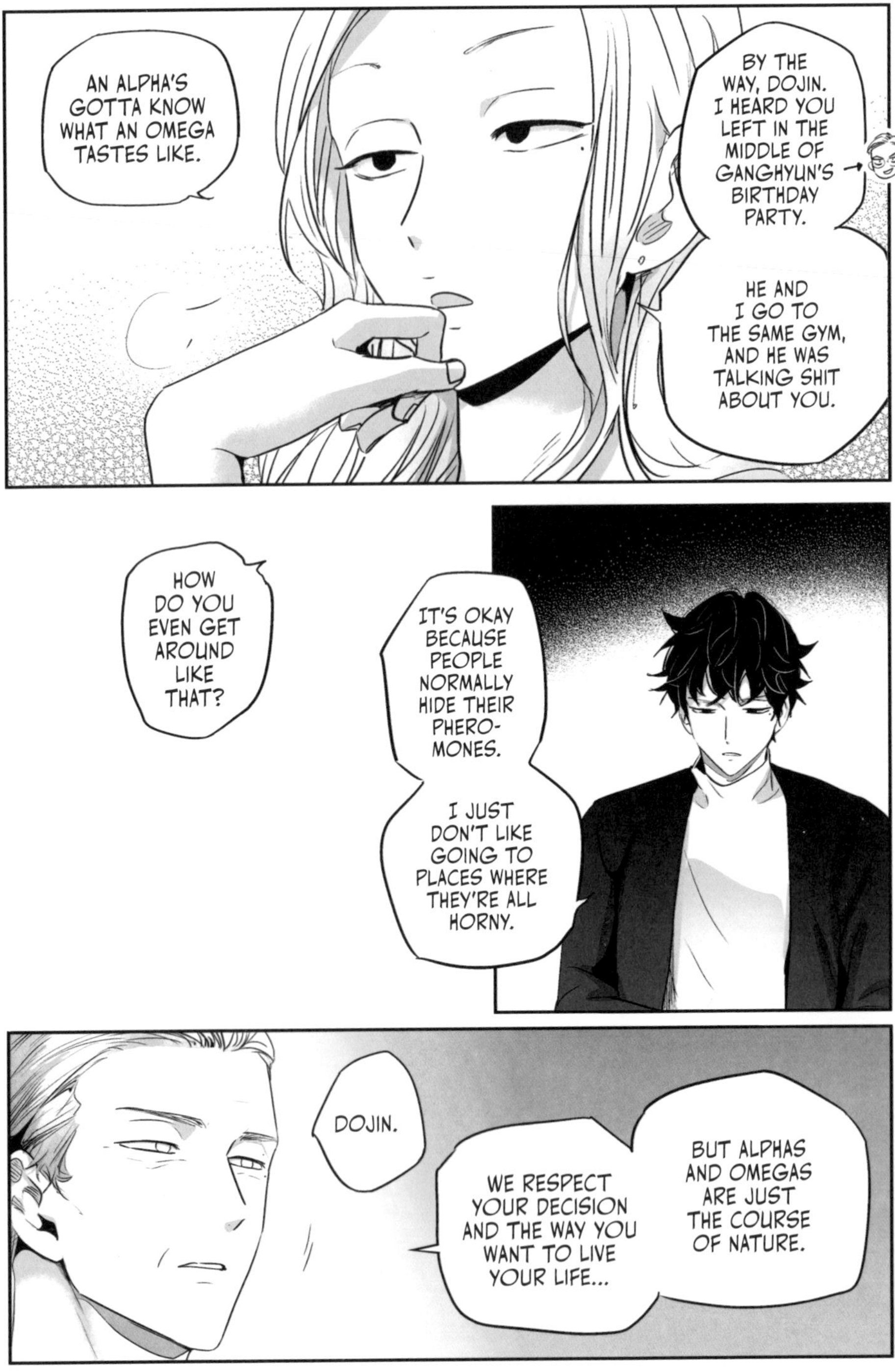
AN ALPHA'S GOTTA KNOW WHAT AN OMEGA TASTES LIKE.
BY THE WAY, DOJIN. I HEARD YOU LEFT IN THE MIDDLE OF GANGHYUN'S BIRTHDAY PARTY.
HE AND I GO TO THE SAME GYM, AND HE WAS TALKING SHIT ABOUT YOU.
HOW DO YOU EVEN GET AROUND LIKE THAT?
IT'S OKAY BECAUSE PEOPLE NORMALLY HIDE THEIR PHERO-MONES.
I JUST DON'T LIKE GOING TO PLACES WHERE THEY'RE ALL HORNY.
DOJIN.
WE RESPECT YOUR DECISION AND THE WAY YOU WANT TO LIVE YOUR LIFE...
BUT ALPHAS AND OMEGAS ARE JUST THE COURSE OF NATURE.

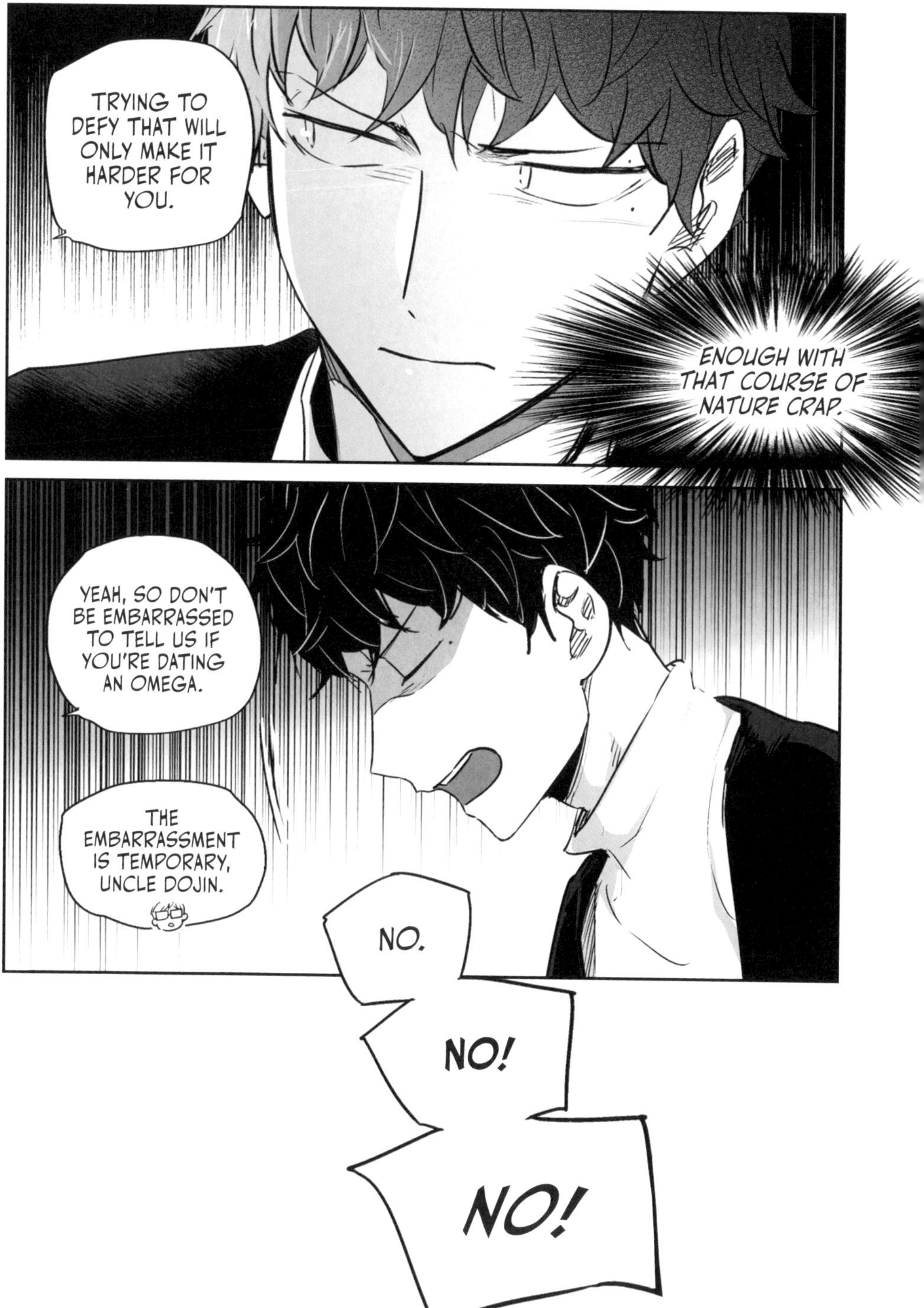
TRYING TO DEFY THAT WILL ONLY MAKE IT HARDER FOR YOU.
ENOUGH WITH THAT COURSE OF NATURE CRAP.
YEAH, SO DON'T BE EMBARRASSED TO TELL US IF YOU'RE DATING AN OMEGA.
THE EMBARRASSMENT IS TEMPORARY, UNCLE DOJIN.
NO.
NO!
NO!

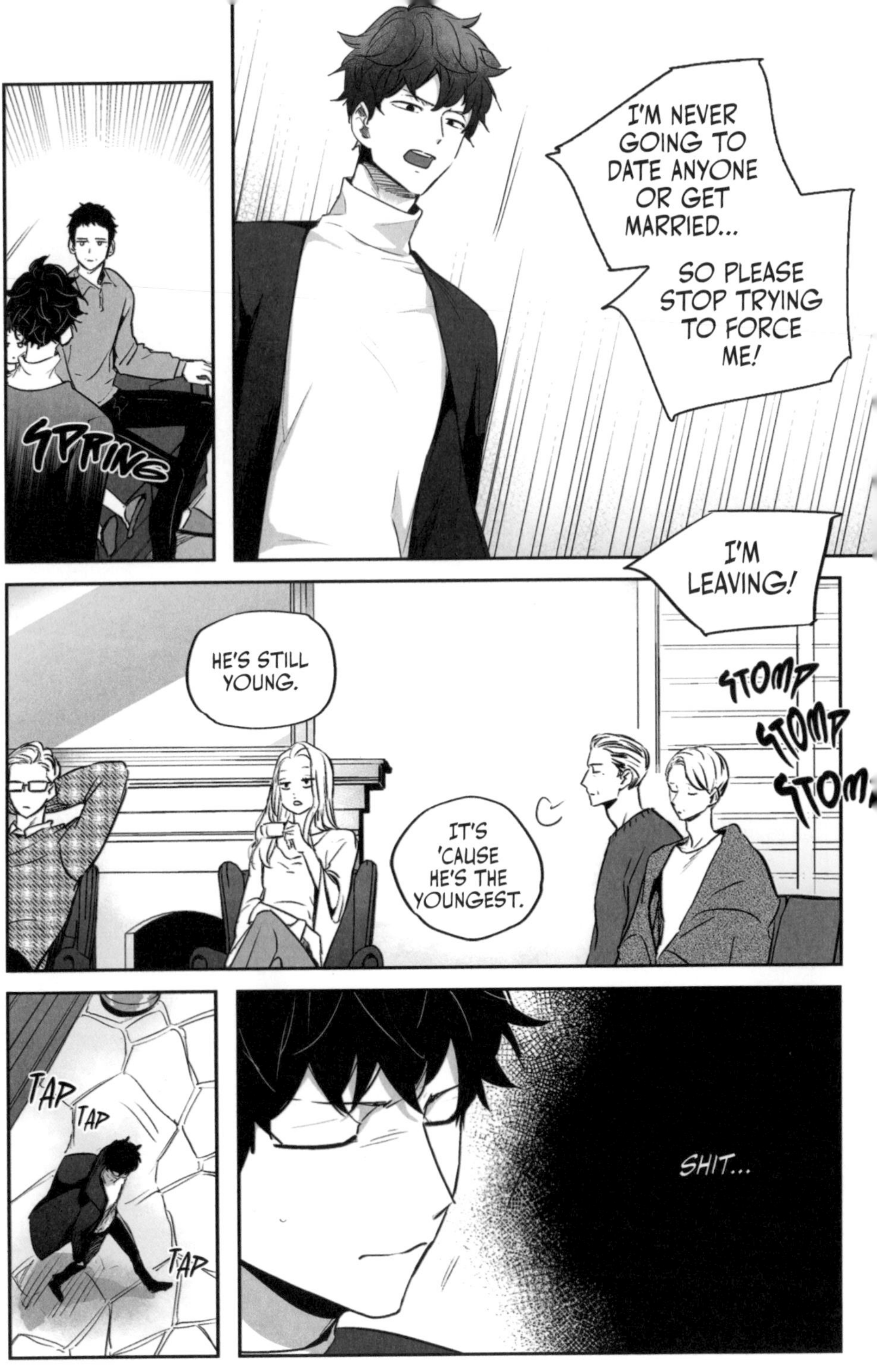
SPRING
I'M NEVER GOING TO DATE ANYONE OR GET MARRIED...
SO PLEASE STOP TRYING TO FORCE ME!
I'M LEAVING!
HE'S STILL YOUNG.
IT'S 'CAUSE HE'S THE YOUNGEST.
STOMP
STOMP
STOMP
TAP
TAP
TAP
SHIT...

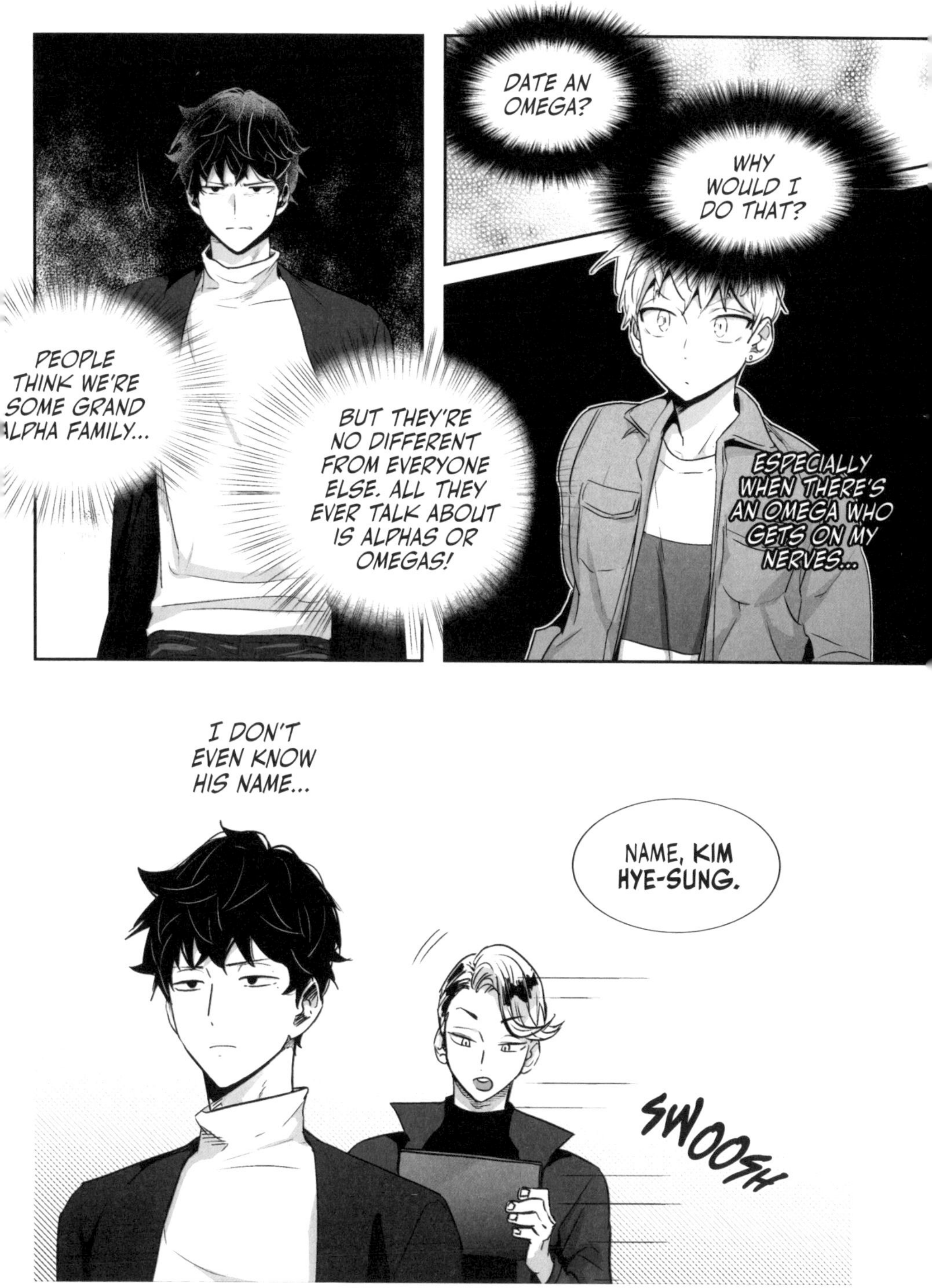
PEOPLE THINK WE'RE SOME GRAND ALPHA FAMILY...
BUT THEY'RE NO DIFFERENT FROM EVERYONE ELSE. ALL THEY EVER TALK ABOUT IS ALPHAS OR OMEGAS!
DATE AN OMEGA?
WHY WOULD I DO THAT?
ESPECIALLY WHEN THERE'S AN OMEGA WHO GETS ON MY NERVES...
I DON'T EVEN KNOW HIS NAME...
NAME, KIM HYE-SUNG.
SWOOSH

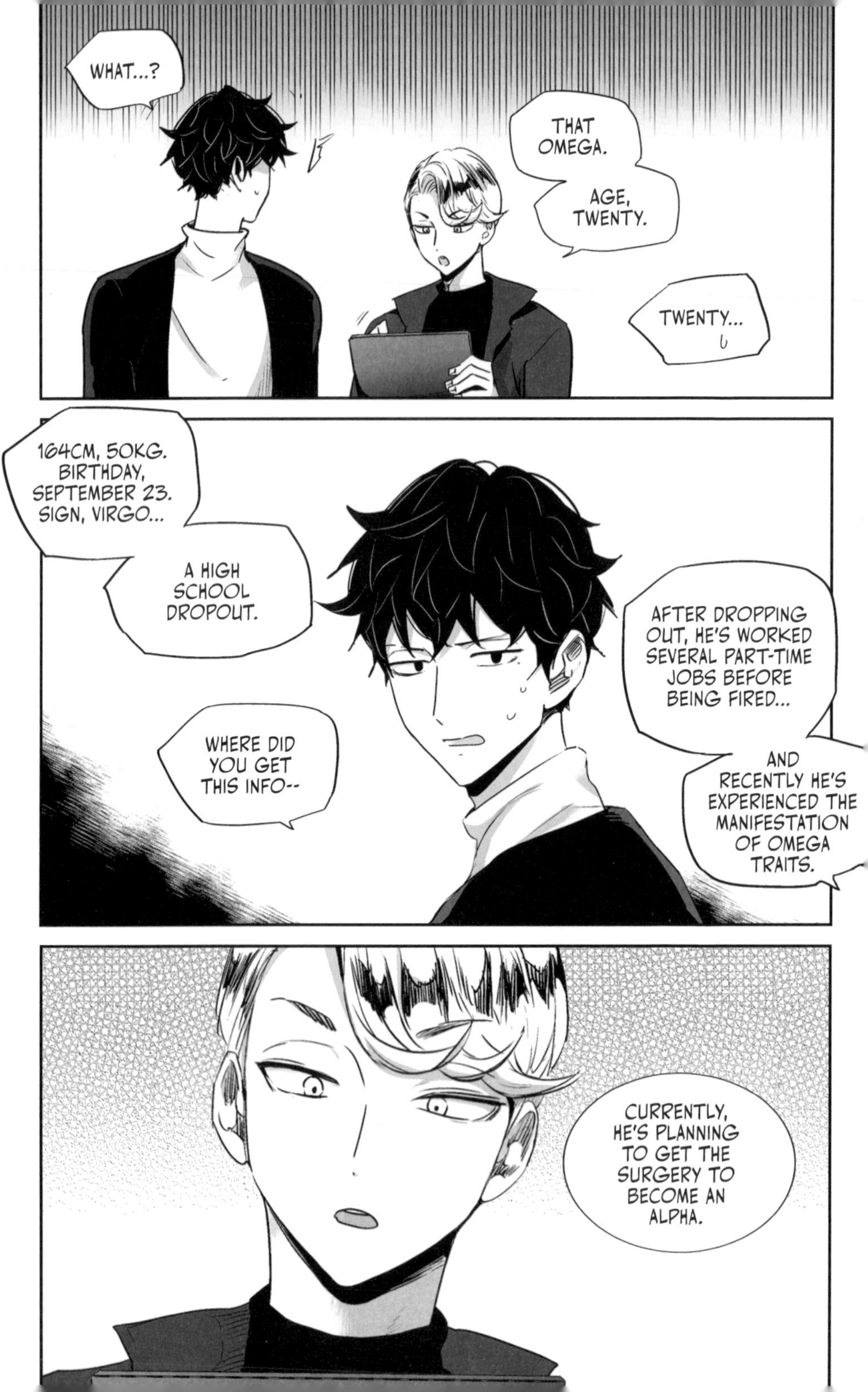

WHAT...?
THAT OMEGA.
AGE, TWENTY.
TWENTY...
164CM, 50KG. BIRTHDAY, SEPTEMBER 23. SIGN, VIRGO...
A HIGH SCHOOL DROPOUT.
WHERE DID YOU GET THIS INFO--
AFTER DROPPING OUT, HE'S WORKED SEVERAL PART-TIME JOBS BEFORE BEING FIRED...
AND RECENTLY HE'S EXPERIENCED THE MANIFESTATION OF OMEGA TRAITS.
CURRENTLY, HE'S PLANNING TO GET THE SURGERY TO BECOME AN ALPHA.

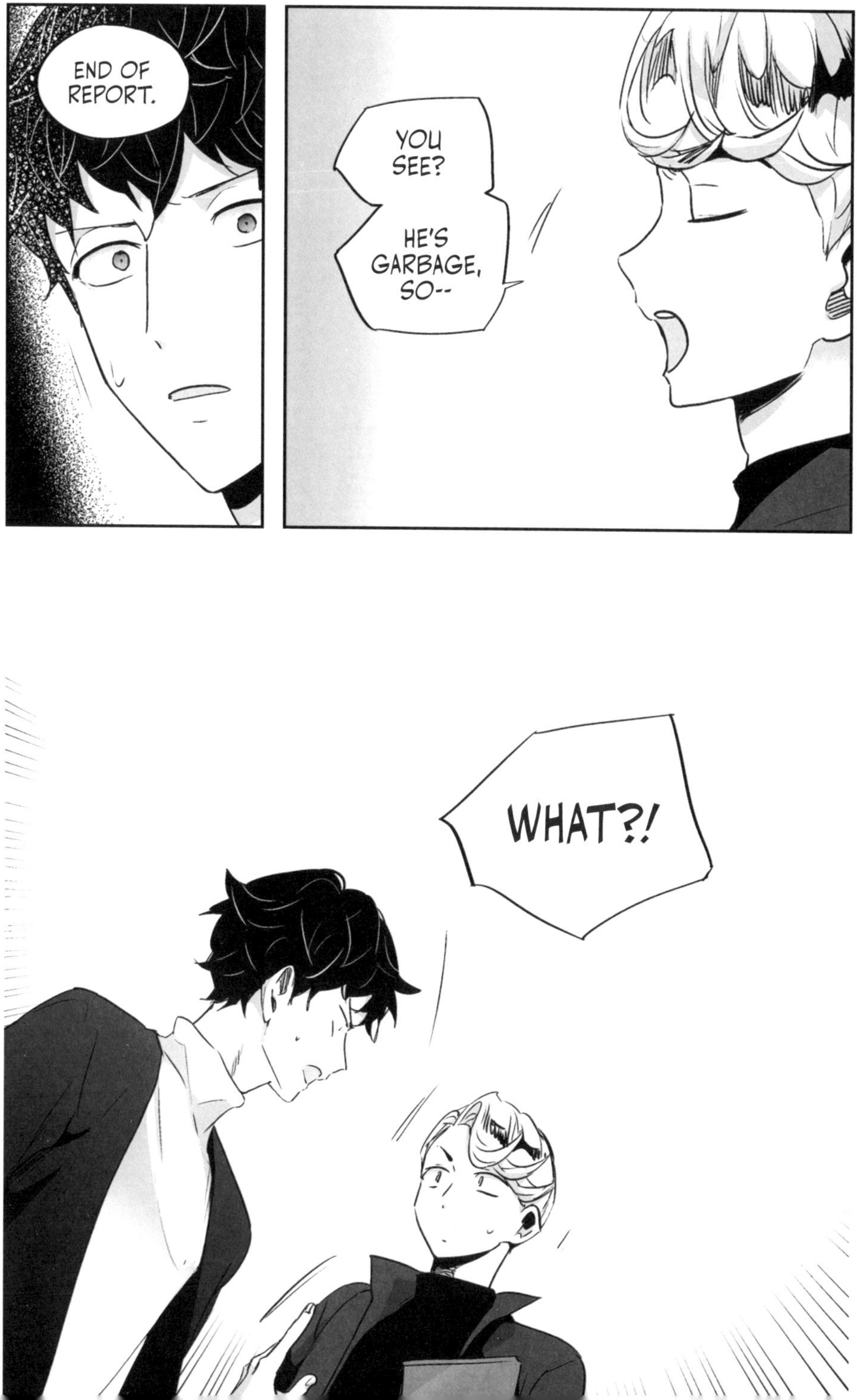
END OF REPORT.
YOU SEE?
HE'S GARBAGE, SO--
WHAT?!

Love is
an Illusion!

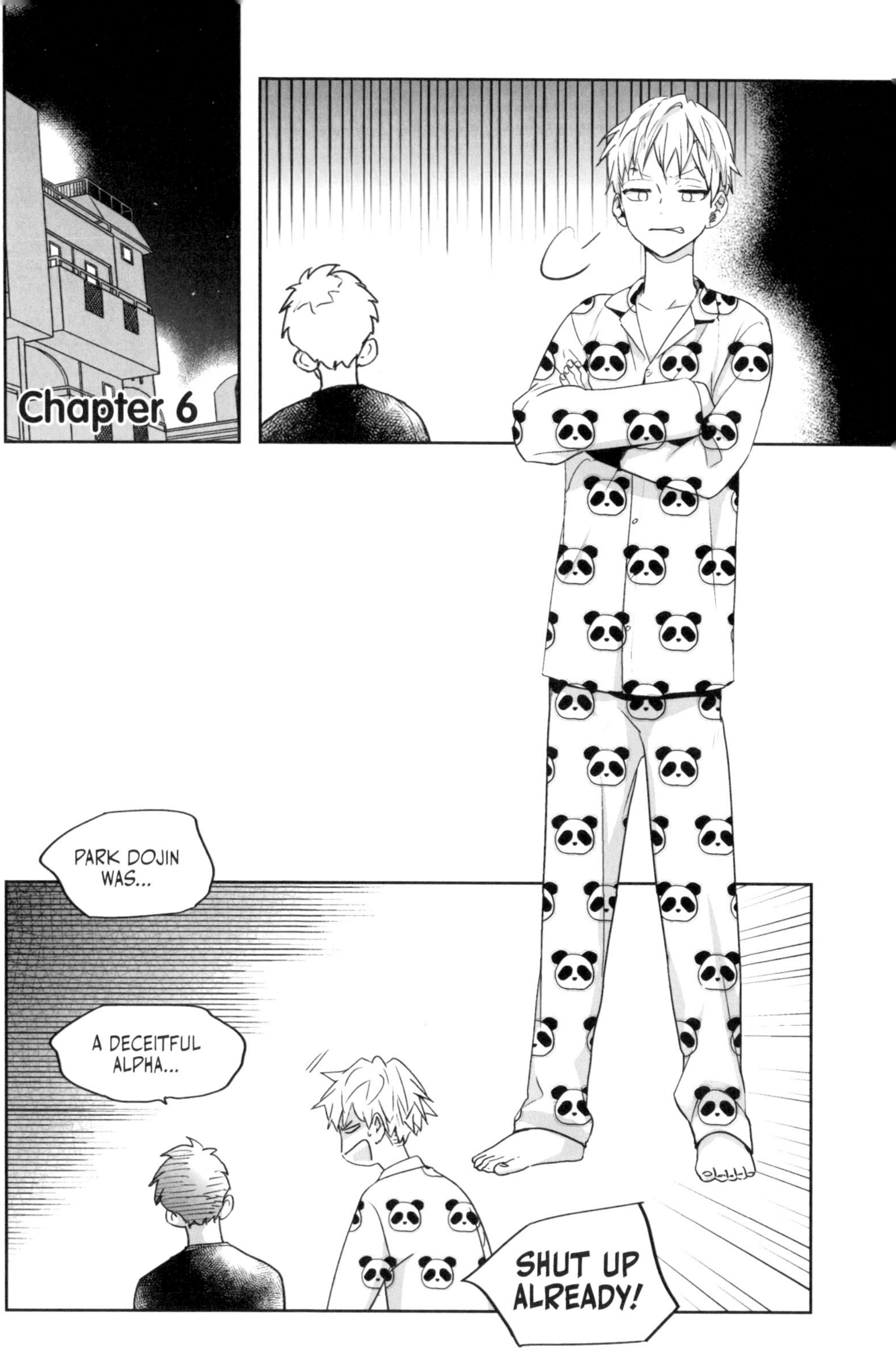
Chapter 6
PARK DOJIN WAS...
A DECEITFUL ALPHA...
SHUT UP ALREADY!

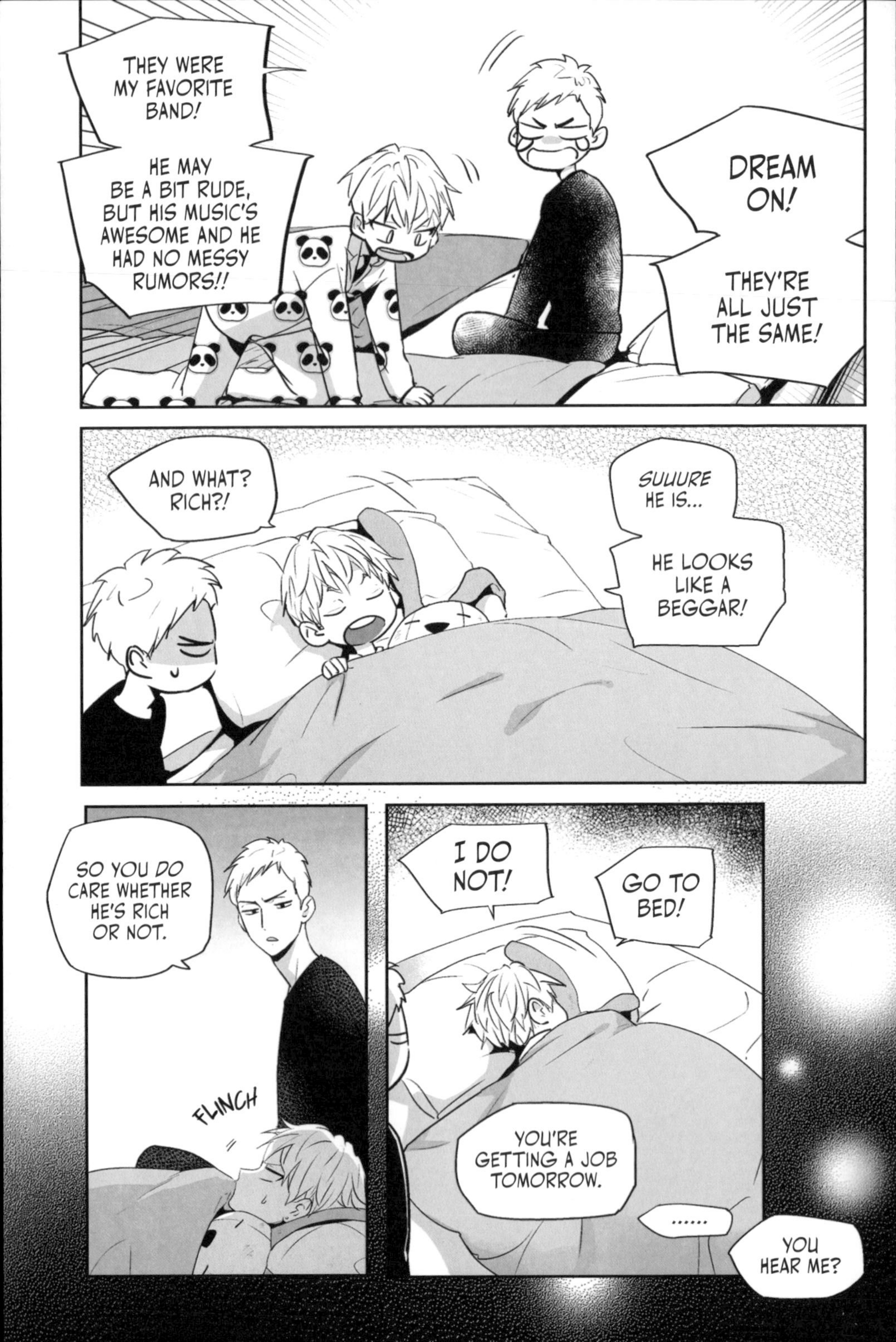
THEY WERE MY FAVORITE BAND!
HE MAY BE A BIT RUDE, BUT HIS MUSIC'S AWESOME AND HE HAD NO MESSY RUMORS!!
DREAM ON!
THEY'RE ALL JUST THE SAME!
AND WHAT? RICH?!
SUUURE HE IS...
HE LOOKS LIKE A BEGGAR!
SO YOU DO CARE WHETHER HE'S RICH OR NOT.
FLINCH
I DO NOT!
GO TO BED!
YOU'RE GETTING A JOB TOMORROW.
......
YOU HEAR ME?

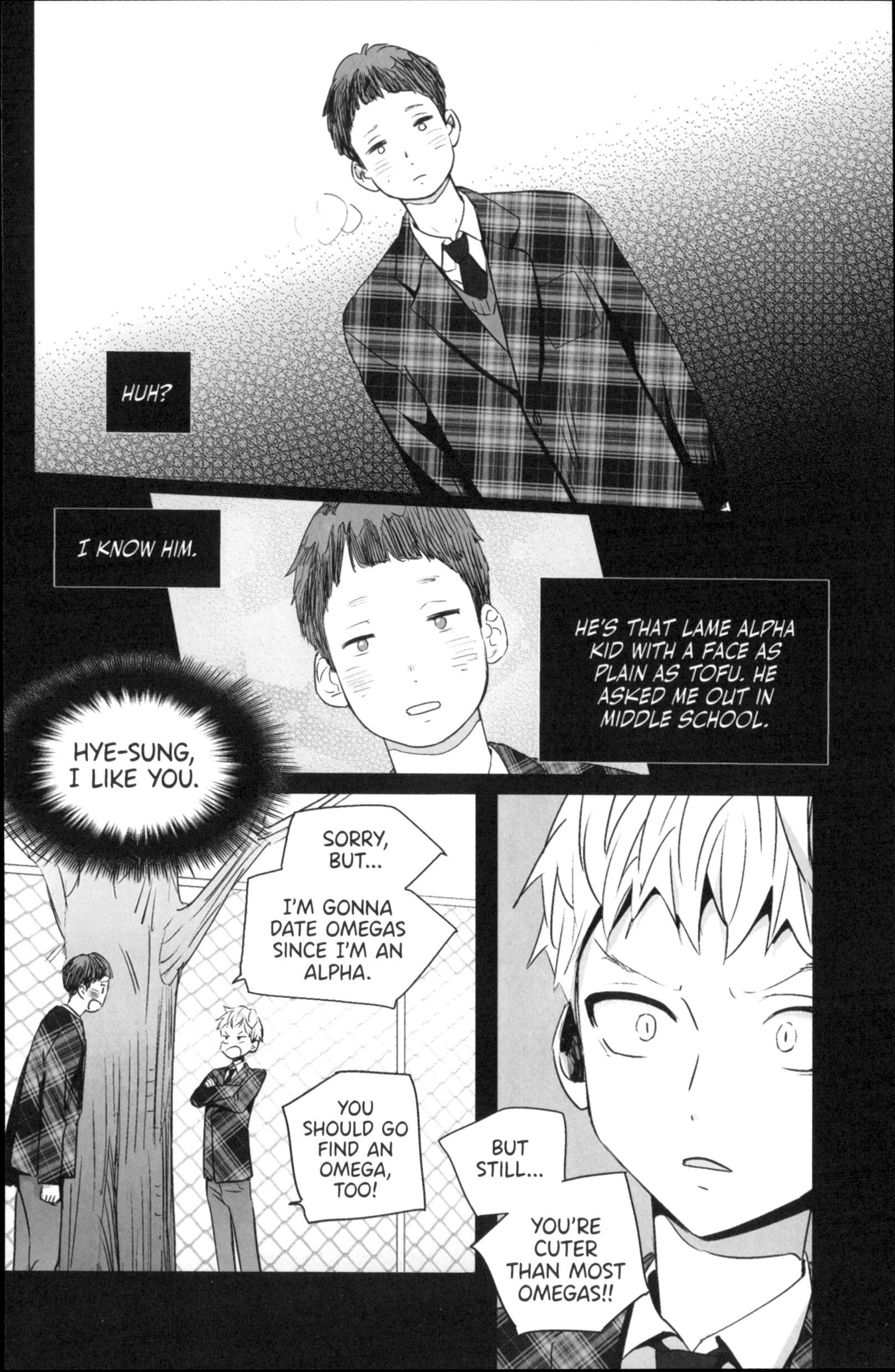
HUH?
I KNOW HIM.
HE'S THAT LAME ALPHA KID WITH A FACE AS PLAIN AS TOFU. HE ASKED ME OUT IN MIDDLE SCHOOL.
HYE-SUNG, I LIKE YOU.
SORRY, BUT...
I'M GONNA DATE OMEGAS SINCE I'M AN ALPHA.
YOU SHOULD GO FIND AN OMEGA, TOO!
BUT STILL...
YOU'RE CUTER THAN MOST OMEGAS!!

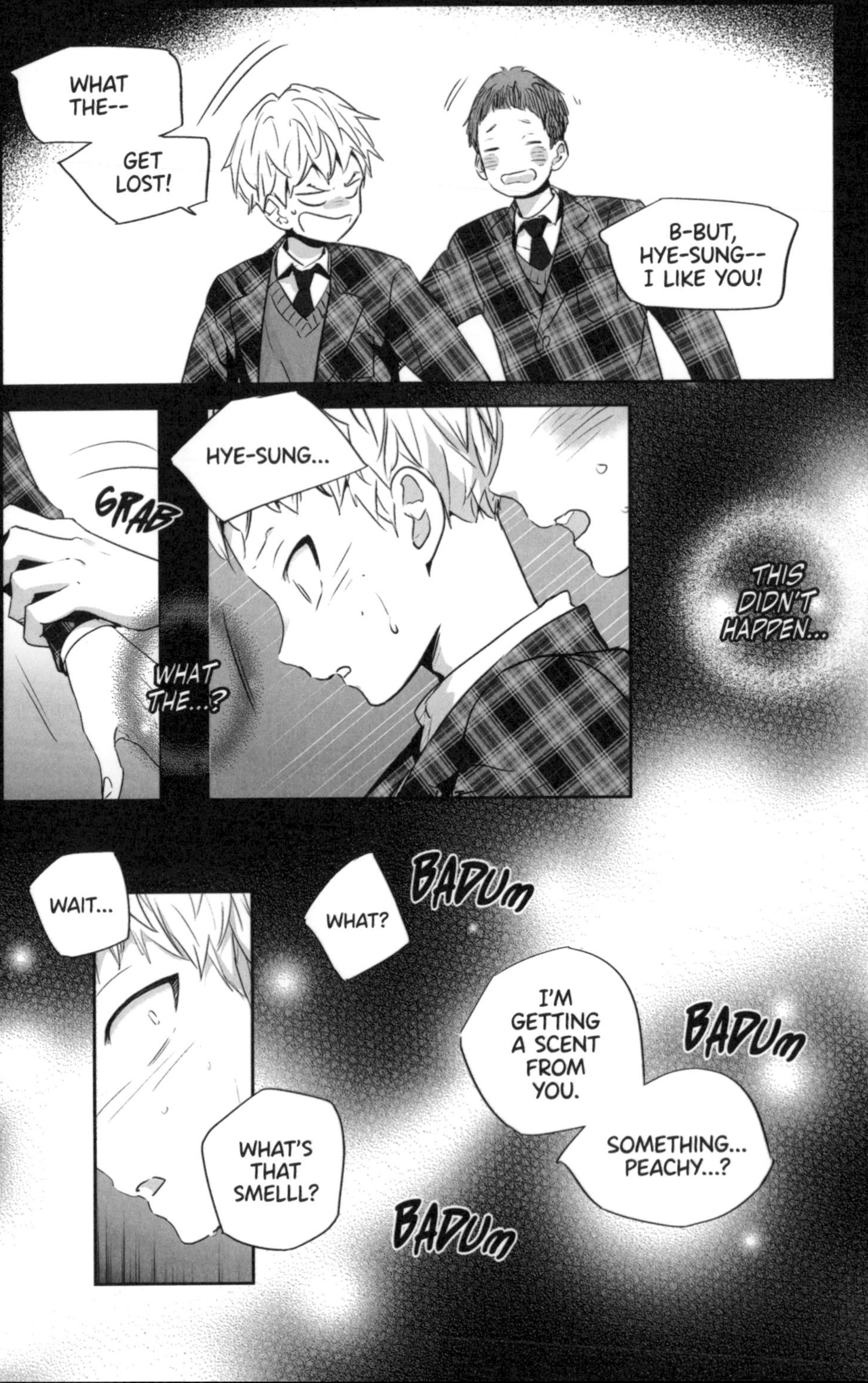
WHAT THE--
GET LOST!
B-BUT, HYE-SUNG-- I LIKE YOU!
GRAB
WHAT THE...?
HYE-SUNG...
THIS DIDN'T HAPPEN...
WAIT...
WHAT?
BADUM
WHAT'S THAT SMELLL?
I'M GETTING A SCENT FROM YOU.
BADUM
SOMETHING... PEACHY...?
BADUM

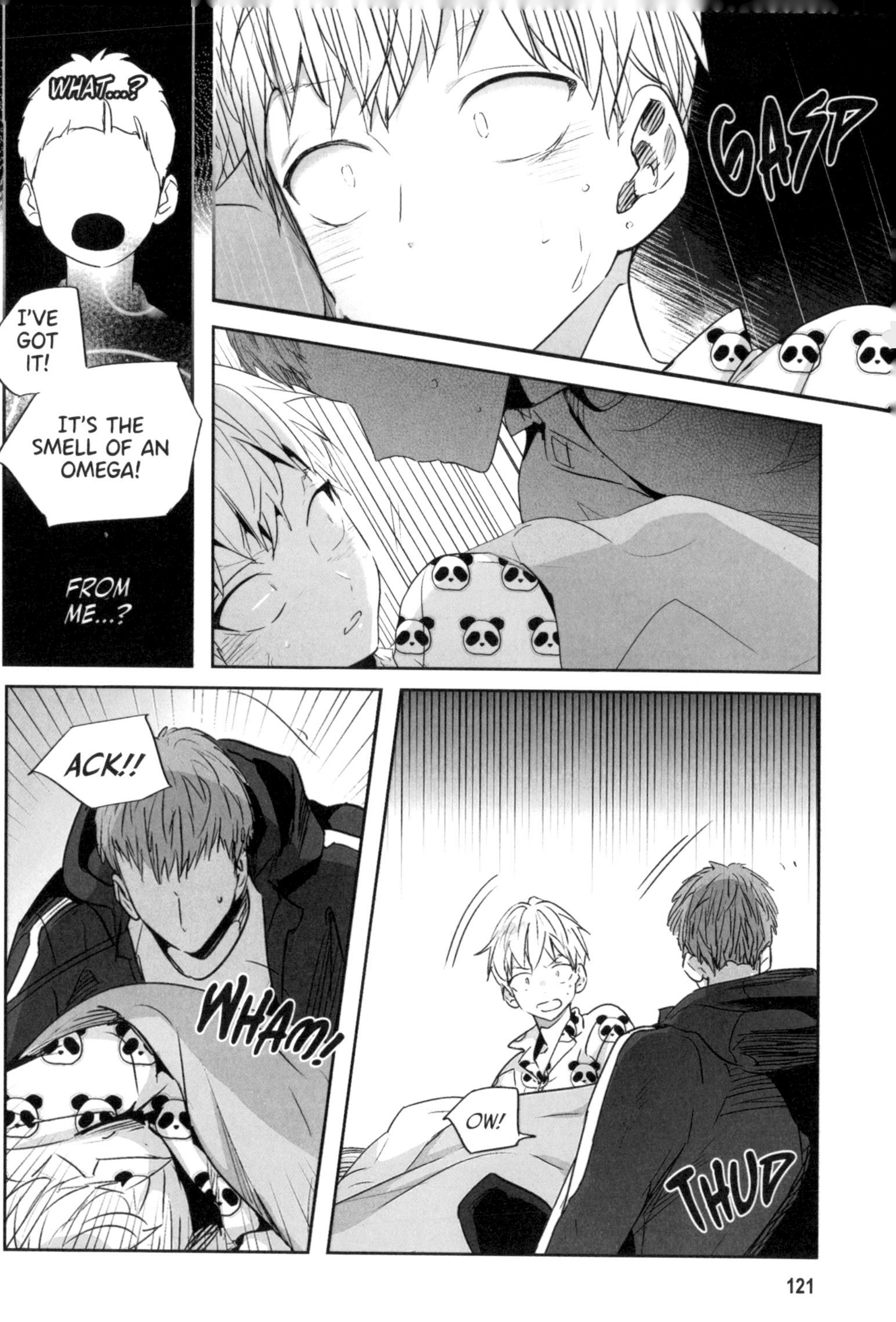
WHAT...?
I'VE GOT IT!
IT'S THE SMELL OF AN OMEGA!
FROM ME...?
GASP
ACK!!
WHAM!
OW!
THUD

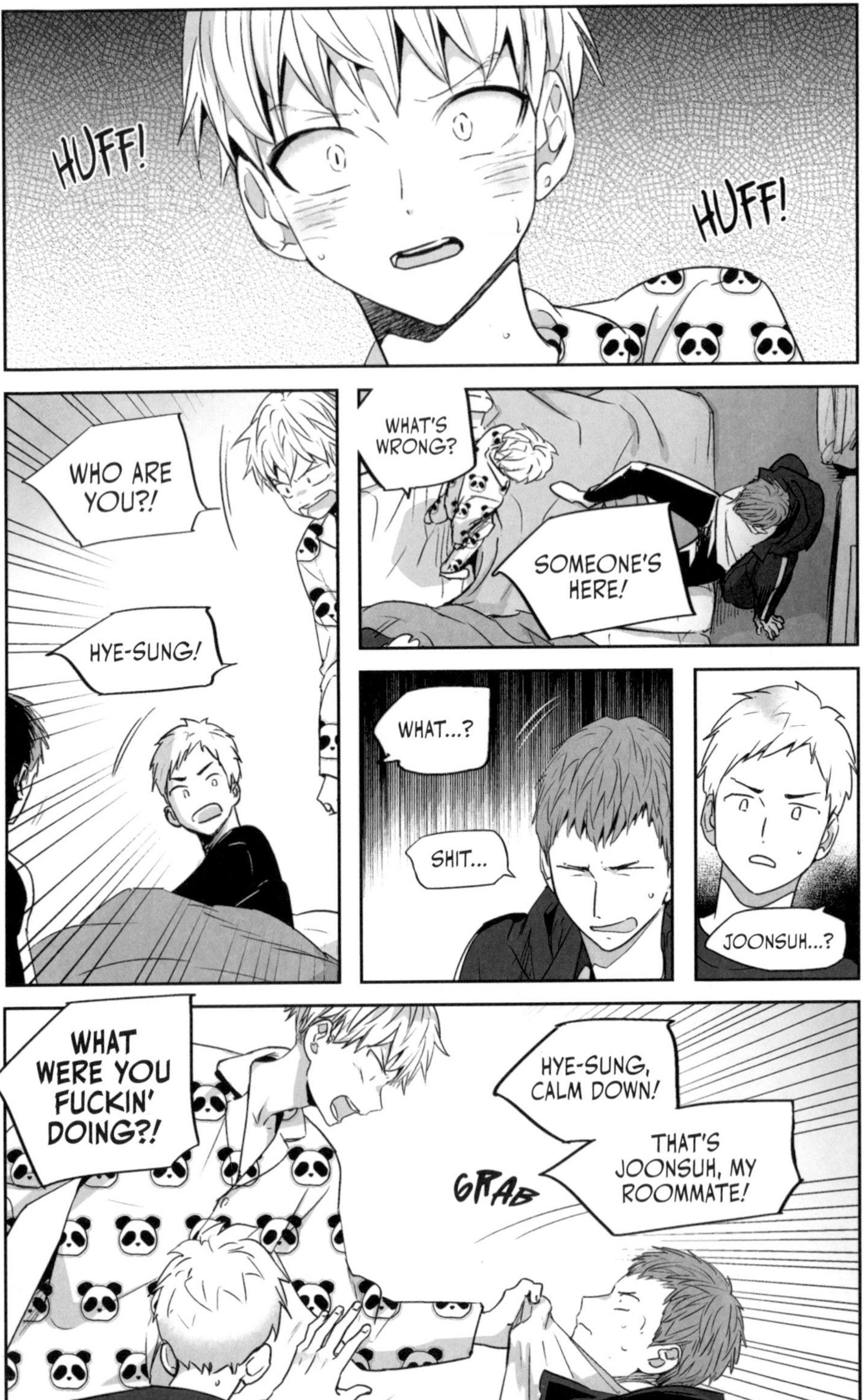
HUFF!
HUFF!
WHO ARE YOU?!
HYE-SUNG!
WHAT'S WRONG?
SOMEONE'S HERE!
WHAT...?
SHIT...
JOONSUH...?
WHAT WERE YOU FUCKIN' DOING?!
HYE-SUNG, CALM DOWN!
THAT'S JOONSUH, MY ROOMMATE!
GRAB

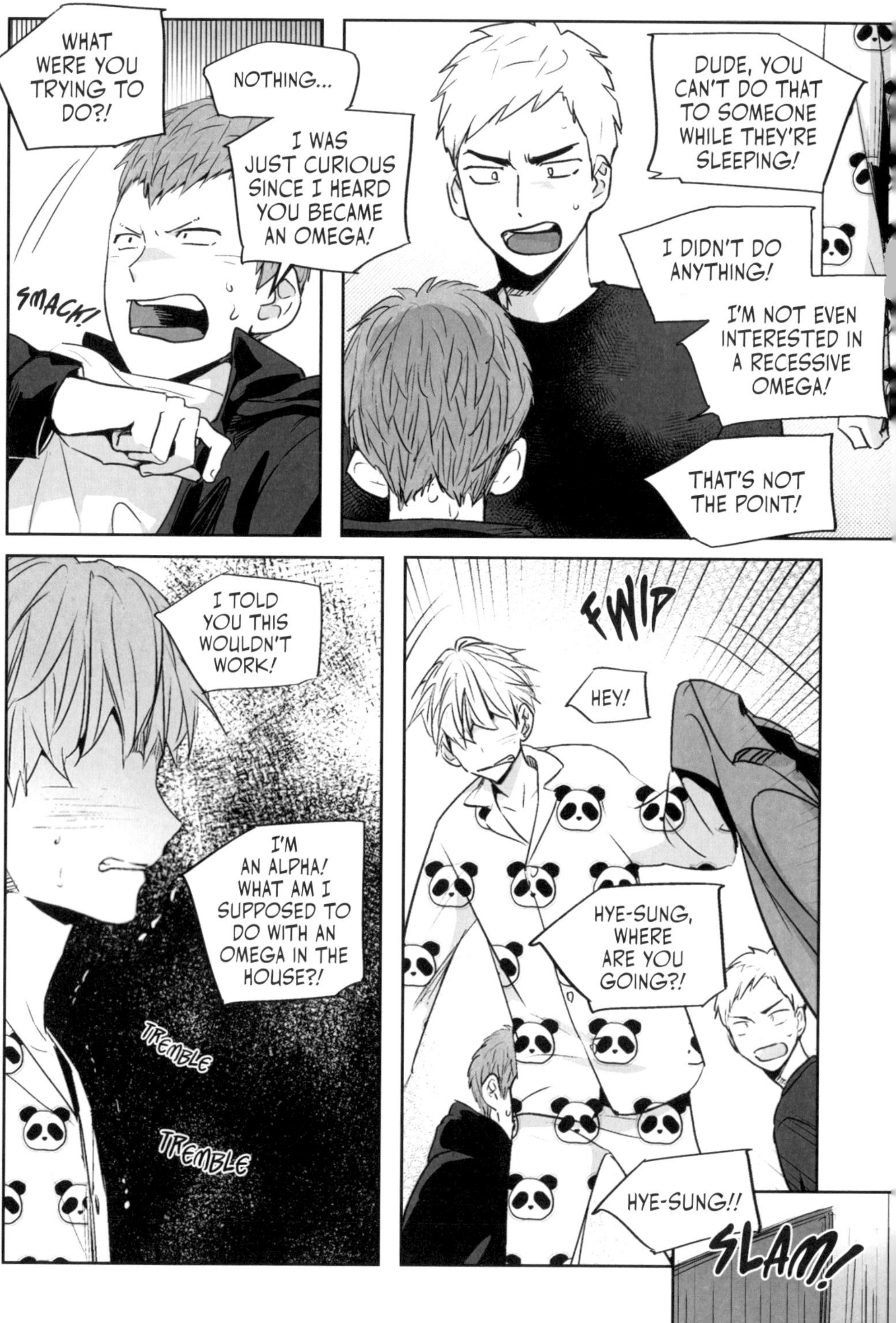
WHAT WERE YOU TRYING TO DO?!
NOTHING...
I WAS JUST CURIOUS SINCE I HEARD YOU BECAME AN OMEGA!
SMACK!
DUDE, YOU CAN'T DO THAT TO SOMEONE WHILE THEY'RE SLEEPING!
I DIDN'T DO ANYTHING!
I'M NOT EVEN INTERESTED IN A RECESSIVE OMEGA!
THAT'S NOT THE POINT!
I TOLD YOU THIS WOULDN'T WORK!
I'M AN ALPHA! WHAT AM I SUPPOSED TO DO WITH AN OMEGA IN THE HOUSE?!
TREMBLE
TREMBLE
FWIP
HEY!
HYE-SUNG, WHERE ARE YOU GOING?!
HYE-SUNG!!
SLAM!

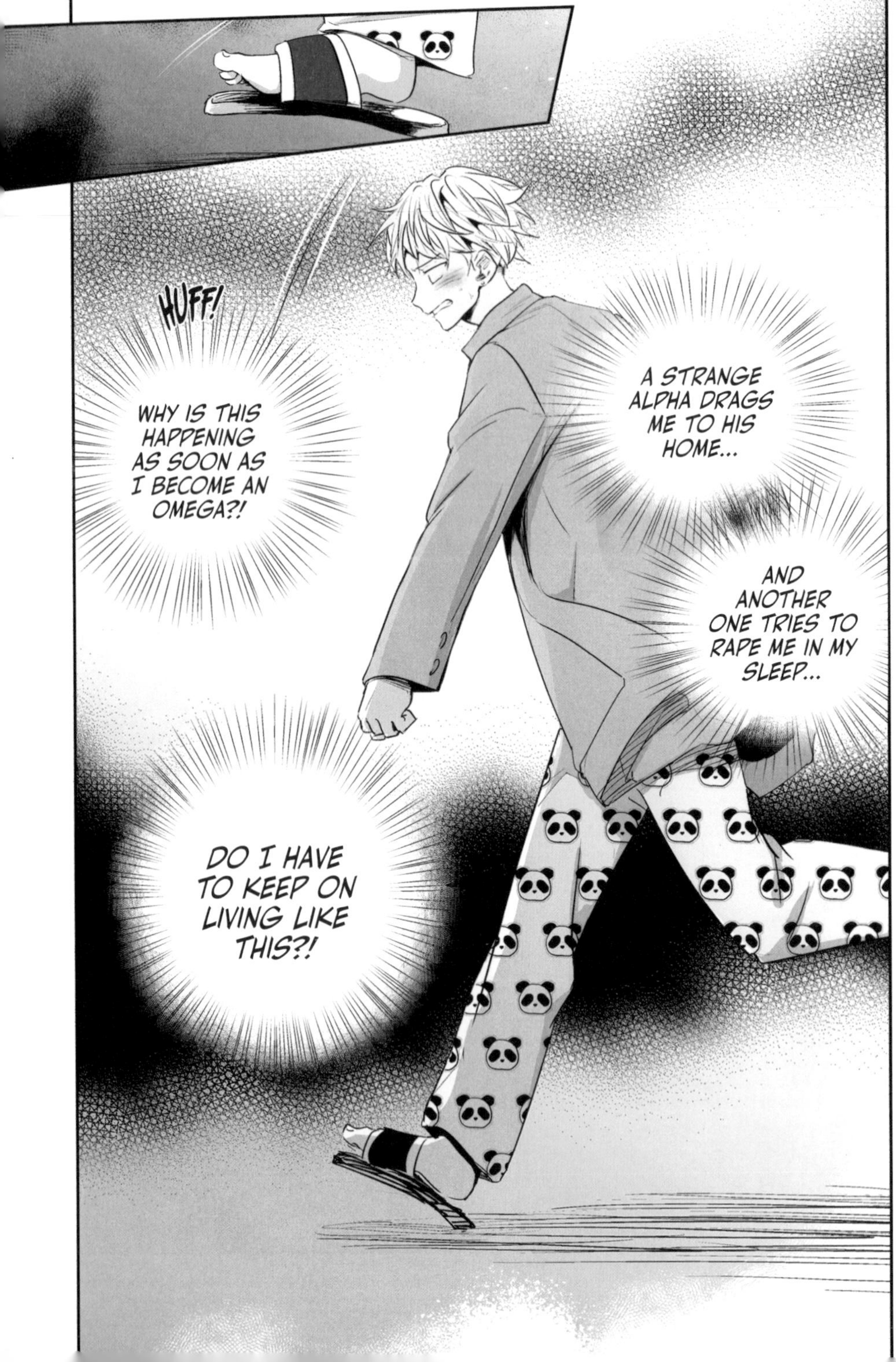
HUFF!
A STRANGE ALPHA DRAGS ME TO HIS HOME...
AND ANOTHER ONE TRIES TO RAPE ME IN MY SLEEP...
WHY IS THIS HAPPENING AS SOON AS I BECOME AN OMEGA?!
DO I HAVE TO KEEP ON LIVING LIKE THIS?!

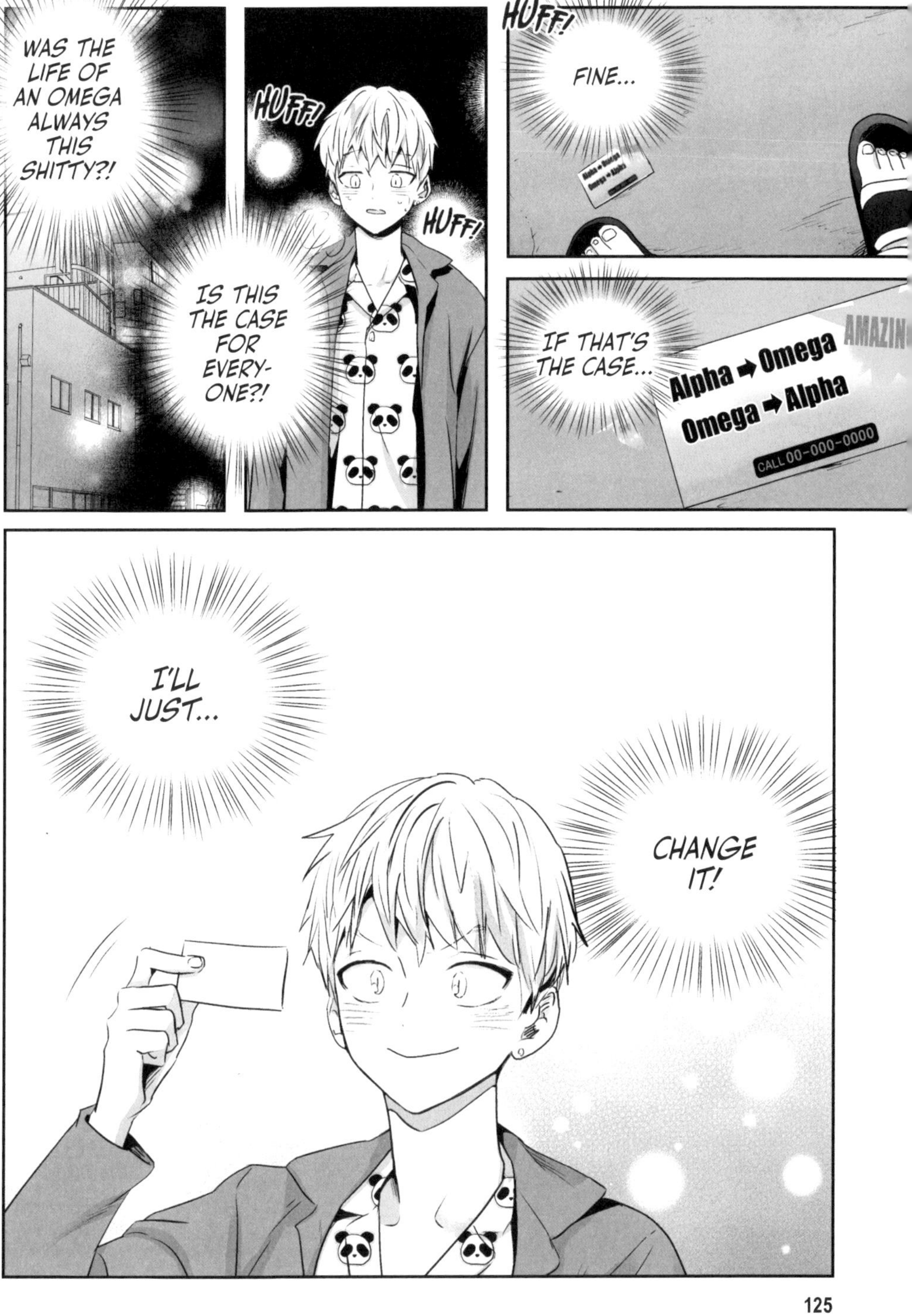
FINE...
HUFF!
IF THAT'S THE CASE...
Alpha ➡ Omega
Omega ➡ Alpha
CALL 00-000-0000
AMAZIN
WAS THE LIFE OF AN OMEGA ALWAYS THIS SHITTY?!
HUFF!
HUFF!
IS THIS THE CASE FOR EVERYONE?!
I'LL JUST...
CHANGE IT!

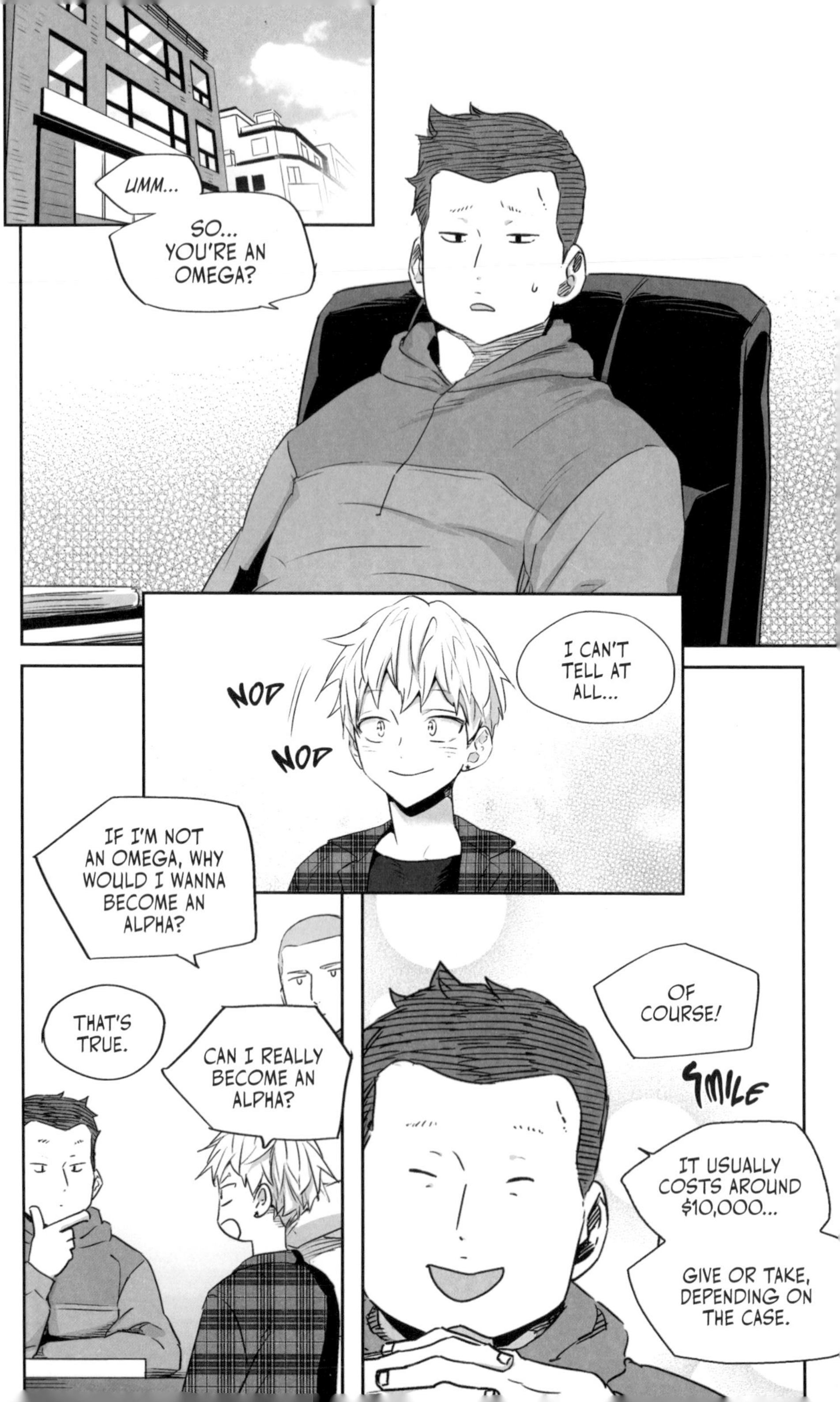
UMM...
SO... YOU'RE AN OMEGA?
NOD
NOD
I CAN'T TELL AT ALL...
IF I'M NOT AN OMEGA, WHY WOULD I WANNA BECOME AN ALPHA?
THAT'S TRUE.
CAN I REALLY BECOME AN ALPHA?
OF COURSE!
SMILE
IT USUALLY COSTS AROUND $10,000...
GIVE OR TAKE, DEPENDING ON THE CASE.

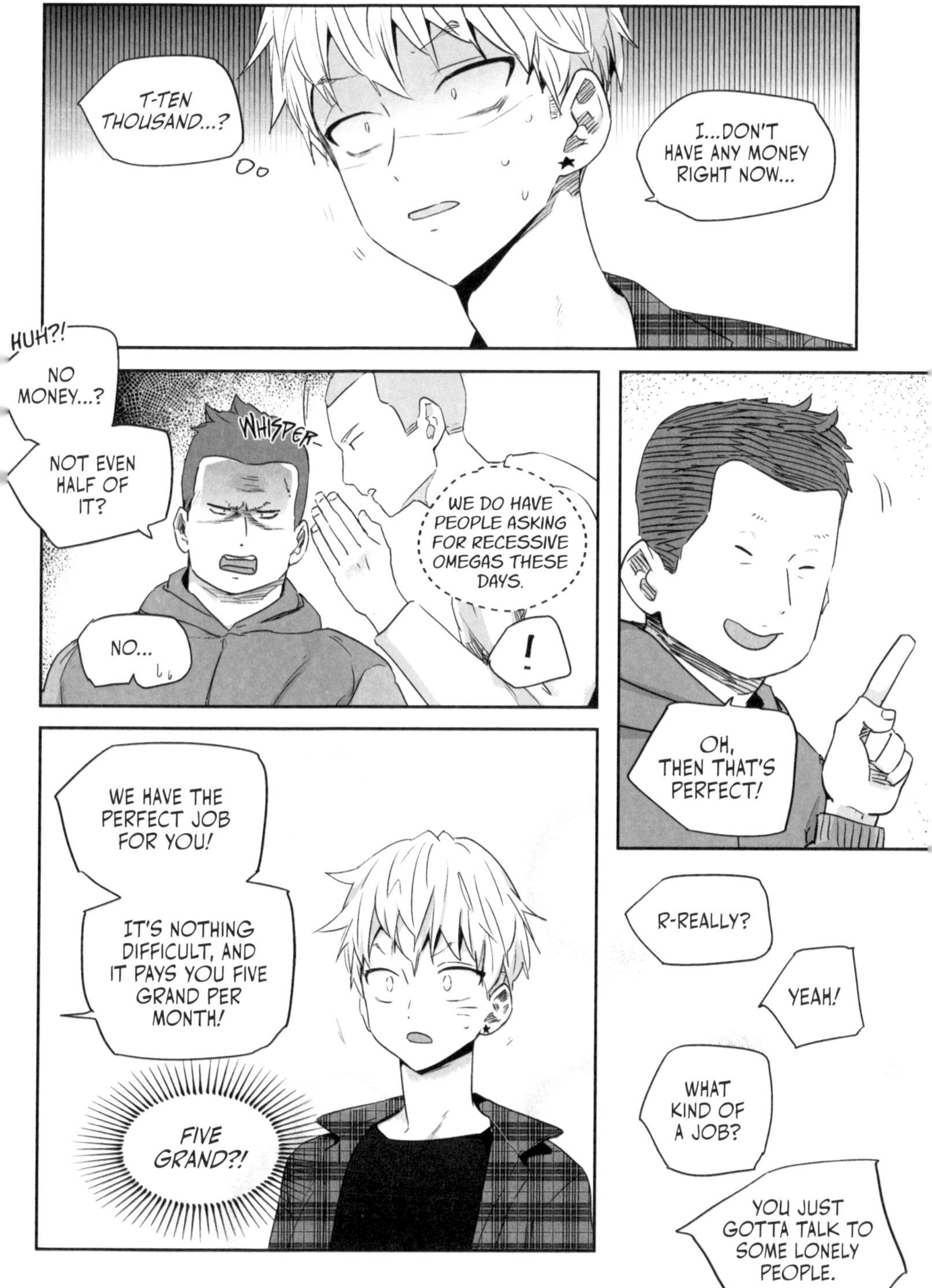
T-TEN THOUSAND...?
I...DON'T HAVE ANY MONEY RIGHT NOW...
HUH?!
NO MONEY...?
NOT EVEN HALF OF IT?
WHISPER
WE DO HAVE PEOPLE ASKING FOR RECESSIVE OMEGAS THESE DAYS.
NO...
!
OH, THEN THAT'S PERFECT!
WE HAVE THE PERFECT JOB FOR YOU!
IT'S NOTHING DIFFICULT, AND IT PAYS YOU FIVE GRAND PER MONTH!
FIVE GRAND?!
R-REALLY?
YEAH!
WHAT KIND OF A JOB?
YOU JUST GOTTA TALK TO SOME LONELY PEOPLE.

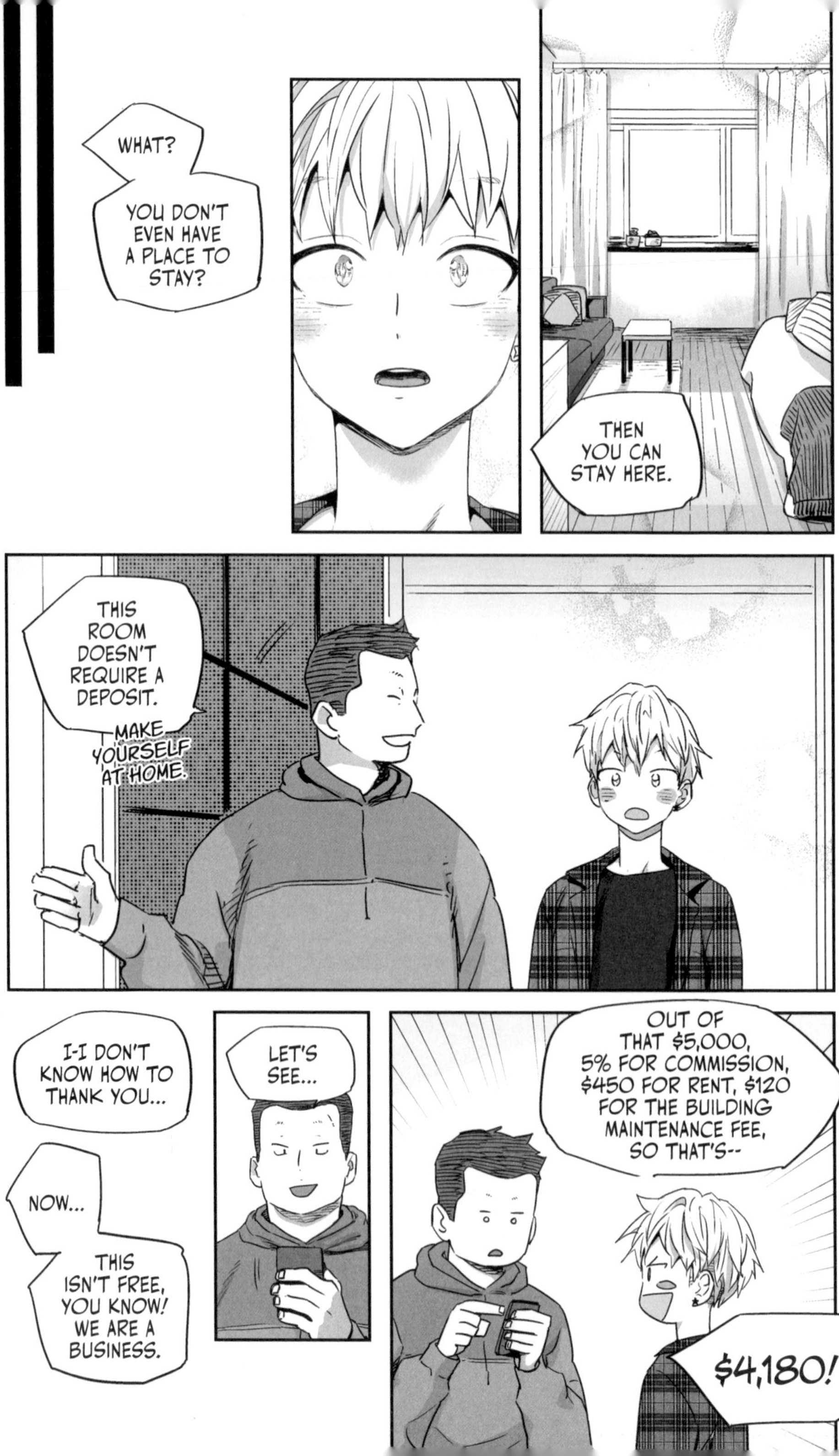
WHAT?
YOU DON'T EVEN HAVE A PLACE TO STAY?
THEN YOU CAN STAY HERE.
THIS ROOM DOESN'T REQUIRE A DEPOSIT.
MAKE YOURSELF AT HOME.
I-I DON'T KNOW HOW TO THANK YOU...
NOW...
THIS ISN'T FREE, YOU KNOW! WE ARE A BUSINESS.
LET'S SEE...
OUT OF THAT $5,000, 5% FOR COMMISSION, $450 FOR RENT, $120 FOR THE BUILDING MAINTENANCE FEE, SO THAT'S--
$4,180!

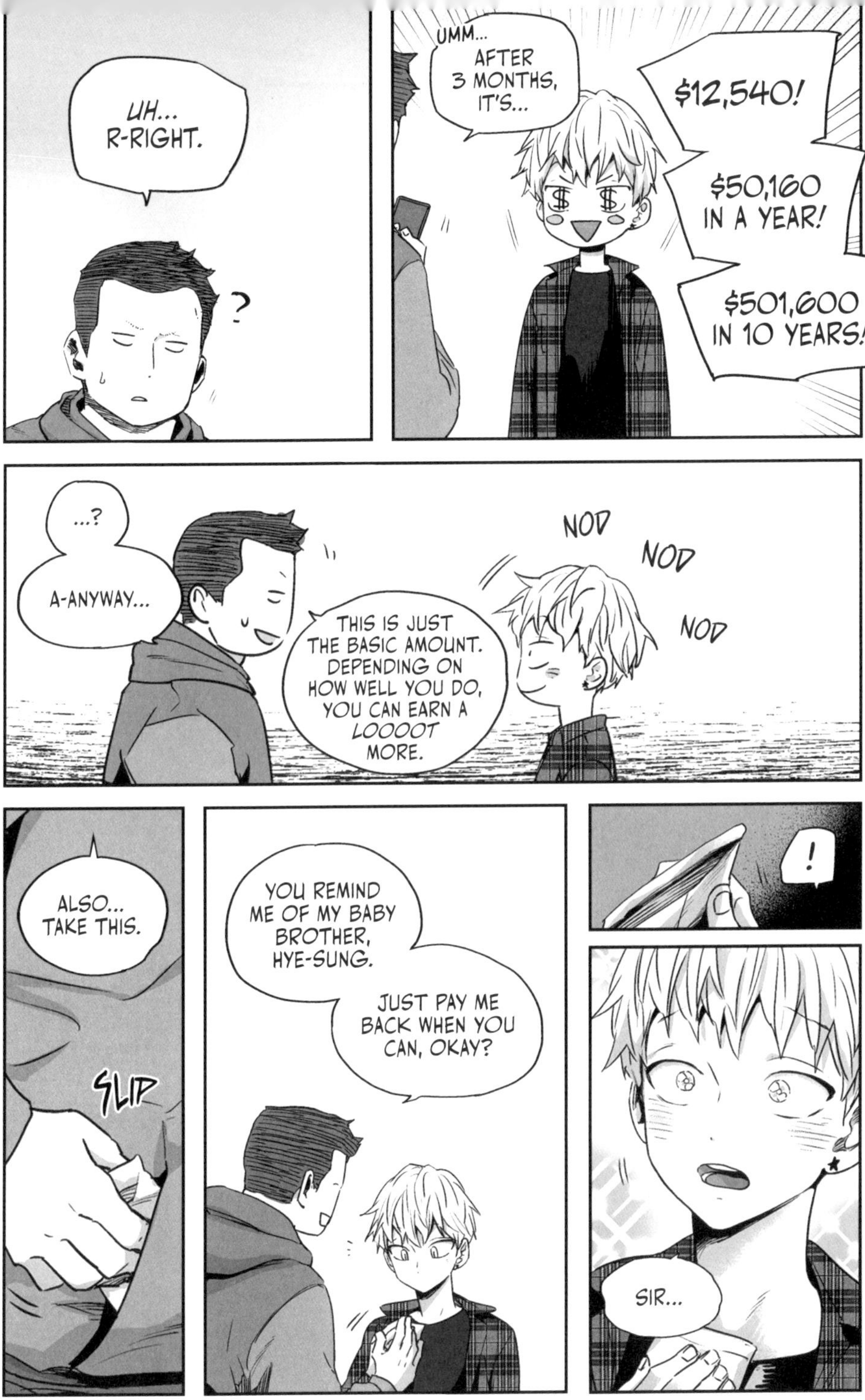
UH... R-RIGHT.
?
UMM... AFTER 3 MONTHS, IT'S...
$12,540!
$50,160 IN A YEAR!
$501,600 IN 10 YEARS!
...?
A-ANYWAY...
THIS IS JUST THE BASIC AMOUNT. DEPENDING ON HOW WELL YOU DO, YOU CAN EARN A LOOOOT MORE.
NOD
NOD
NOD
ALSO... TAKE THIS.
SLIP
YOU REMIND ME OF MY BABY BROTHER, HYE-SUNG.
JUST PAY ME BACK WHEN YOU CAN, OKAY?
!
SIR...

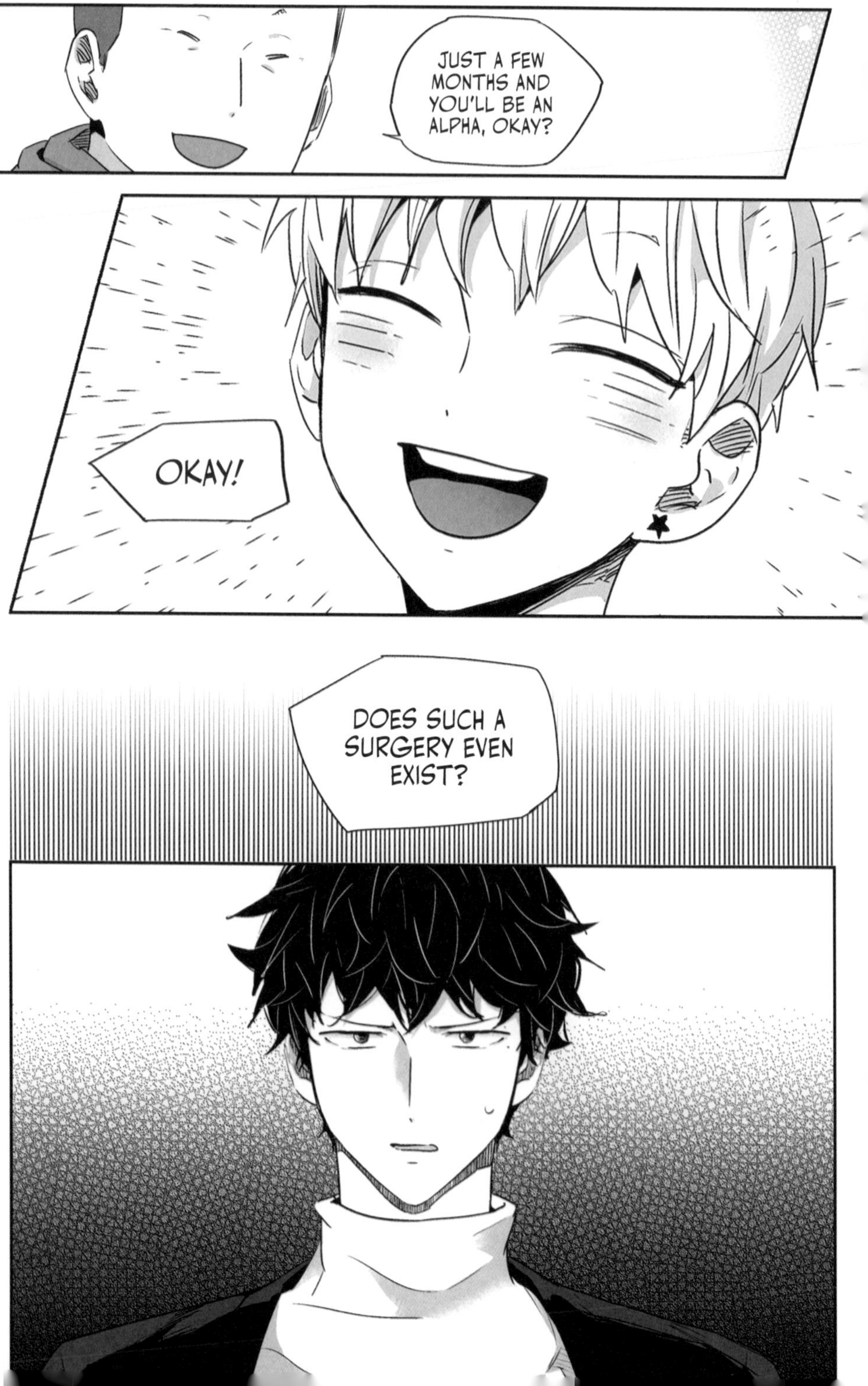
JUST A FEW MONTHS AND YOU'LL BE AN ALPHA, OKAY?
OKAY!
DOES SUCH A SURGERY EVEN EXIST?

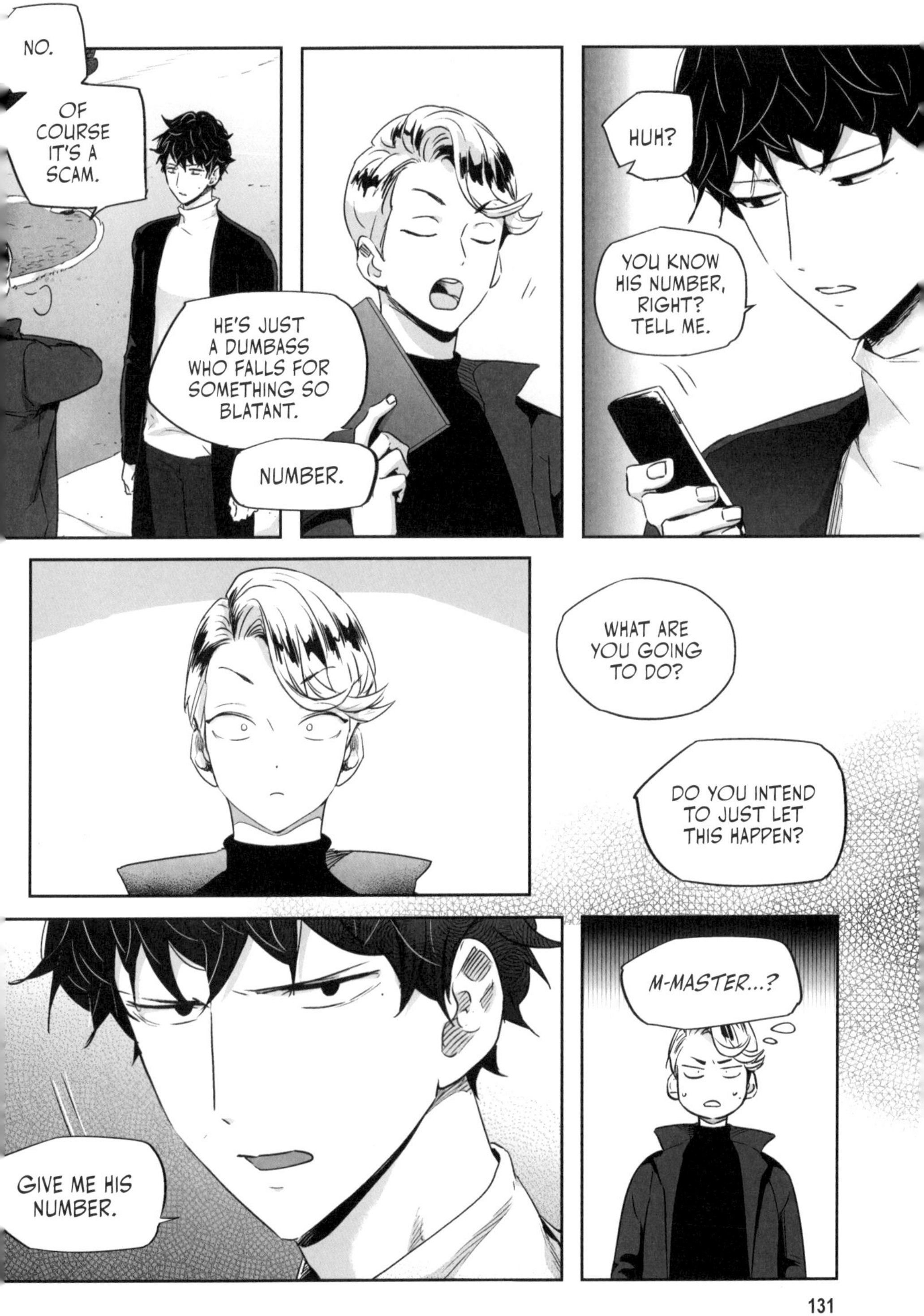
NO.
OF COURSE IT'S A SCAM.
HE'S JUST A DUMBASS WHO FALLS FOR SOMETHING SO BLATANT.
NUMBER.
HUH?
YOU KNOW HIS NUMBER, RIGHT? TELL ME.
WHAT ARE YOU GOING TO DO?
DO YOU INTEND TO JUST LET THIS HAPPEN?
GIVE ME HIS NUMBER.
M-MASTER...?

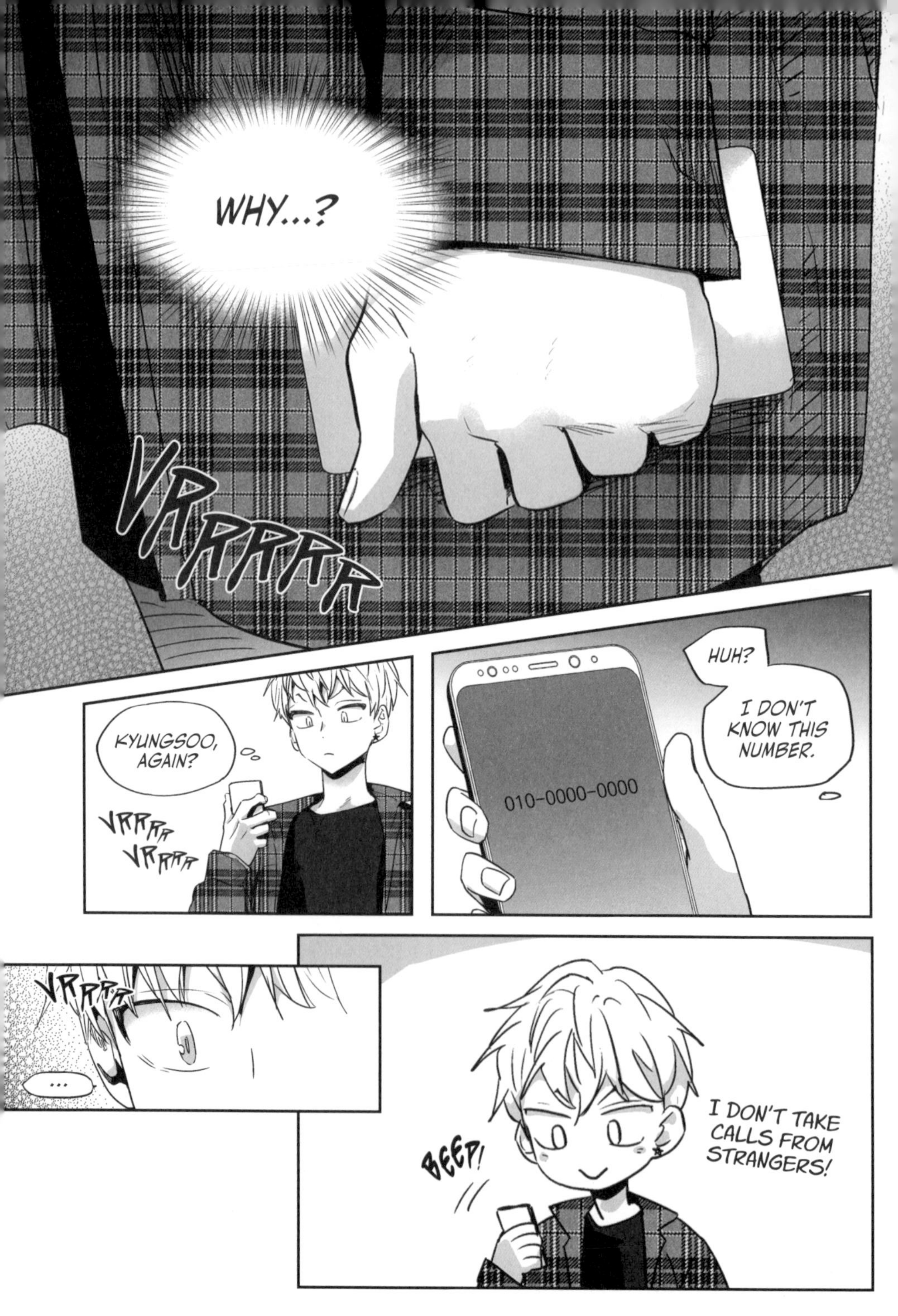

WHY...?
VRRRRRR
KYUNGSOO, AGAIN?
VRRRR VRRRR
010-0000-0000
HUH?
I DON'T KNOW THIS NUMBER.
VRRRR
...
BEEP!
I DON'T TAKE CALLS FROM STRANGERS!

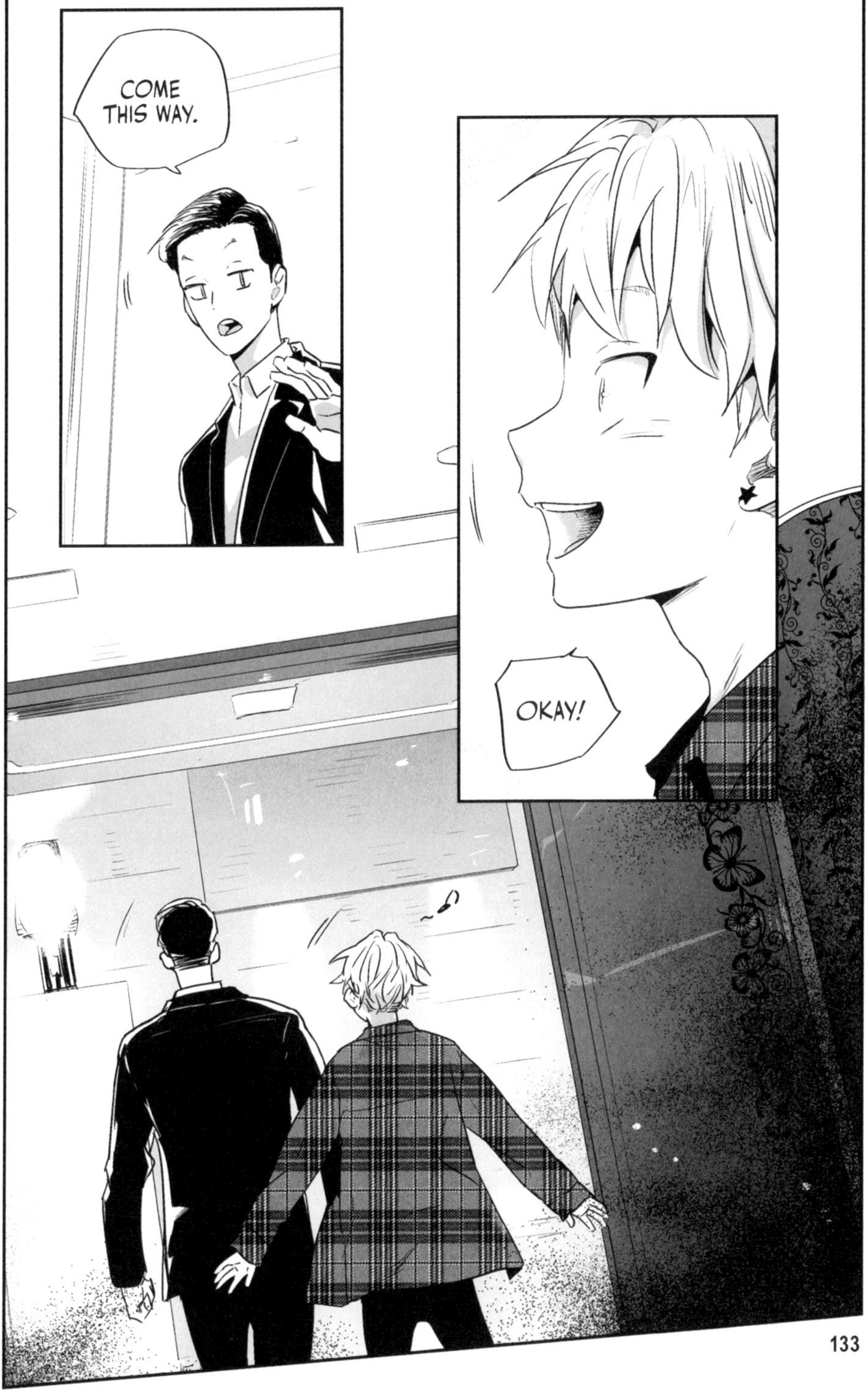
COME THIS WAY.
OKAY!

Love is an Illusion!

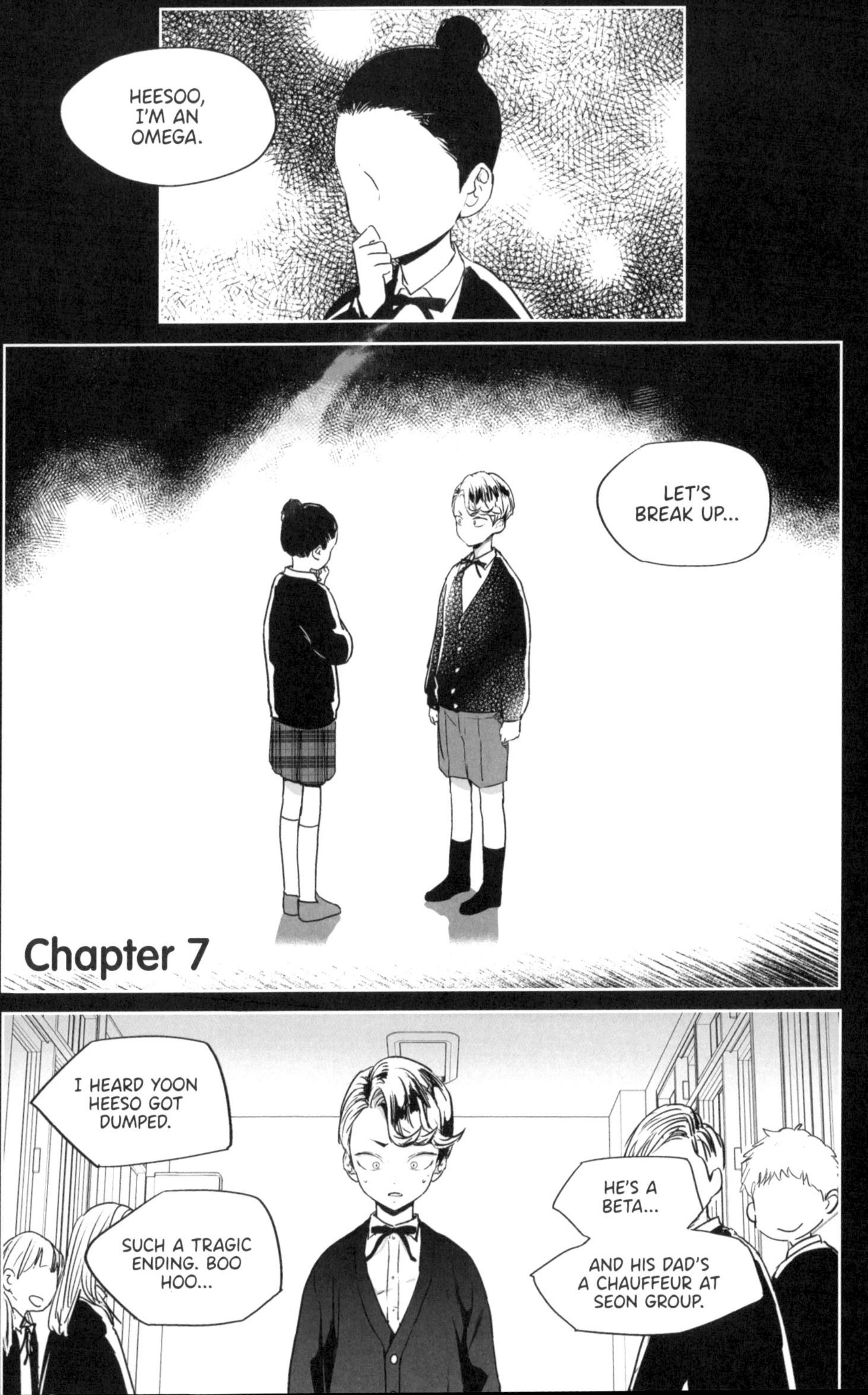
HEESOO, I'M AN OMEGA.
LET'S BREAK UP...
Chapter 7
I HEARD YOON HEESO GOT DUMPED.
SUCH A TRAGIC ENDING. BOO HOO...
HE'S A BETA...
AND HIS DAD'S A CHAUFFEUR AT SEON GROUP.

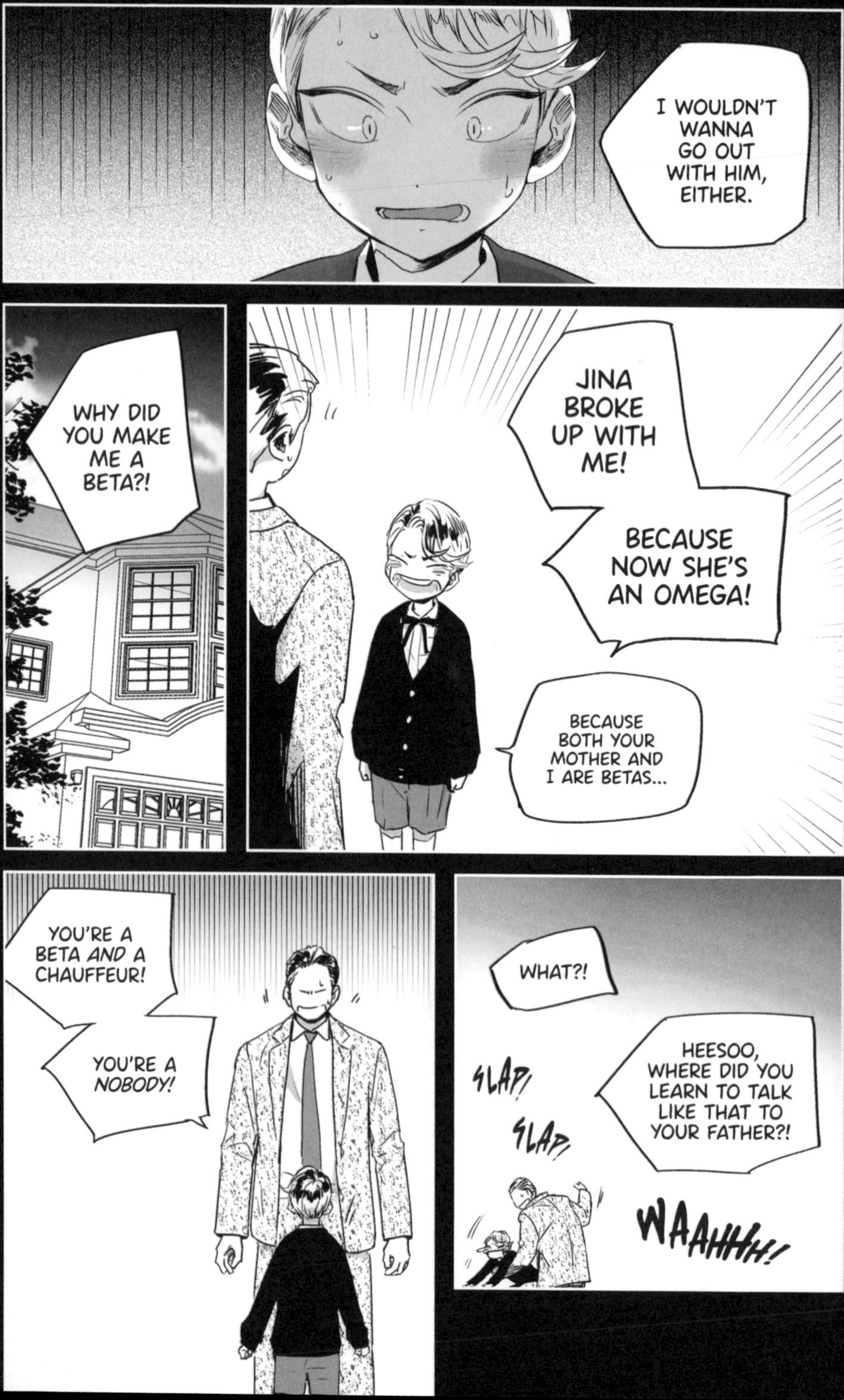
I WOULDN'T WANNA GO OUT WITH HIM, EITHER.
WHY DID YOU MAKE ME A BETA?!
JINA BROKE UP WITH ME!
BECAUSE NOW SHE'S AN OMEGA!
BECAUSE BOTH YOUR MOTHER AND I ARE BETAS...
YOU'RE A BETA AND A CHAUFFEUR!
YOU'RE A NOBODY!
WHAT?!
HEESOO, WHERE DID YOU LEARN TO TALK LIKE THAT TO YOUR FATHER?!
SLAP!
SLAP!
WAAHHHH!

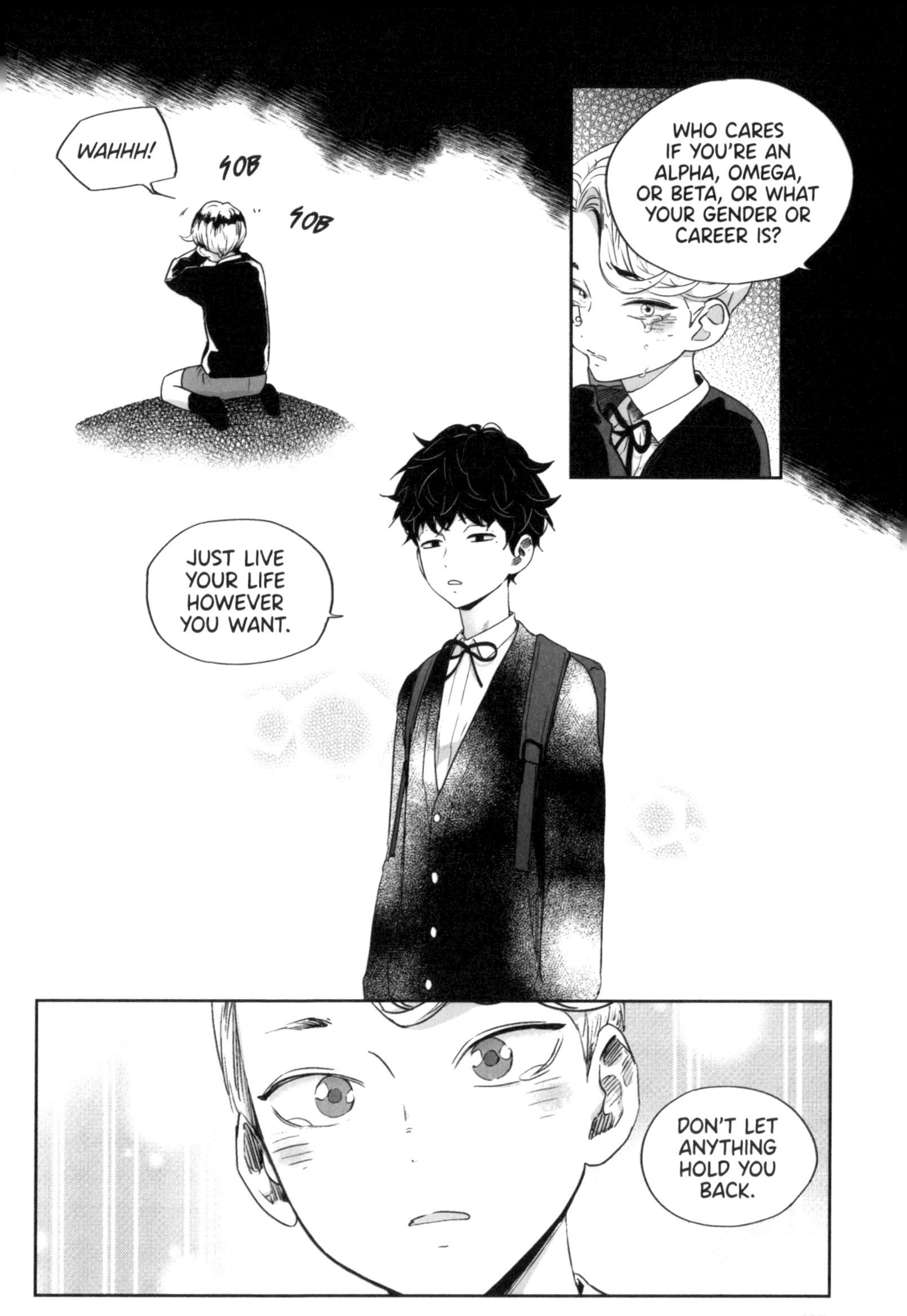
WAHHH!
SOB
SOB
WHO CARES IF YOU'RE AN ALPHA, OMEGA, OR BETA, OR WHAT YOUR GENDER OR CAREER IS?
JUST LIVE YOUR LIFE HOWEVER YOU WANT.
DON'T LET ANYTHING HOLD YOU BACK.

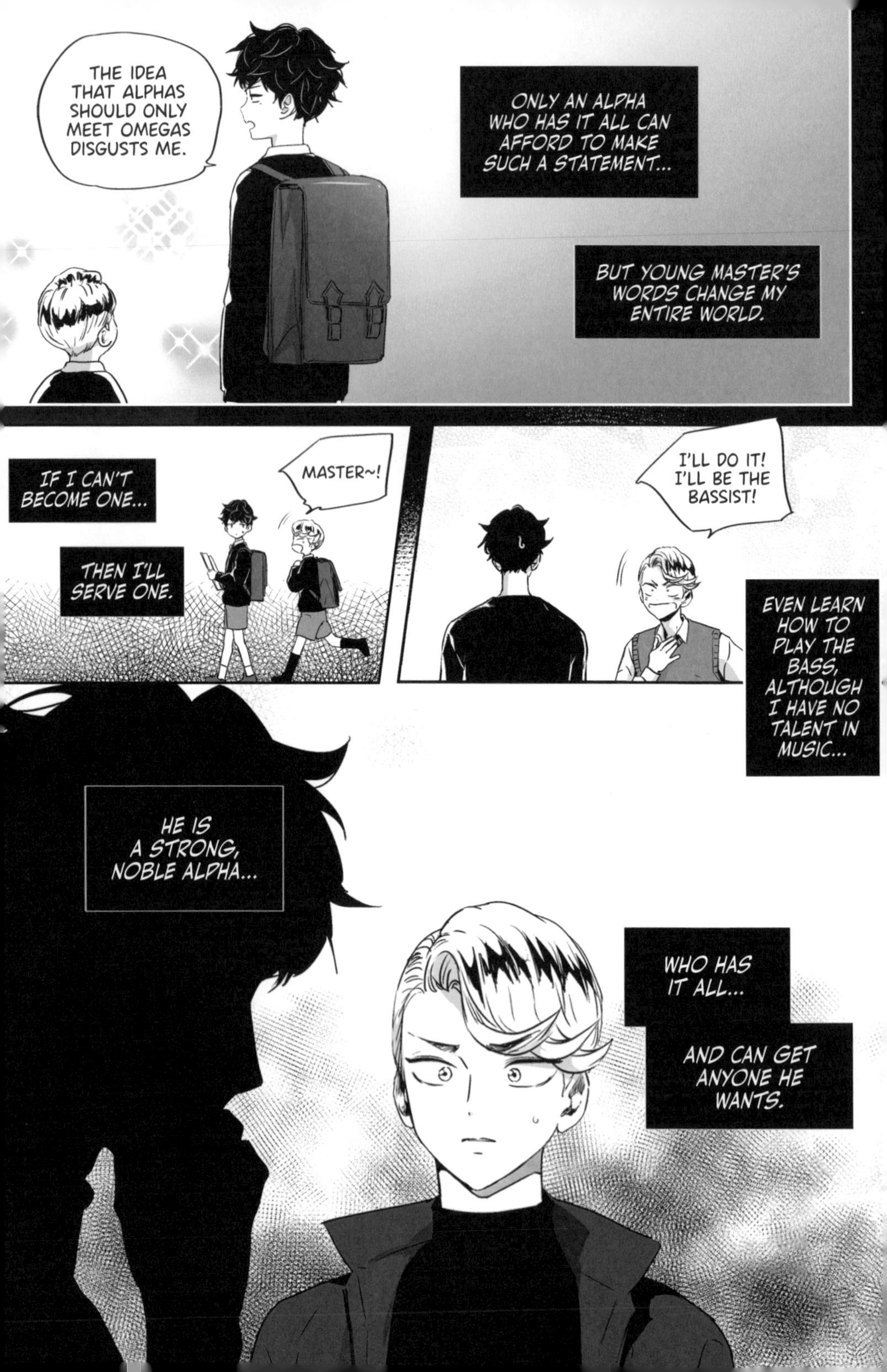
THE IDEA THAT ALPHAS SHOULD ONLY MEET OMEGAS DISGUSTS ME.
ONLY AN ALPHA WHO HAS IT ALL CAN AFFORD TO MAKE SUCH A STATEMENT...
BUT YOUNG MASTER'S WORDS CHANGE MY ENTIRE WORLD.
IF I CAN'T BECOME ONE...
THEN I'LL SERVE ONE.
MASTER~!
I'LL DO IT! I'LL BE THE BASSIST!
EVEN LEARN HOW TO PLAY THE BASS, ALTHOUGH I HAVE NO TALENT IN MUSIC...
HE IS A STRONG, NOBLE ALPHA...
WHO HAS IT ALL...
AND CAN GET ANYONE HE WANTS.

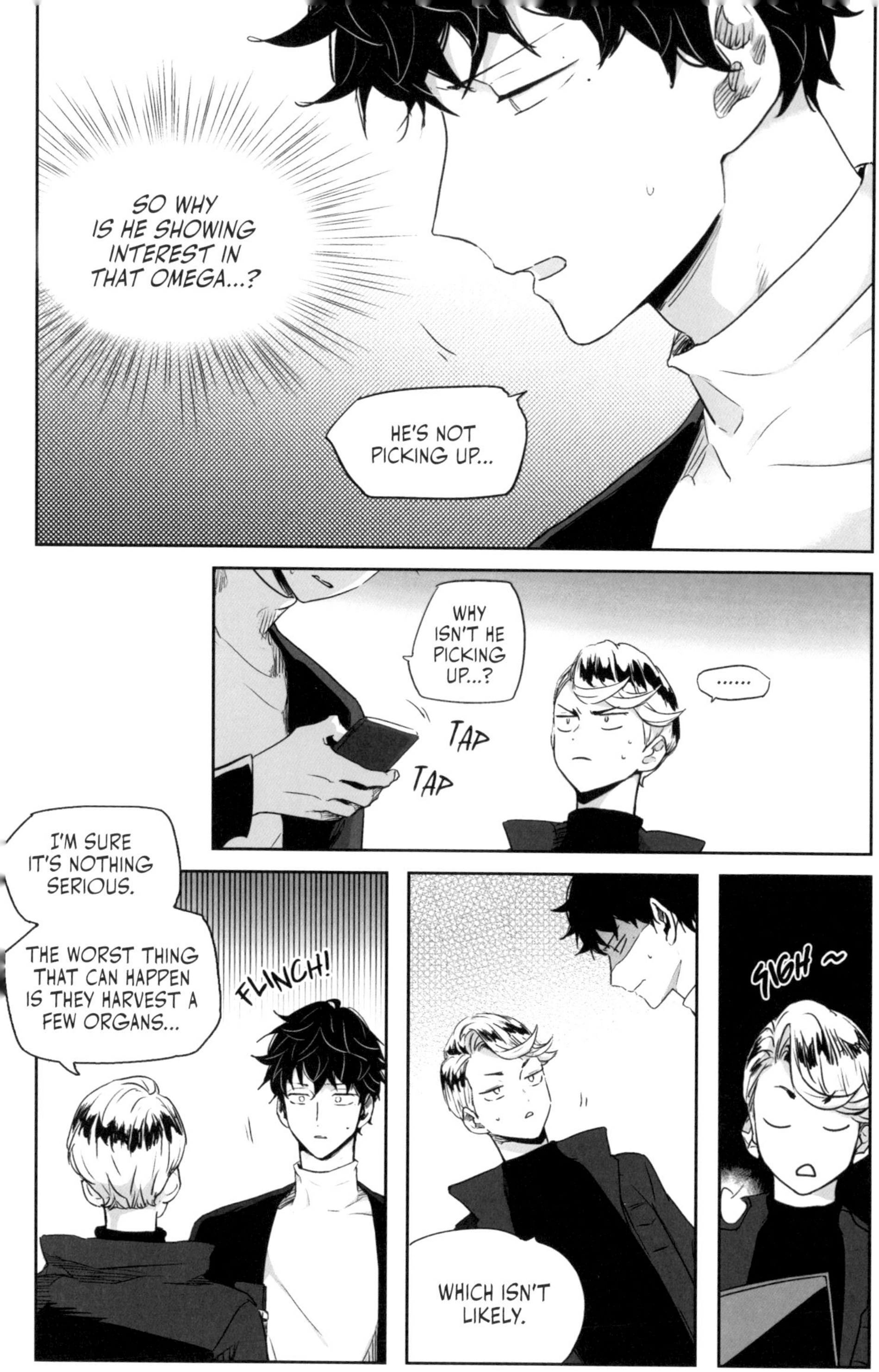

SO WHY IS HE SHOWING INTEREST IN THAT OMEGA...?
HE'S NOT PICKING UP...
WHY ISN'T HE PICKING UP...?
......
TAP
TAP
I'M SURE IT'S NOTHING SERIOUS.
THE WORST THING THAT CAN HAPPEN IS THEY HARVEST A FEW ORGANS...
FLINCH!
WHICH ISN'T LIKELY.
SIGH ~

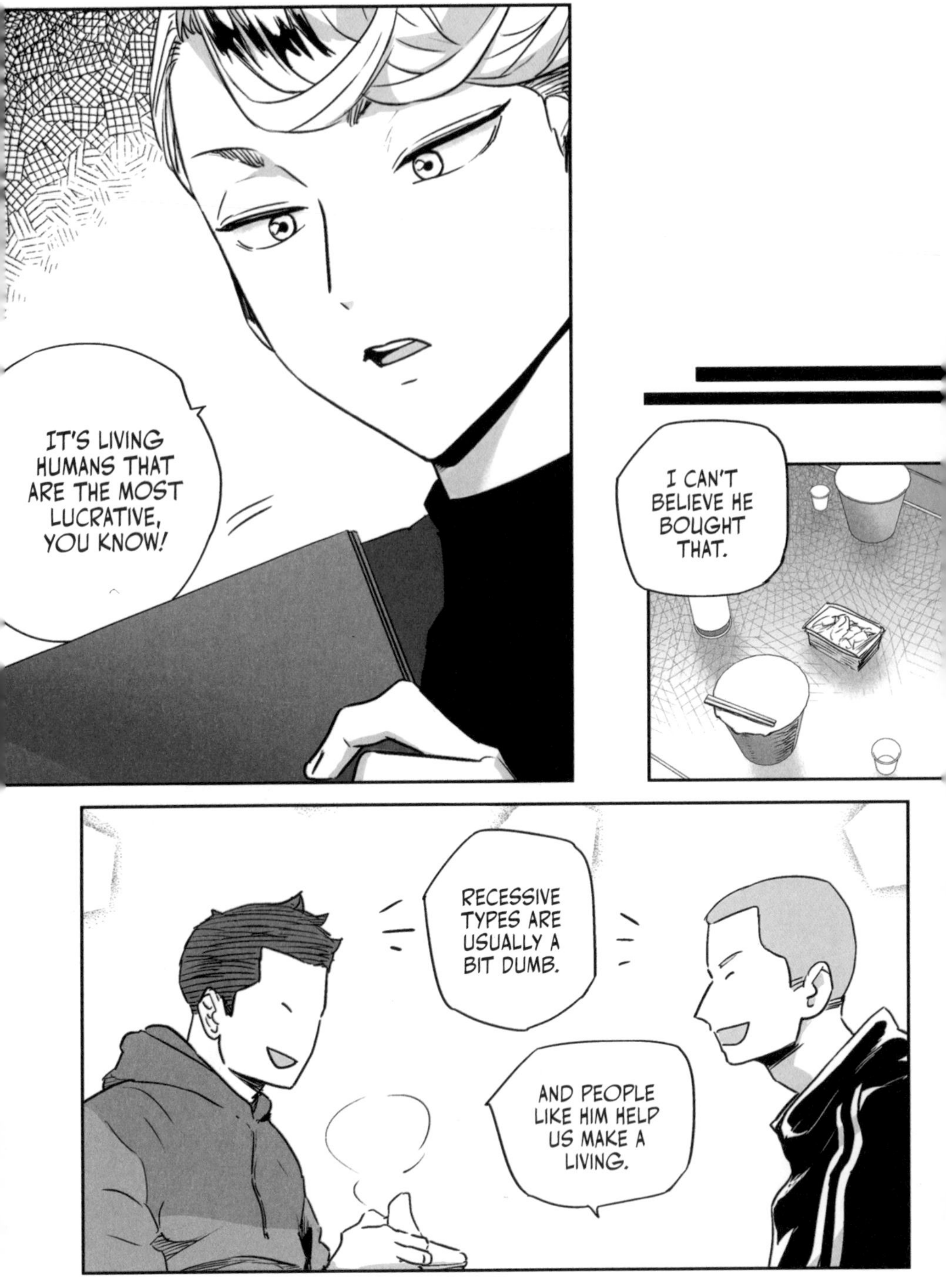
IT'S LIVING HUMANS THAT ARE THE MOST LUCRATIVE, YOU KNOW!
I CAN'T BELIEVE HE BOUGHT THAT.
RECESSIVE TYPES ARE USUALLY A BIT DUMB.
AND PEOPLE LIKE HIM HELP US MAKE A LIVING.

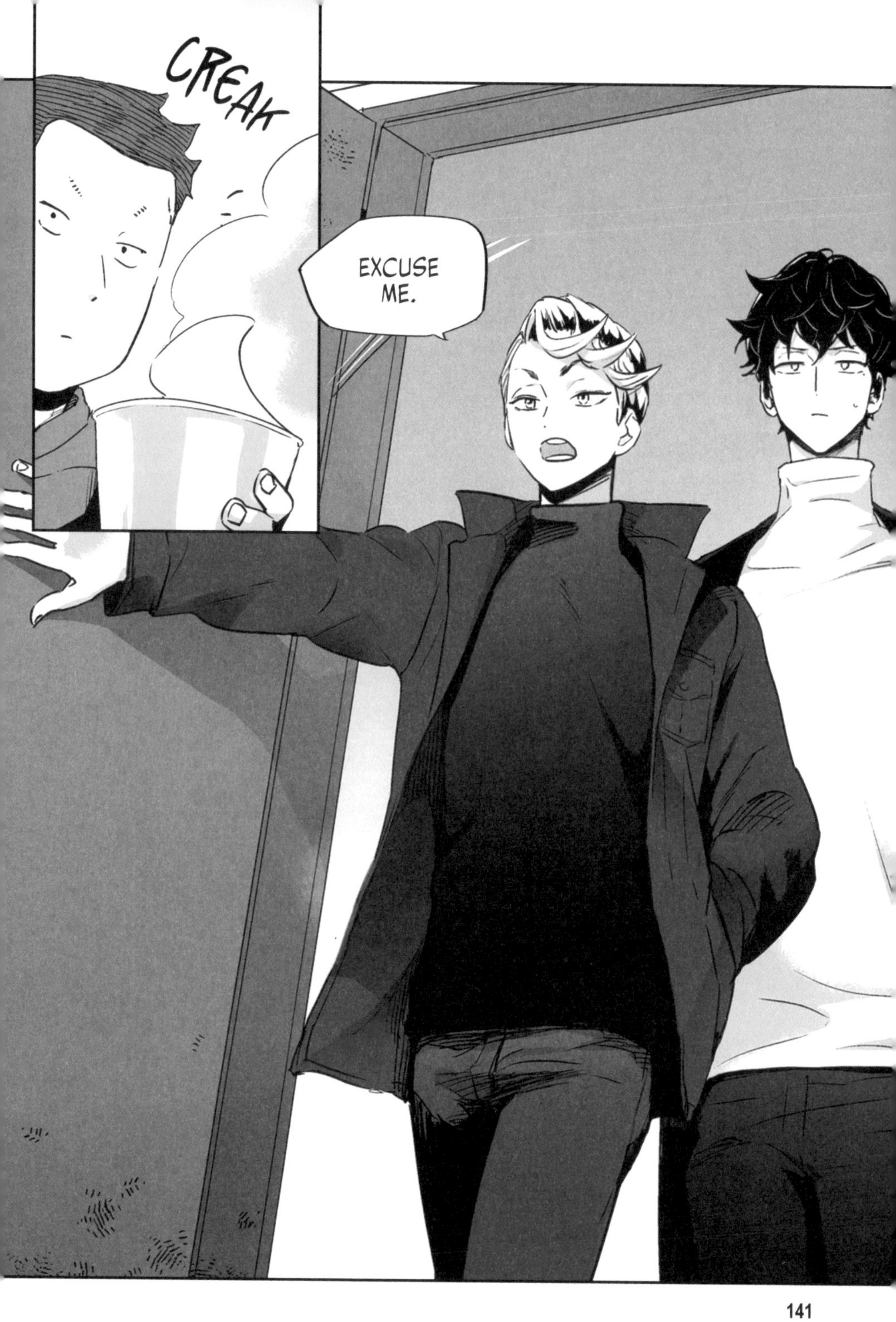
CREAK
EXCUSE ME.

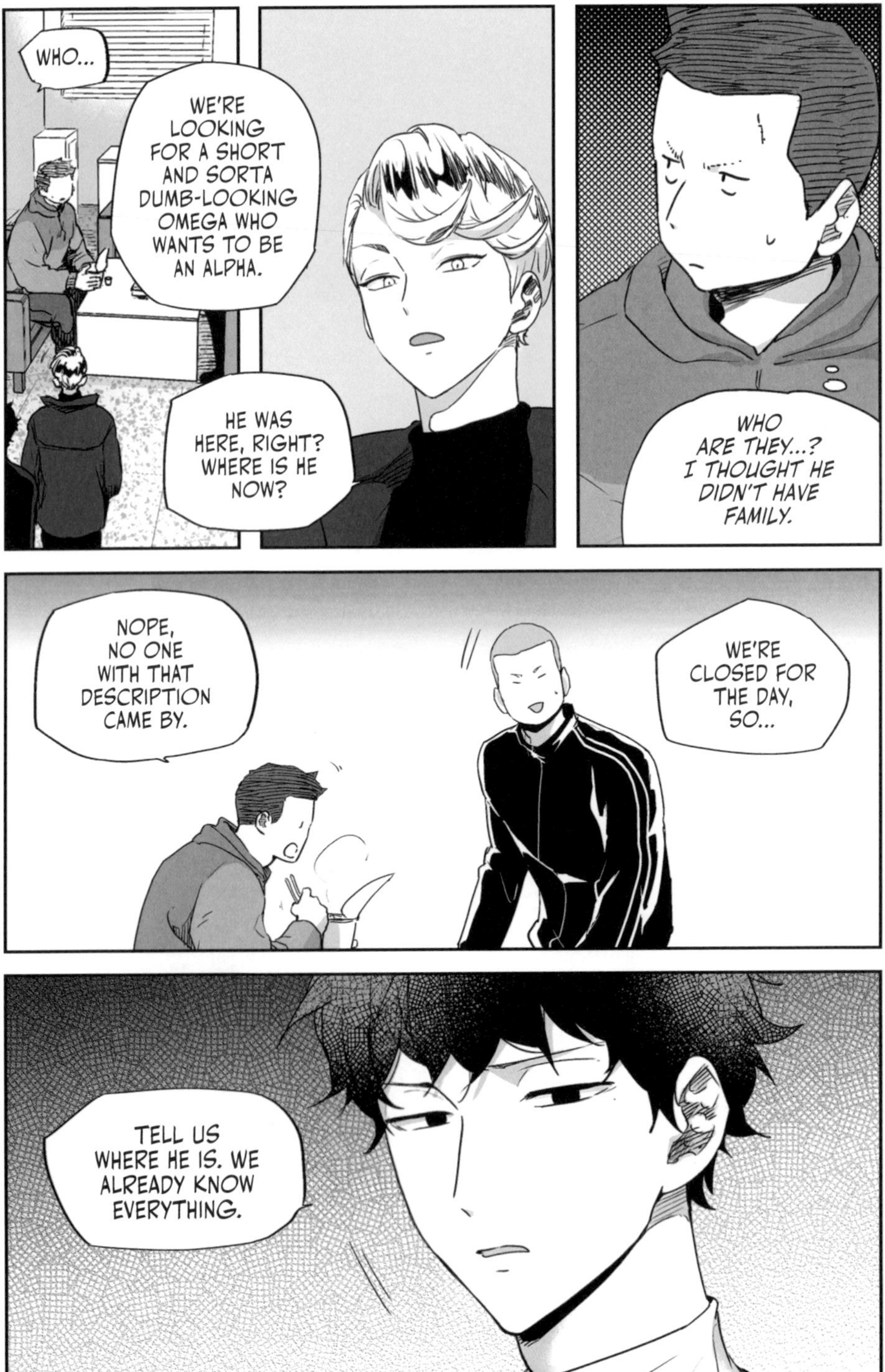
WHO...
WE'RE LOOKING FOR A SHORT AND SORTA DUMB-LOOKING OMEGA WHO WANTS TO BE AN ALPHA.
HE WAS HERE, RIGHT? WHERE IS HE NOW?
WHO ARE THEY...? I THOUGHT HE DIDN'T HAVE FAMILY.
NOPE, NO ONE WITH THAT DESCRIPTION CAME BY.
WE'RE CLOSED FOR THE DAY, SO...
TELL US WHERE HE IS. WE ALREADY KNOW EVERYTHING.

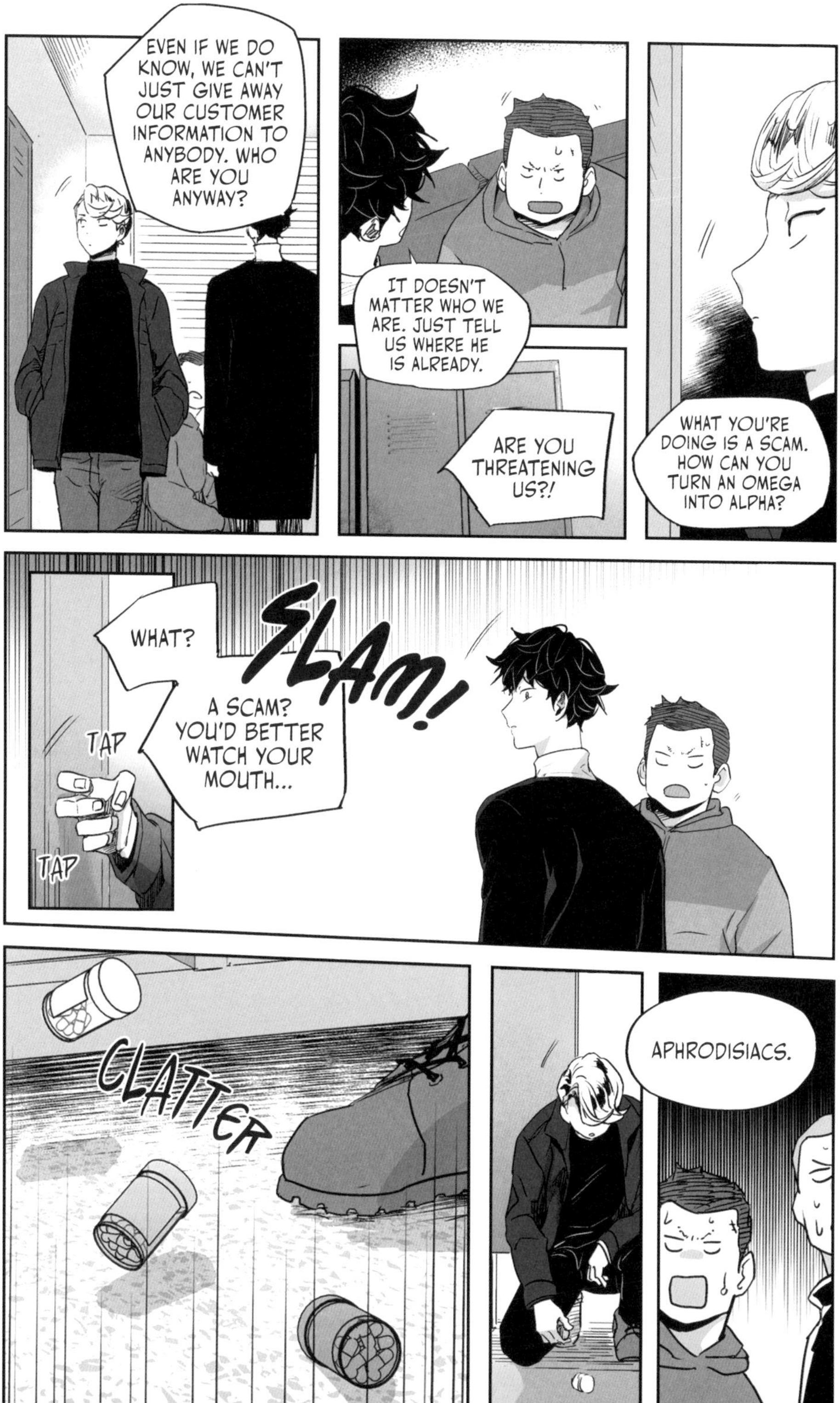
EVEN IF WE DO KNOW, WE CAN'T JUST GIVE AWAY OUR CUSTOMER INFORMATION TO ANYBODY. WHO ARE YOU ANYWAY?
IT DOESN'T MATTER WHO WE ARE. JUST TELL US WHERE HE IS ALREADY.
ARE YOU THREATENING US?!
WHAT YOU'RE DOING IS A SCAM. HOW CAN YOU TURN AN OMEGA INTO ALPHA?
WHAT?
A SCAM? YOU'D BETTER WATCH YOUR MOUTH...
TAP
TAP
SLAM!
CLATTER
APHRODISIACS.

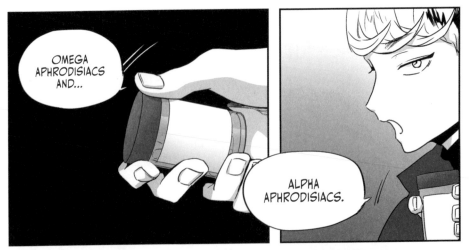

OMEGA APHRODISIACS AND...

ALPHA APHRODISIACS.

AND JUST WHAT ARE THESE FOR?

GRAB!

TELL US...

NOW!

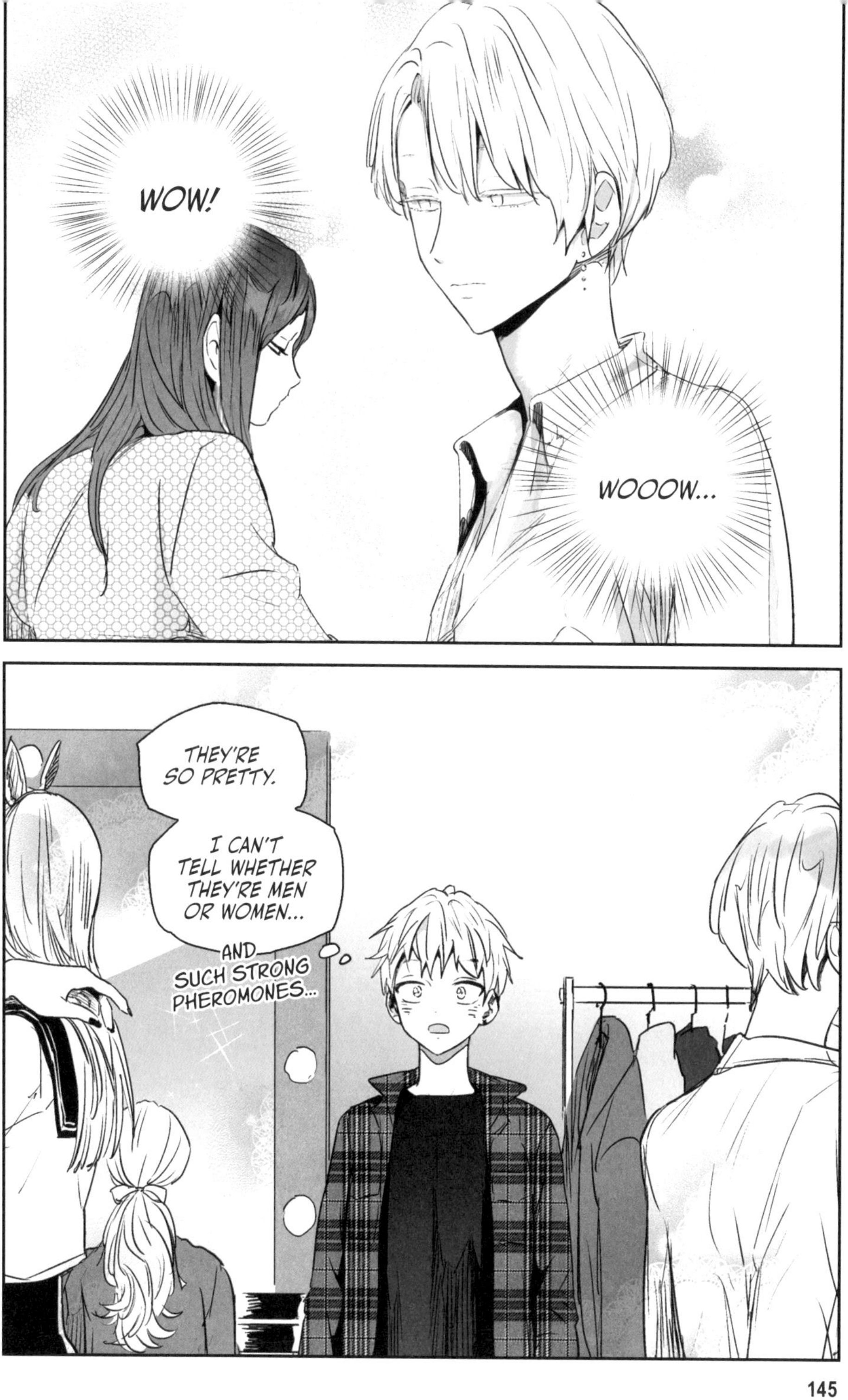

WOW!
WOOOW...
THEY'RE SO PRETTY.
I CAN'T TELL WHETHER THEY'RE MEN OR WOMEN...
AND SUCH STRONG PHEROMONES...

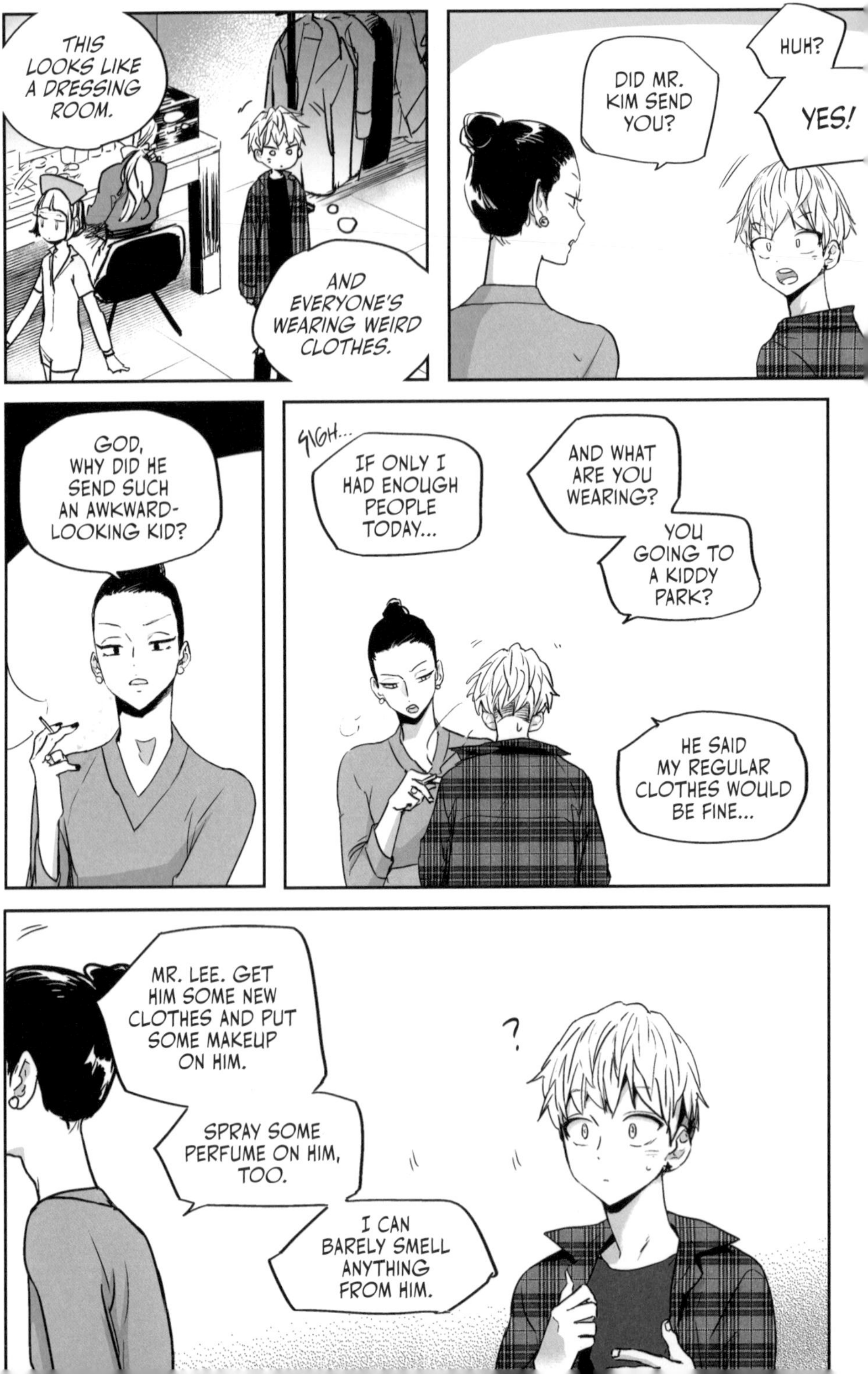
THIS LOOKS LIKE A DRESSING ROOM.
AND EVERYONE'S WEARING WEIRD CLOTHES.
DID MR. KIM SEND YOU?
HUH?
YES!
GOD, WHY DID HE SEND SUCH AN AWKWARD-LOOKING KID?
SIGH...
IF ONLY I HAD ENOUGH PEOPLE TODAY...
AND WHAT ARE YOU WEARING?
YOU GOING TO A KIDDY PARK?
HE SAID MY REGULAR CLOTHES WOULD BE FINE...
MR. LEE. GET HIM SOME NEW CLOTHES AND PUT SOME MAKEUP ON HIM.
SPRAY SOME PERFUME ON HIM, TOO.
I CAN BARELY SMELL ANYTHING FROM HIM.
?

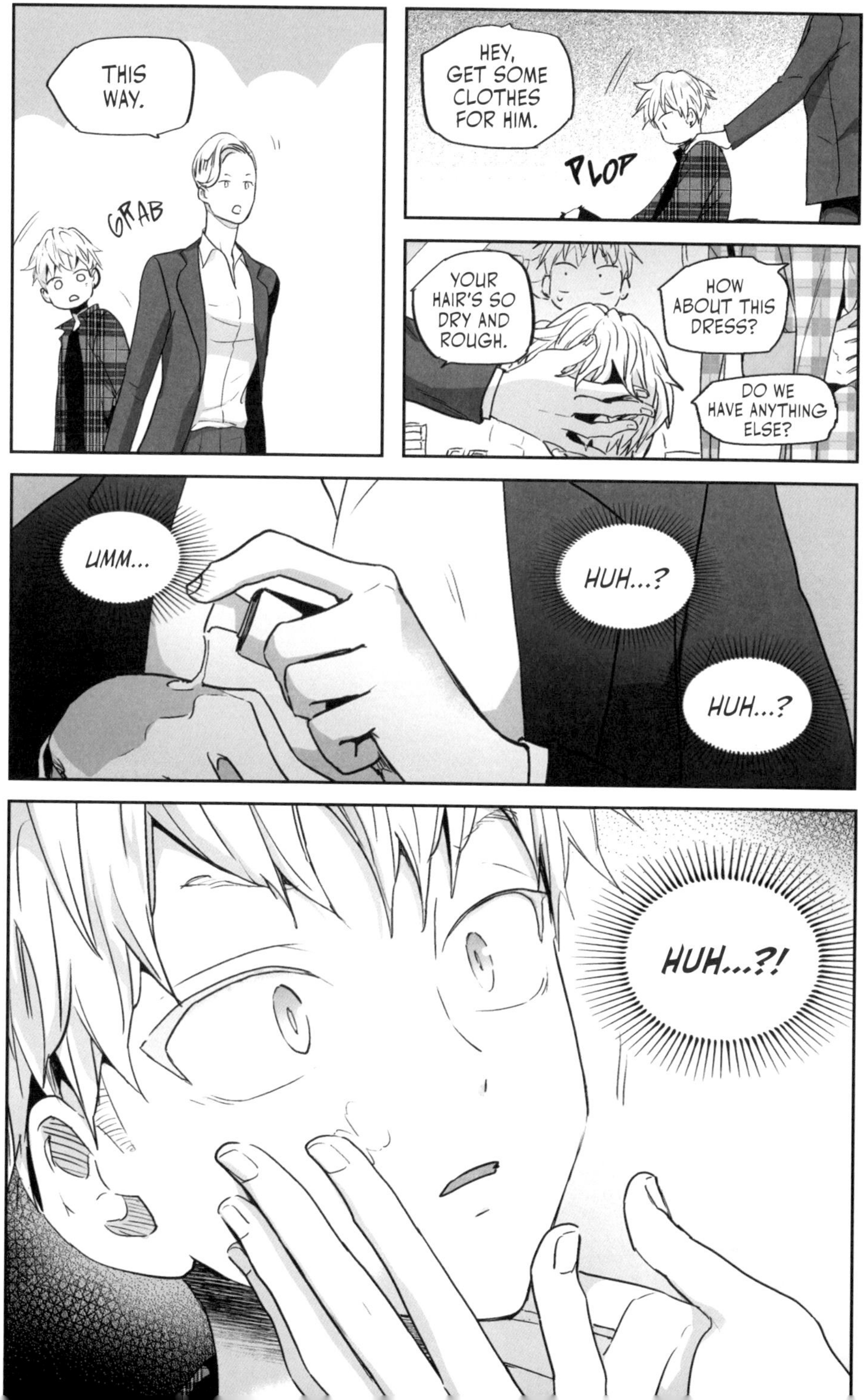
THIS WAY.
GRAB
HEY, GET SOME CLOTHES FOR HIM.
PLOP
YOUR HAIR'S SO DRY AND ROUGH.
HOW ABOUT THIS DRESS?
DO WE HAVE ANYTHING ELSE?
UMM...
HUH...?
HUH...?
HUH...?!

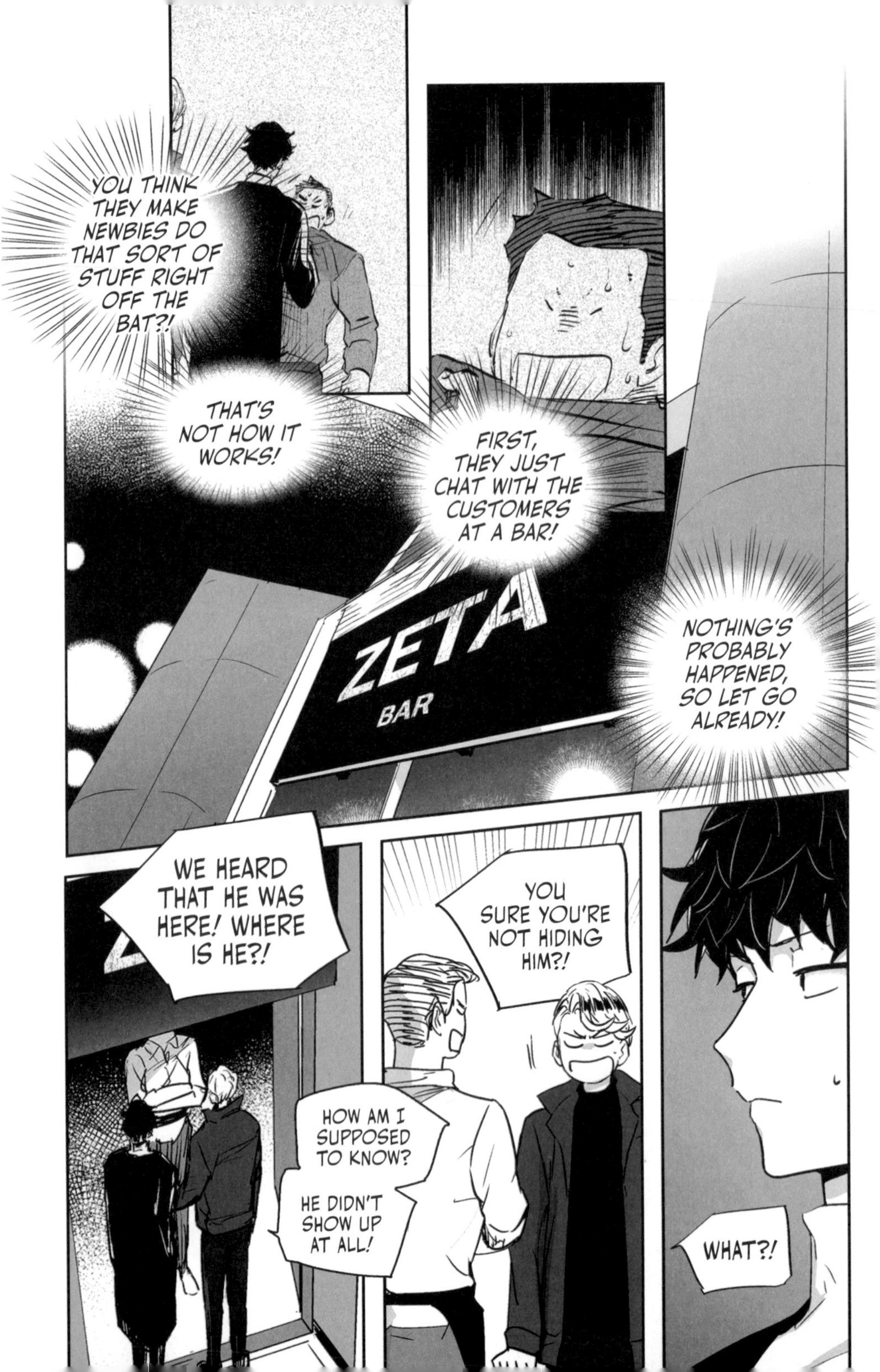
YOU THINK THEY MAKE NEWBIES DO THAT SORT OF STUFF RIGHT OFF THE BAT?!
THAT'S NOT HOW IT WORKS!
FIRST, THEY JUST CHAT WITH THE CUSTOMERS AT A BAR!
ZETA
BAR
NOTHING'S PROBABLY HAPPENED, SO LET GO ALREADY!
WE HEARD THAT HE WAS HERE! WHERE IS HE?!
YOU SURE YOU'RE NOT HIDING HIM?!
HOW AM I SUPPOSED TO KNOW?
HE DIDN'T SHOW UP AT ALL!
WHAT?!

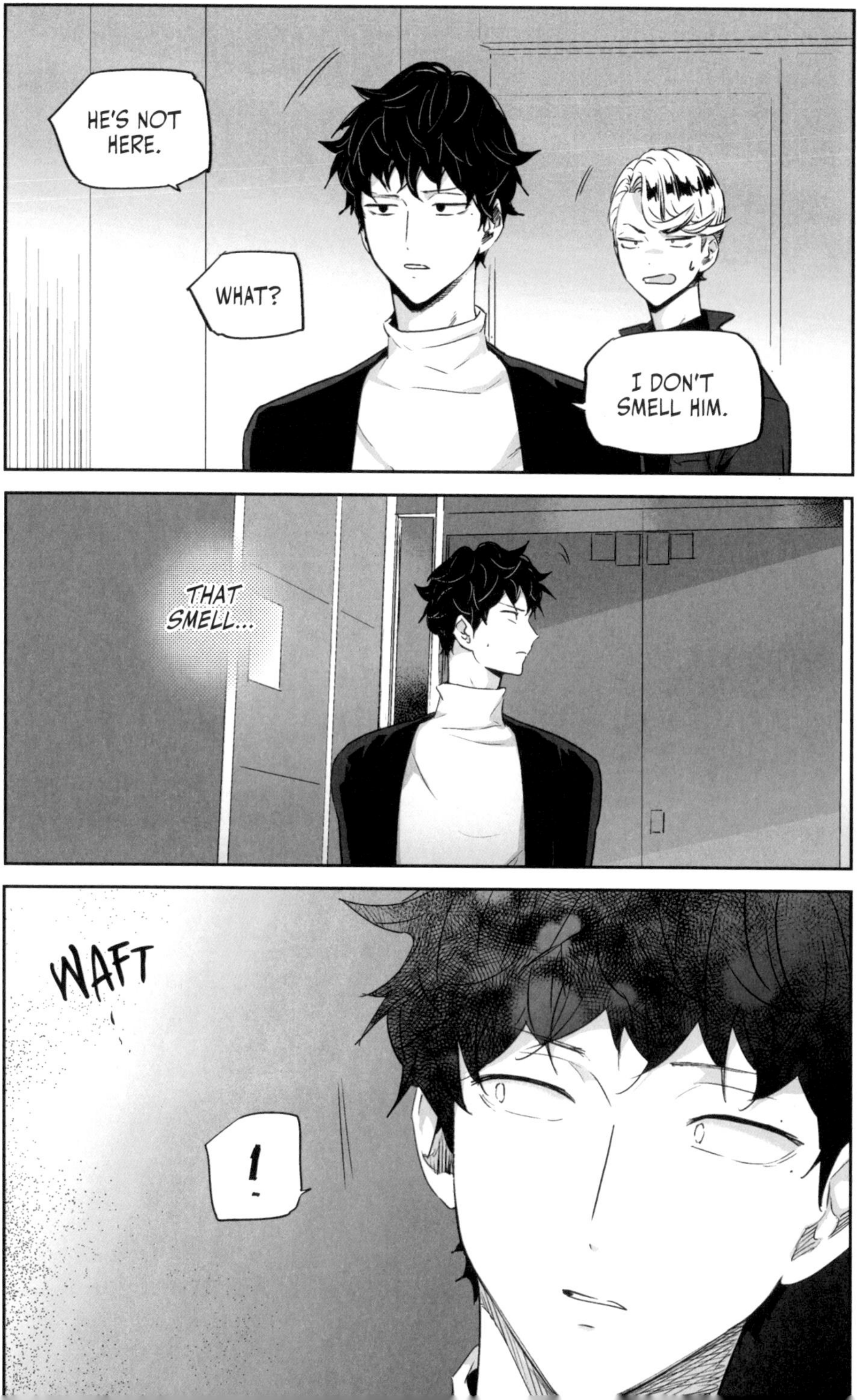
HE'S NOT HERE.
WHAT?
I DON'T SMELL HIM.
THAT SMELL...
WAFT
!

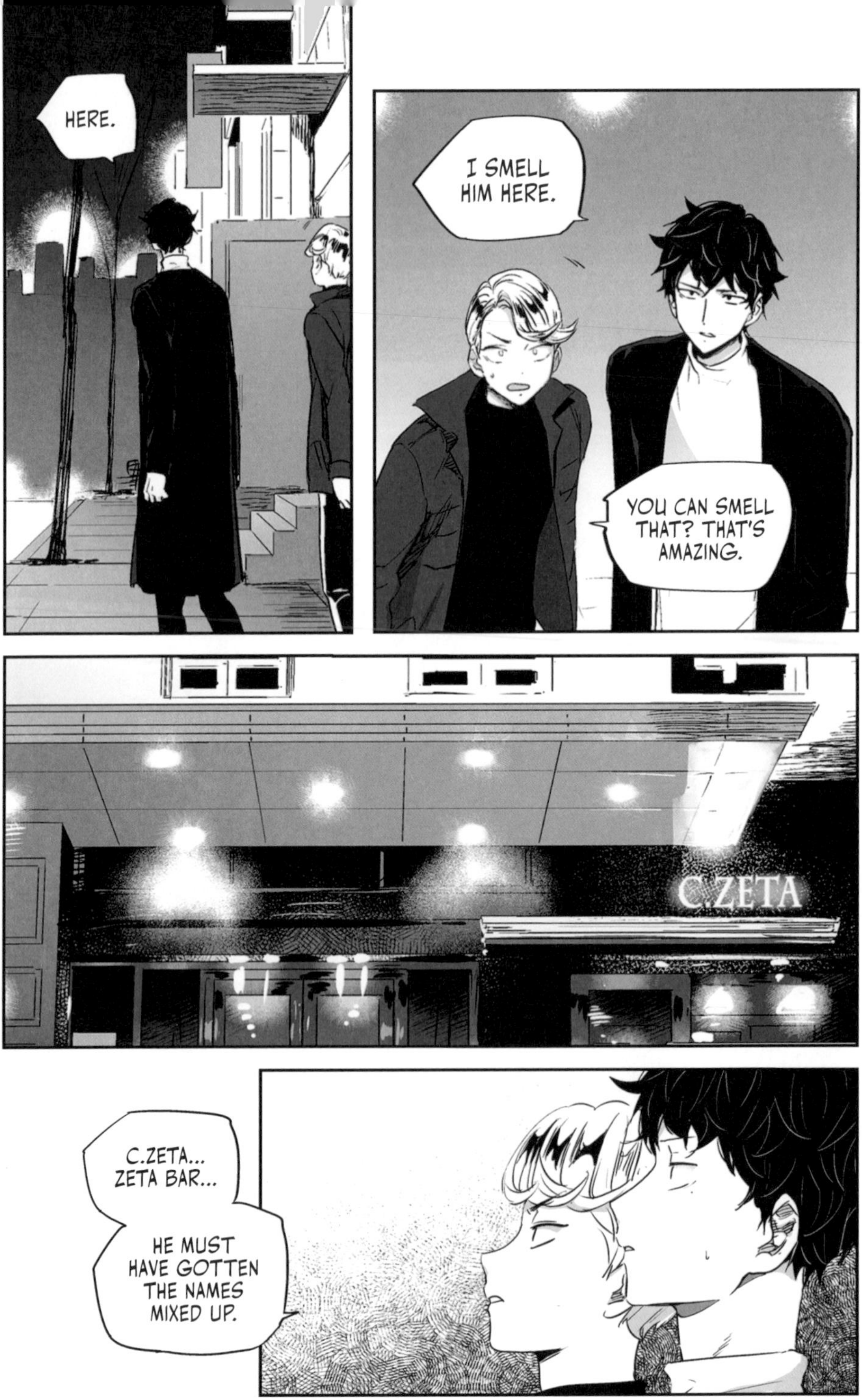
HERE.
I SMELL HIM HERE.
YOU CAN SMELL THAT? THAT'S AMAZING.
C.ZETA
C.ZETA... ZETA BAR...
HE MUST HAVE GOTTEN THE NAMES MIXED UP.

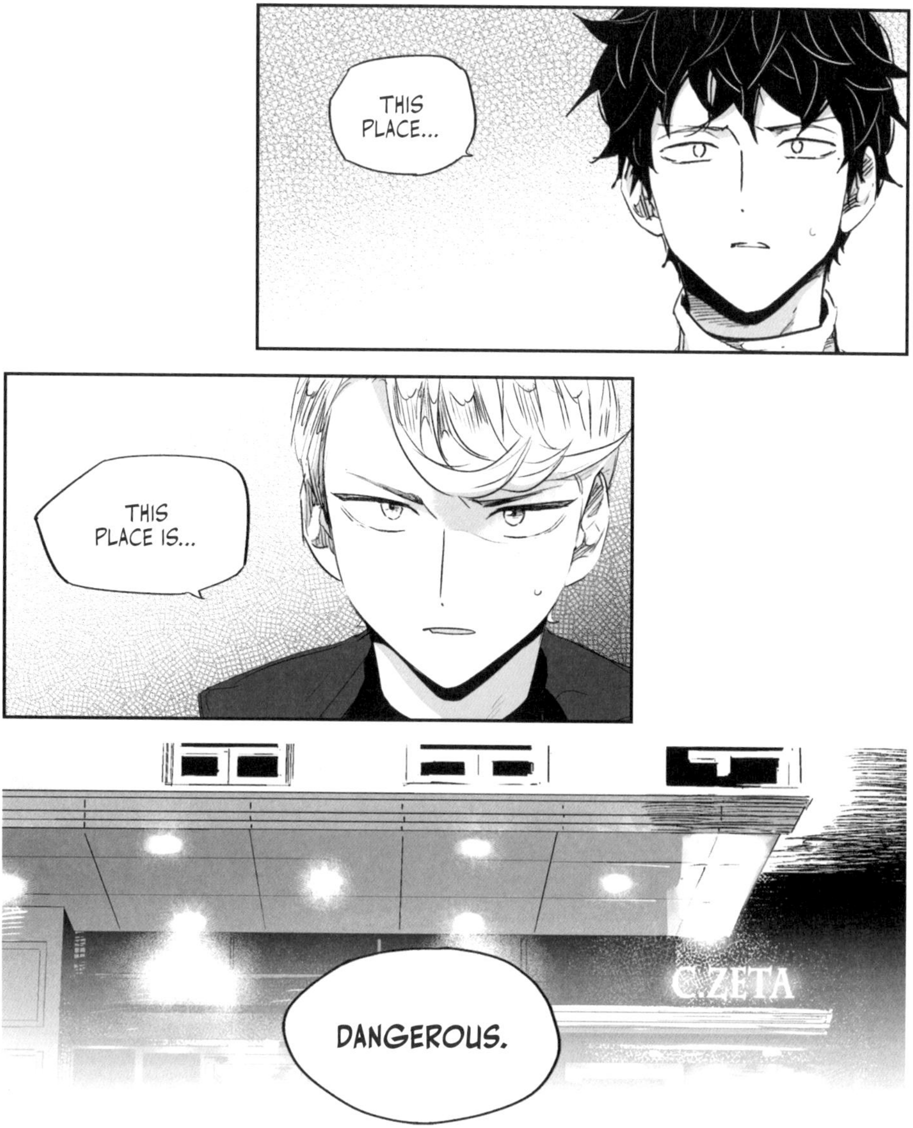
THIS PLACE...
THIS PLACE IS...
C.ZETA
DANGEROUS.

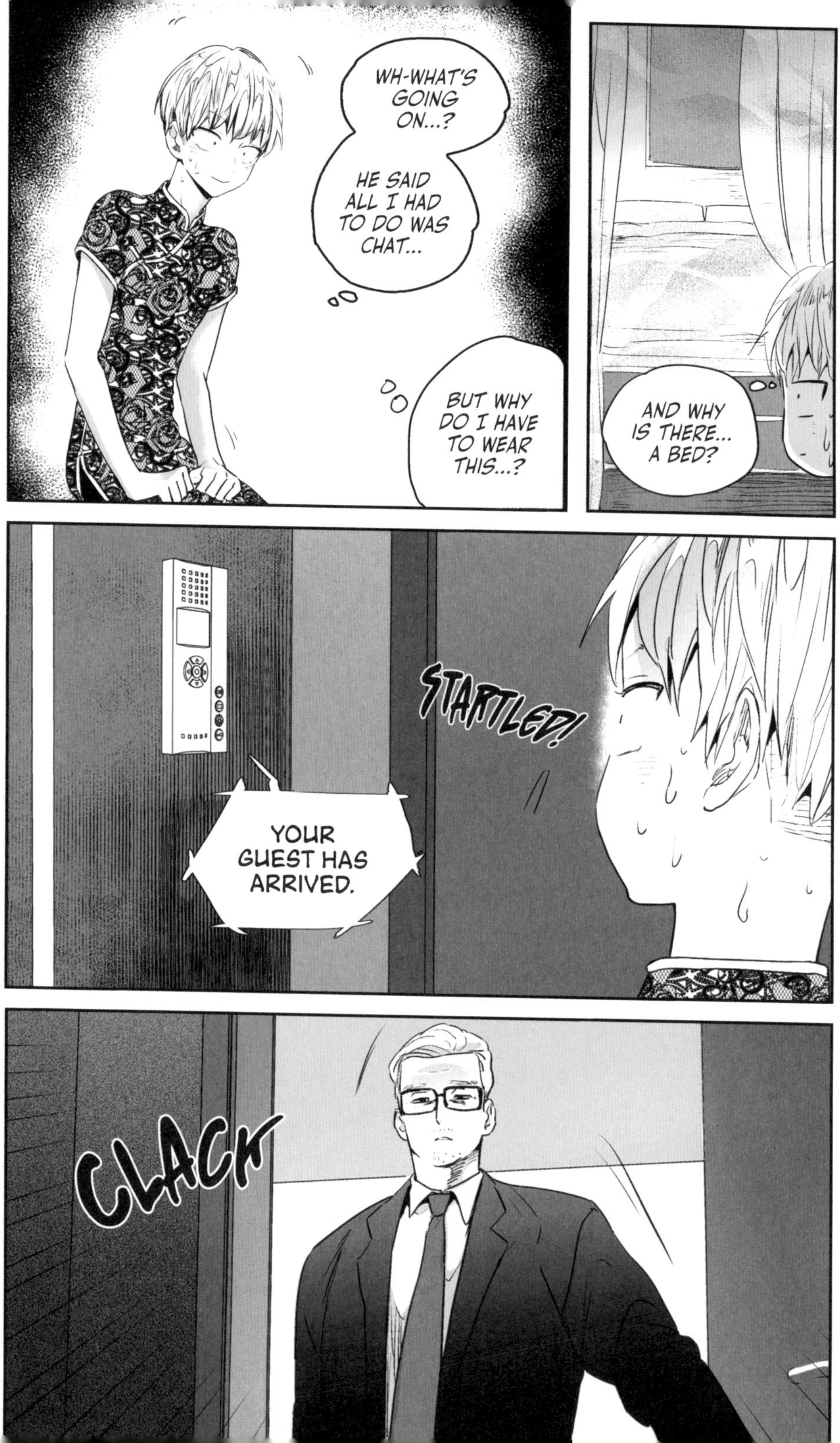
WH-WHAT'S GOING ON...?
HE SAID ALL I HAD TO DO WAS CHAT...
BUT WHY DO I HAVE TO WEAR THIS...?
AND WHY IS THERE... A BED?
YOUR GUEST HAS ARRIVED.
STARTLED!
CLACK

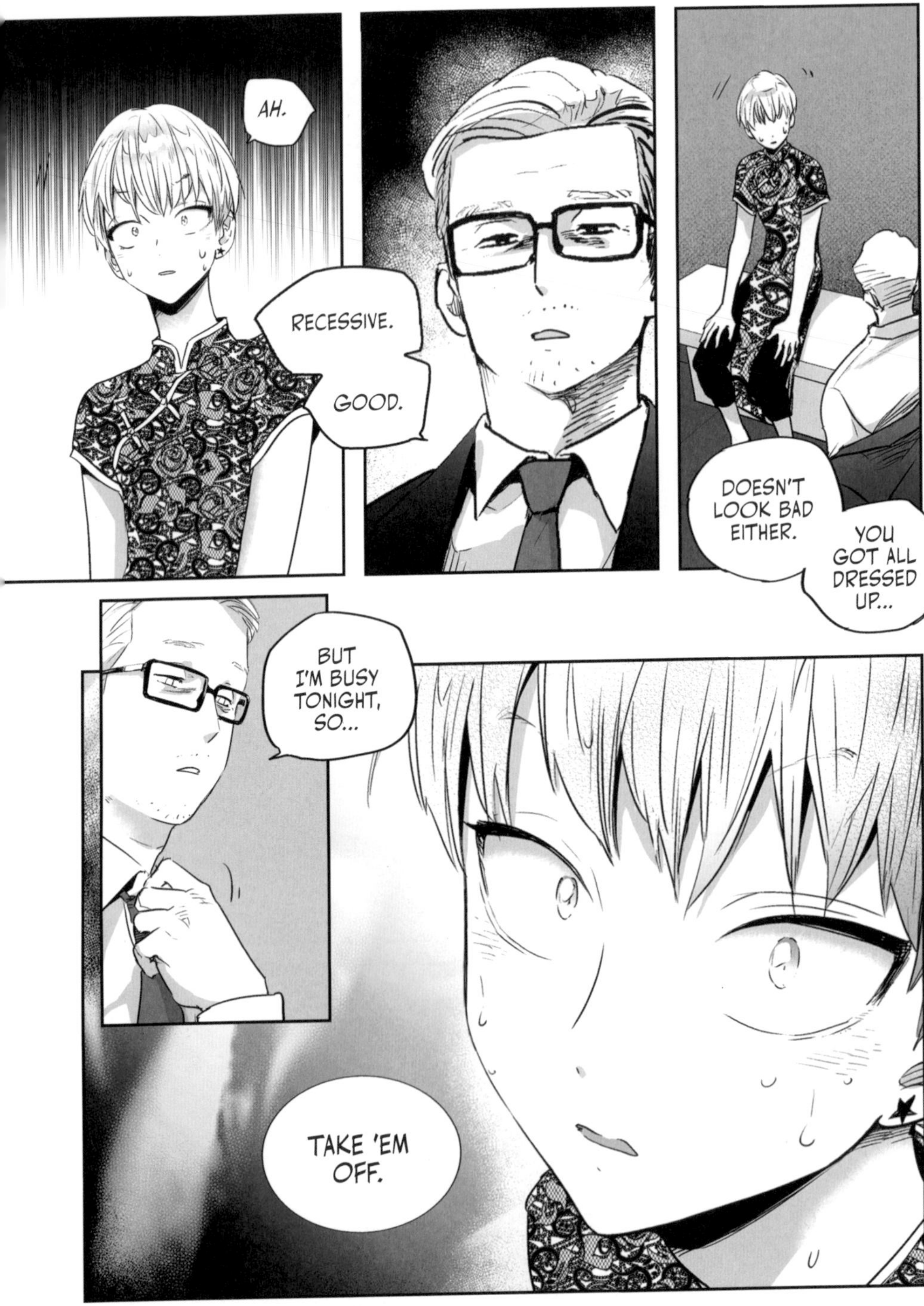
AH.
RECESSIVE.
GOOD.
DOESN'T LOOK BAD EITHER.
YOU GOT ALL DRESSED UP...
BUT I'M BUSY TONIGHT, SO...
TAKE 'EM OFF.

Love is
an Illusion!

Love is
an Illusion!

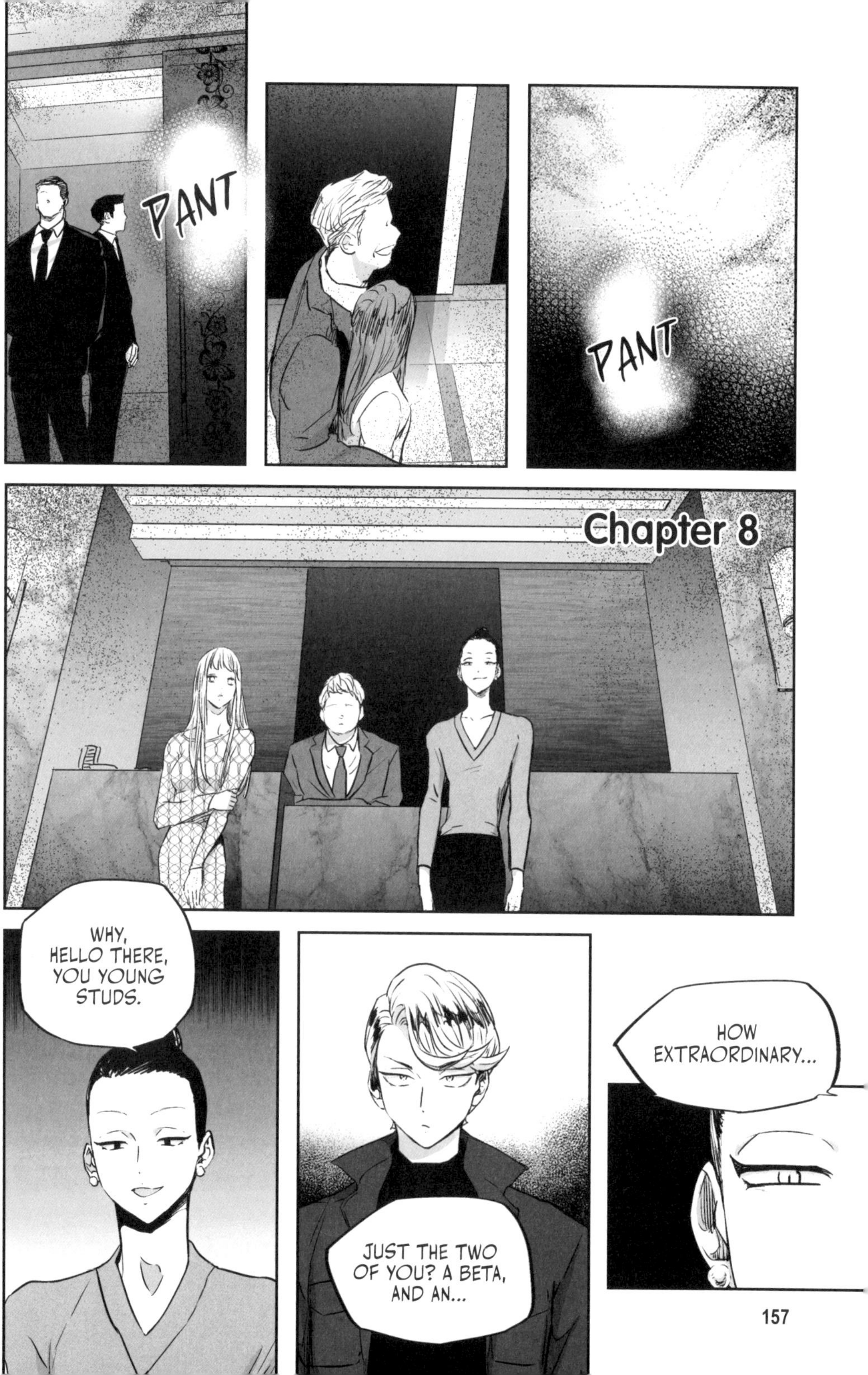
PANT
PANT
Chapter 8
WHY, HELLO THERE, YOU YOUNG STUDS.
JUST THE TWO OF YOU? A BETA, AND AN...
HOW EXTRAORDINARY...

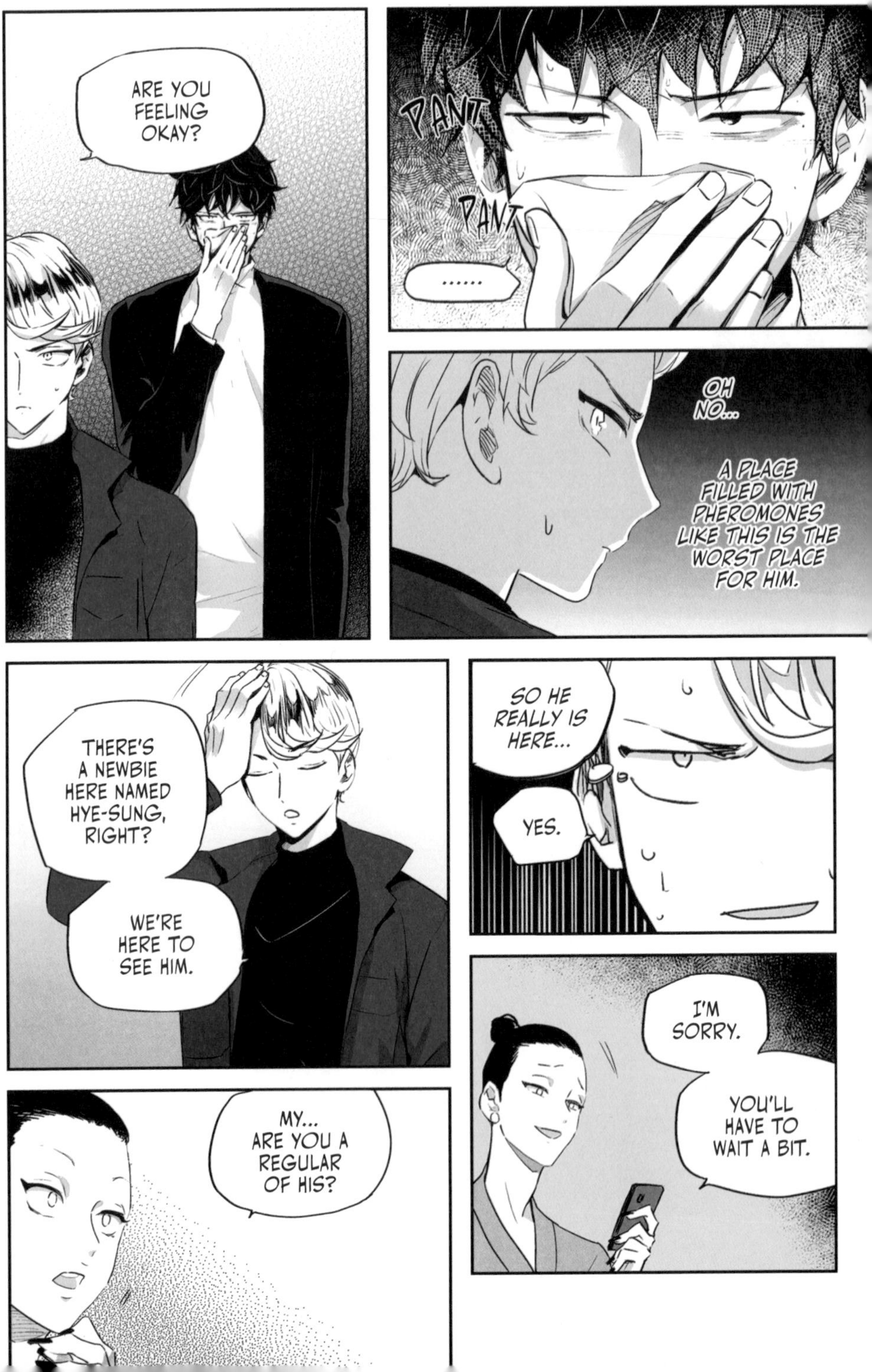

ARE YOU FEELING OKAY?
PANT
PANT
......
OH NO...
A PLACE FILLED WITH PHEROMONES LIKE THIS IS THE WORST PLACE FOR HIM.
THERE'S A NEWBIE HERE NAMED HYE-SUNG, RIGHT?
WE'RE HERE TO SEE HIM.
SO HE REALLY IS HERE...
YES.
MY... ARE YOU A REGULAR OF HIS?
I'M SORRY.
YOU'LL HAVE TO WAIT A BIT.

*Oppa: Honorific title used by females to address elder brothers or other males older than themselves.

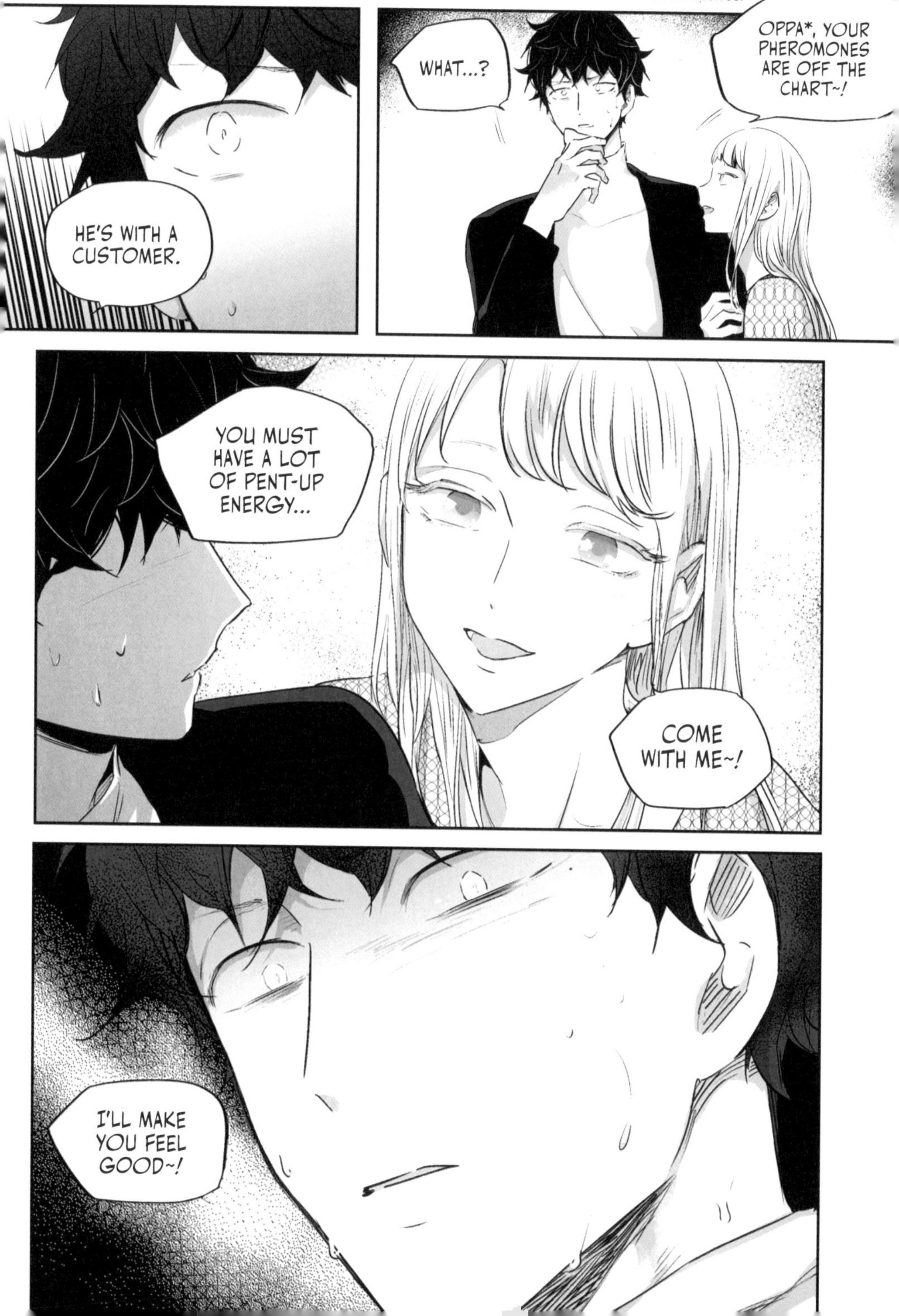
HE'S WITH A CUSTOMER.
WHAT...?
OPPA*, YOUR PHEROMONES ARE OFF THE CHART~!
YOU MUST HAVE A LOT OF PENT-UP ENERGY...
COME WITH ME~!
I'LL MAKE YOU FEEL GOOD~!

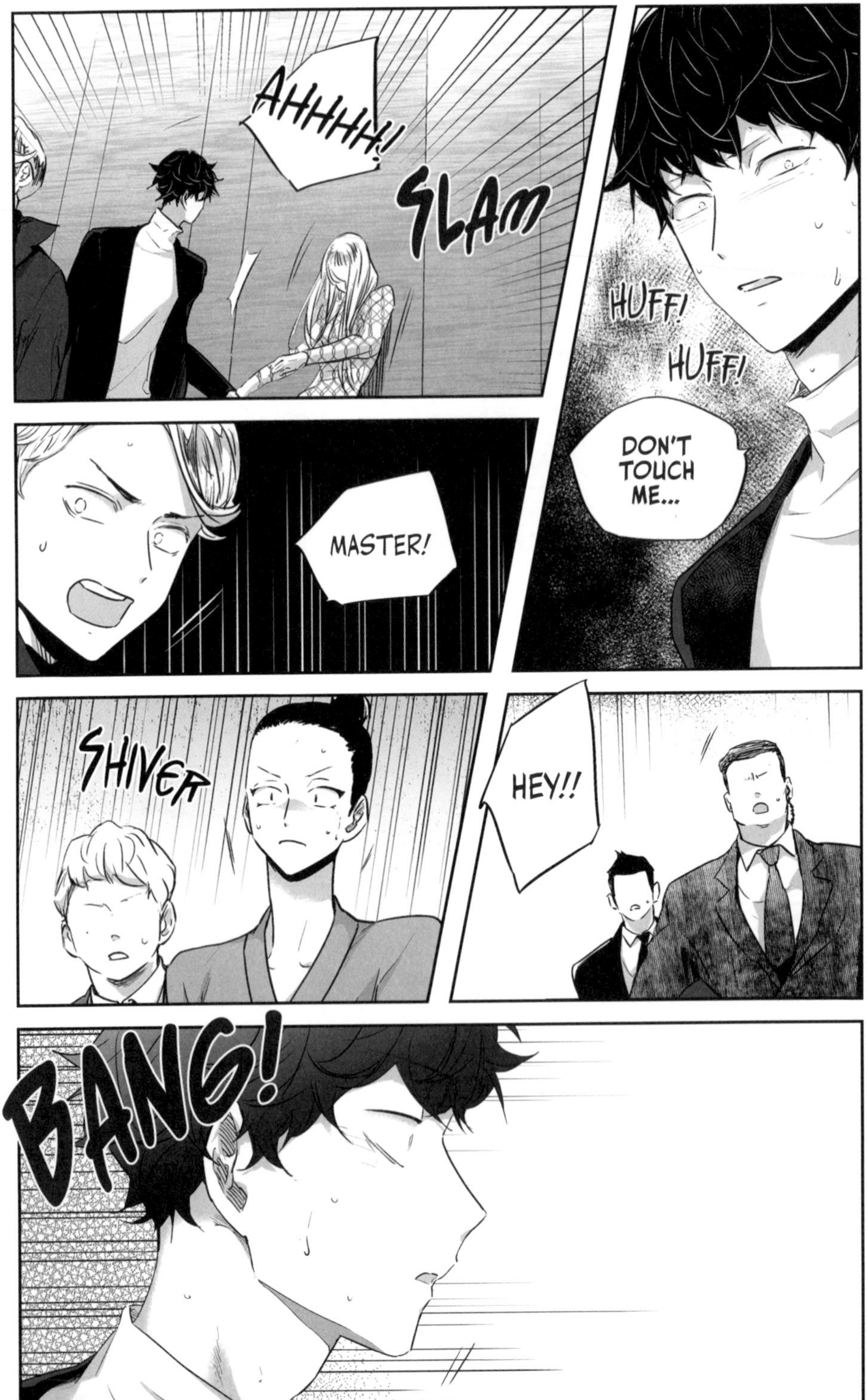
AHHHH!
SLAM
HUFF!
HUFF!
DON'T TOUCH ME...
MASTER!
SHIVER
HEY!!
BANG!

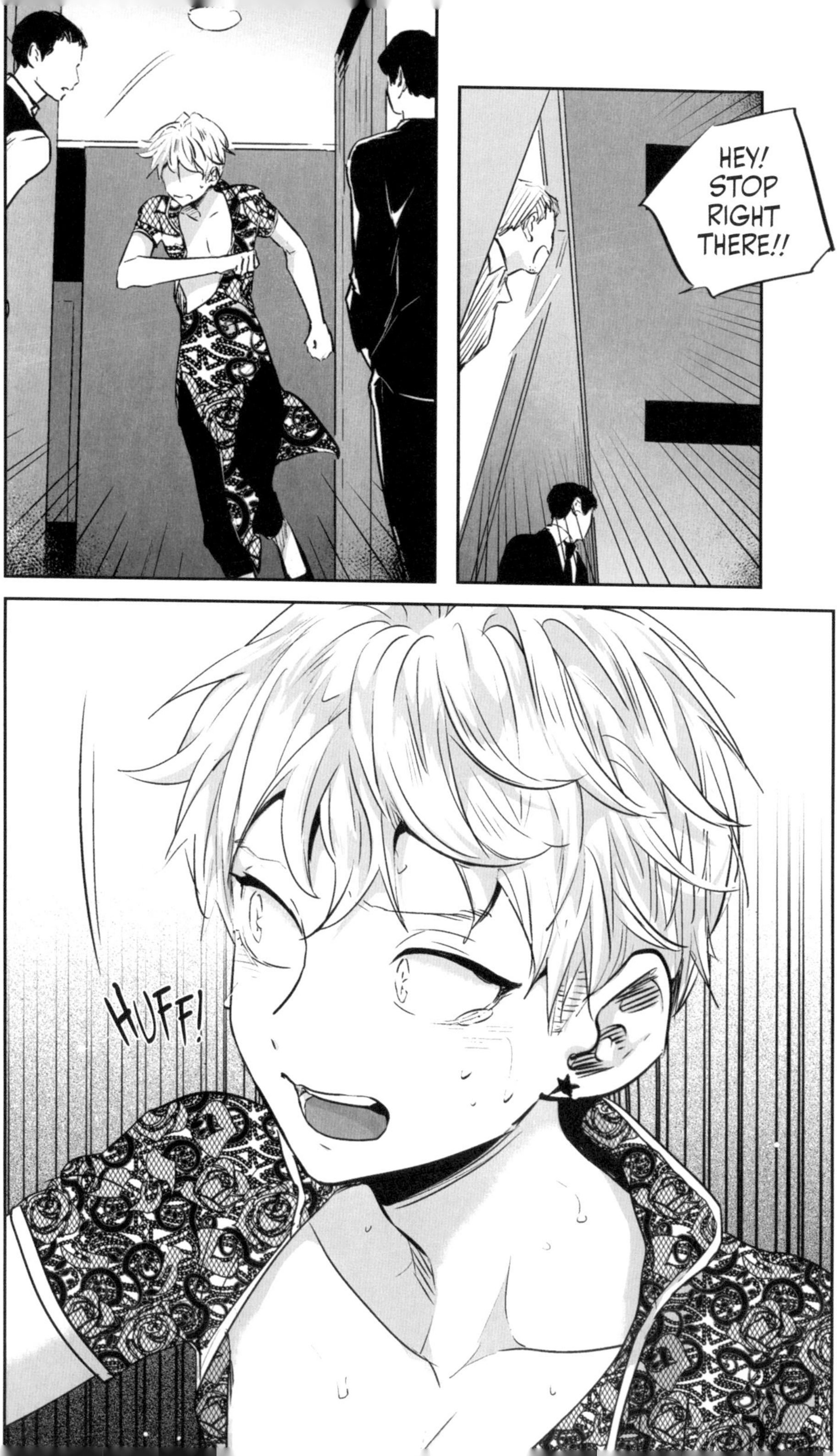
HEY! STOP RIGHT THERE!!
HUFF!

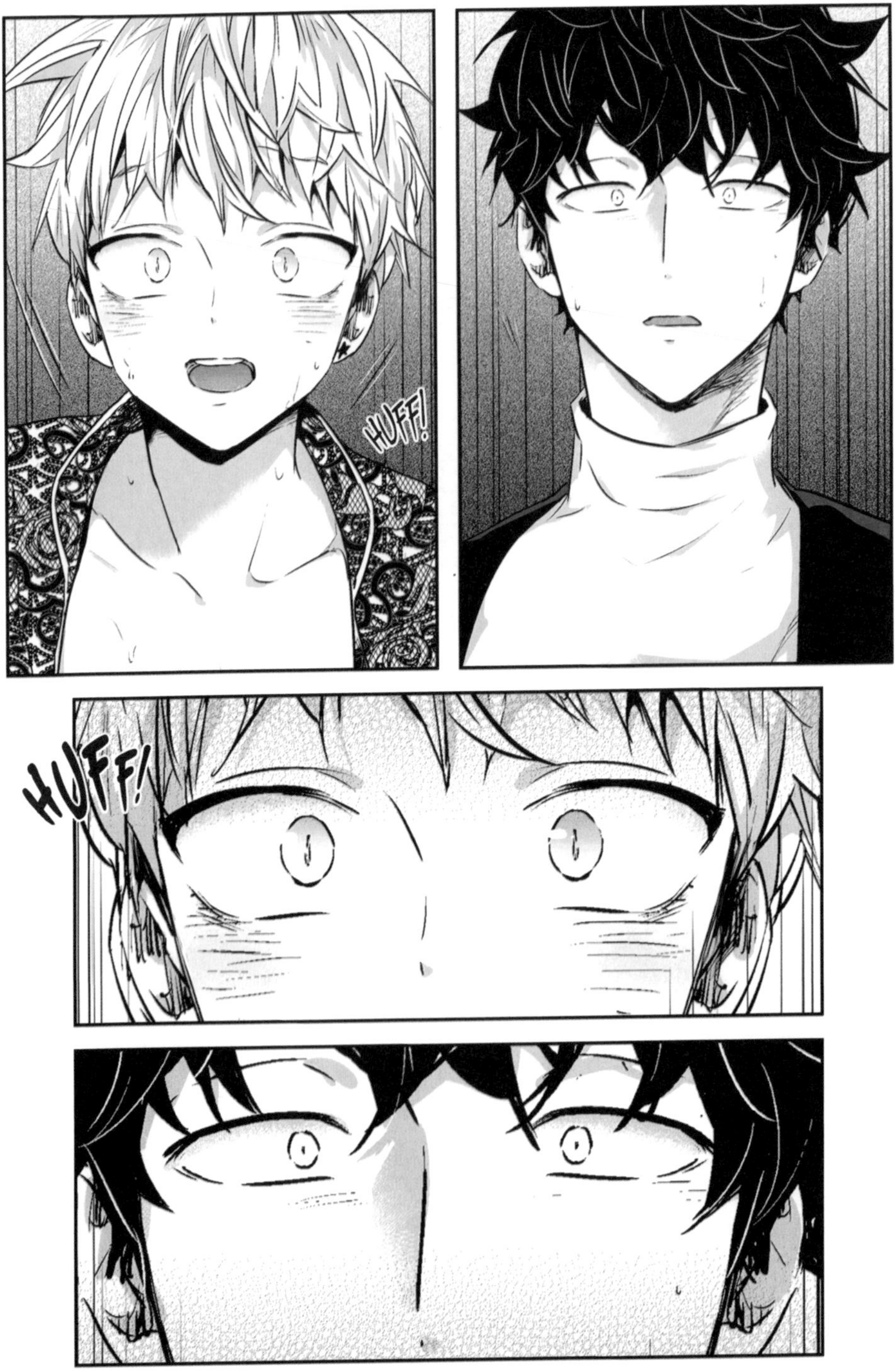
HUFF!
HUFF!

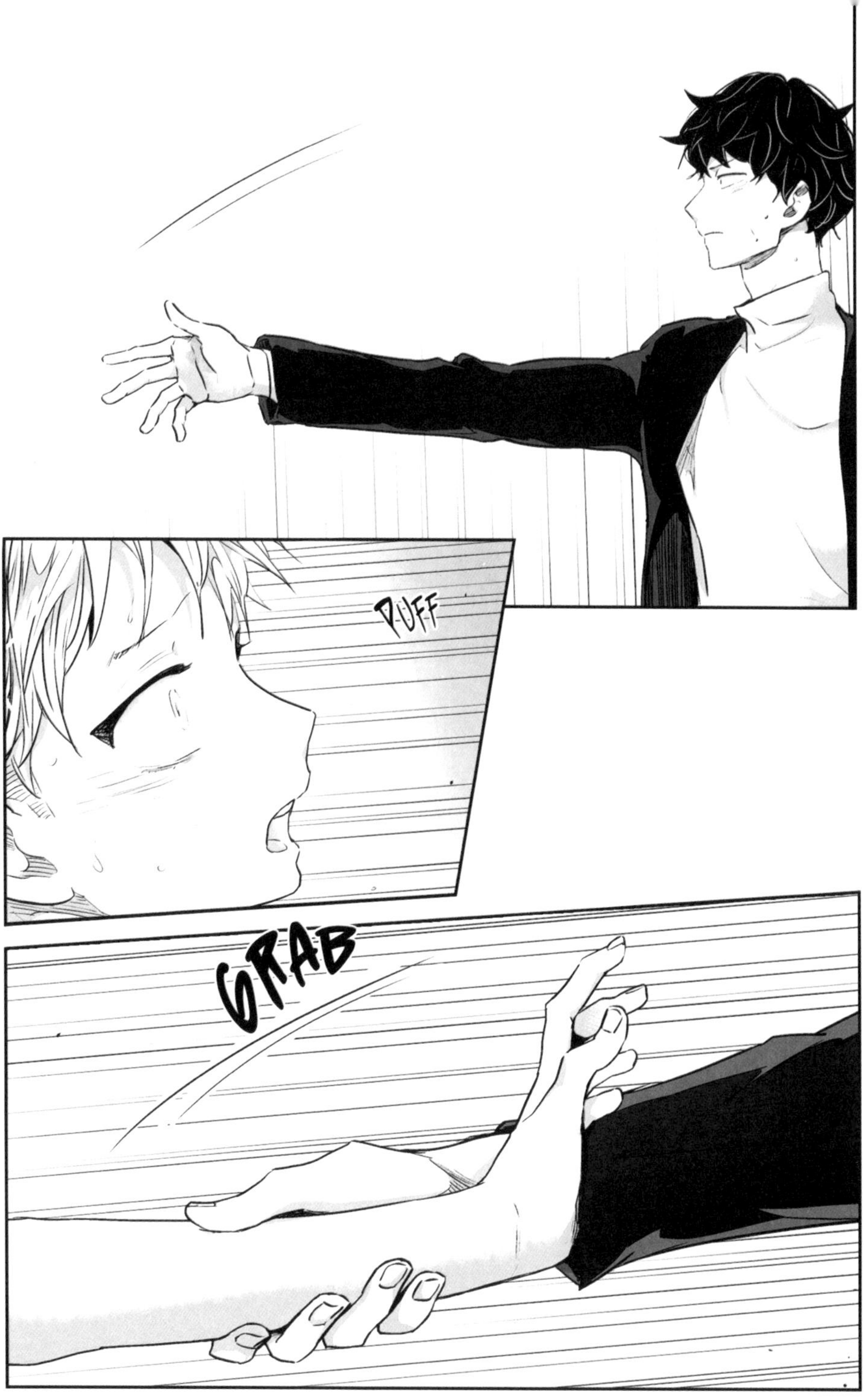
DUFF
GRAB

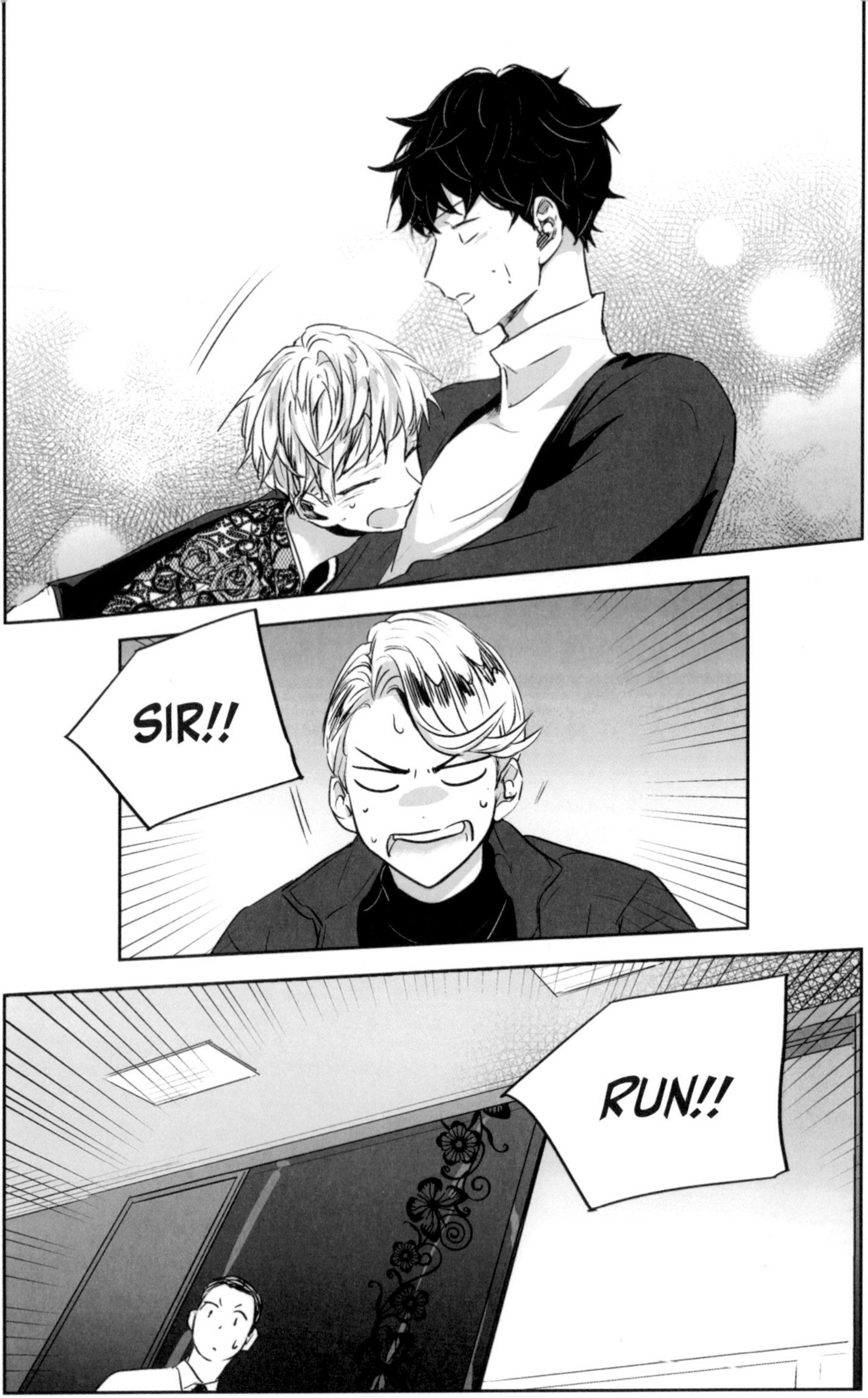
SIR!!
RUN!!

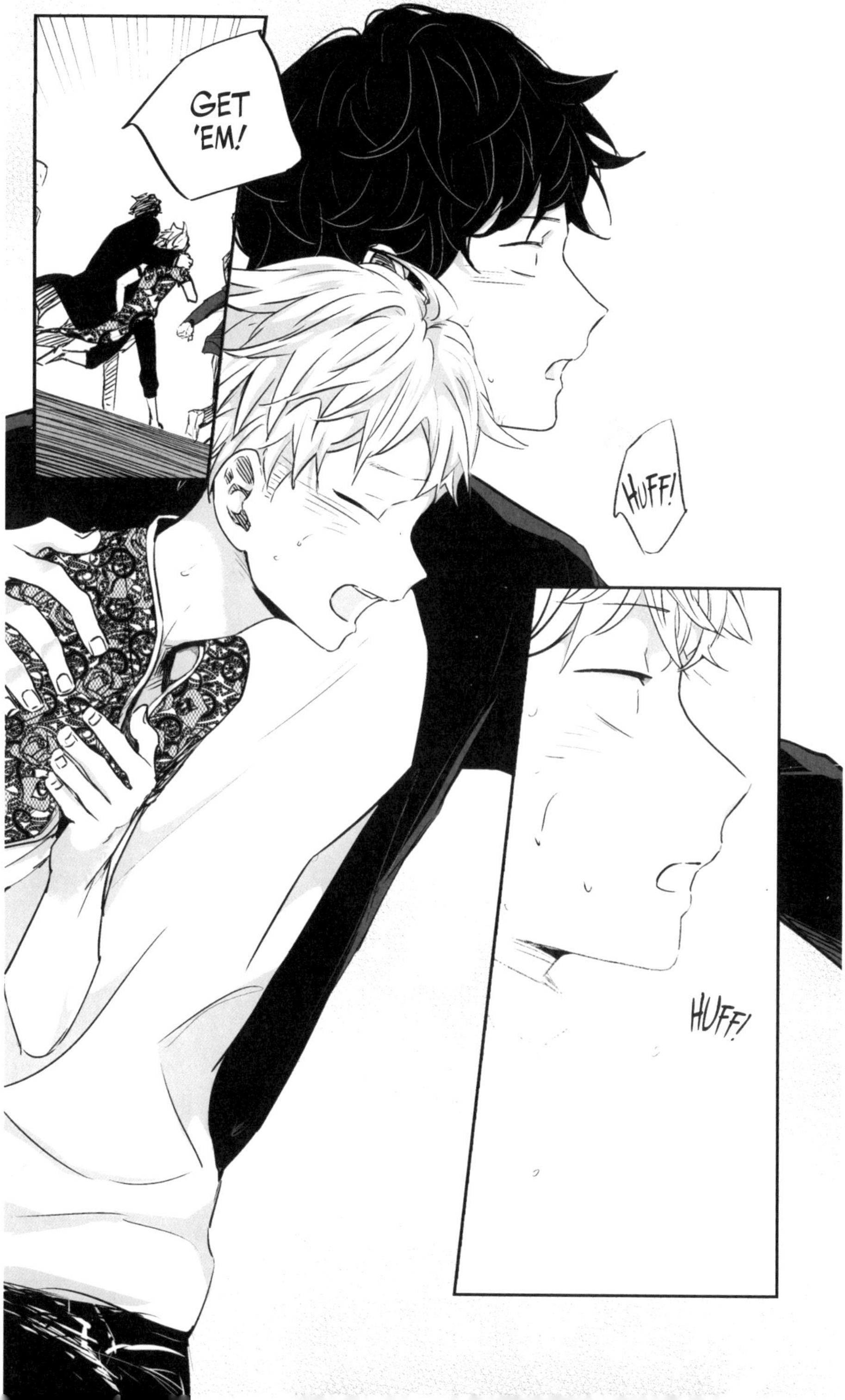
GET 'EM!
HUFF!
HUFF!

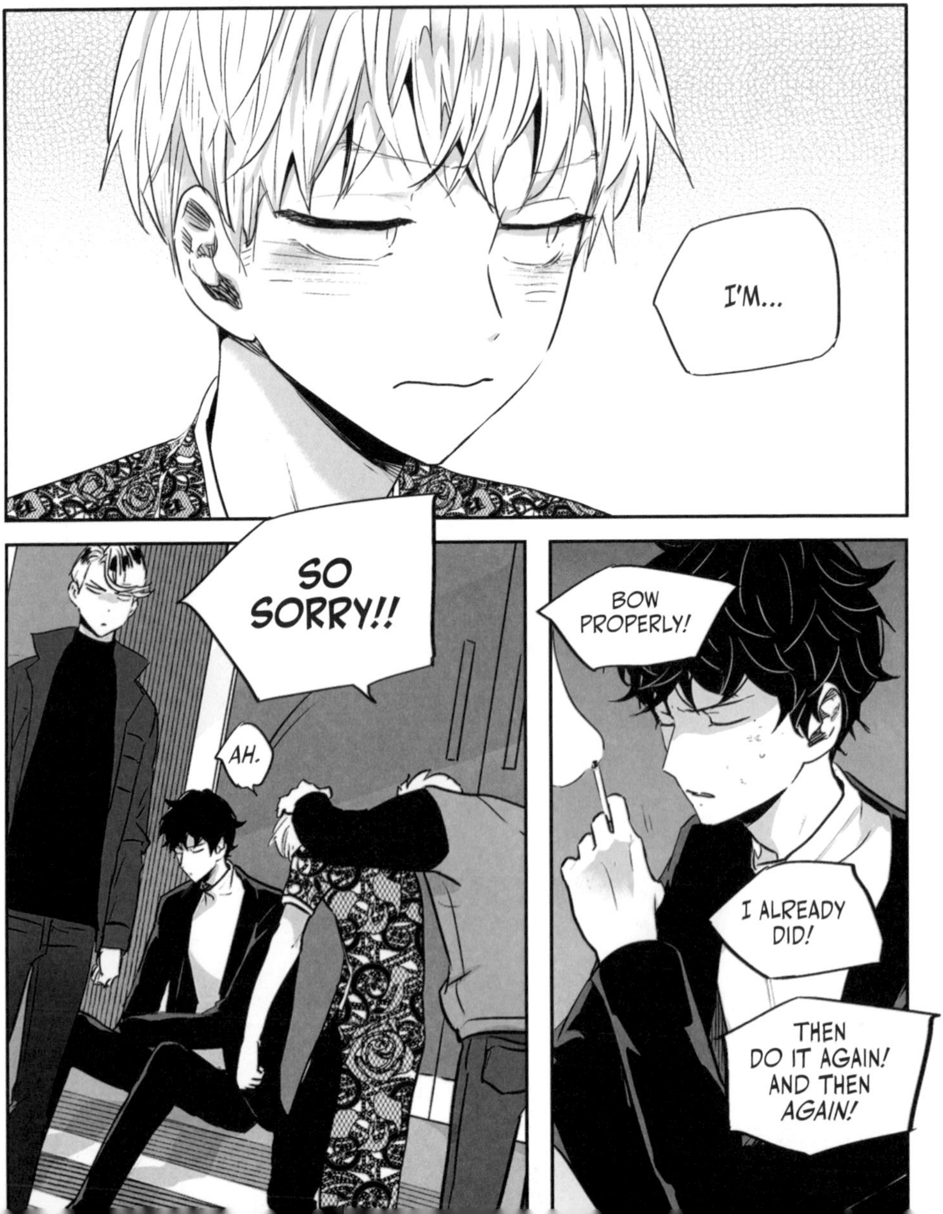
I'M...
SO SORRY!!
AH.
BOW PROPERLY!
I ALREADY DID!
THEN DO IT AGAIN! AND THEN AGAIN!

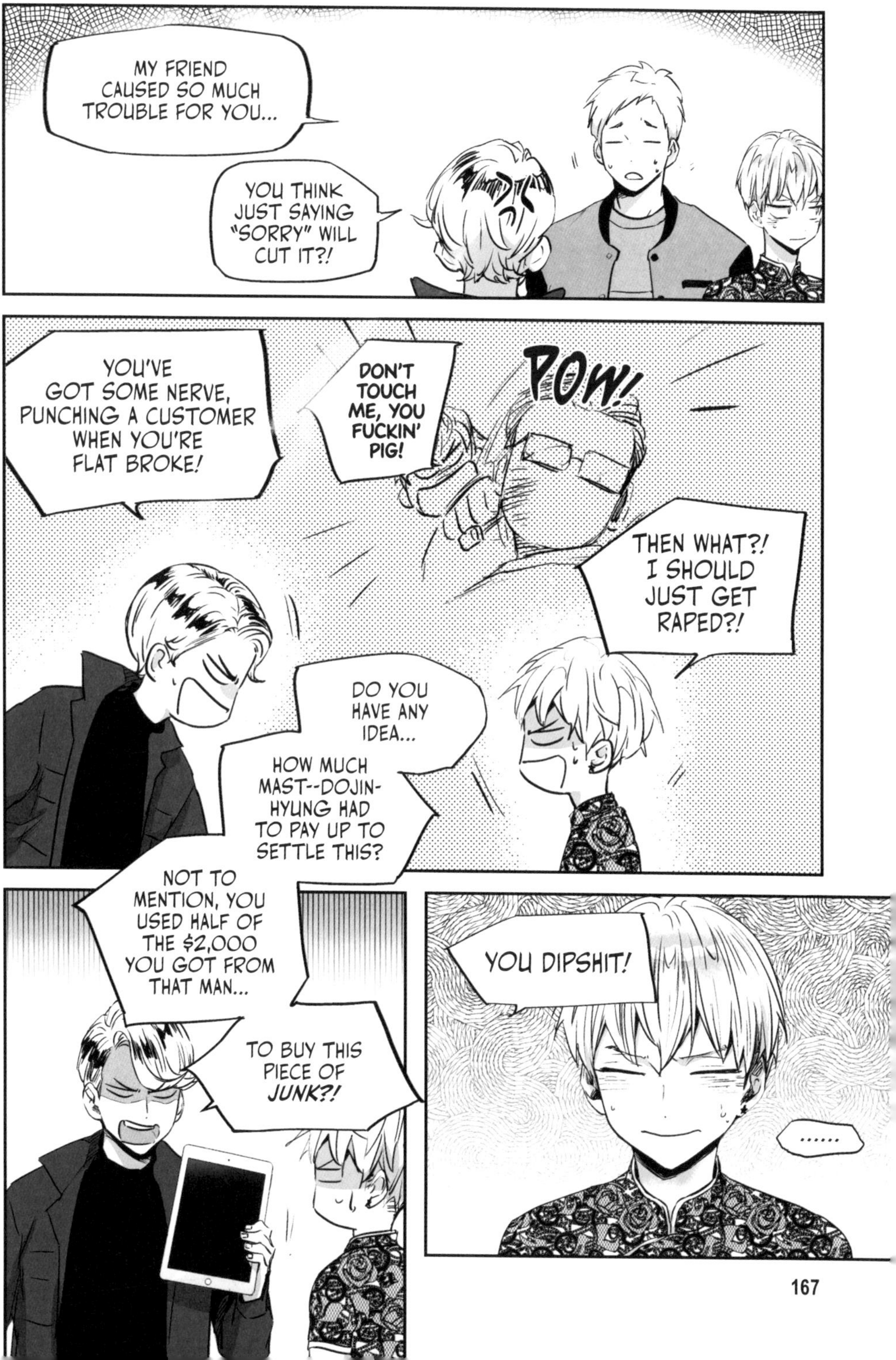
MY FRIEND CAUSED SO MUCH TROUBLE FOR YOU...
YOU THINK JUST SAYING "SORRY" WILL CUT IT?!
YOU'VE GOT SOME NERVE, PUNCHING A CUSTOMER WHEN YOU'RE FLAT BROKE!
DON'T TOUCH ME, YOU FUCKIN' PIG!
POW!
THEN WHAT?! I SHOULD JUST GET RAPED?!
DO YOU HAVE ANY IDEA...
HOW MUCH MAST--DOJIN-HYUNG HAD TO PAY UP TO SETTLE THIS?
NOT TO MENTION, YOU USED HALF OF THE $2,000 YOU GOT FROM THAT MAN...
TO BUY THIS PIECE OF JUNK?!
YOU DIPSHIT!
......

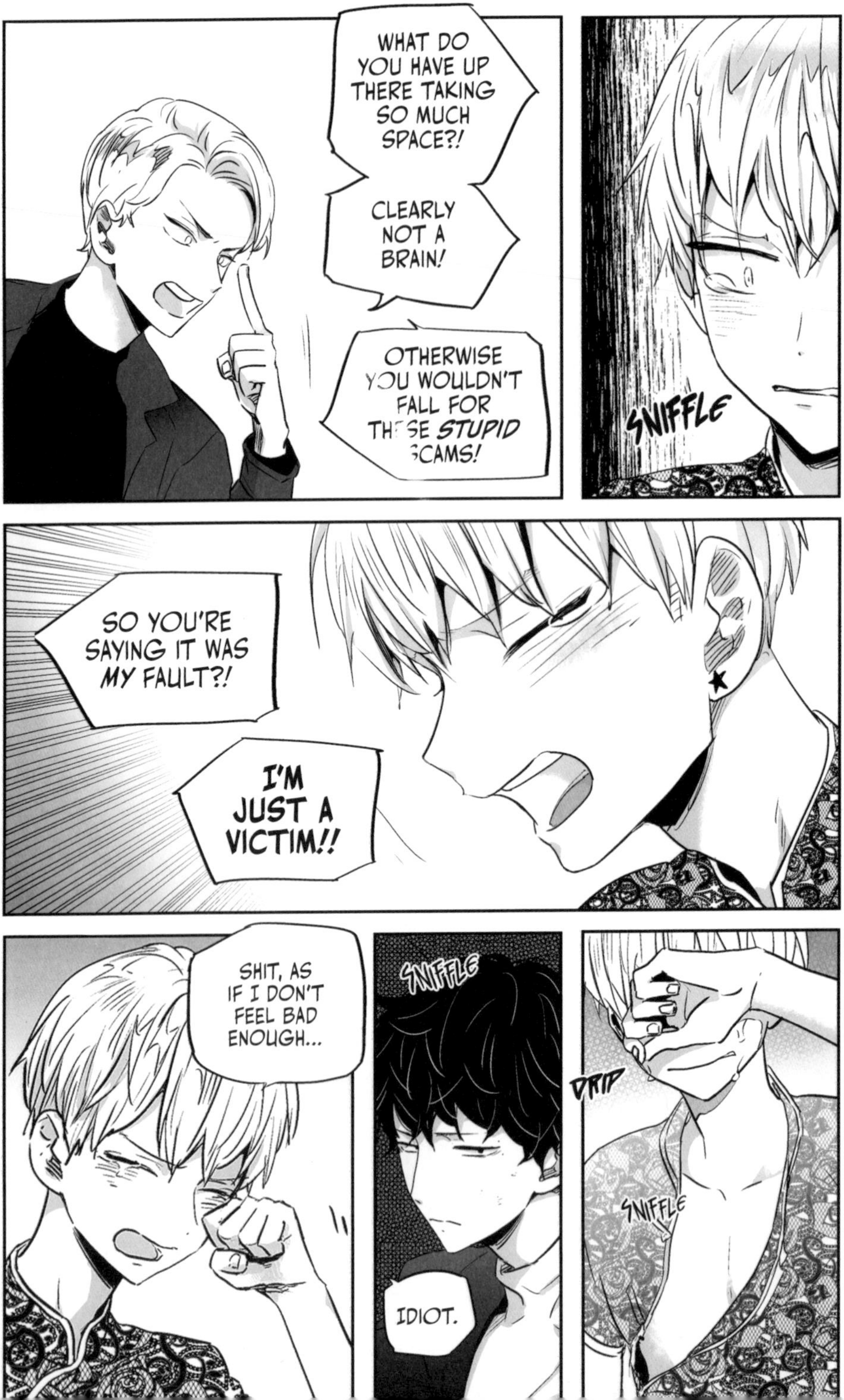
WHAT DO YOU HAVE UP THERE TAKING SO MUCH SPACE?!
CLEARLY NOT A BRAIN!
OTHERWISE YOU WOULDN'T FALL FOR THESE STUPID SCAMS!
SNIFFLE
SO YOU'RE SAYING IT WAS MY FAULT?!
I'M JUST A VICTIM!!
SHIT, AS IF I DON'T FEEL BAD ENOUGH...
SNIFFLE
IDIOT.
DRIP
SNIFFLE

HAA...

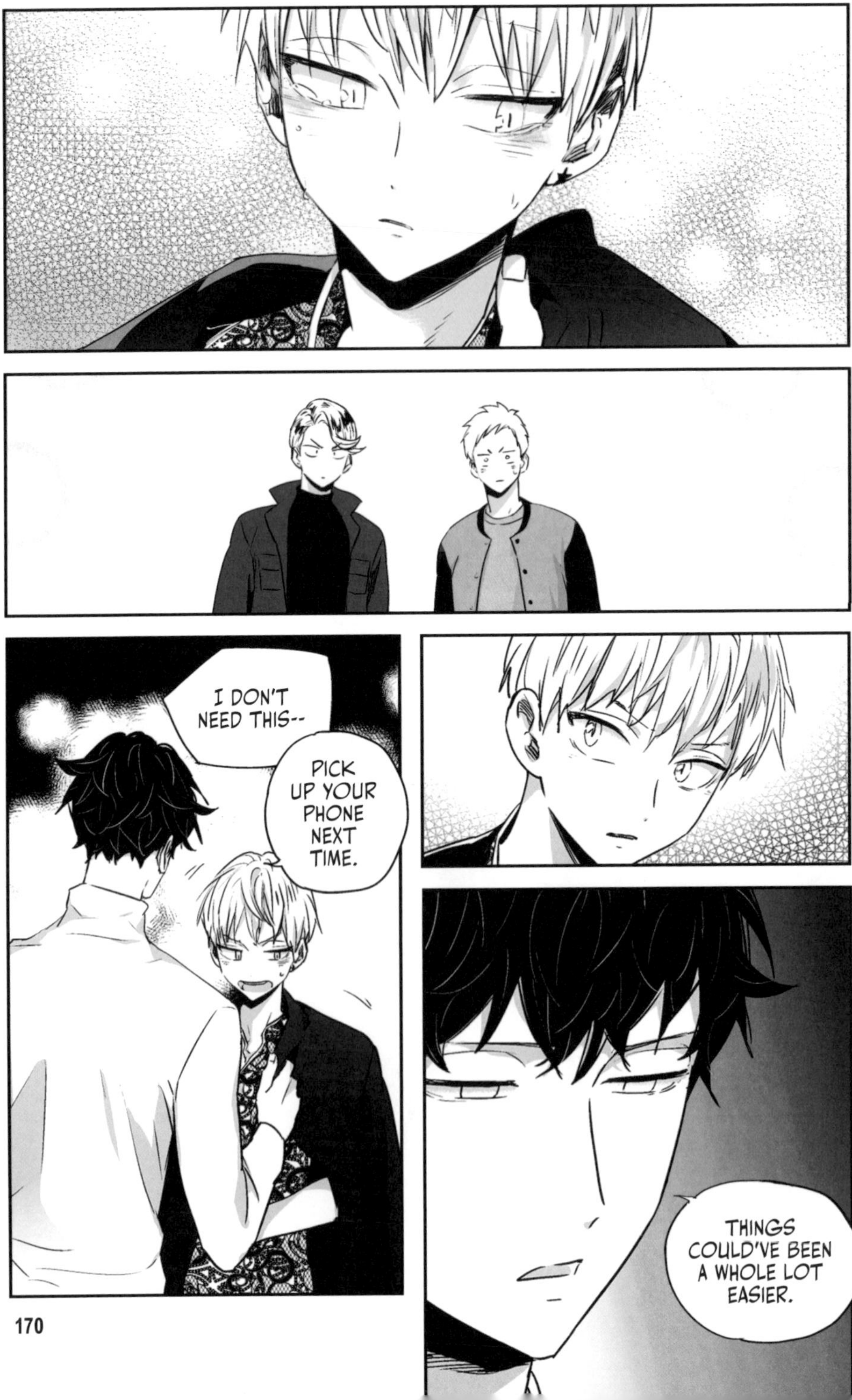
I DON'T NEED THIS--
PICK UP YOUR PHONE NEXT TIME.
THINGS COULD'VE BEEN A WHOLE LOT EASIER.

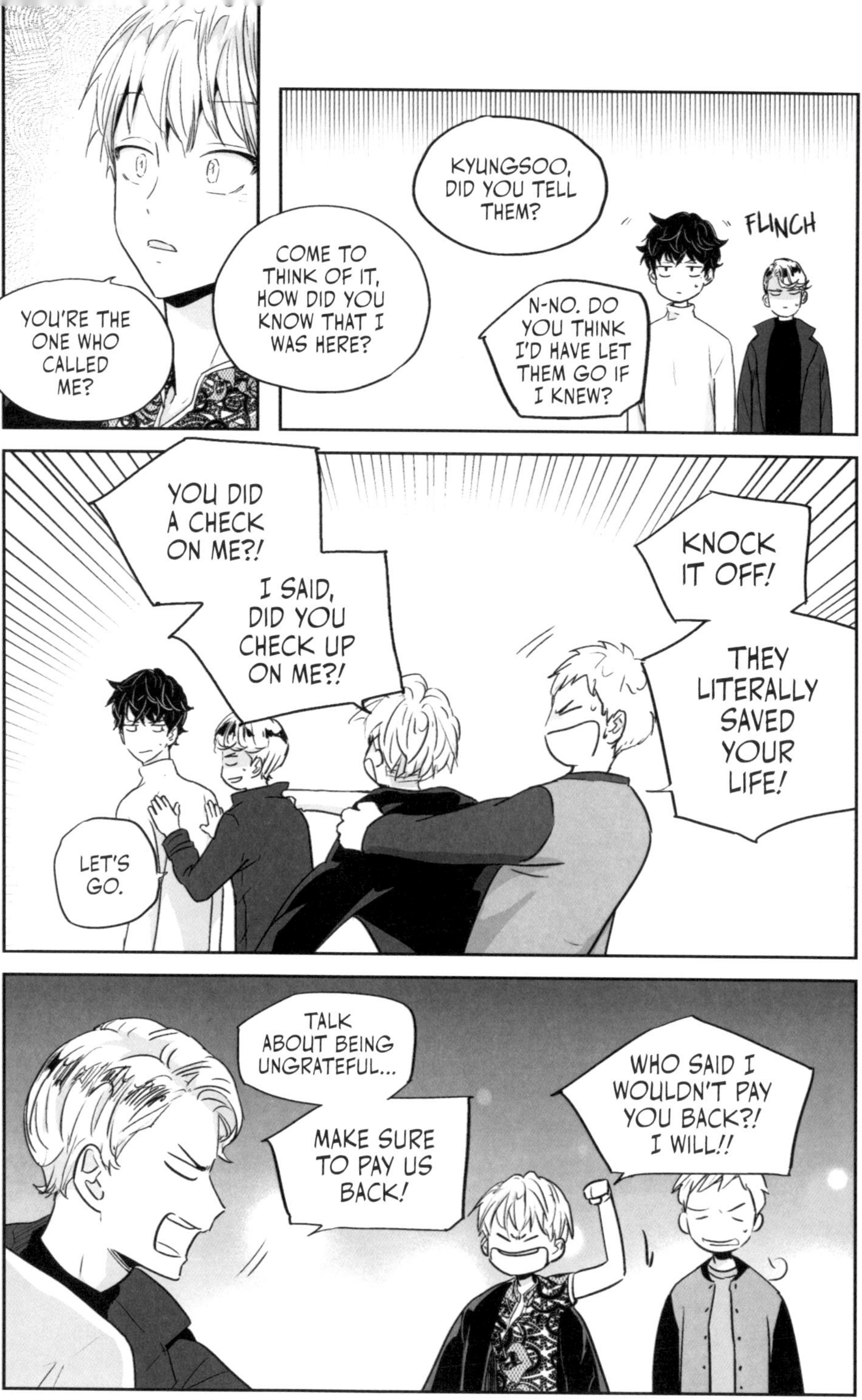
YOU'RE THE ONE WHO CALLED ME?
COME TO THINK OF IT, HOW DID YOU KNOW THAT I WAS HERE?
KYUNGSOO, DID YOU TELL THEM?
FLINCH
N-NO. DO YOU THINK I'D HAVE LET THEM GO IF I KNEW?
YOU DID A CHECK ON ME?!
I SAID, DID YOU CHECK UP ON ME?!
LET'S GO.
KNOCK IT OFF!
THEY LITERALLY SAVED YOUR LIFE!
TALK ABOUT BEING UNGRATEFUL...
MAKE SURE TO PAY US BACK!
WHO SAID I WOULDN'T PAY YOU BACK?! I WILL!!

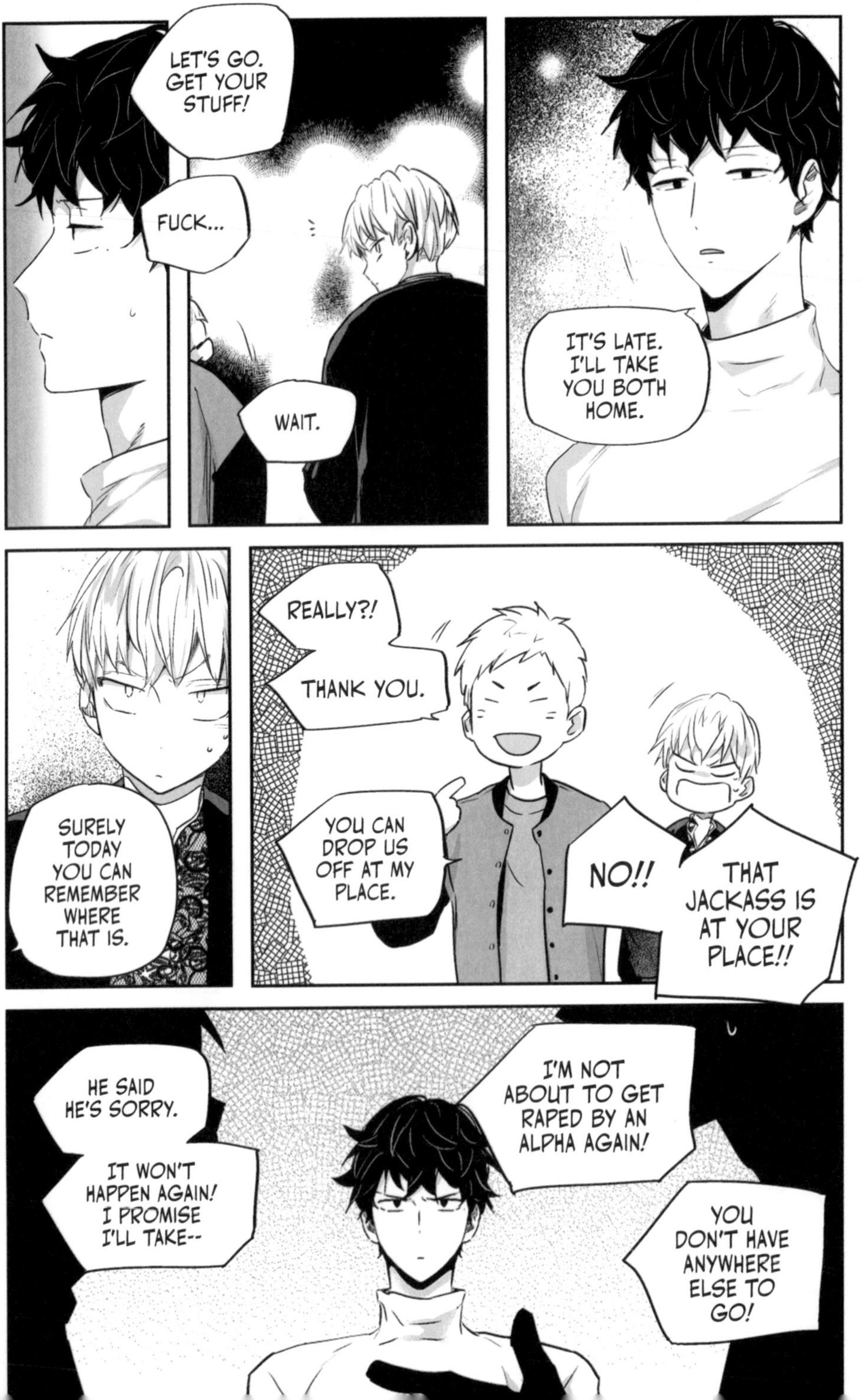
LET'S GO. GET YOUR STUFF!
FUCK...
WAIT.
IT'S LATE. I'LL TAKE YOU BOTH HOME.
SURELY TODAY YOU CAN REMEMBER WHERE THAT IS.
REALLY?!
THANK YOU.
YOU CAN DROP US OFF AT MY PLACE.
NO!!
THAT JACKASS IS AT YOUR PLACE!!
HE SAID HE'S SORRY.
IT WON'T HAPPEN AGAIN! I PROMISE I'LL TAKE--
I'M NOT ABOUT TO GET RAPED BY AN ALPHA AGAIN!
YOU DON'T HAVE ANYWHERE ELSE TO GO!

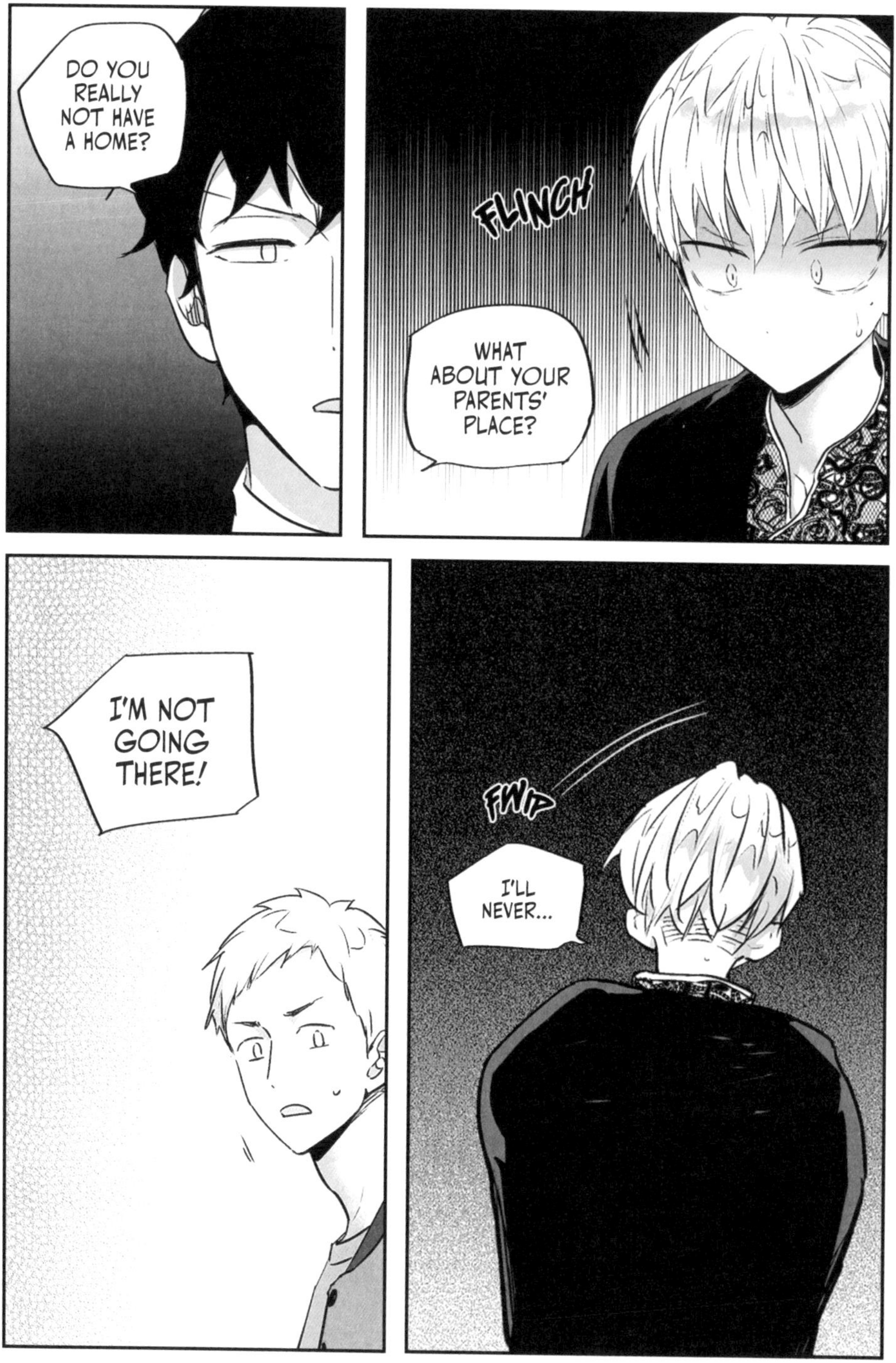
DO YOU REALLY NOT HAVE A HOME?
FLINCH
WHAT ABOUT YOUR PARENTS' PLACE?
I'M NOT GOING THERE!
FWIP
I'LL NEVER...

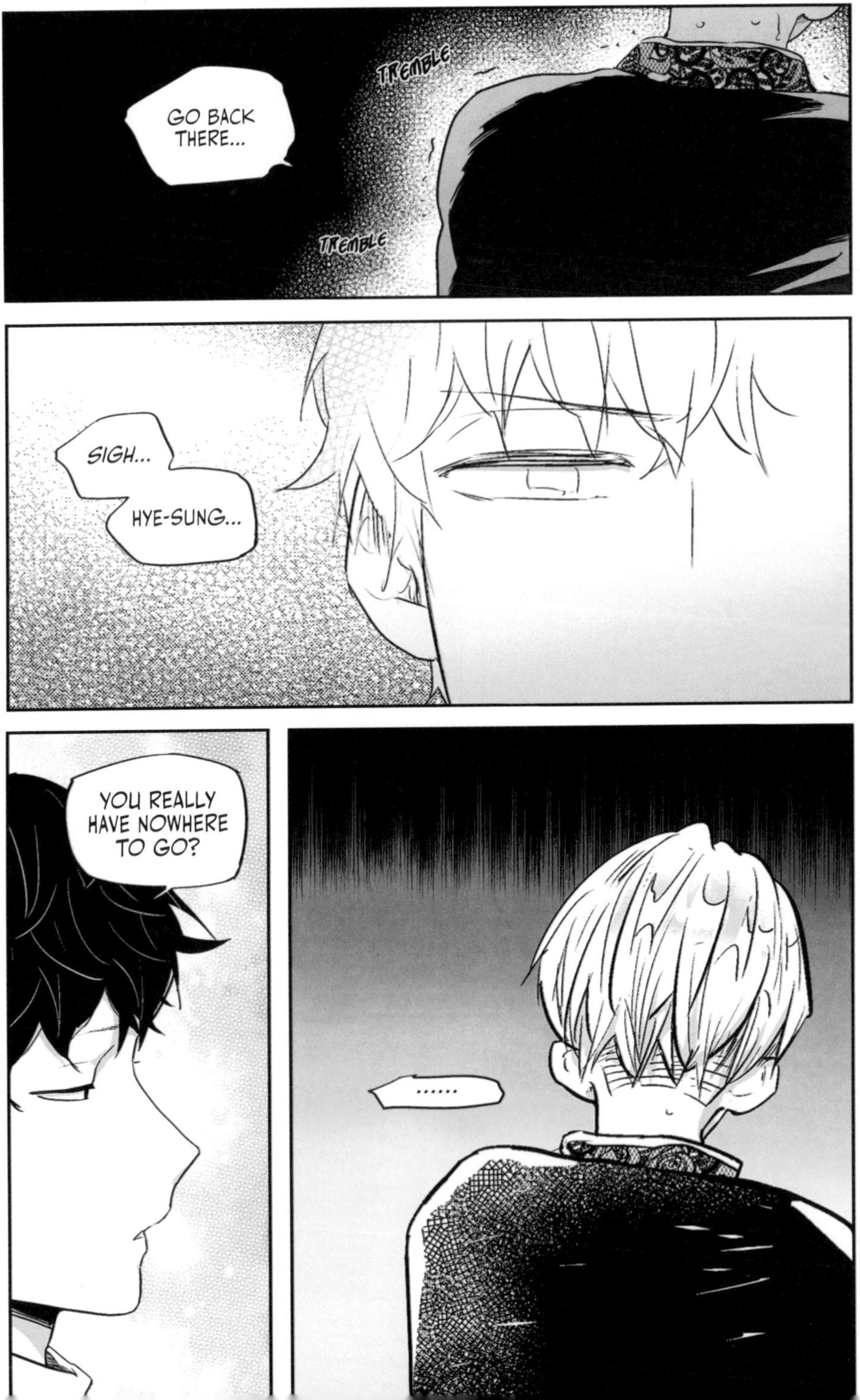

GO BACK THERE...
TREMBLE
TREMBLE
SIGH...
HYE-SUNG...
YOU REALLY HAVE NOWHERE TO GO?
......

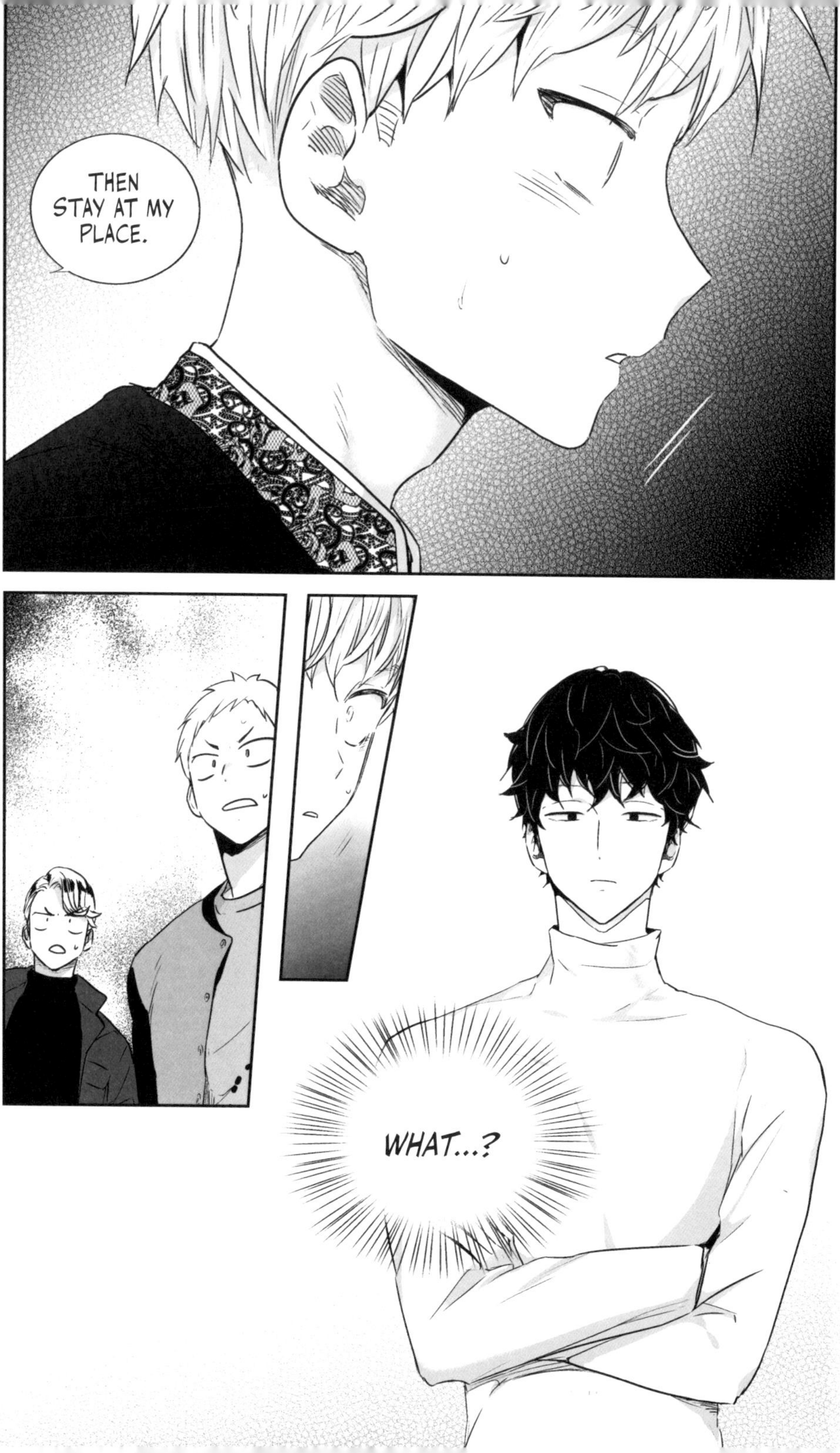
THEN STAY AT MY PLACE.
WHAT...?

Love is
an Illusion!

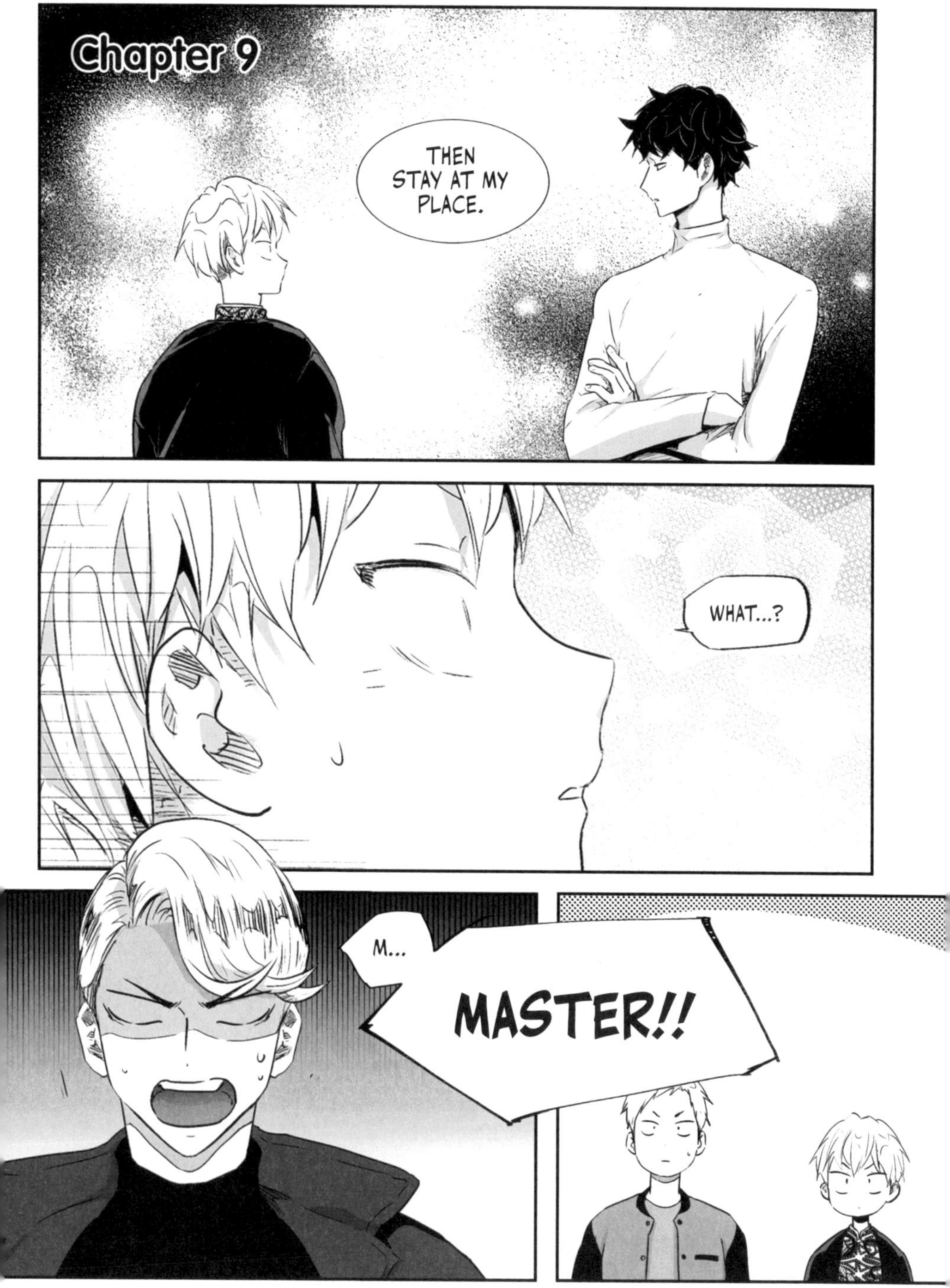
Chapter 9
THEN STAY AT MY PLACE.
WHAT...?
M...
MASTER!!

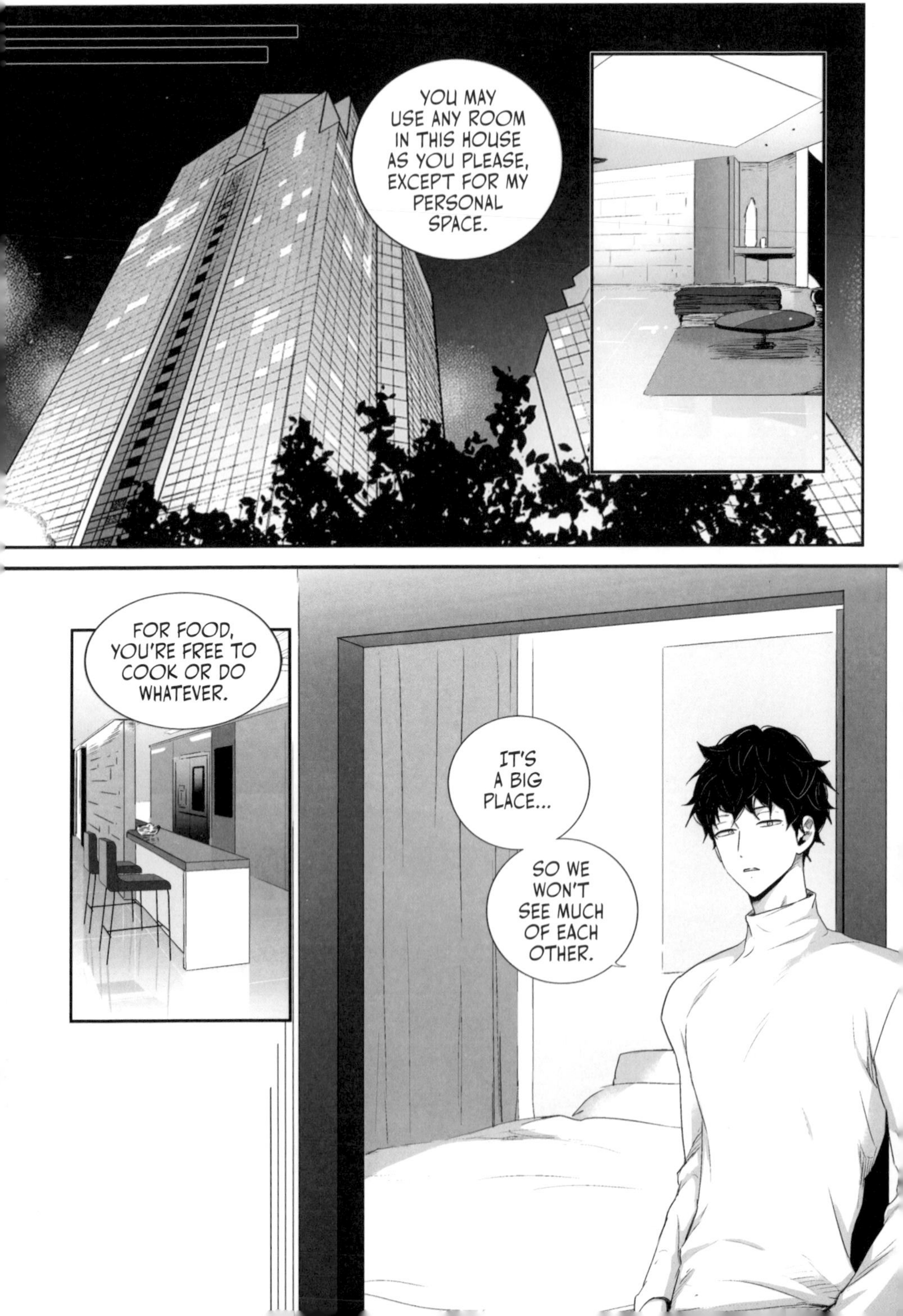
YOU MAY USE ANY ROOM IN THIS HOUSE AS YOU PLEASE, EXCEPT FOR MY PERSONAL SPACE.
FOR FOOD, YOU'RE FREE TO COOK OR DO WHATEVER.
IT'S A BIG PLACE...
SO WE WON'T SEE MUCH OF EACH OTHER.

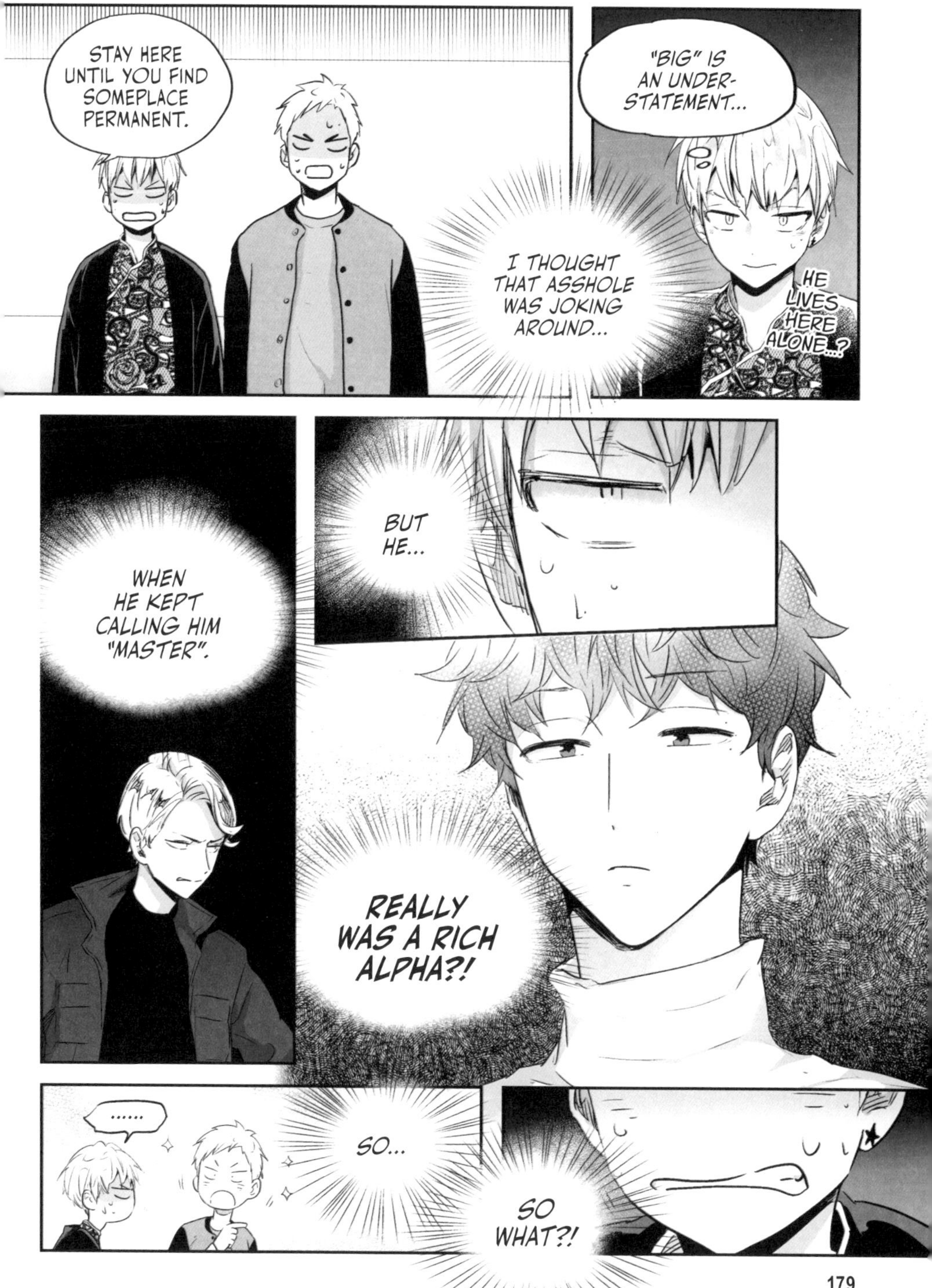
STAY HERE UNTIL YOU FIND SOMEPLACE PERMANENT.
"BIG" IS AN UNDER-STATEMENT...
I THOUGHT THAT ASSHOLE WAS JOKING AROUND...
HE LIVES HERE ALONE...?
WHEN HE KEPT CALLING HIM "MASTER".
BUT HE...
REALLY WAS A RICH ALPHA?!
......
SO...
SO WHAT?!

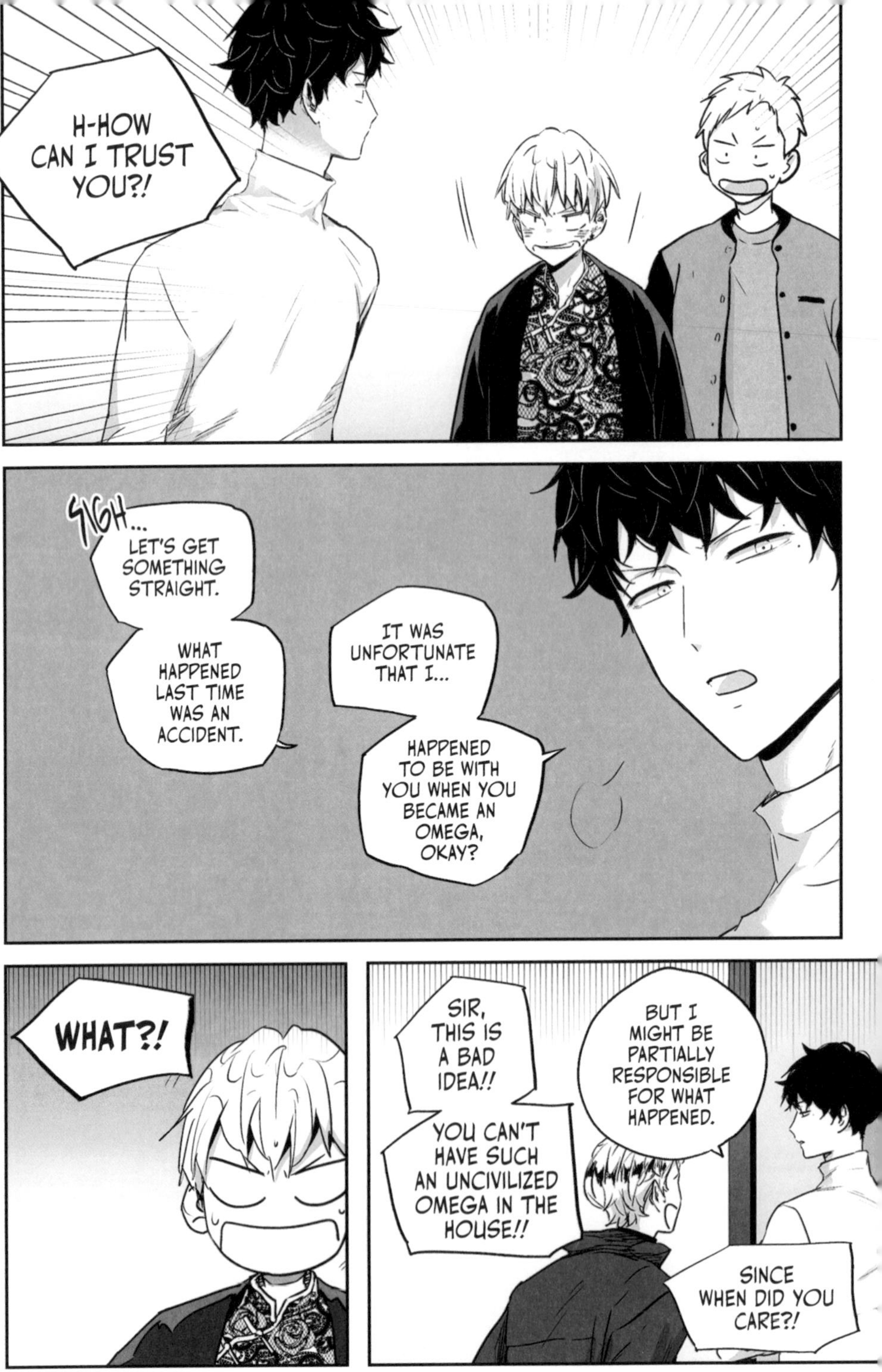

H-HOW CAN I TRUST YOU?!
SIGH...
LET'S GET SOMETHING STRAIGHT.
WHAT HAPPENED LAST TIME WAS AN ACCIDENT.
IT WAS UNFORTUNATE THAT I...
HAPPENED TO BE WITH YOU WHEN YOU BECAME AN OMEGA, OKAY?
WHAT?!
SIR, THIS IS A BAD IDEA!!
YOU CAN'T HAVE SUCH AN UNCIVILIZED OMEGA IN THE HOUSE!!
BUT I MIGHT BE PARTIALLY RESPONSIBLE FOR WHAT HAPPENED.
SINCE WHEN DID YOU CARE?!

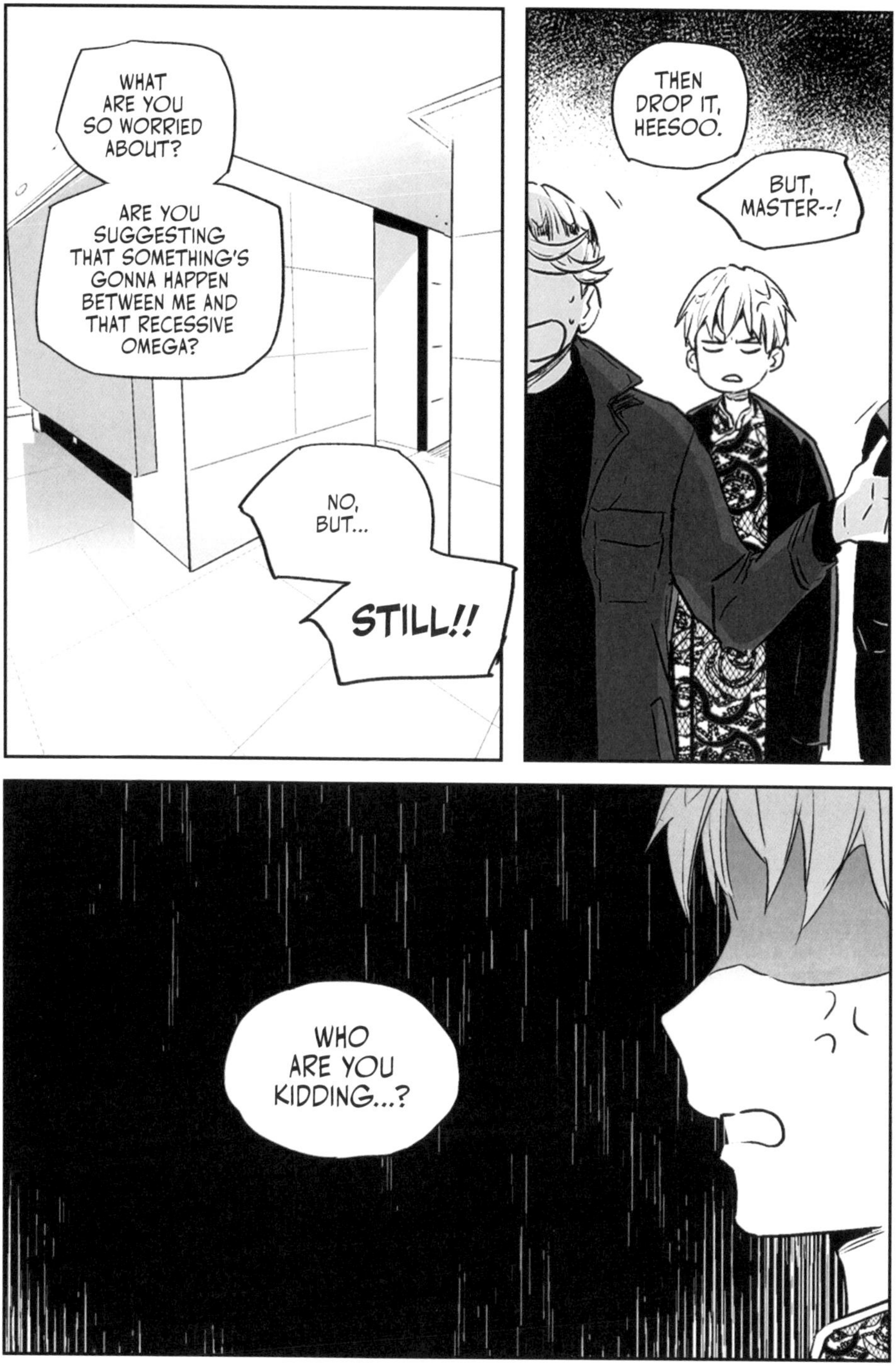
WHAT ARE YOU SO WORRIED ABOUT?
ARE YOU SUGGESTING THAT SOMETHING'S GONNA HAPPEN BETWEEN ME AND THAT RECESSIVE OMEGA?
NO, BUT...
STILL!!
THEN DROP IT, HEESOO.
BUT, MASTER--!
WHO ARE YOU KIDDING...?

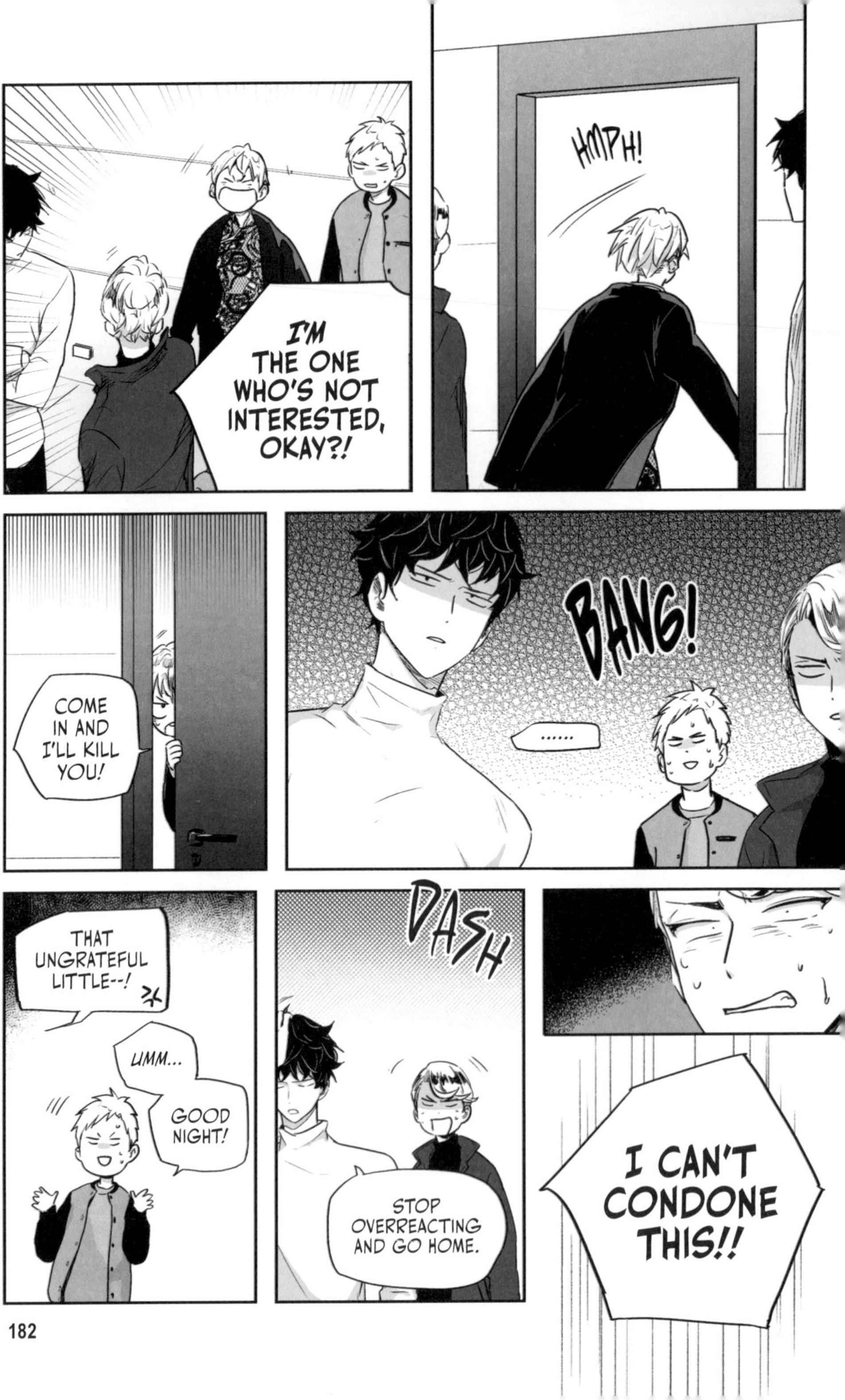
I'M THE ONE WHO'S NOT INTERESTED, OKAY?!
HMPH!
COME IN AND I'LL KILL YOU!
BANG!
......
THAT UNGRATEFUL LITTLE--!
UMM...
GOOD NIGHT!
DASH
STOP OVERREACTING AND GO HOME.
I CAN'T CONDONE THIS!!

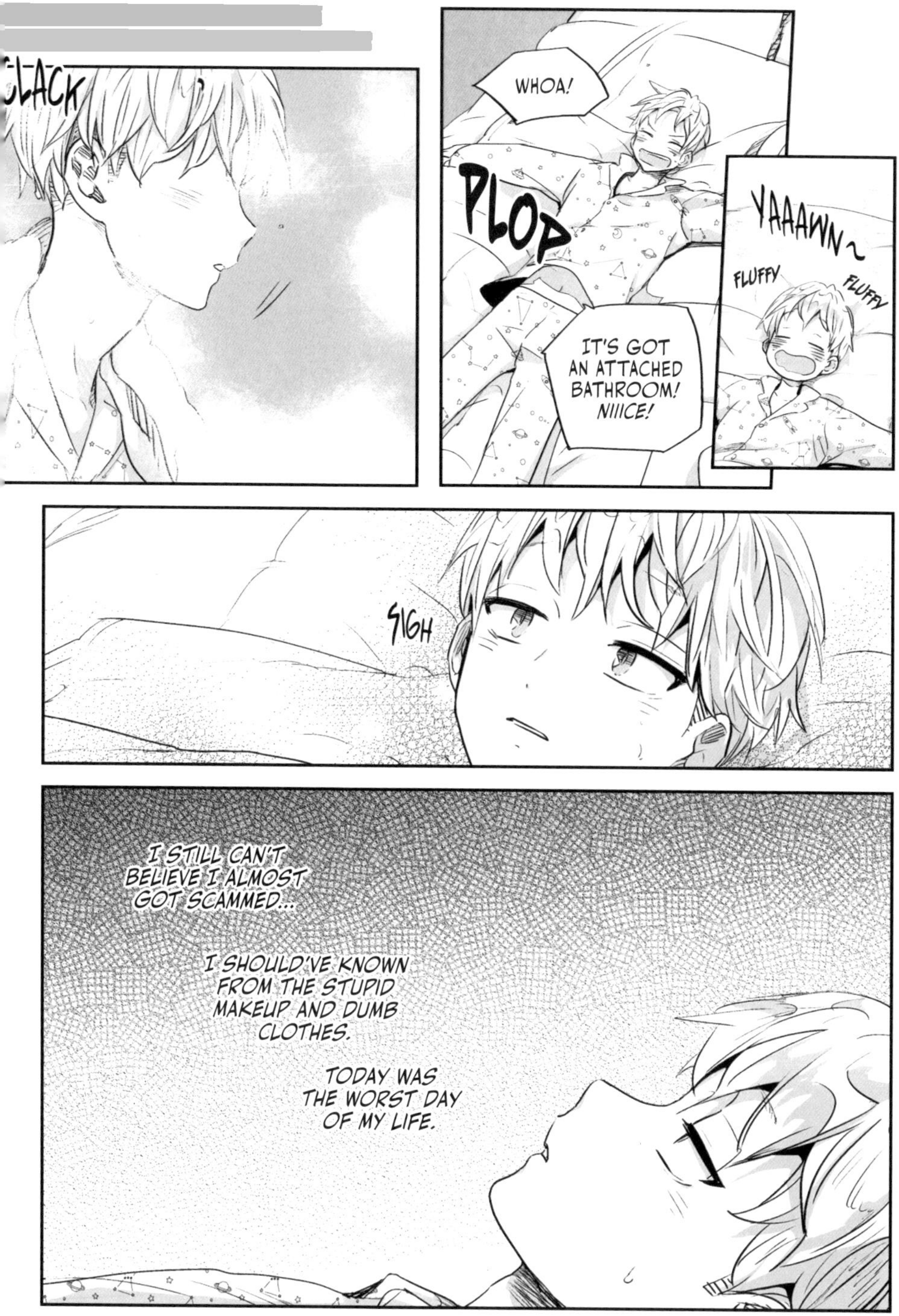
CLACK
WHOA!
PLOP
IT'S GOT AN ATTACHED BATHROOM! NIIICE!
YAAAWN~
FLUFFY
FLUFFY
SIGH
I STILL CAN'T BELIEVE I ALMOST GOT SCAMMED...
I SHOULD'VE KNOWN FROM THE STUPID MAKEUP AND DUMB CLOTHES.
TODAY WAS THE WORST DAY OF MY LIFE.

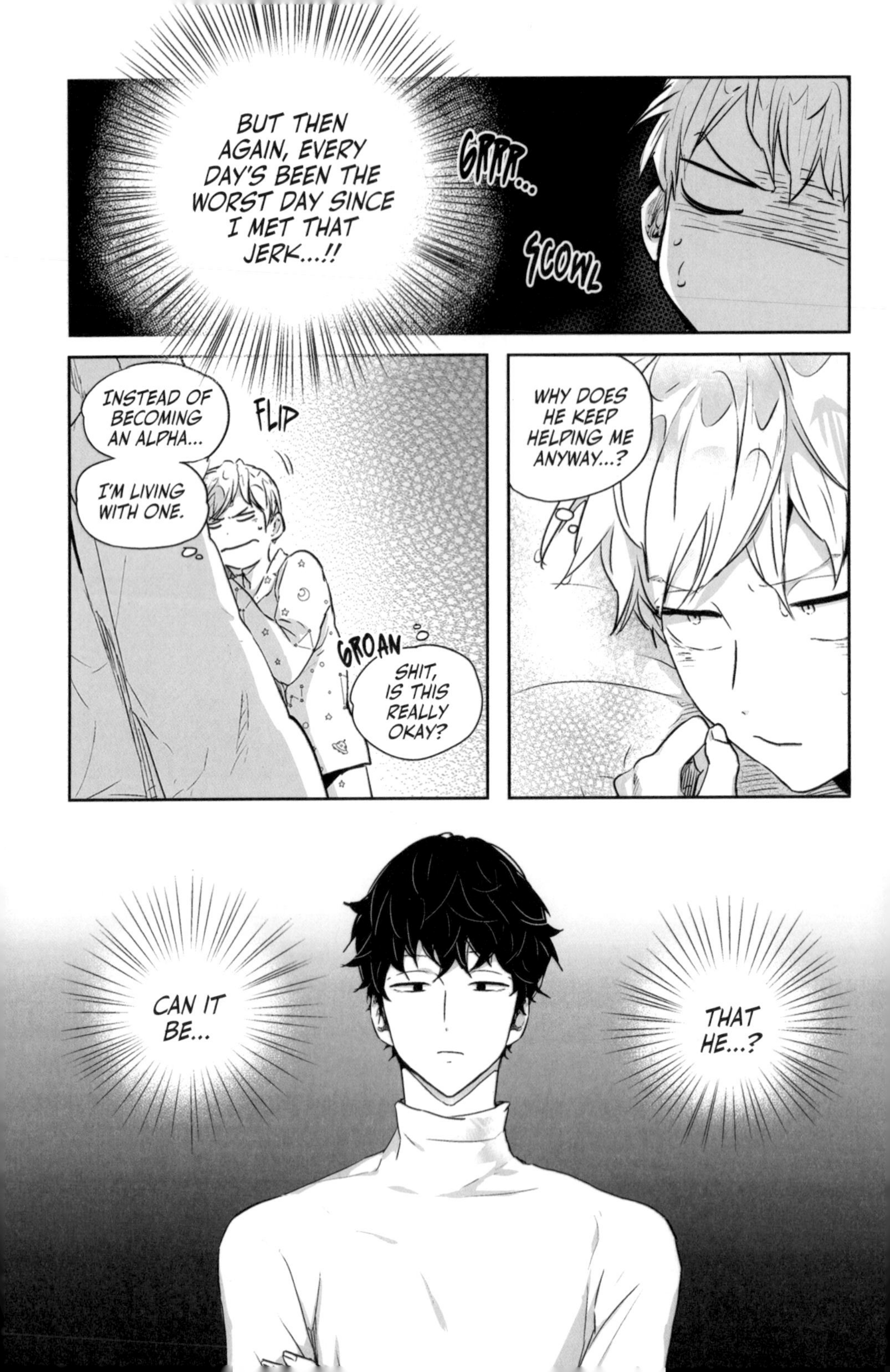
BUT THEN AGAIN, EVERY DAY'S BEEN THE WORST DAY SINCE I MET THAT JERK...!!
GRRR...
SCOWL
INSTEAD OF BECOMING AN ALPHA...
I'M LIVING WITH ONE.
FLIP
GROAN
SHIT, IS THIS REALLY OKAY?
WHY DOES HE KEEP HELPING ME ANYWAY...?
CAN IT BE...
THAT HE...?

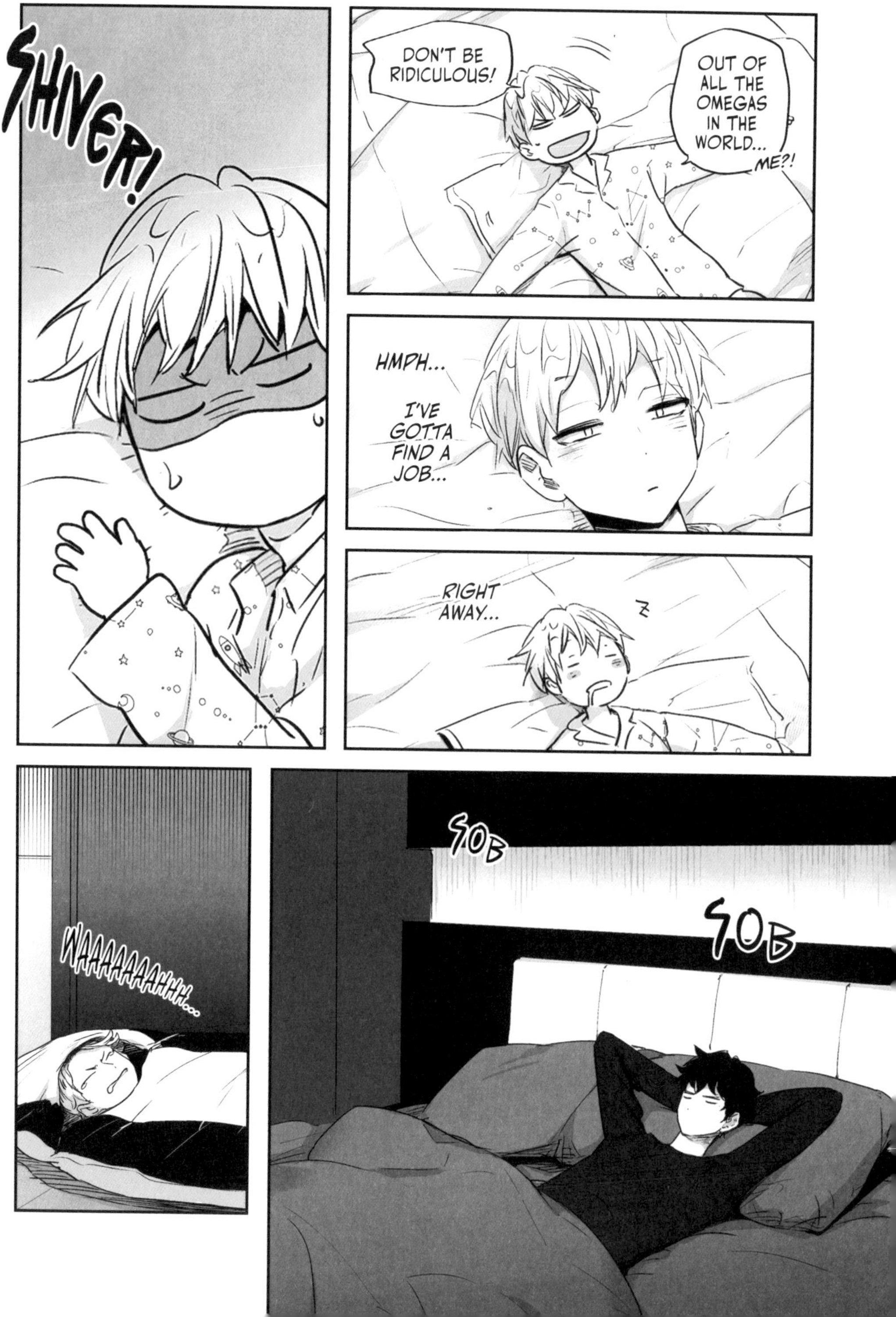
SHIVER!
DON'T BE RIDICULOUS!
OUT OF ALL THE OMEGAS IN THE WORLD... ME?!
HMPH...
I'VE GOTTA FIND A JOB...
RIGHT AWAY...
Z
WAAAAAAAAHHH...
SOB
SOB

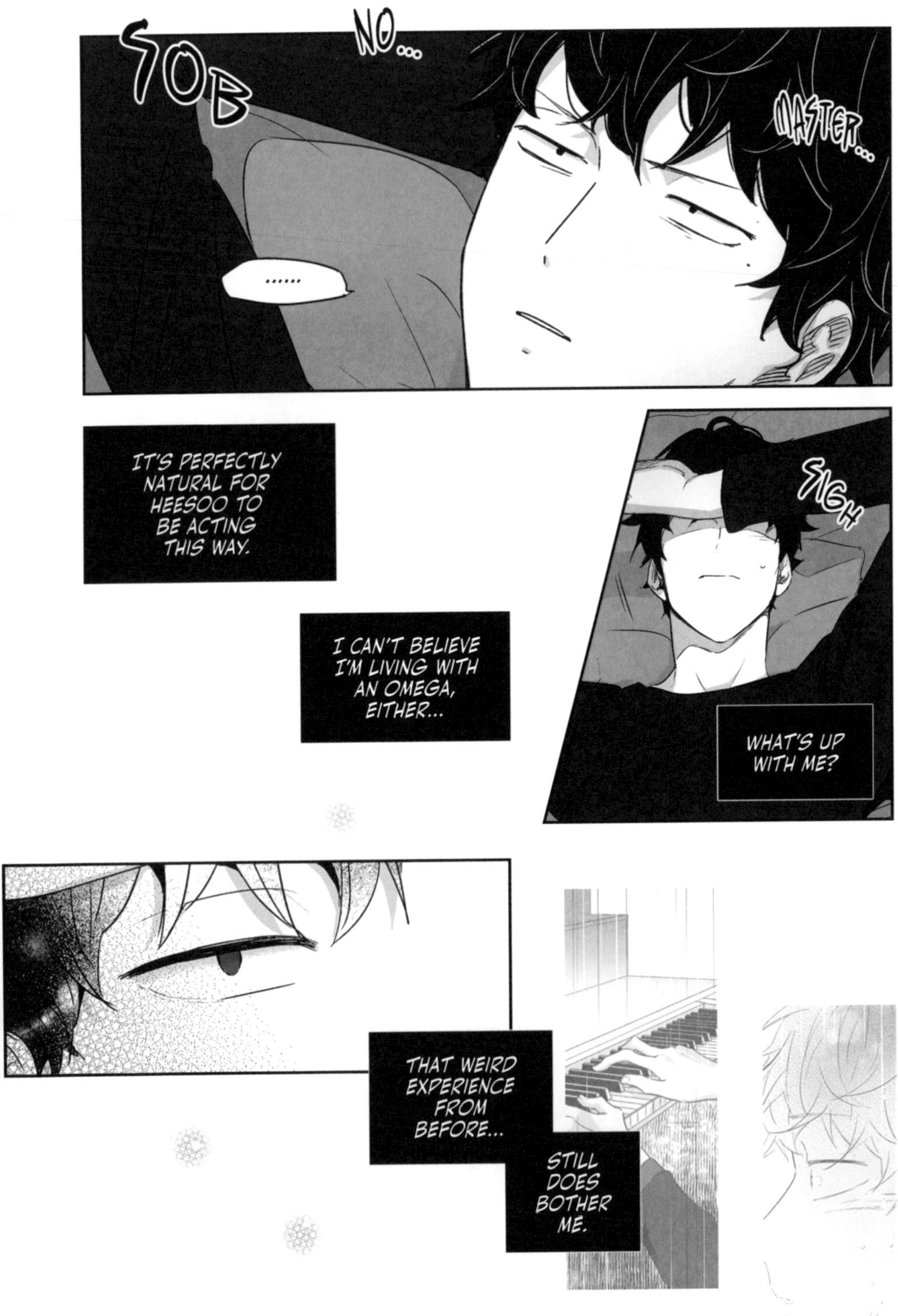
SOB
NO...
MASTER...
......
IT'S PERFECTLY NATURAL FOR HEESOO TO BE ACTING THIS WAY.
SIGH
I CAN'T BELIEVE I'M LIVING WITH AN OMEGA, EITHER...
WHAT'S UP WITH ME?
THAT WEIRD EXPERIENCE FROM BEFORE...
STILL DOES BOTHER ME.

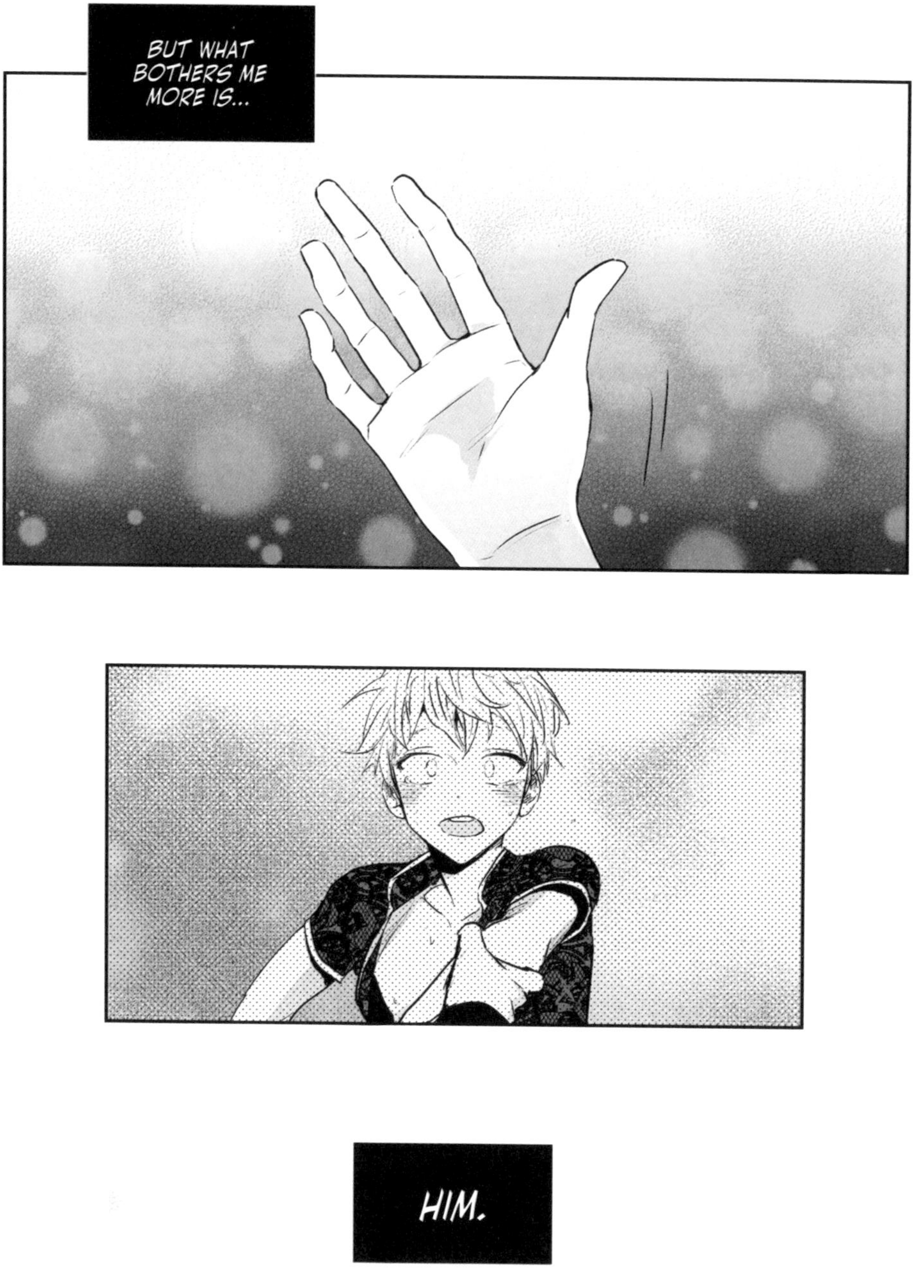
BUT WHAT BOTHERS ME MORE IS...
HIM.

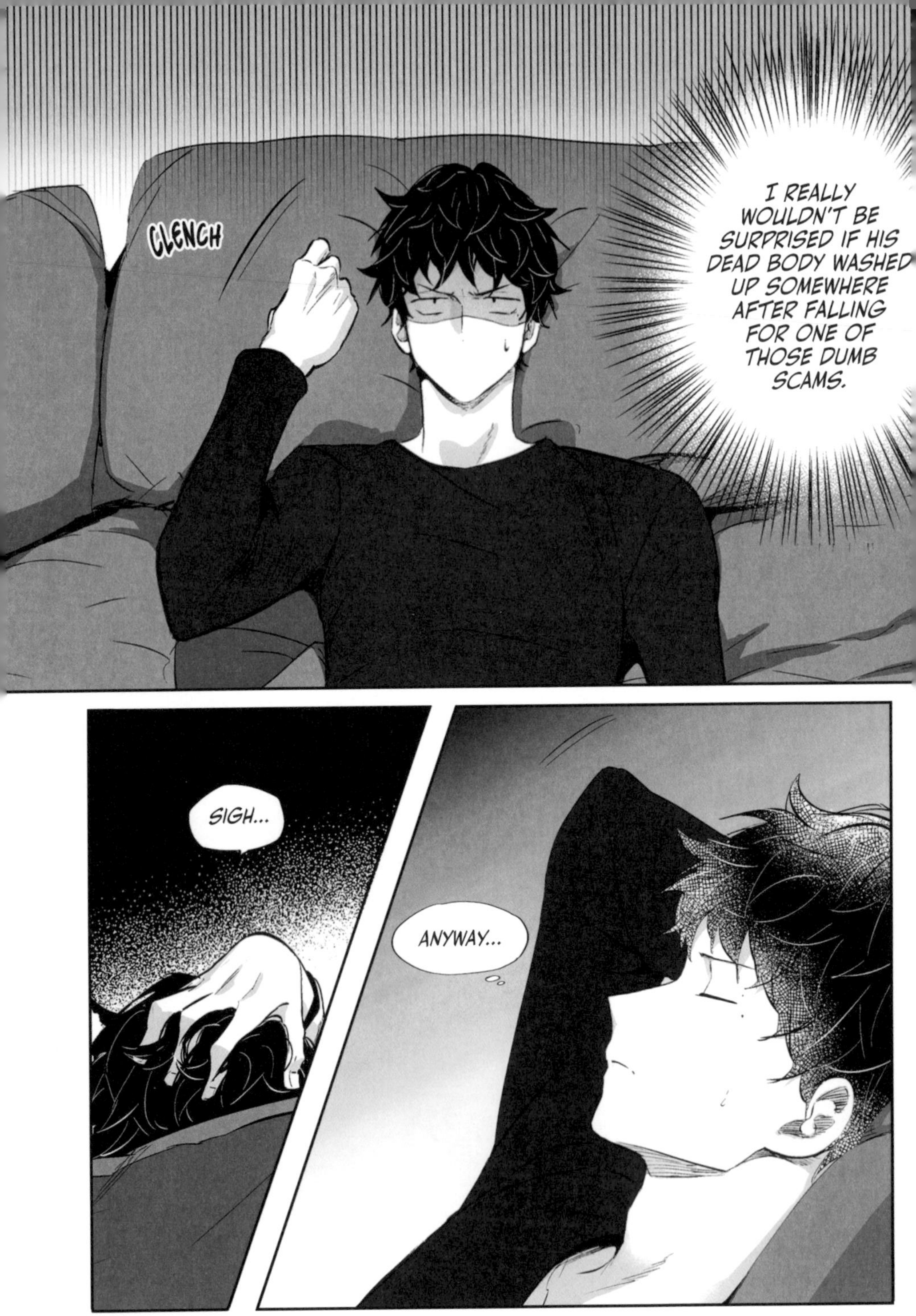
CLENCH
I REALLY WOULDN'T BE SURPRISED IF HIS DEAD BODY WASHED UP SOMEWHERE AFTER FALLING FOR ONE OF THOSE DUMB SCAMS.
SIGH...
ANYWAY...

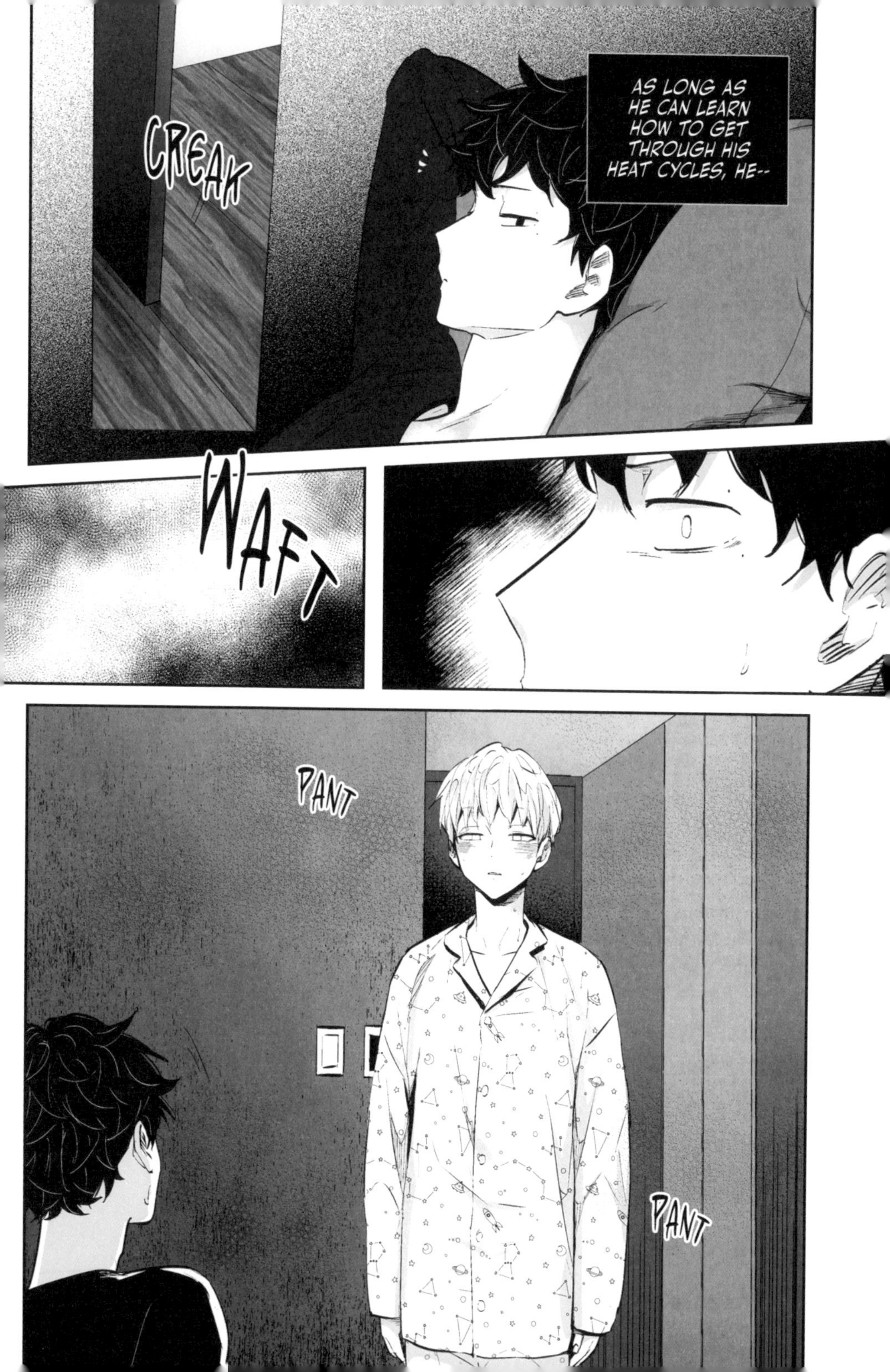
CREAK
AS LONG AS HE CAN LEARN HOW TO GET THROUGH HIS HEAT CYCLES, HE--
WAFT
PANT
PANT

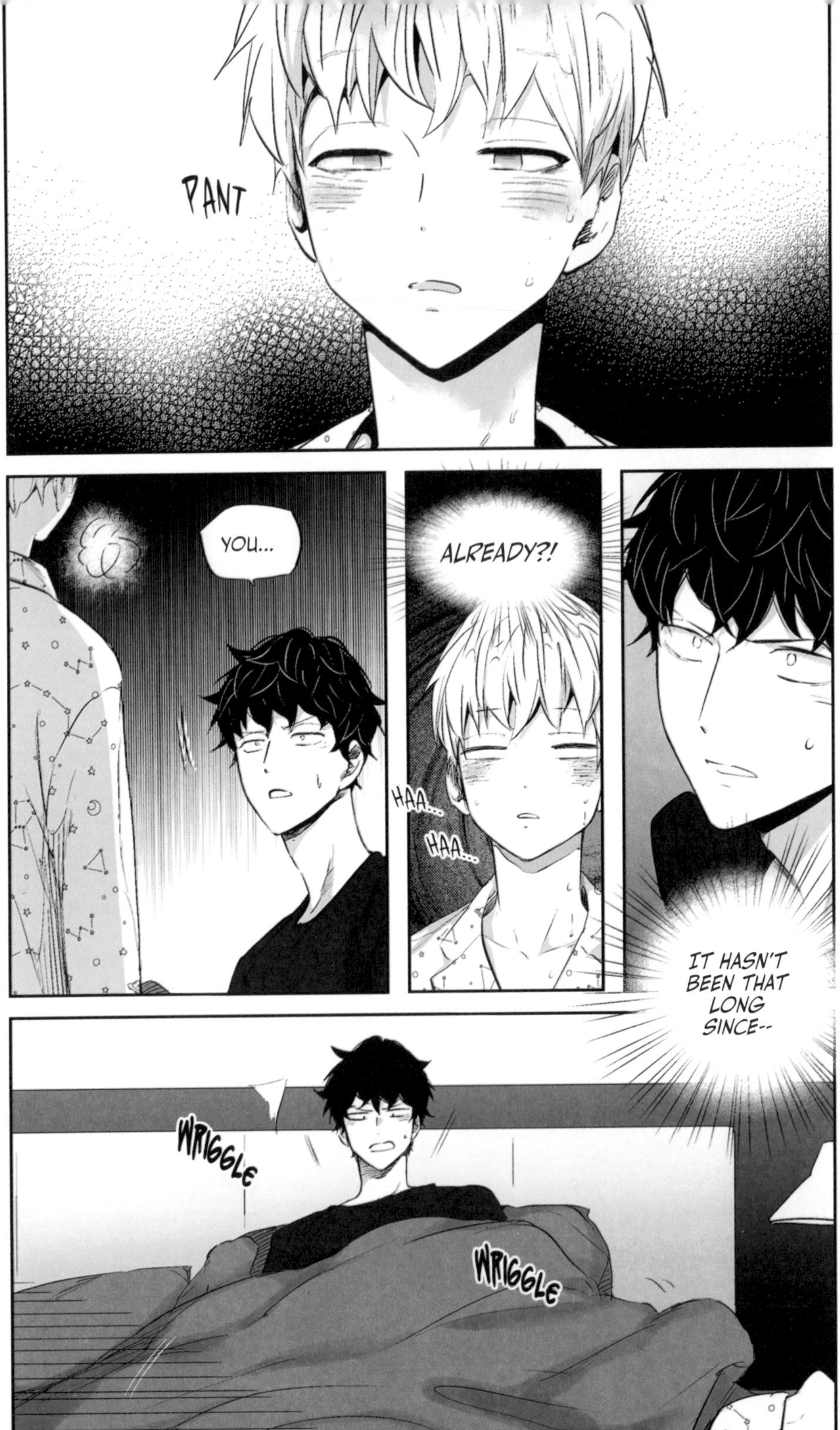
PANT
YOU...
ALREADY?!
HAA...
HAA...
IT HASN'T BEEN THAT LONG SINCE--
WRIGGLE
WRIGGLE

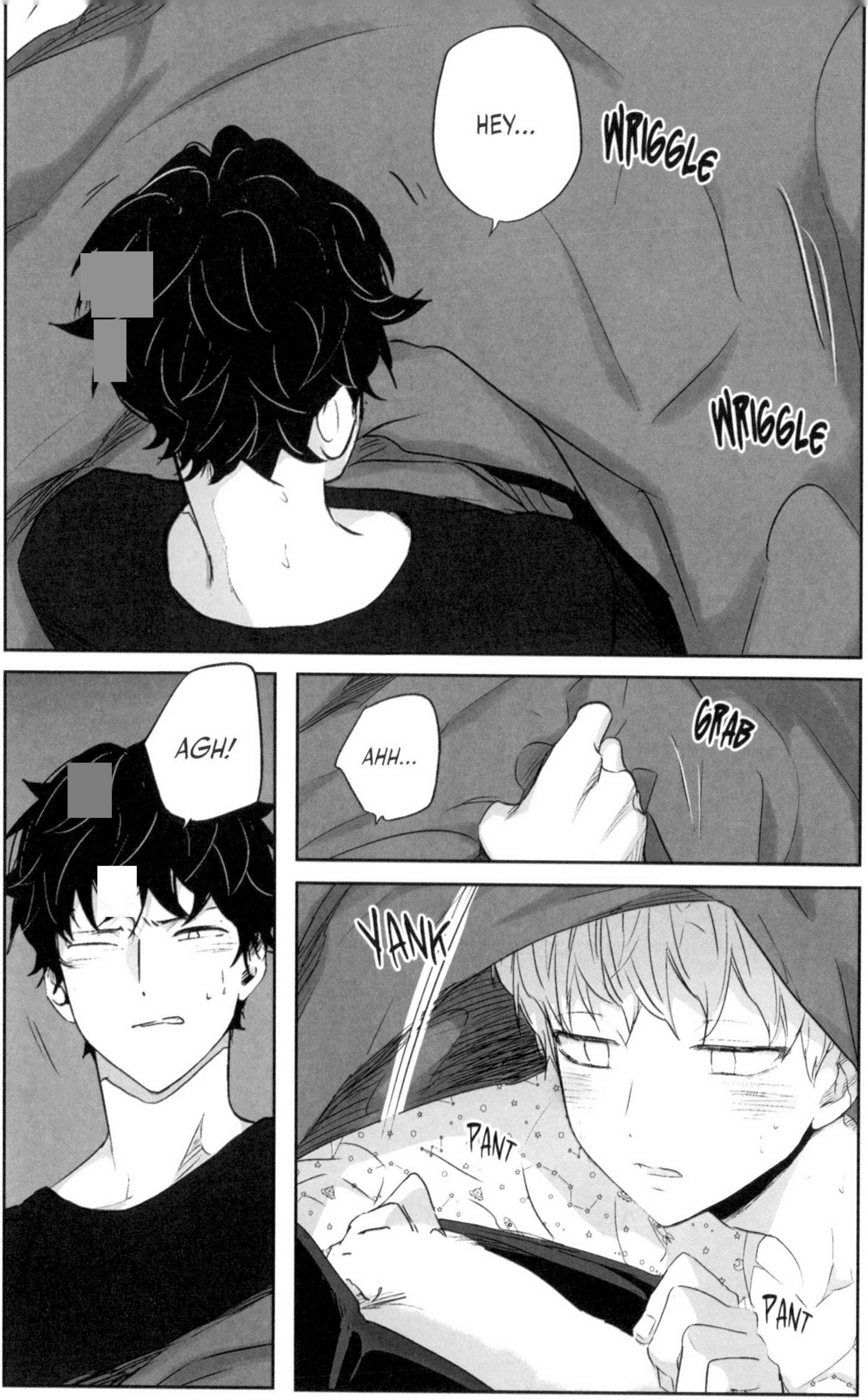
HEY...
WRIGGLE
WRIGGLE
AGH!
AHH...
GRAB
YANK
PANT
PANT

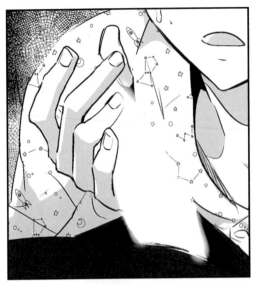

IT'S NOT HARD...

BLINK

IT NEEDS TO GET BIGGER...

MMPH...

THROB

UNGH...

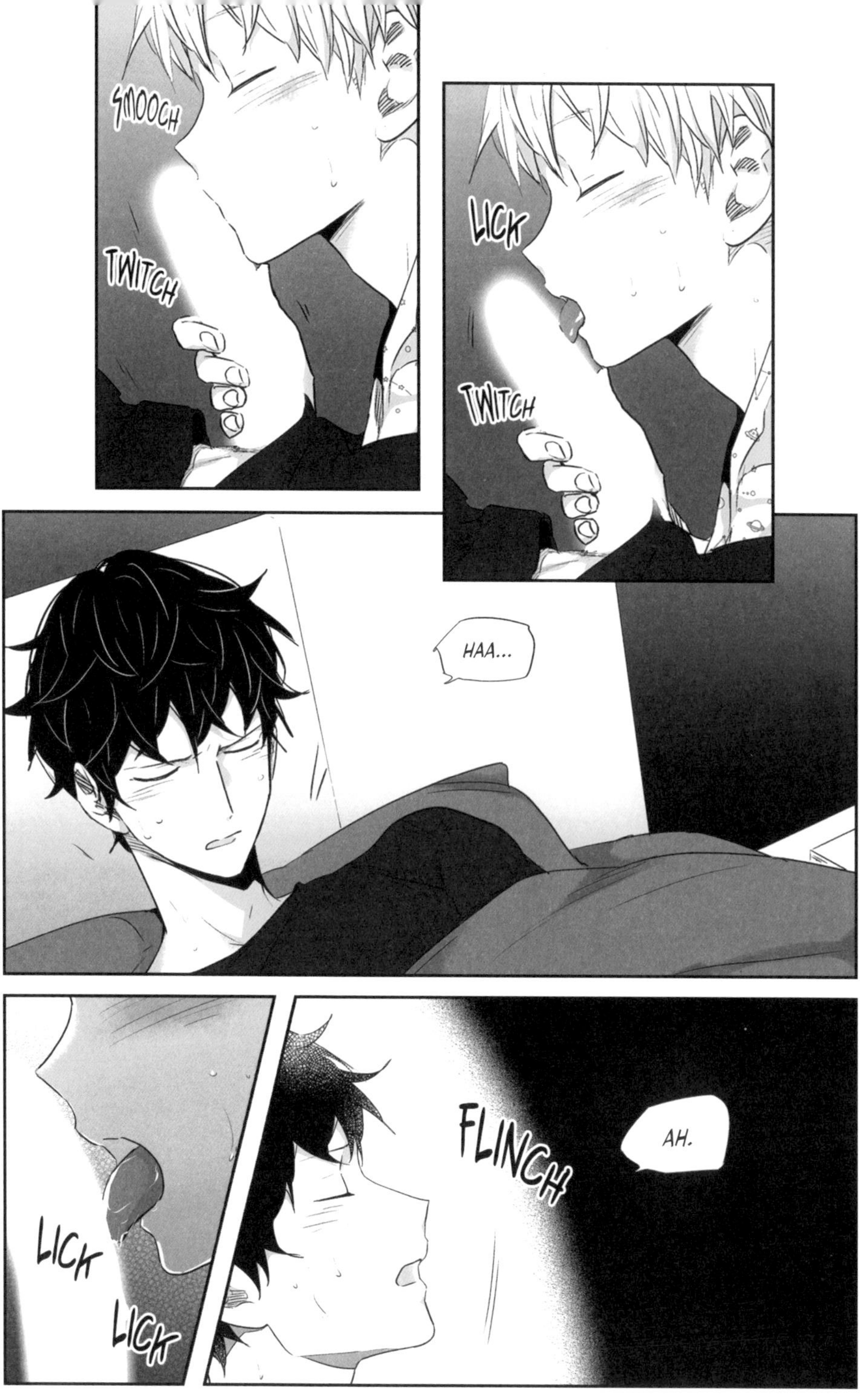
SMOOCH
TWITCH
LICK
TWITCH
HAA...
LICK
LICK
FLINCH
AH.

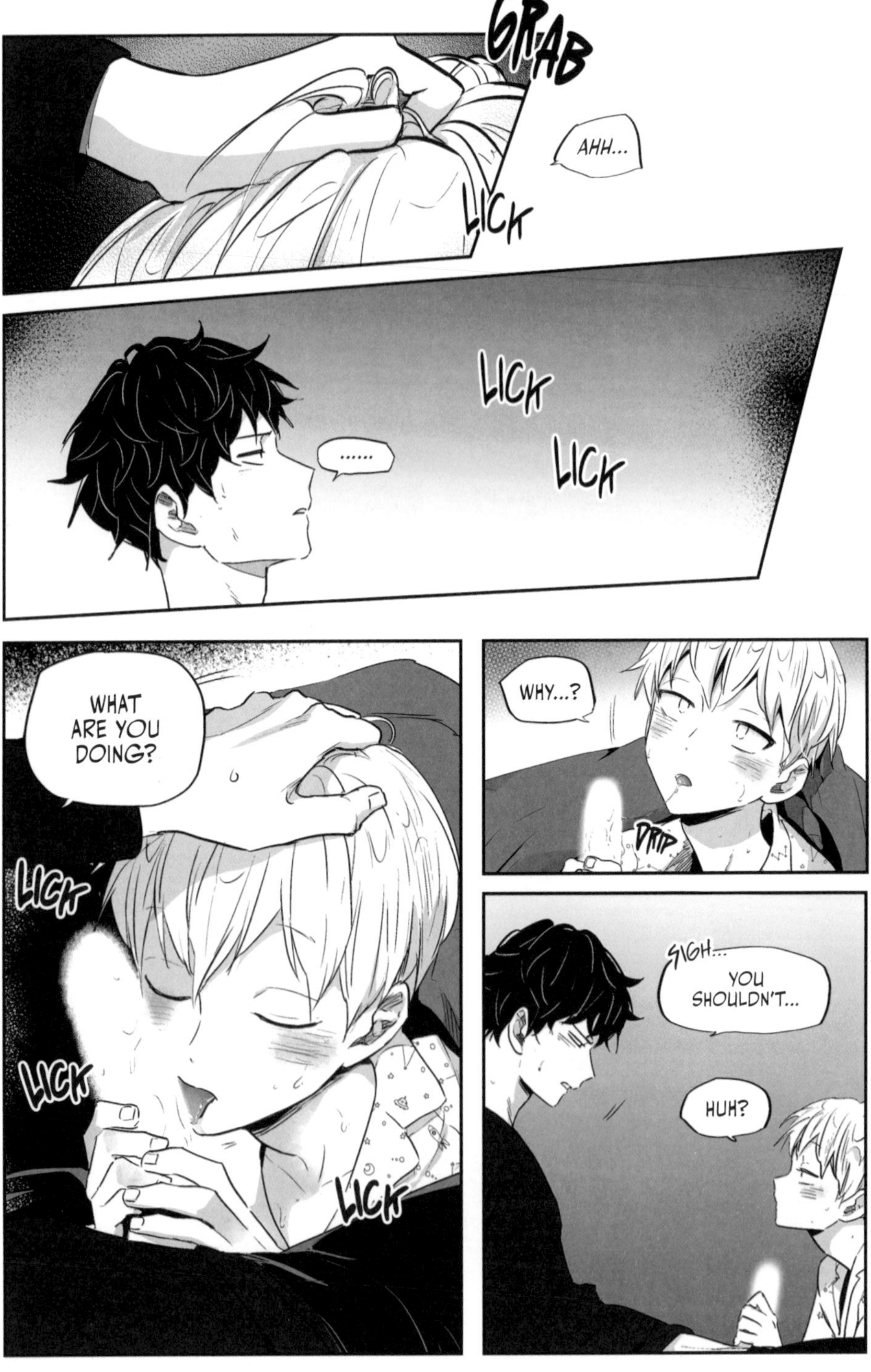
GRAB
AHH...
LICK
LICK
......
LICK
WHAT ARE YOU DOING?
LICK
LICK
LICK
WHY...?
DRIP
SIGH...
YOU SHOULDN'T...
HUH?

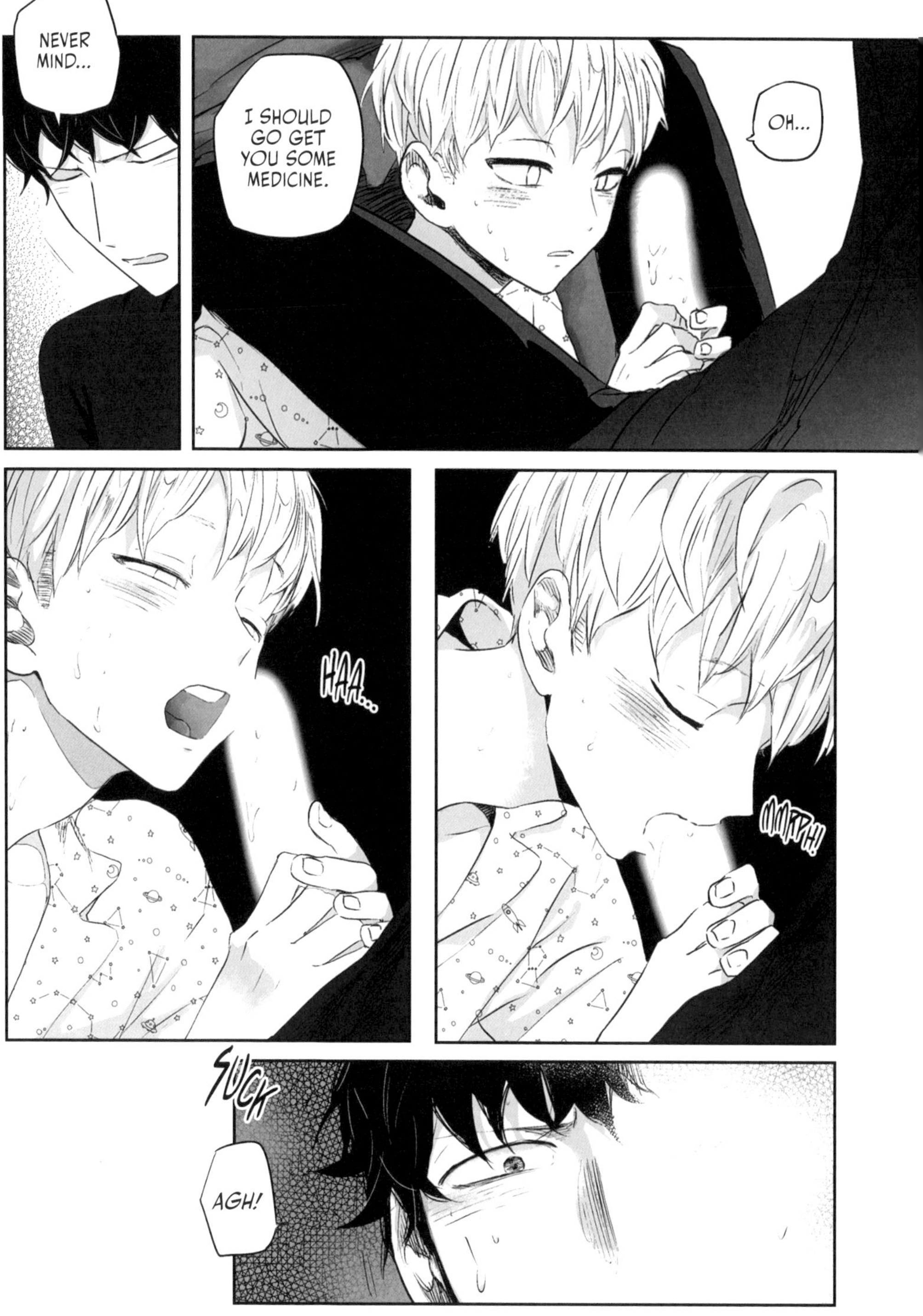
NEVER MIND...
I SHOULD GO GET YOU SOME MEDICINE.
OH...
HAA...
MMRPH!
SUCK
AGH!

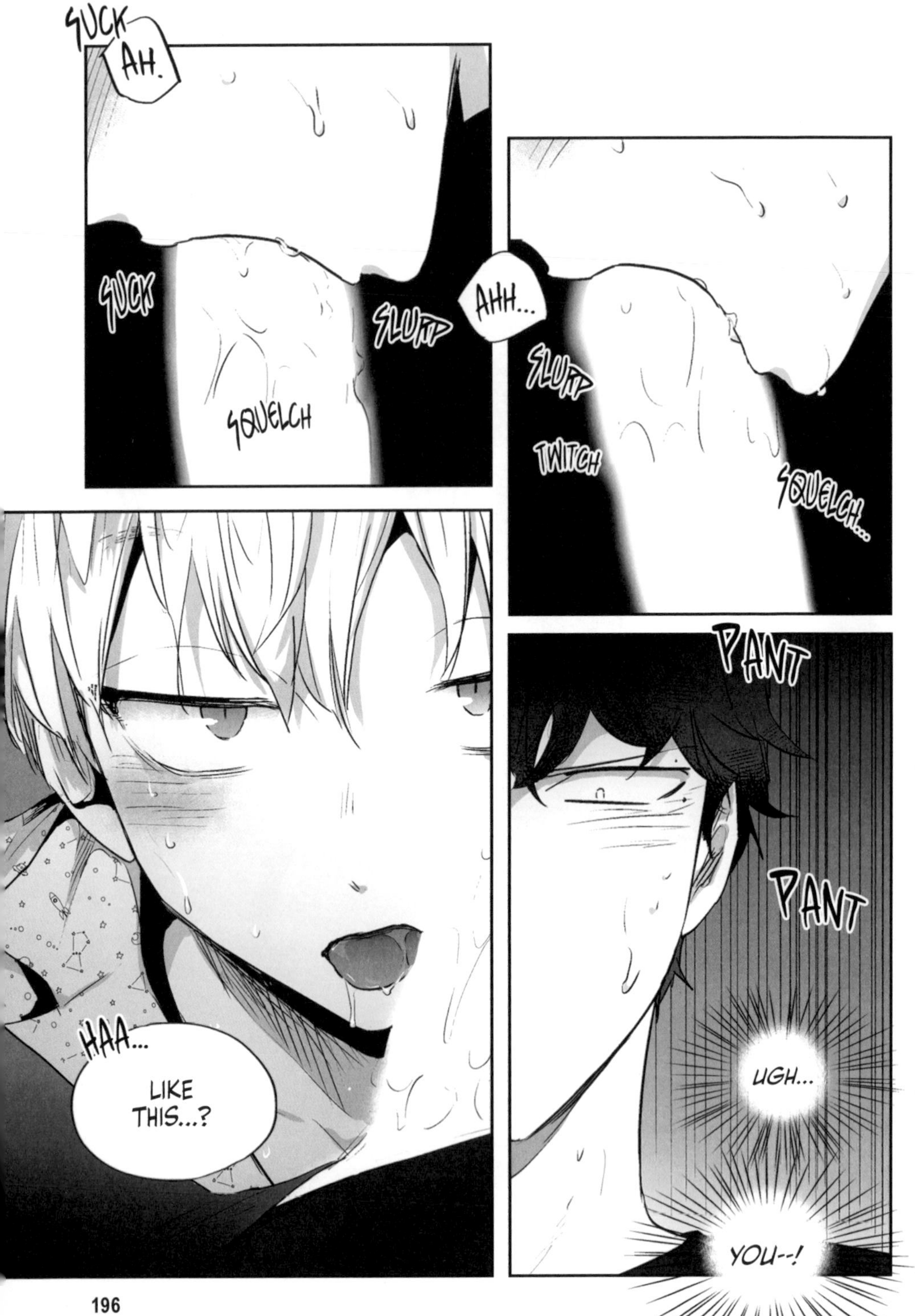
SUCK
AH.
SUCK
SLURP
SQUELCH
AHH...
SLURP
TWITCH
SQUELCH...
HAA...
LIKE THIS...?
PANT
PANT
UGH...
YOU--!

Love is an Illusion!

Love is
an Illusion!

Chapter 10

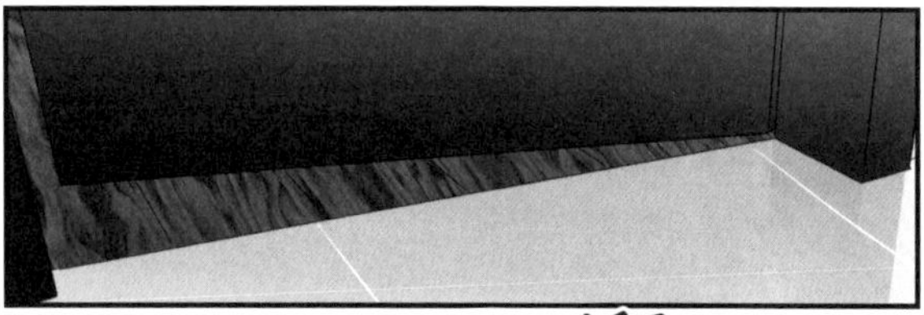

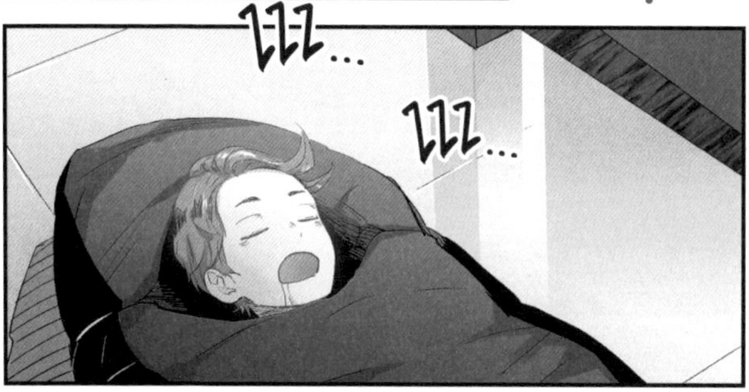
ZZZ...
ZZZ...

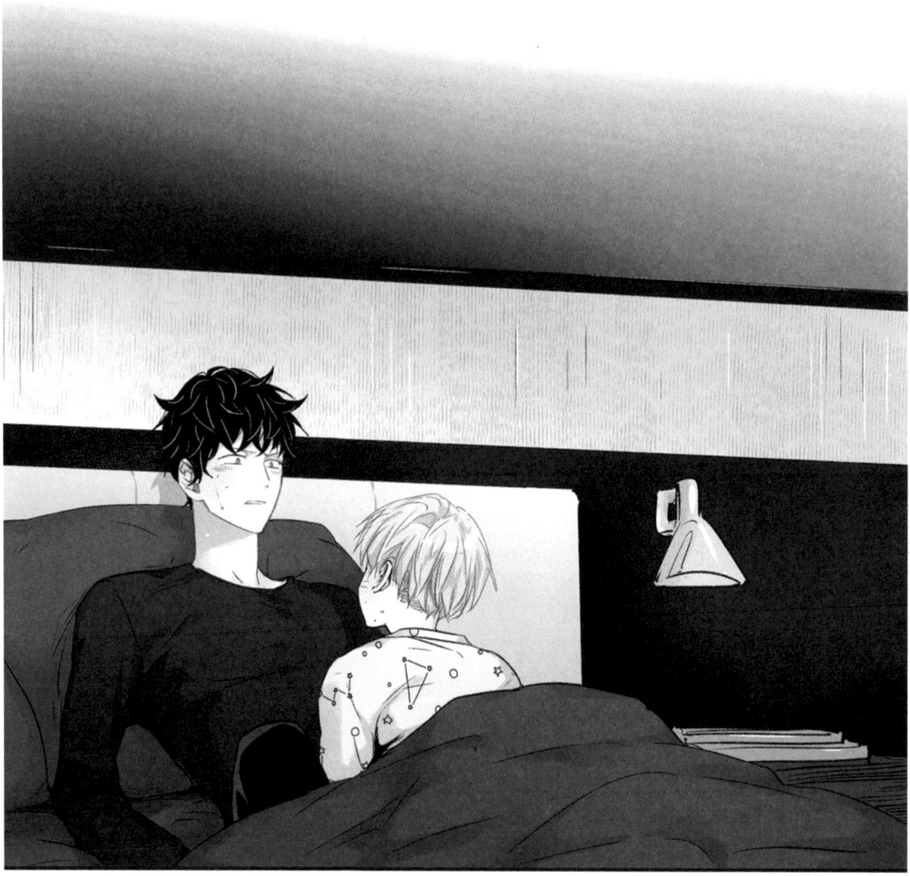

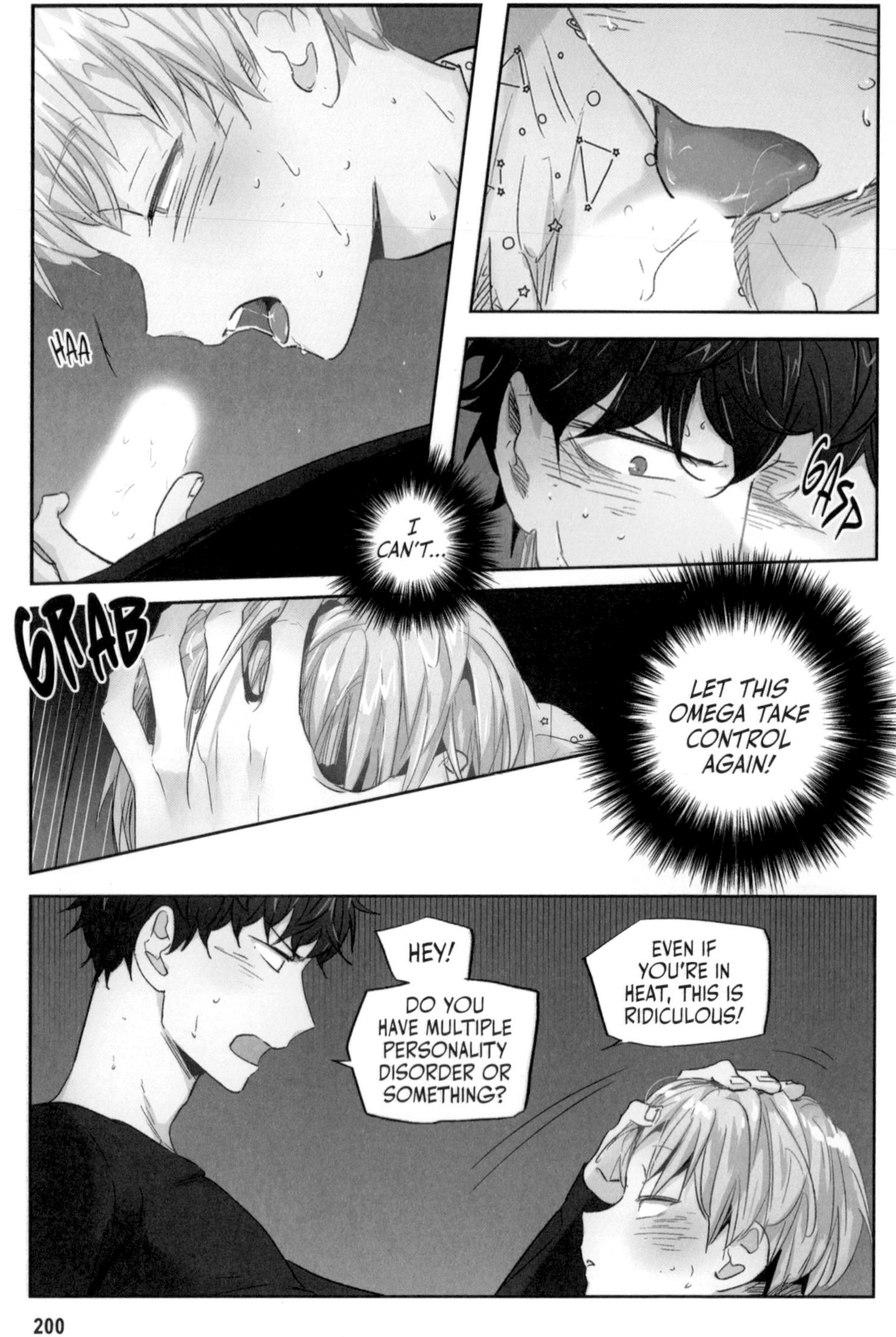
HAA
GASP
I CAN'T...
GRAB
LET THIS OMEGA TAKE CONTROL AGAIN!
HEY!
DO YOU HAVE MULTIPLE PERSONALITY DISORDER OR SOMETHING?
EVEN IF YOU'RE IN HEAT, THIS IS RIDICULOUS!

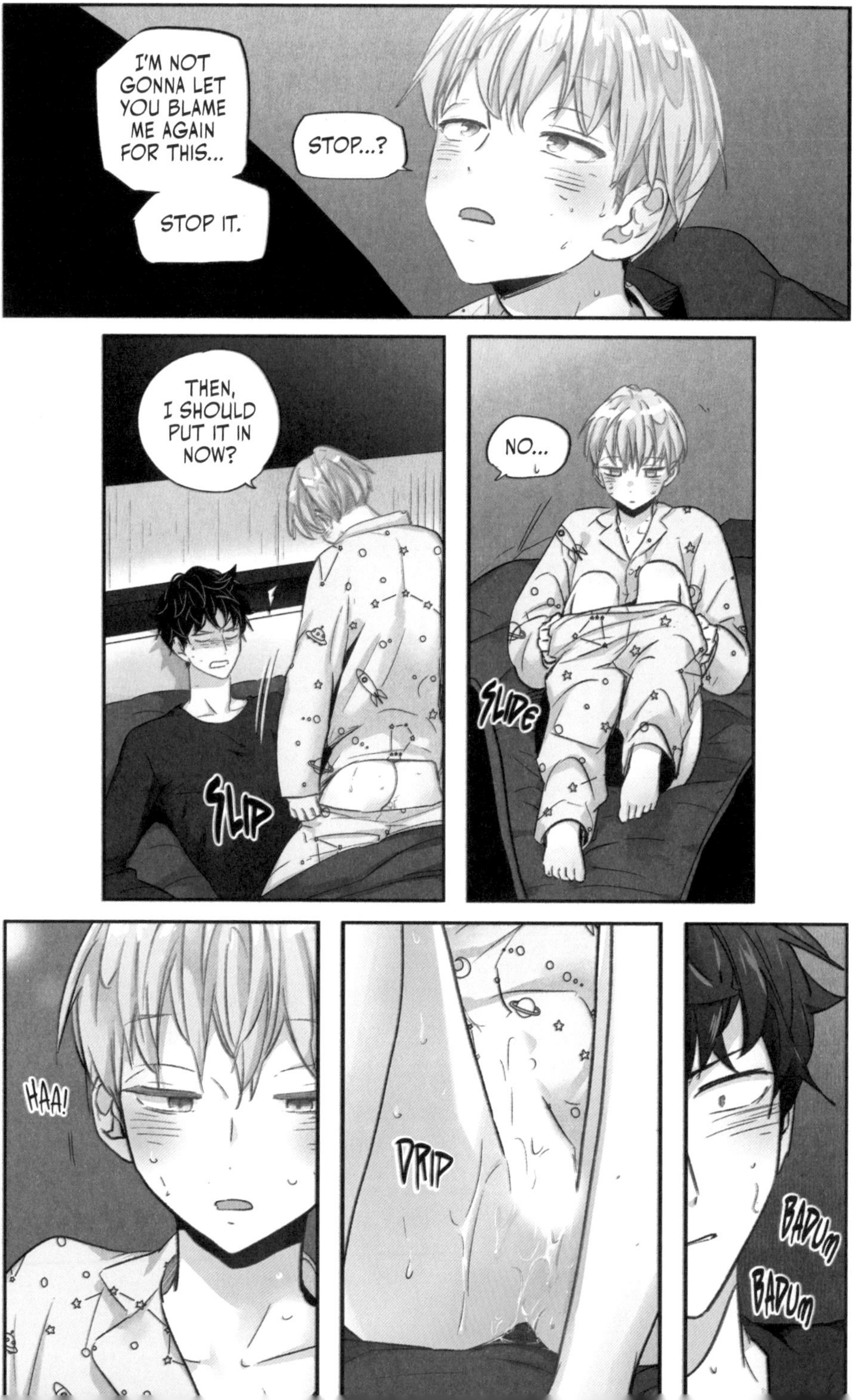
I'M NOT GONNA LET YOU BLAME ME AGAIN FOR THIS...
STOP IT.
STOP...?
THEN, I SHOULD PUT IT IN NOW?
SLIP
NO...
SLIDE
HAA!
DRIP
BADUM
BADUM

SLIP

CREAK

HAA...

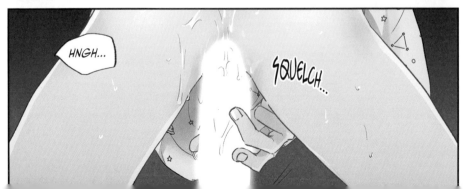

HNGH...

SQUELCH...

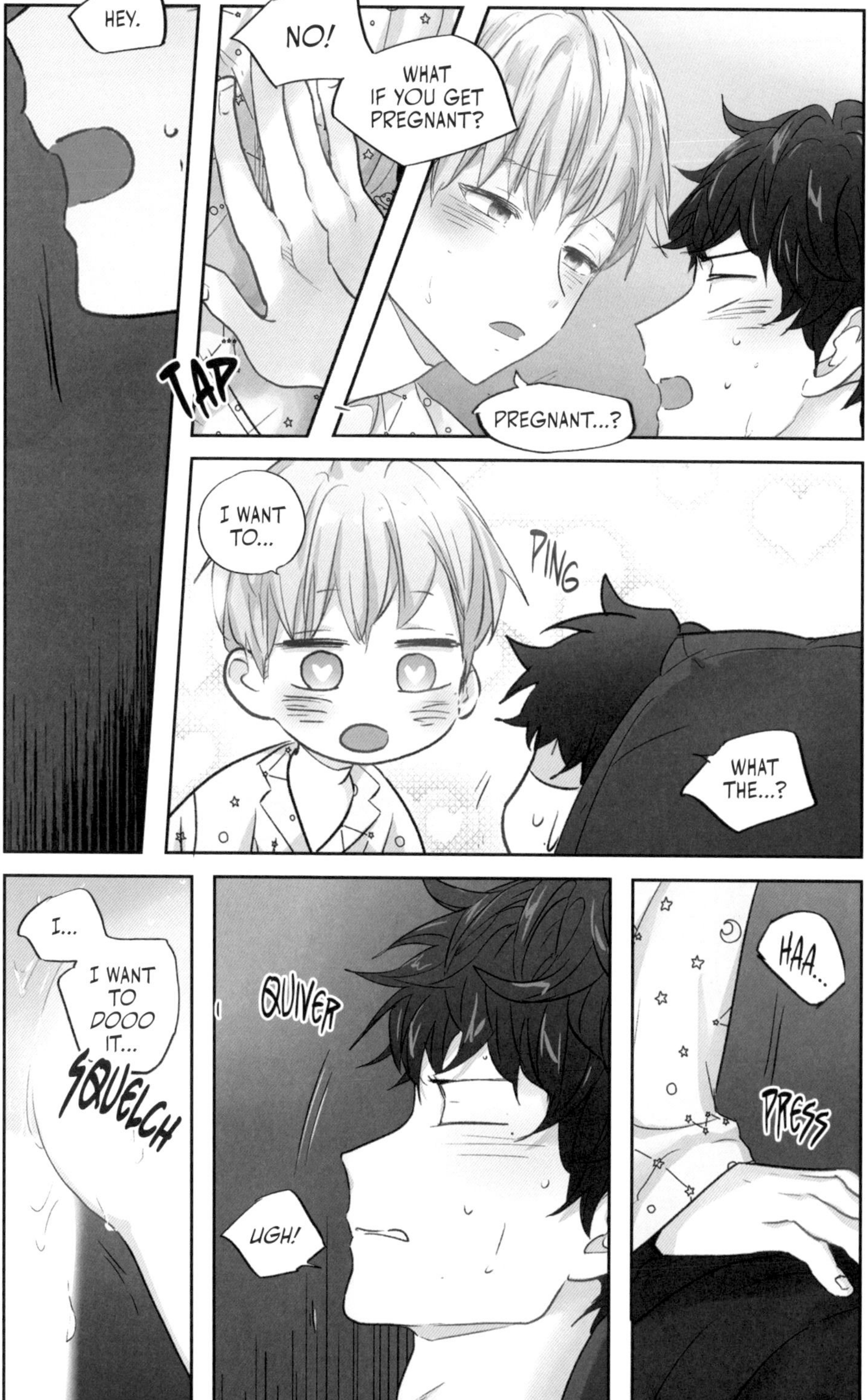
HEY.
NO!
TAP
WHAT IF YOU GET PREGNANT?
PREGNANT...?
I WANT TO...
PING
WHAT THE...?
I...
I WANT TO DOOO IT...
SQUELCH
QUIVER
UGH!
HAA...
PRESS

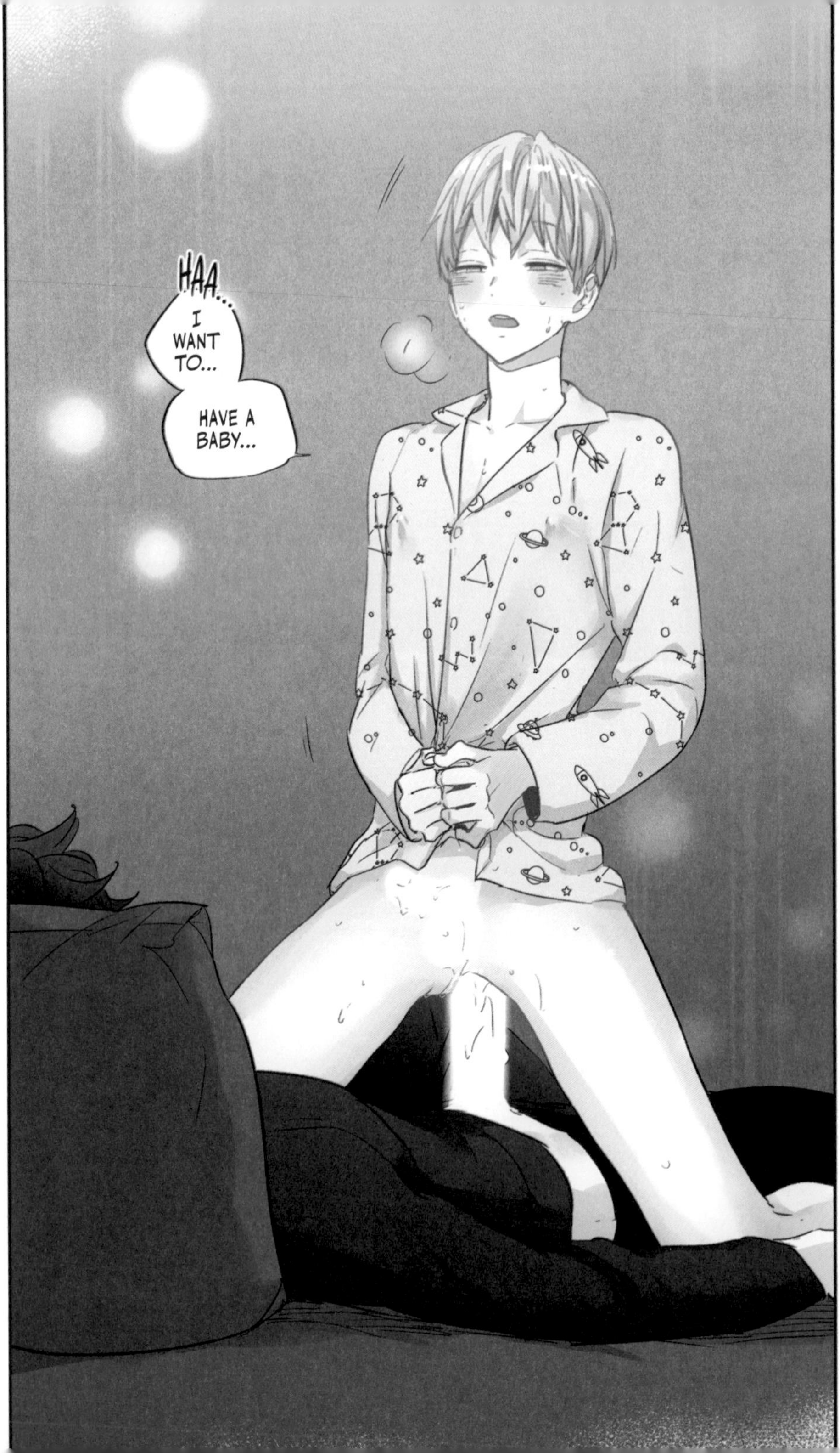
HAA...
I WANT TO...
HAVE A BABY...

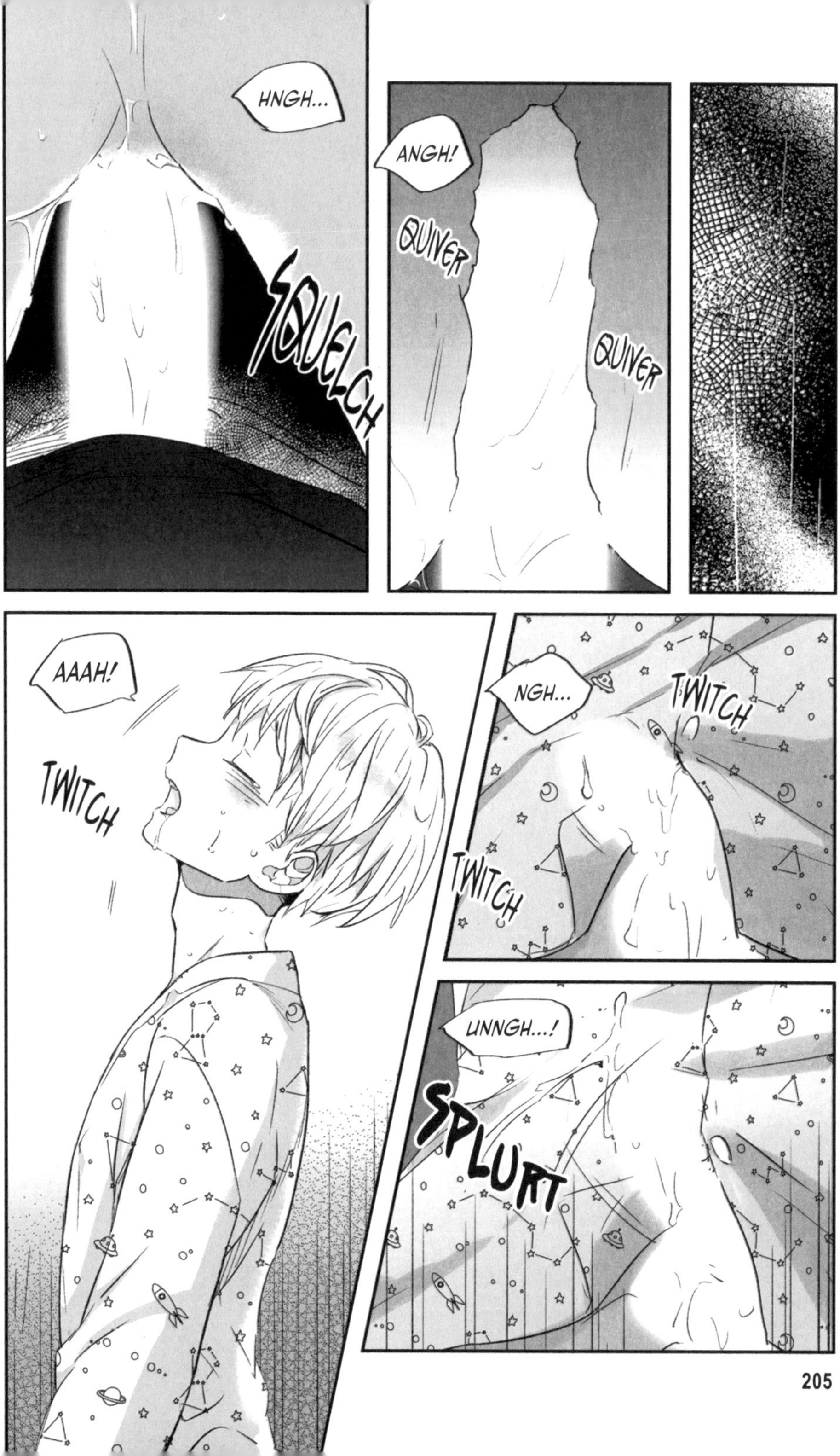
HNGH...
SQUELCH
ANGH!
QUIVER
QUIVER
AAAH!
TWITCH
NGH...
TWITCH
TWITCH
UNNGH...!
SPLURT

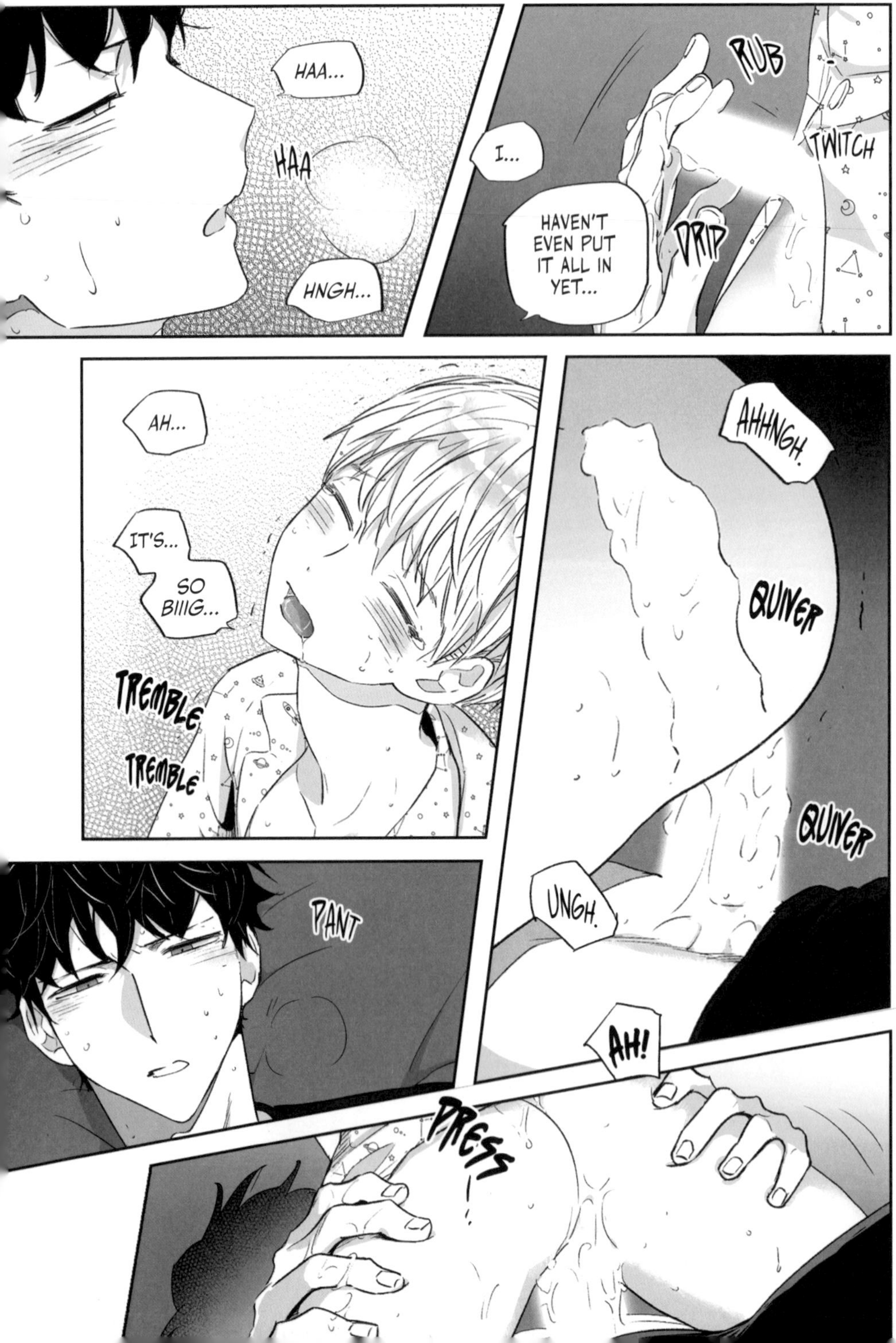
HAA...
HAA
HNGH...
RUB
I...
HAVEN'T EVEN PUT IT ALL IN YET...
TWITCH
DRIP
AH...
IT'S... SO BIIIG...
TREMBLE
TREMBLE
AHHNGH.
QUIVER
QUIVER
UNGH.
PANT
AH!
PRESS

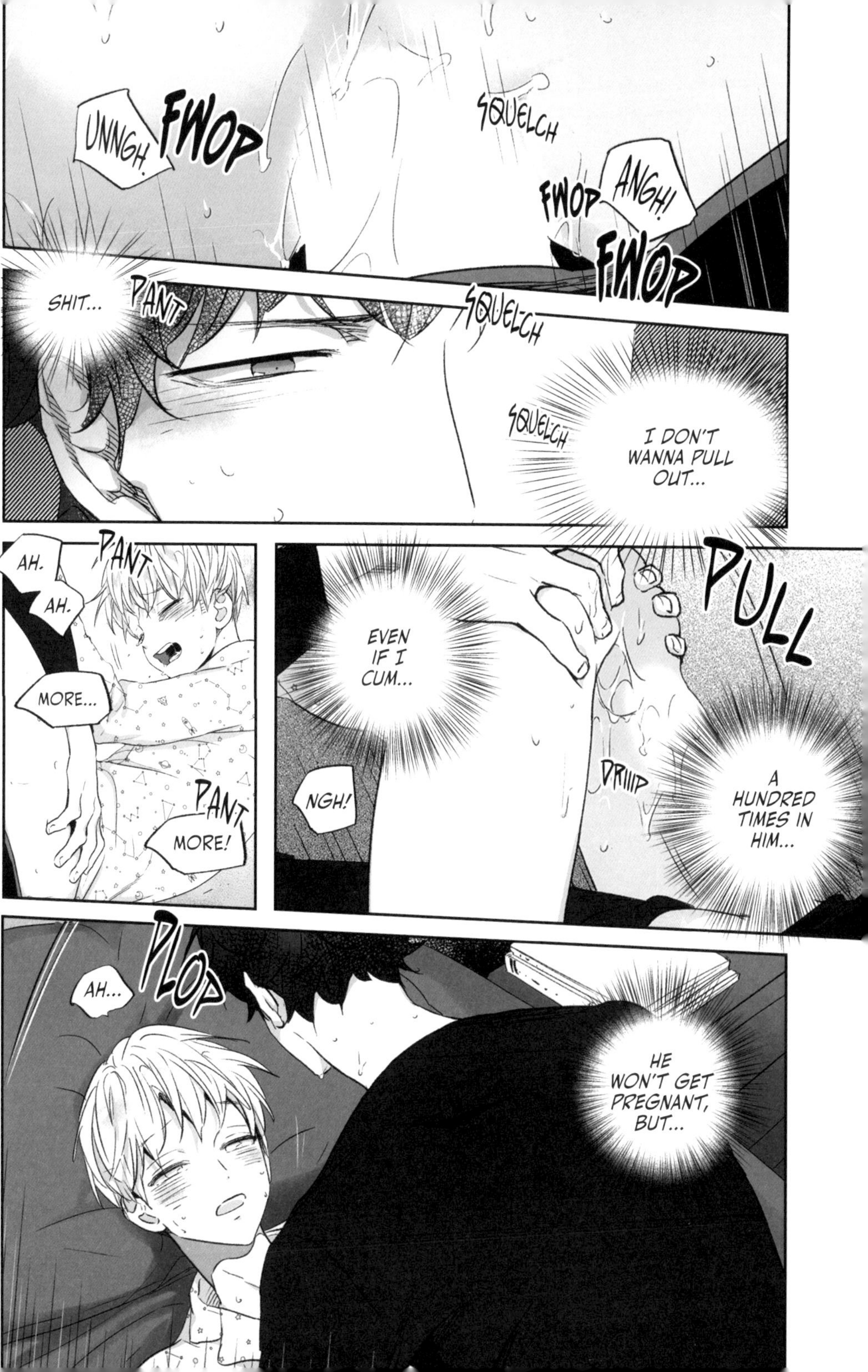

UNNGH.
FWOP
SQUELCH
FWOP
ANGH!
FWOP
SHIT...
PANT
SQUELCH
SQUELCH
I DON'T WANNA PULL OUT...
AH.
PANT
AH.
MORE...
PANT
MORE!
EVEN IF I CUM...
PULL
NGH!
DRIIIP
A HUNDRED TIMES IN HIM...
AH...
PLOP
HE WON'T GET PREGNANT, BUT...

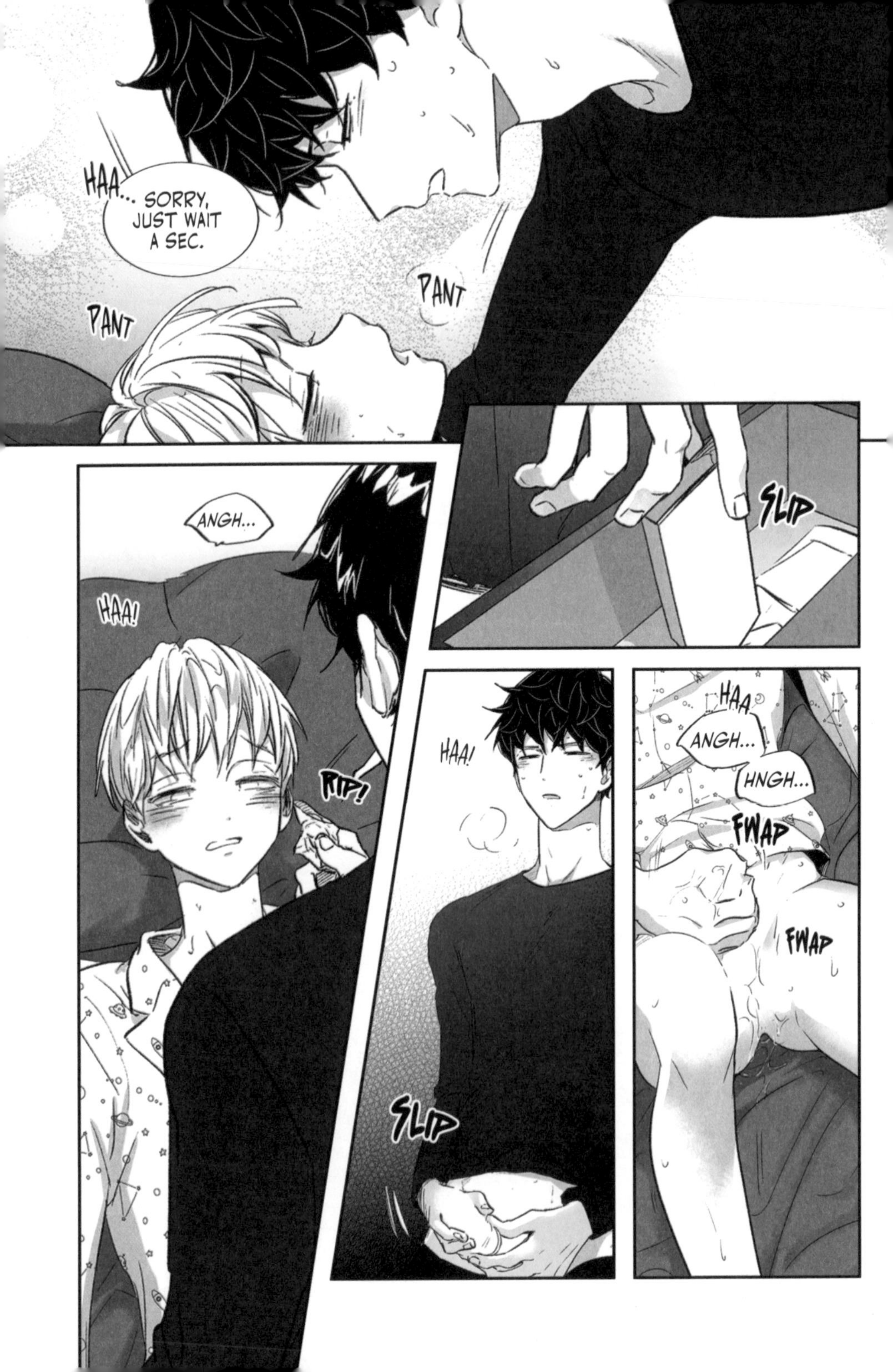

HAA... SORRY, JUST WAIT A SEC.
PANT
PANT
ANGH...
HAA!
RIP!
SLIP
HAA!
SLIP
HAA
ANGH...
HNGH...
FWAP
FWAP

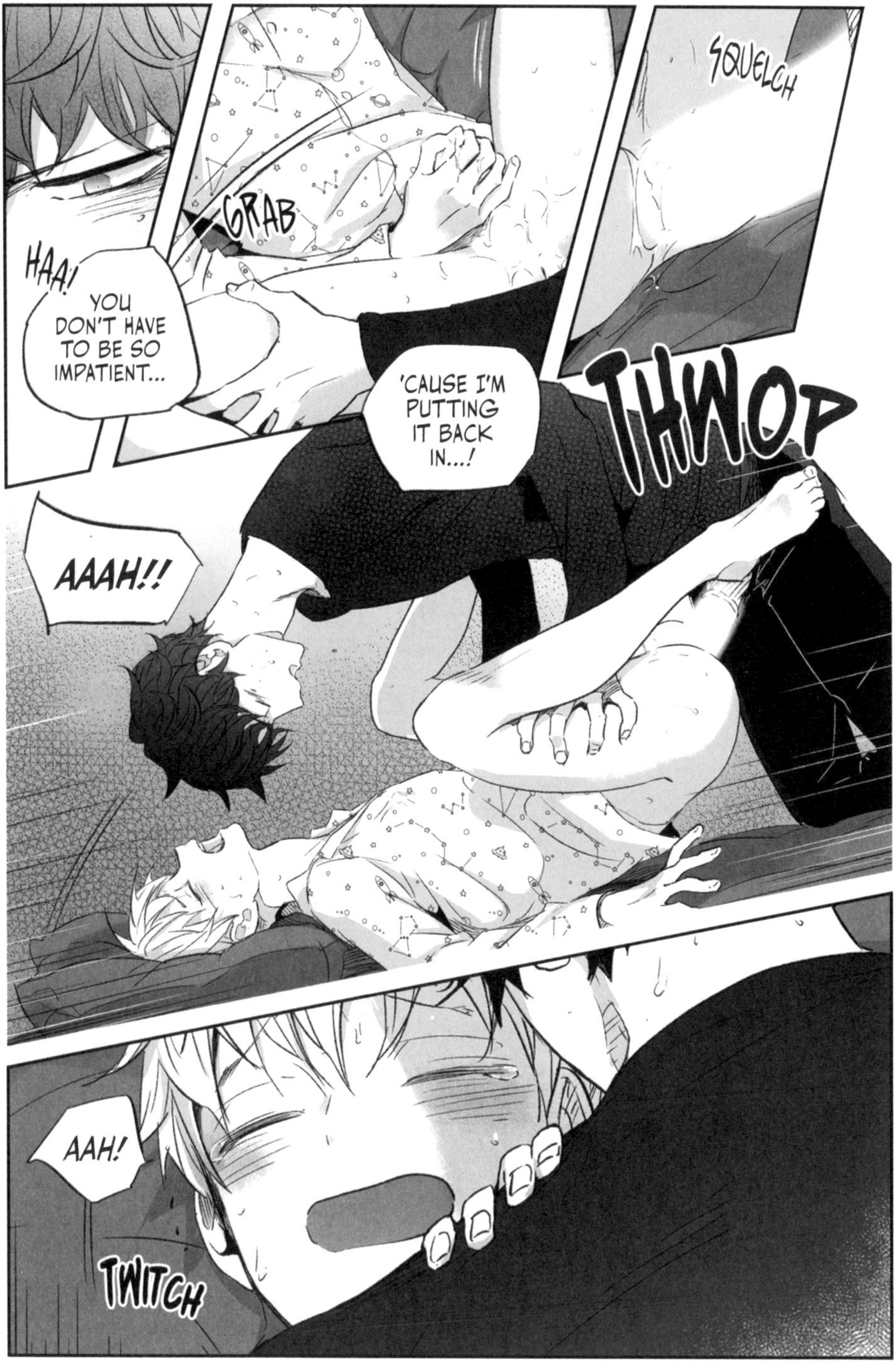
HAA!
YOU DON'T HAVE TO BE SO IMPATIENT...
GRAB
SQUELCH
'CAUSE I'M PUTTING IT BACK IN...!
THWOP
AAAH!!
AAH!
TWITCH

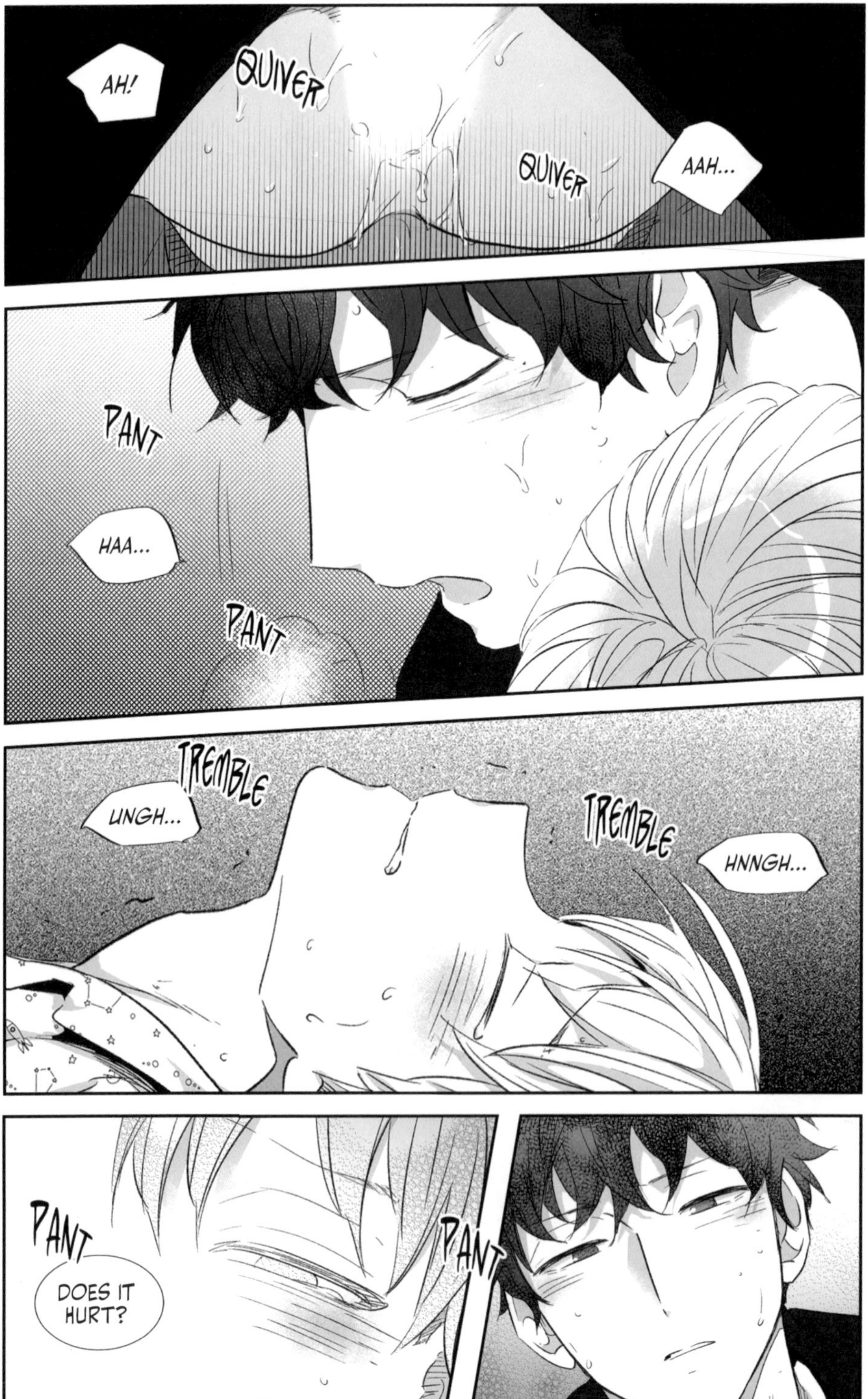
AH!
QUIVER
QUIVER
AAH...
PANT
HAA...
PANT
TREMBLE
UNGH...
TREMBLE
HNNGH...
PANT
DOES IT HURT?
PANT

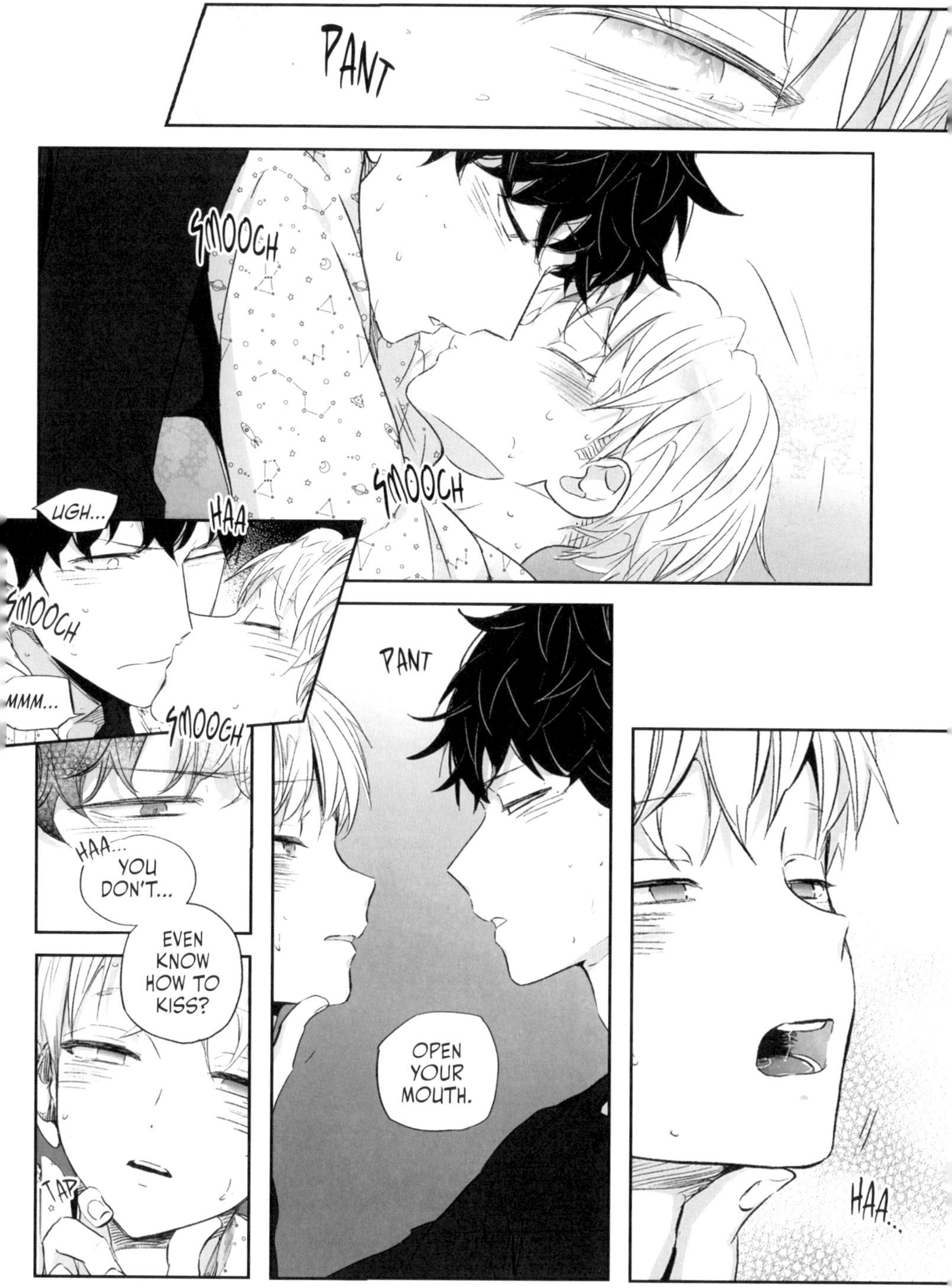
PANT
SMOOCH
SMOOCH
UGH...
HAA
SMOOCH
MMM...
SMOOCH
HAA... YOU DON'T...
EVEN KNOW HOW TO KISS?
TAP
PANT
OPEN YOUR MOUTH.
HAA...

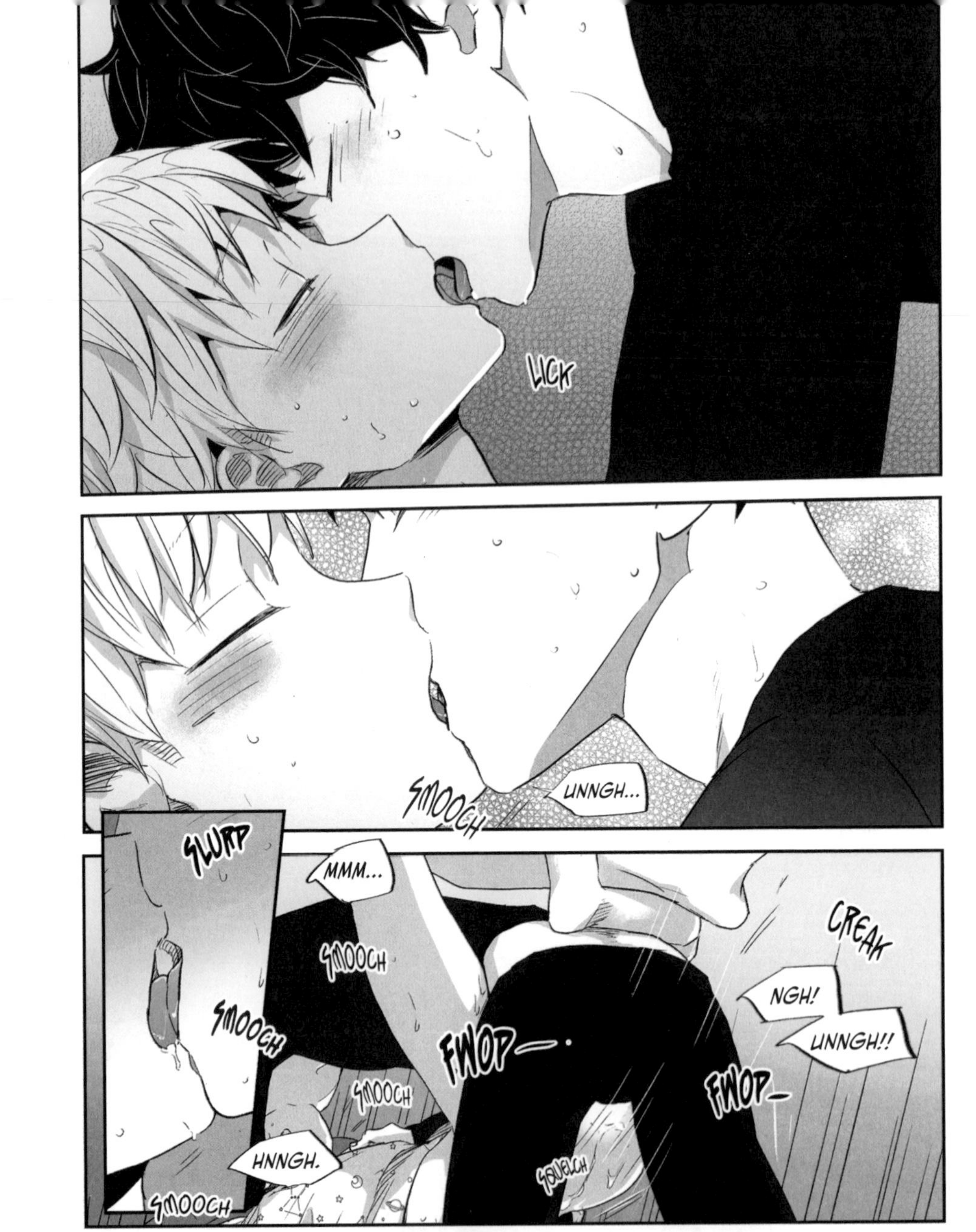
LICK
SMOOCH
UNNGH...
SLURP
SMOOCH
SMOOCH
MMM...
SMOOCH
SMOOCH
HNNGH.
FWOP—.
SQUELCH
FWOP_
CREAK
NGH!
UNNGH!!
TICK
TICK
CREAK
HAA...
PANT

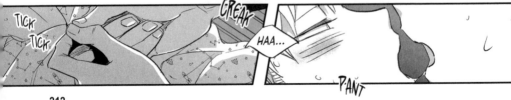

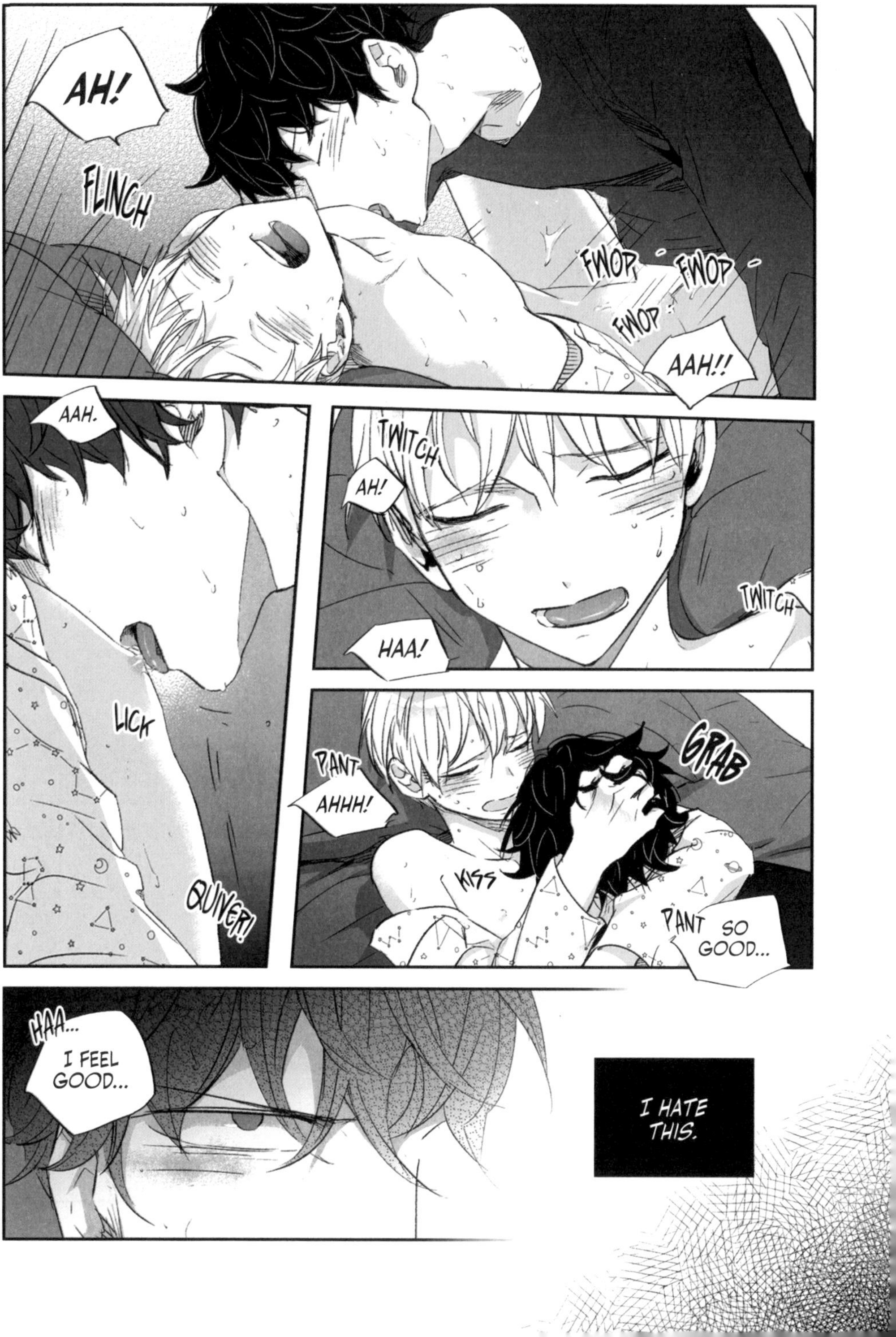
AH!
FLINCH
FWOP
FWOP
FWOP
AAH!!
AAH.
LICK
QUIVER!
TWITCH
AH!
TWITCH
HAA!
PANT
AHHH!
GRAB
KISS
PANT
SO GOOD...
HAA...
I FEEL GOOD...
I HATE THIS.

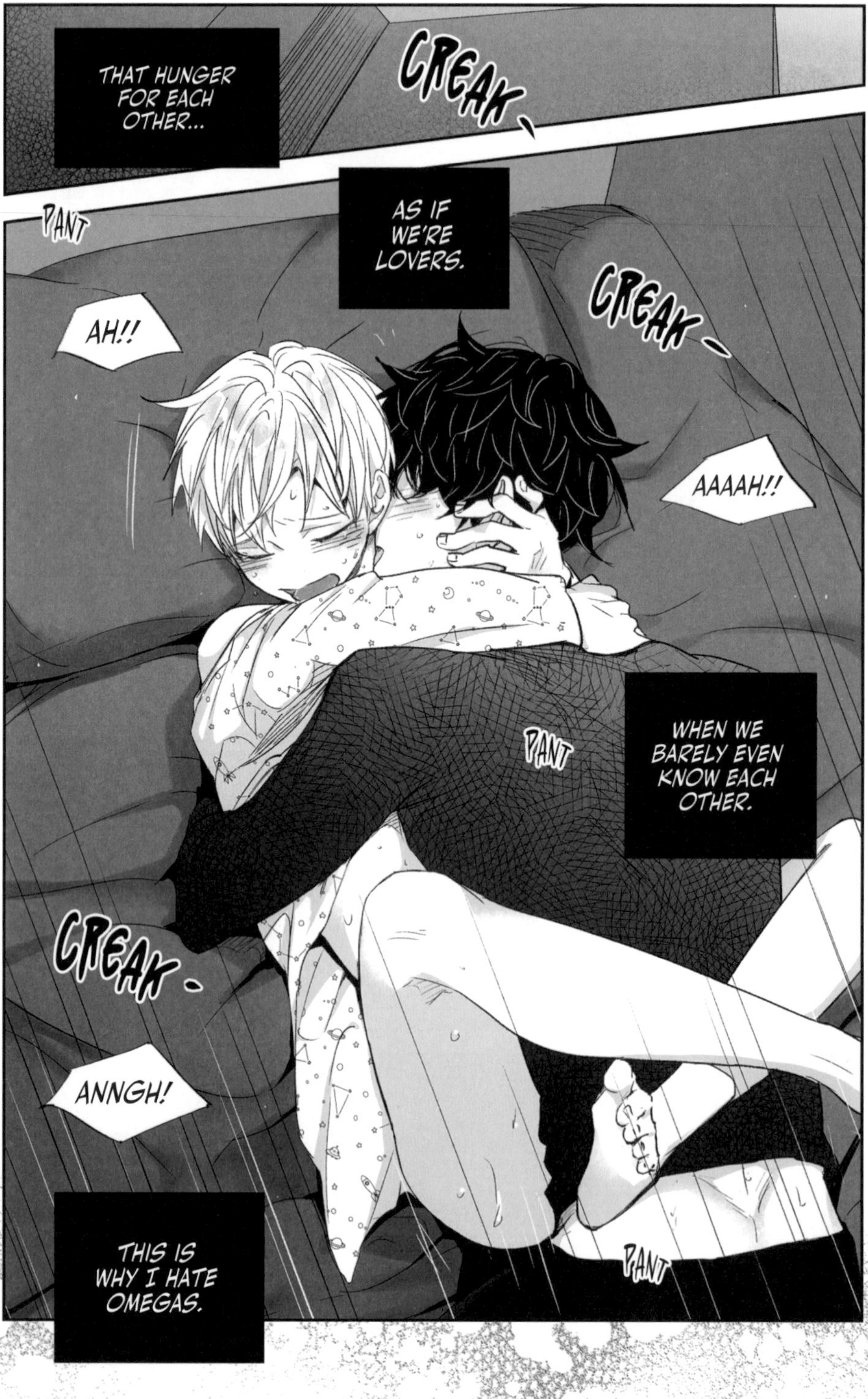
THAT HUNGER FOR EACH OTHER...
CREAK-
PANT
AS IF WE'RE LOVERS.
CREAK-
AH!!
AAAAH!!
WHEN WE BARELY EVEN KNOW EACH OTHER.
PANT
CREAK-
ANNGH!
THIS IS WHY I HATE OMEGAS.
PANT

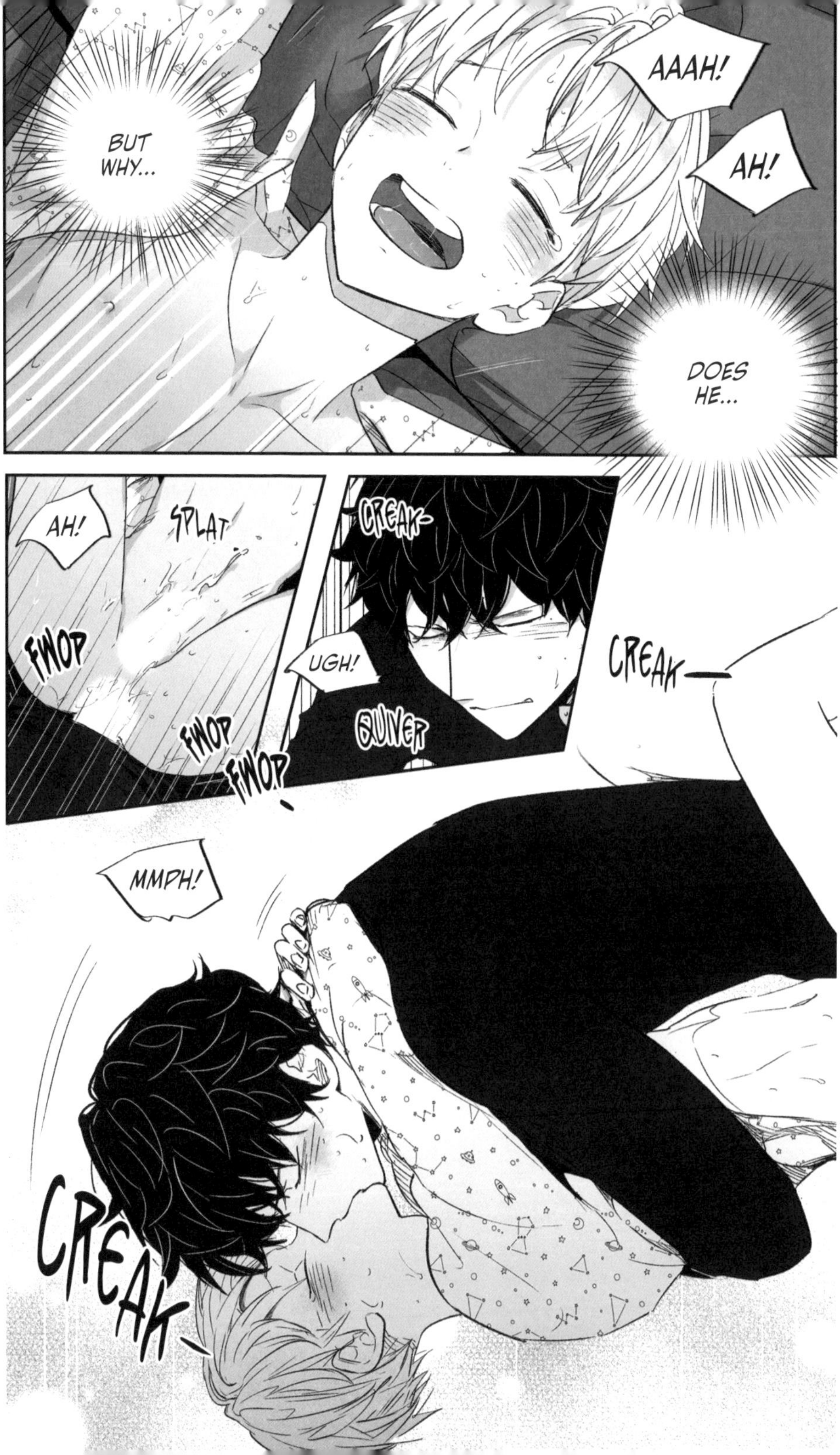
BUT WHY...
AAAH!
AH!
DOES HE...
AH!
SPLAT
FWOP
FWOP
FWOP
CREAK-
UGH!
QUIVER
CREAK—
MMPH!
CREAK-

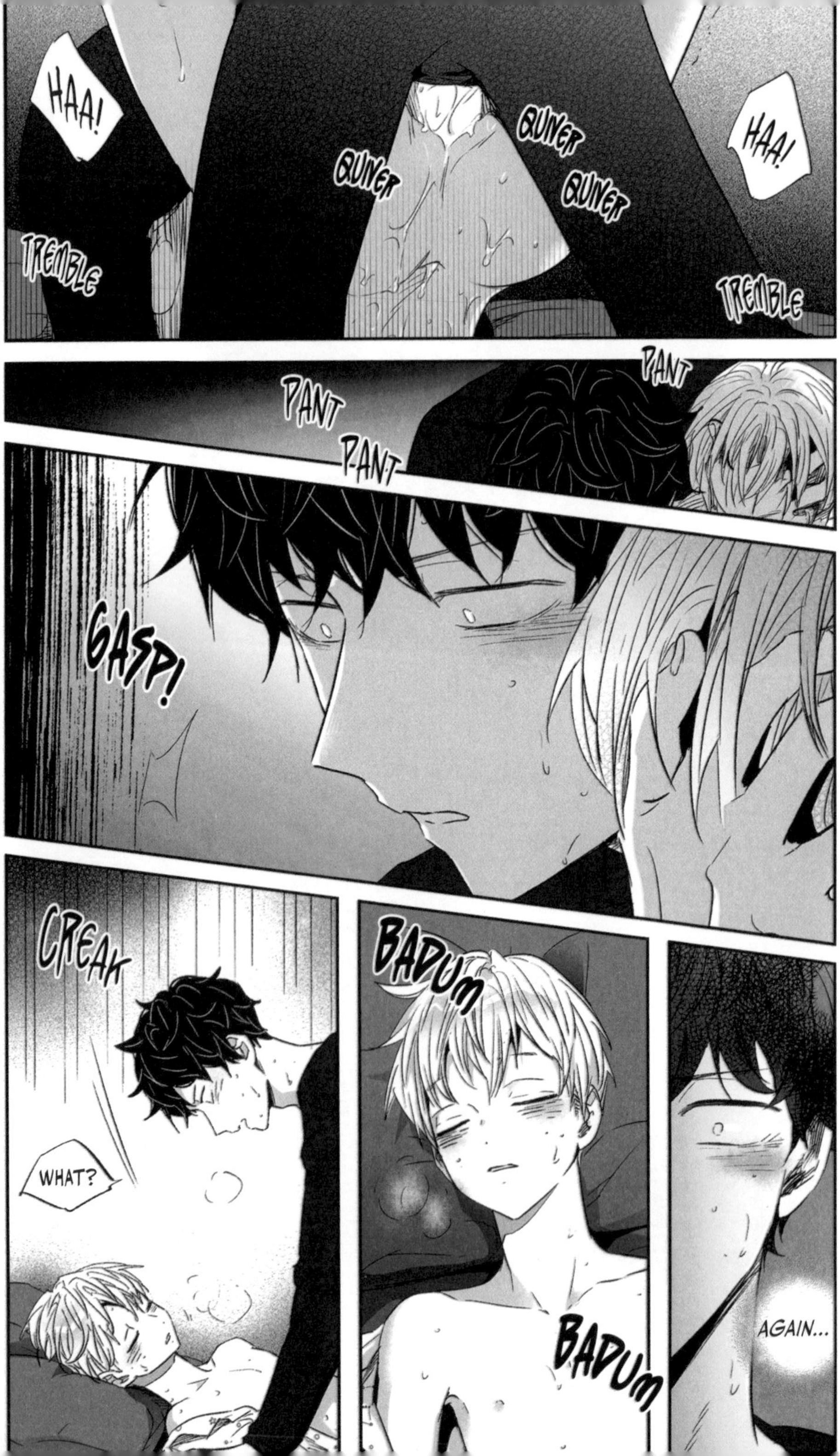
HAA!
TREMBLE
QUIVER
QUIVER
QUIVER
HAA!
TREMBLE
PANT
PANT
PANT
GASP!
CREAK
WHAT?
BADUM
BADUM
AGAIN...

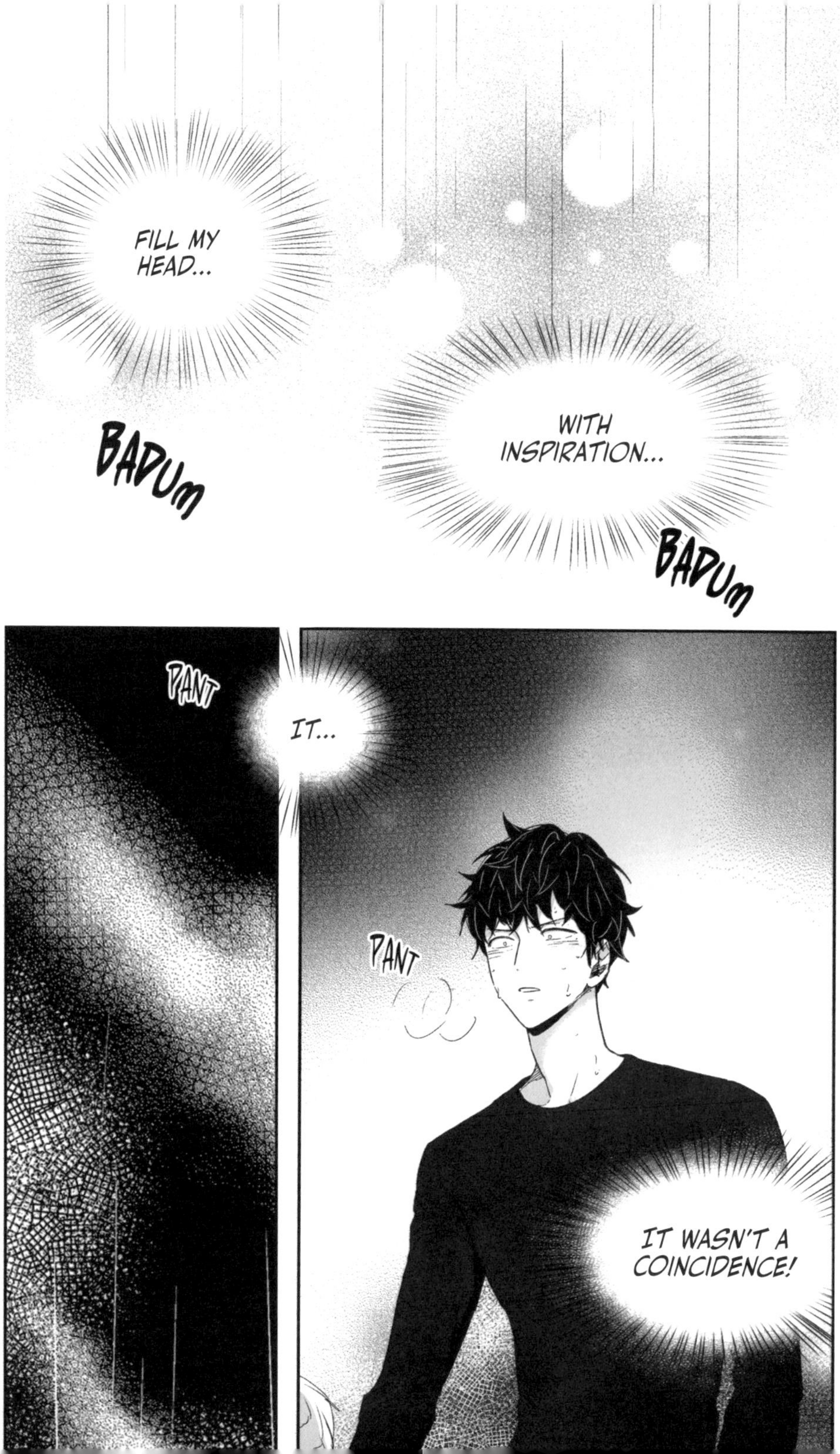
FILL MY HEAD...
BADUM
WITH INSPIRATION...
BADUM
PANT
IT...
PANT
IT WASN'T A COINCIDENCE!

Love is
an Illusion!

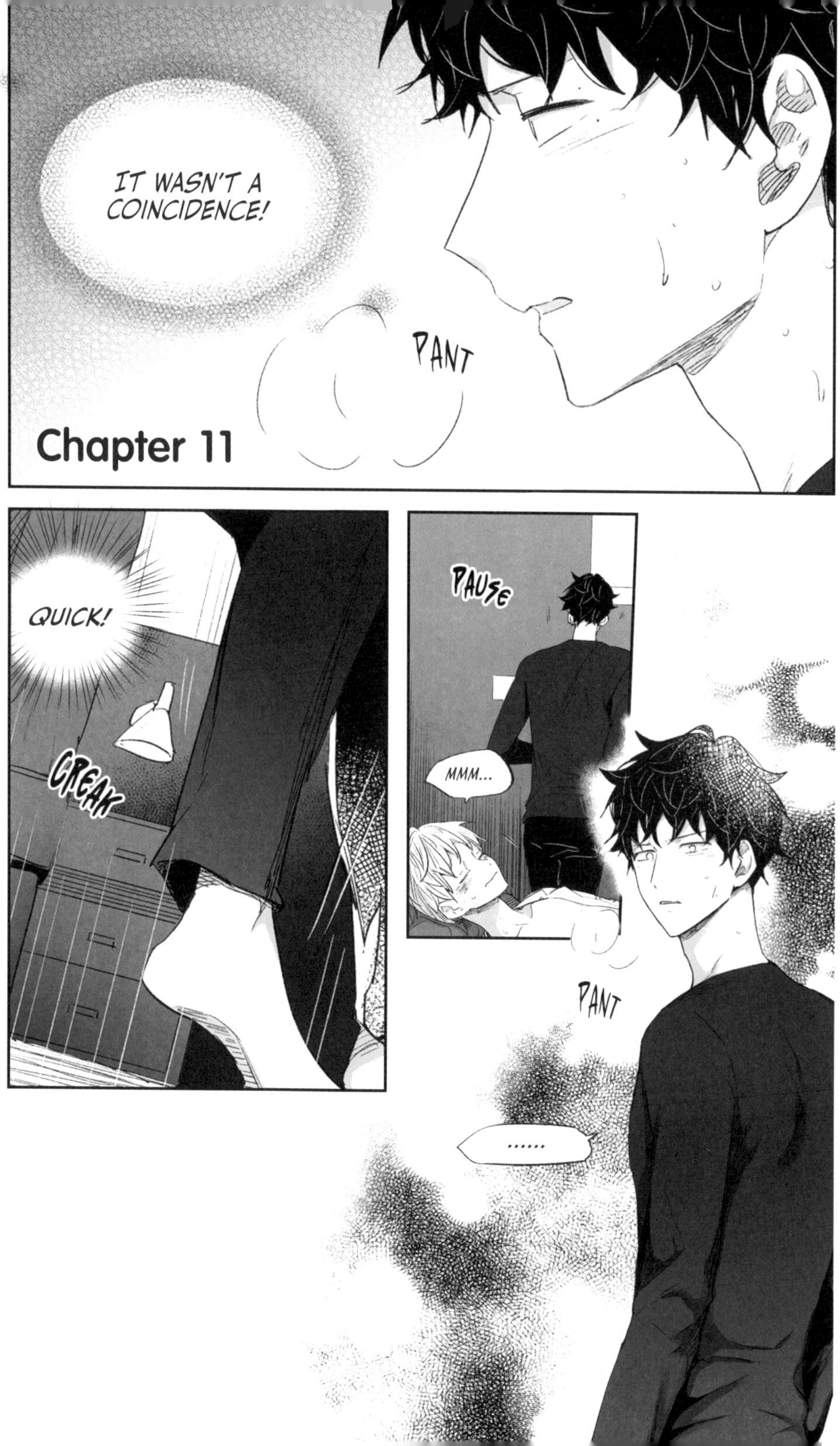
IT WASN'T A COINCIDENCE!
PANT
Chapter 11
QUICK!
CREAK
PAUSE
MMM...
PANT
......

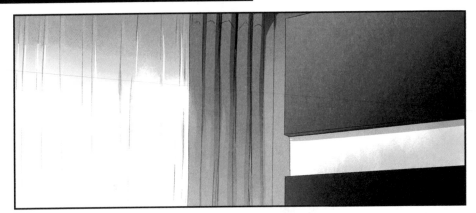

CLICK
CLICK
CLICK

ZZZz
ZZZz

PHEW...

I HAD A FEELING THAT...

IF I LEFT, HE'D DISAPPEAR AGAIN.

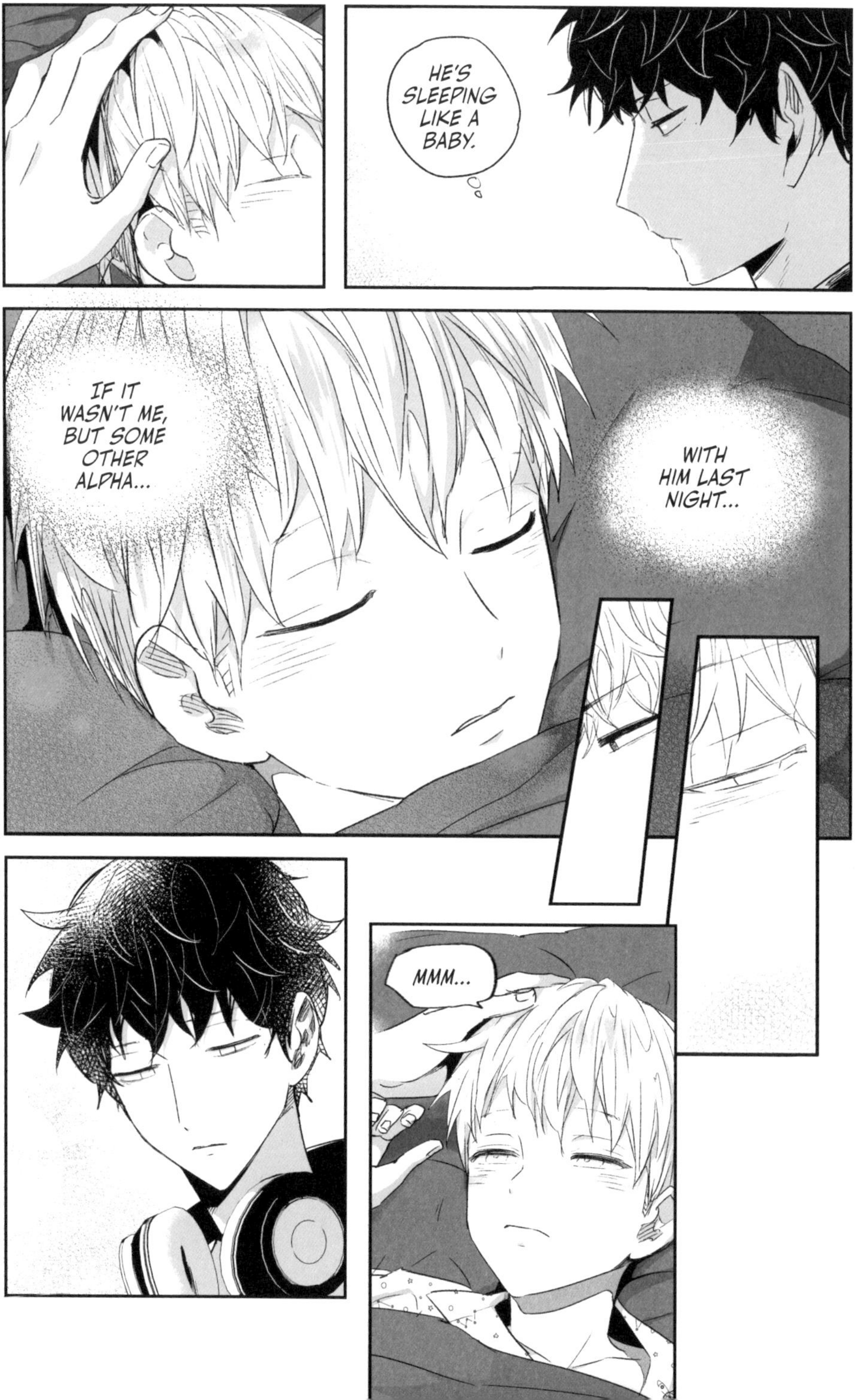
HE'S SLEEPING LIKE A BABY.
IF IT WASN'T ME, BUT SOME OTHER ALPHA...
WITH HIM LAST NIGHT...
MMM...

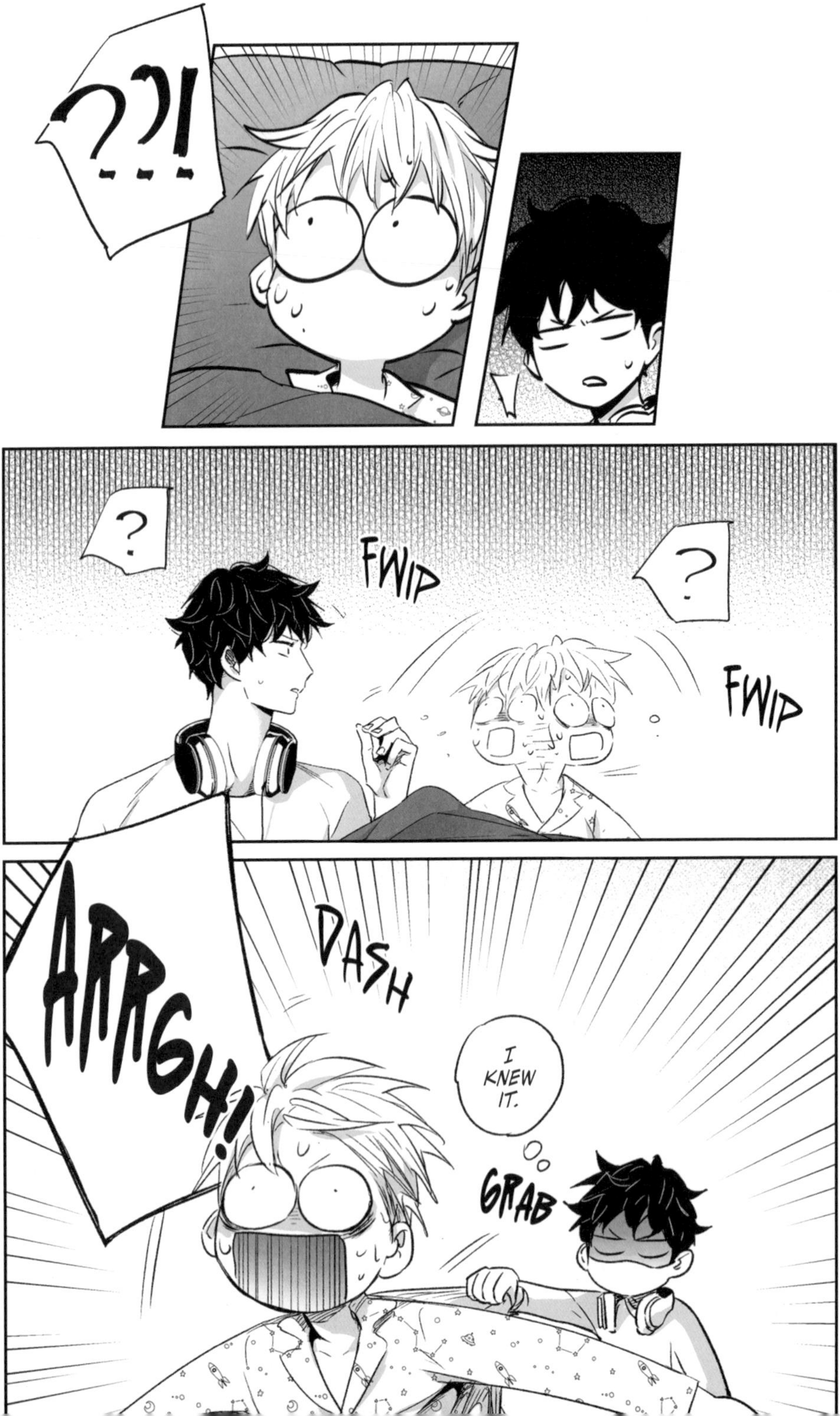
??!
?
FWIP
?
FWIP
ARRGH!!
DASH
I KNEW IT.
GRAB

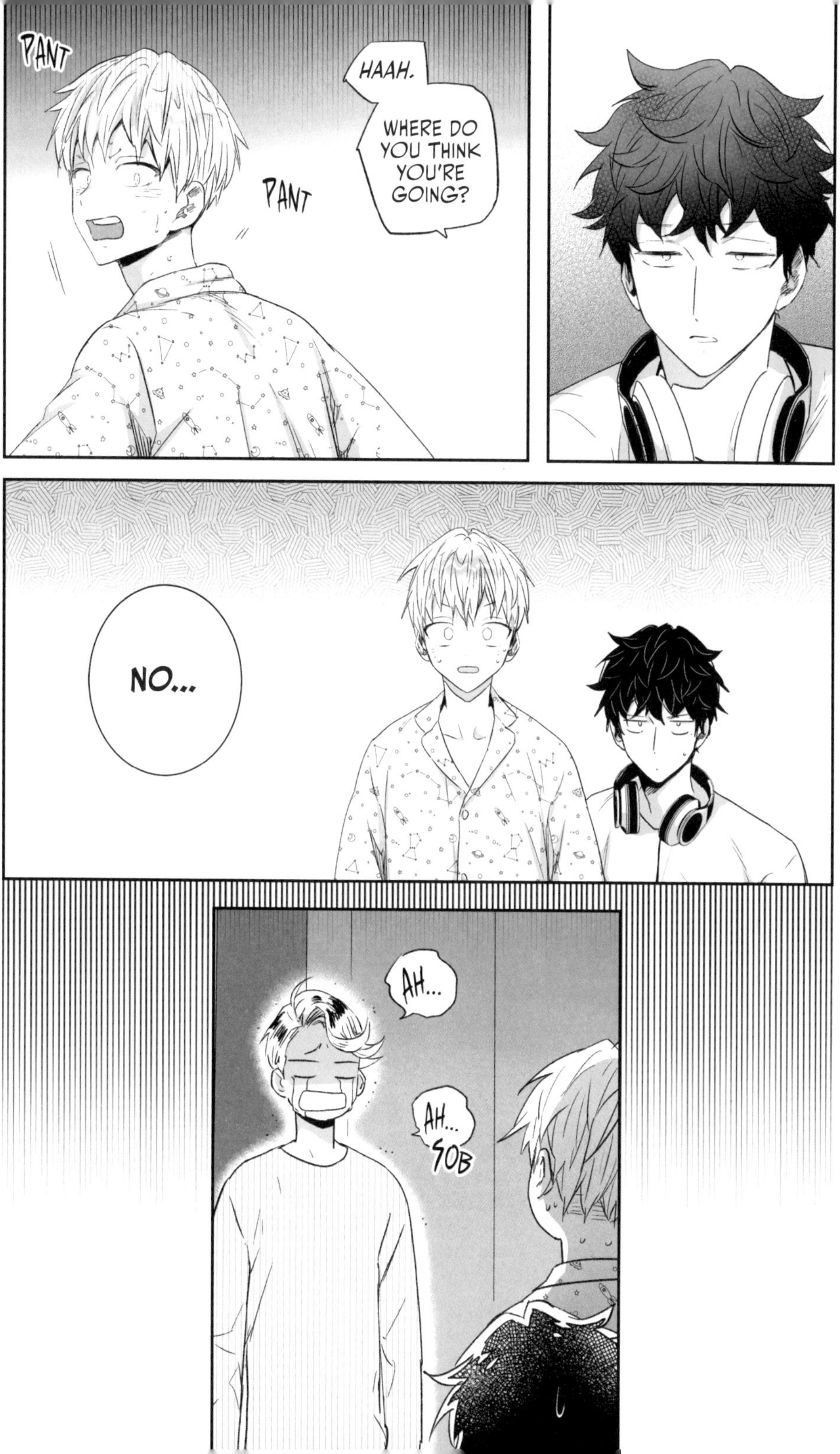
PANT
PANT
HAAH.
WHERE DO YOU THINK YOU'RE GOING?
NO...
AH...
AH... SOB

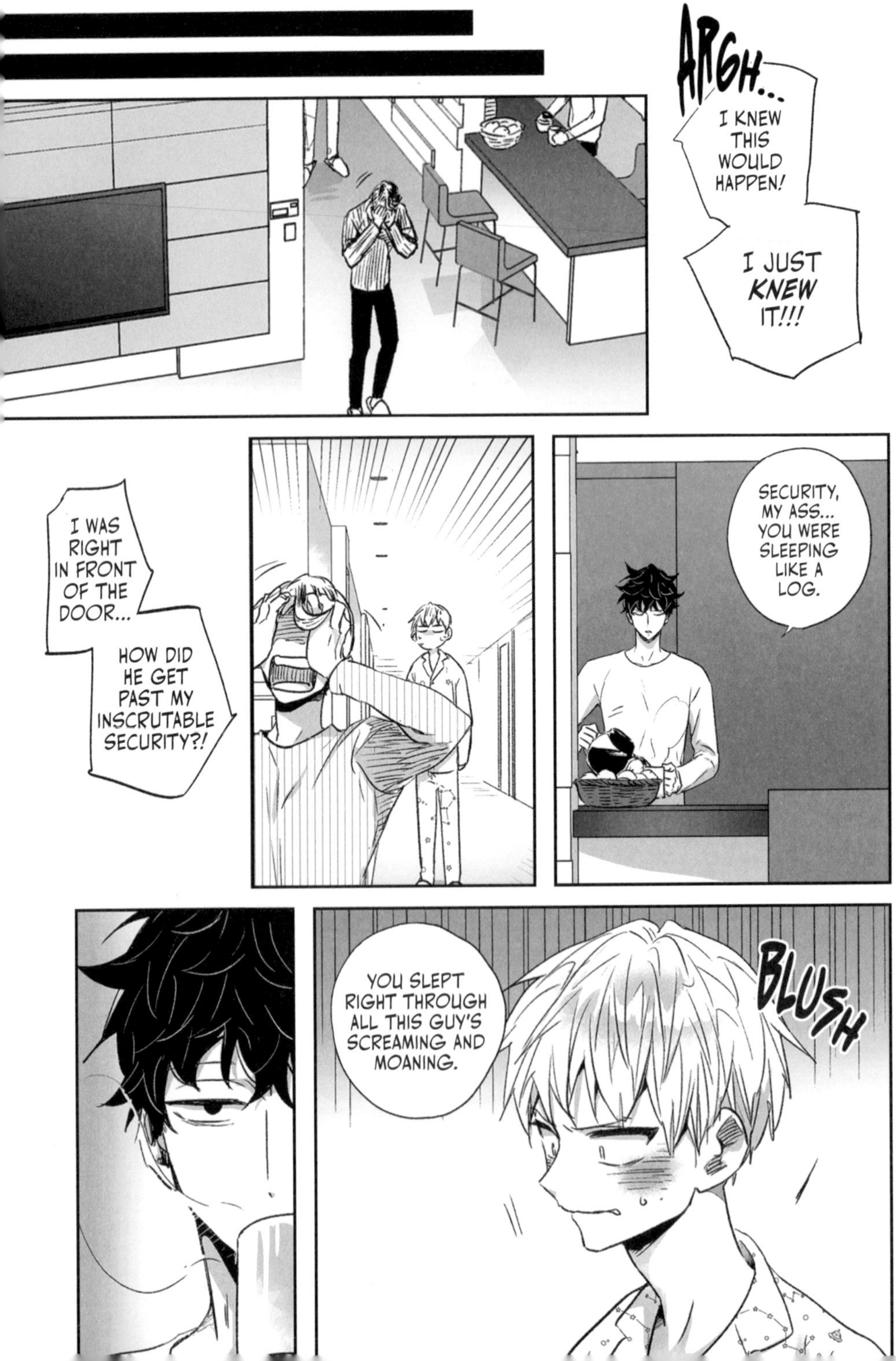
ARGH...
I KNEW THIS WOULD HAPPEN!
I JUST KNEW IT!!!
I WAS RIGHT IN FRONT OF THE DOOR...
HOW DID HE GET PAST MY INSCRUTABLE SECURITY?!
SECURITY, MY ASS... YOU WERE SLEEPING LIKE A LOG.
YOU SLEPT RIGHT THROUGH ALL THIS GUY'S SCREAMING AND MOANING.
BLUSH

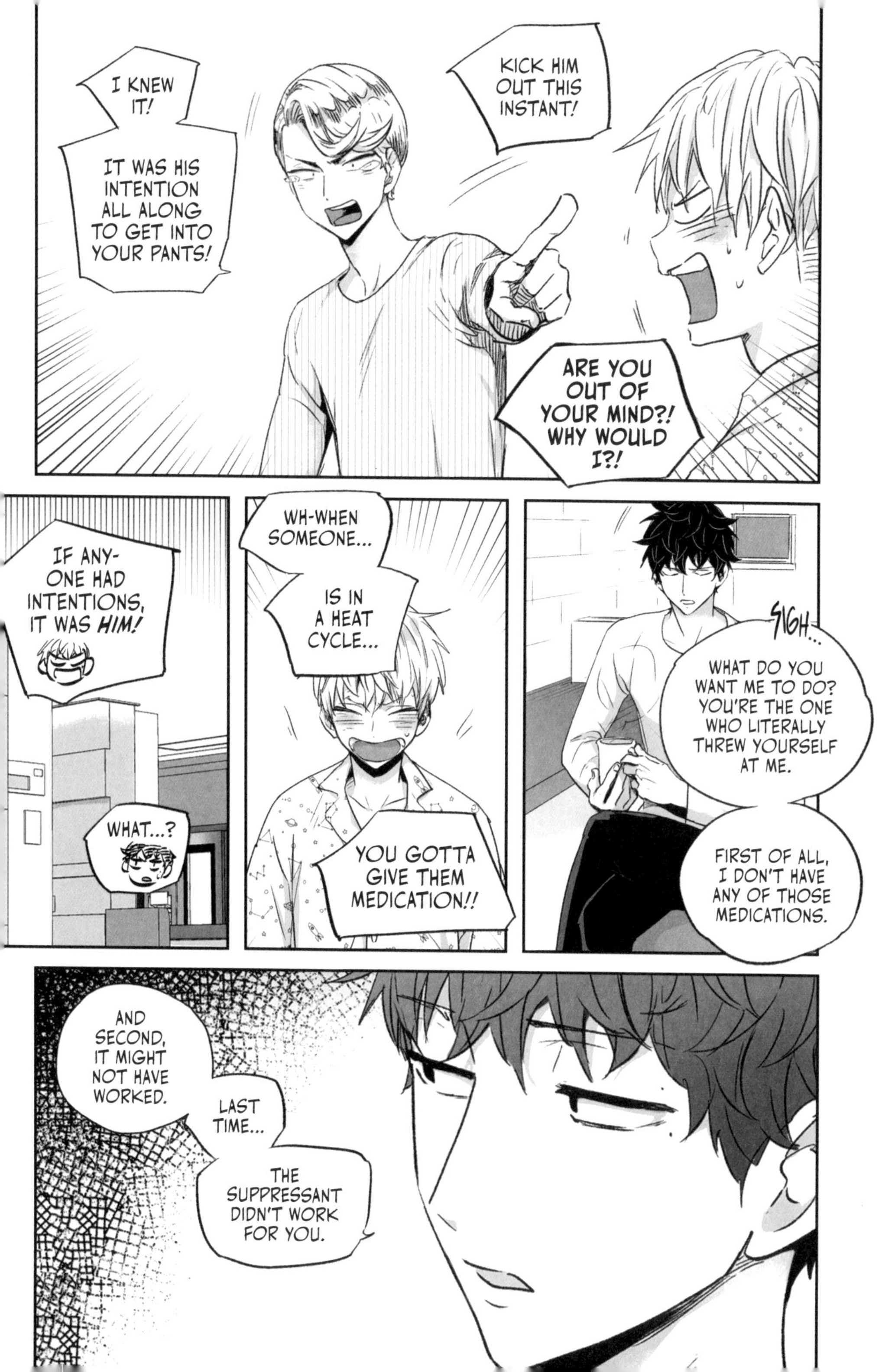
I KNEW IT!
IT WAS HIS INTENTION ALL ALONG TO GET INTO YOUR PANTS!
KICK HIM OUT THIS INSTANT!
ARE YOU OUT OF YOUR MIND?! WHY WOULD I?!
IF ANY-ONE HAD INTENTIONS, IT WAS *HIM!*
WHAT...?
WH-WHEN SOMEONE...
IS IN A HEAT CYCLE...
YOU GOTTA GIVE THEM MEDICATION!!
SIGH...
WHAT DO YOU WANT ME TO DO? YOU'RE THE ONE WHO LITERALLY THREW YOURSELF AT ME.
FIRST OF ALL, I DON'T HAVE ANY OF THOSE MEDICATIONS.
AND SECOND, IT MIGHT NOT HAVE WORKED.
LAST TIME...
THE SUPPRESSANT DIDN'T WORK FOR YOU.

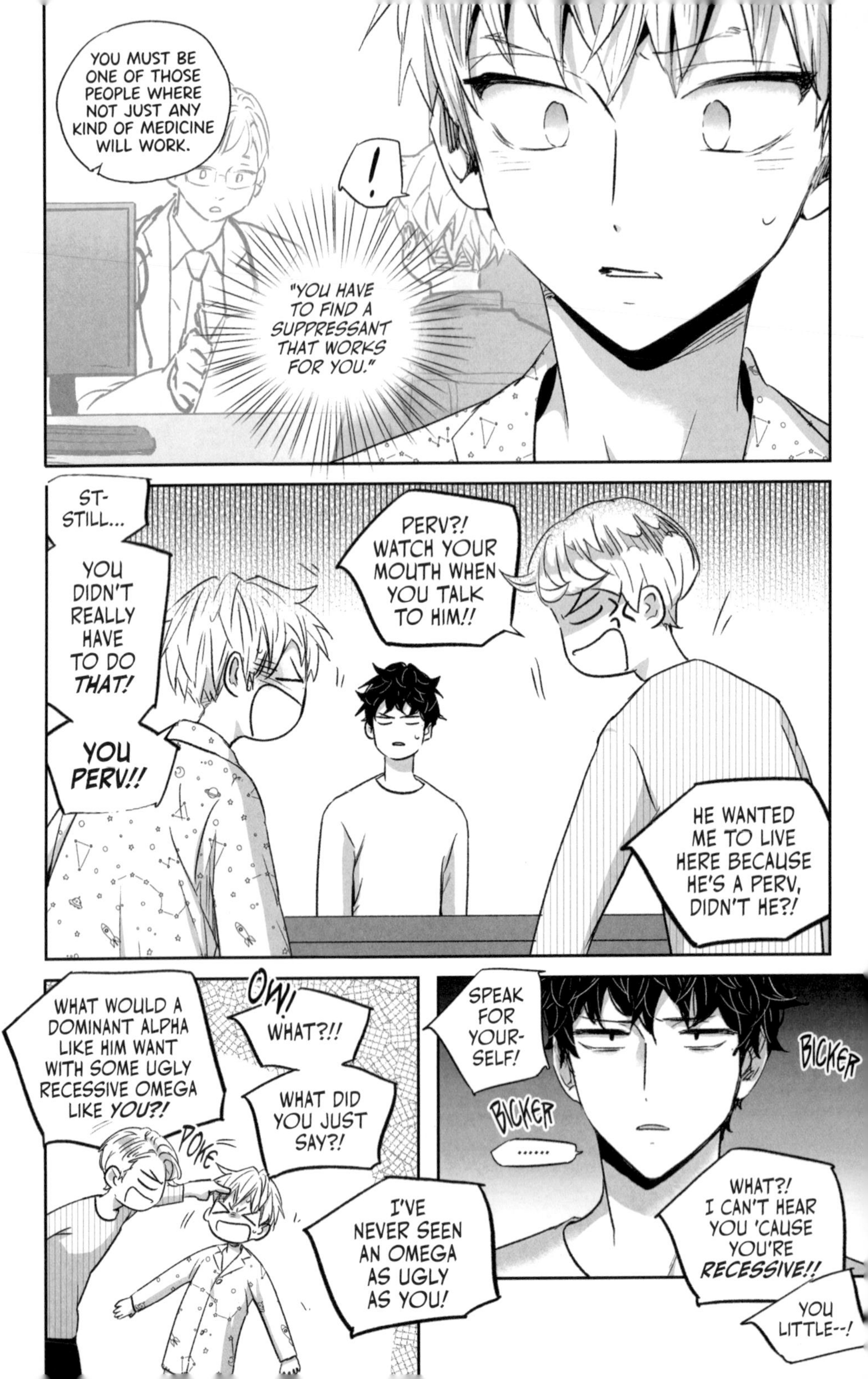
YOU MUST BE ONE OF THOSE PEOPLE WHERE NOT JUST ANY KIND OF MEDICINE WILL WORK.
!
"YOU HAVE TO FIND A SUPPRESSANT THAT WORKS FOR YOU."
ST-STILL...
YOU DIDN'T REALLY HAVE TO DO THAT!
YOU PERV!!
PERV?! WATCH YOUR MOUTH WHEN YOU TALK TO HIM!!
HE WANTED ME TO LIVE HERE BECAUSE HE'S A PERV, DIDN'T HE?!
WHAT WOULD A DOMINANT ALPHA LIKE HIM WANT WITH SOME UGLY RECESSIVE OMEGA LIKE YOU?!
OW!
WHAT?!!
WHAT DID YOU JUST SAY?!
POKE
I'VE NEVER SEEN AN OMEGA AS UGLY AS YOU!
SPEAK FOR YOUR-SELF!
BICKER
BICKER
......
WHAT?! I CAN'T HEAR YOU 'CAUSE YOU'RE RECESSIVE!!
YOU LITTLE--!

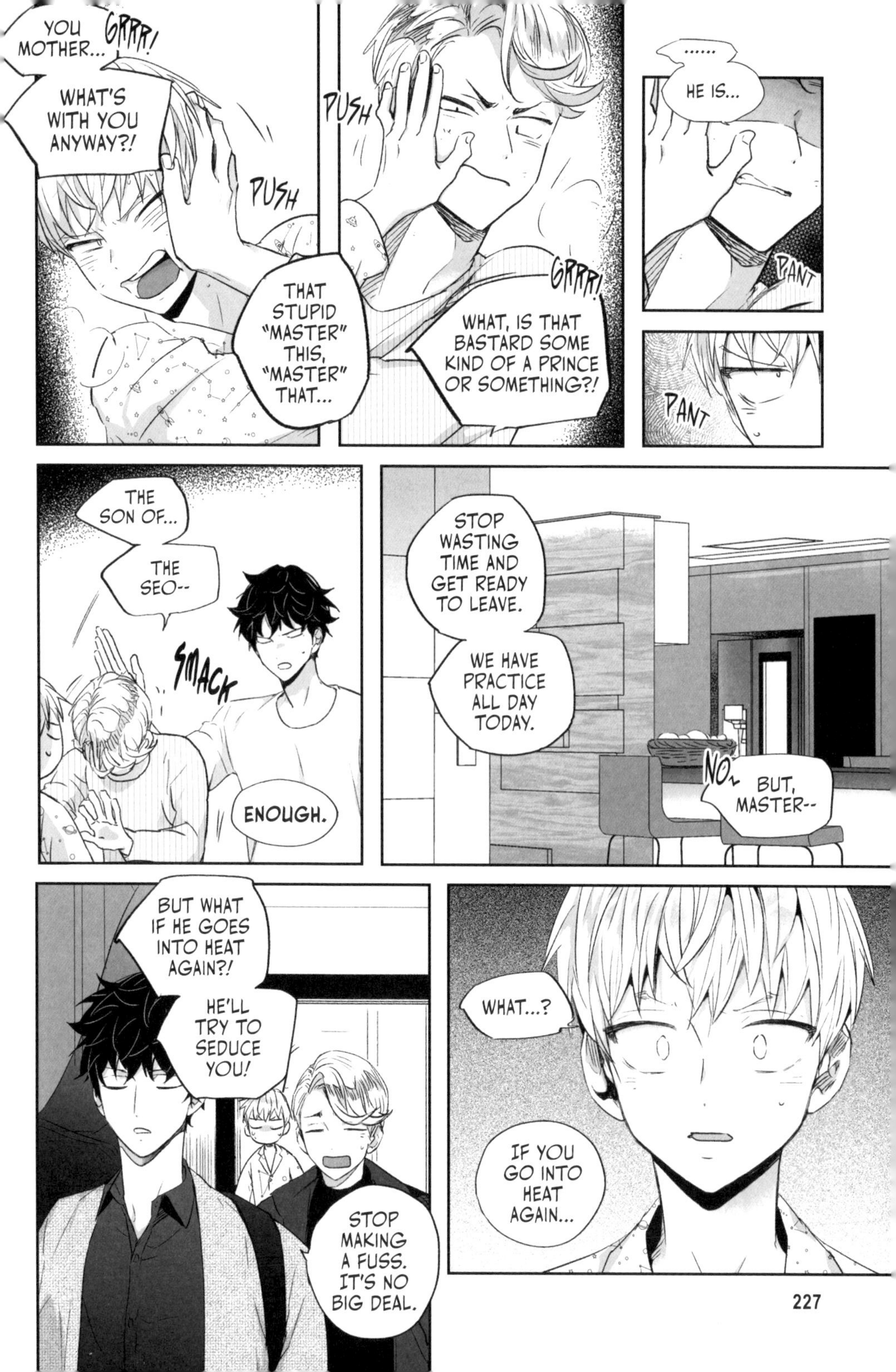
YOU MOTHER...
GRRR!
WHAT'S WITH YOU ANYWAY?!
PUSH
PUSH
THAT STUPID "MASTER" THIS, "MASTER" THAT...
GRRR!
WHAT, IS THAT BASTARD SOME KIND OF A PRINCE OR SOMETHING?!
......
HE IS...
PANT
PANT
THE SON OF...
THE SEO--
SMACK
ENOUGH.
STOP WASTING TIME AND GET READY TO LEAVE.
WE HAVE PRACTICE ALL DAY TODAY.
NO~
BUT, MASTER--
BUT WHAT IF HE GOES INTO HEAT AGAIN?!
HE'LL TRY TO SEDUCE YOU!
STOP MAKING A FUSS. IT'S NO BIG DEAL.
WHAT...?
IF YOU GO INTO HEAT AGAIN...

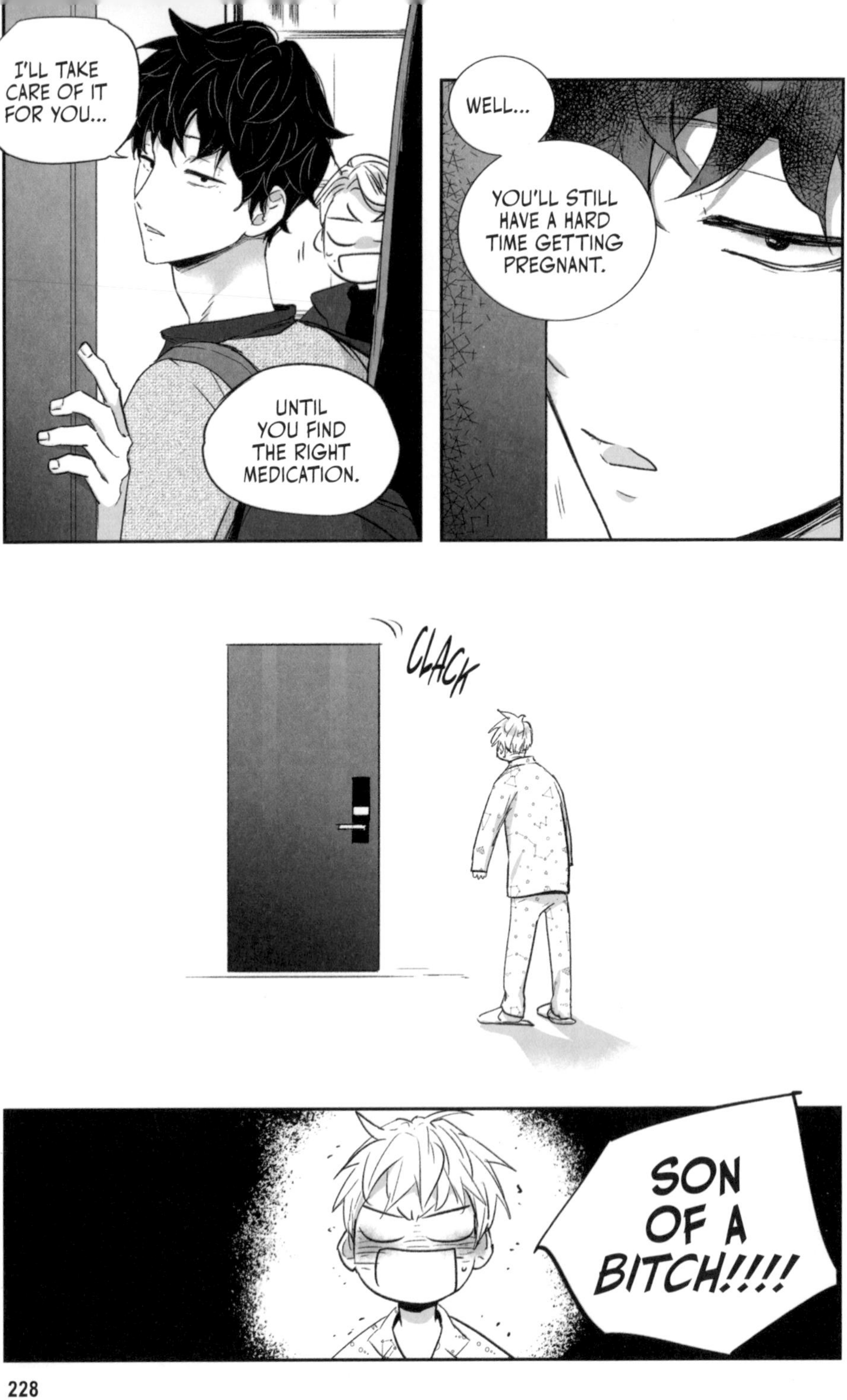
I'LL TAKE CARE OF IT FOR YOU...
UNTIL YOU FIND THE RIGHT MEDICATION.
WELL...
YOU'LL STILL HAVE A HARD TIME GETTING PREGNANT.
CLACK
SON OF A BITCH!!!!

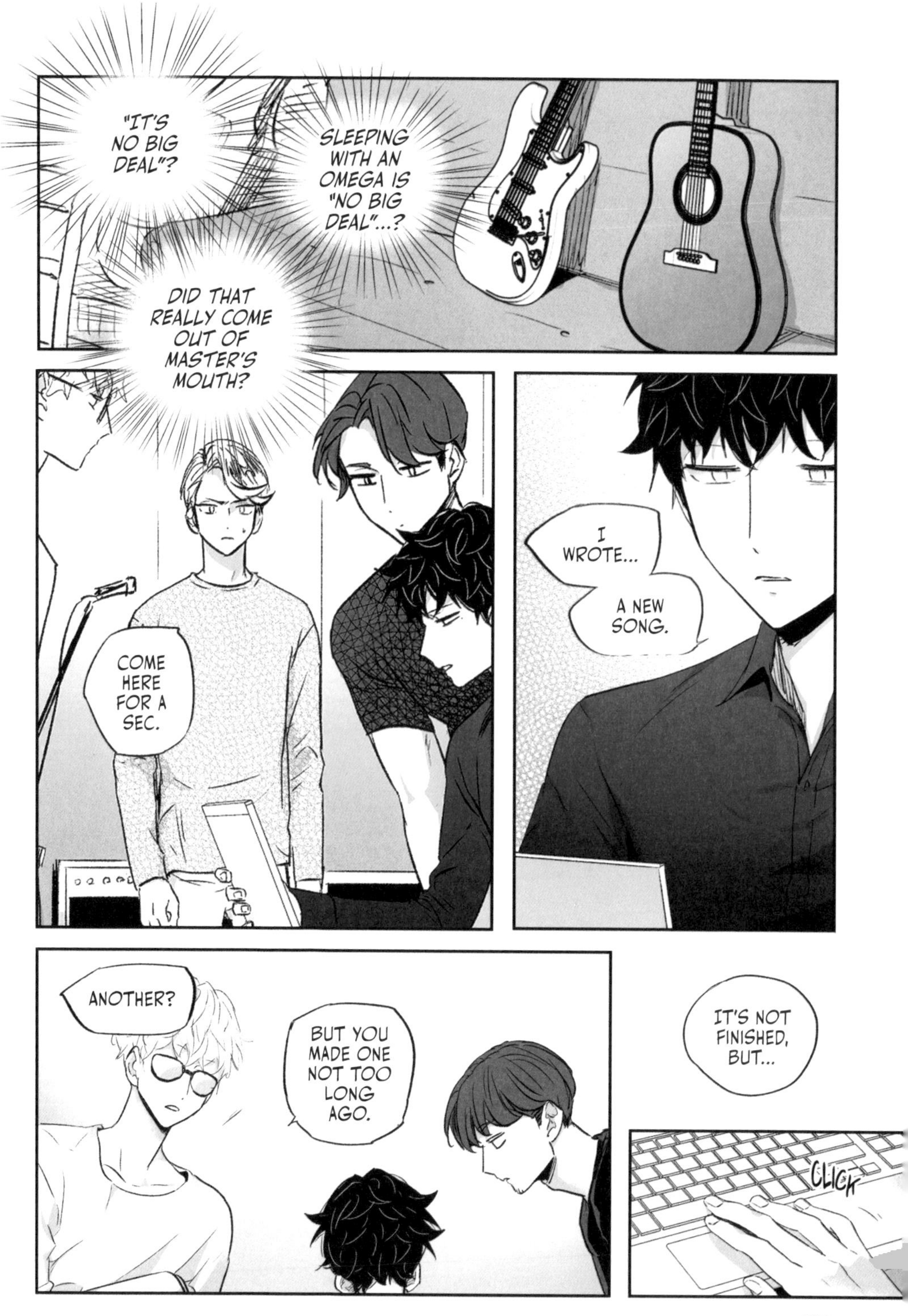
"IT'S NO BIG DEAL"?
SLEEPING WITH AN OMEGA IS "NO BIG DEAL"...?
DID THAT REALLY COME OUT OF MASTER'S MOUTH?
COME HERE FOR A SEC.
I WROTE...
A NEW SONG.
ANOTHER?
BUT YOU MADE ONE NOT TOO LONG AGO.
IT'S NOT FINISHED, BUT...
CLICK

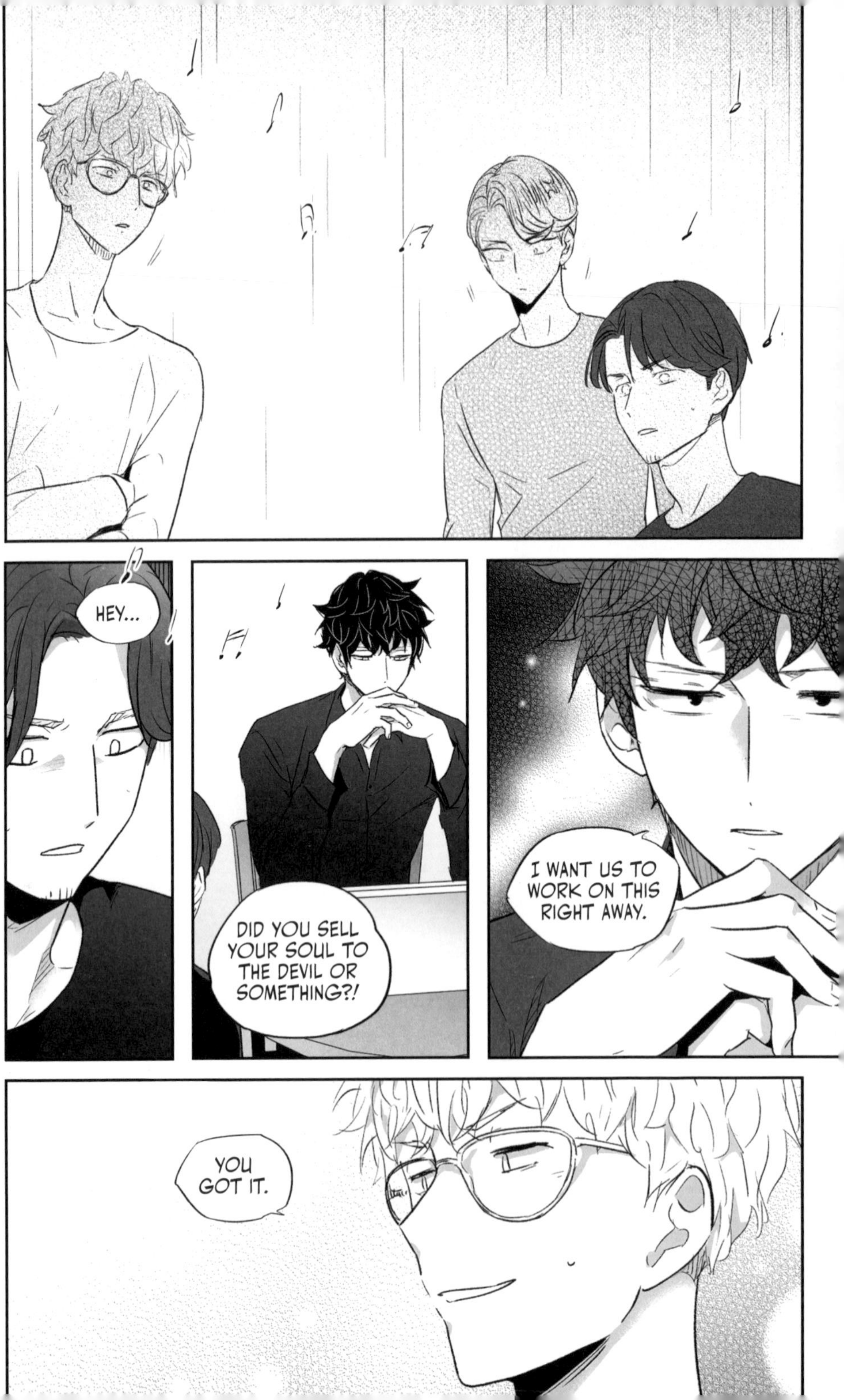
HEY...
DID YOU SELL YOUR SOUL TO THE DEVIL OR SOMETHING?!
I WANT US TO WORK ON THIS RIGHT AWAY.
YOU GOT IT.

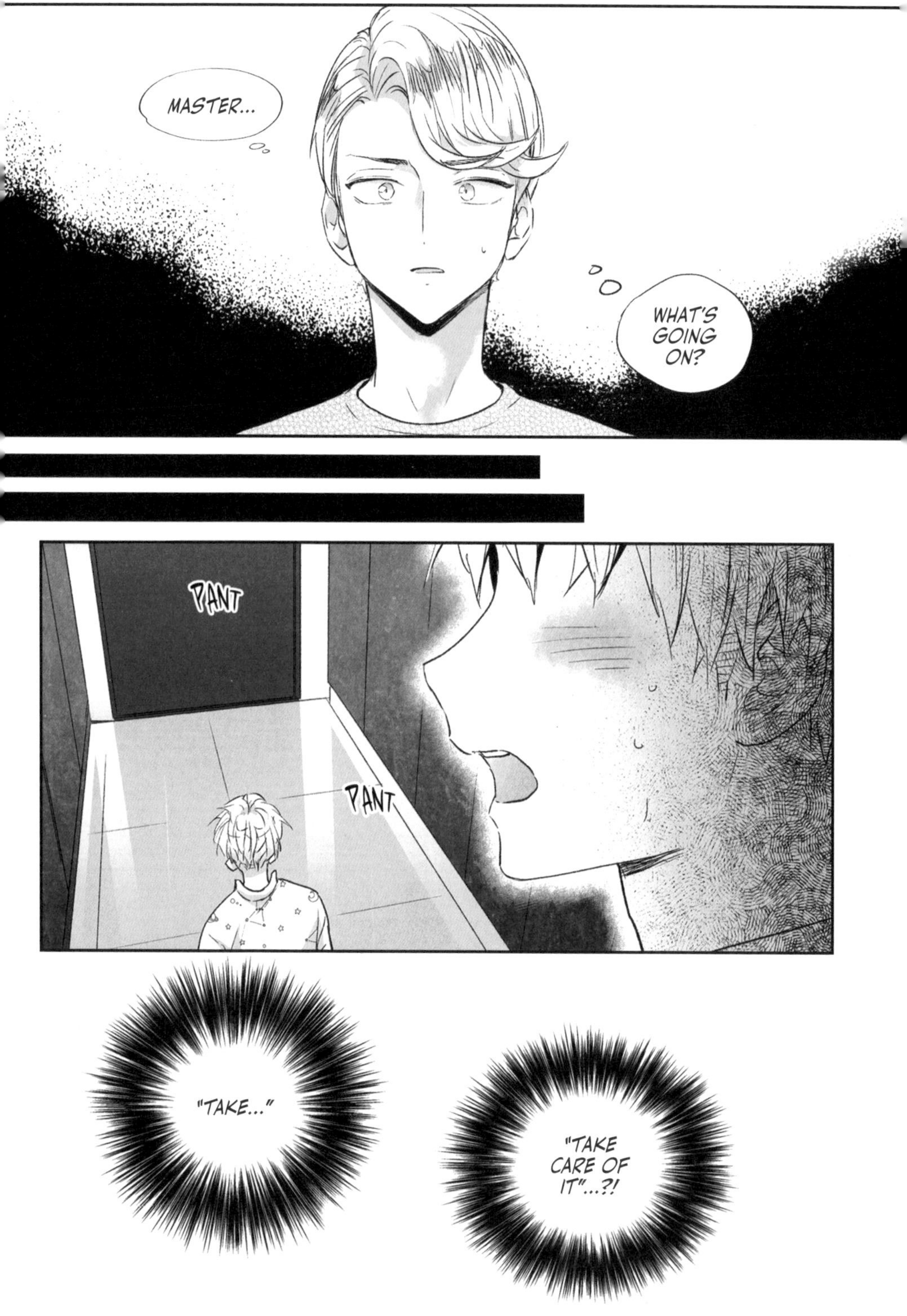
MASTER...
WHAT'S GOING ON?
PANT
PANT
"TAKE..."
"TAKE CARE OF IT"...?!

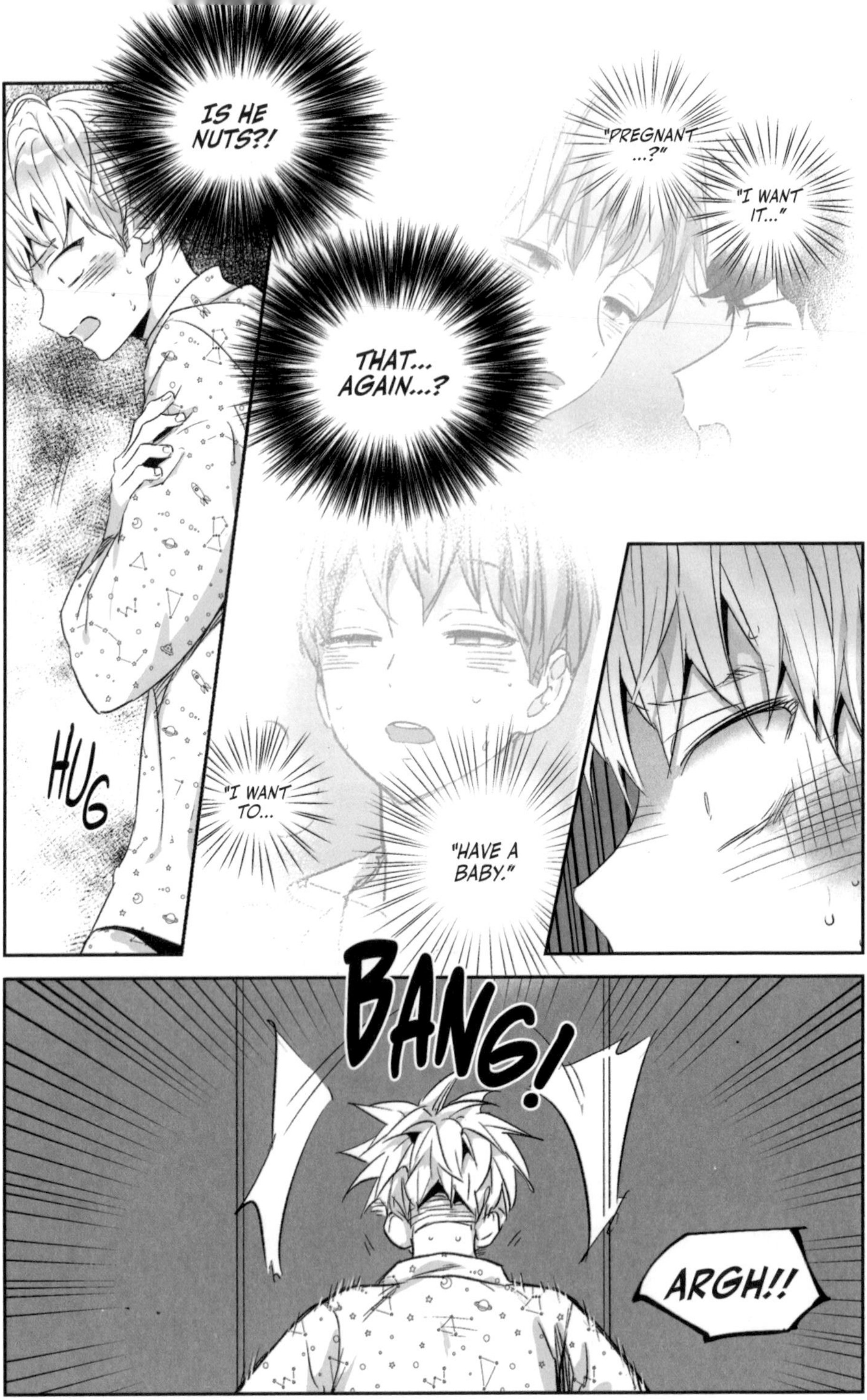
IS HE NUTS?!
"PREGNANT ...?"
"I WANT IT..."
THAT... AGAIN...?
HUG
"I WANT TO...
"HAVE A BABY."
BANG!
ARGH!!

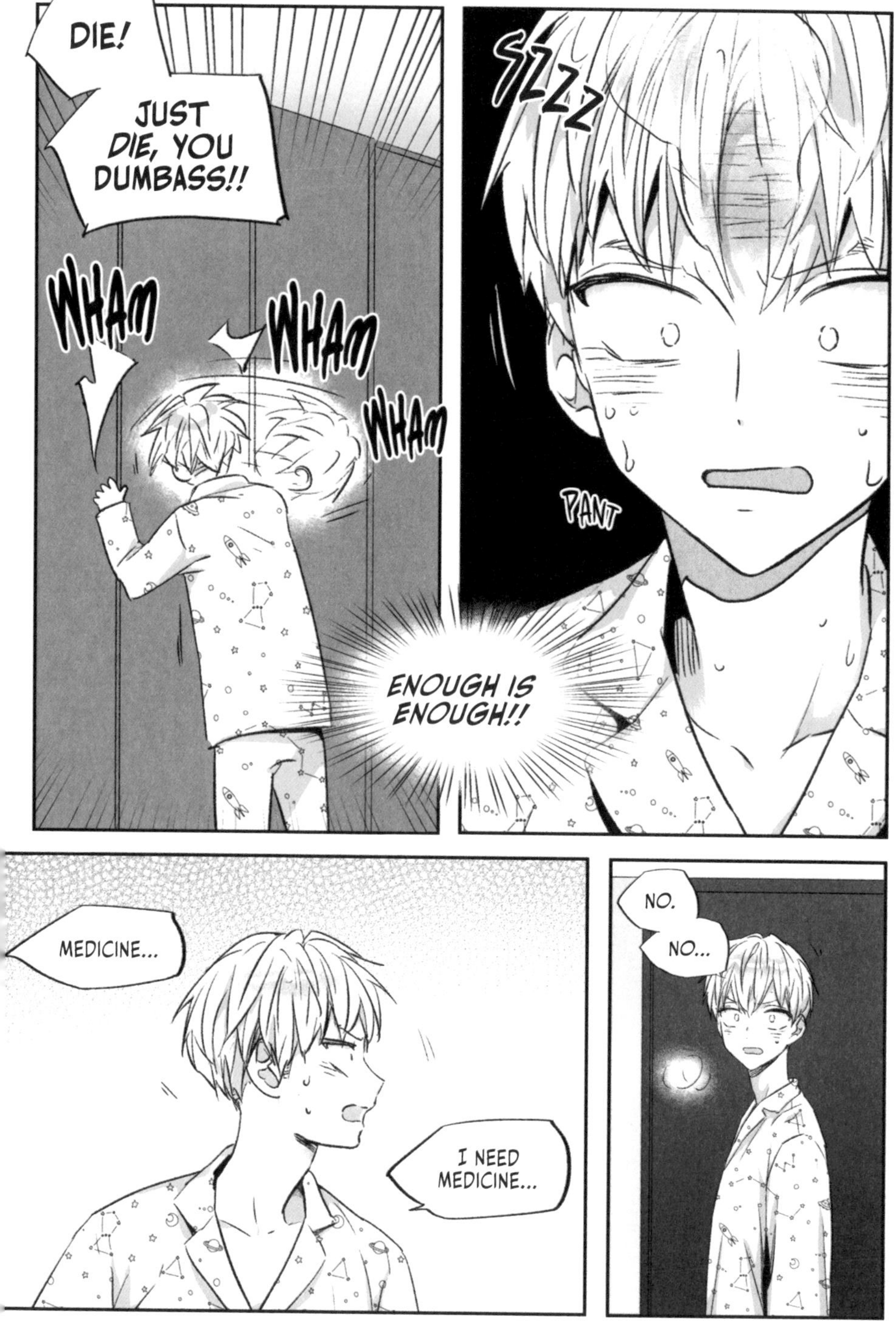
DIE!
JUST DIE, YOU DUMBASS!!
WHAM
WHAM
WHAM
SZZZ
PANT
ENOUGH IS ENOUGH!!
MEDICINE...
I NEED MEDICINE...
NO.
NO...

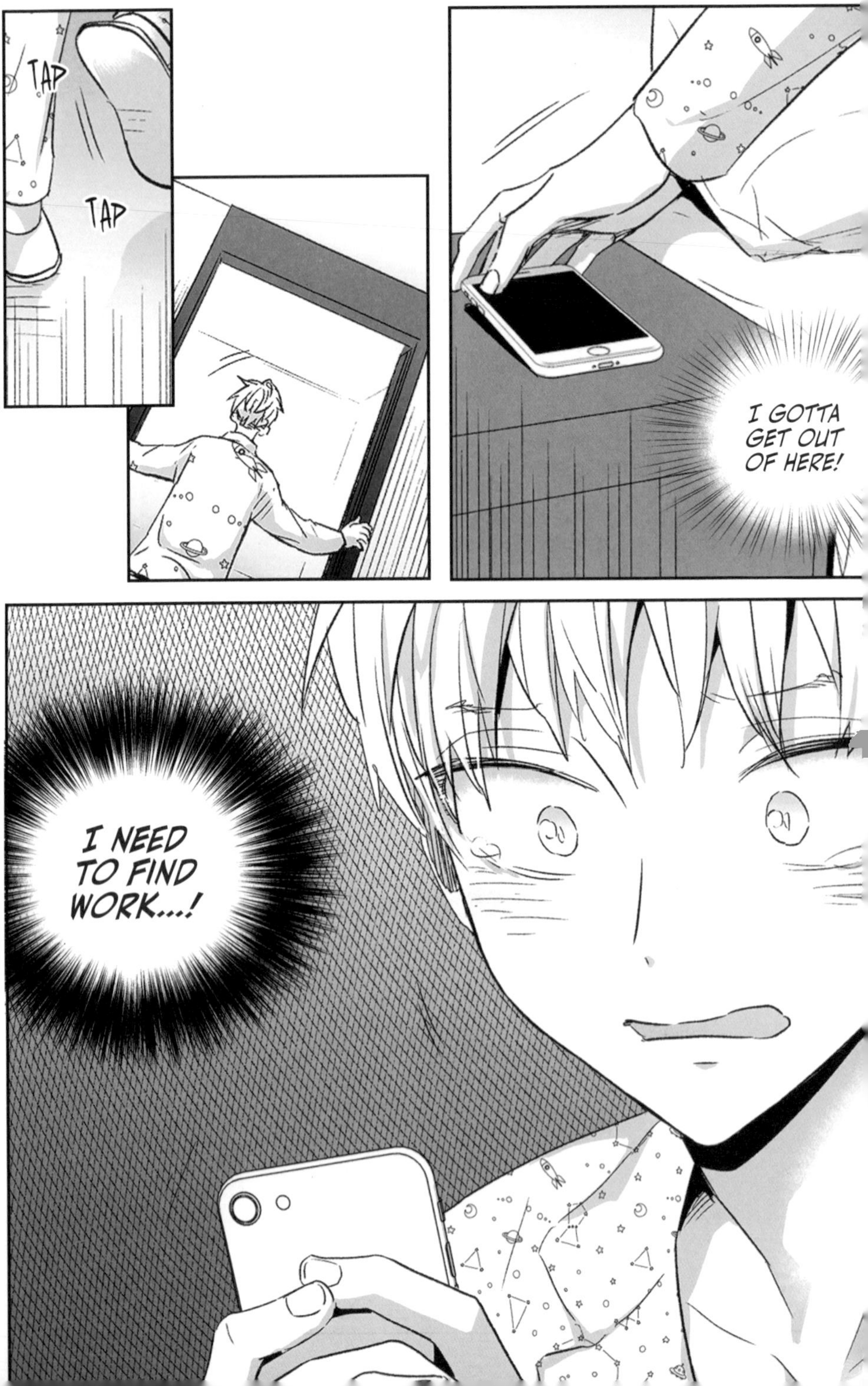
TAP
TAP
I GOTTA GET OUT OF HERE!
I NEED TO FIND WORK...!

Love is an Illusion!

Love is an Illusion!

Chapter 12

OMEGAS...

DESERVE TO BE LOVED!

Protect omegas

PROTECT...

Protect omegas

PRECIOUS...

OMEGAS!

Omegas deserve t... b... lov...

REASONS I LIKE OMEGAS

Smell nice	Pretty face
Tender heart	Soft skin

OMEGAS ARE LIKE FLOWERS.

PROTECT THEM!

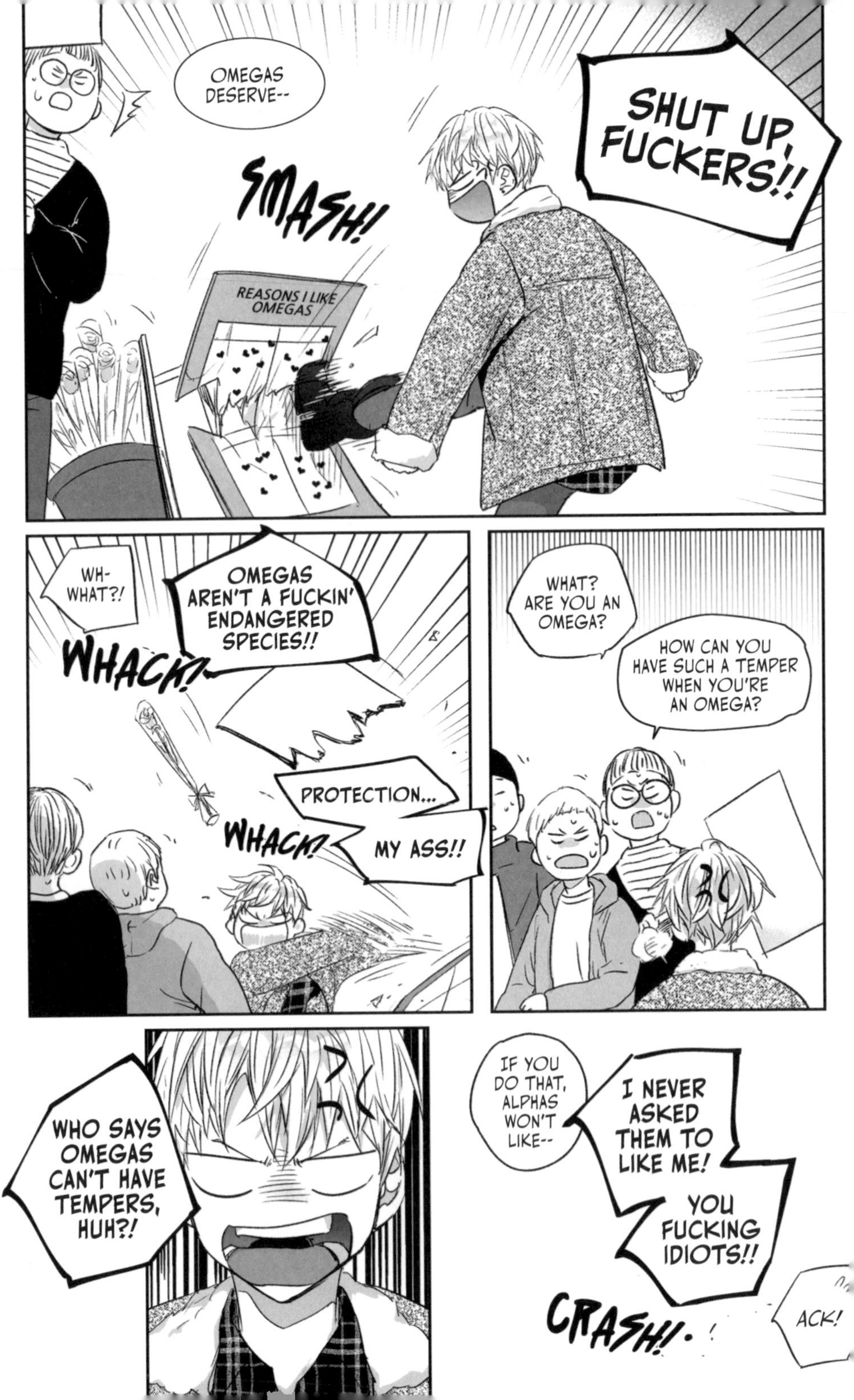
OMEGAS DESERVE--
SHUT UP, FUCKERS!!
SMASH!
REASONS I LIKE OMEGAS
WH- WHAT?!
OMEGAS AREN'T A FUCKIN' ENDANGERED SPECIES!!
WHACK!
PROTECTION...
WHACK!
MY ASS!!
WHAT? ARE YOU AN OMEGA?
HOW CAN YOU HAVE SUCH A TEMPER WHEN YOU'RE AN OMEGA?
WHO SAYS OMEGAS CAN'T HAVE TEMPERS, HUH?!
IF YOU DO THAT, ALPHAS WON'T LIKE--
I NEVER ASKED THEM TO LIKE ME!
YOU FUCKING IDIOTS!!
CRASH!
ACK!

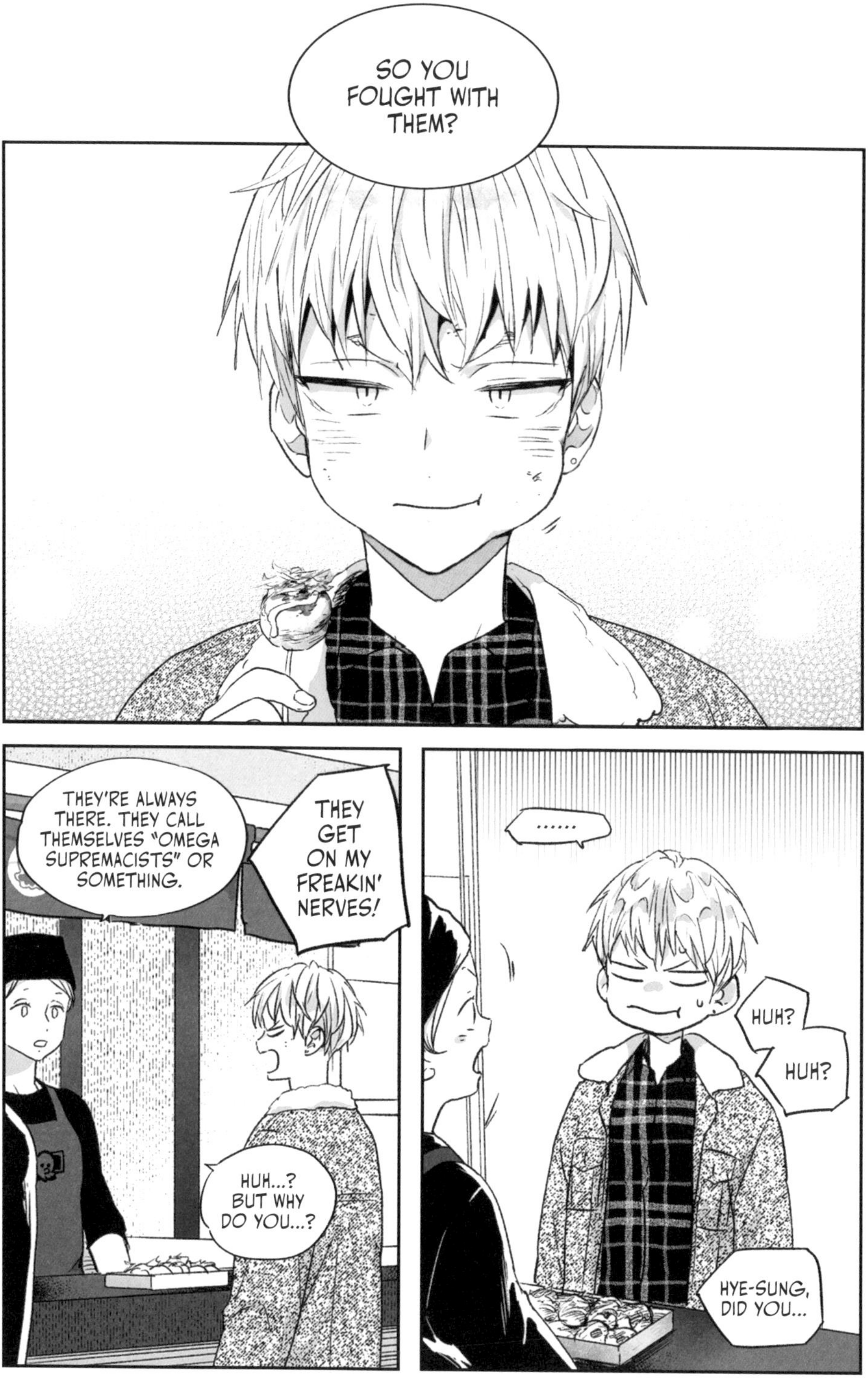
SO YOU FOUGHT WITH THEM?
THEY'RE ALWAYS THERE. THEY CALL THEMSELVES "OMEGA SUPREMACISTS" OR SOMETHING.
THEY GET ON MY FREAKIN' NERVES!
HUH...? BUT WHY DO YOU...?
......
HUH?
HUH?
HYE-SUNG, DID YOU...

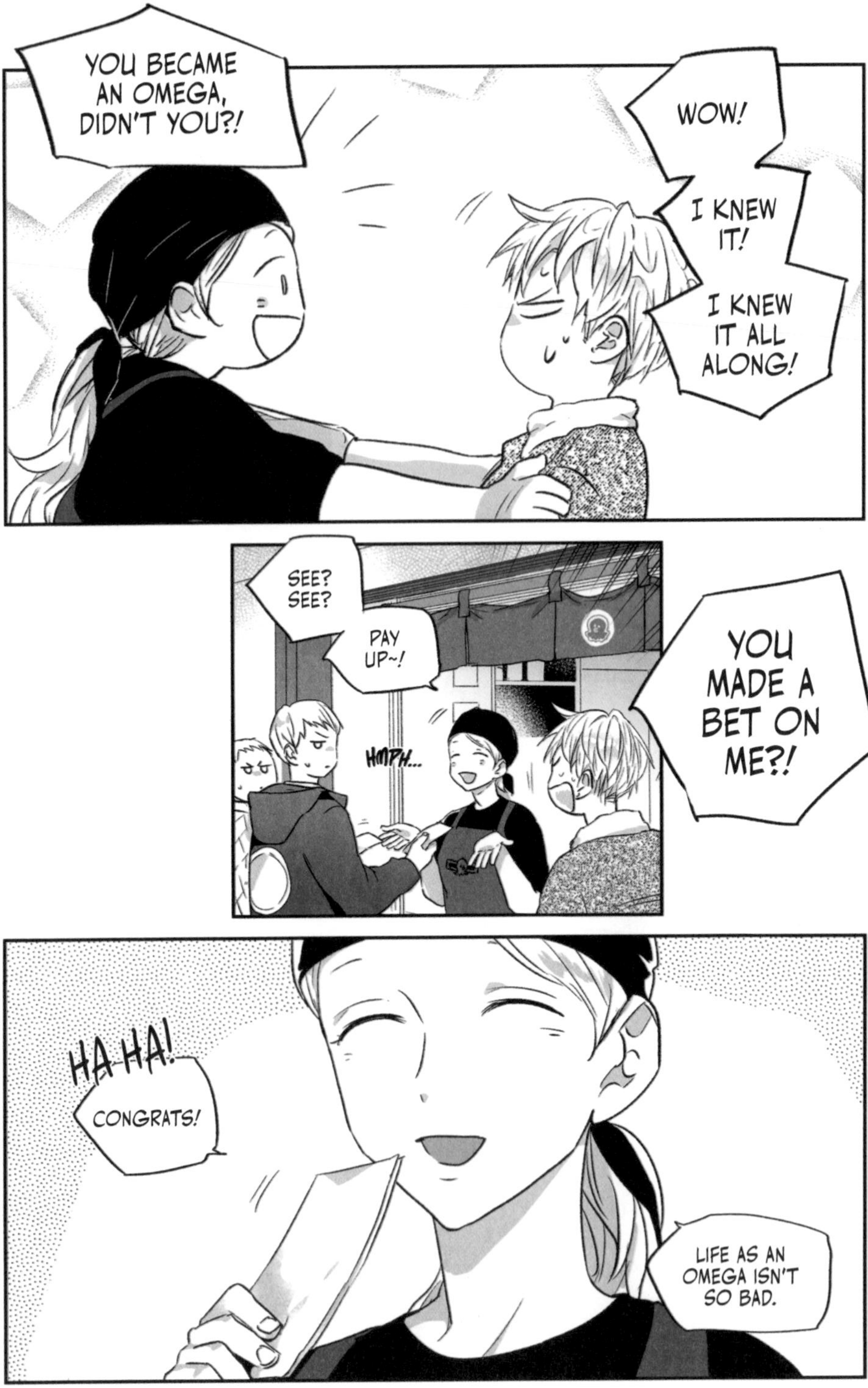
YOU BECAME AN OMEGA, DIDN'T YOU?!
WOW!
I KNEW IT!
I KNEW IT ALL ALONG!
SEE? SEE?
PAY UP~!
HMPH...
YOU MADE A BET ON ME?!
HA HA!
CONGRATS!
LIFE AS AN OMEGA ISN'T SO BAD.

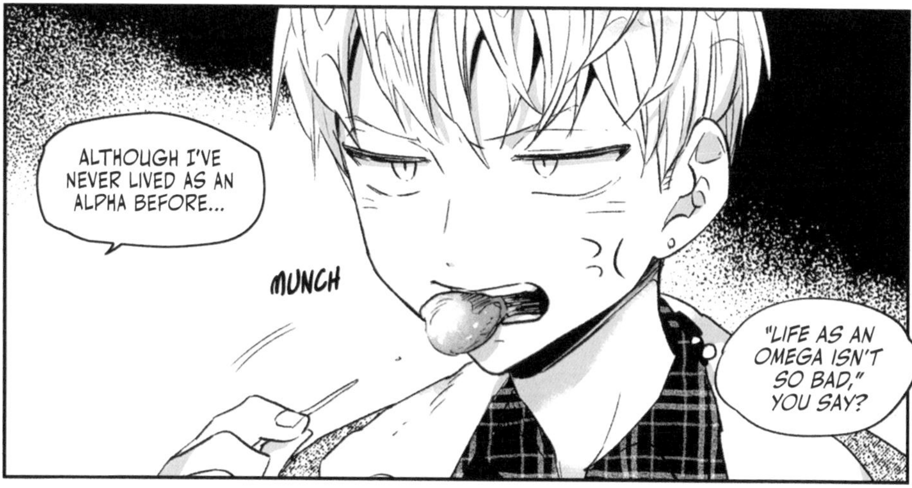
ALTHOUGH I'VE NEVER LIVED AS AN ALPHA BEFORE...
MUNCH
"LIFE AS AN OMEGA ISN'T SO BAD," YOU SAY?
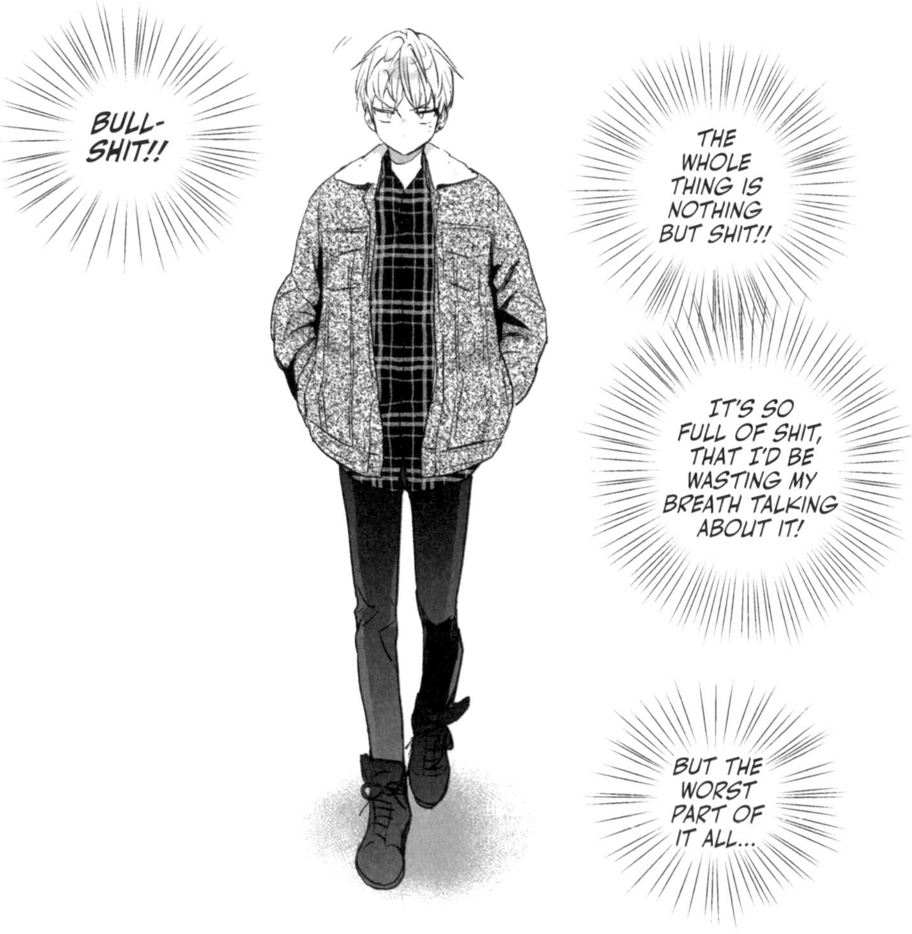
BULL-SHIT!!
THE WHOLE THING IS NOTHING BUT SHIT!!
IT'S SO FULL OF SHIT, THAT I'D BE WASTING MY BREATH TALKING ABOUT IT!
BUT THE WORST PART OF IT ALL...

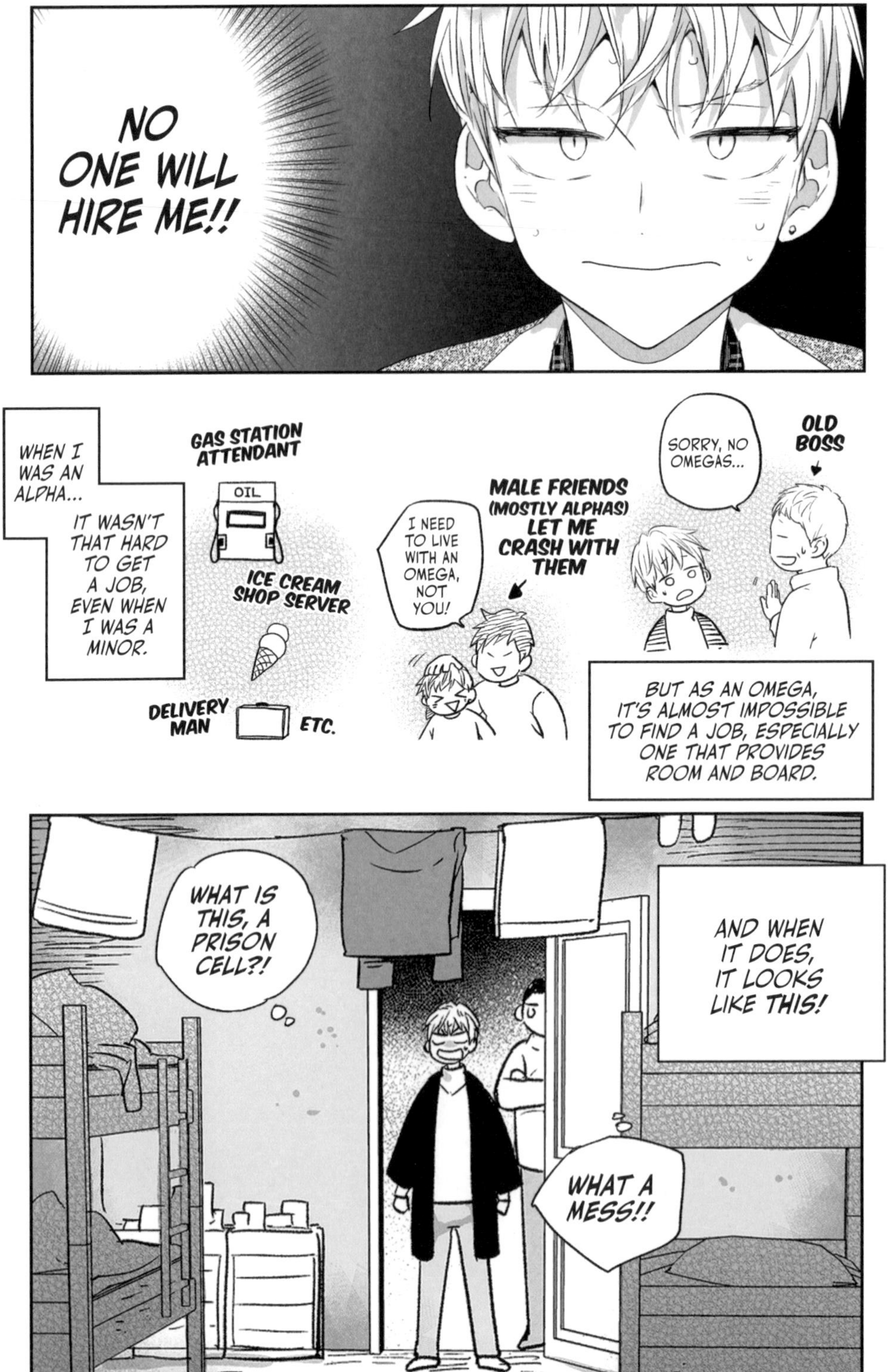
NO ONE WILL HIRE ME!!
WHEN I WAS AN ALPHA...
IT WASN'T THAT HARD TO GET A JOB, EVEN WHEN I WAS A MINOR.
GAS STATION ATTENDANT
OIL
ICE CREAM SHOP SERVER
DELIVERY MAN
ETC.
MALE FRIENDS (MOSTLY ALPHAS) LET ME CRASH WITH THEM
I NEED TO LIVE WITH AN OMEGA, NOT YOU!
SORRY, NO OMEGAS...
OLD BOSS
BUT AS AN OMEGA, IT'S ALMOST IMPOSSIBLE TO FIND A JOB, ESPECIALLY ONE THAT PROVIDES ROOM AND BOARD.
AND WHEN IT DOES, IT LOOKS LIKE THIS!
WHAT IS THIS, A PRISON CELL?!
WHAT A MESS!!

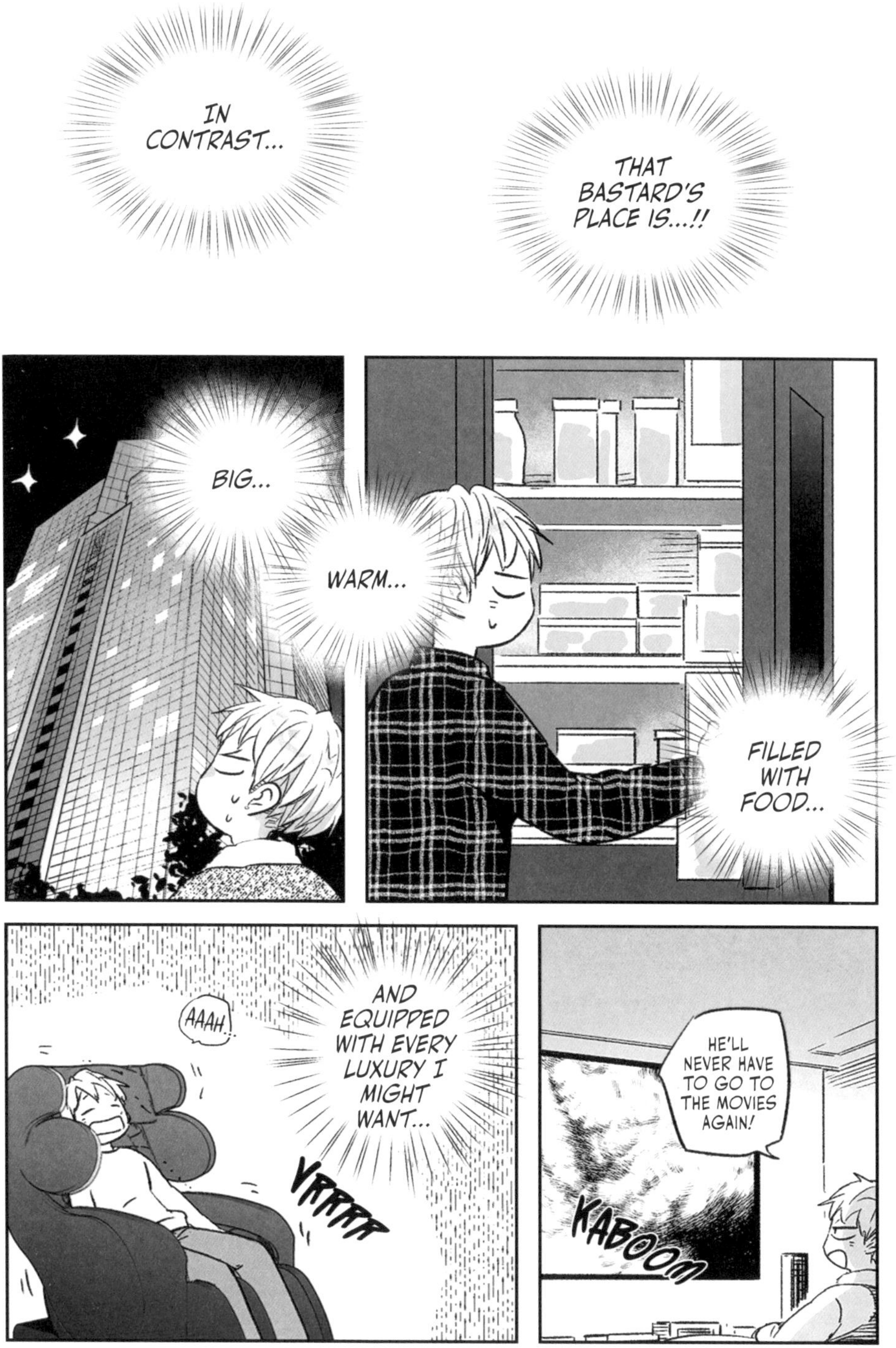
IN CONTRAST...
THAT BASTARD'S PLACE IS...!!
BIG...
WARM...
FILLED WITH FOOD...
AAAH...
AND EQUIPPED WITH EVERY LUXURY I MIGHT WANT...
VRRRRR
HE'LL NEVER HAVE TO GO TO THE MOVIES AGAIN!
KABOOM

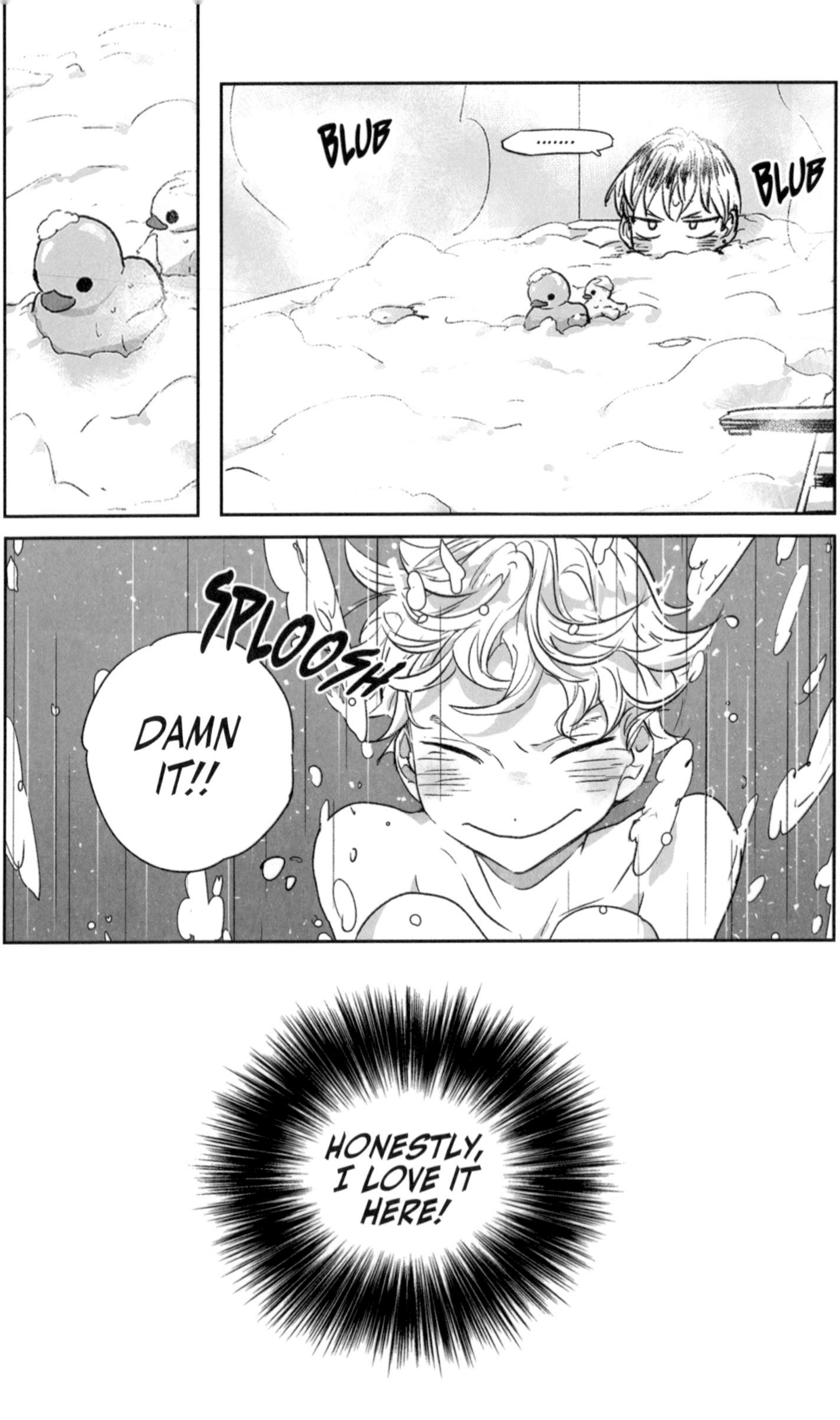
BLUB
......
BLUB
SPLOOSH
DAMN IT!!
HONESTLY, I LOVE IT HERE!

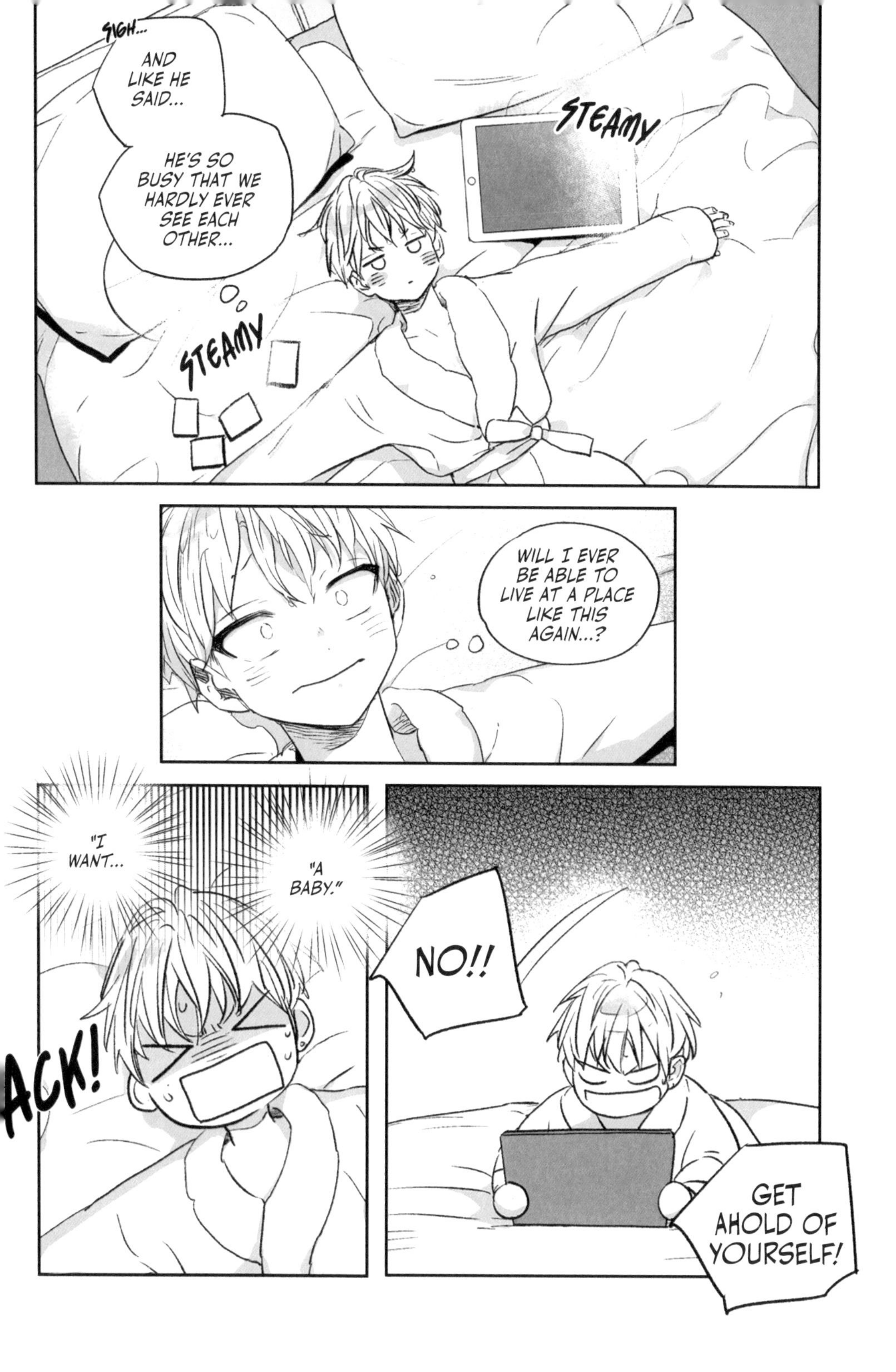
SIGH...
AND LIKE HE SAID...
HE'S SO BUSY THAT WE HARDLY EVER SEE EACH OTHER...
STEAMY
STEAMY
WILL I EVER BE ABLE TO LIVE AT A PLACE LIKE THIS AGAIN...?
"I WANT...
"A BABY."
ACK!
NO!!
GET AHOLD OF YOURSELF!

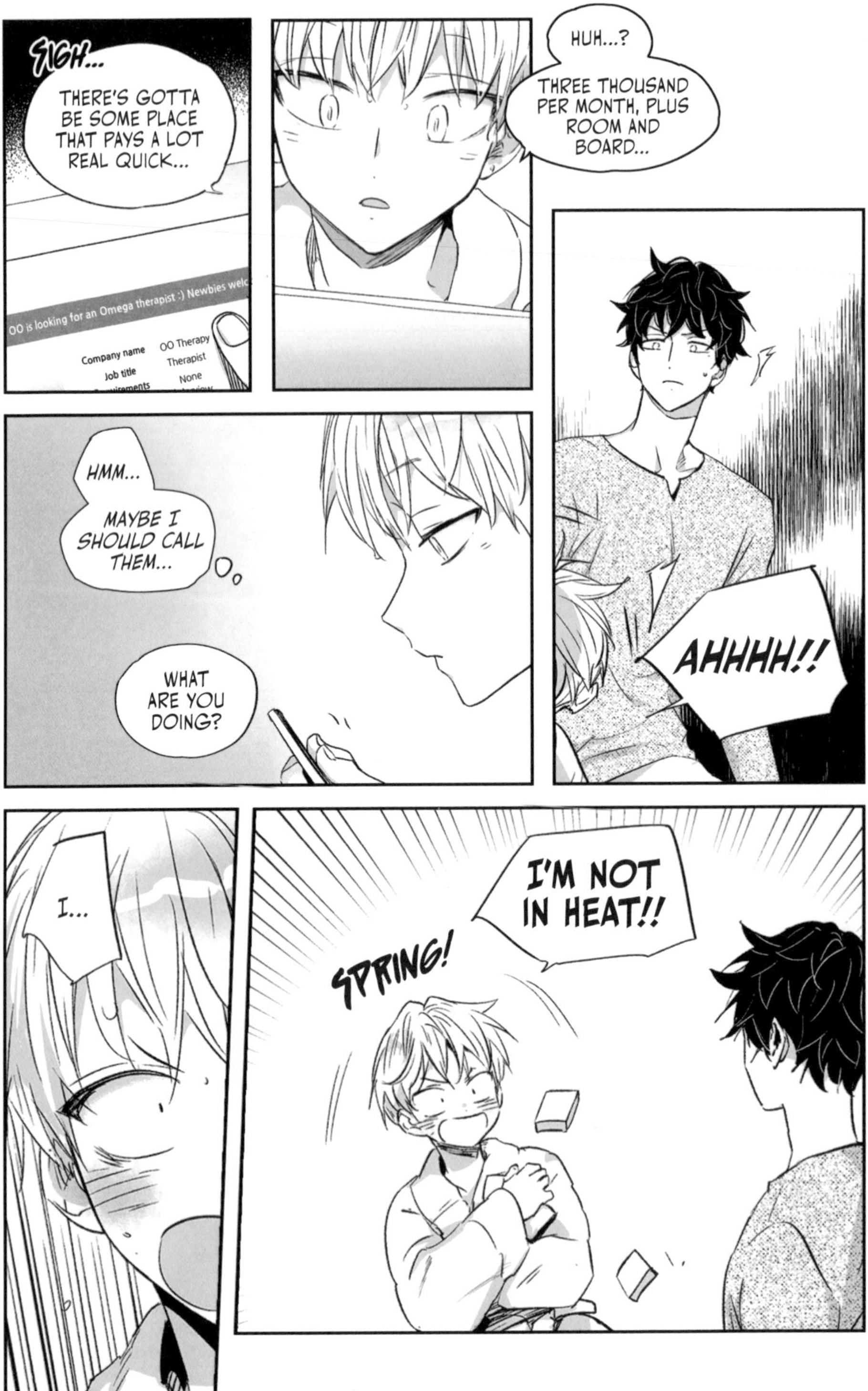
SIGH...
THERE'S GOTTA BE SOME PLACE THAT PAYS A LOT REAL QUICK...
OO is looking for an Omega therapist :) Newbies welc
Company name OO Therapy
Job title Therapist
None
HUH...?
THREE THOUSAND PER MONTH, PLUS ROOM AND BOARD...
HMM...
MAYBE I SHOULD CALL THEM...
WHAT ARE YOU DOING?
AHHHH!!
I...
SPRING!
I'M NOT IN HEAT!!

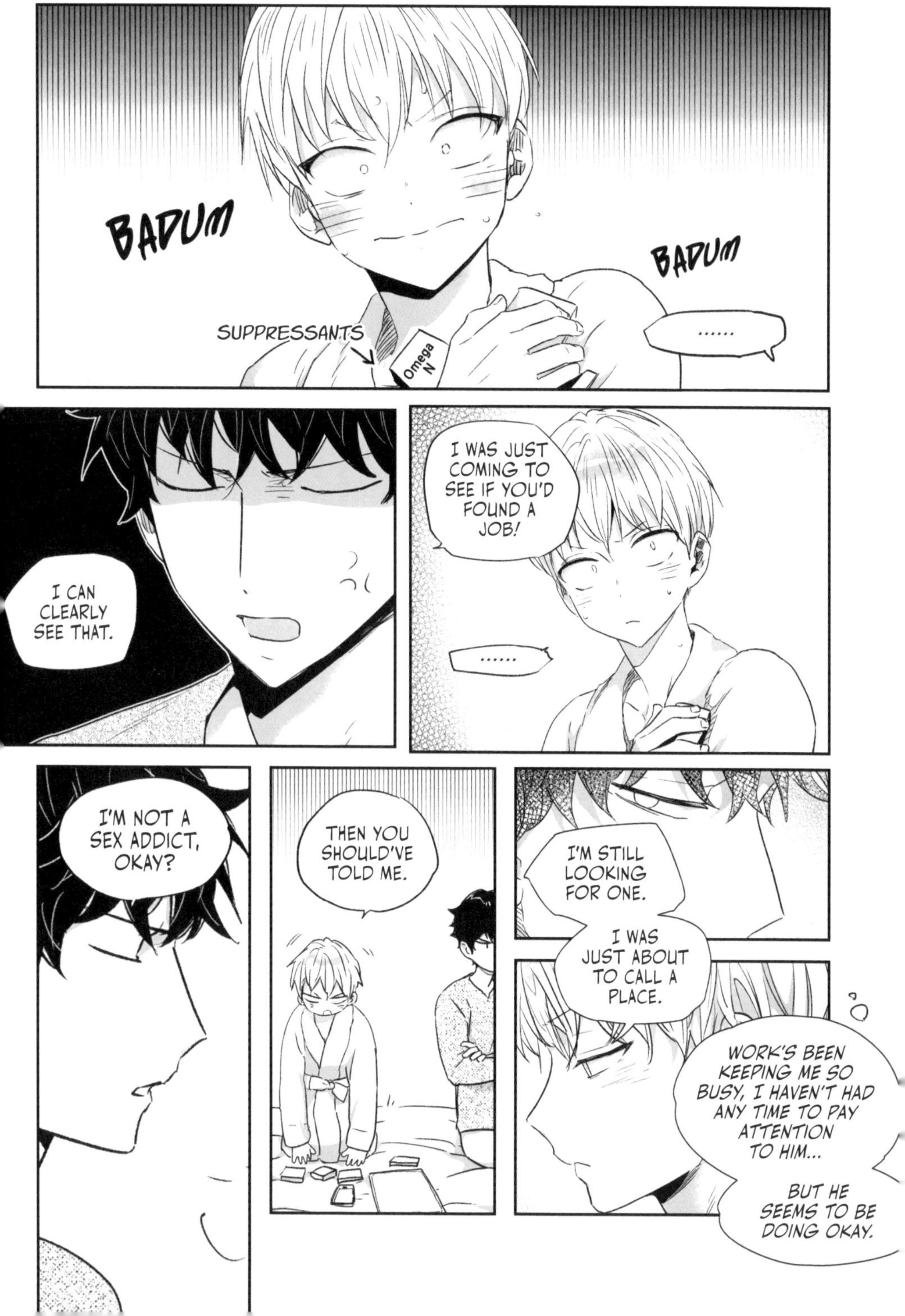
BADUM
BADUM
SUPPRESSANTS
Omega N
......
I CAN CLEARLY SEE THAT.
I WAS JUST COMING TO SEE IF YOU'D FOUND A JOB!
......
I'M NOT A SEX ADDICT, OKAY?
THEN YOU SHOULD'VE TOLD ME.
I'M STILL LOOKING FOR ONE.
I WAS JUST ABOUT TO CALL A PLACE.
WORK'S BEEN KEEPING ME SO BUSY, I HAVEN'T HAD ANY TIME TO PAY ATTENTION TO HIM...
BUT HE SEEMS TO BE DOING OKAY.

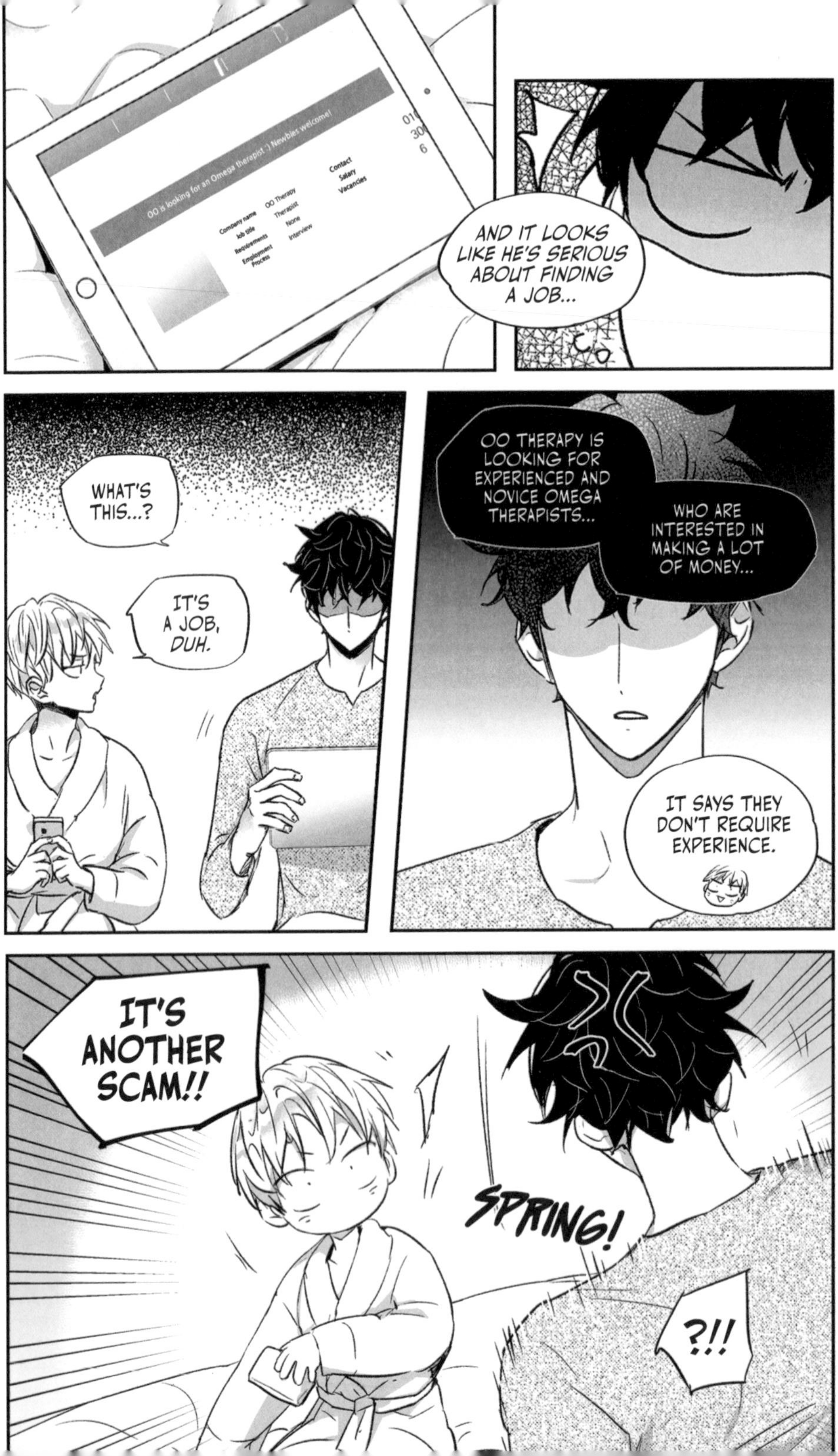
OO is looking for an Omega therapist :) Newbies welcome!
Company name OO Therapy
Job title Therapist
Requirements None
Employment Process Interview
Contact
Salary
Vacancies
AND IT LOOKS LIKE HE'S SERIOUS ABOUT FINDING A JOB...
WHAT'S THIS...?
IT'S A JOB, DUH.
OO THERAPY IS LOOKING FOR EXPERIENCED AND NOVICE OMEGA THERAPISTS...
WHO ARE INTERESTED IN MAKING A LOT OF MONEY...
IT SAYS THEY DON'T REQUIRE EXPERIENCE.
IT'S ANOTHER SCAM!!
SPRING!
?!!

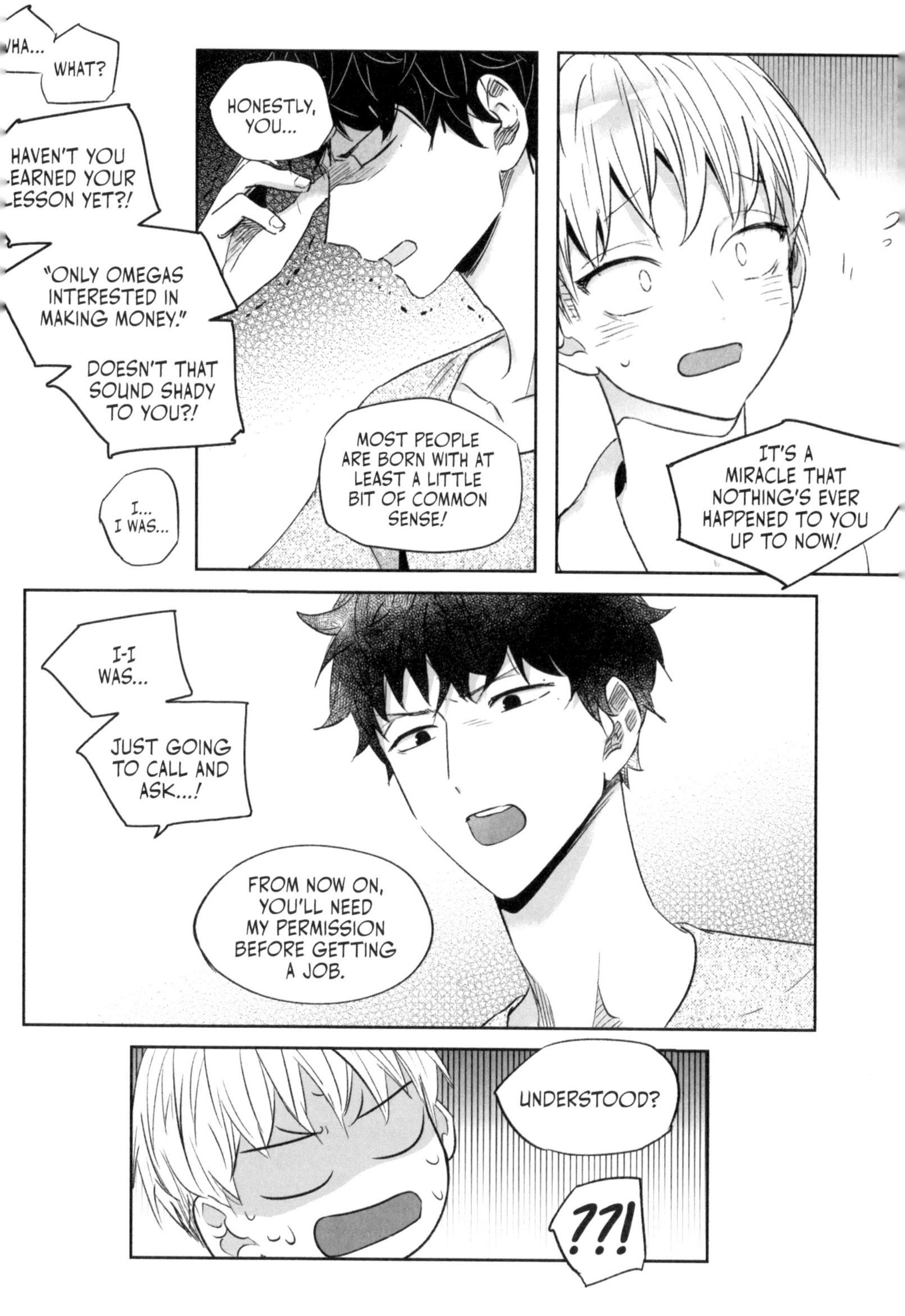
WHA... WHAT?
HAVEN'T YOU LEARNED YOUR LESSON YET?!
"ONLY OMEGAS INTERESTED IN MAKING MONEY."
DOESN'T THAT SOUND SHADY TO YOU?!
I... I WAS...
HONESTLY, YOU...
MOST PEOPLE ARE BORN WITH AT LEAST A LITTLE BIT OF COMMON SENSE!
IT'S A MIRACLE THAT NOTHING'S EVER HAPPENED TO YOU UP TO NOW!
I-I WAS...
JUST GOING TO CALL AND ASK...!
FROM NOW ON, YOU'LL NEED MY PERMISSION BEFORE GETTING A JOB.
UNDERSTOOD?
??!

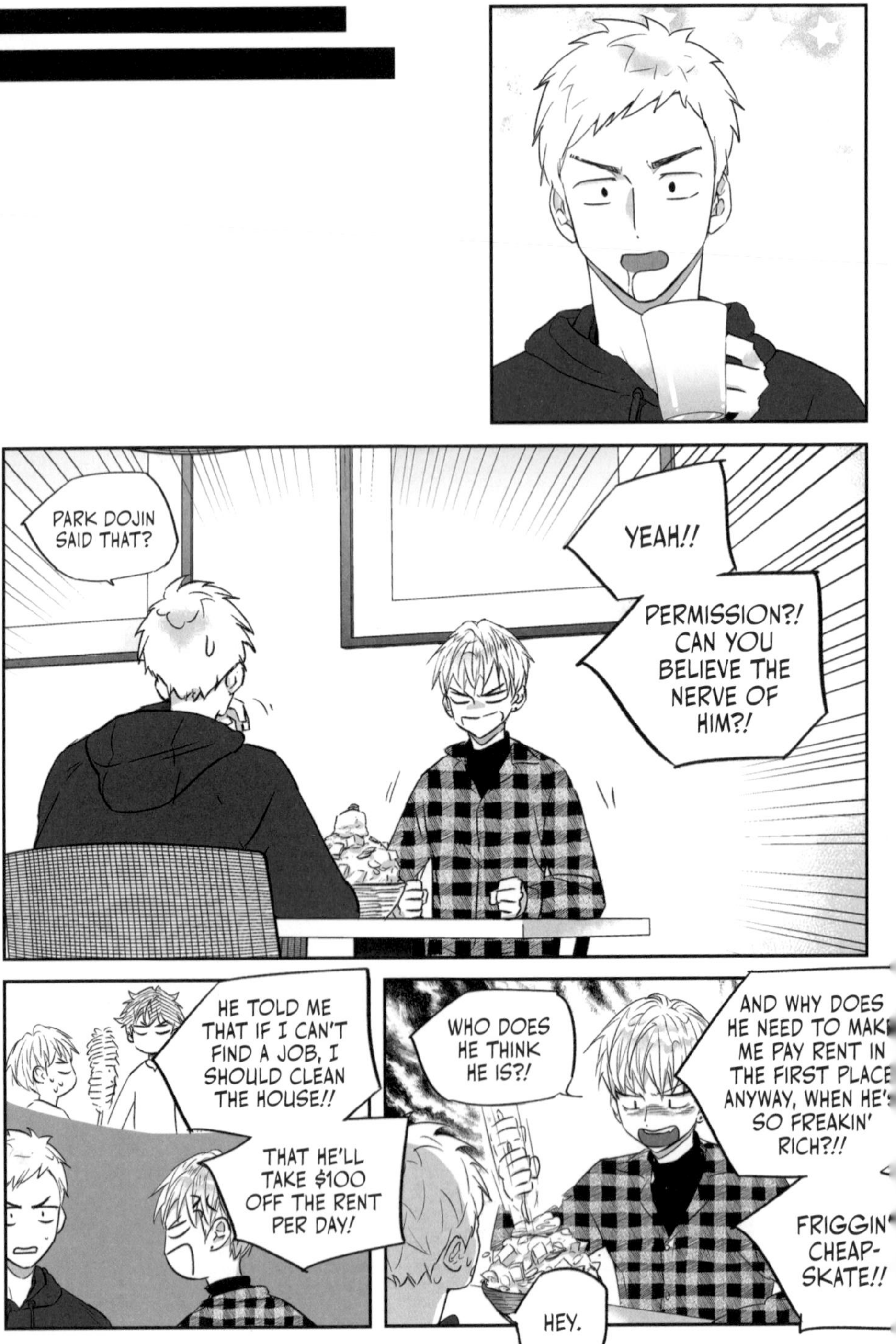
PARK DOJIN SAID THAT?
YEAH!!
PERMISSION?! CAN YOU BELIEVE THE NERVE OF HIM?!
HE TOLD ME THAT IF I CAN'T FIND A JOB, I SHOULD CLEAN THE HOUSE!!
THAT HE'LL TAKE $100 OFF THE RENT PER DAY!
WHO DOES HE THINK HE IS?!
AND WHY DOES HE NEED TO MAKE ME PAY RENT IN THE FIRST PLACE ANYWAY, WHEN HE'S SO FREAKIN' RICH?!!
FRIGGIN' CHEAP-SKATE!!
HEY.

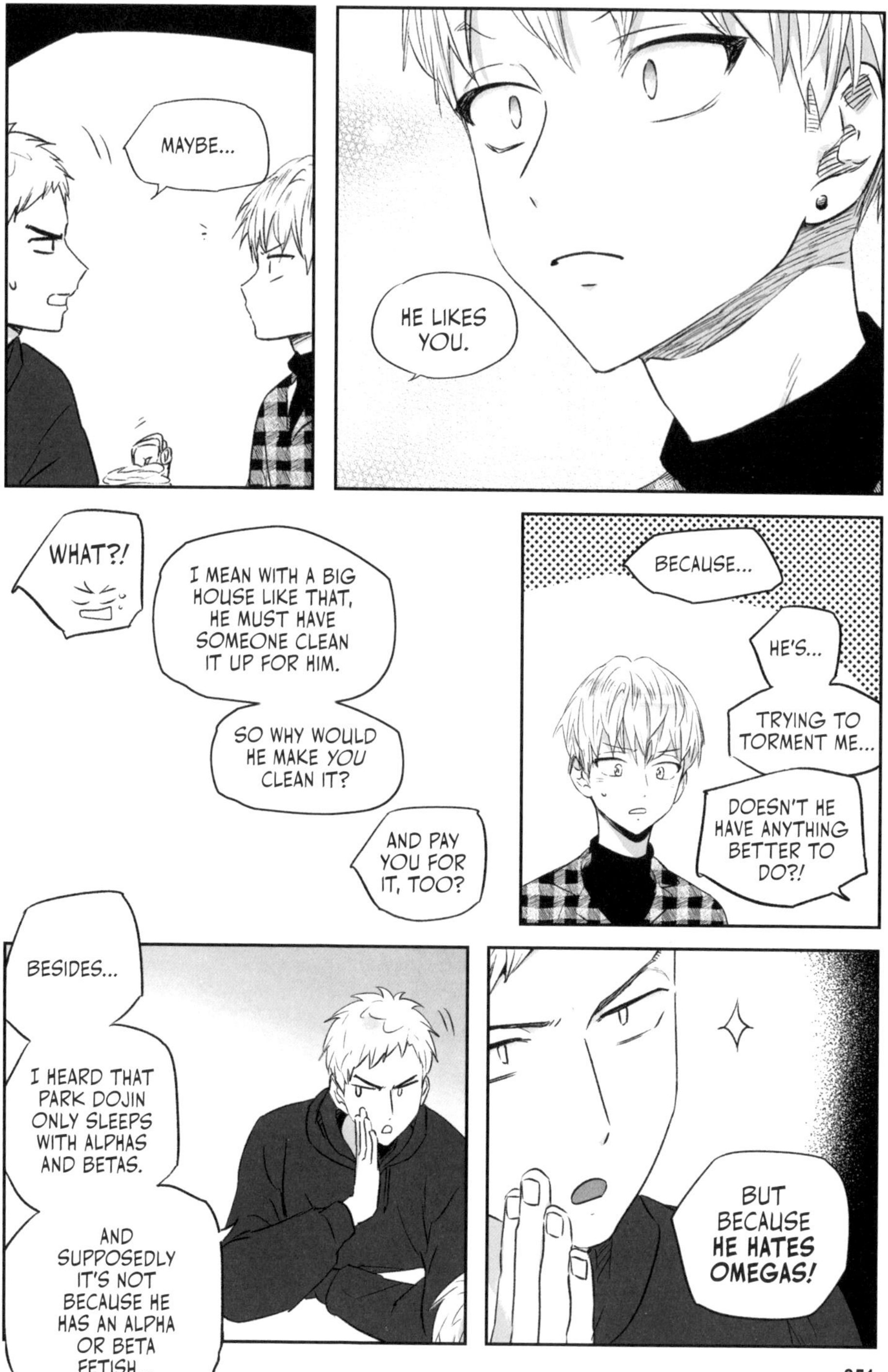
MAYBE...
HE LIKES YOU.
WHAT?!
I MEAN WITH A BIG HOUSE LIKE THAT, HE MUST HAVE SOMEONE CLEAN IT UP FOR HIM.
SO WHY WOULD HE MAKE *YOU* CLEAN IT?
AND PAY YOU FOR IT, TOO?
BECAUSE...
HE'S...
TRYING TO TORMENT ME...
DOESN'T HE HAVE ANYTHING BETTER TO DO?!
BESIDES...
I HEARD THAT PARK DOJIN ONLY SLEEPS WITH ALPHAS AND BETAS.
AND SUPPOSEDLY IT'S NOT BECAUSE HE HAS AN ALPHA OR BETA FETISH...
BUT BECAUSE **HE HATES OMEGAS!**

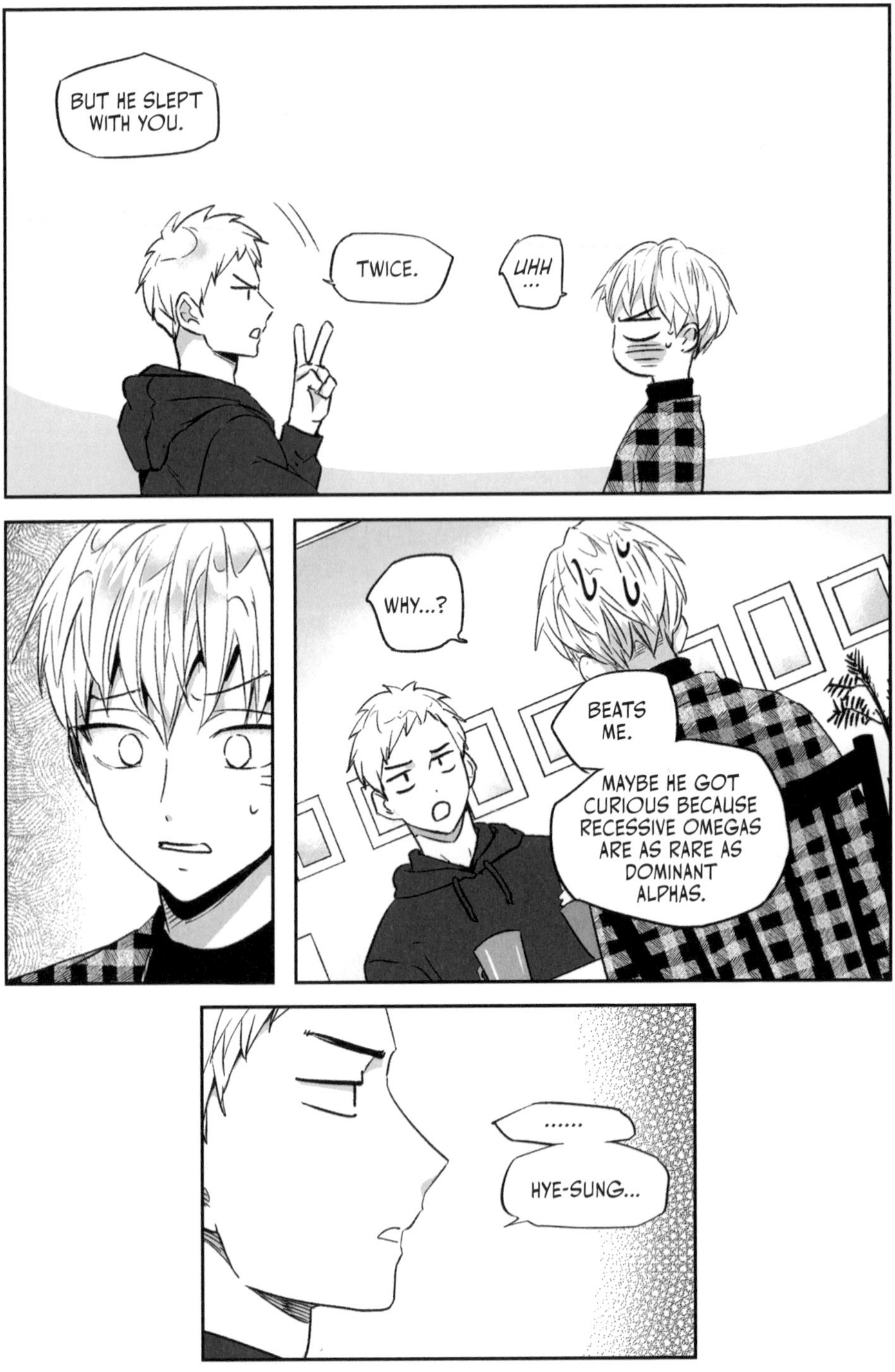
BUT HE SLEPT WITH YOU.
TWICE.
UHH ...
WHY...?
BEATS ME.
MAYBE HE GOT CURIOUS BECAUSE RECESSIVE OMEGAS ARE AS RARE AS DOMINANT ALPHAS.
......
HYE-SUNG...

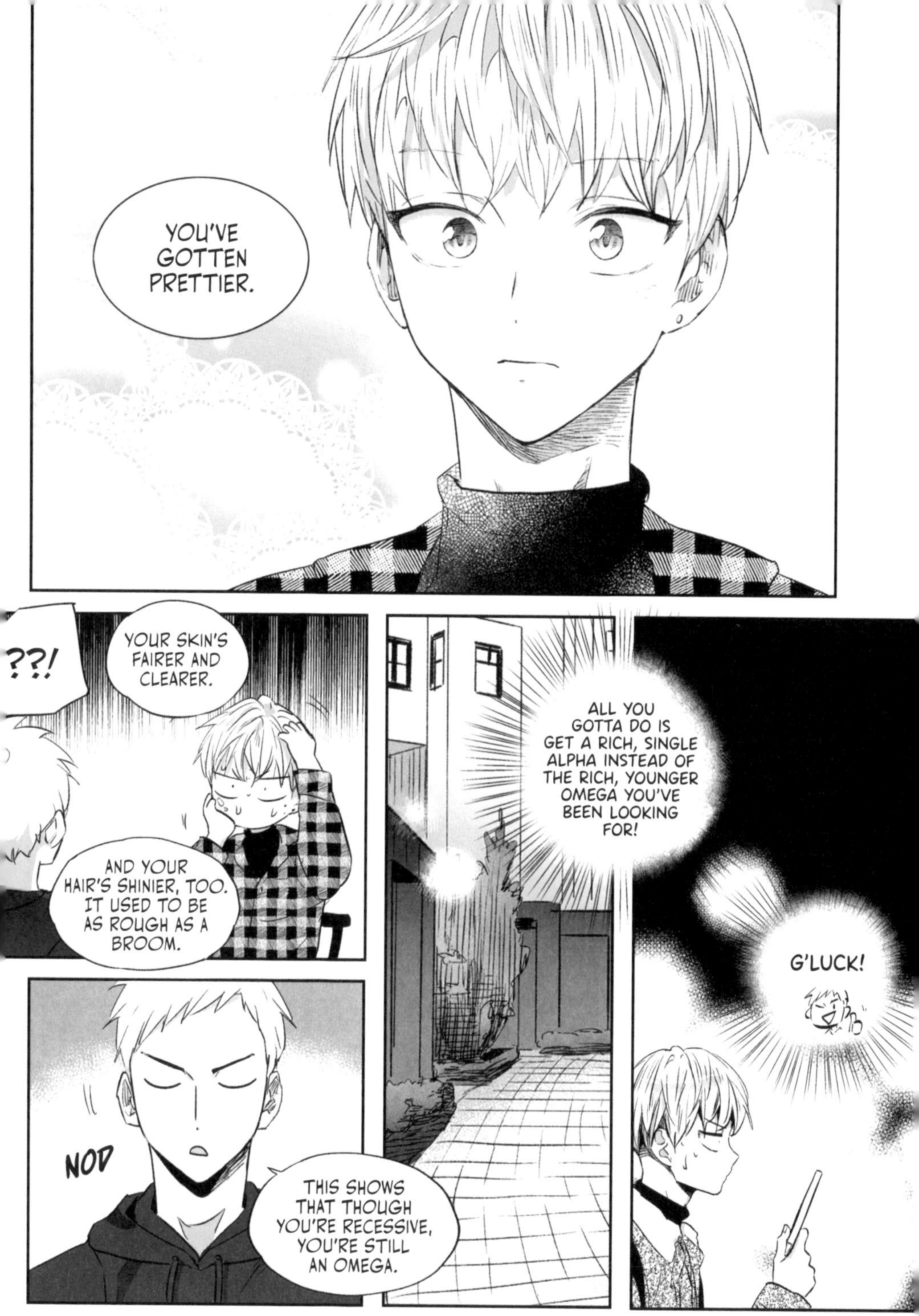
YOU'VE GOTTEN PRETTIER.
??!
YOUR SKIN'S FAIRER AND CLEARER.
AND YOUR HAIR'S SHINIER, TOO. IT USED TO BE AS ROUGH AS A BROOM.
NOD
THIS SHOWS THAT THOUGH YOU'RE RECESSIVE, YOU'RE STILL AN OMEGA.
ALL YOU GOTTA DO IS GET A RICH, SINGLE ALPHA INSTEAD OF THE RICH, YOUNGER OMEGA YOU'VE BEEN LOOKING FOR!
G'LUCK!

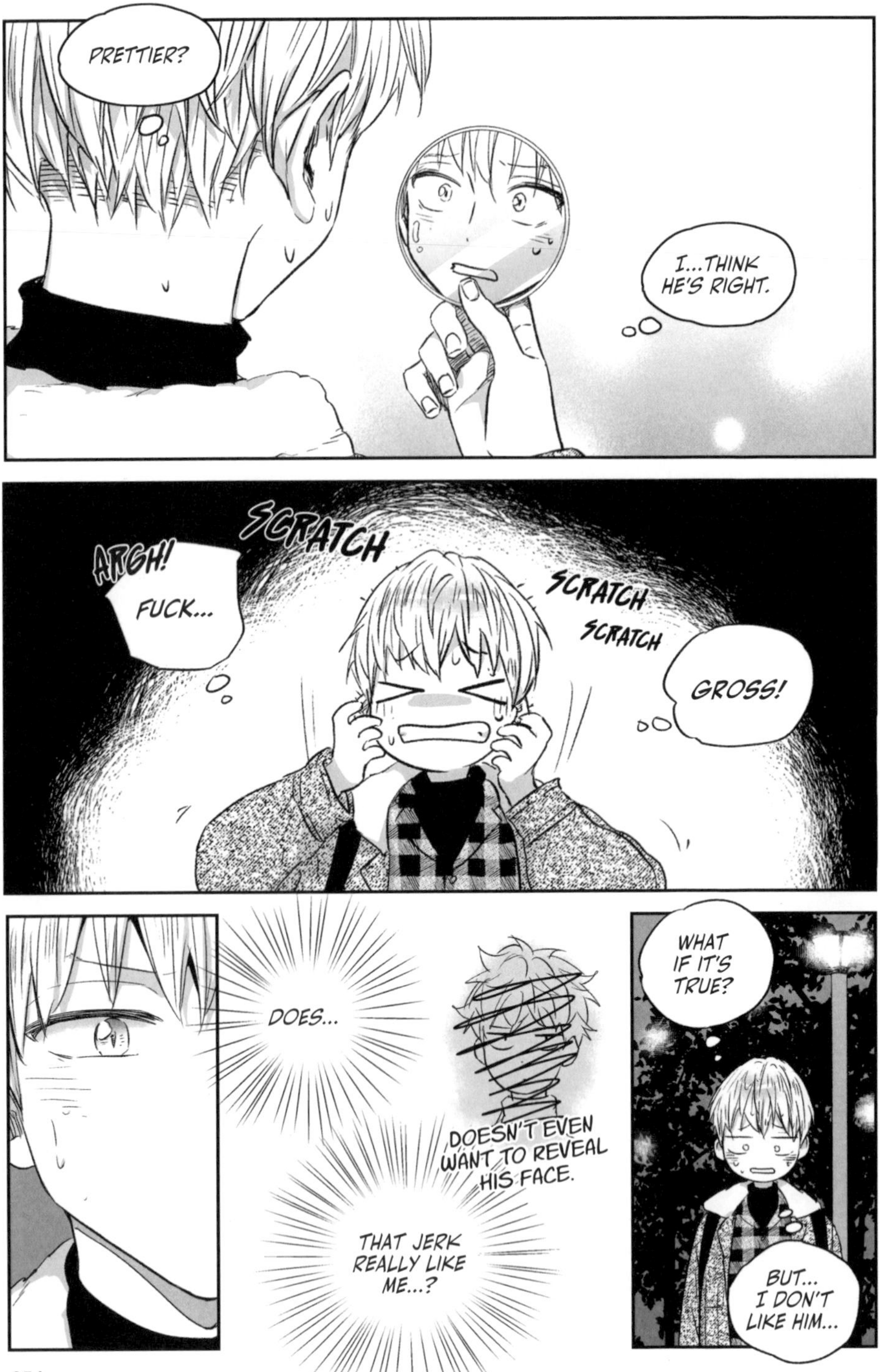
PRETTIER?
I...THINK HE'S RIGHT.
ARGH!
SCRATCH
FUCK...
SCRATCH
SCRATCH
GROSS!
DOES...
DOESN'T EVEN WANT TO REVEAL HIS FACE.
THAT JERK REALLY LIKE ME...?
WHAT IF IT'S TRUE?
BUT... I DON'T LIKE HIM...

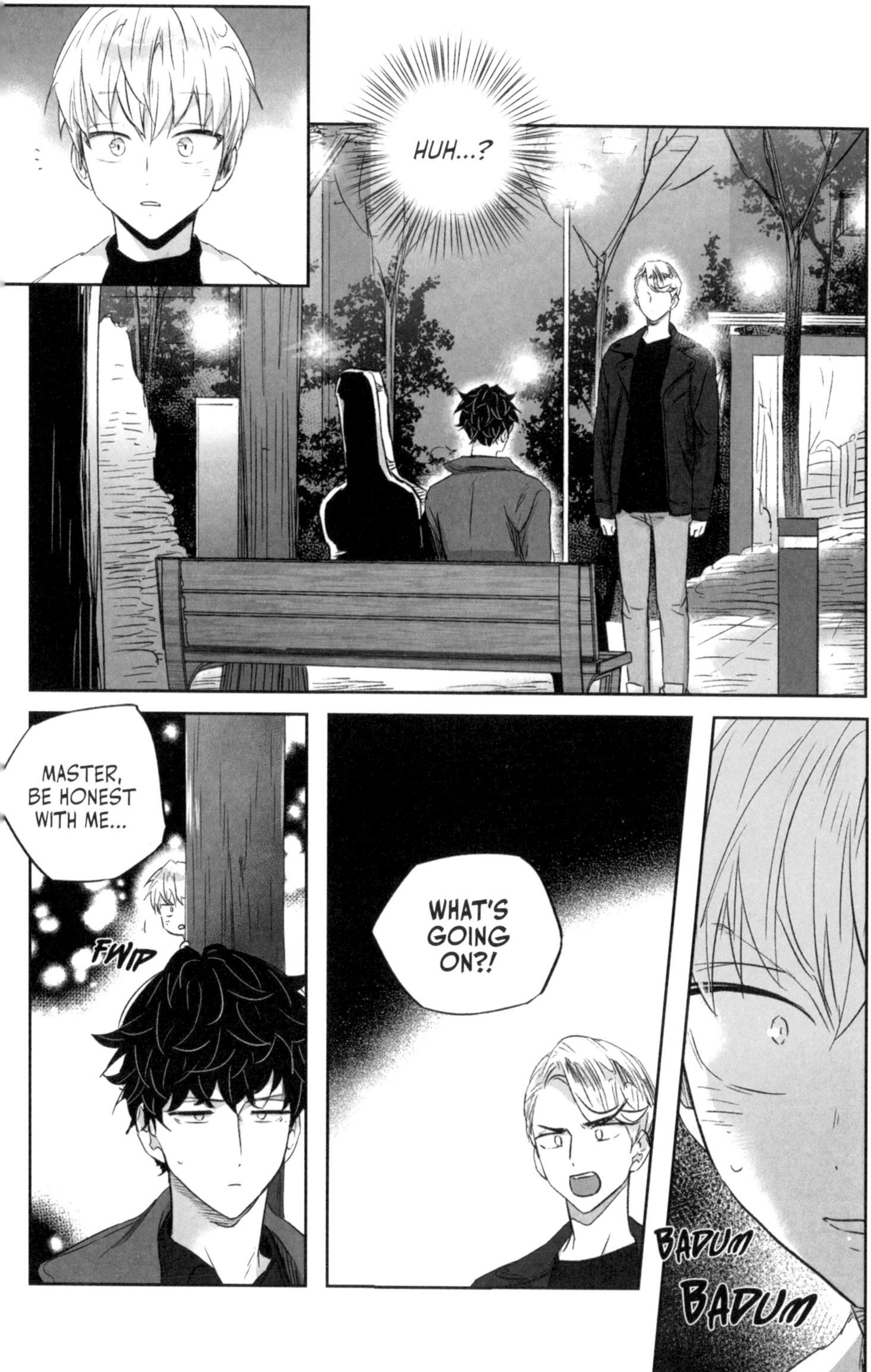
HUH...?
MASTER, BE HONEST WITH ME...
FWIP
WHAT'S GOING ON?!
BADUM
BADUM

Love is an Illusion!

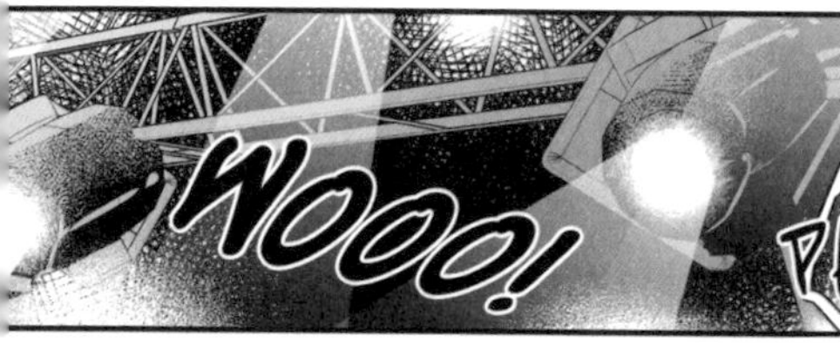
WOOO!
PANT

Chapter 13

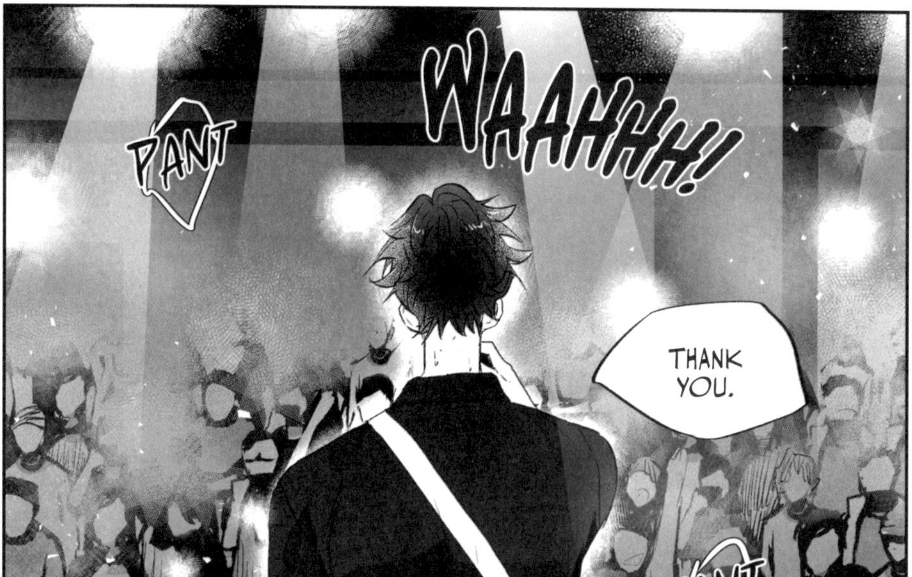
WAAHHH!
PANT
THANK YOU.
PANT

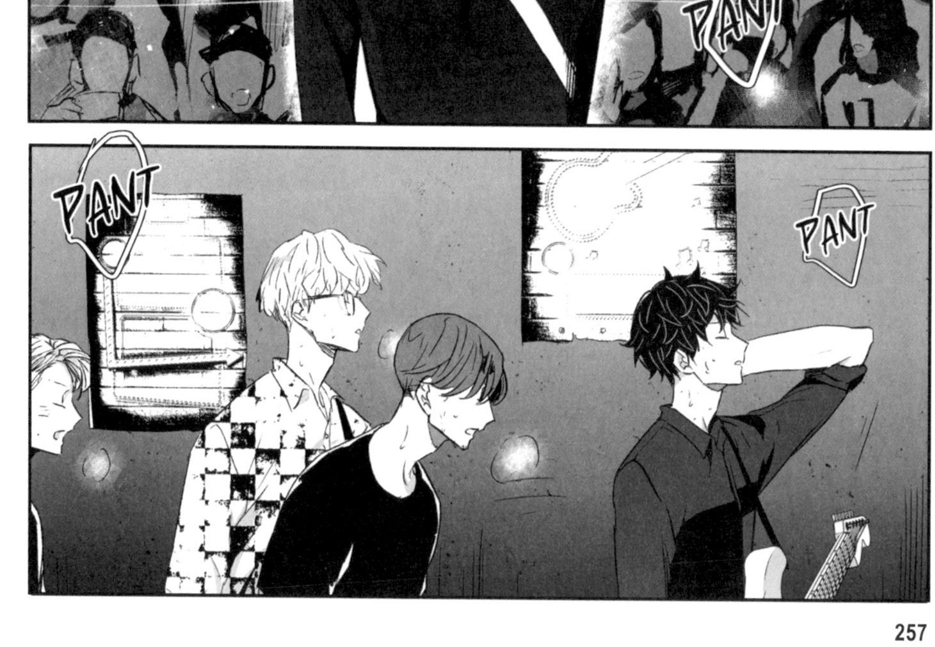
PANT
PANT

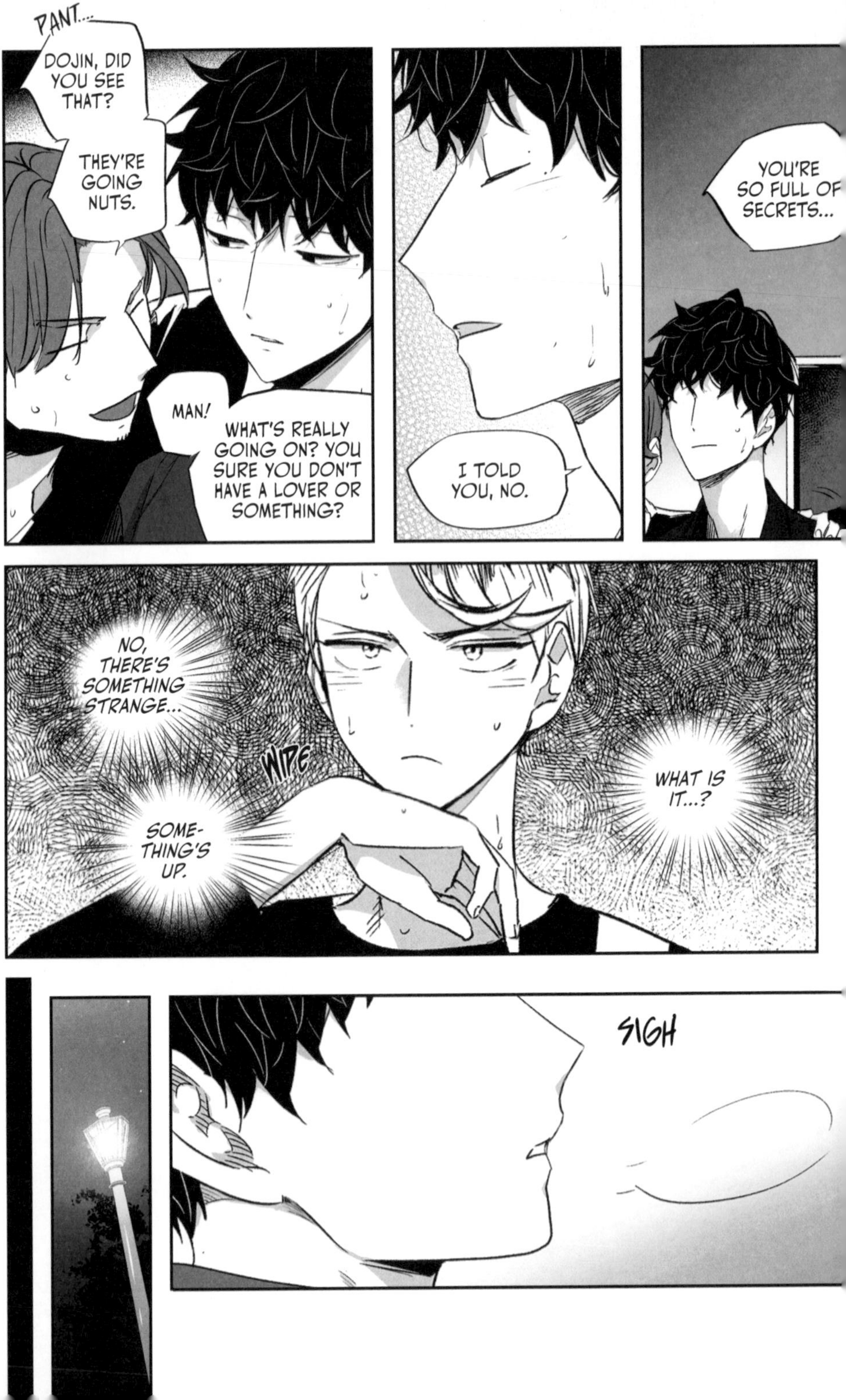
PANT...
DOJIN, DID YOU SEE THAT?
THEY'RE GOING NUTS.
MAN!
WHAT'S REALLY GOING ON? YOU SURE YOU DON'T HAVE A LOVER OR SOMETHING?
I TOLD YOU, NO.
YOU'RE SO FULL OF SECRETS...
NO, THERE'S SOMETHING STRANGE...
WIPE
SOME-THING'S UP.
WHAT IS IT...?
SIGH

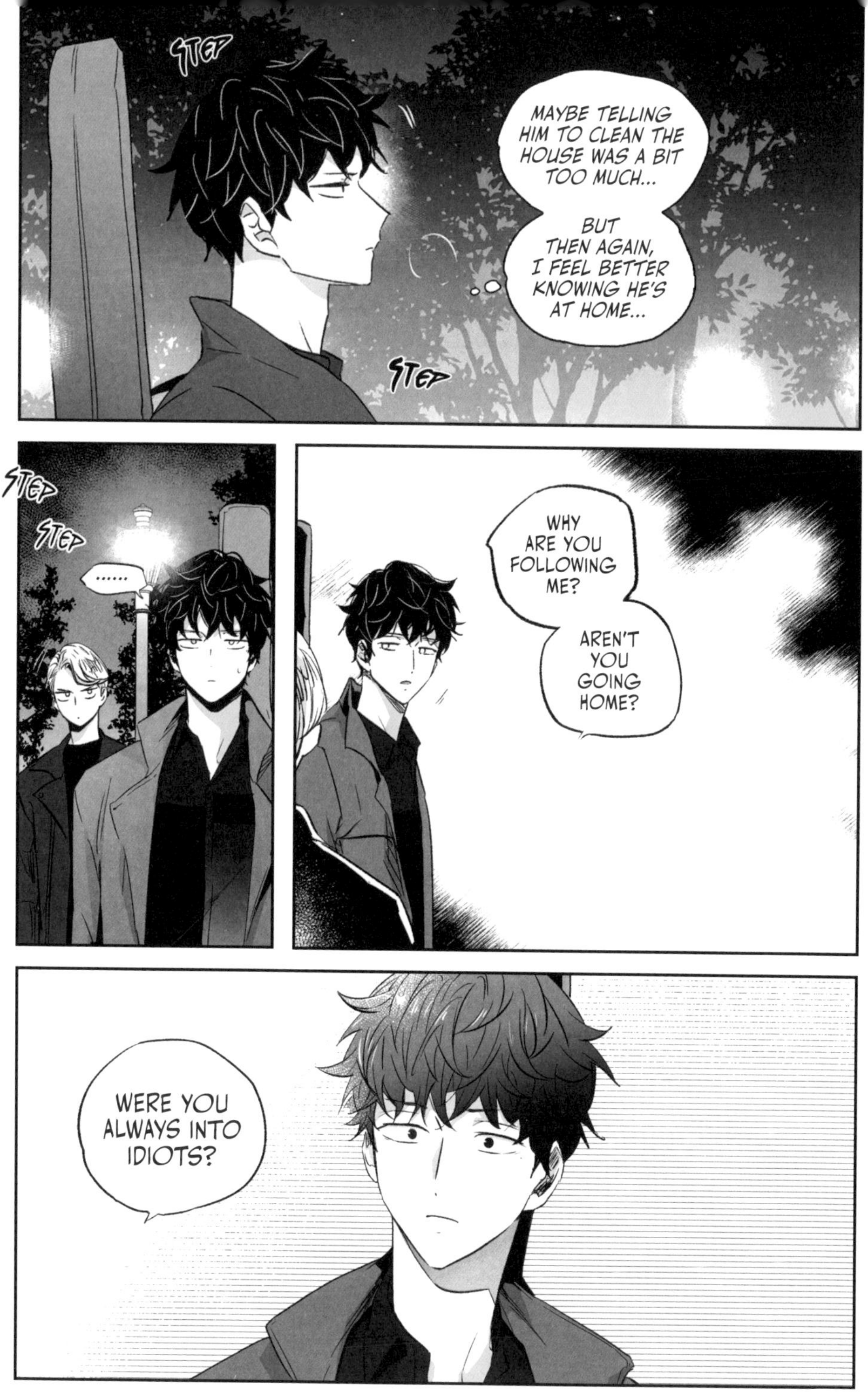
STEP
MAYBE TELLING HIM TO CLEAN THE HOUSE WAS A BIT TOO MUCH...
BUT THEN AGAIN, I FEEL BETTER KNOWING HE'S AT HOME...
STEP
STEP
STEP
......
WHY ARE YOU FOLLOWING ME?
AREN'T YOU GOING HOME?
WERE YOU ALWAYS INTO IDIOTS?

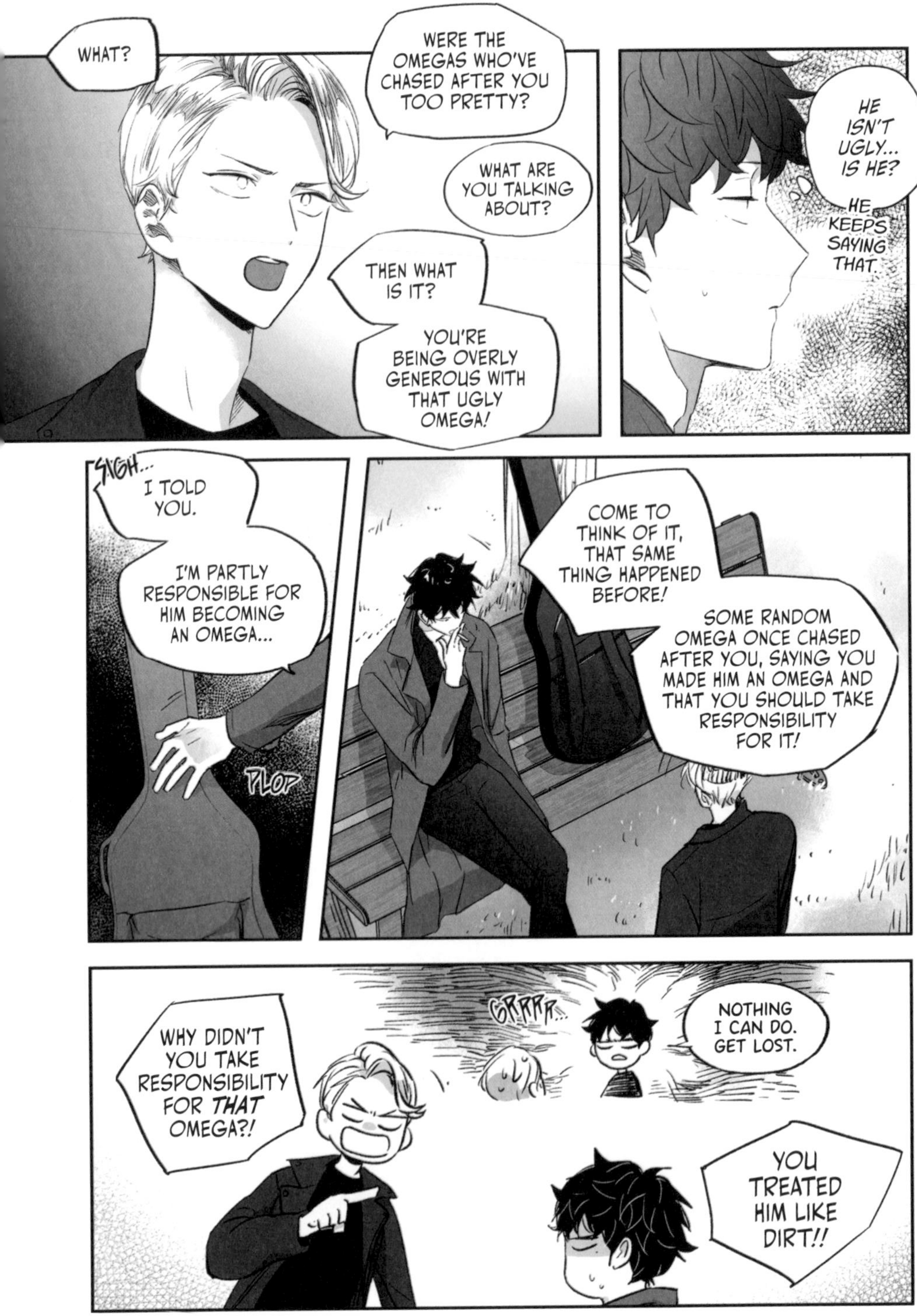
WHAT?
WERE THE OMEGAS WHO'VE CHASED AFTER YOU TOO PRETTY?
WHAT ARE YOU TALKING ABOUT?
THEN WHAT IS IT?
YOU'RE BEING OVERLY GENEROUS WITH THAT UGLY OMEGA!
HE ISN'T UGLY... IS HE?
HE KEEPS SAYING THAT.
SIGH...
I TOLD YOU.
I'M PARTLY RESPONSIBLE FOR HIM BECOMING AN OMEGA...
PLOP
COME TO THINK OF IT, THAT SAME THING HAPPENED BEFORE!
SOME RANDOM OMEGA ONCE CHASED AFTER YOU, SAYING YOU MADE HIM AN OMEGA AND THAT YOU SHOULD TAKE RESPONSIBILITY FOR IT!
WHY DIDN'T YOU TAKE RESPONSIBILITY FOR *THAT* OMEGA?!
GRRRR...
NOTHING I CAN DO. GET LOST.
YOU TREATED HIM LIKE DIRT!!

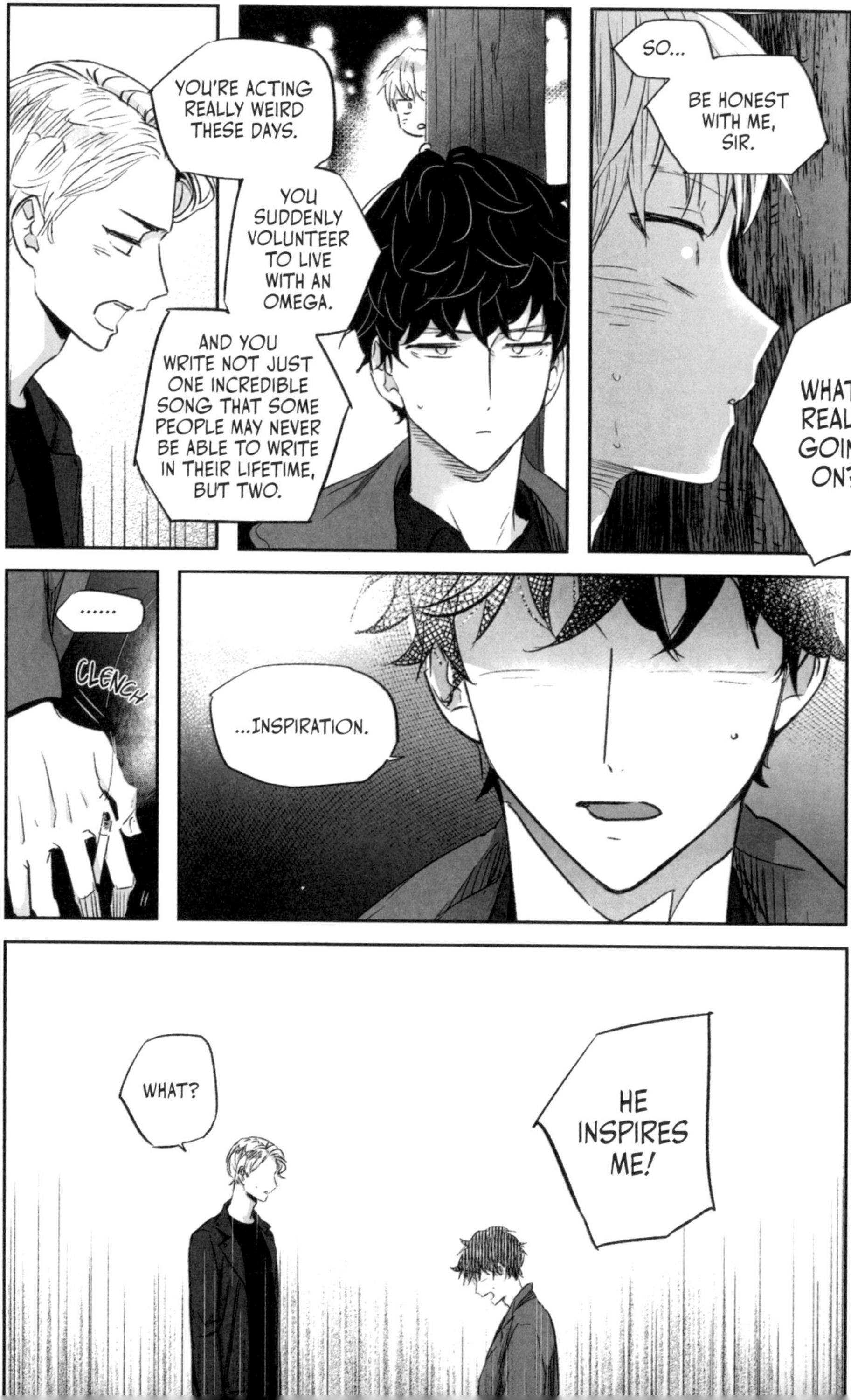
YOU'RE ACTING REALLY WEIRD THESE DAYS.
YOU SUDDENLY VOLUNTEER TO LIVE WITH AN OMEGA.
AND YOU WRITE NOT JUST ONE INCREDIBLE SONG THAT SOME PEOPLE MAY NEVER BE ABLE TO WRITE IN THEIR LIFETIME, BUT TWO.
SO...
BE HONEST WITH ME, SIR.
WHAT'S REALLY GOING ON?!
......
CLENCH
...INSPIRATION.
WHAT?
HE INSPIRES ME!

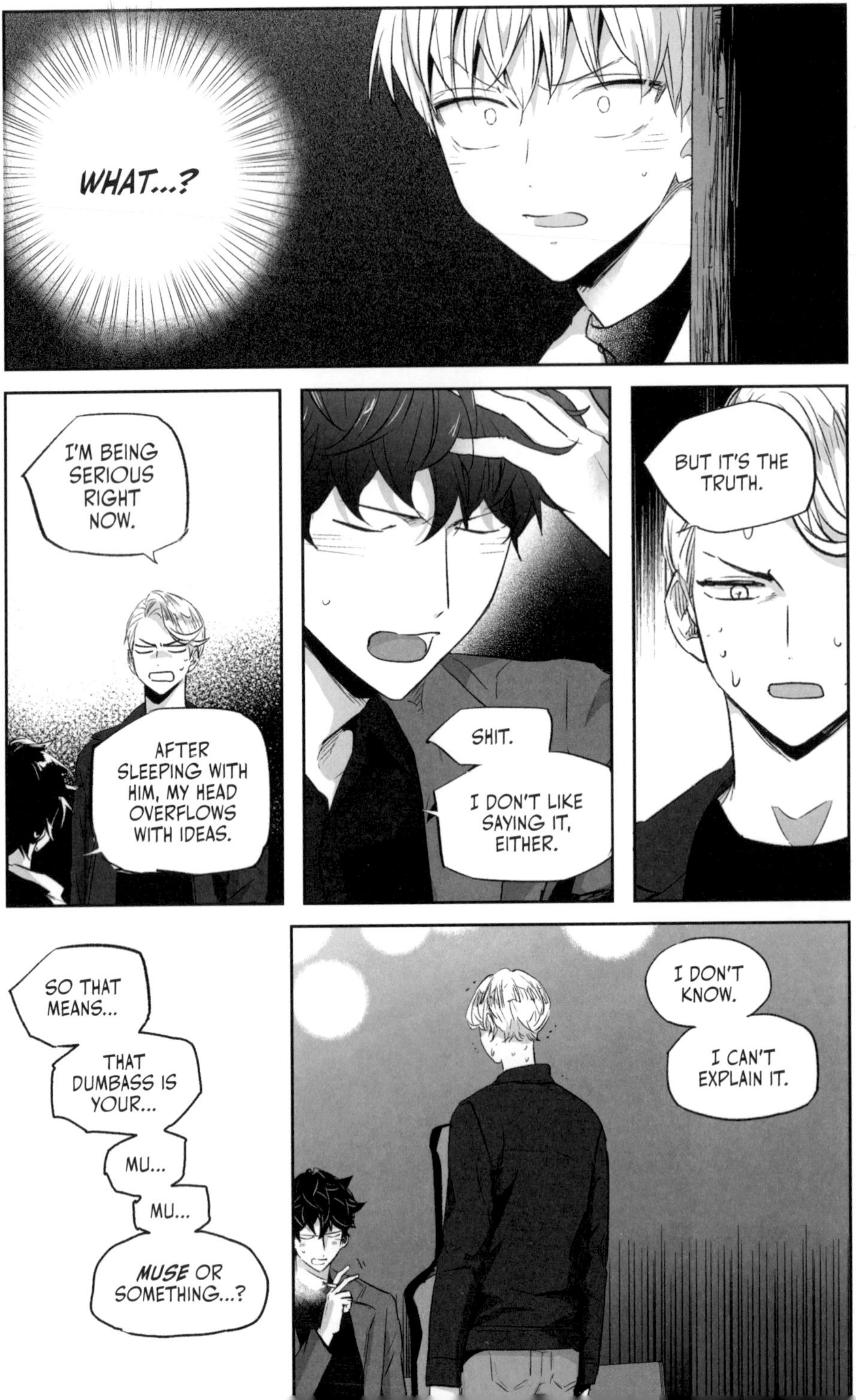
WHAT...?
I'M BEING SERIOUS RIGHT NOW.
AFTER SLEEPING WITH HIM, MY HEAD OVERFLOWS WITH IDEAS.
SHIT.
I DON'T LIKE SAYING IT, EITHER.
BUT IT'S THE TRUTH.
SO THAT MEANS...
THAT DUMBASS IS YOUR...
MU...
MU...
MUSE OR SOMETHING...?
I DON'T KNOW.
I CAN'T EXPLAIN IT.

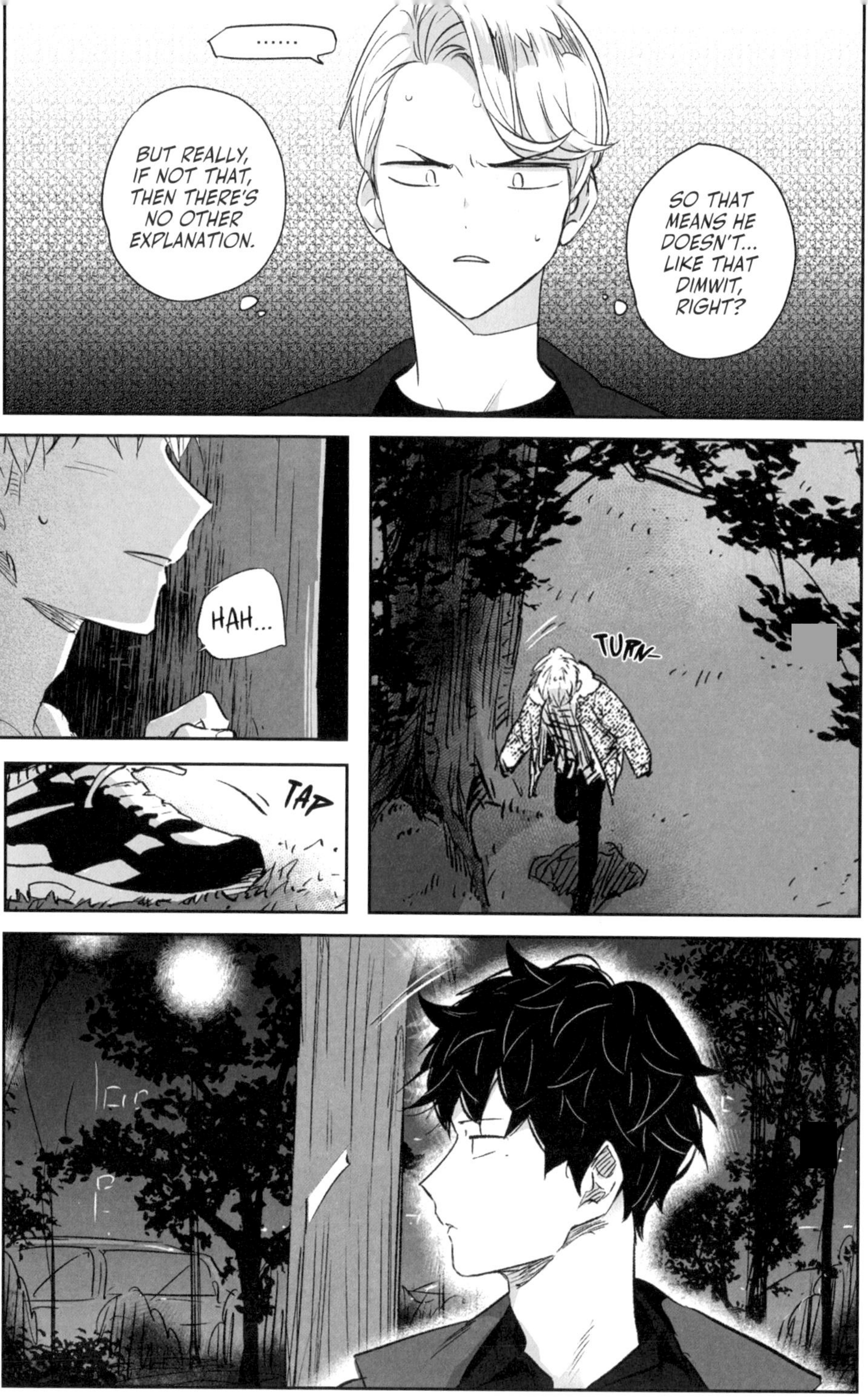
......
BUT REALLY, IF NOT THAT, THEN THERE'S NO OTHER EXPLANATION.
SO THAT MEANS HE DOESN'T... LIKE THAT DIMWIT, RIGHT?
HAH...
TAP
TURN-

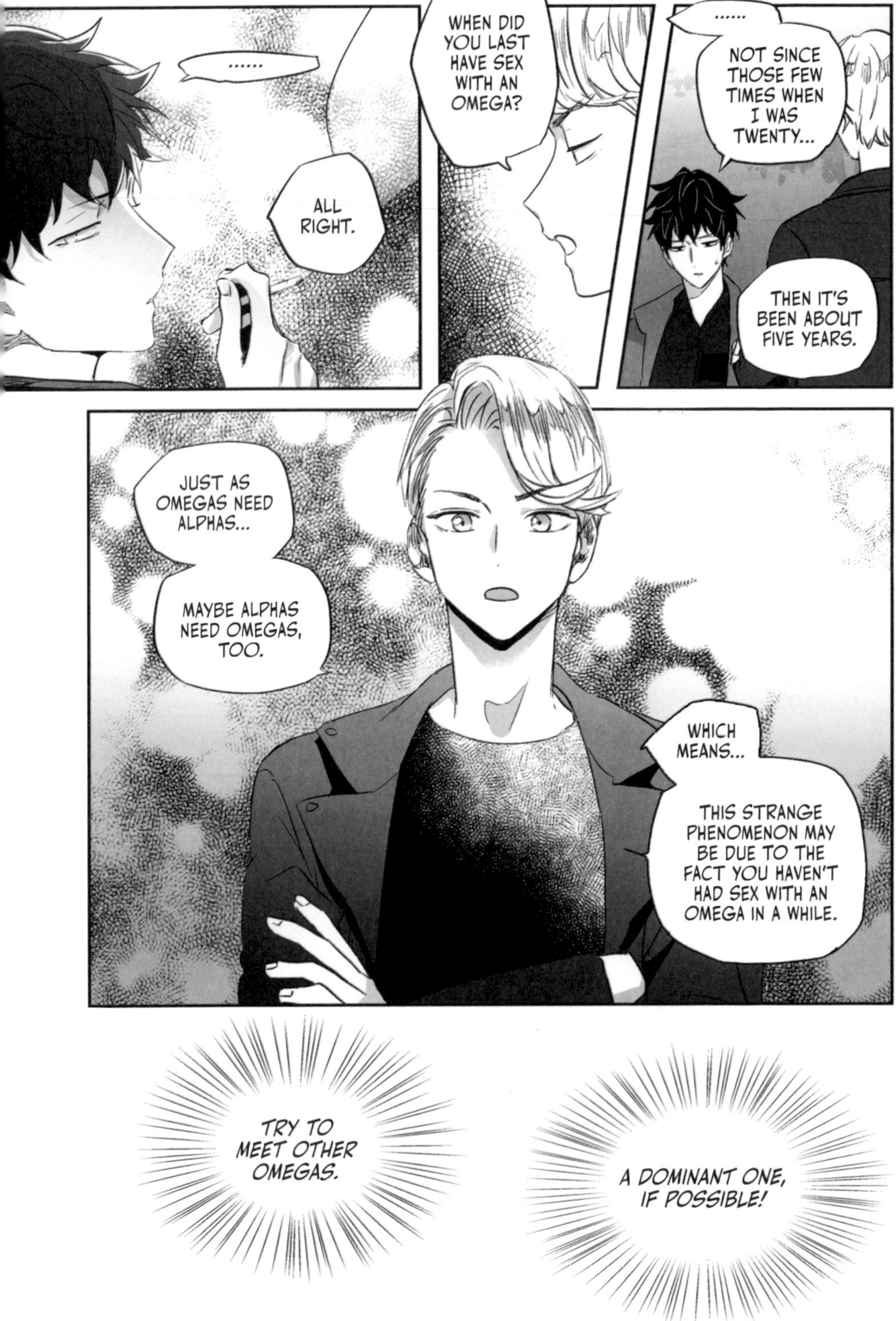
......
ALL RIGHT.
WHEN DID YOU LAST HAVE SEX WITH AN OMEGA?
......
NOT SINCE THOSE FEW TIMES WHEN I WAS TWENTY...
THEN IT'S BEEN ABOUT FIVE YEARS.
JUST AS OMEGAS NEED ALPHAS...
MAYBE ALPHAS NEED OMEGAS, TOO.
WHICH MEANS...
THIS STRANGE PHENOMENON MAY BE DUE TO THE FACT YOU HAVEN'T HAD SEX WITH AN OMEGA IN A WHILE.
TRY TO MEET OTHER OMEGAS.
A DOMINANT ONE, IF POSSIBLE!

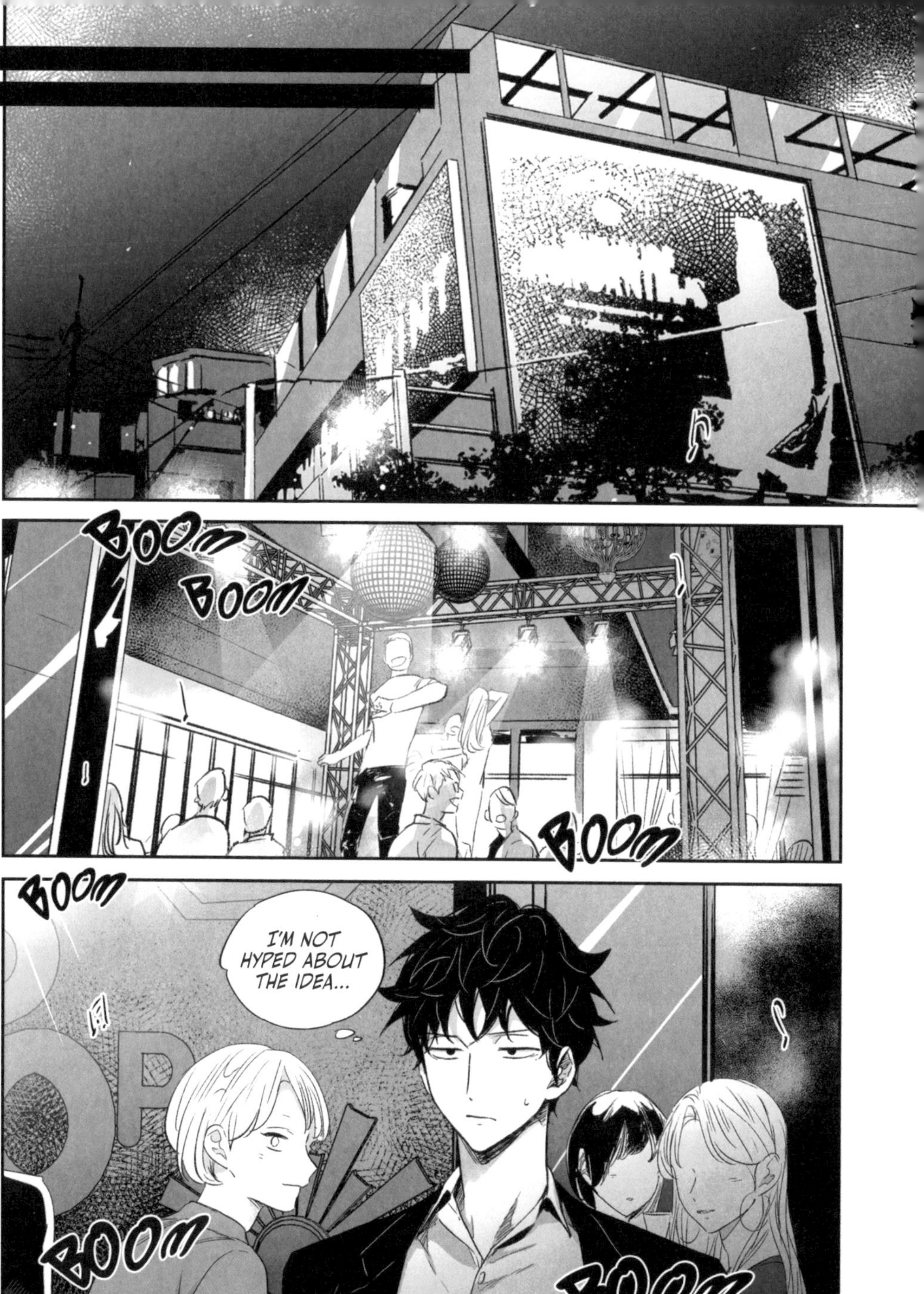
BOOM
BOOM
BOOM
BOOM
I'M NOT HYPED ABOUT THE IDEA...
BOOM
BOOM

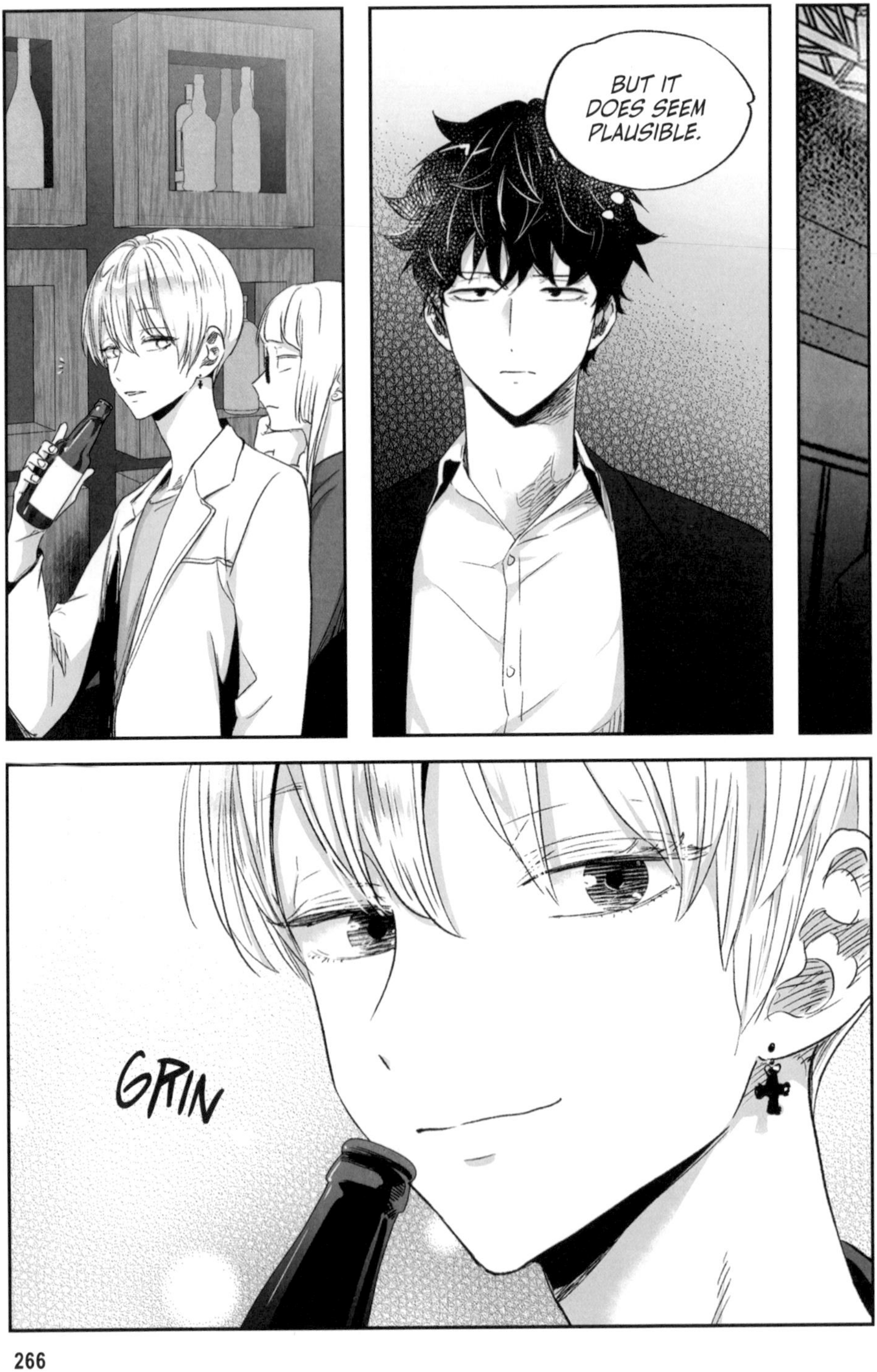
BUT IT DOES SEEM PLAUSIBLE.
GRIN

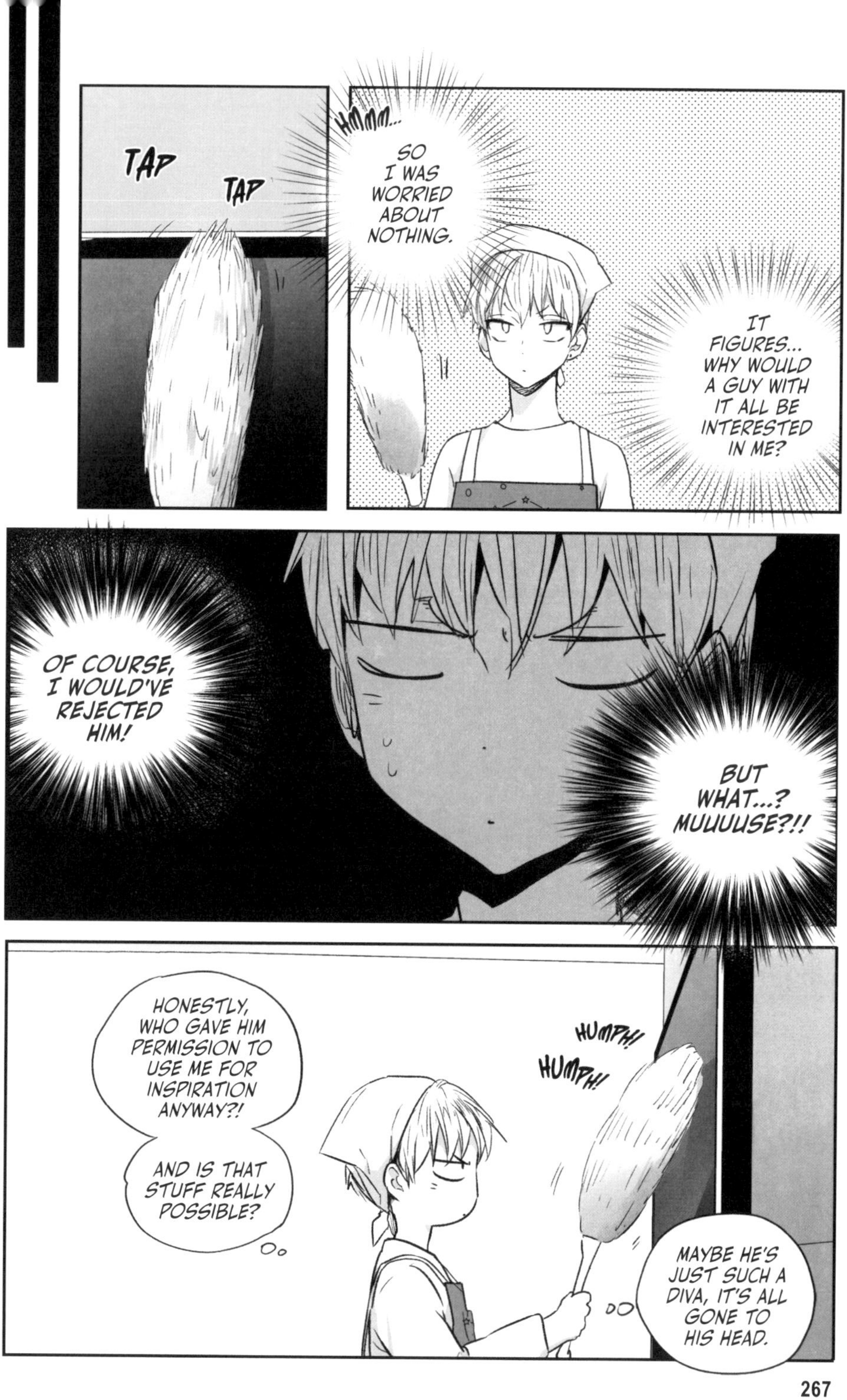
TAP
TAP
HMMM...
SO I WAS WORRIED ABOUT NOTHING.
IT FIGURES... WHY WOULD A GUY WITH IT ALL BE INTERESTED IN ME?
OF COURSE, I WOULD'VE REJECTED HIM!
BUT WHAT...? MUUUUSE?!!
HONESTLY, WHO GAVE HIM PERMISSION TO USE ME FOR INSPIRATION ANYWAY?!
AND IS THAT STUFF REALLY POSSIBLE?
HUMPH!
HUMPH!
MAYBE HE'S JUST SUCH A DIVA, IT'S ALL GONE TO HIS HEAD.

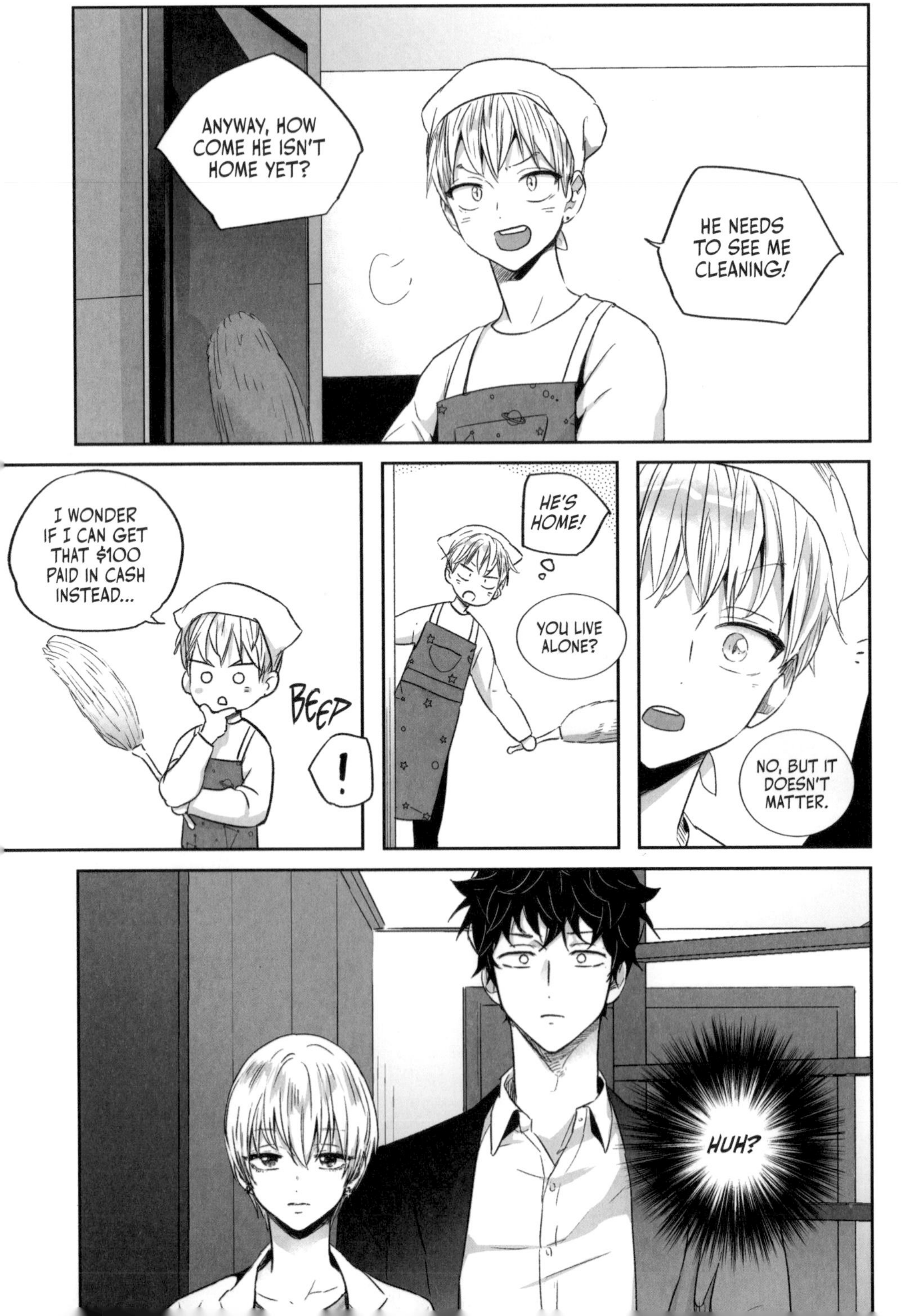
ANYWAY, HOW COME HE ISN'T HOME YET?
HE NEEDS TO SEE ME CLEANING!
I WONDER IF I CAN GET THAT $100 PAID IN CASH INSTEAD...
BEEP
!
HE'S HOME!
YOU LIVE ALONE?
NO, BUT IT DOESN'T MATTER.
HUH?

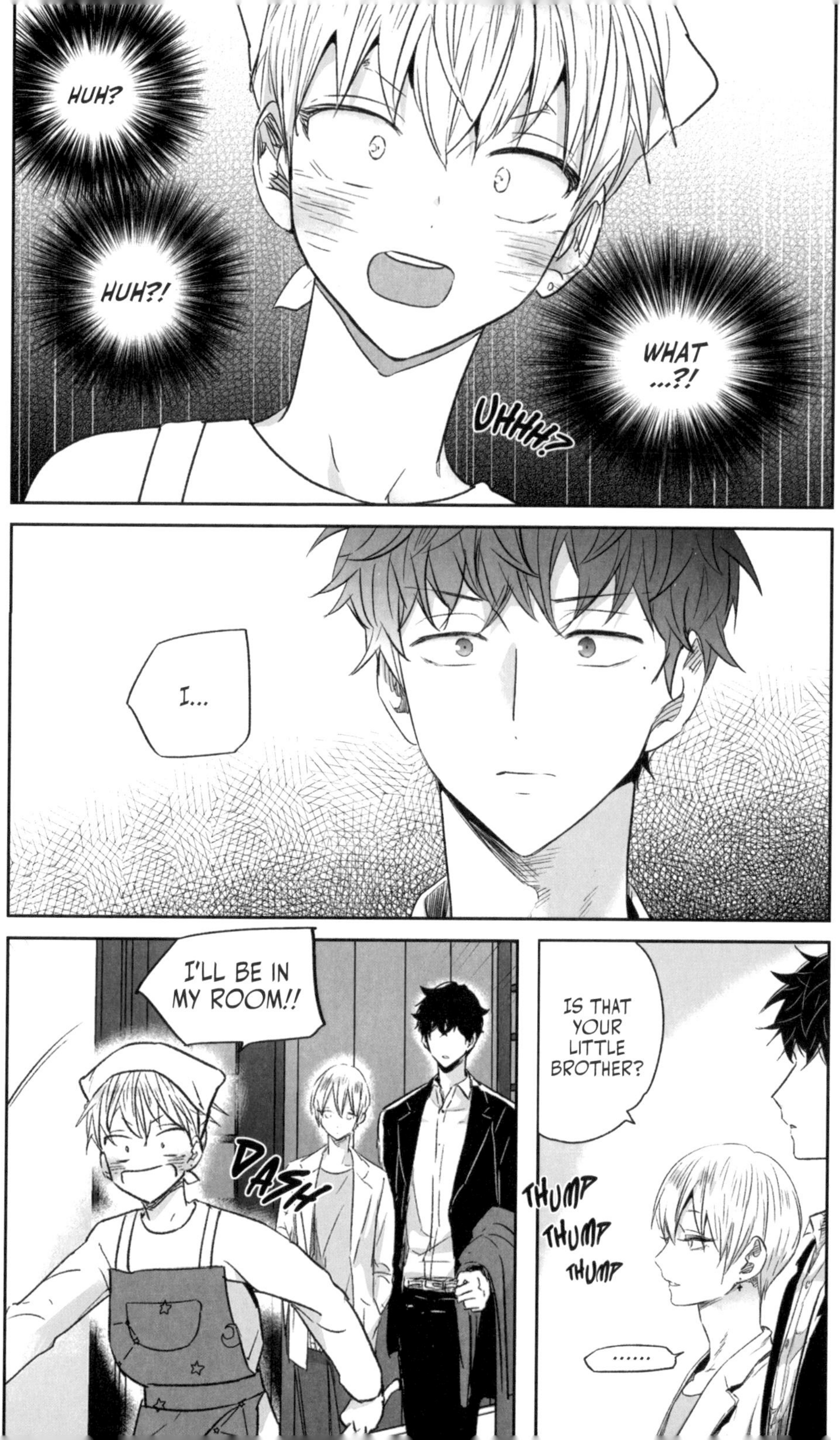
HUH?
HUH?!
WHAT ...?!
UHHH?
I...
I'LL BE IN MY ROOM!!
DASH
IS THAT YOUR LITTLE BROTHER?
THUMP THUMP THUMP
......

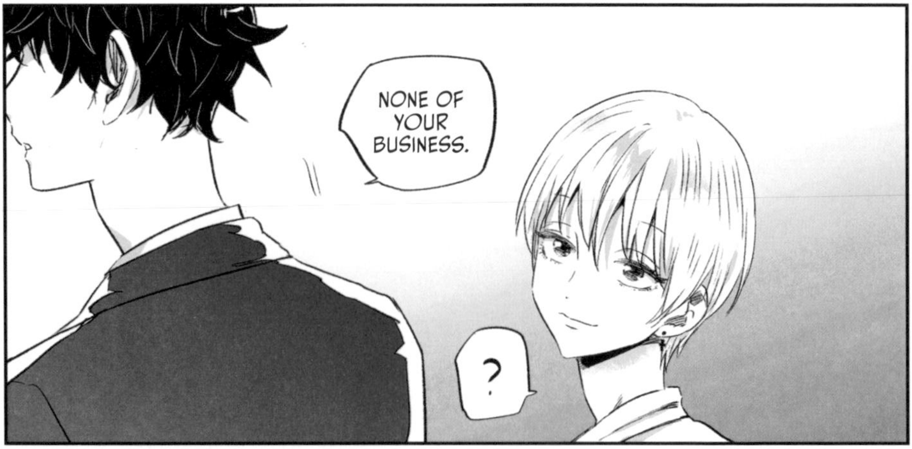
NONE OF YOUR BUSINESS.
?

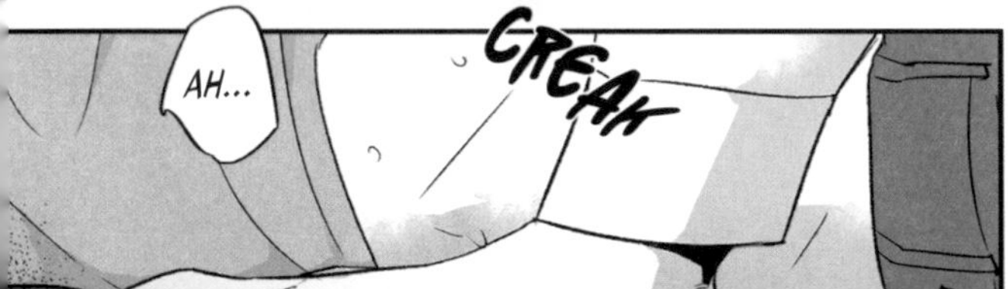
AH...
CREAK

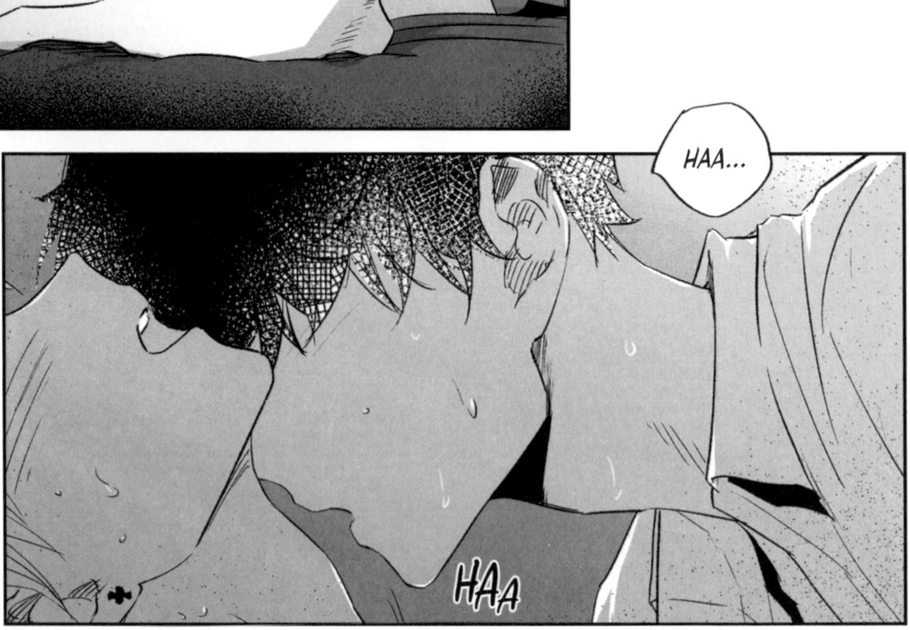
HAA...
HAA

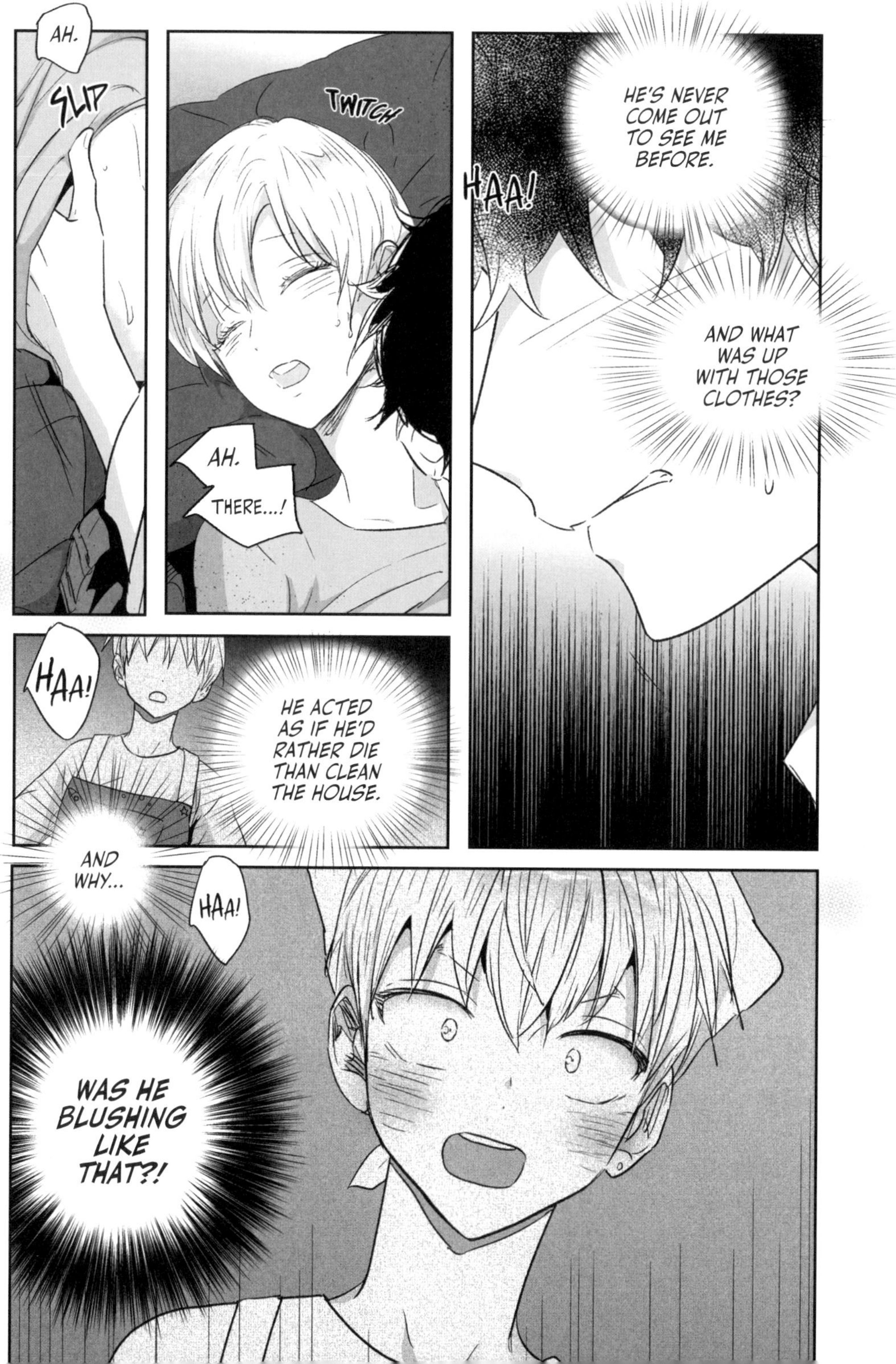

AH.
SLIP
TWITCH
AH.
THERE...!
HAA!
HE ACTED AS IF HE'D RATHER DIE THAN CLEAN THE HOUSE.
HAA!
HE'S NEVER COME OUT TO SEE ME BEFORE.
AND WHAT WAS UP WITH THOSE CLOTHES?
AND WHY...
HAA!
WAS HE BLUSHING LIKE THAT?!

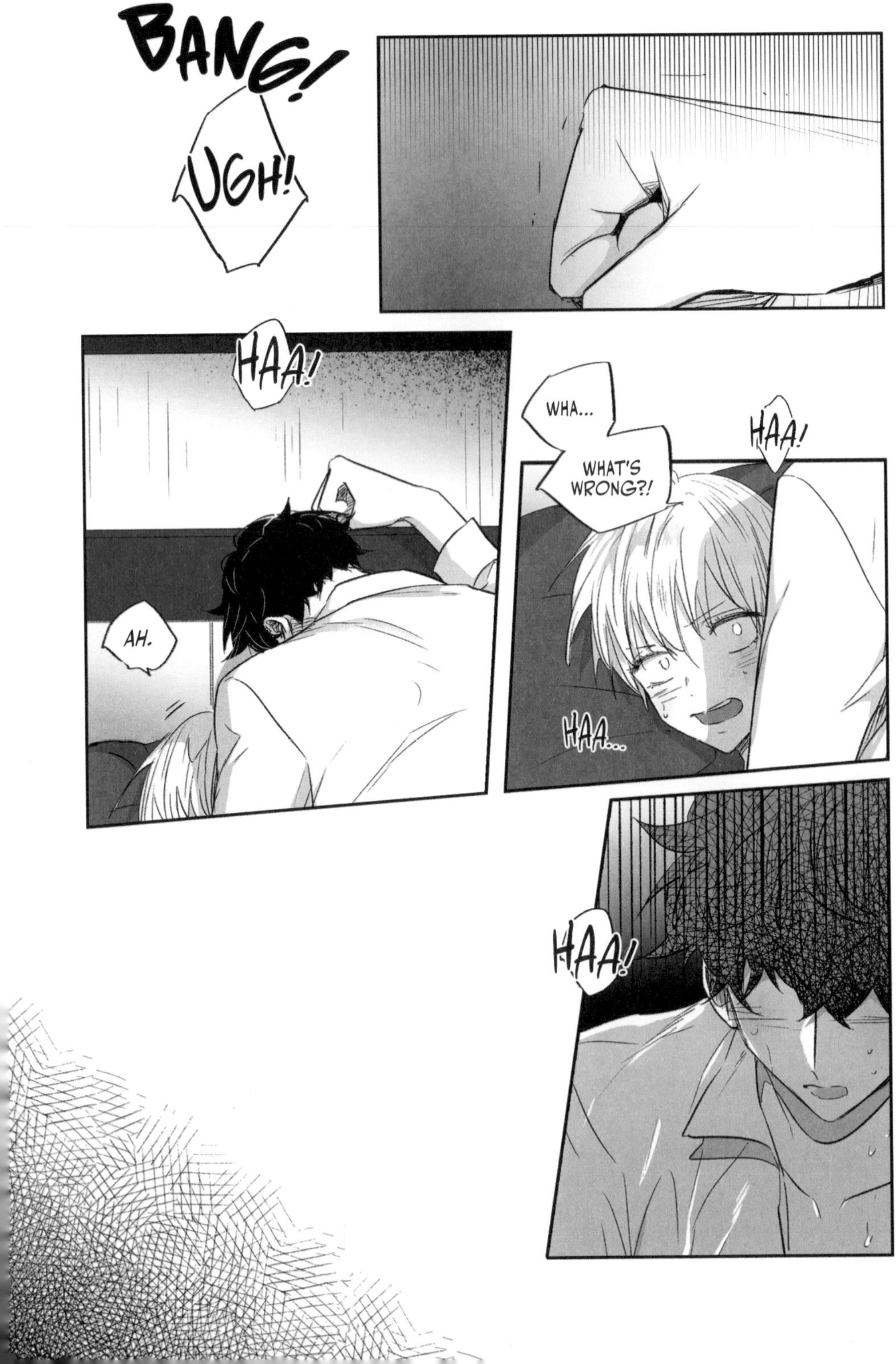
BANG!
UGH!
HAA!
AH.
WHA...
WHAT'S WRONG?!
HAA!
HAA...
HAA!

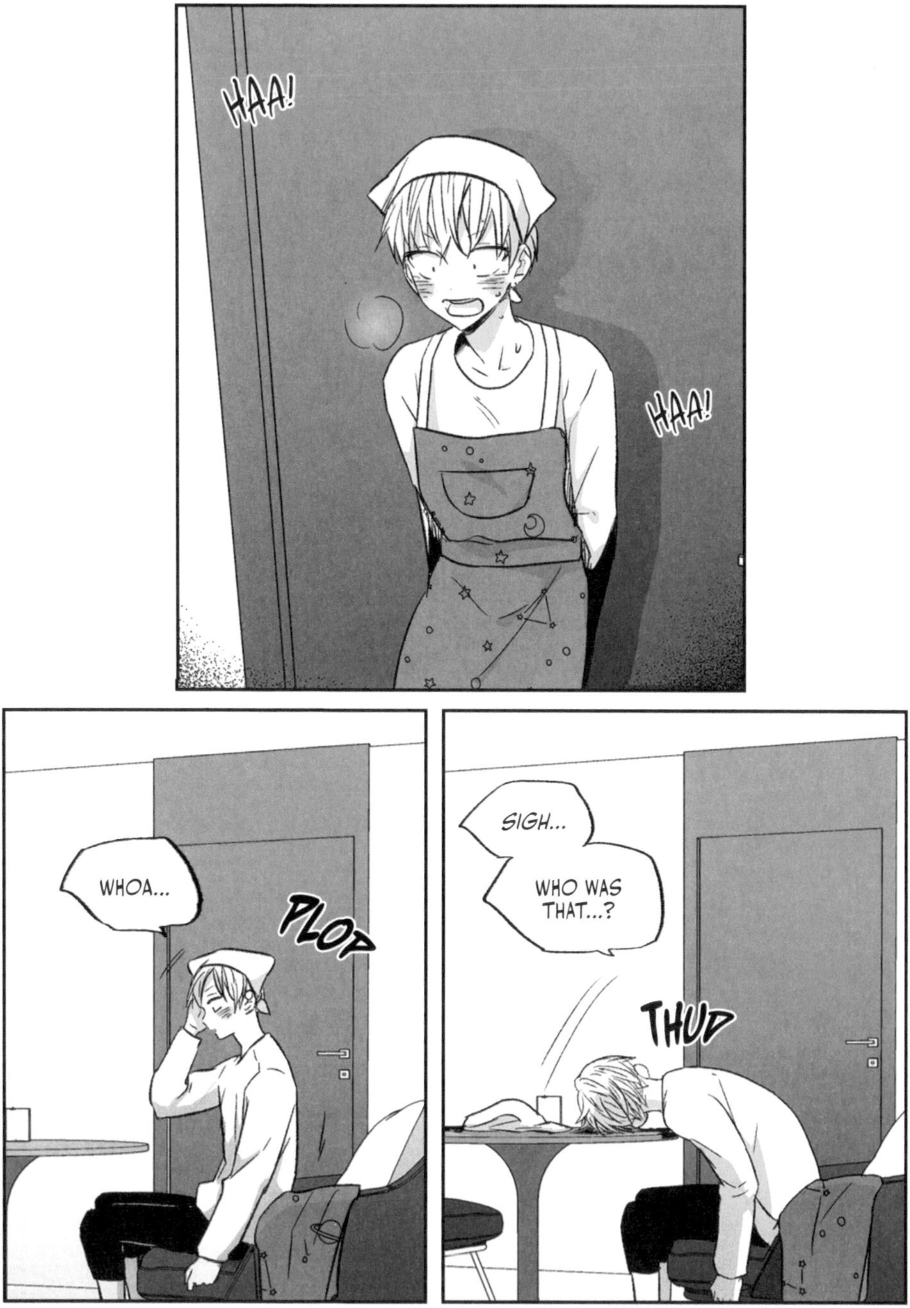
HAA!
HAA!
WHOA...
PLOP
SIGH...
WHO WAS THAT...?
THUD

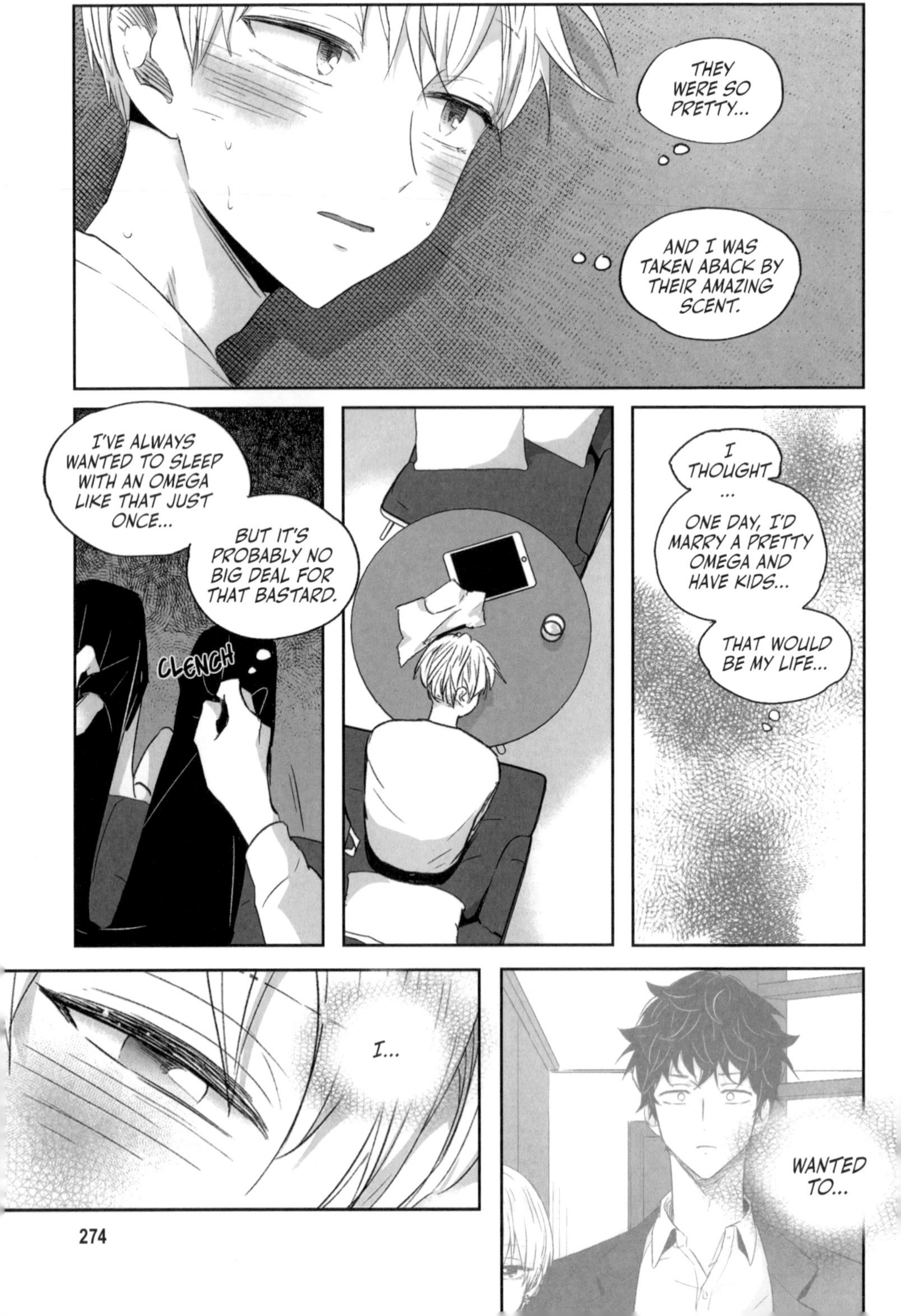
THEY WERE SO PRETTY...
AND I WAS TAKEN ABACK BY THEIR AMAZING SCENT.
I'VE ALWAYS WANTED TO SLEEP WITH AN OMEGA LIKE THAT JUST ONCE...
BUT IT'S PROBABLY NO BIG DEAL FOR THAT BASTARD.
CLENCH
I THOUGHT...
ONE DAY, I'D MARRY A PRETTY OMEGA AND HAVE KIDS...
THAT WOULD BE MY LIFE...
I...
WANTED TO...

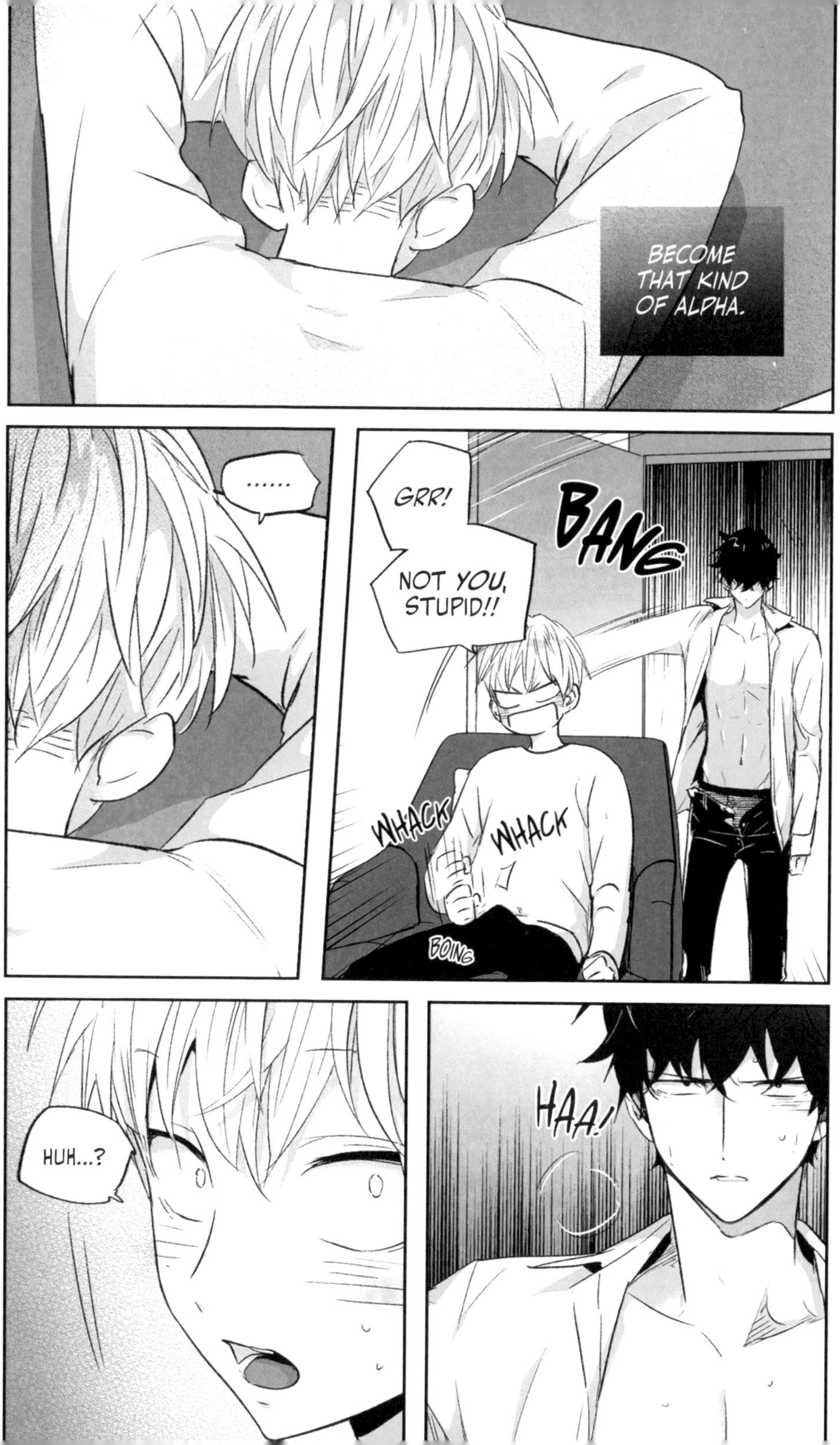
BECOME THAT KIND OF ALPHA.
......
GRR!
NOT YOU, STUPID!!
BANG
WHACK
WHACK
BOING
HUH...?
HAA!

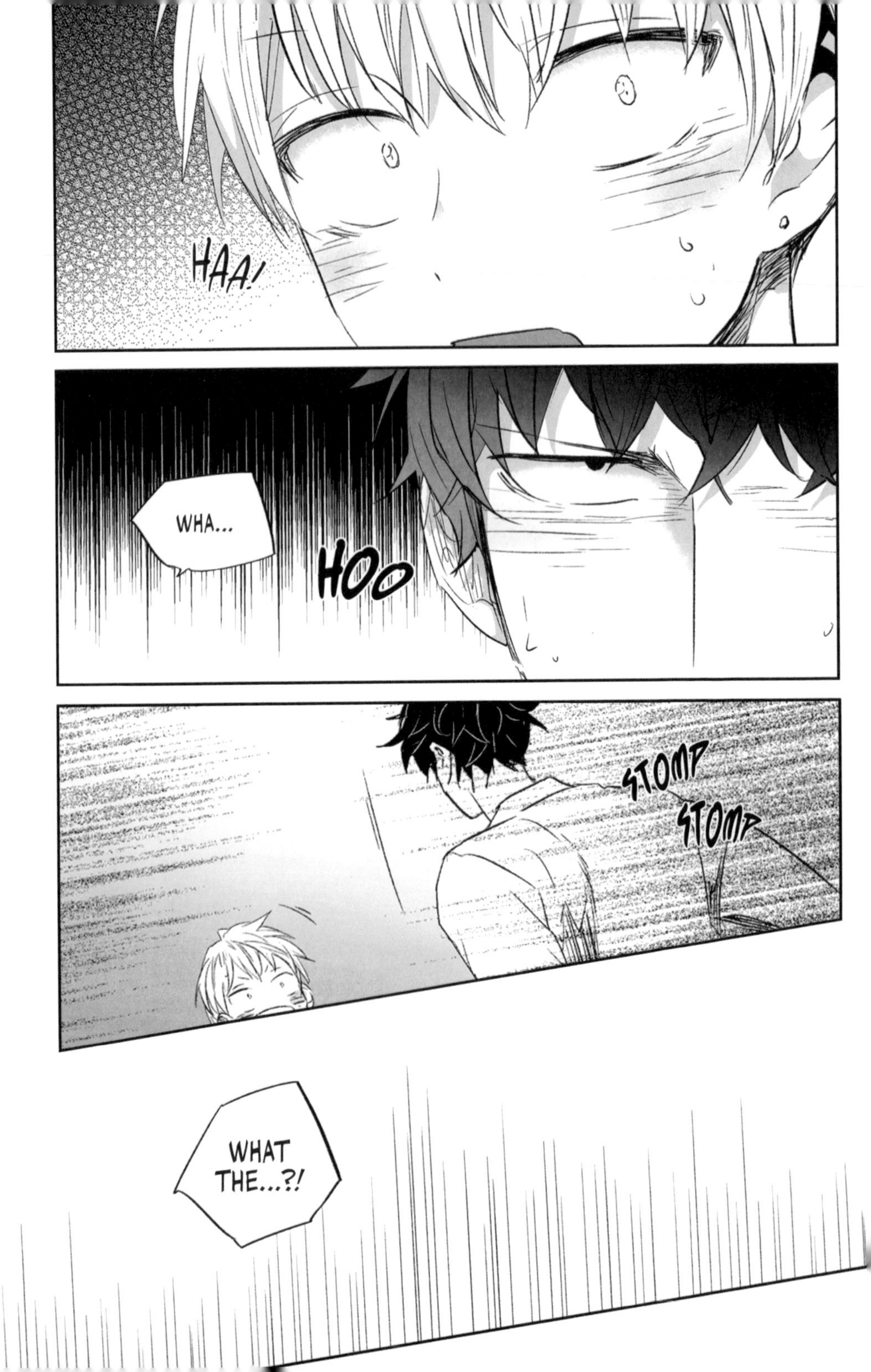
HAA!
WHA...
HOO
STOMP
STOMP
WHAT THE...?!

Love is
an Illusion!

Love is
an Illusion!

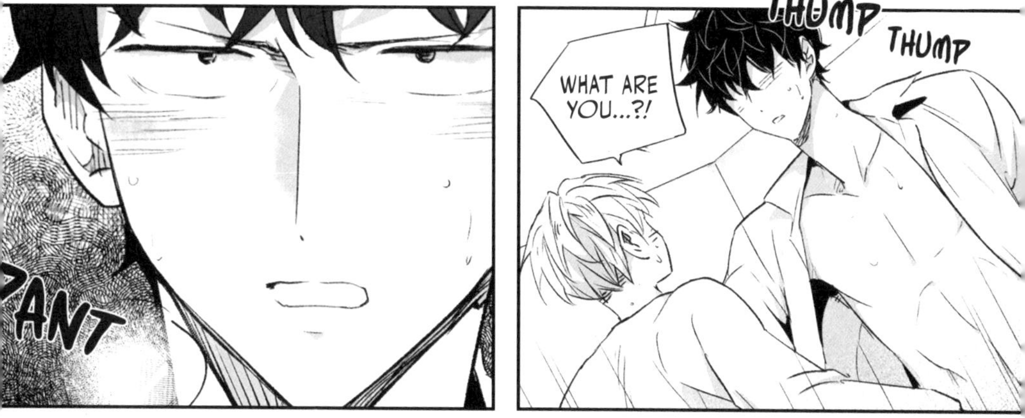
PANT
THUMP
THUMP
WHAT ARE YOU...?!

Chapter 14

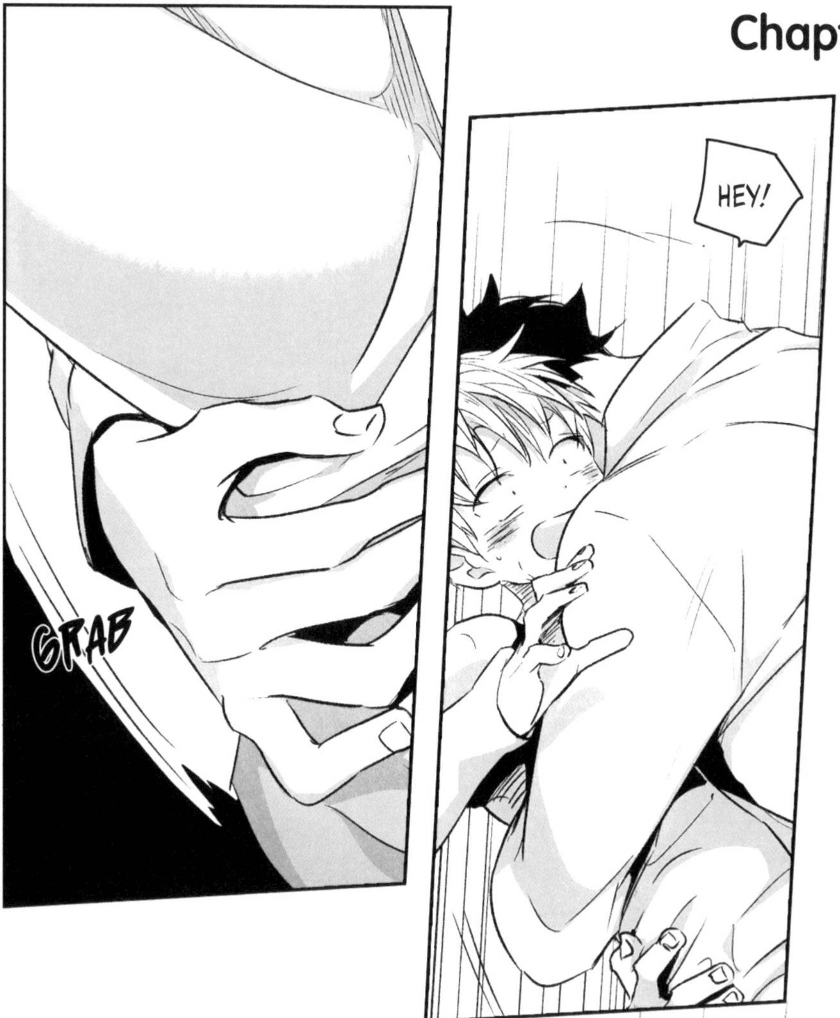
GRAB
HEY!

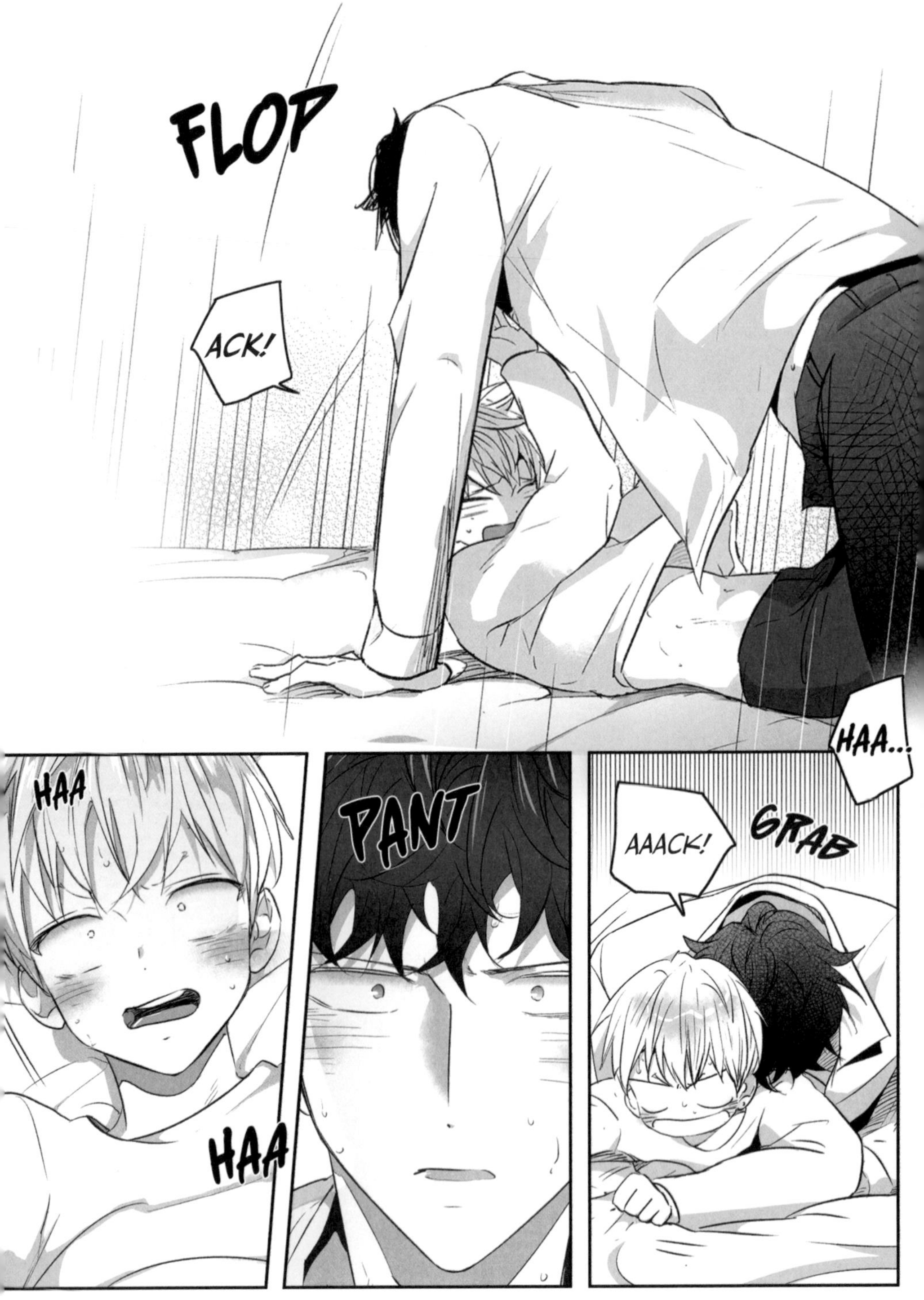
FLOP
ACK!
HAA...
HAA
HAA
PANT
AAACK!
GRAB

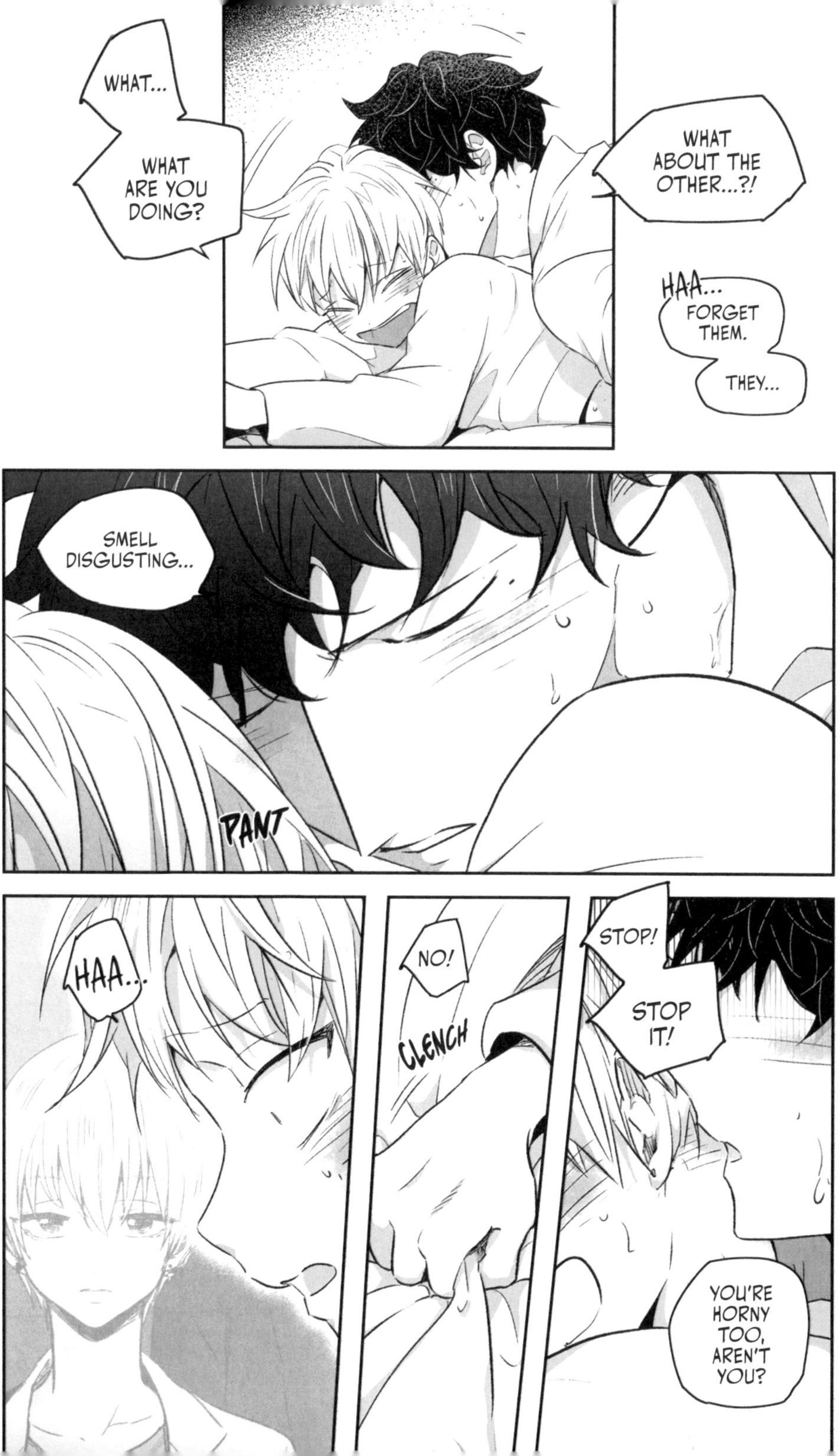
WHAT...
WHAT ARE YOU DOING?
WHAT ABOUT THE OTHER...?!
HAA... FORGET THEM.
THEY...
SMELL DISGUSTING...
PANT
HAA...
NO!
CLENCH
STOP!
STOP IT!
YOU'RE HORNY TOO, AREN'T YOU?

YOU'VE BEEN HORNY SINCE I GOT HOME.
HAA
I CAN FEEL IT.
YOU CAN'T HIDE YOUR PHEROMONES.
HAA
NO...!
NO!!
RUB
ACK!
SLIP
BOING
YANK
AH...!
DRIP

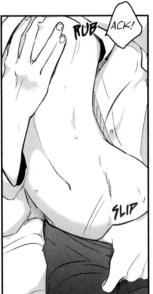

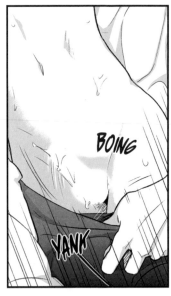

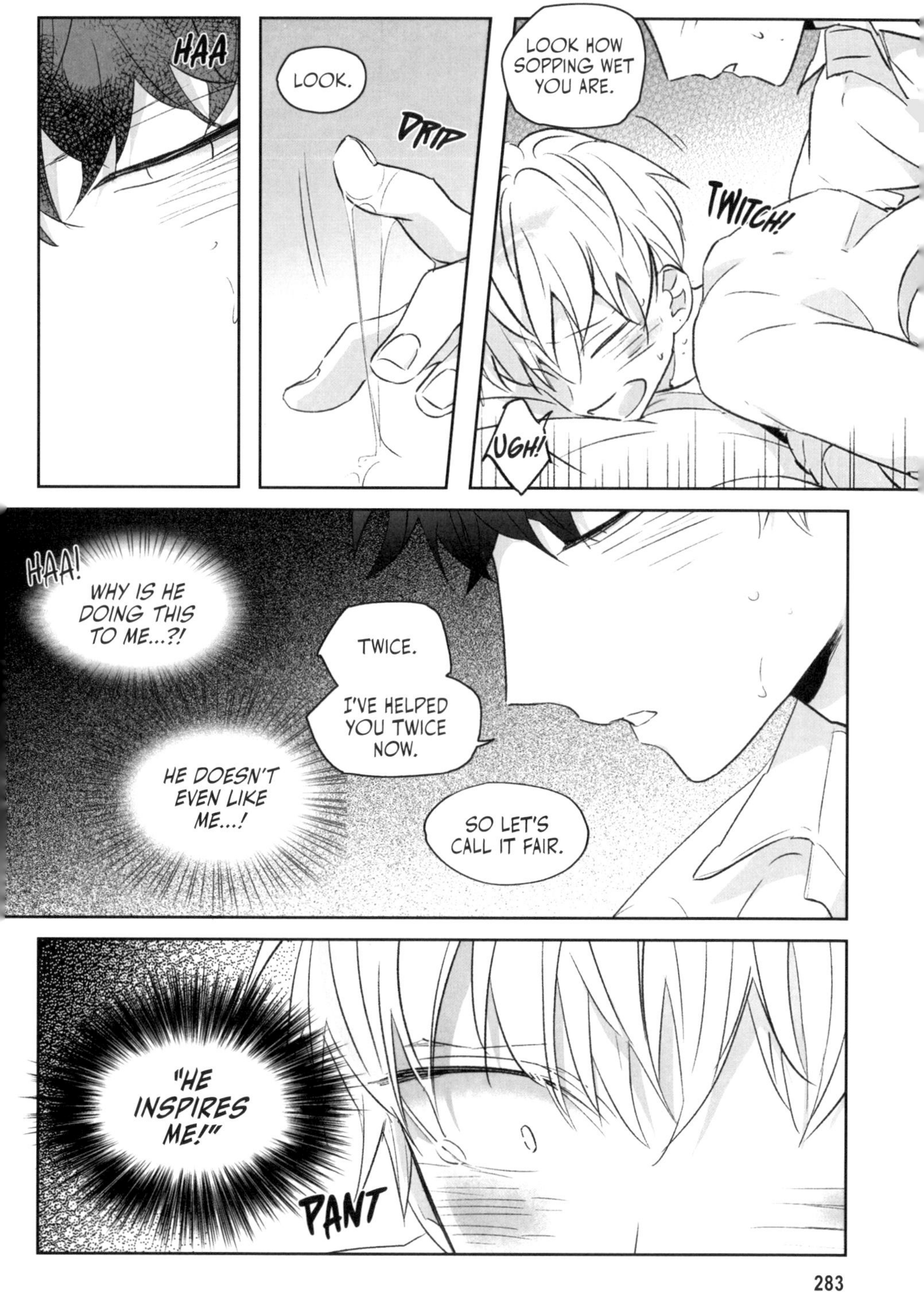
HAA
LOOK.
DRIP
LOOK HOW SOPPING WET YOU ARE.
TWITCH!
UGH!
HAA!
WHY IS HE DOING THIS TO ME...?!
TWICE.
I'VE HELPED YOU TWICE NOW.
HE DOESN'T EVEN LIKE ME...!
SO LET'S CALL IT FAIR.
"HE INSPIRES ME!"
PANT

......
HAA...
UGH...
GROPE
AH...
STRETCH
SQUELCH
ACK!
SQUELCH

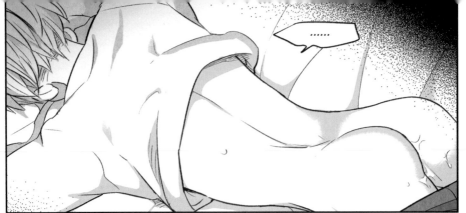

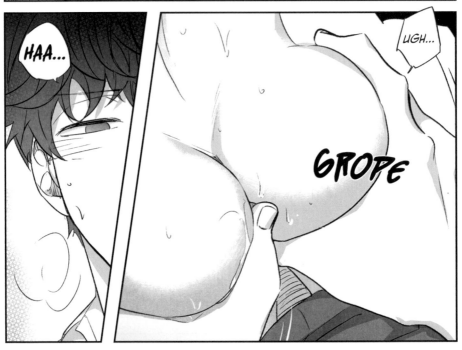

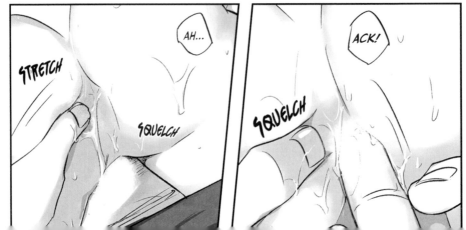

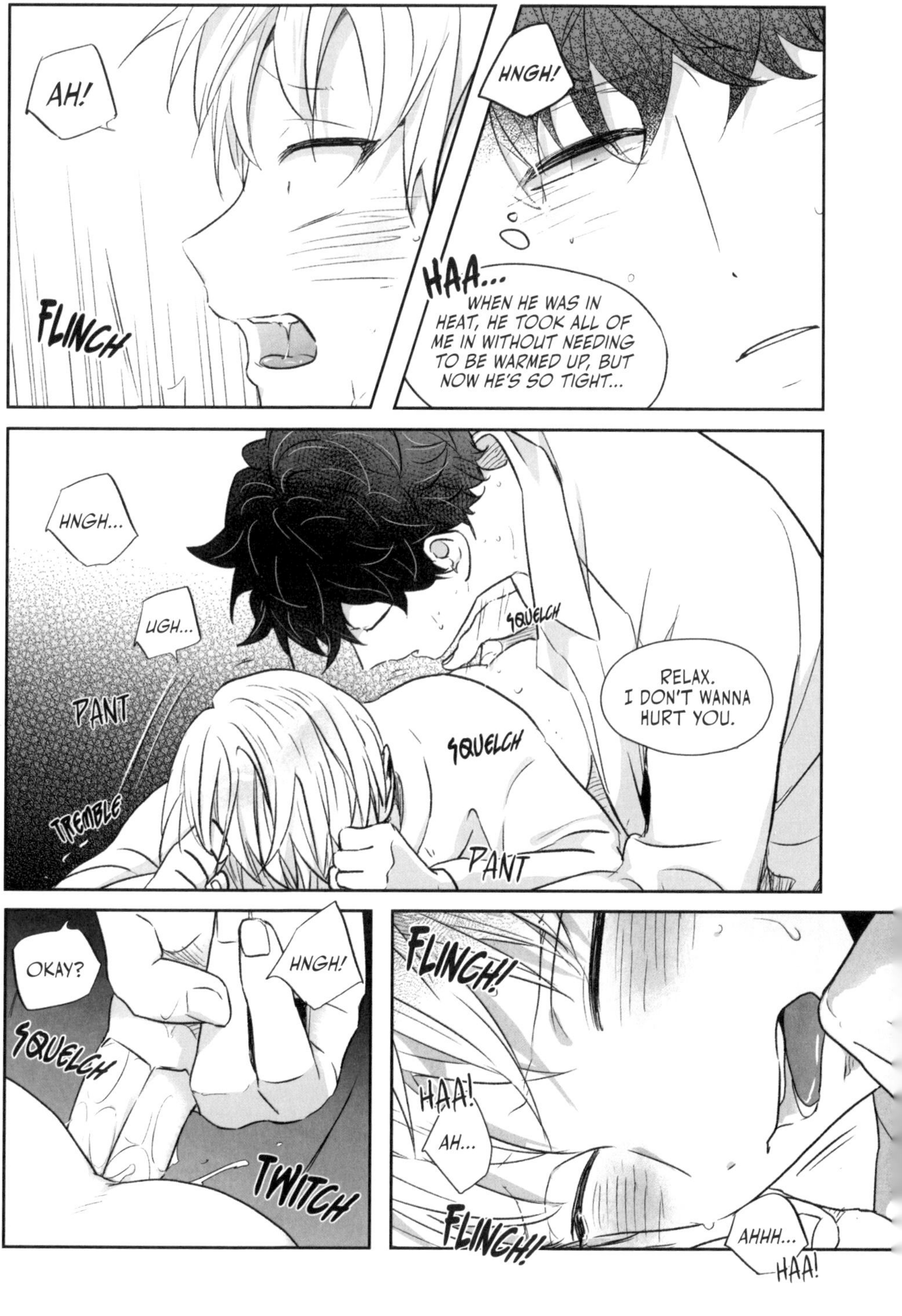
AH!
FLINCH
HNGH!
HAA...
WHEN HE WAS IN HEAT, HE TOOK ALL OF ME IN WITHOUT NEEDING TO BE WARMED UP, BUT NOW HE'S SO TIGHT...
HNGH...
UGH...
SQUELCH
RELAX. I DON'T WANNA HURT YOU.
PANT
SQUELCH
TREMBLE
PANT
OKAY?
HNGH!
SQUELCH
TWITCH
FLINCH!
HAA!
AH...
FLINCH!
AHHH...
HAA!

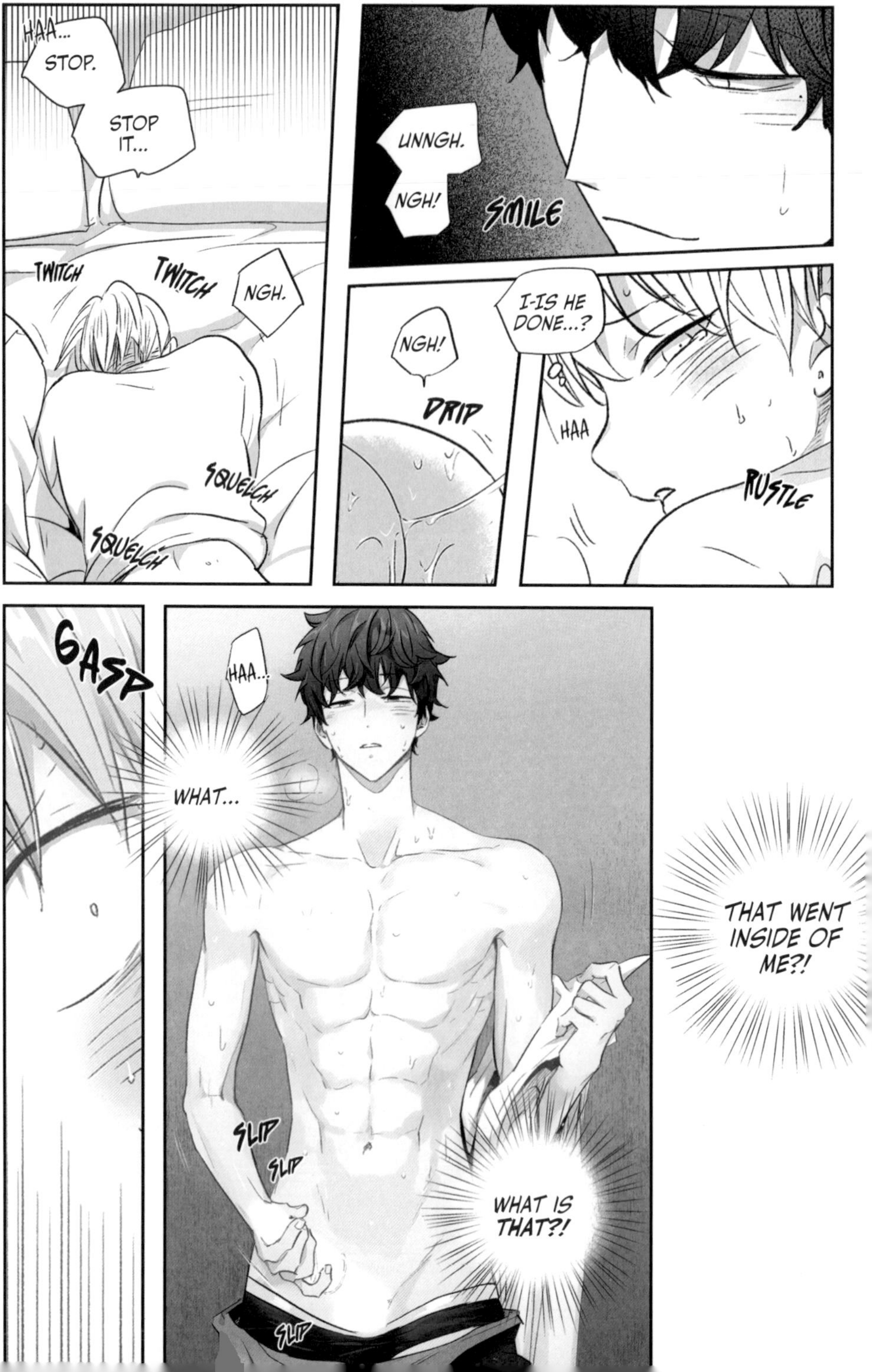
HAA...
STOP.
STOP IT...
UNNGH.
NGH!
SMILE
TWITCH
TWITCH
NGH.
SQUELCH
SQUELCH
NGH!
DRIP
I-IS HE DONE...?
HAA
RUSTLE
GASP
HAA...
WHAT...
SLIP
SLIP
SLIP
WHAT IS THAT?!
THAT WENT INSIDE OF ME?!

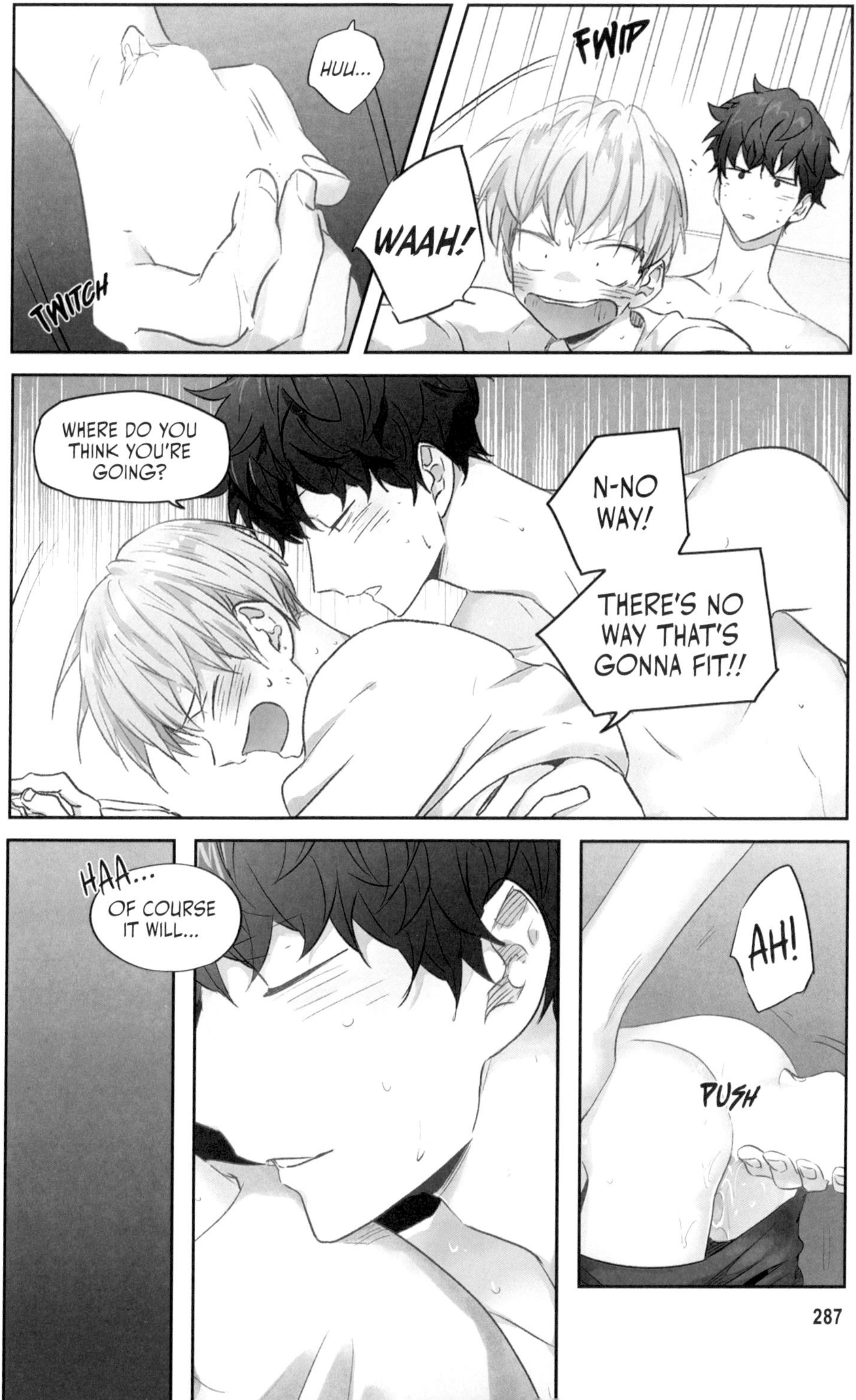
HUU...
TWITCH
FWIP
WAAH!
WHERE DO YOU THINK YOU'RE GOING?
N-NO WAY!
THERE'S NO WAY THAT'S GONNA FIT!!
HAA...
OF COURSE IT WILL...
AH!
PUSH

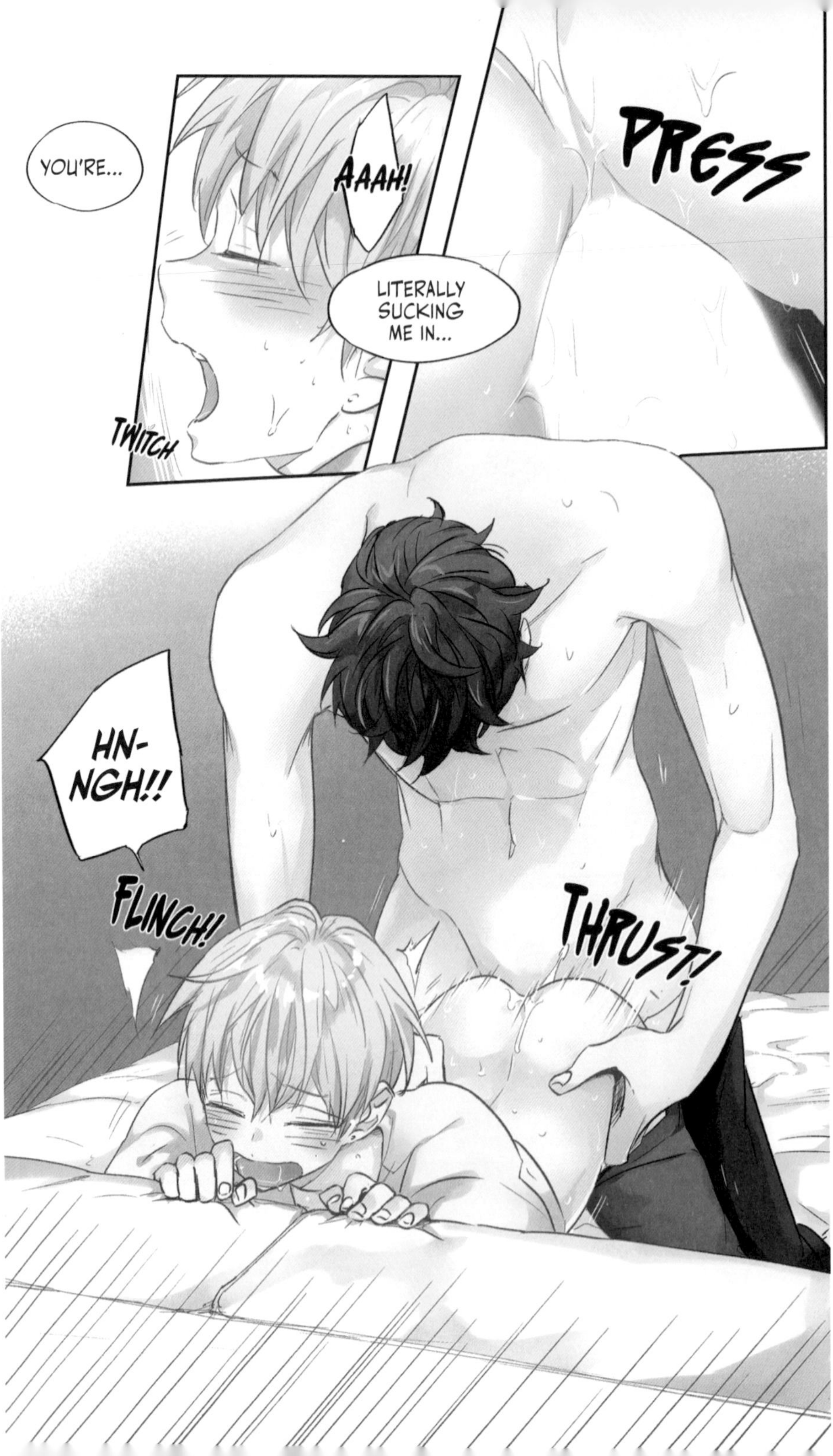
YOU'RE...
AAAH!
LITERALLY SUCKING ME IN...
TWITCH
PRESS
HN-NGH!!
FLINCH!
THRUST!

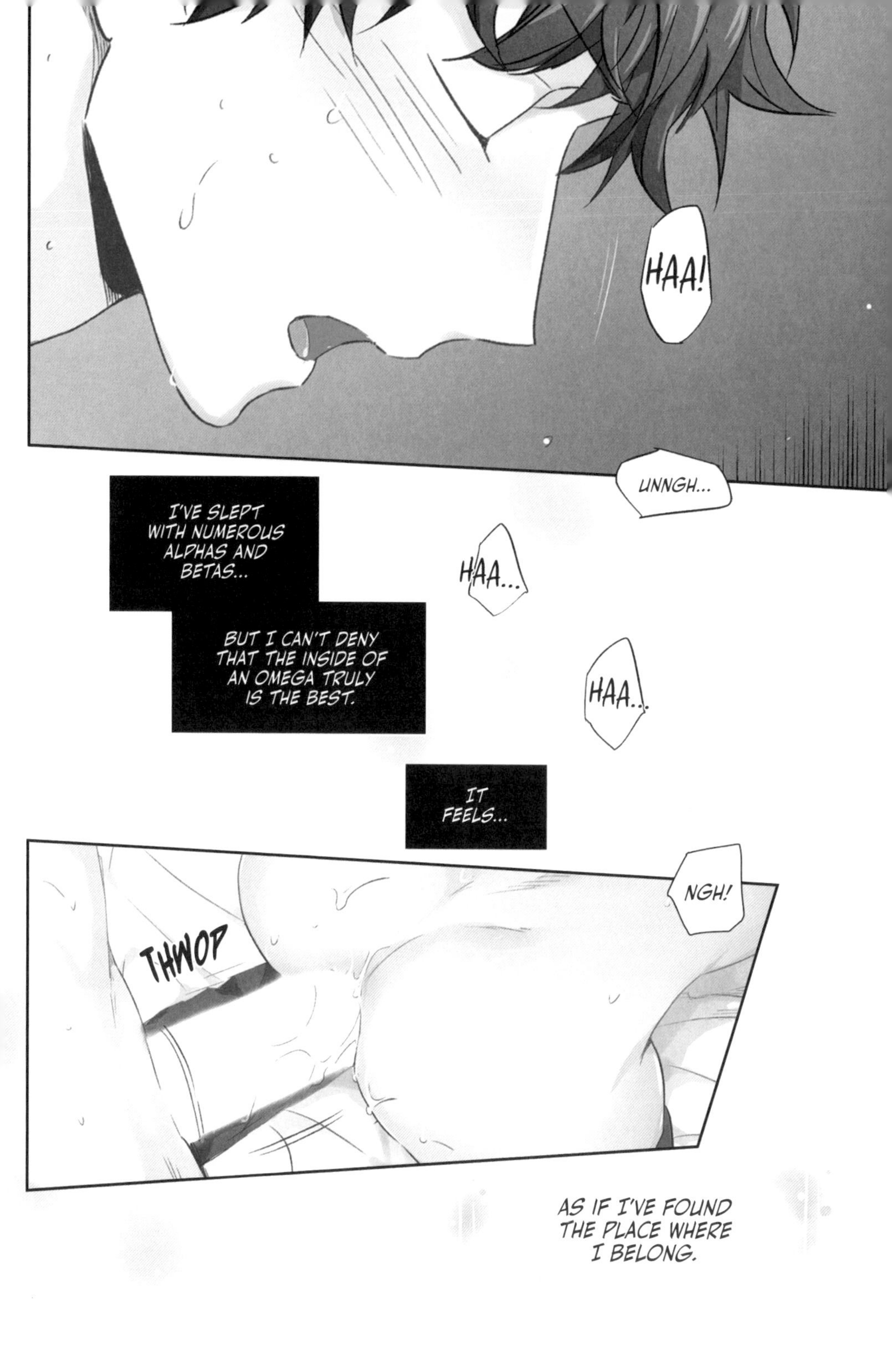
HAA!
UNNGH...
I'VE SLEPT WITH NUMEROUS ALPHAS AND BETAS...
HAA...
BUT I CAN'T DENY THAT THE INSIDE OF AN OMEGA TRULY IS THE BEST.
HAA...
IT FEELS...
NGH!
THWOP
AS IF I'VE FOUND THE PLACE WHERE I BELONG.

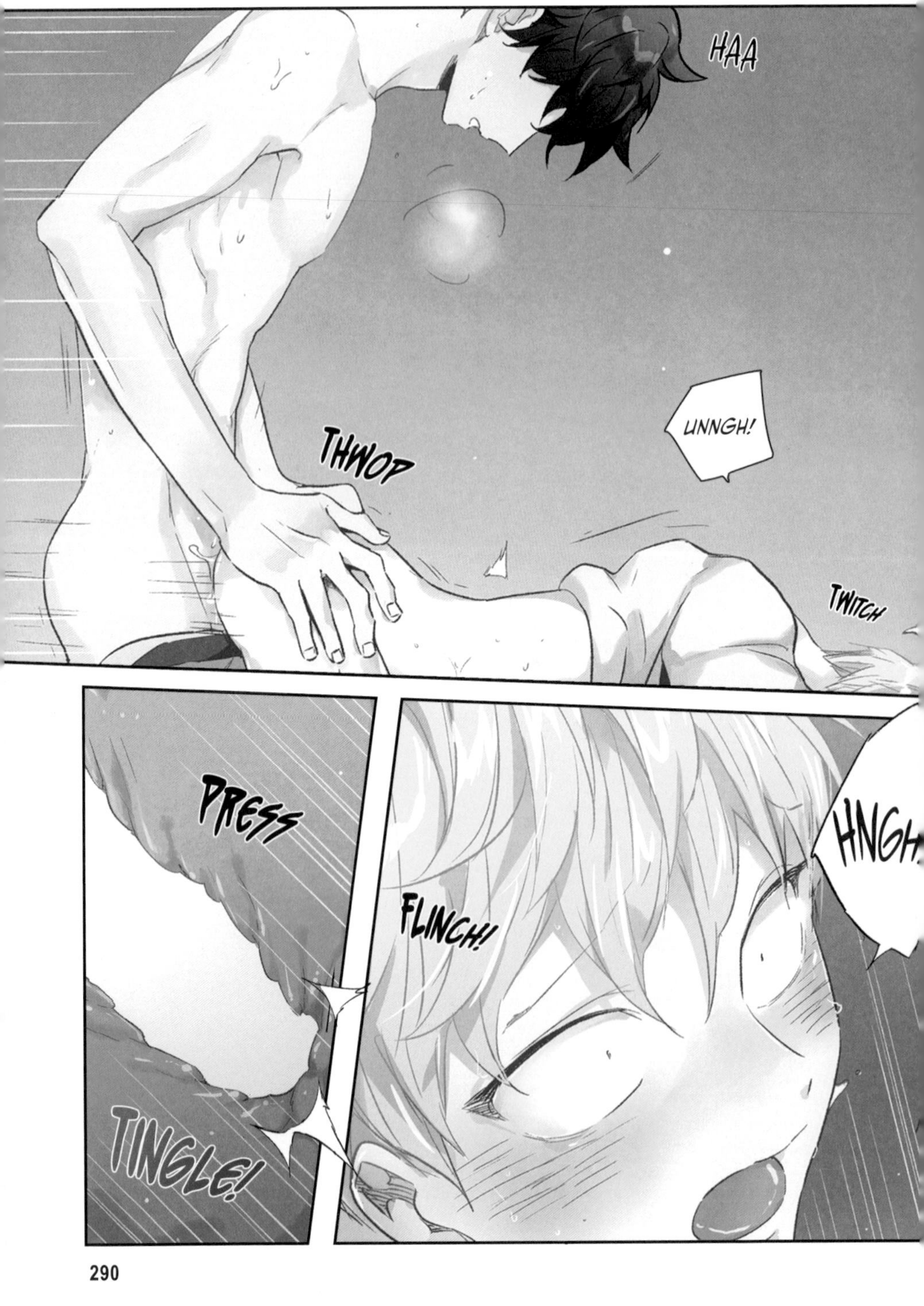
HAA
UNNGH!
THWOP
TWITCH
PRESS
TINGLE!
FLINCH!
HNGH

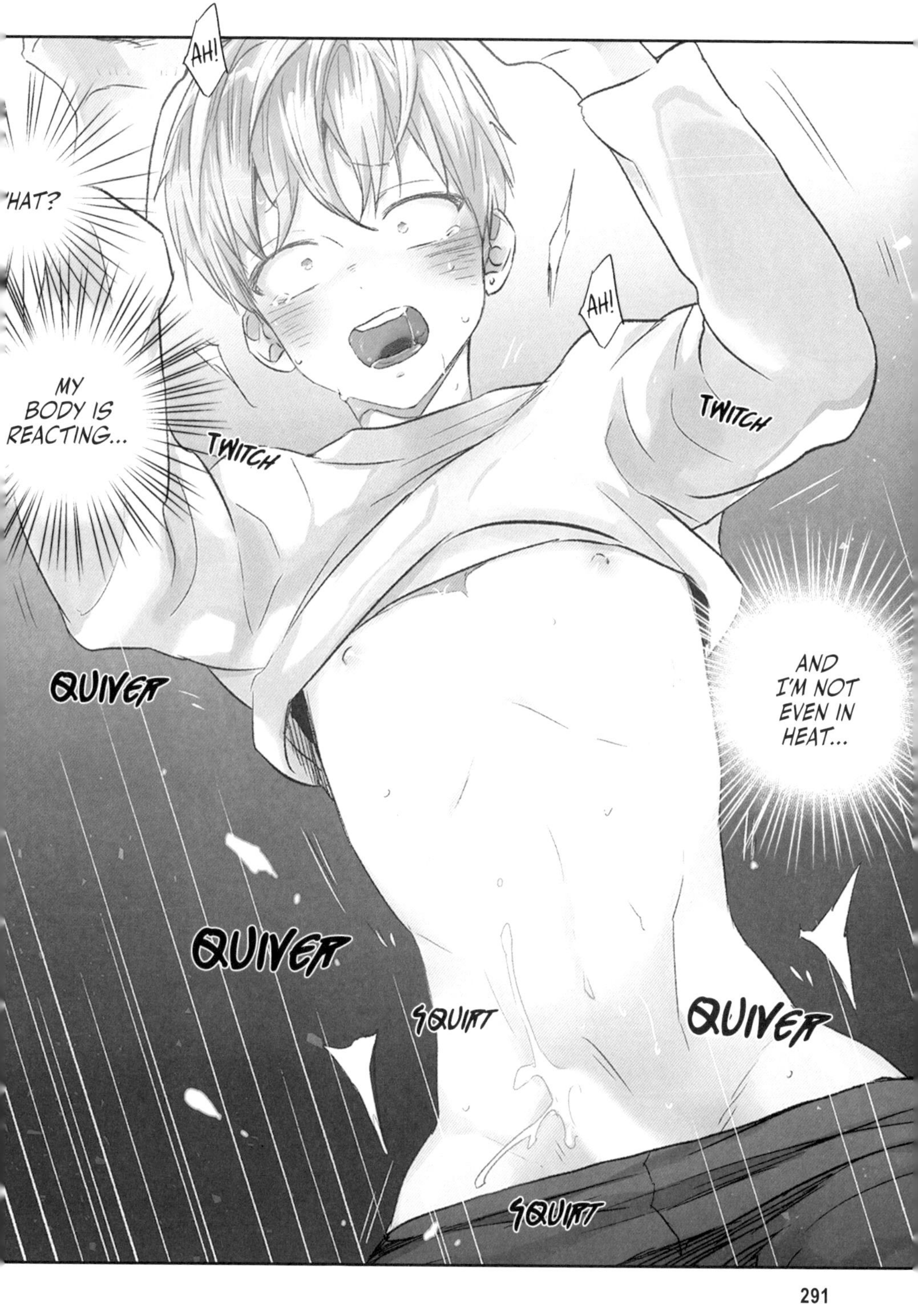
AH!
AH!
'HAT?
MY BODY IS REACTING...
TWITCH
TWITCH
AND I'M NOT EVEN IN HEAT...
QUIVER
QUIVER
QUIVER
SQUIRT
SQUIRT

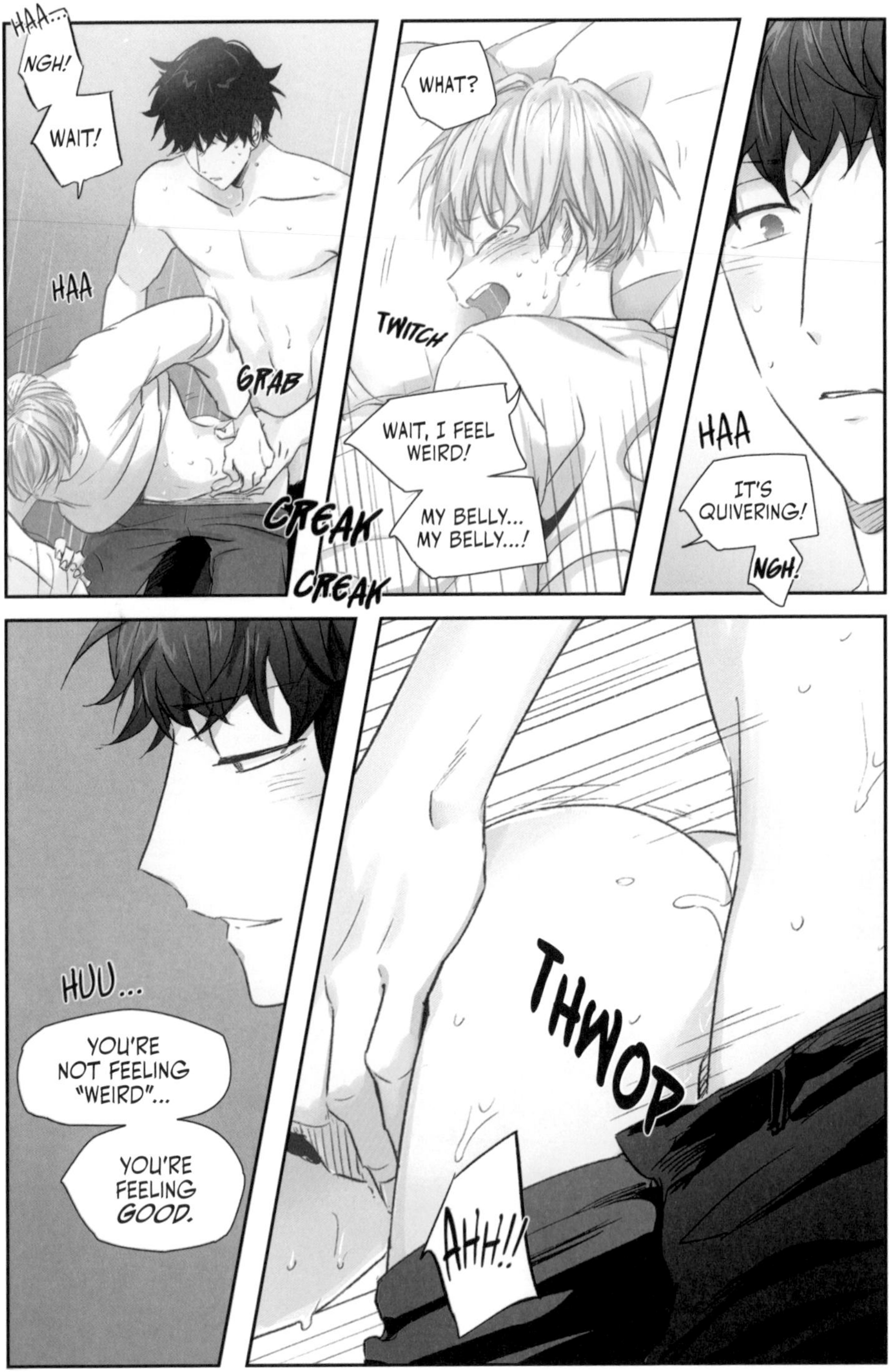
HAA...
NGH!
WAIT!
HAA
GRAB
CREAK
CREAK
WHAT?
TWITCH
WAIT, I FEEL WEIRD!
MY BELLY... MY BELLY...!
HAA
IT'S QUIVERING!
NGH.
HUU...
YOU'RE NOT FEELING "WEIRD"...
YOU'RE FEELING *GOOD.*
THWOP
AHH!!

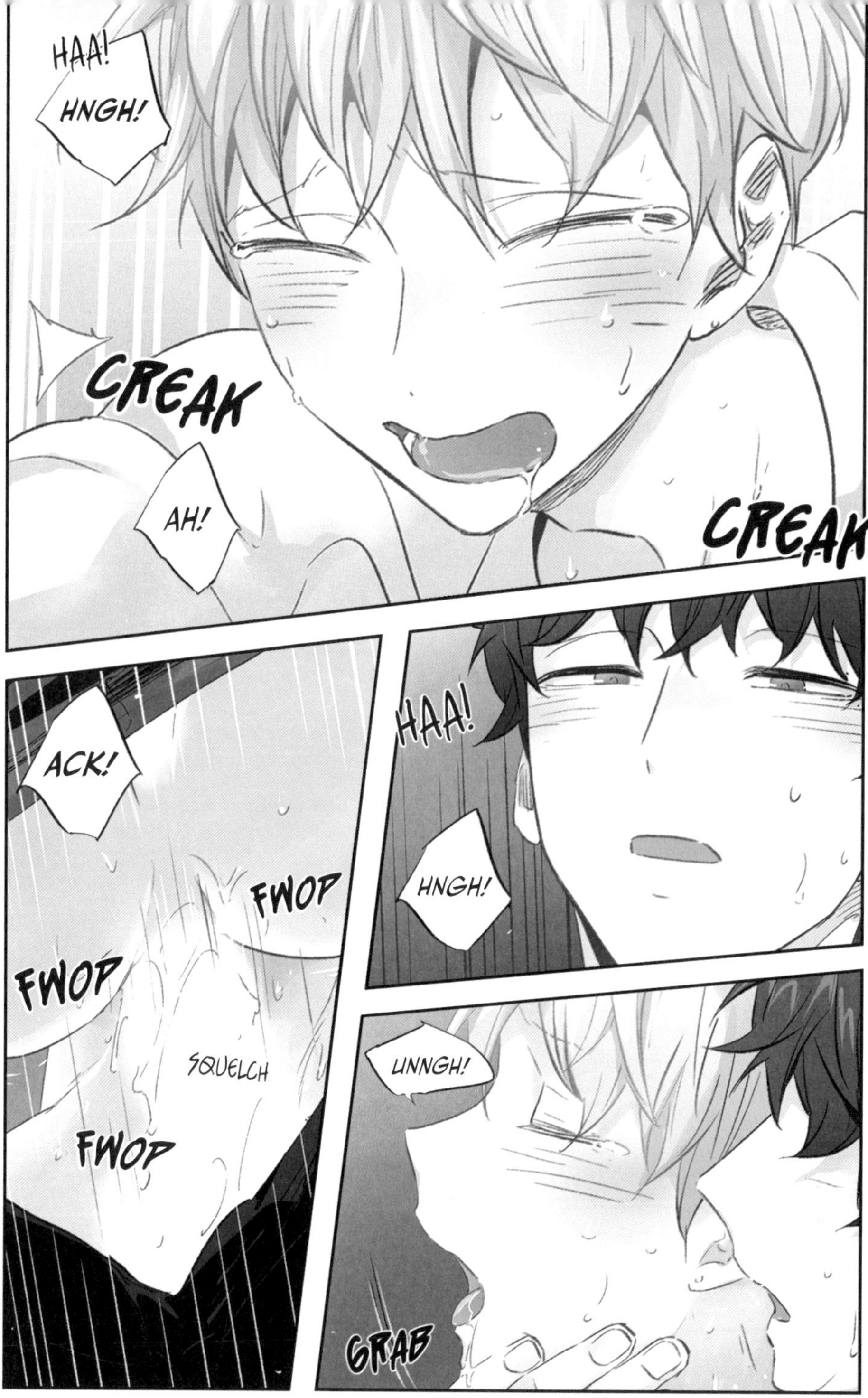
HAA!
HNGH!
CREAK
AH!
CREAK
ACK!
FWOP
FWOP
SQUELCH
FWOP
HAA!
HNGH!
UNNGH!
GRAB

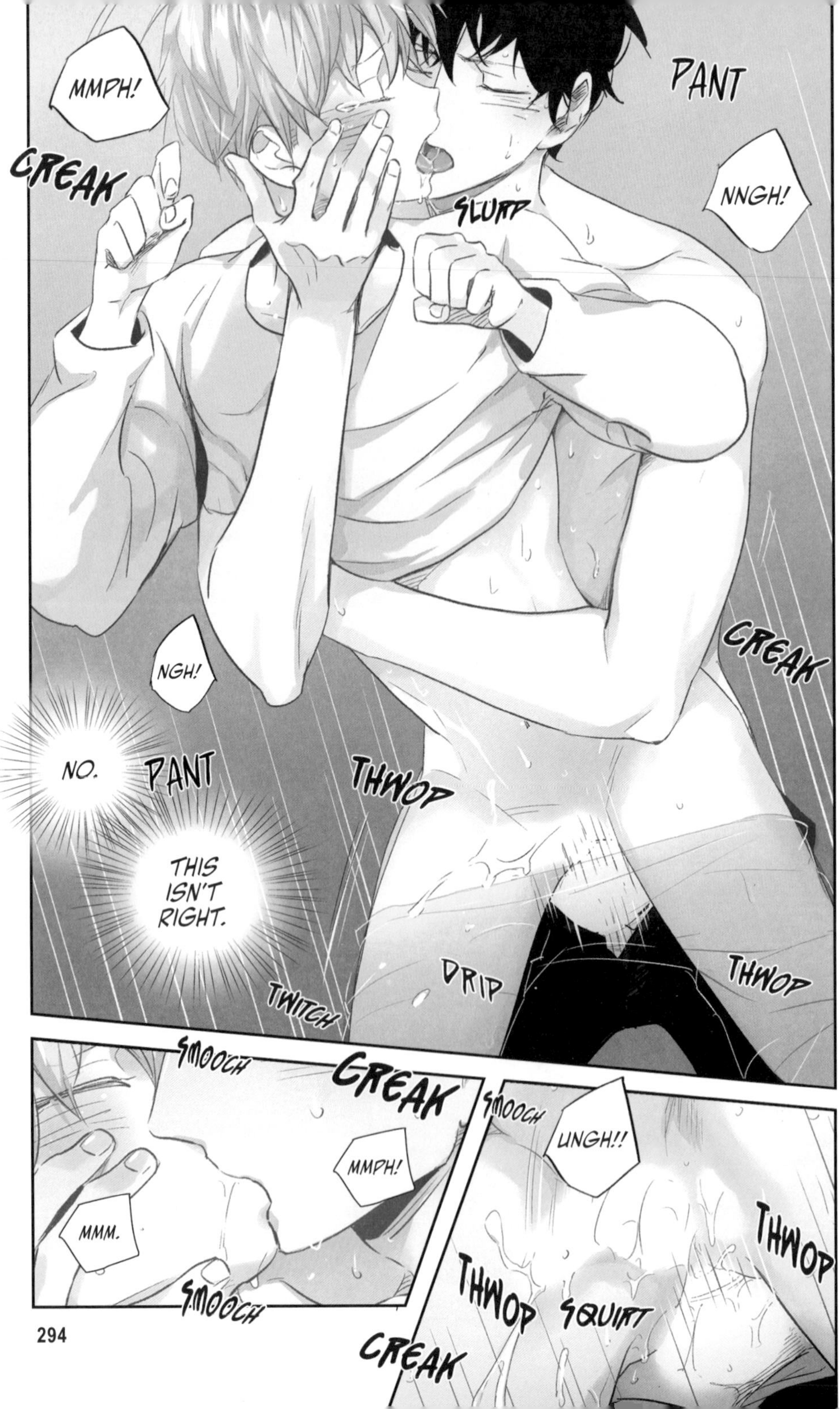
MMPH!
PANT
CREAK
NNGH!
SLURP
CREAK
NGH!
NO.
PANT
THWOP
THIS ISN'T RIGHT.
DRIP
THWOP
TWITCH
SMOOCH
CREAK
MMPH!
MMM.
SMOOCH
SMOOCH
UNGH!!
THWOP
THWOP
SQUIRT
CREAK

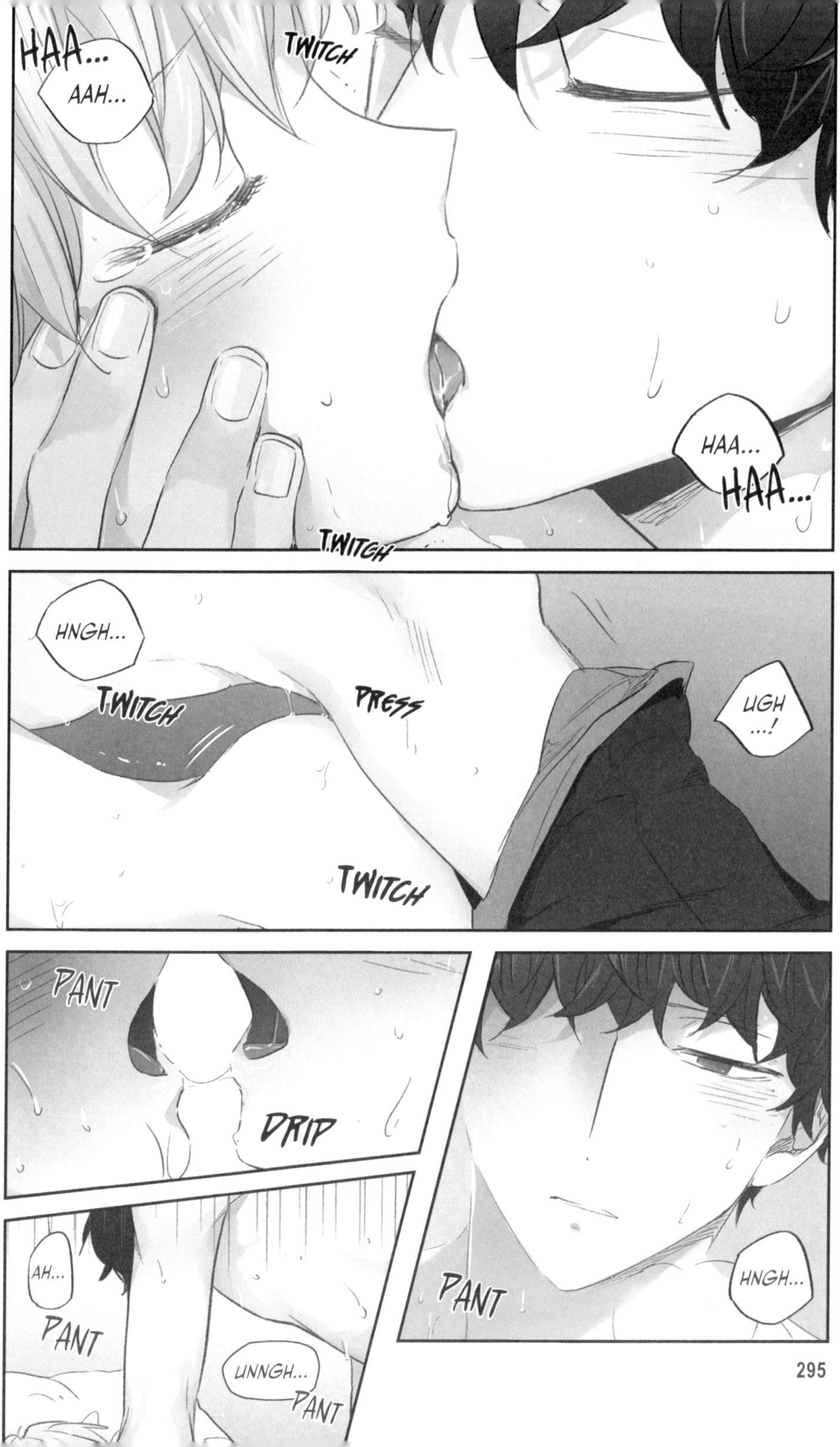
HAA...
AAH...
TWITCH
HAA...
HAA...
TWITCH
HNGH...
TWITCH
PRESS
UGH ...!
TWITCH
PANT
DRIP
AH...
PANT
UNNGH...
PANT
PANT
HNGH...

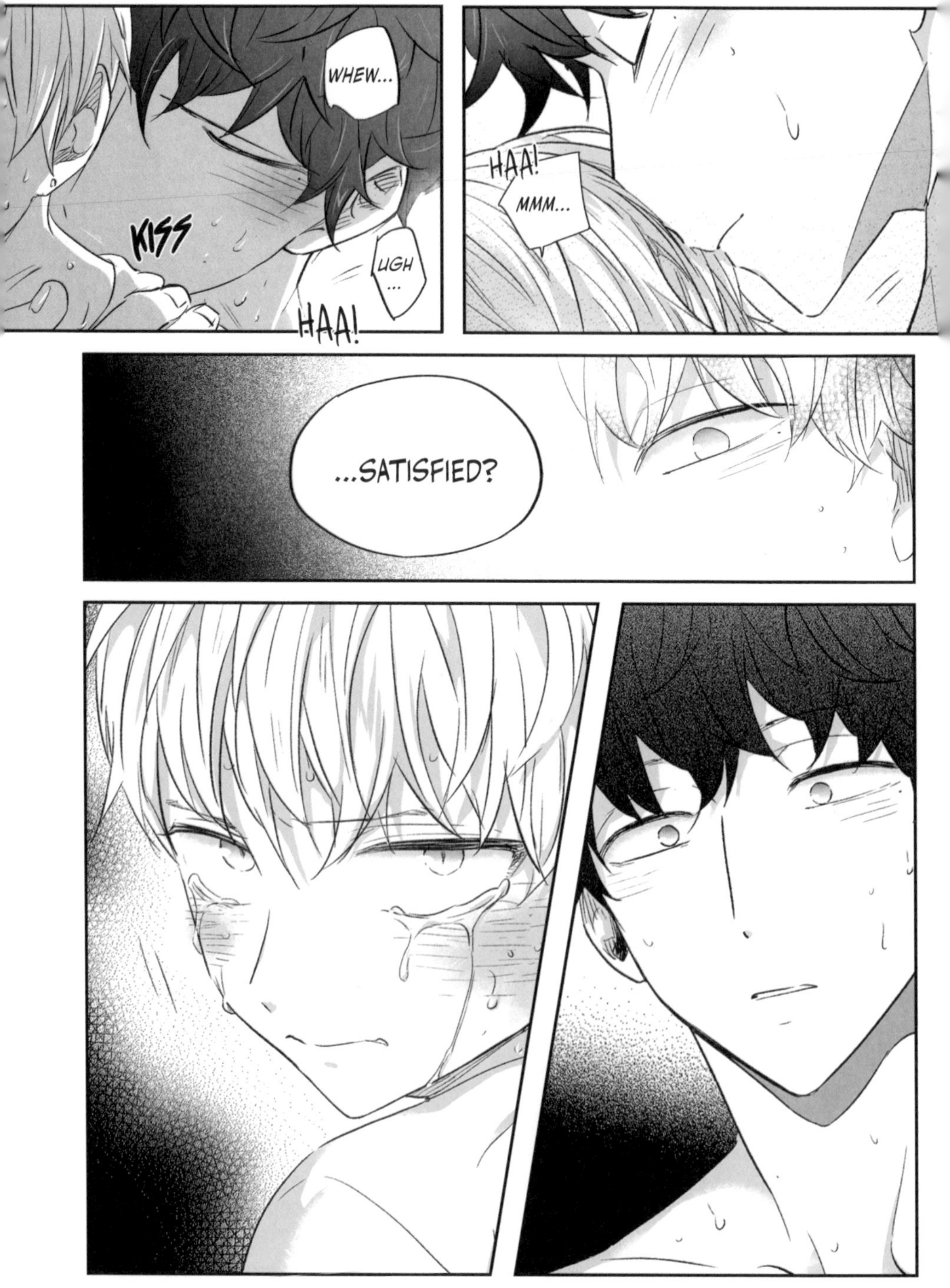
WHEW...
KISS
UGH...
HAA!
HAA!
MMM...
...SATISFIED?

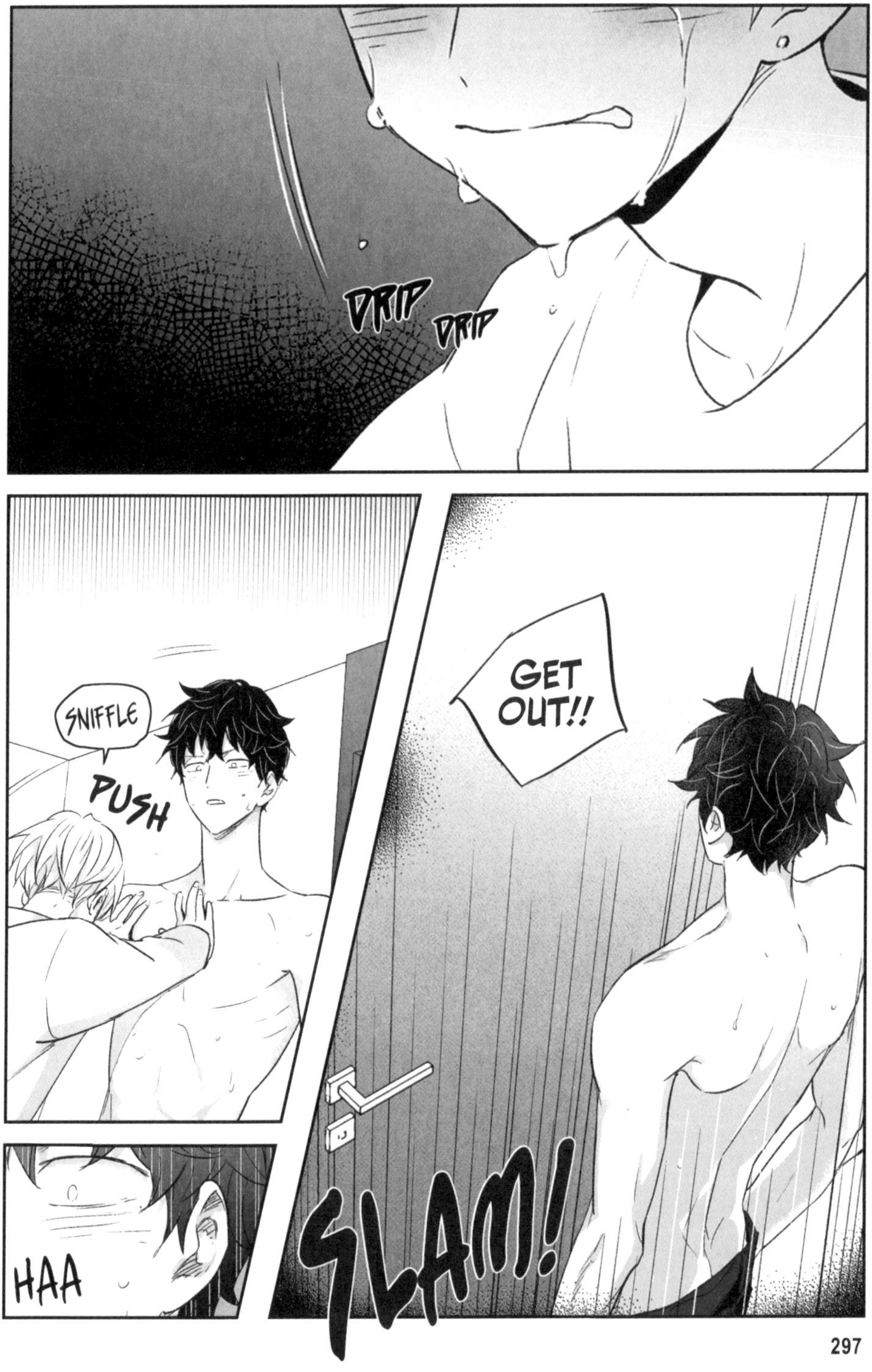
DRIP
DRIP
SNIFFLE
PUSH
GET OUT!!
HAA
SLAM!

Love is
an Illusion!

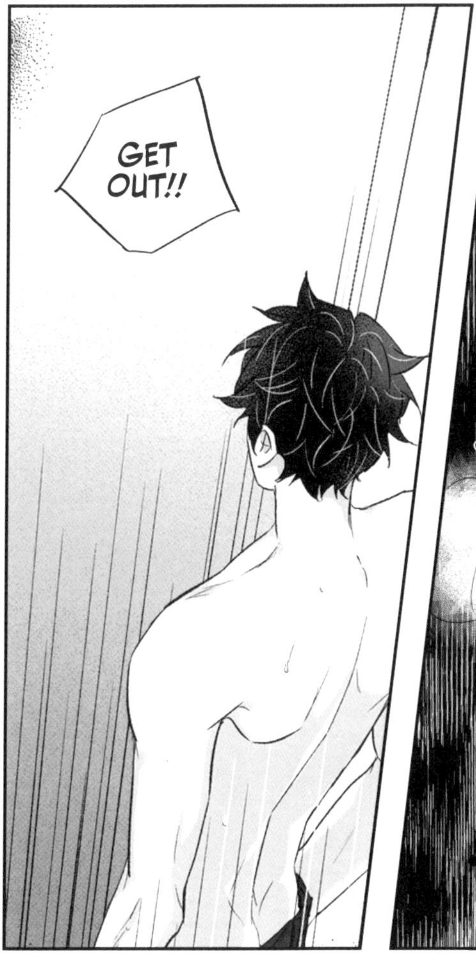
GET OUT!!
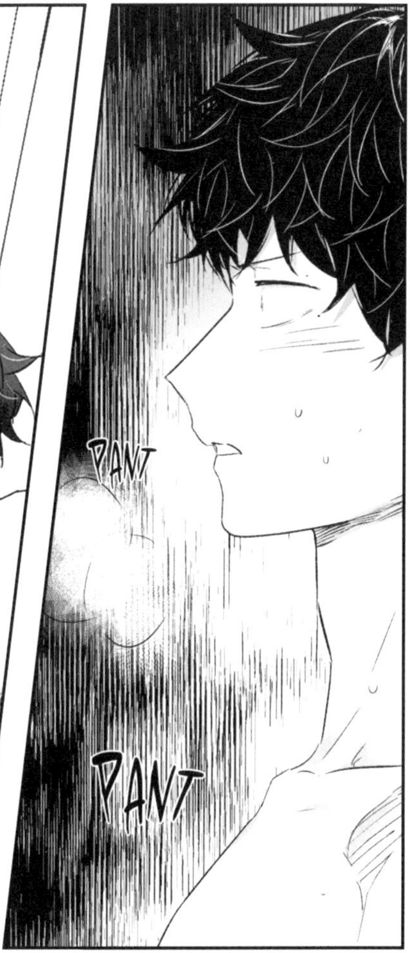
PANT
PANT

Chapter 15

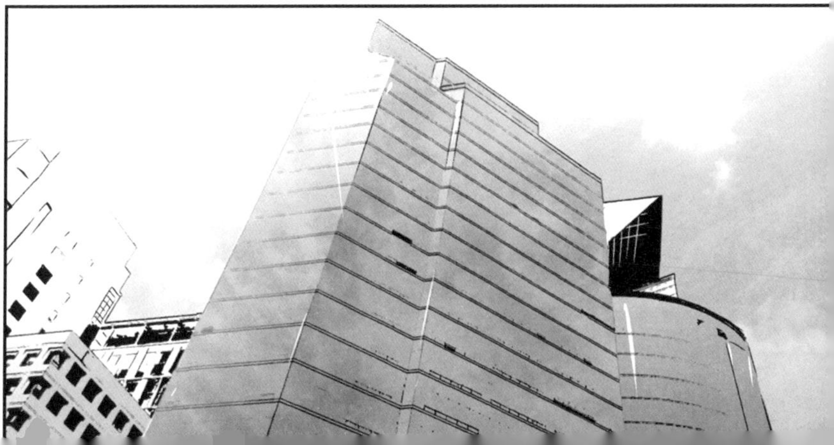

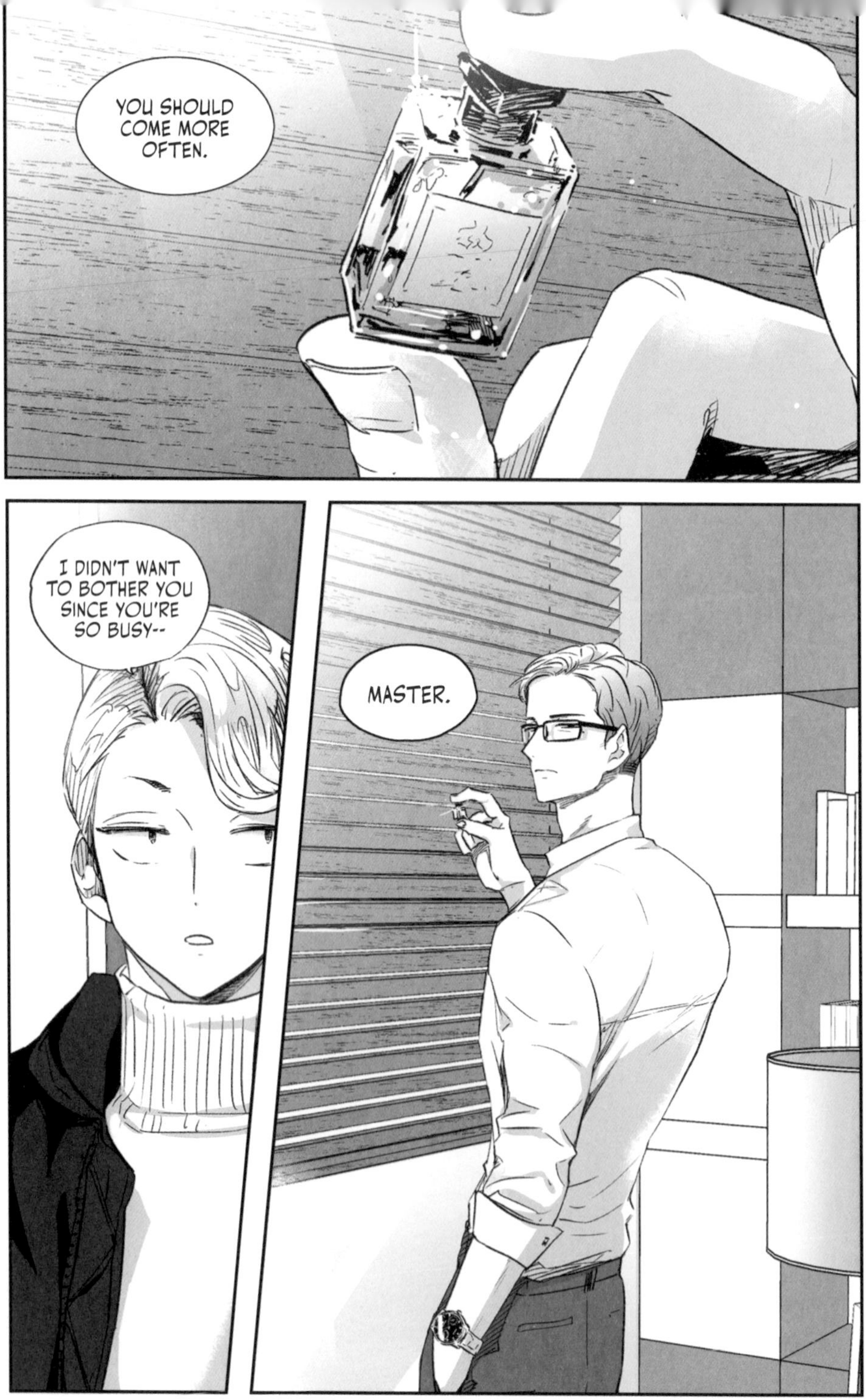
YOU SHOULD COME MORE OFTEN.
I DIDN'T WANT TO BOTHER YOU SINCE YOU'RE SO BUSY--
MASTER.

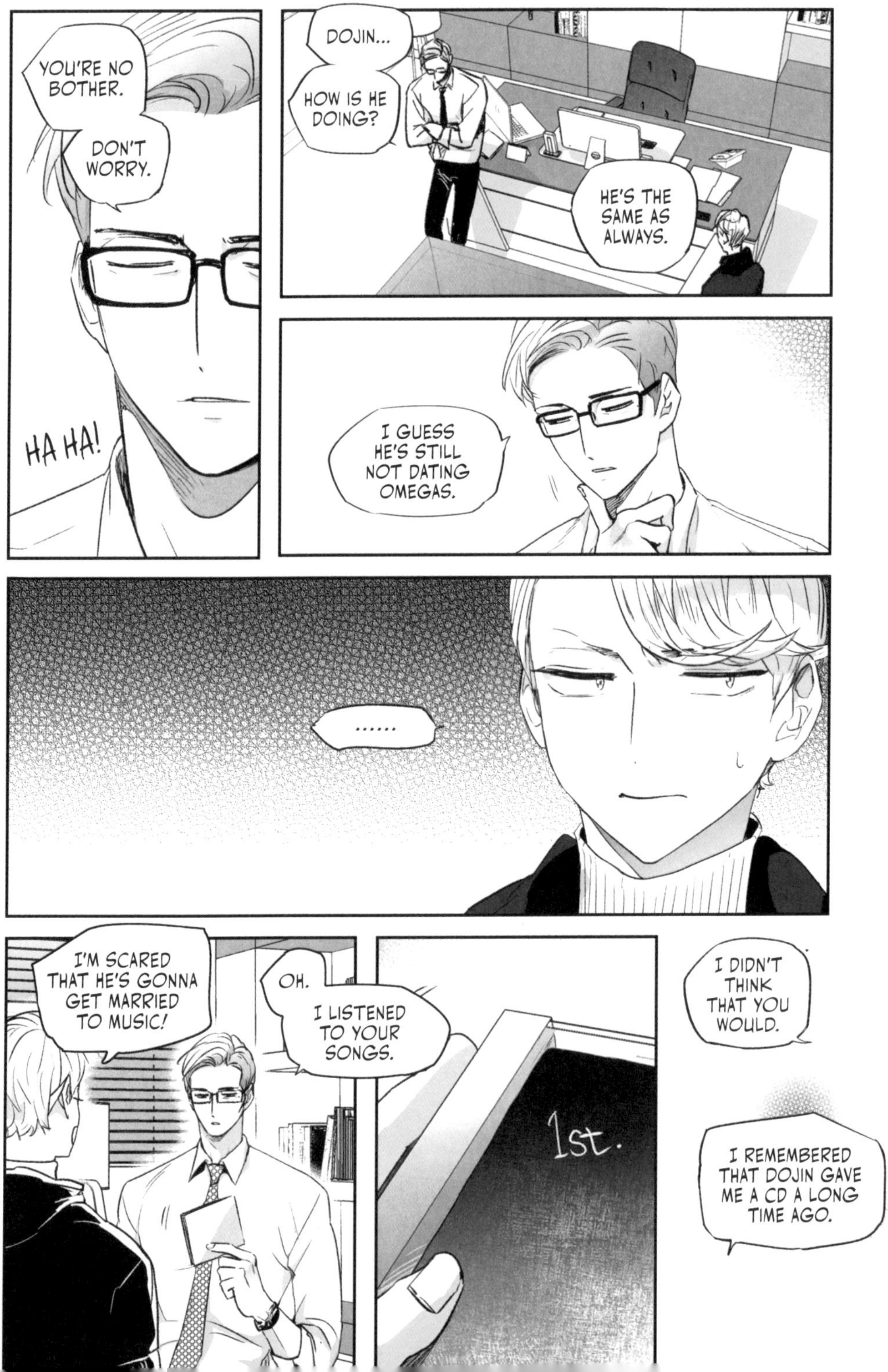
YOU'RE NO BOTHER.
DON'T WORRY.
HA HA!
DOJIN...
HOW IS HE DOING?
HE'S THE SAME AS ALWAYS.
I GUESS HE'S STILL NOT DATING OMEGAS.
......
I'M SCARED THAT HE'S GONNA GET MARRIED TO MUSIC!
OH.
I LISTENED TO YOUR SONGS.
1st.
I DIDN'T THINK THAT YOU WOULD.
I REMEMBERED THAT DOJIN GAVE ME A CD A LONG TIME AGO.

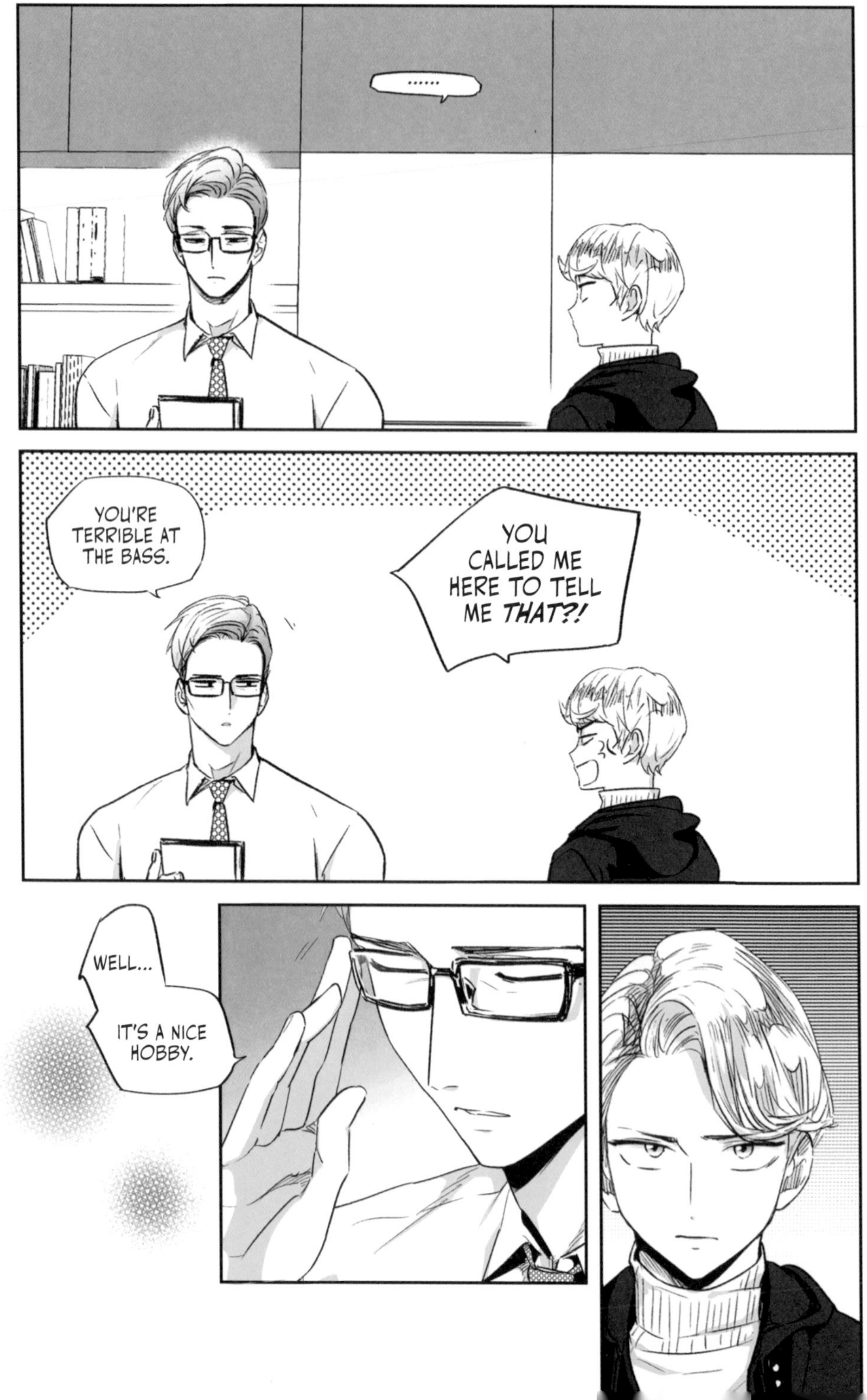
......
YOU'RE TERRIBLE AT THE BASS.
YOU CALLED ME HERE TO TELL ME *THAT?!*
WELL...
IT'S A NICE HOBBY.

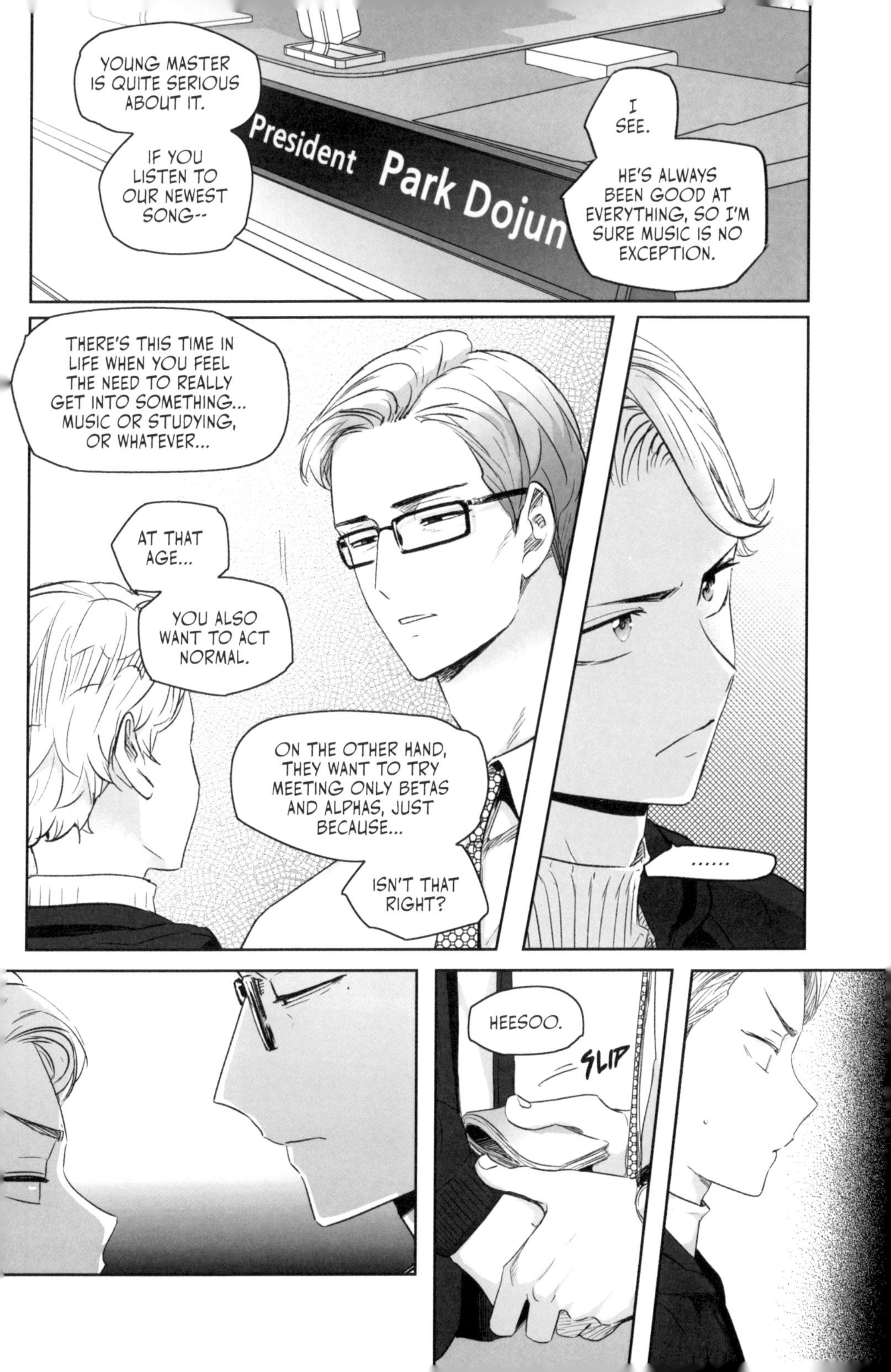
YOUNG MASTER IS QUITE SERIOUS ABOUT IT.
IF YOU LISTEN TO OUR NEWEST SONG--
President Park Dojun
I SEE.
HE'S ALWAYS BEEN GOOD AT EVERYTHING, SO I'M SURE MUSIC IS NO EXCEPTION.
THERE'S THIS TIME IN LIFE WHEN YOU FEEL THE NEED TO REALLY GET INTO SOMETHING... MUSIC OR STUDYING, OR WHATEVER...
AT THAT AGE...
YOU ALSO WANT TO ACT NORMAL.
ON THE OTHER HAND, THEY WANT TO TRY MEETING ONLY BETAS AND ALPHAS, JUST BECAUSE...
ISN'T THAT RIGHT?
......
HEESOO.
SLIP

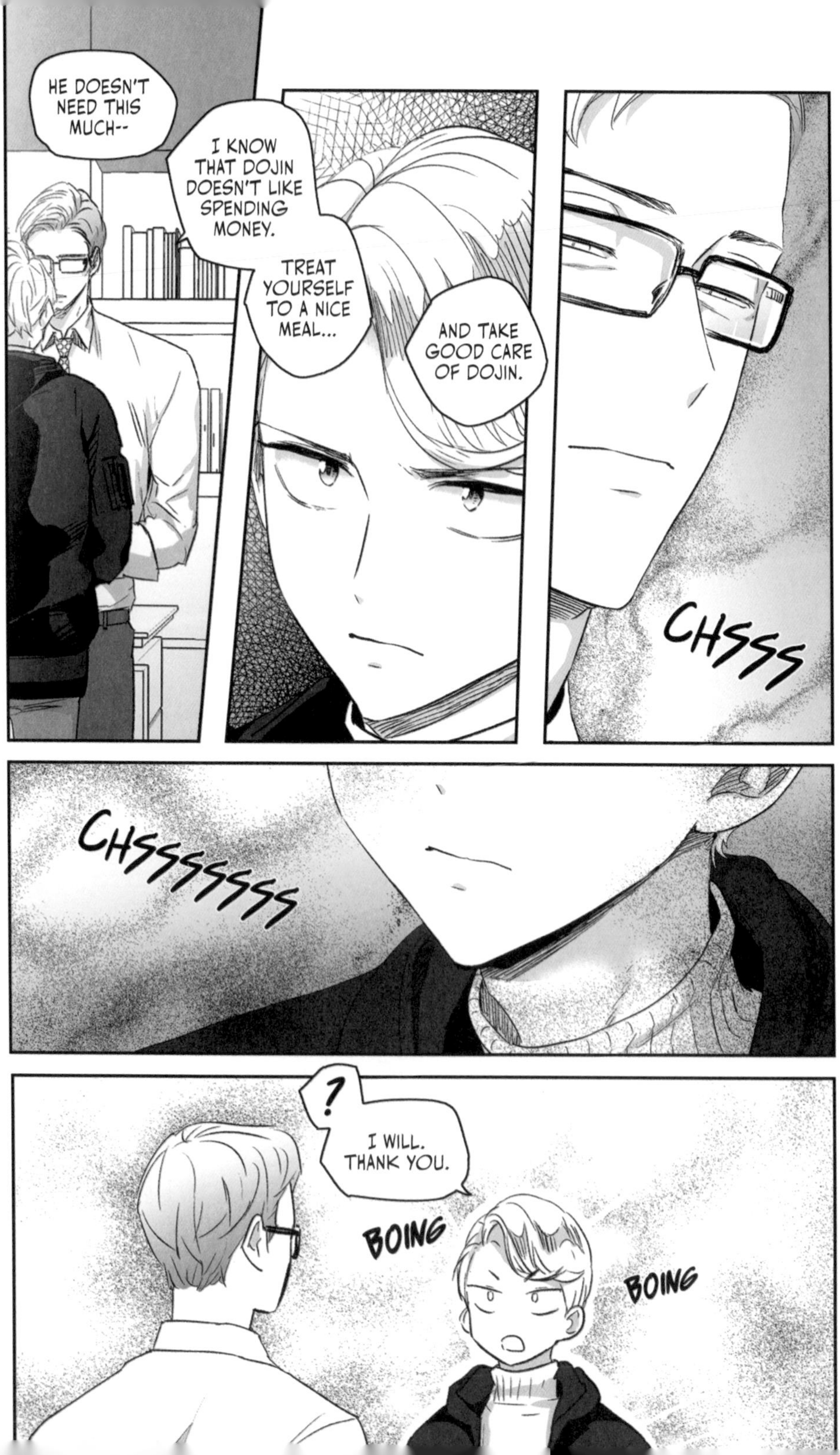
HE DOESN'T NEED THIS MUCH--
I KNOW THAT DOJIN DOESN'T LIKE SPENDING MONEY.
TREAT YOURSELF TO A NICE MEAL...
AND TAKE GOOD CARE OF DOJIN.
CHSSS
CHSSSSSSSS
?
I WILL. THANK YOU.
BOING
BOING

HAVE A GOOD DAY.

......

BOW

SIGH...

PLOP

BETAS...

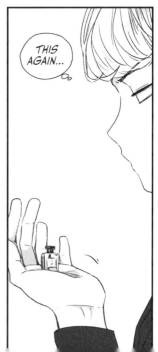

THIS AGAIN...

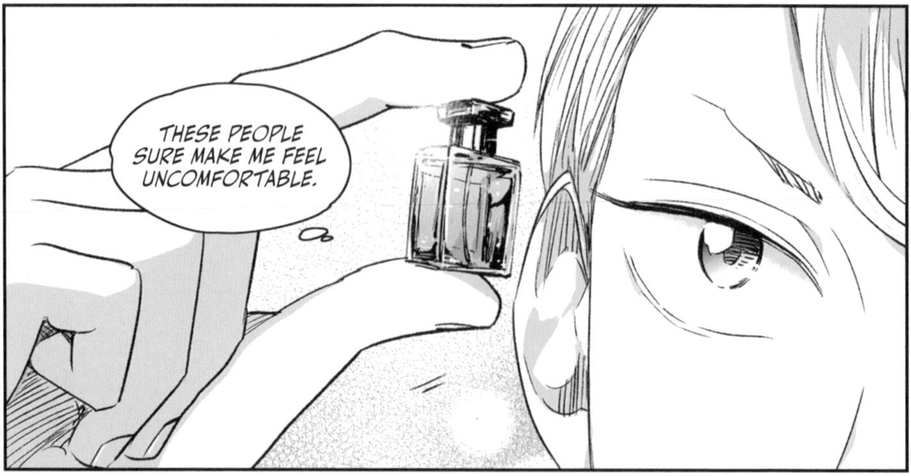
THESE PEOPLE SURE MAKE ME FEEL UNCOMFORTABLE.

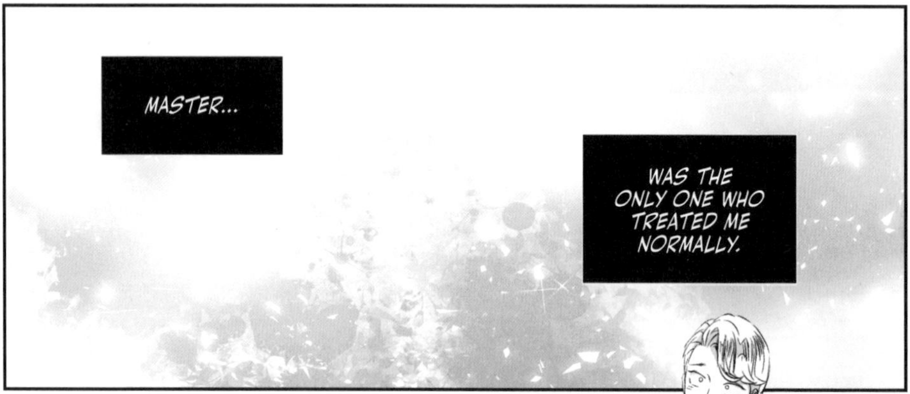
MASTER...
WAS THE ONLY ONE WHO TREATED ME NORMALLY.

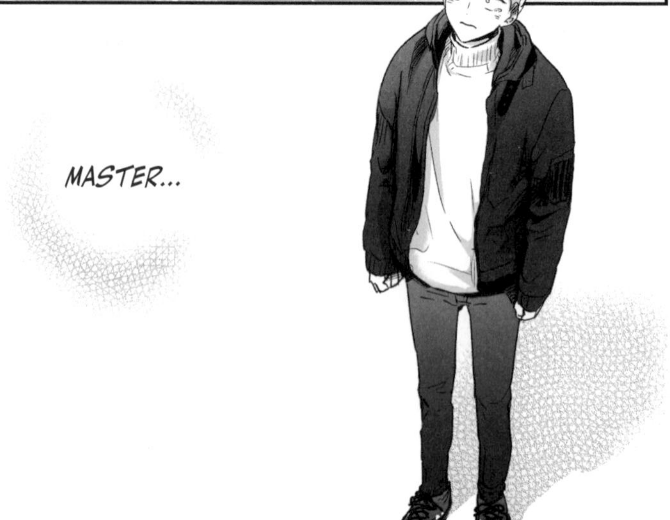
MASTER...

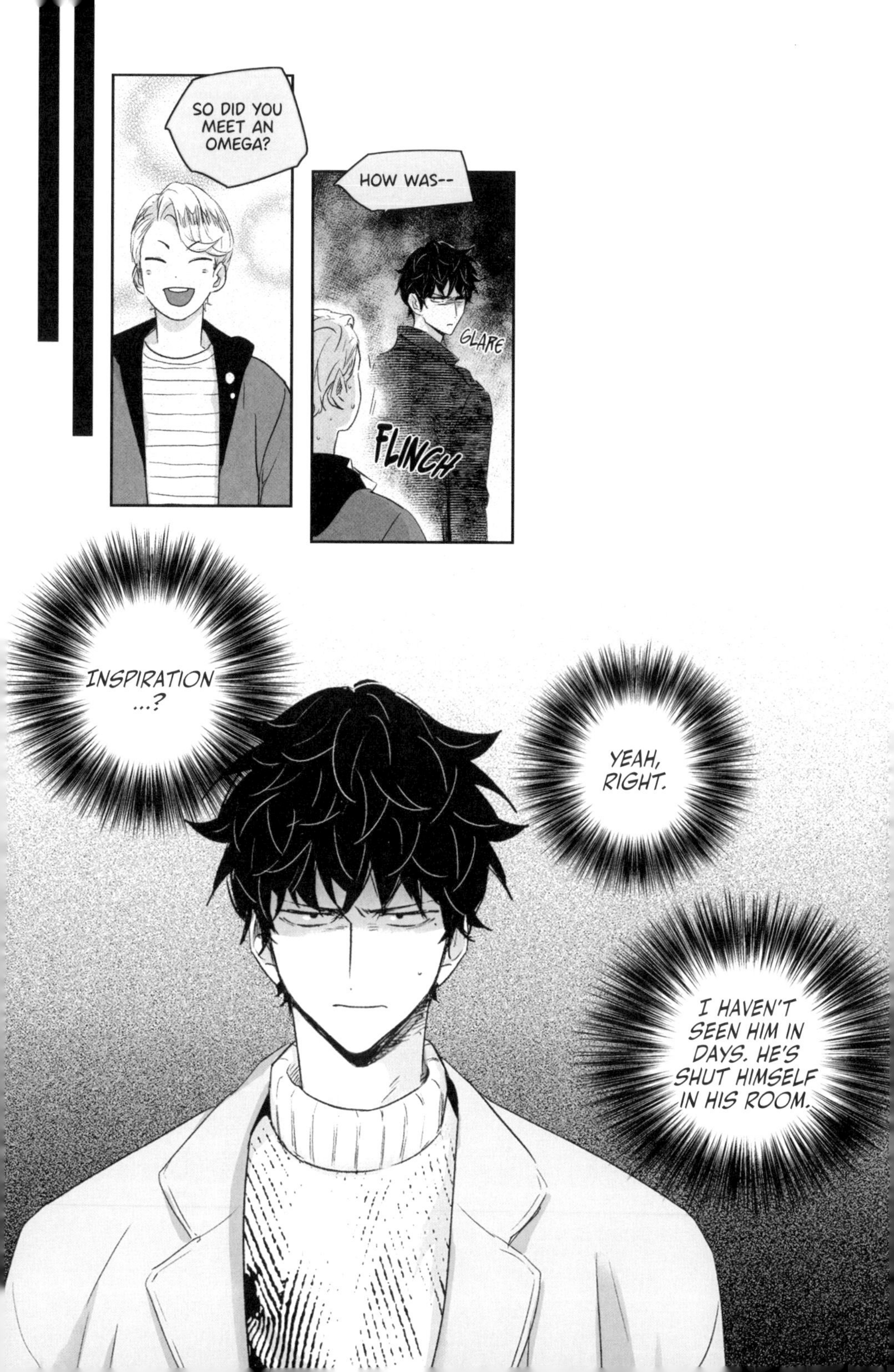
SO DID YOU MEET AN OMEGA?
HOW WAS--
GLARE
FLINCH
INSPIRATION ...?
YEAH, RIGHT.
I HAVEN'T SEEN HIM IN DAYS. HE'S SHUT HIMSELF IN HIS ROOM.

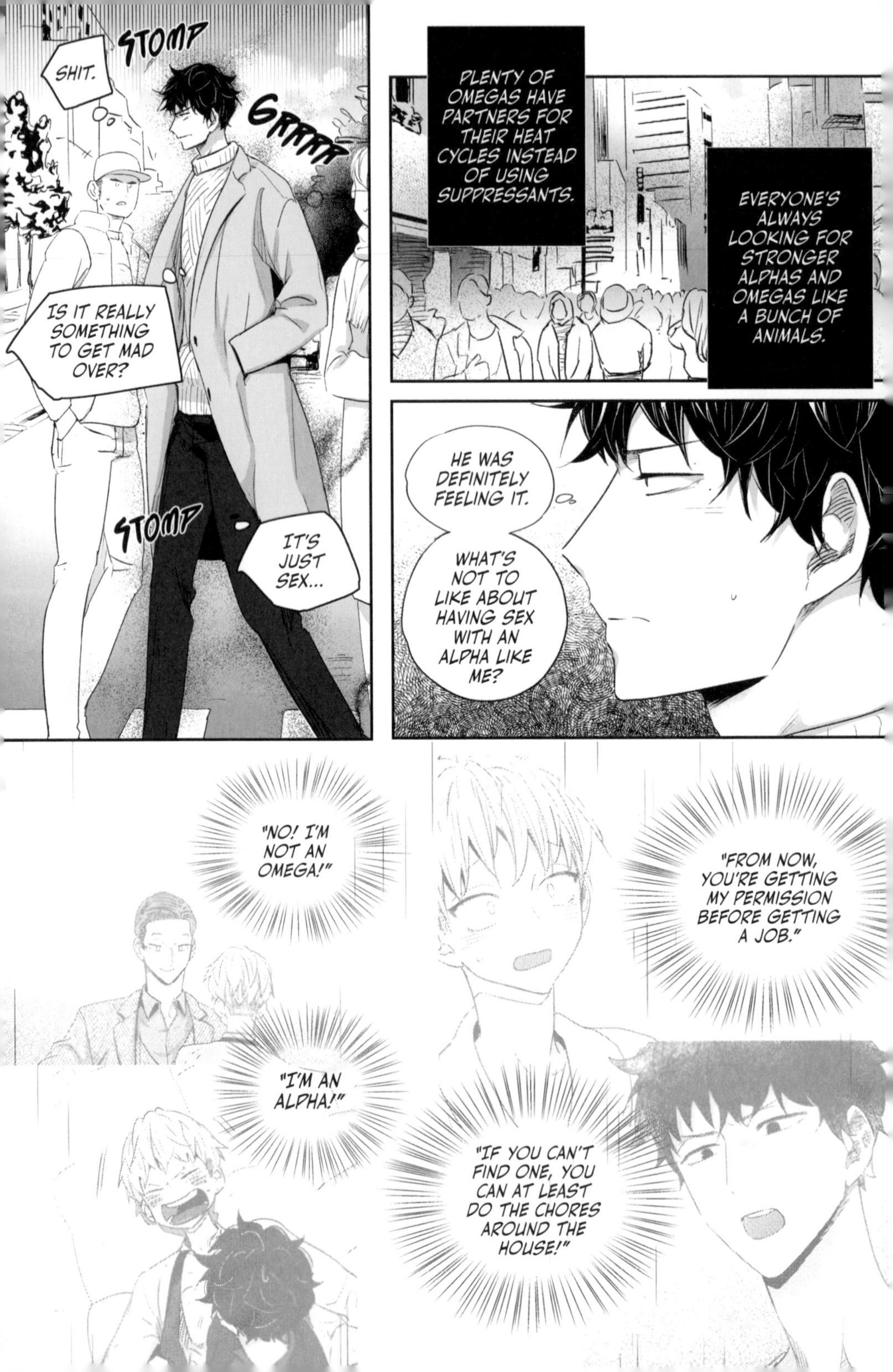
STOMP
SHIT.
GRRRRR
IS IT REALLY SOMETHING TO GET MAD OVER?
STOMP
IT'S JUST SEX...
PLENTY OF OMEGAS HAVE PARTNERS FOR THEIR HEAT CYCLES INSTEAD OF USING SUPPRESSANTS.
EVERYONE'S ALWAYS LOOKING FOR STRONGER ALPHAS AND OMEGAS LIKE A BUNCH OF ANIMALS.
HE WAS DEFINITELY FEELING IT.
WHAT'S NOT TO LIKE ABOUT HAVING SEX WITH AN ALPHA LIKE ME?
"NO! I'M NOT AN OMEGA!"
"FROM NOW, YOU'RE GETTING MY PERMISSION BEFORE GETTING A JOB."
"I'M AN ALPHA!"
"IF YOU CAN'T FIND ONE, YOU CAN AT LEAST DO THE CHORES AROUND THE HOUSE!"

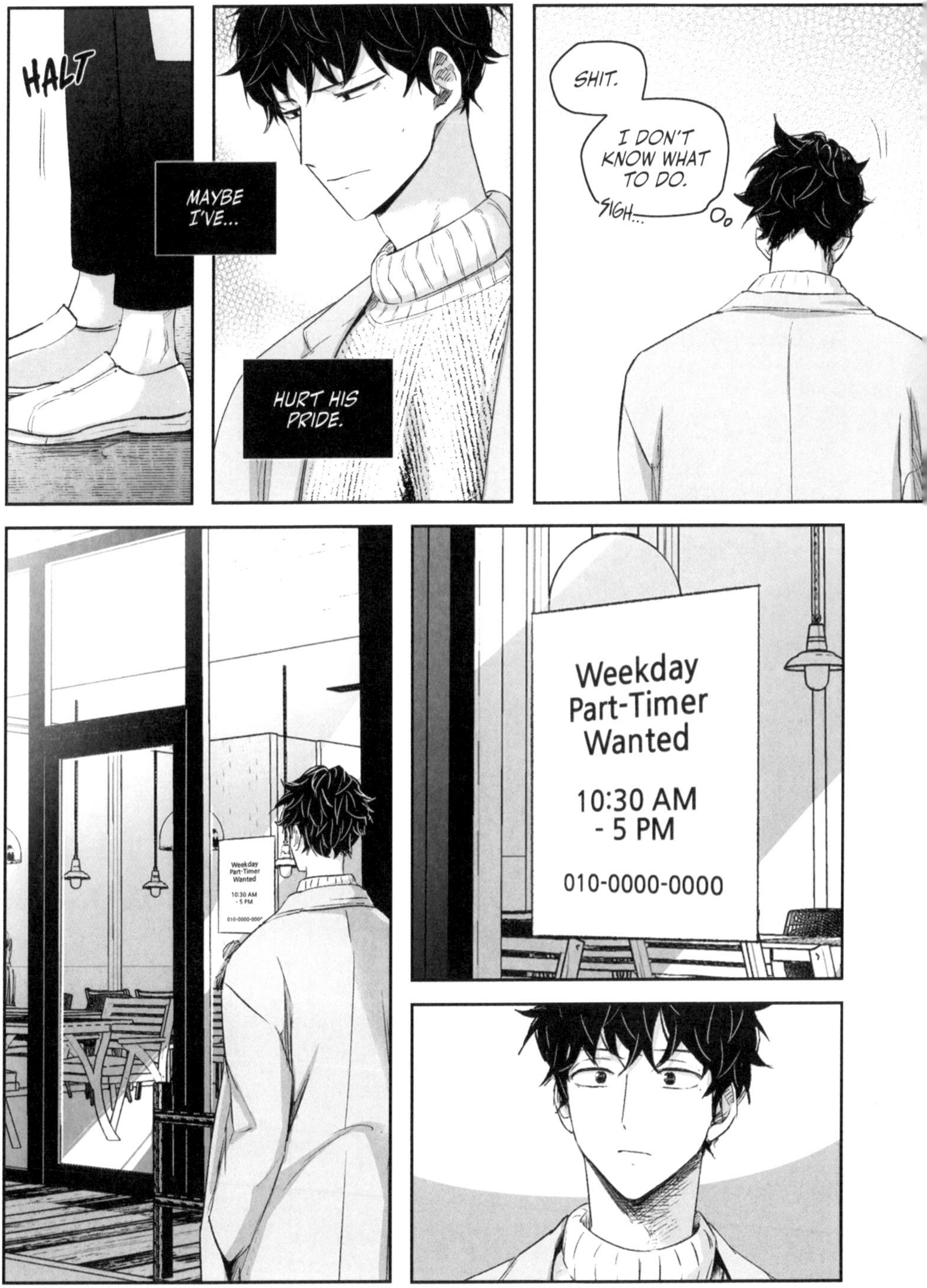
HALT
MAYBE I'VE...
HURT HIS PRIDE.
SHIT.
I DON'T KNOW WHAT TO DO.
SIGH...
Weekday Part-Timer Wanted
10:30 AM - 5 PM
010-0000-0000
Weekday Part-Timer Wanted
10:30 AM - 5 PM
010-0000-0000

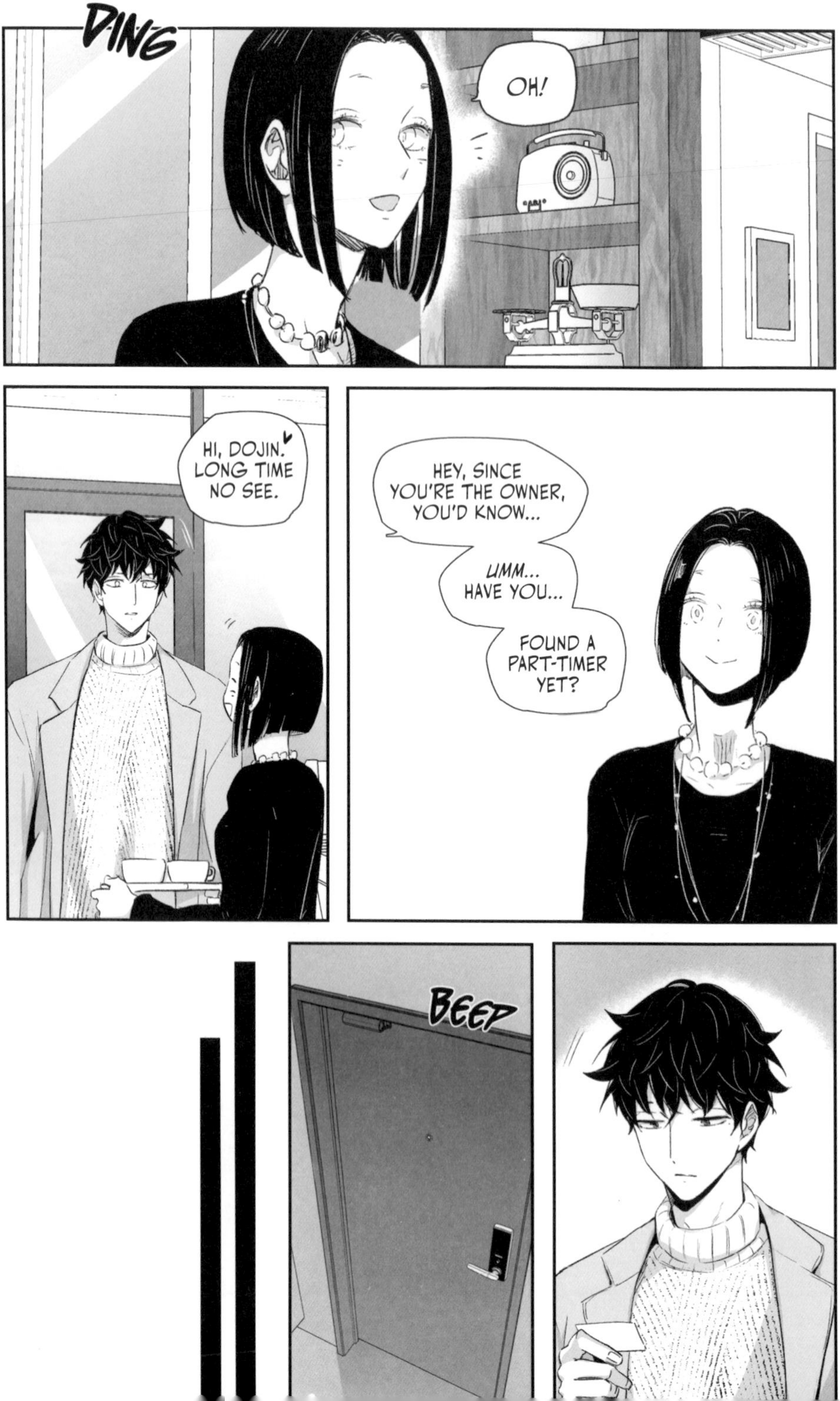
DING
OH!
HI, DOJIN. LONG TIME NO SEE.
HEY, SINCE YOU'RE THE OWNER, YOU'D KNOW...
UMM... HAVE YOU...
FOUND A PART-TIMER YET?
BEEP

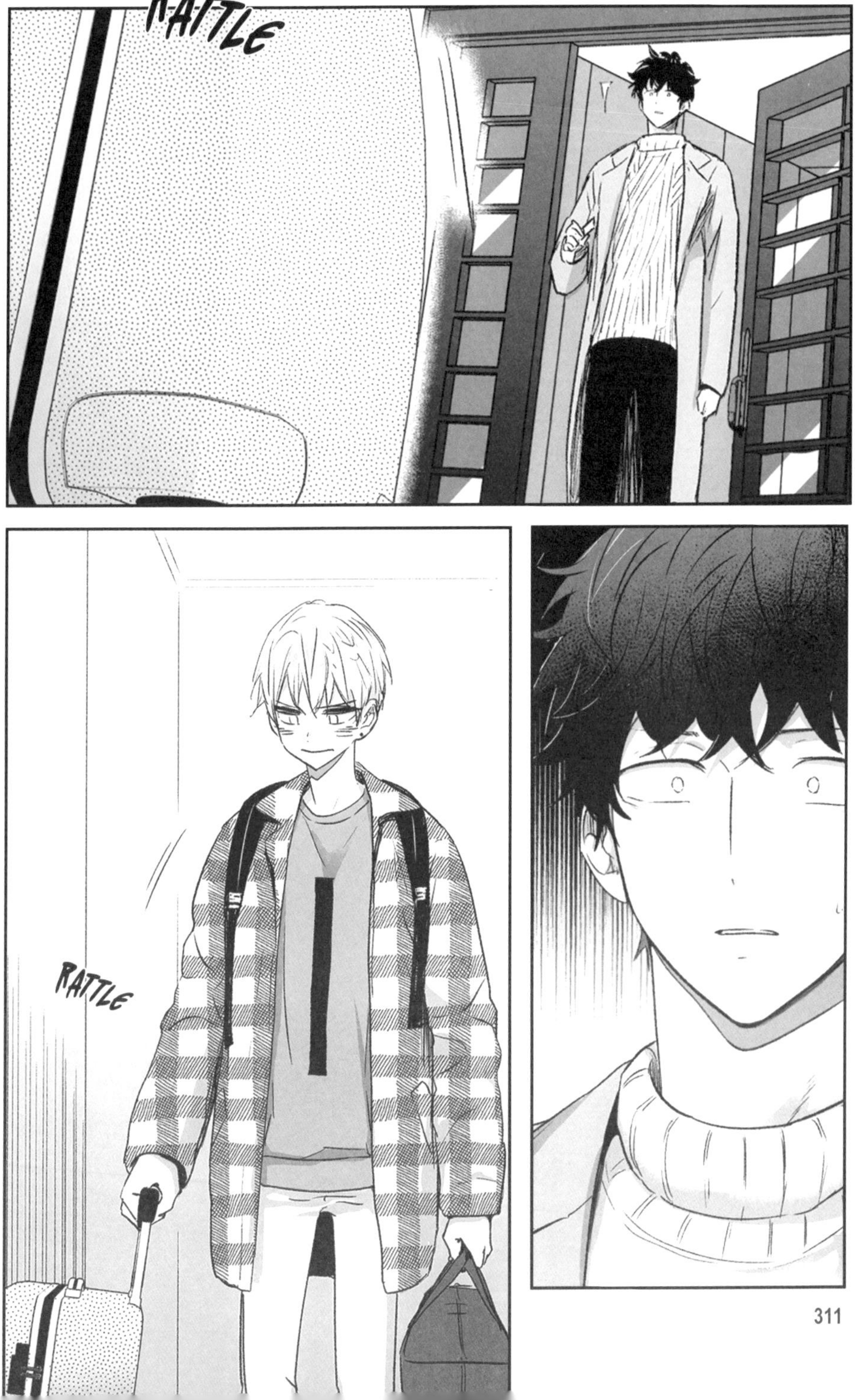
RATTLE
RATTLE

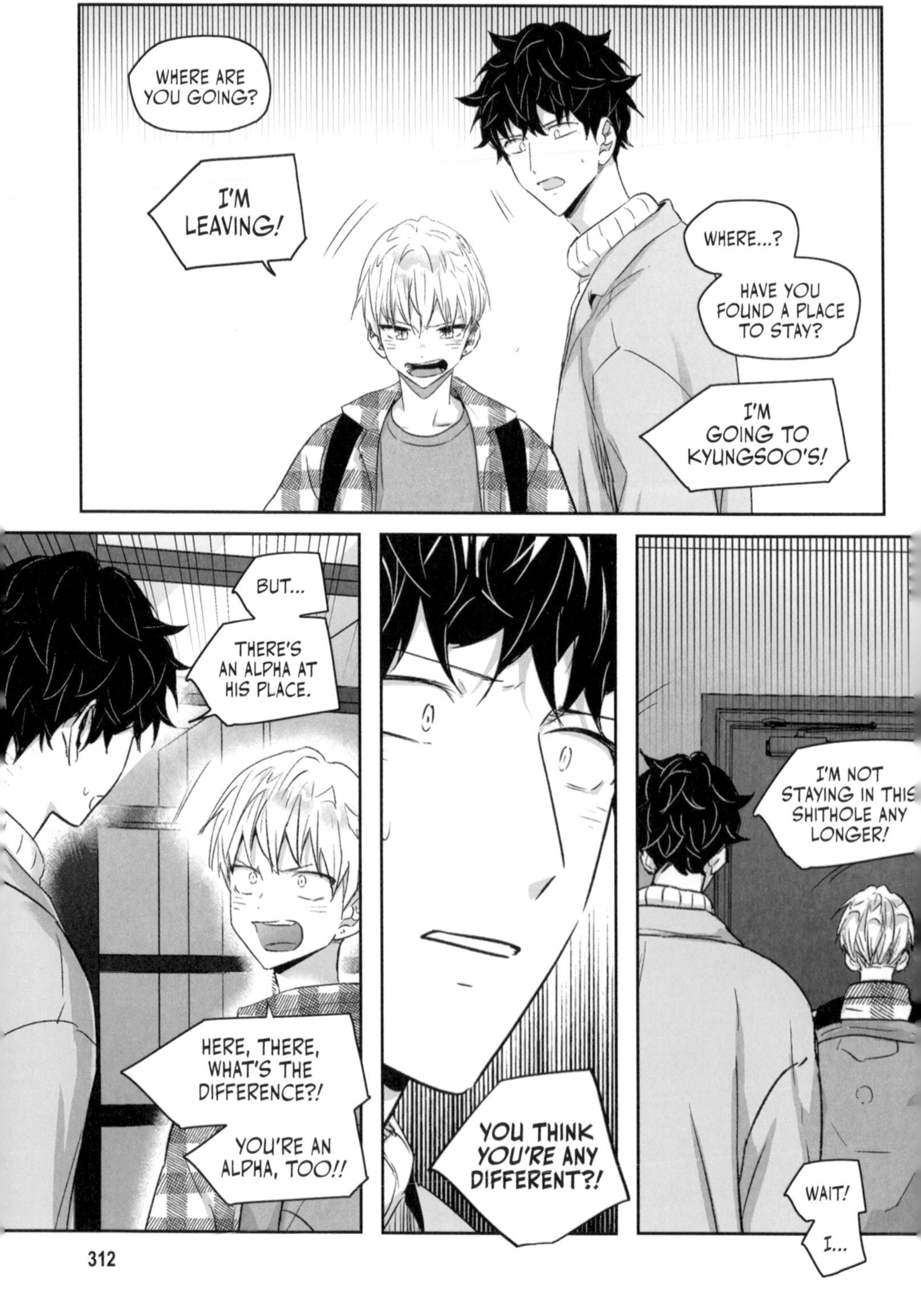
WHERE ARE YOU GOING?
I'M LEAVING!
WHERE...?
HAVE YOU FOUND A PLACE TO STAY?
I'M GOING TO KYUNGSOO'S!
BUT...
THERE'S AN ALPHA AT HIS PLACE.
HERE, THERE, WHAT'S THE DIFFERENCE?!
YOU'RE AN ALPHA, TOO!!
YOU THINK YOU'RE ANY DIFFERENT?!
I'M NOT STAYING IN THIS SHITHOLE ANY LONGER!
WAIT!
I...

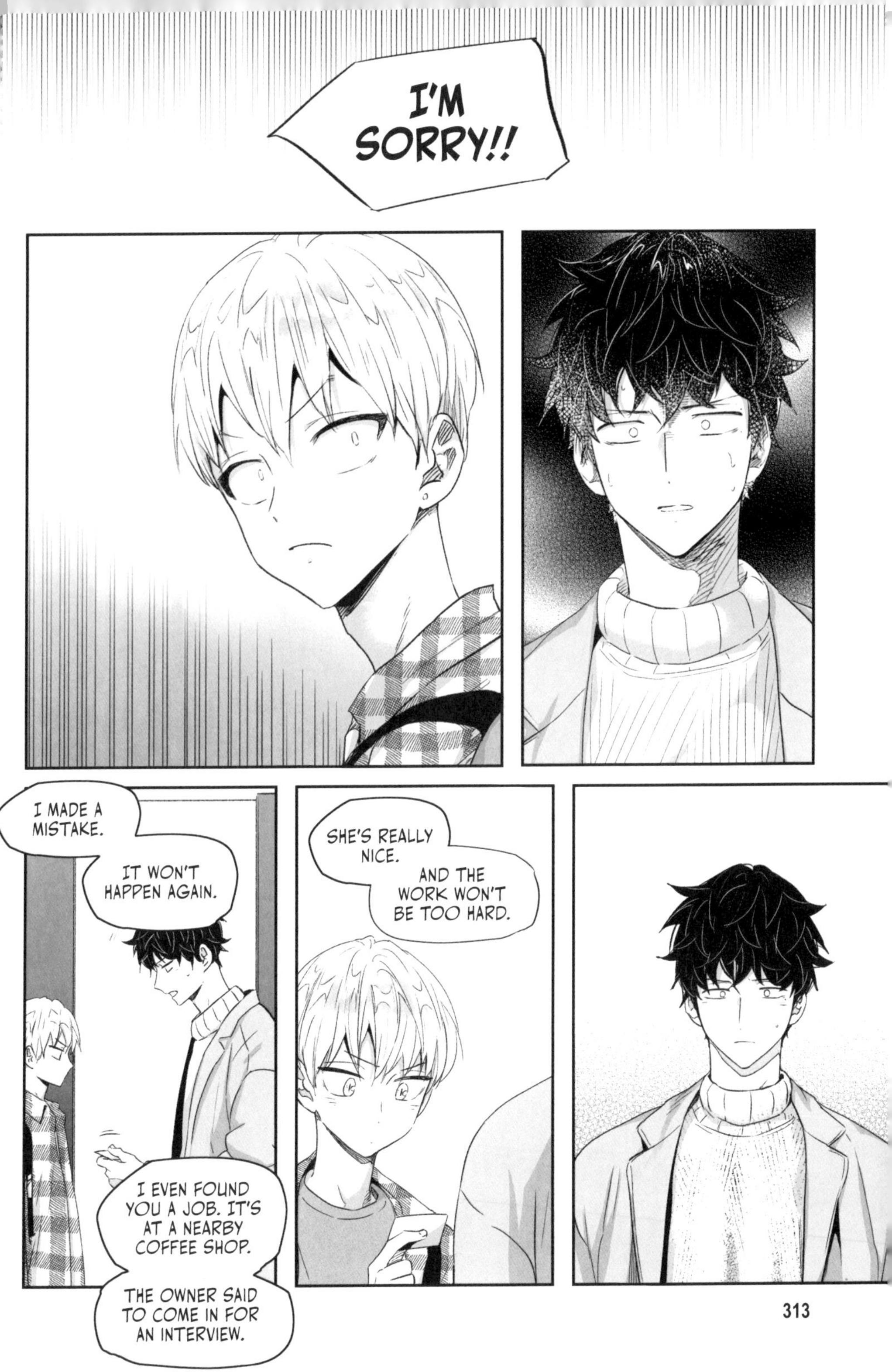
I'M SORRY!!
I MADE A MISTAKE.
IT WON'T HAPPEN AGAIN.
I EVEN FOUND YOU A JOB. IT'S AT A NEARBY COFFEE SHOP.
THE OWNER SAID TO COME IN FOR AN INTERVIEW.
SHE'S REALLY NICE.
AND THE WORK WON'T BE TOO HARD.

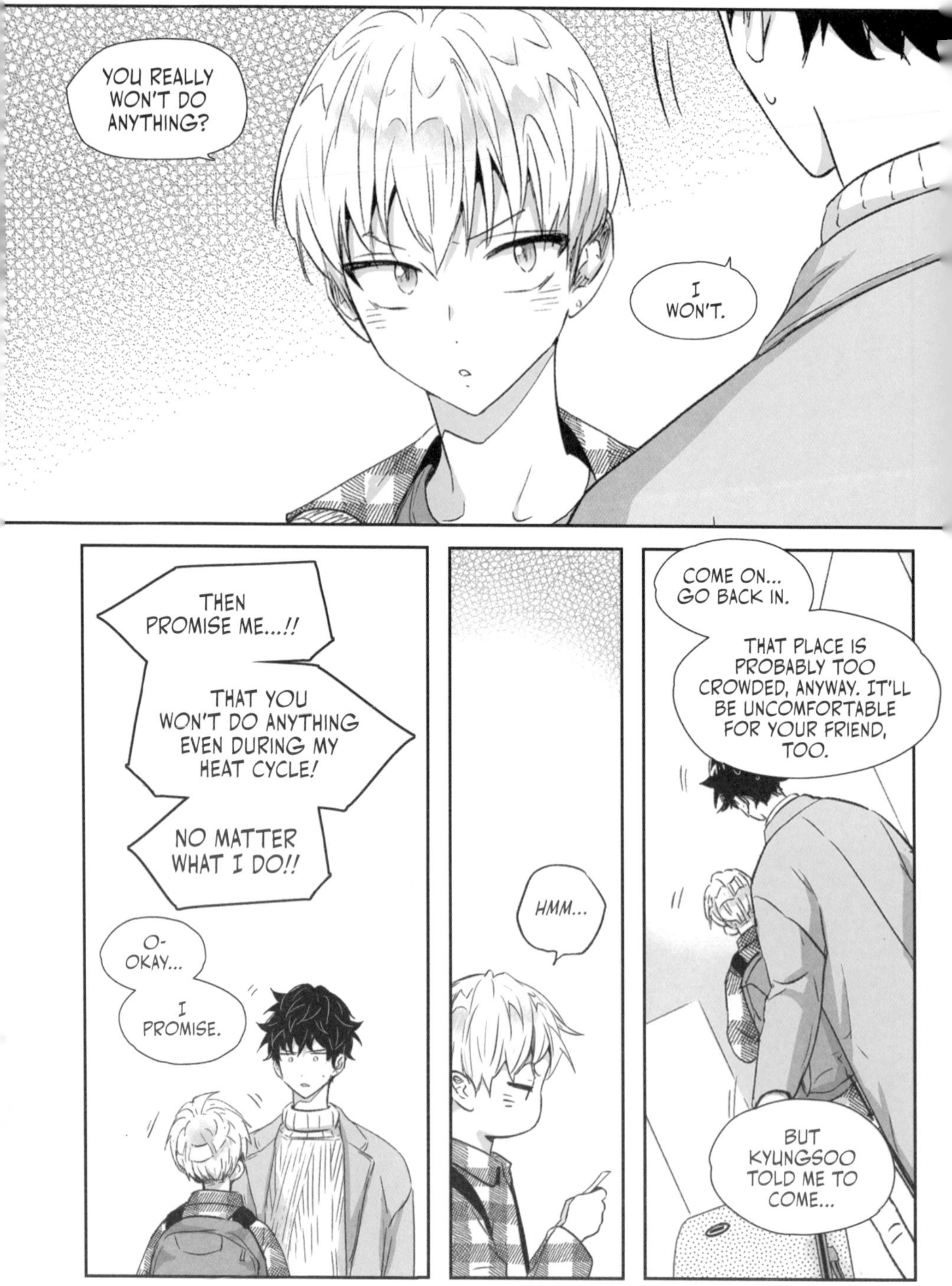
YOU REALLY WON'T DO ANYTHING?
I WON'T.
THEN PROMISE ME...!!
THAT YOU WON'T DO ANYTHING EVEN DURING MY HEAT CYCLE!
NO MATTER WHAT I DO!!
O-OKAY...
I PROMISE.
HMM...
COME ON... GO BACK IN.
THAT PLACE IS PROBABLY TOO CROWDED, ANYWAY. IT'LL BE UNCOMFORTABLE FOR YOUR FRIEND, TOO.
BUT KYUNGSOO TOLD ME TO COME...

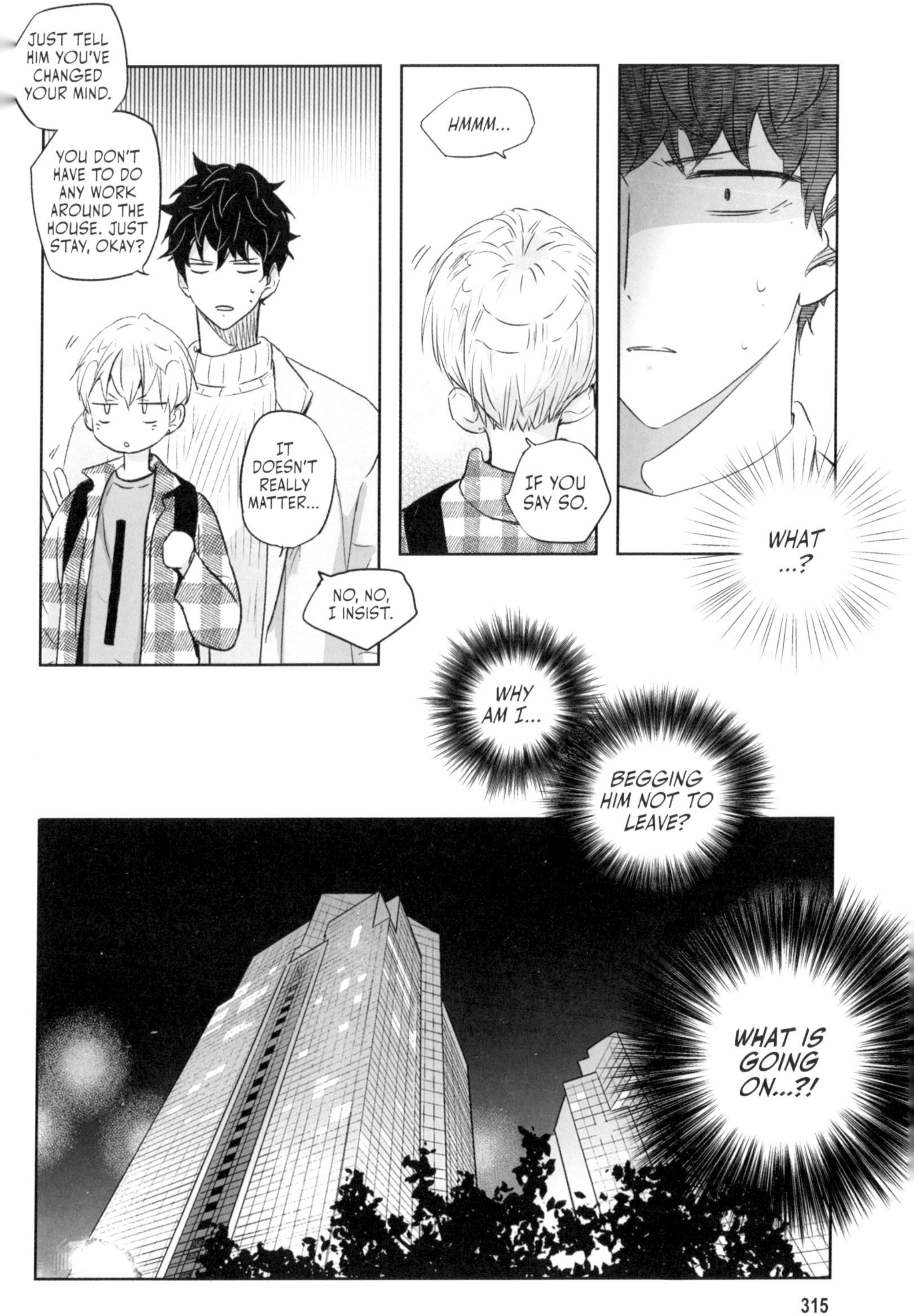
JUST TELL HIM YOU'VE CHANGED YOUR MIND.
YOU DON'T HAVE TO DO ANY WORK AROUND THE HOUSE. JUST STAY, OKAY?
IT DOESN'T REALLY MATTER...
NO, NO, I INSIST.
HMMM...
IF YOU SAY SO.
WHAT ...?
WHY AM I...
BEGGING HIM NOT TO LEAVE?
WHAT IS GOING ON...?!

Love is
an Illusion!

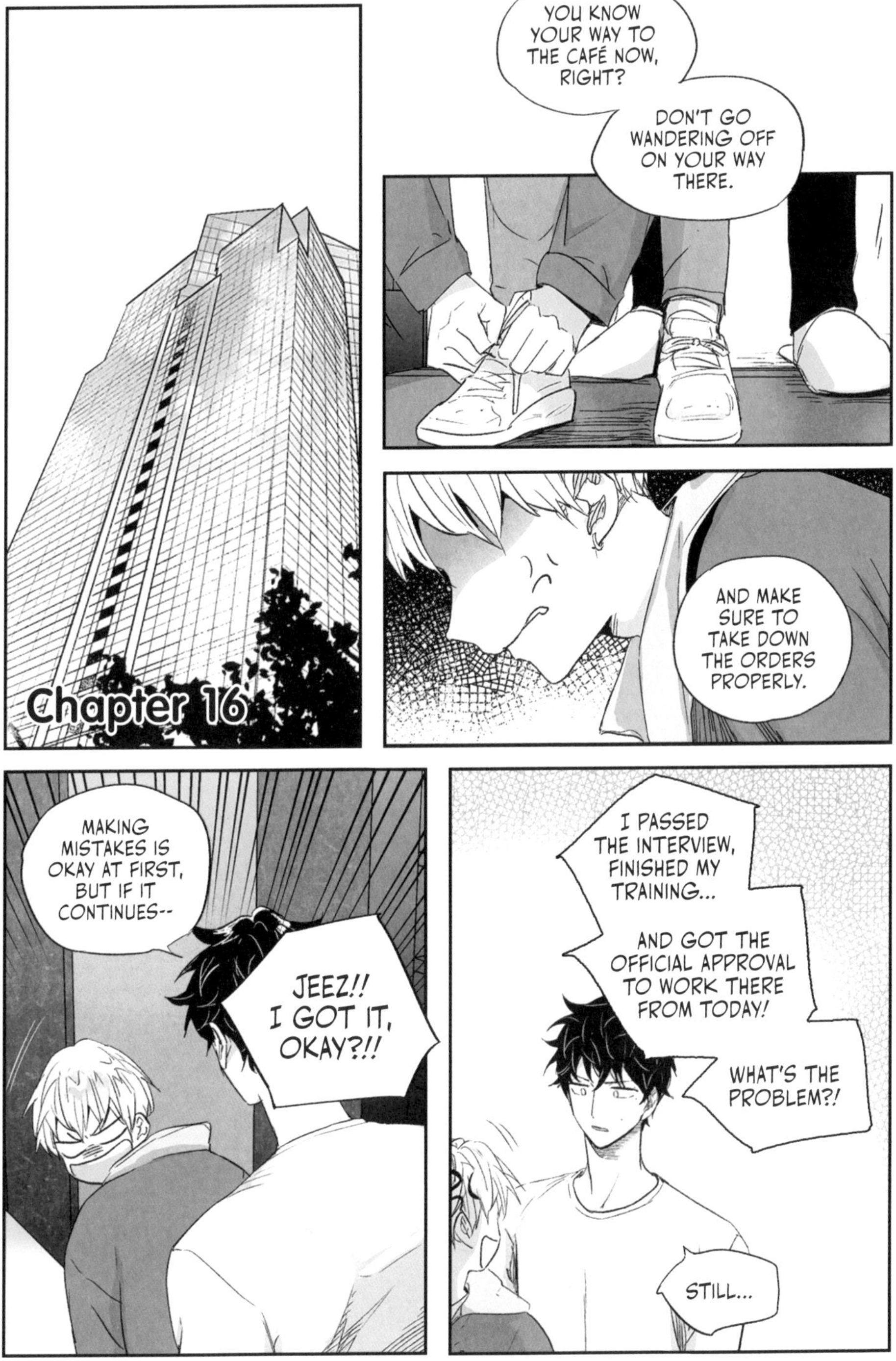
Chapter 16
YOU KNOW YOUR WAY TO THE CAFÉ NOW, RIGHT?
DON'T GO WANDERING OFF ON YOUR WAY THERE.
AND MAKE SURE TO TAKE DOWN THE ORDERS PROPERLY.
MAKING MISTAKES IS OKAY AT FIRST, BUT IF IT CONTINUES--
JEEZ!! I GOT IT, OKAY?!!
I PASSED THE INTERVIEW, FINISHED MY TRAINING...
AND GOT THE OFFICIAL APPROVAL TO WORK THERE FROM TODAY!
WHAT'S THE PROBLEM?!
STILL...

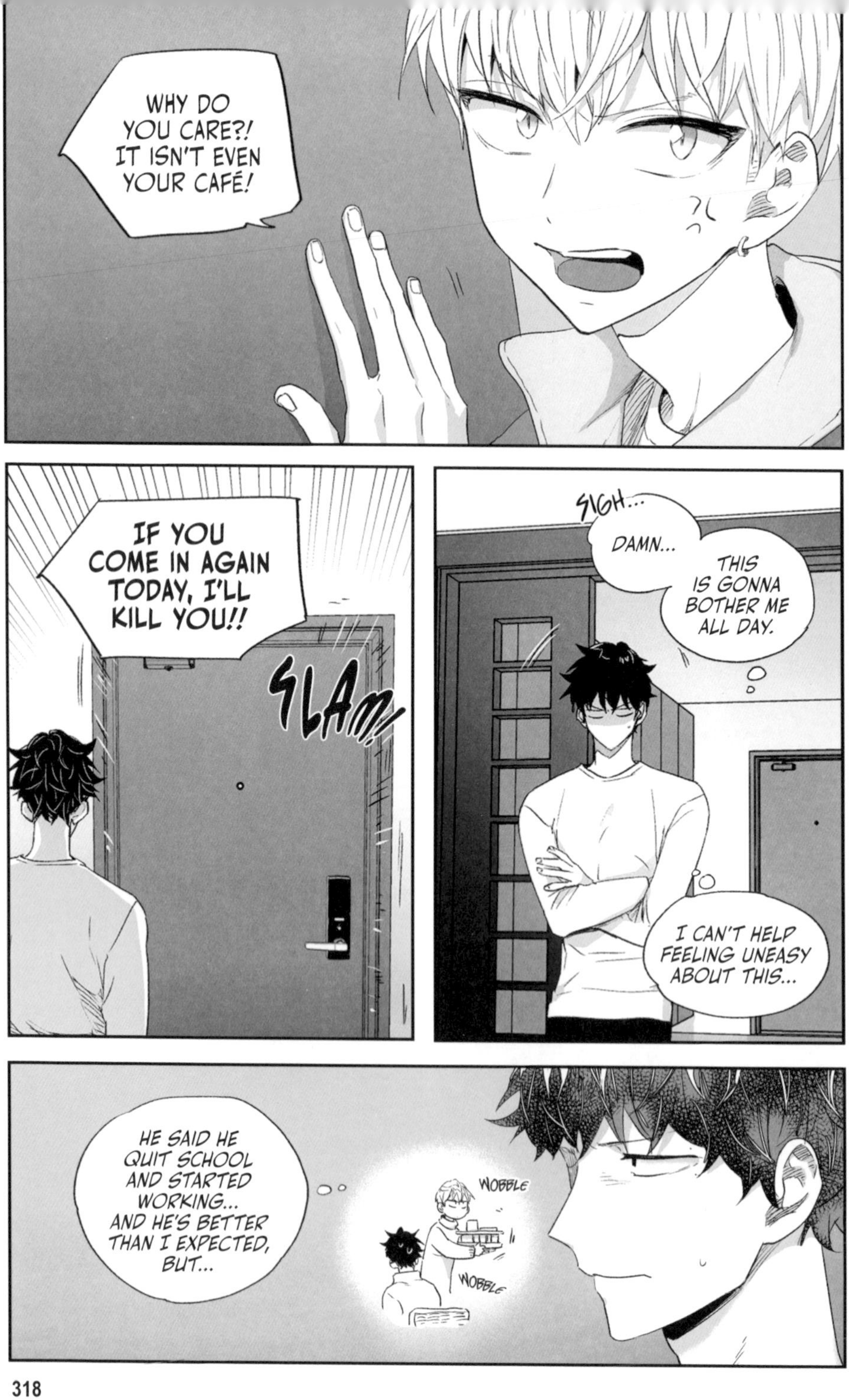
WHY DO YOU CARE?! IT ISN'T EVEN YOUR CAFÉ!
IF YOU COME IN AGAIN TODAY, I'LL KILL YOU!!
SLAM!!
SIGH...
DAMN...
THIS IS GONNA BOTHER ME ALL DAY.
I CAN'T HELP FEELING UNEASY ABOUT THIS...
HE SAID HE QUIT SCHOOL AND STARTED WORKING... AND HE'S BETTER THAN I EXPECTED, BUT...
WOBBLE
WOBBLE

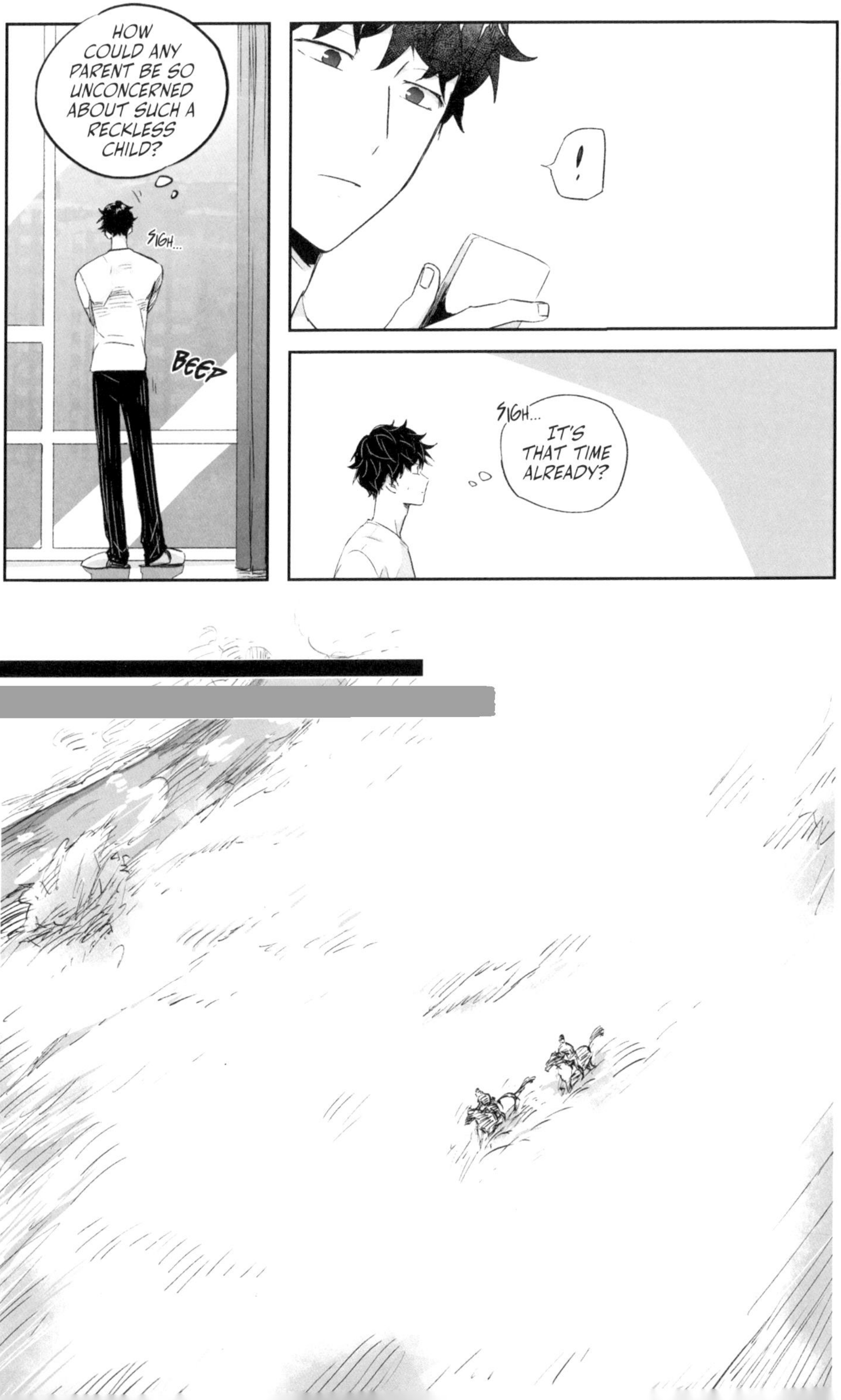
HOW COULD ANY PARENT BE SO UNCONCERNED ABOUT SUCH A RECKLESS CHILD?
SIGH...
BEEP
!
SIGH...
IT'S THAT TIME ALREADY?

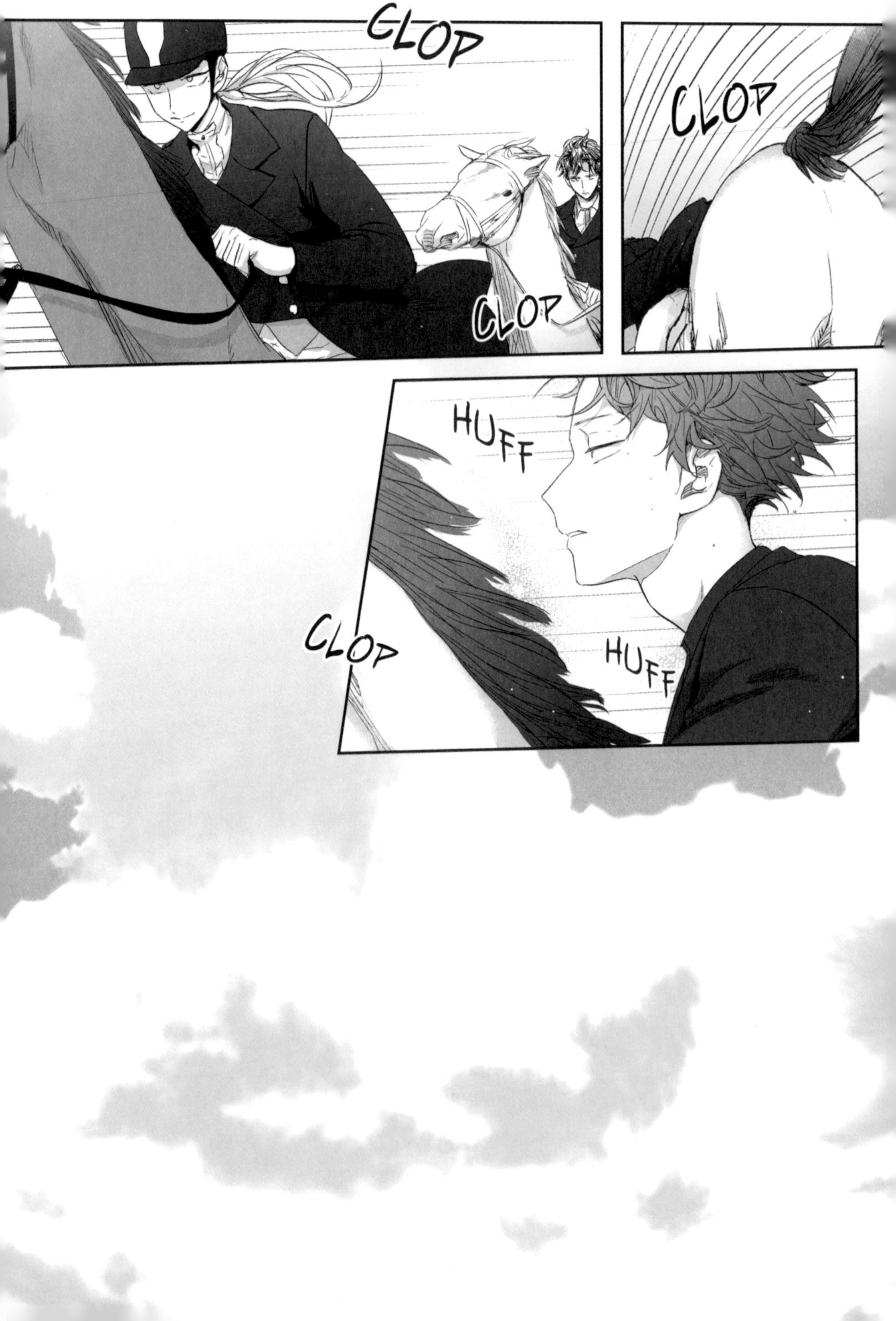
CLOP
CLOP
CLOP
HUFF
CLOP
HUFF

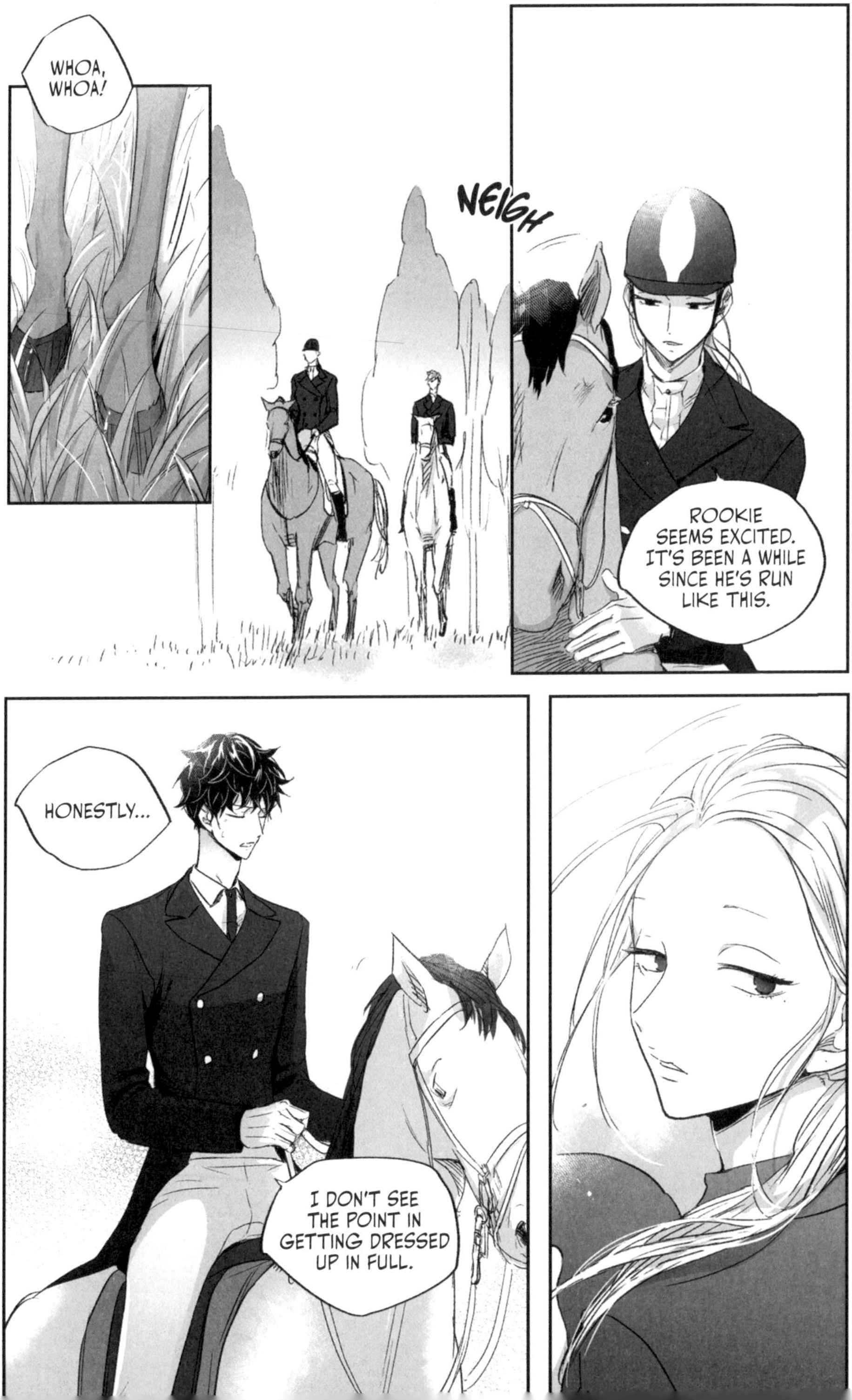
WHOA, WHOA!
NEIGH
ROOKIE SEEMS EXCITED. IT'S BEEN A WHILE SINCE HE'S RUN LIKE THIS.
HONESTLY...
I DON'T SEE THE POINT IN GETTING DRESSED UP IN FULL.

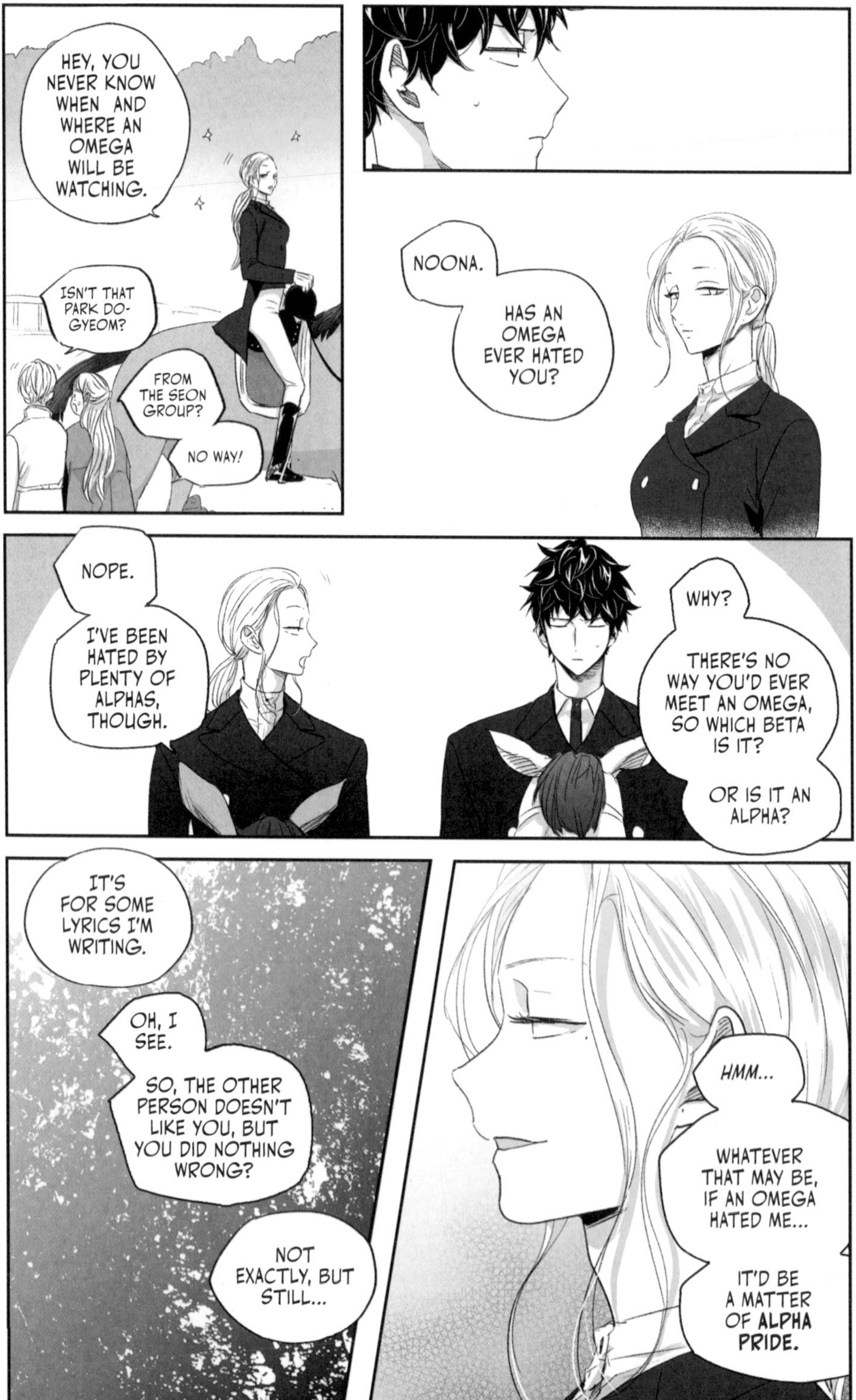
HEY, YOU NEVER KNOW WHEN AND WHERE AN OMEGA WILL BE WATCHING.
ISN'T THAT PARK DO-GYEOM?
FROM THE SEON GROUP?
NO WAY!
NOONA.
HAS AN OMEGA EVER HATED YOU?
NOPE.
I'VE BEEN HATED BY PLENTY OF ALPHAS, THOUGH.
WHY?
THERE'S NO WAY YOU'D EVER MEET AN OMEGA, SO WHICH BETA IS IT?
OR IS IT AN ALPHA?
IT'S FOR SOME LYRICS I'M WRITING.
OH, I SEE.
SO, THE OTHER PERSON DOESN'T LIKE YOU, BUT YOU DID NOTHING WRONG?
NOT EXACTLY, BUT STILL...
HMM...
WHATEVER THAT MAY BE, IF AN OMEGA HATED ME...
IT'D BE A MATTER OF ALPHA PRIDE.

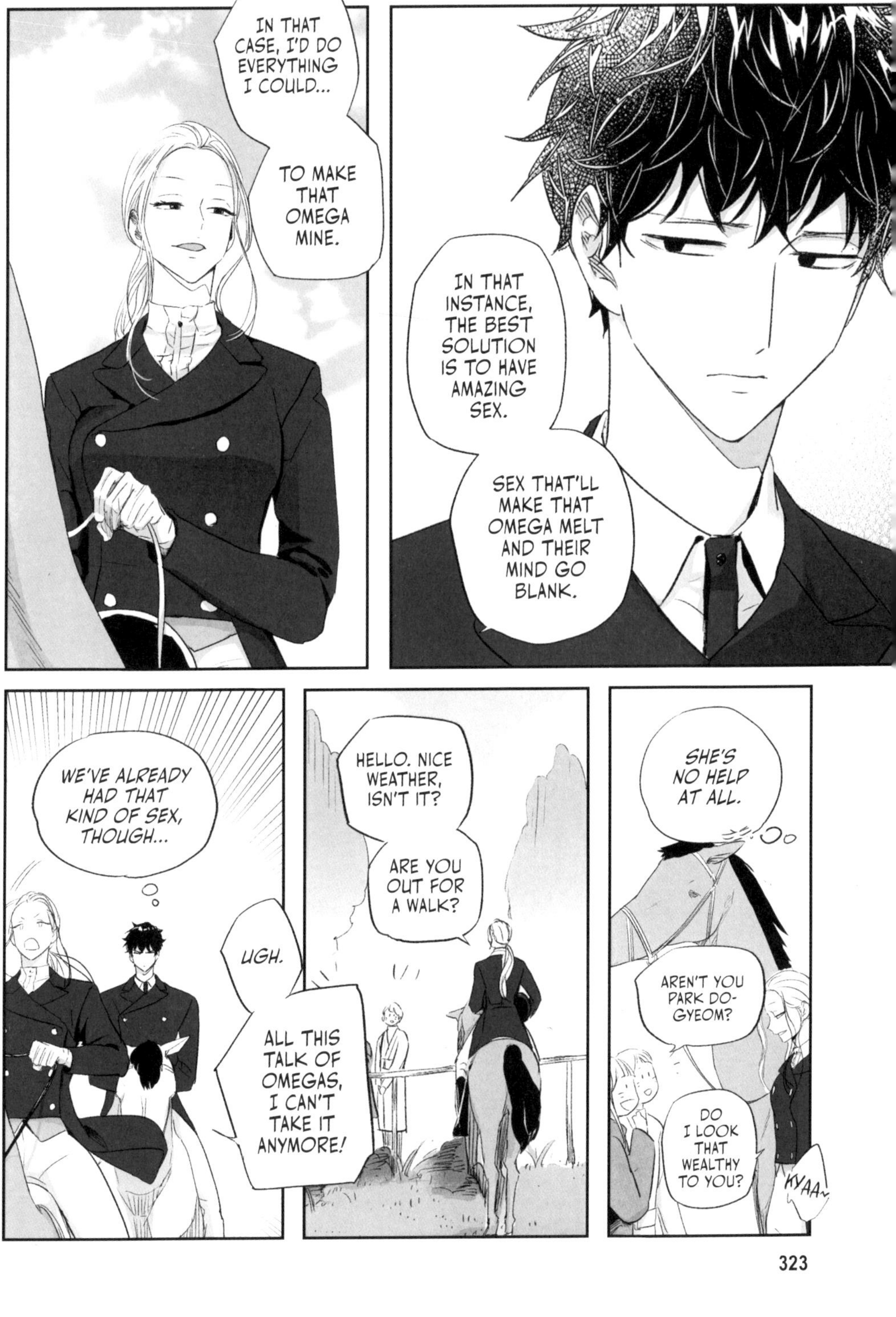
IN THAT CASE, I'D DO EVERYTHING I COULD...
TO MAKE THAT OMEGA MINE.
IN THAT INSTANCE, THE BEST SOLUTION IS TO HAVE AMAZING SEX.
SEX THAT'LL MAKE THAT OMEGA MELT AND THEIR MIND GO BLANK.
WE'VE ALREADY HAD THAT KIND OF SEX, THOUGH...
UGH.
ALL THIS TALK OF OMEGAS, I CAN'T TAKE IT ANYMORE!
HELLO. NICE WEATHER, ISN'T IT?
ARE YOU OUT FOR A WALK?
SHE'S NO HELP AT ALL.
AREN'T YOU PARK DO-GYEOM?
DO I LOOK THAT WEALTHY TO YOU?
KYAA~

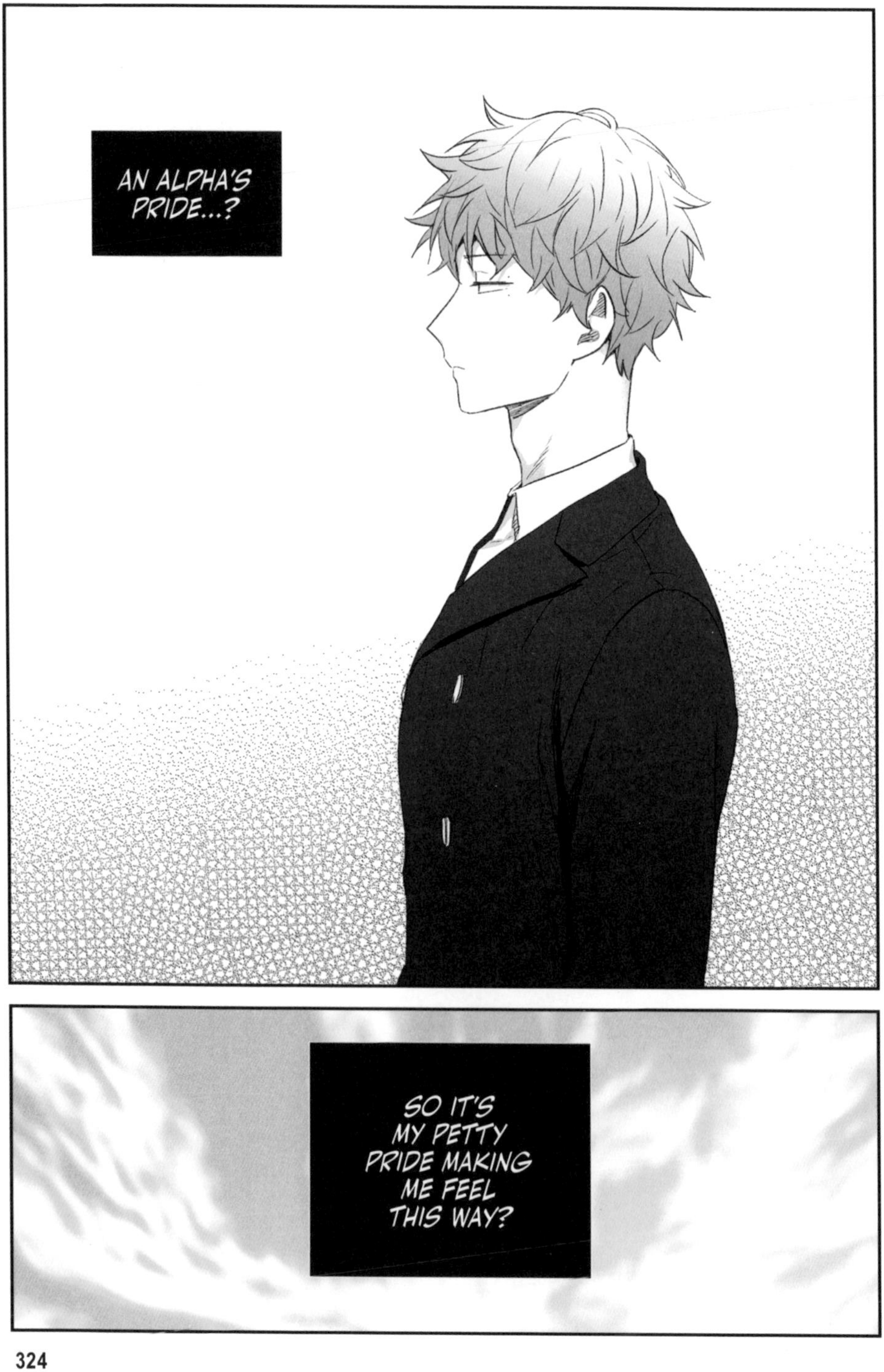
AN ALPHA'S PRIDE...?
SO IT'S MY PETTY PRIDE MAKING ME FEEL THIS WAY?

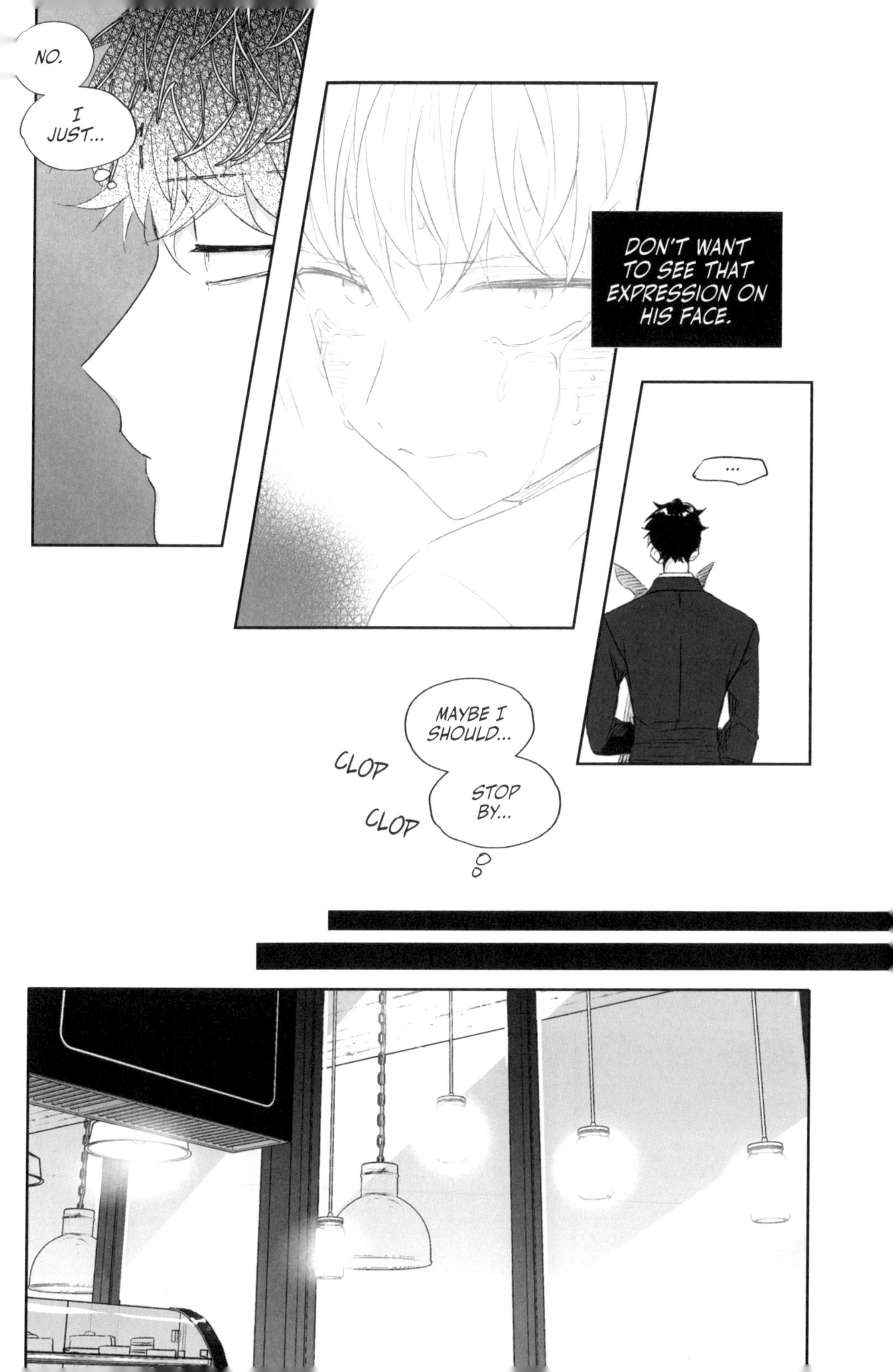
NO.
I JUST...
DON'T WANT TO SEE THAT EXPRESSION ON HIS FACE.
...
MAYBE I SHOULD...
CLOP
CLOP
STOP BY...

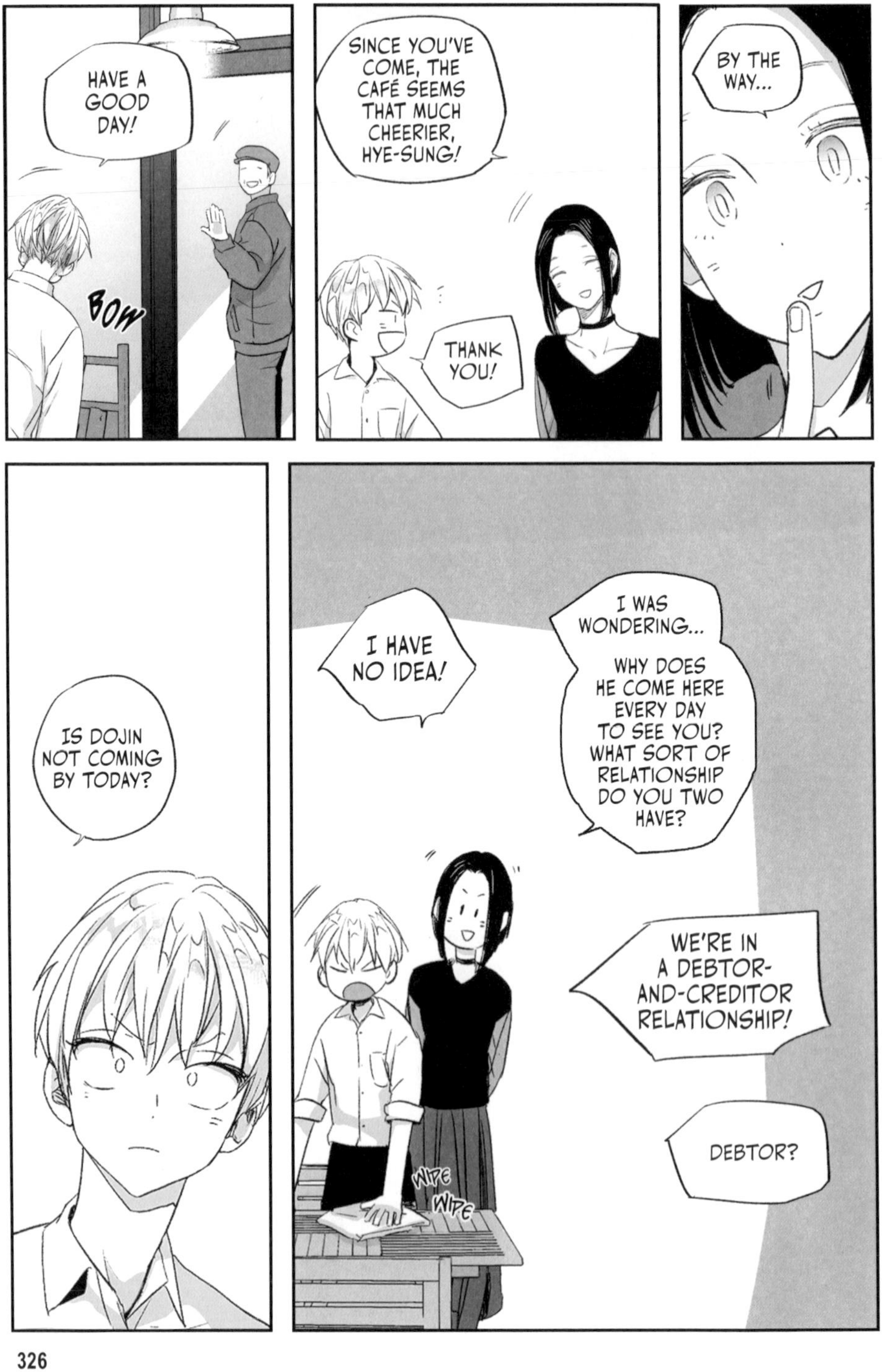
HAVE A GOOD DAY!
BOW
SINCE YOU'VE COME, THE CAFÉ SEEMS THAT MUCH CHEERIER, HYE-SUNG!
THANK YOU!
BY THE WAY...
IS DOJIN NOT COMING BY TODAY?
I HAVE NO IDEA!
I WAS WONDERING... WHY DOES HE COME HERE EVERY DAY TO SEE YOU? WHAT SORT OF RELATIONSHIP DO YOU TWO HAVE?
WE'RE IN A DEBTOR-AND-CREDITOR RELATIONSHIP!
DEBTOR?
WIPE WIPE

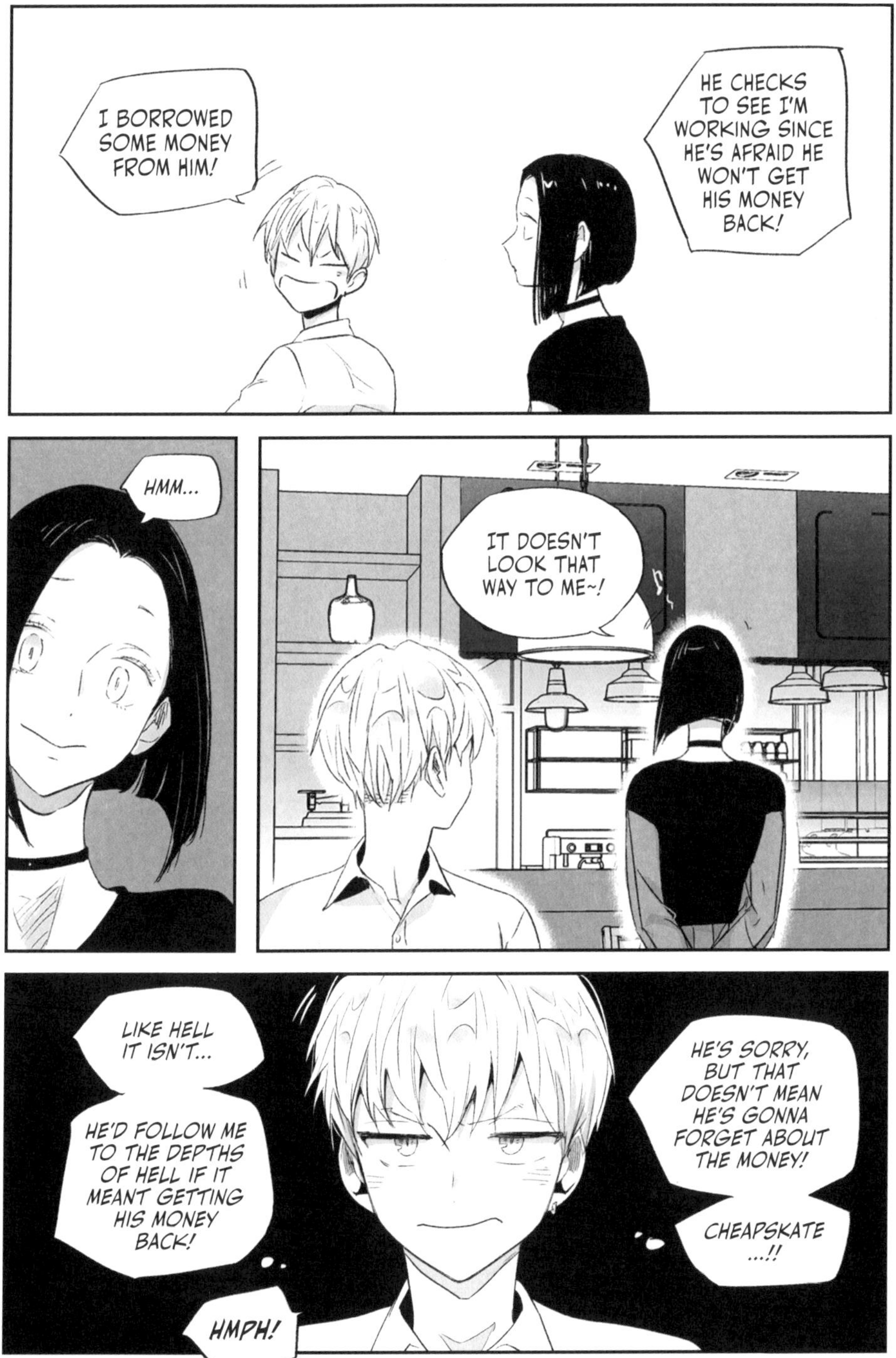
I BORROWED SOME MONEY FROM HIM!
HE CHECKS TO SEE I'M WORKING SINCE HE'S AFRAID HE WON'T GET HIS MONEY BACK!
HMM...
IT DOESN'T LOOK THAT WAY TO ME~!
LIKE HELL IT ISN'T...
HE'D FOLLOW ME TO THE DEPTHS OF HELL IF IT MEANT GETTING HIS MONEY BACK!
HE'S SORRY, BUT THAT DOESN'T MEAN HE'S GONNA FORGET ABOUT THE MONEY!
CHEAPSKATE ...!!
HMPH!

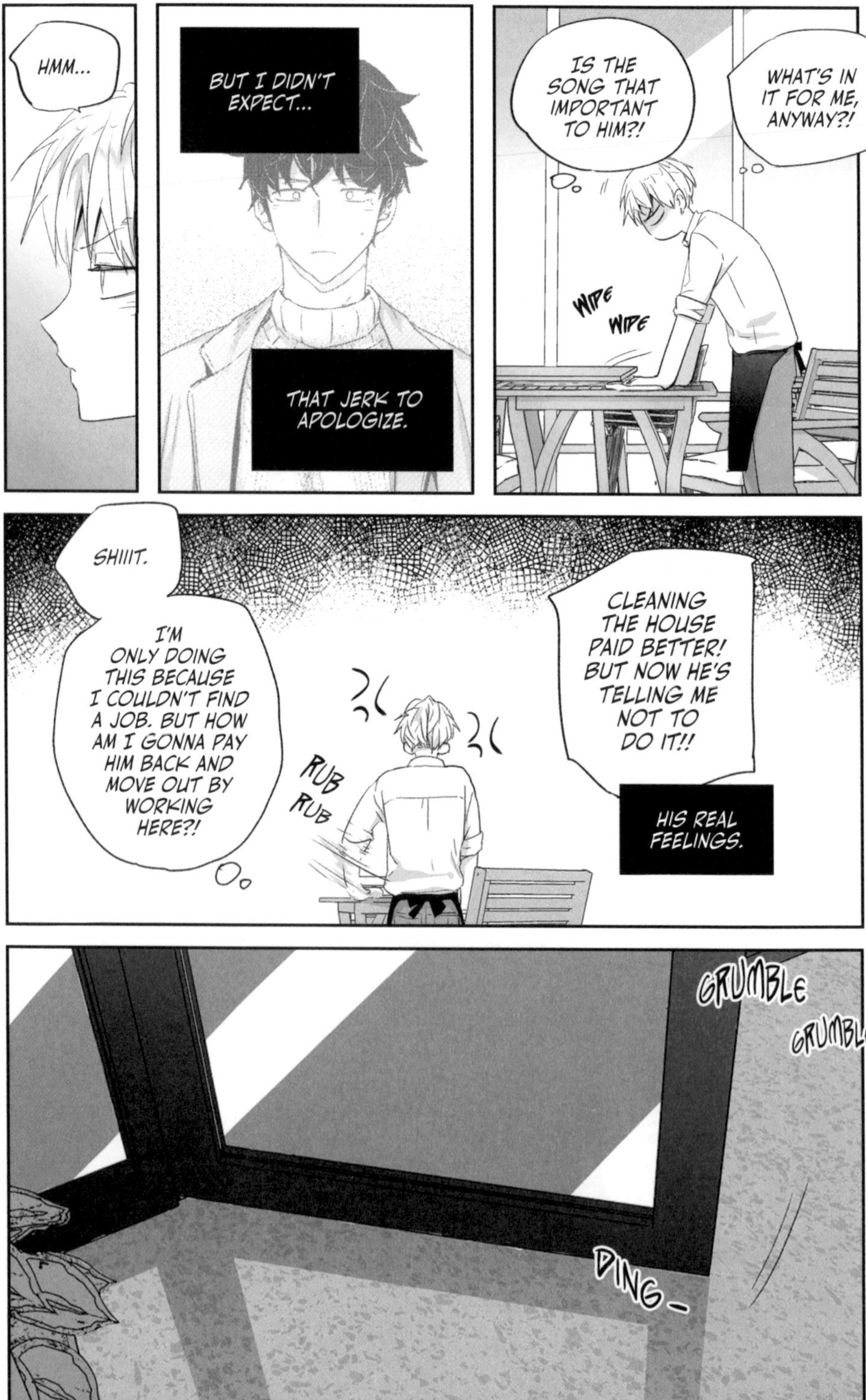
HMM...
BUT I DIDN'T EXPECT...
THAT JERK TO APOLOGIZE.
IS THE SONG THAT IMPORTANT TO HIM?!
WHAT'S IN IT FOR ME, ANYWAY?!
WIPE
WIPE
SHIIIT.
I'M ONLY DOING THIS BECAUSE I COULDN'T FIND A JOB. BUT HOW AM I GONNA PAY HIM BACK AND MOVE OUT BY WORKING HERE?!
RUB
RUB
CLEANING THE HOUSE PAID BETTER! BUT NOW HE'S TELLING ME NOT TO DO IT!!
HIS REAL FEELINGS.
GRUMBLE
GRUMBLE
DING—

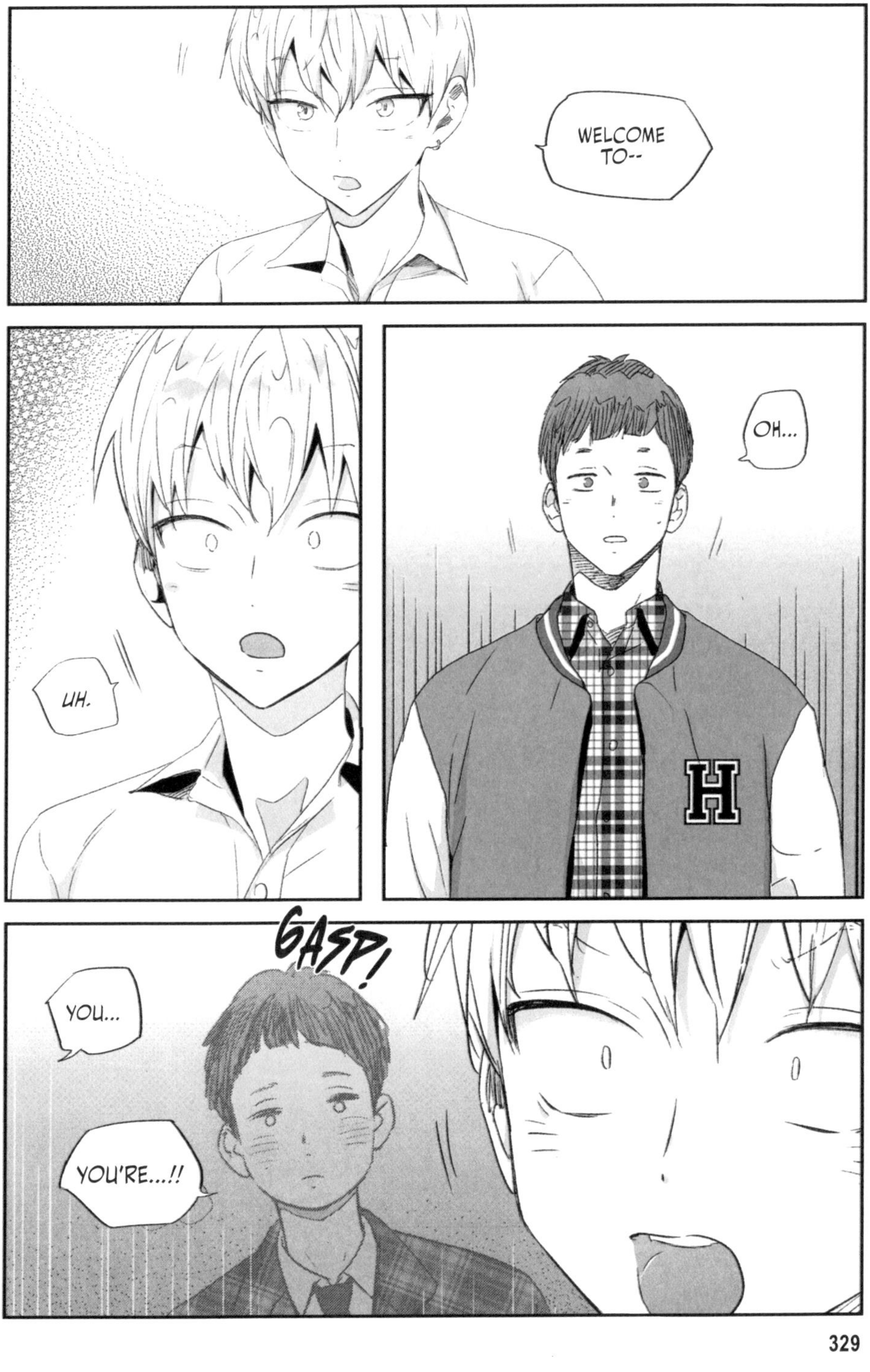
WELCOME TO--
UH.
OH...
GASP!
YOU...
YOU'RE...!!

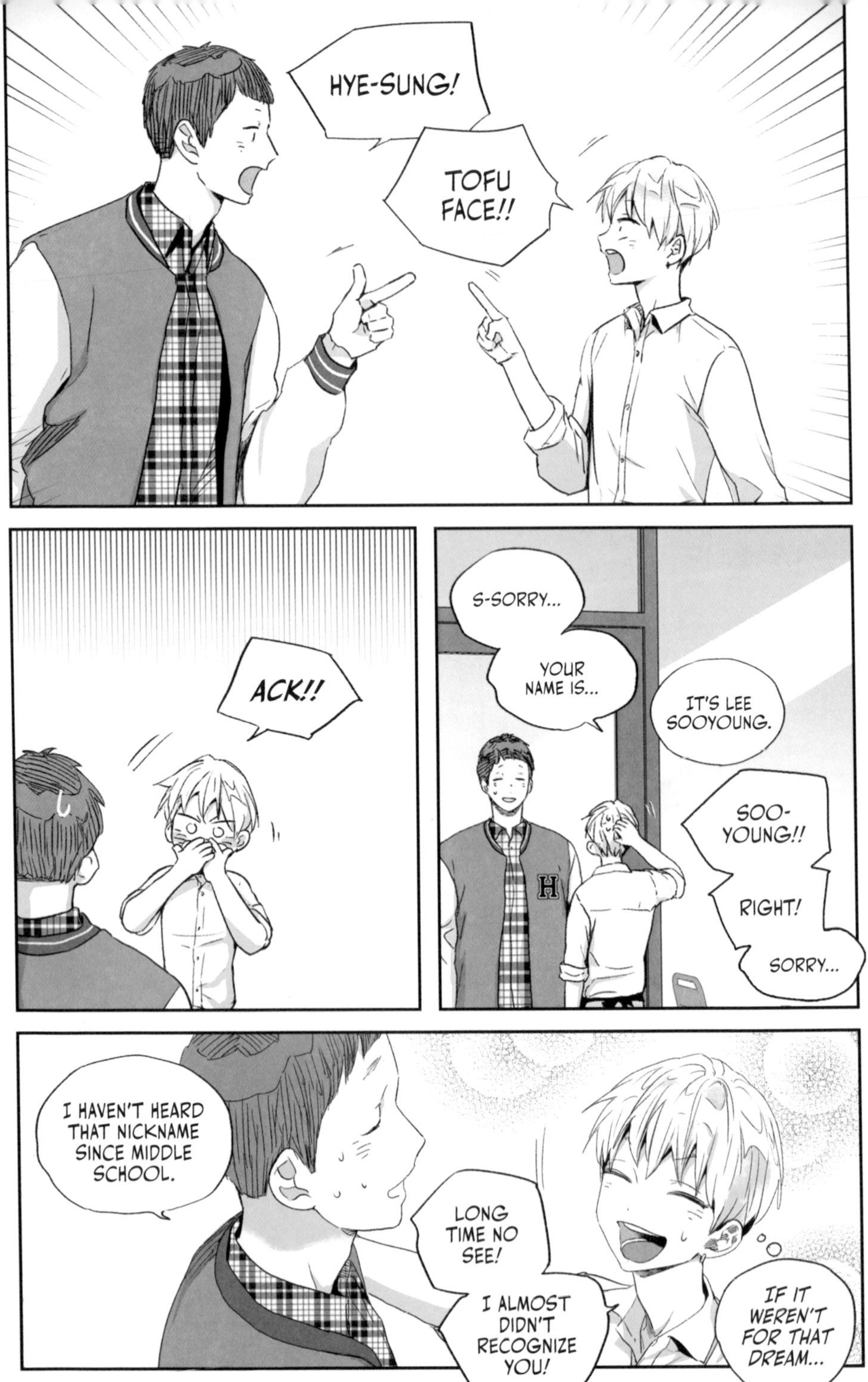
HYE-SUNG!
TOFU FACE!!
ACK!!
S-SORRY...
YOUR NAME IS...
IT'S LEE SOOYOUNG.
SOO-YOUNG!!
RIGHT!
SORRY...
I HAVEN'T HEARD THAT NICKNAME SINCE MIDDLE SCHOOL.
LONG TIME NO SEE!
I ALMOST DIDN'T RECOGNIZE YOU!
IF IT WEREN'T FOR THAT DREAM...

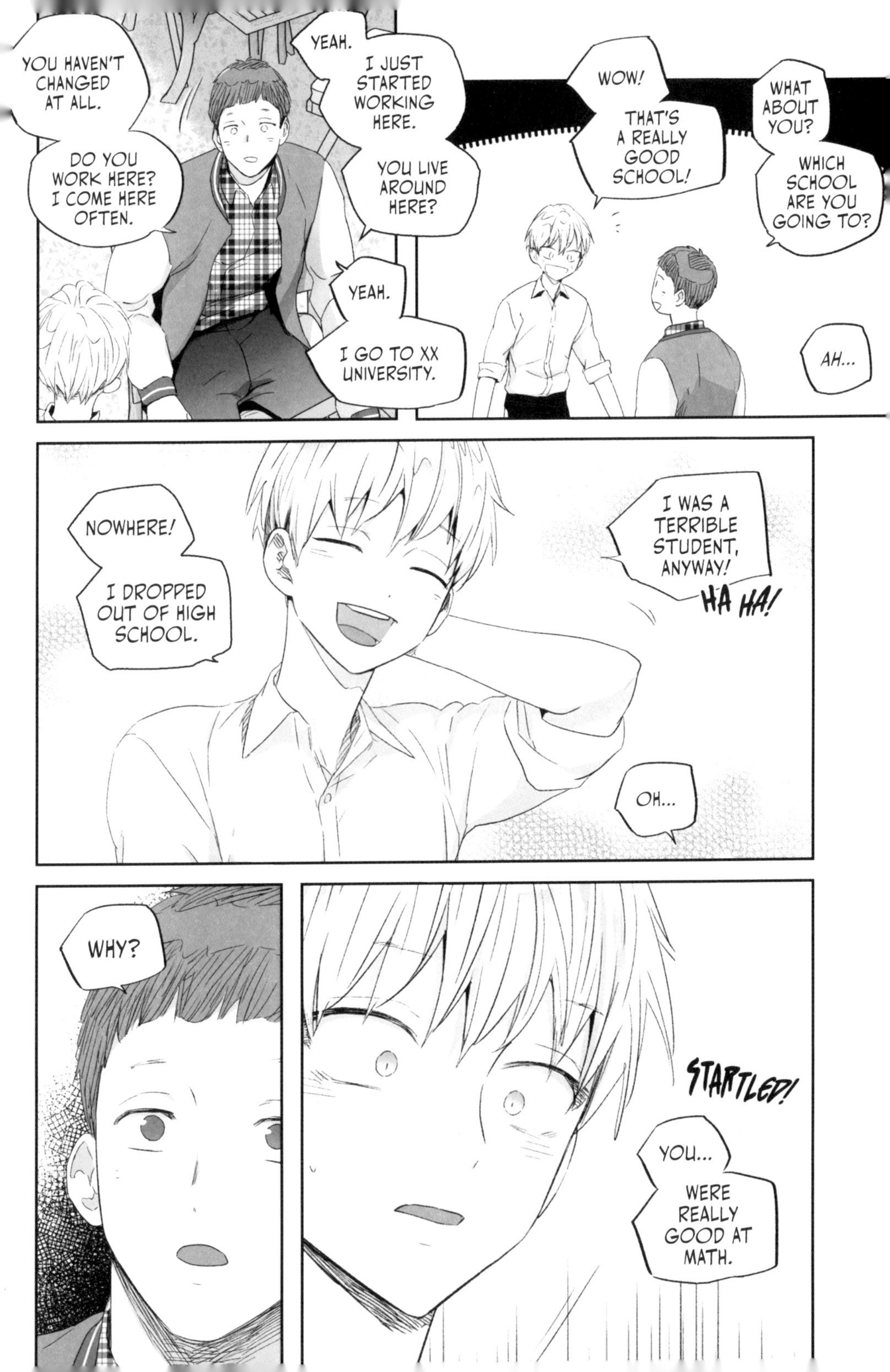
YOU HAVEN'T CHANGED AT ALL.
DO YOU WORK HERE? I COME HERE OFTEN.
YEAH.
I JUST STARTED WORKING HERE.
YOU LIVE AROUND HERE?
YEAH.
I GO TO XX UNIVERSITY.
WOW!
THAT'S A REALLY GOOD SCHOOL!
WHAT ABOUT YOU?
WHICH SCHOOL ARE YOU GOING TO?
AH...
NOWHERE!
I DROPPED OUT OF HIGH SCHOOL.
I WAS A TERRIBLE STUDENT, ANYWAY!
HA HA!
OH...
WHY?
STARTLED!
YOU...
WERE REALLY GOOD AT MATH.

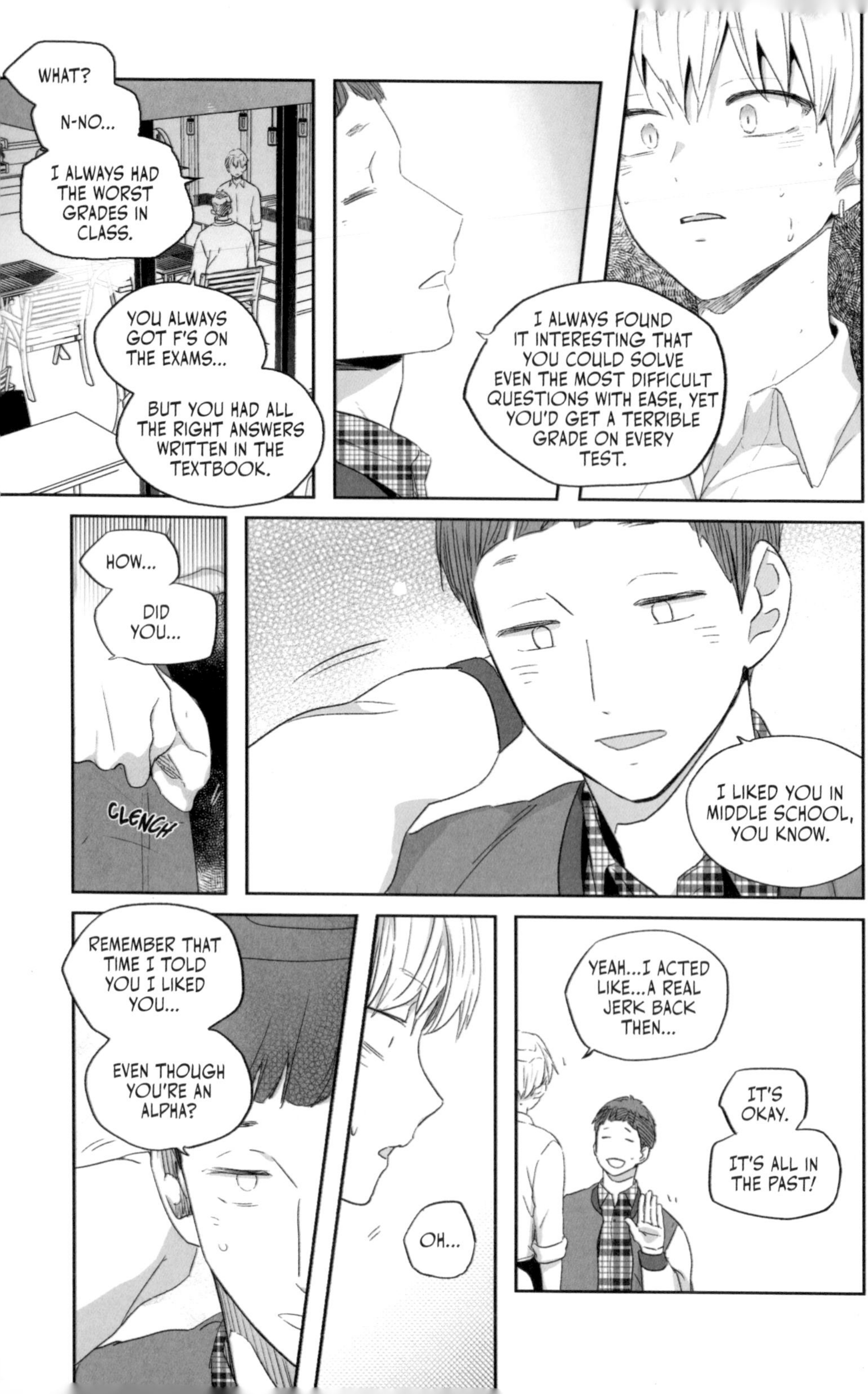
WHAT?
N-NO...
I ALWAYS HAD THE WORST GRADES IN CLASS.
YOU ALWAYS GOT F'S ON THE EXAMS...
BUT YOU HAD ALL THE RIGHT ANSWERS WRITTEN IN THE TEXTBOOK.
I ALWAYS FOUND IT INTERESTING THAT YOU COULD SOLVE EVEN THE MOST DIFFICULT QUESTIONS WITH EASE, YET YOU'D GET A TERRIBLE GRADE ON EVERY TEST.
HOW...
DID YOU...
CLENCH
I LIKED YOU IN MIDDLE SCHOOL, YOU KNOW.
REMEMBER THAT TIME I TOLD YOU I LIKED YOU...
EVEN THOUGH YOU'RE AN ALPHA?
OH...
YEAH...I ACTED LIKE...A REAL JERK BACK THEN...
IT'S OKAY.
IT'S ALL IN THE PAST!

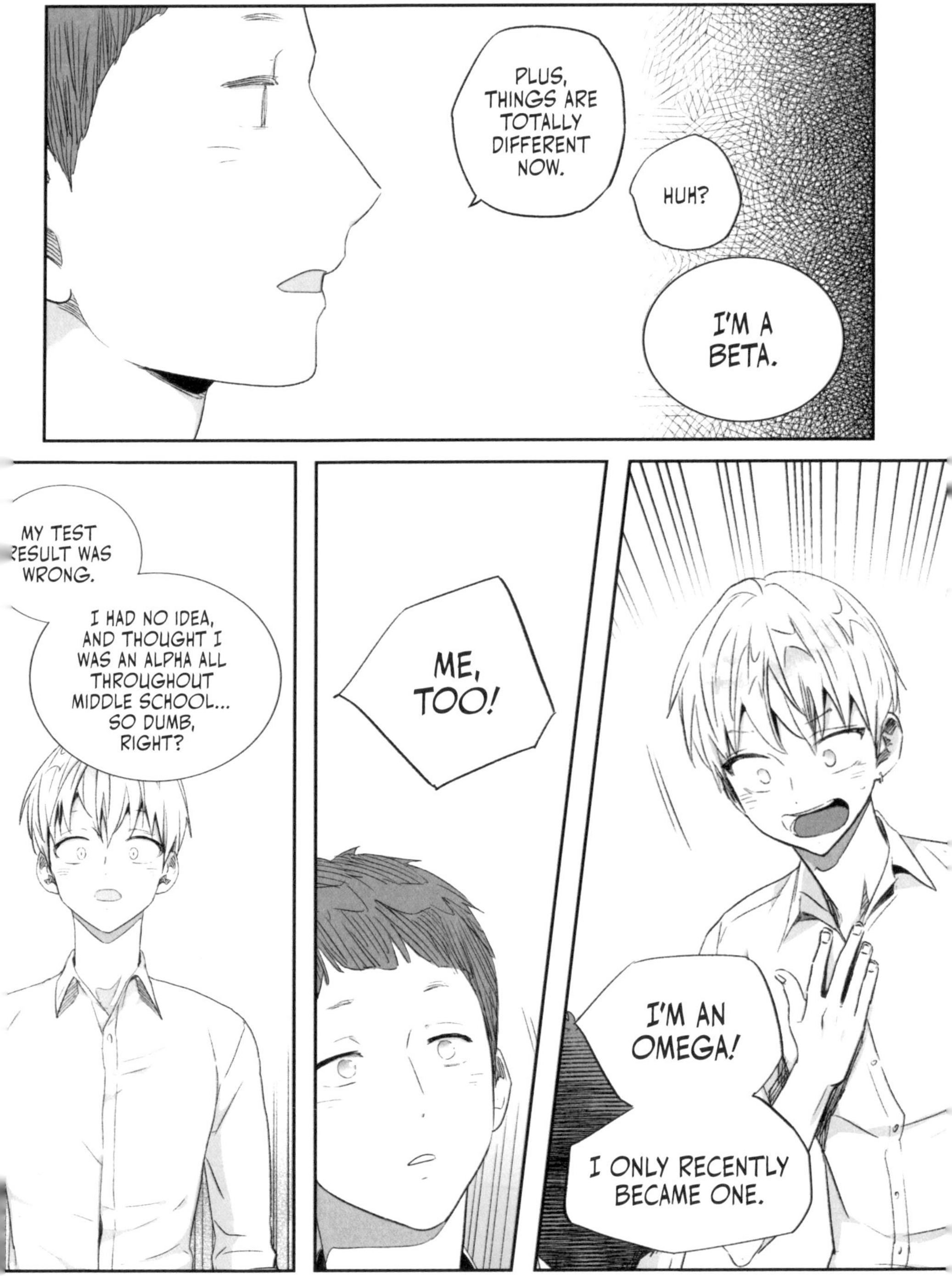
PLUS, THINGS ARE TOTALLY DIFFERENT NOW.
HUH?
I'M A BETA.
MY TEST RESULT WAS WRONG.
I HAD NO IDEA, AND THOUGHT I WAS AN ALPHA ALL THROUGHOUT MIDDLE SCHOOL... SO DUMB, RIGHT?
ME, TOO!
I'M AN OMEGA!
I ONLY RECENTLY BECAME ONE.

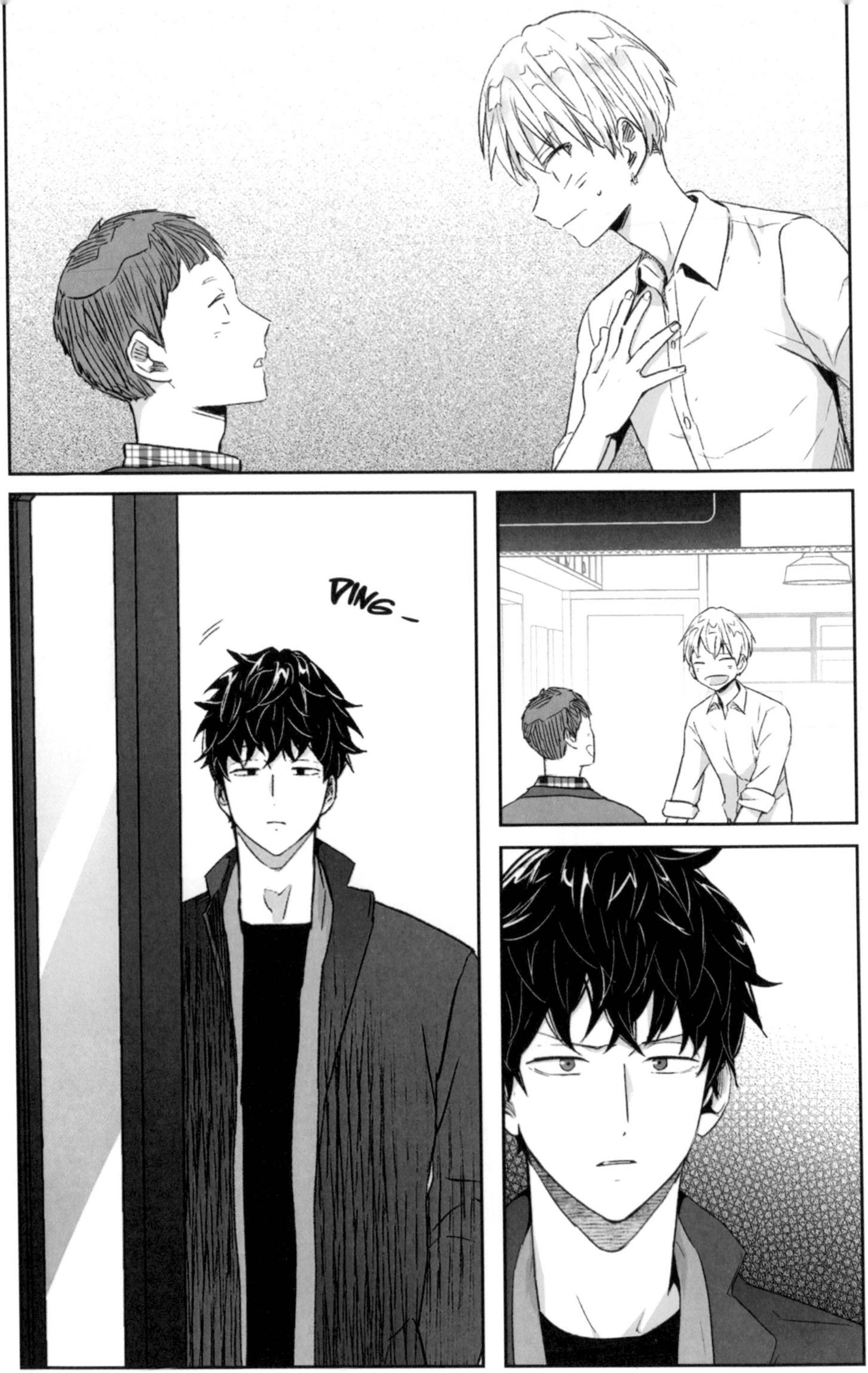
DING –

Love is an Illusion!

Love is an Illusion!

Chapter 17

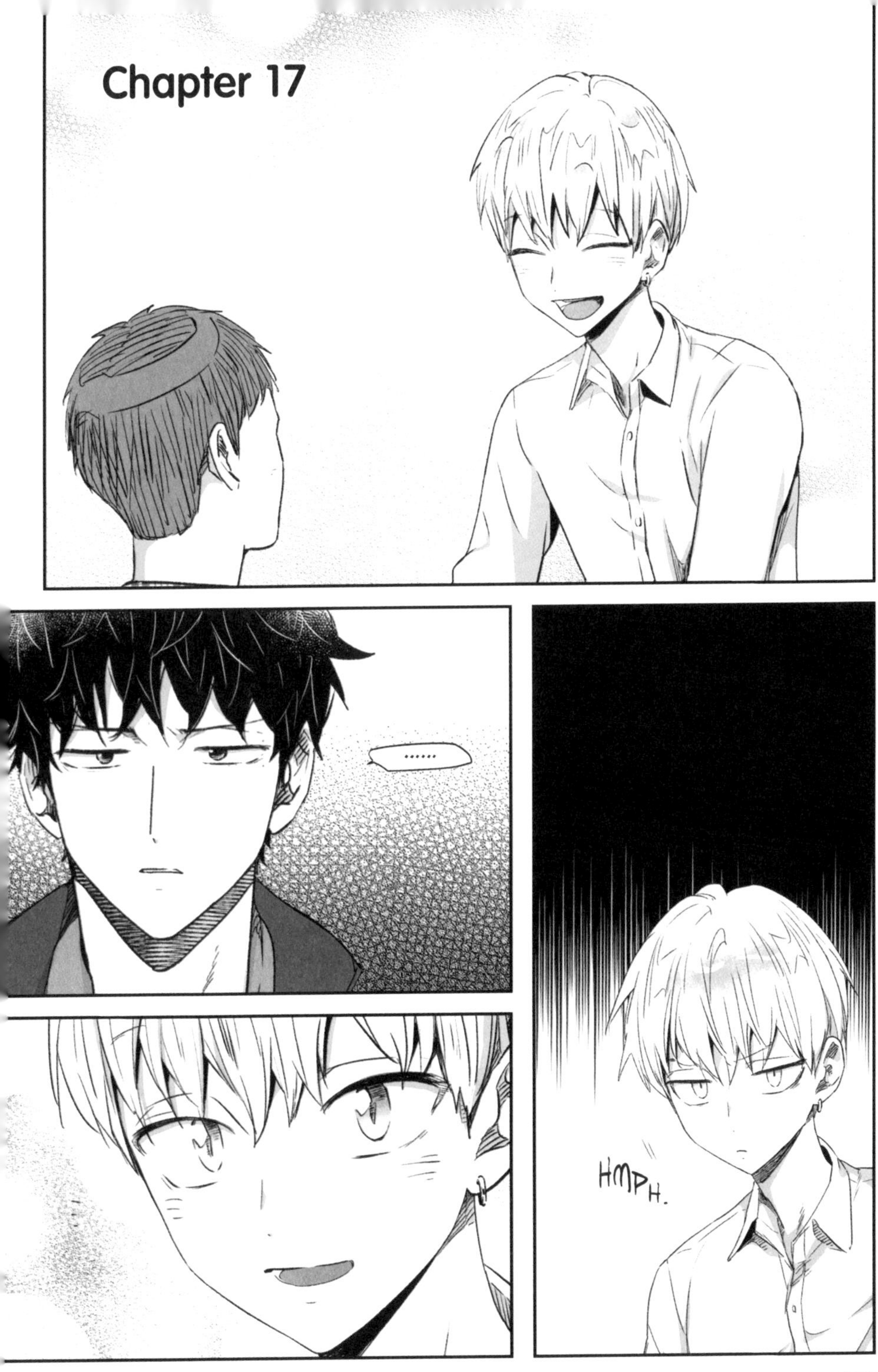
......
HMPH.

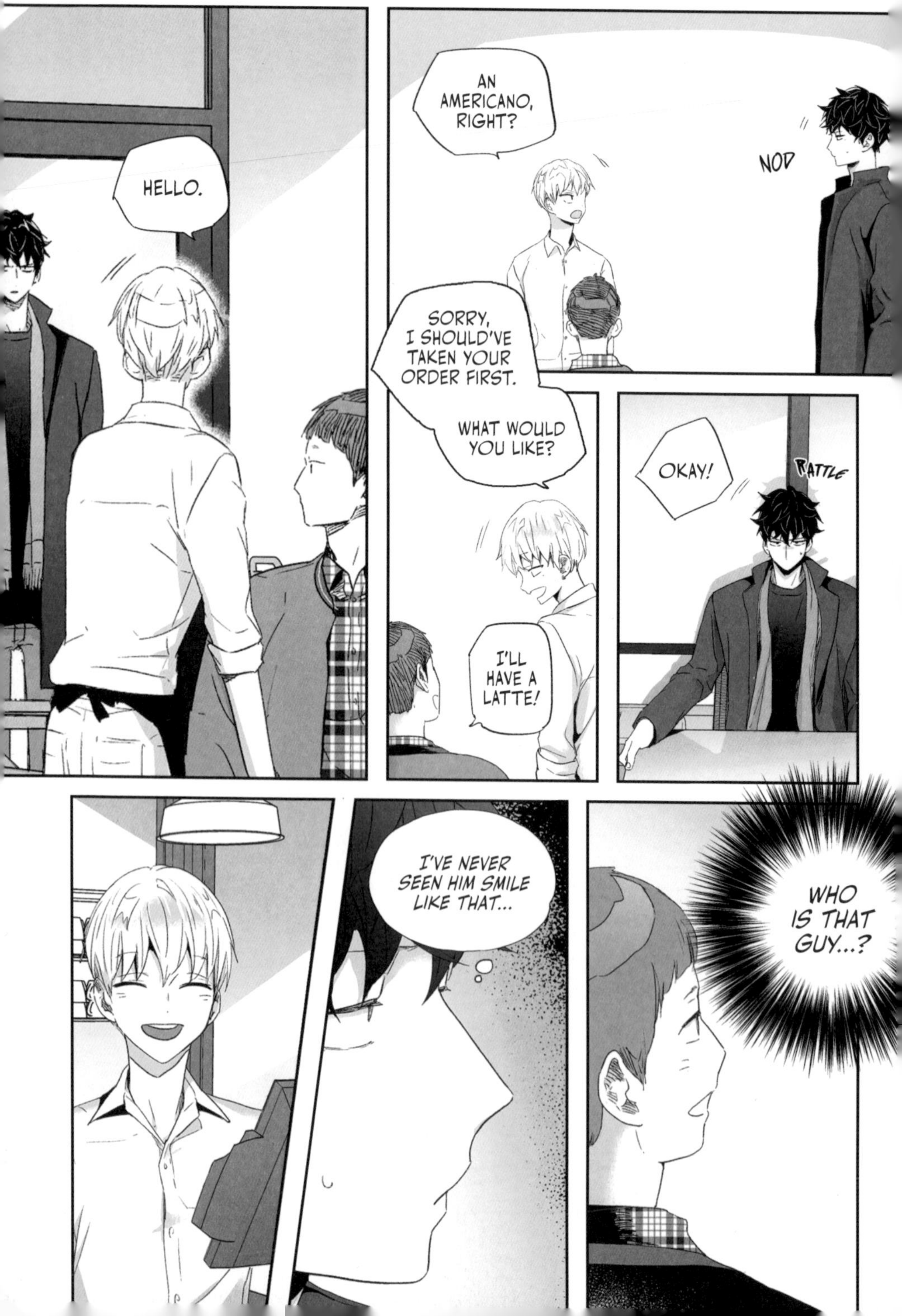

HELLO.
AN AMERICANO, RIGHT?
NOD
SORRY, I SHOULD'VE TAKEN YOUR ORDER FIRST.
WHAT WOULD YOU LIKE?
I'LL HAVE A LATTE!
OKAY!
RATTLE
I'VE NEVER SEEN HIM SMILE LIKE THAT...
WHO IS THAT GUY...?

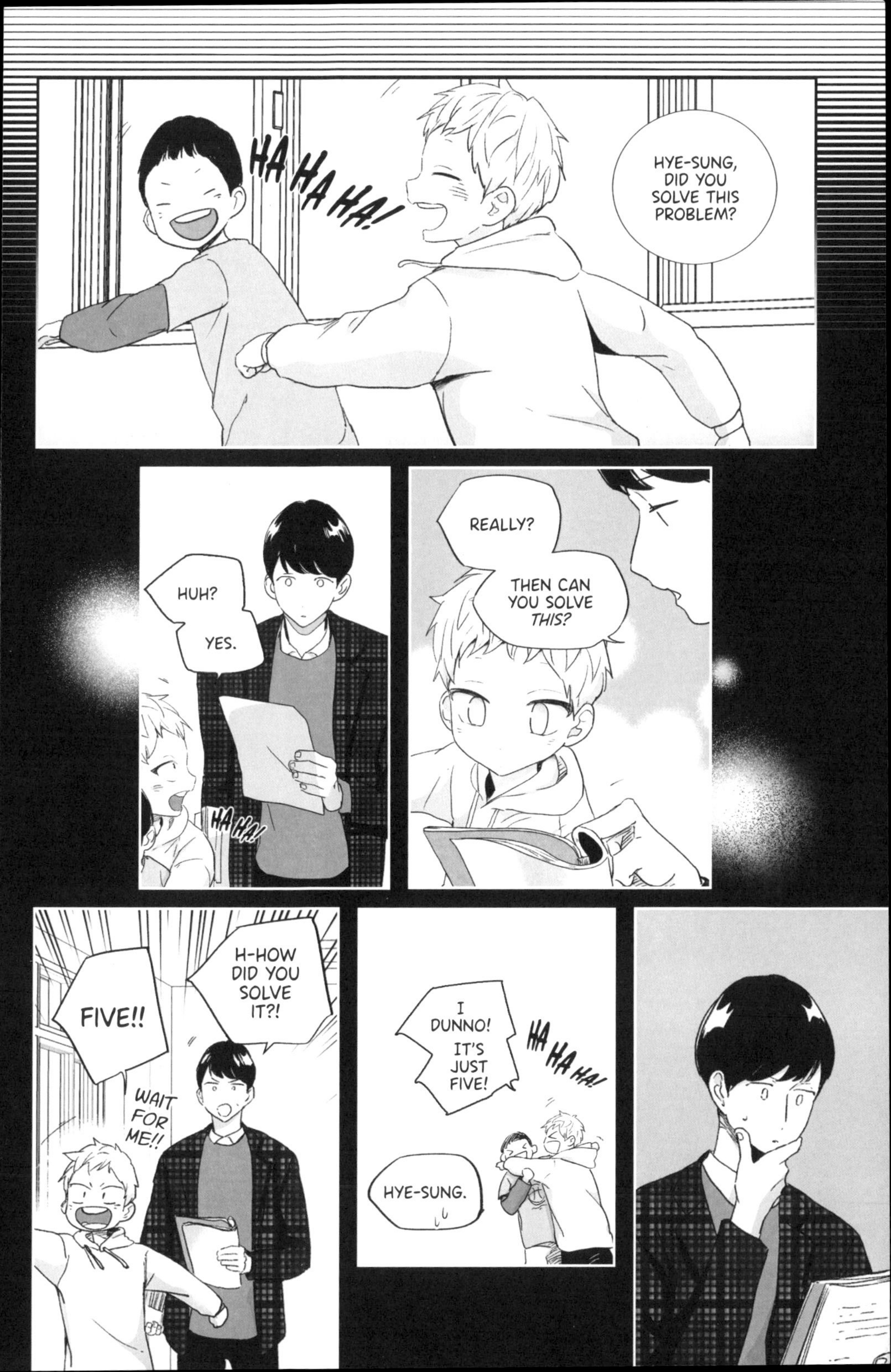
HA HA HA HA!
HYE-SUNG, DID YOU SOLVE THIS PROBLEM?
HUH?
YES.
HA HA!
REALLY?
THEN CAN YOU SOLVE *THIS*?
FIVE!!
H-HOW DID YOU SOLVE IT?!
WAIT FOR ME!!
I DUNNO! IT'S JUST FIVE!
HA HA HA!
HYE-SUNG.

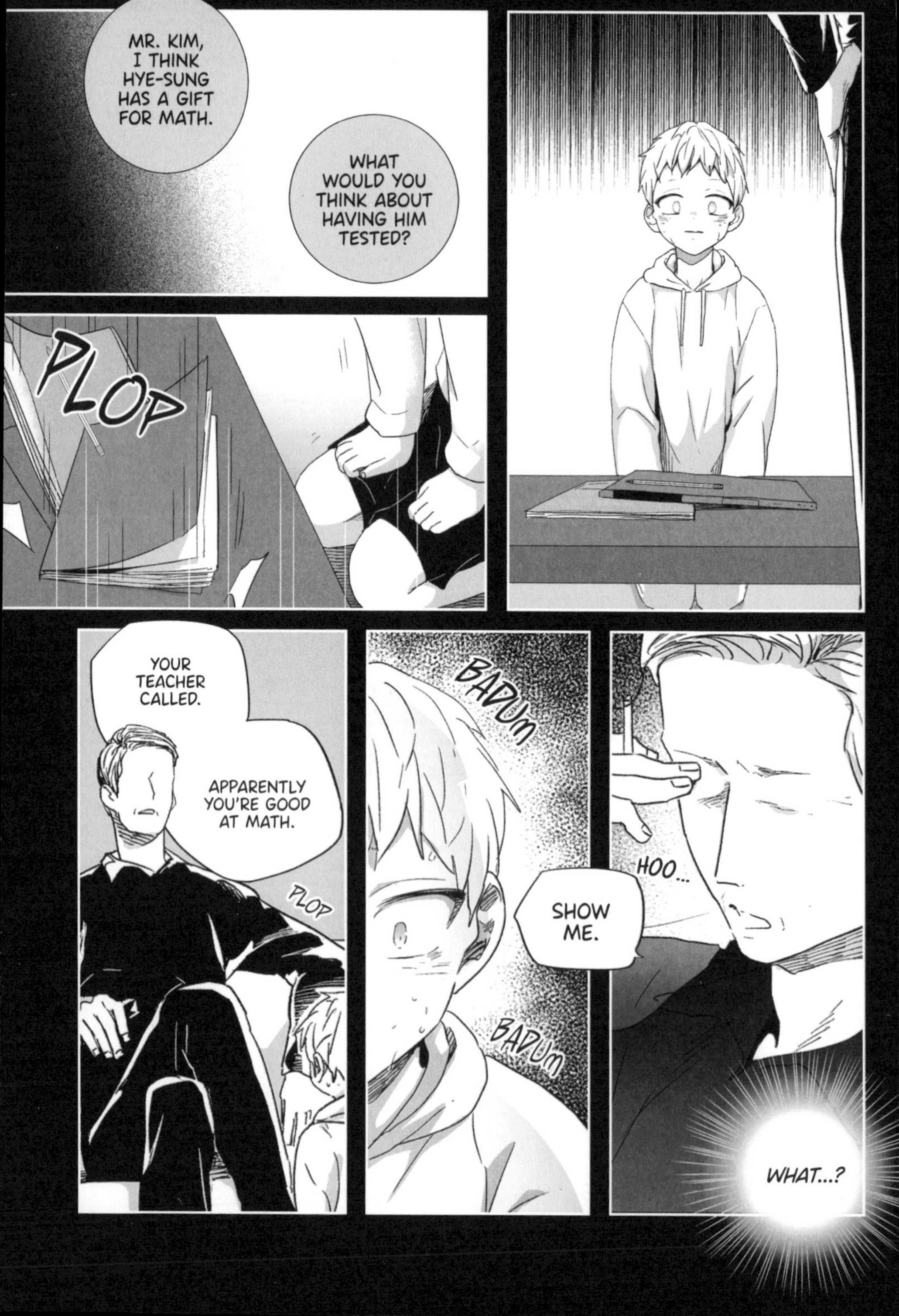
MR. KIM, I THINK HYE-SUNG HAS A GIFT FOR MATH.
WHAT WOULD YOU THINK ABOUT HAVING HIM TESTED?
PLOP
YOUR TEACHER CALLED.
APPARENTLY YOU'RE GOOD AT MATH.
PLOP
BADUM
BADUM
SHOW ME.
HOO...
WHAT...?

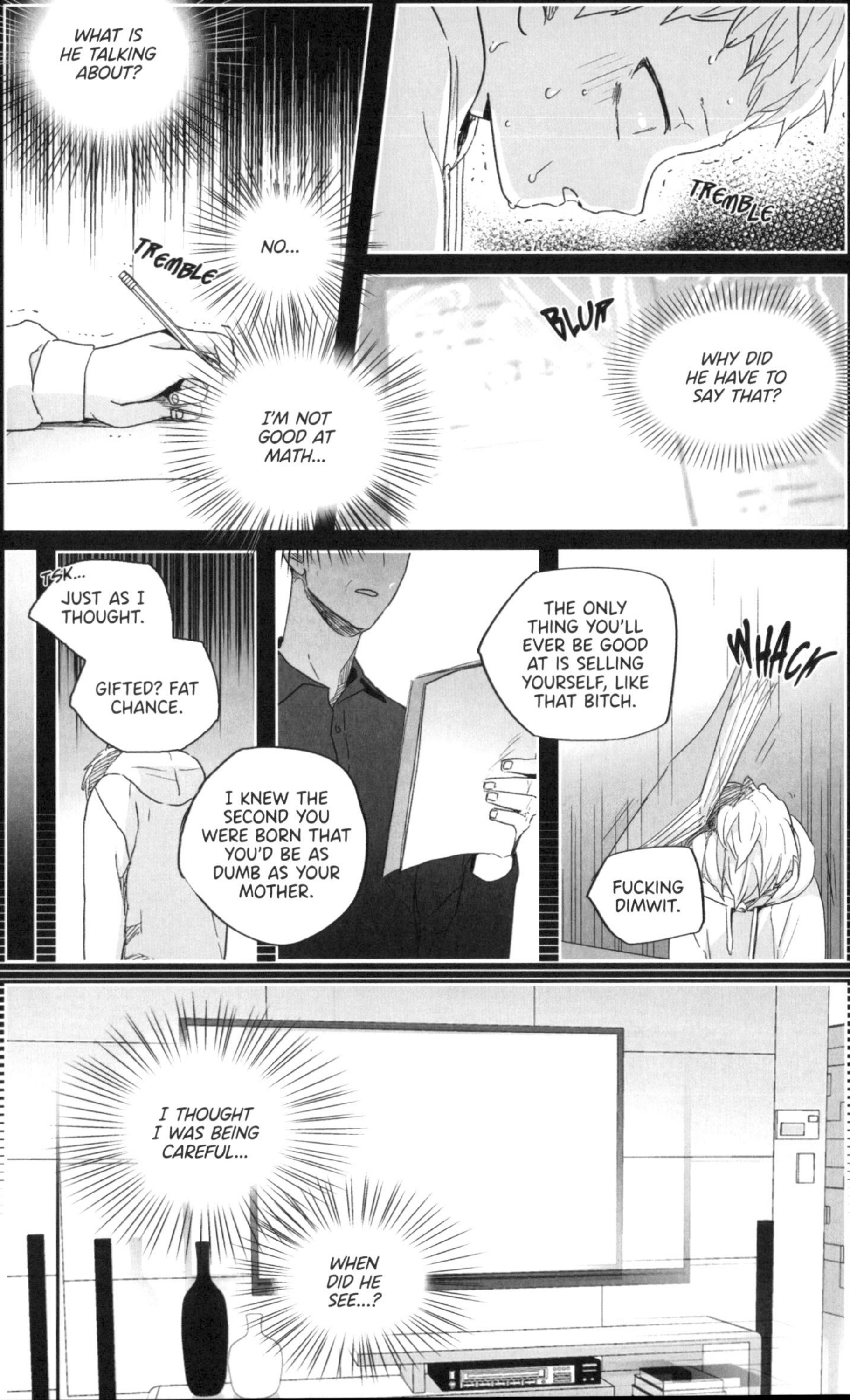
WHAT IS HE TALKING ABOUT?
TREMBLE
TREMBLE
NO...
I'M NOT GOOD AT MATH...
BLUR
WHY DID HE HAVE TO SAY THAT?
TSK...
JUST AS I THOUGHT.
GIFTED? FAT CHANCE.
I KNEW THE SECOND YOU WERE BORN THAT YOU'D BE AS DUMB AS YOUR MOTHER.
THE ONLY THING YOU'LL EVER BE GOOD AT IS SELLING YOURSELF, LIKE THAT BITCH.
WHACK
FUCKING DIMWIT.
I THOUGHT I WAS BEING CAREFUL...
WHEN DID HE SEE...?

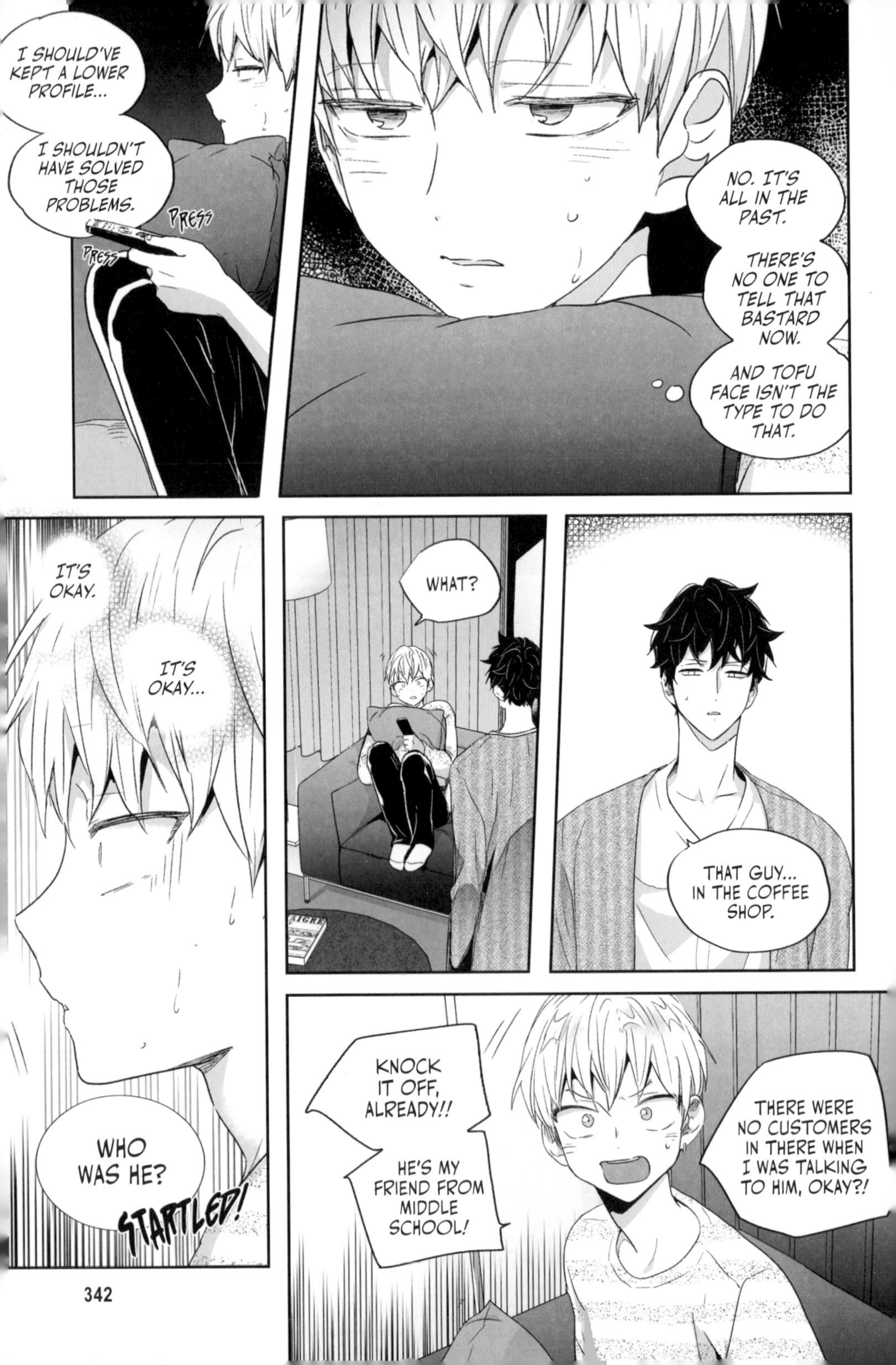
I SHOULD'VE KEPT A LOWER PROFILE...
I SHOULDN'T HAVE SOLVED THOSE PROBLEMS.
PRESS
PRESS
NO. IT'S ALL IN THE PAST.
THERE'S NO ONE TO TELL THAT BASTARD NOW.
AND TOFU FACE ISN'T THE TYPE TO DO THAT.
IT'S OKAY.
IT'S OKAY...
WHO WAS HE?
STARTLED!
WHAT?
THAT GUY... IN THE COFFEE SHOP.
KNOCK IT OFF, ALREADY!!
HE'S MY FRIEND FROM MIDDLE SCHOOL!
THERE WERE NO CUSTOMERS IN THERE WHEN I WAS TALKING TO HIM, OKAY?!

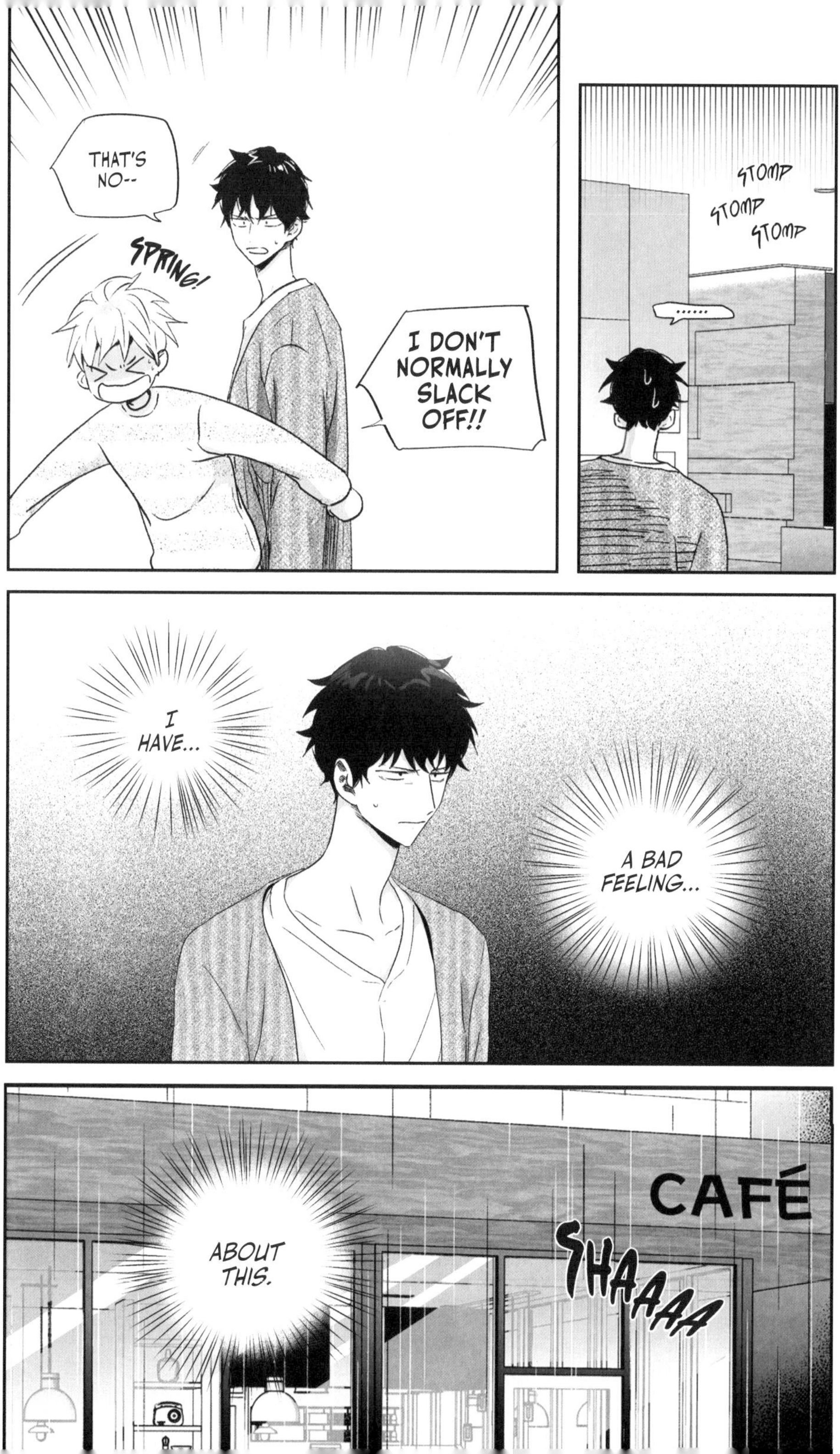
THAT'S NO--
SPRING!
I DON'T NORMALLY SLACK OFF!!
STOMP
STOMP
STOMP
......
I HAVE...
A BAD FEELING...
ABOUT THIS.
CAFÉ
SHAAAA

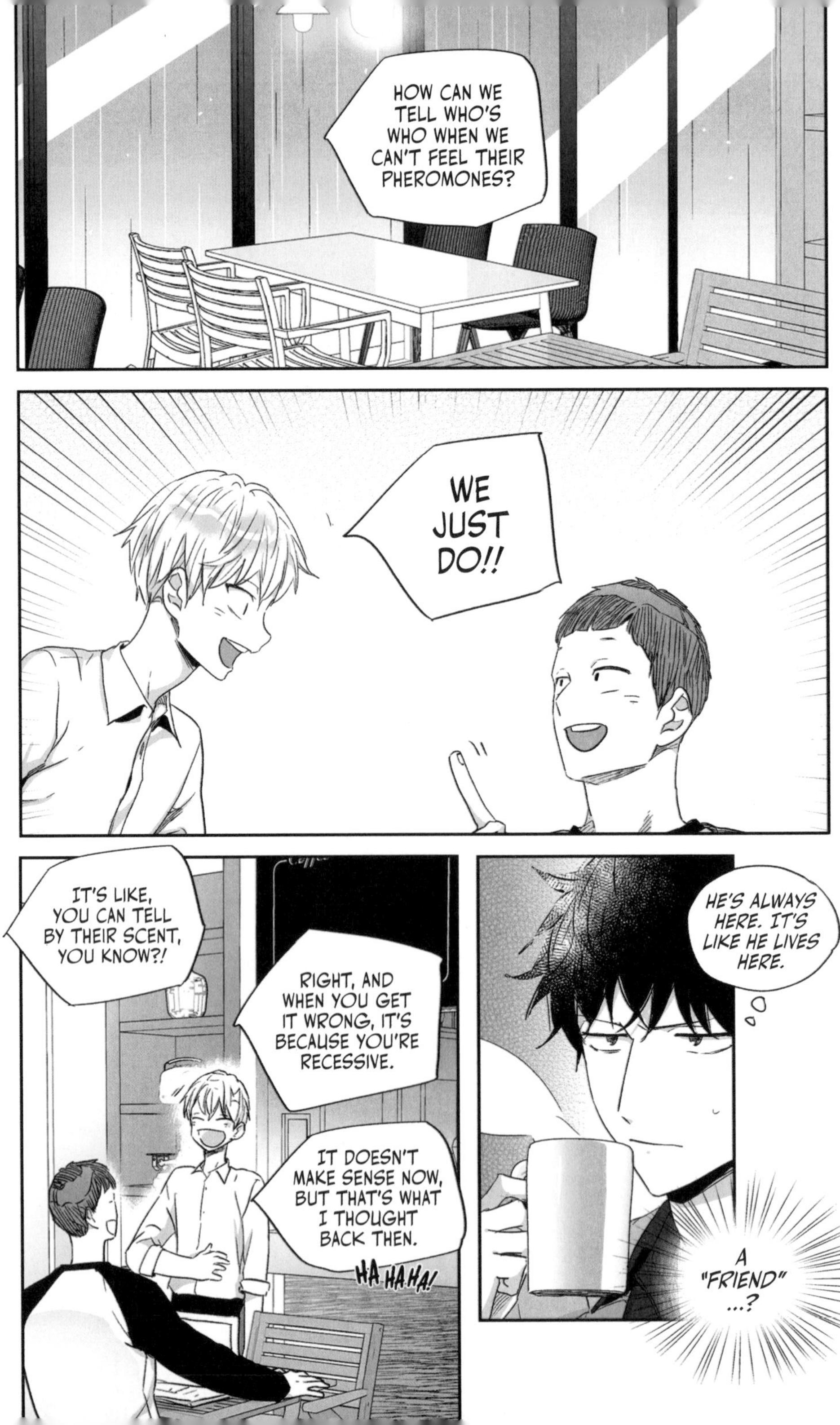
HOW CAN WE TELL WHO'S WHO WHEN WE CAN'T FEEL THEIR PHEROMONES?
WE JUST DO!!
IT'S LIKE, YOU CAN TELL BY THEIR SCENT, YOU KNOW?!
RIGHT, AND WHEN YOU GET IT WRONG, IT'S BECAUSE YOU'RE RECESSIVE.
IT DOESN'T MAKE SENSE NOW, BUT THAT'S WHAT I THOUGHT BACK THEN.
HA HA HA!
HE'S ALWAYS HERE. IT'S LIKE HE LIVES HERE.
A "FRIEND" ...?

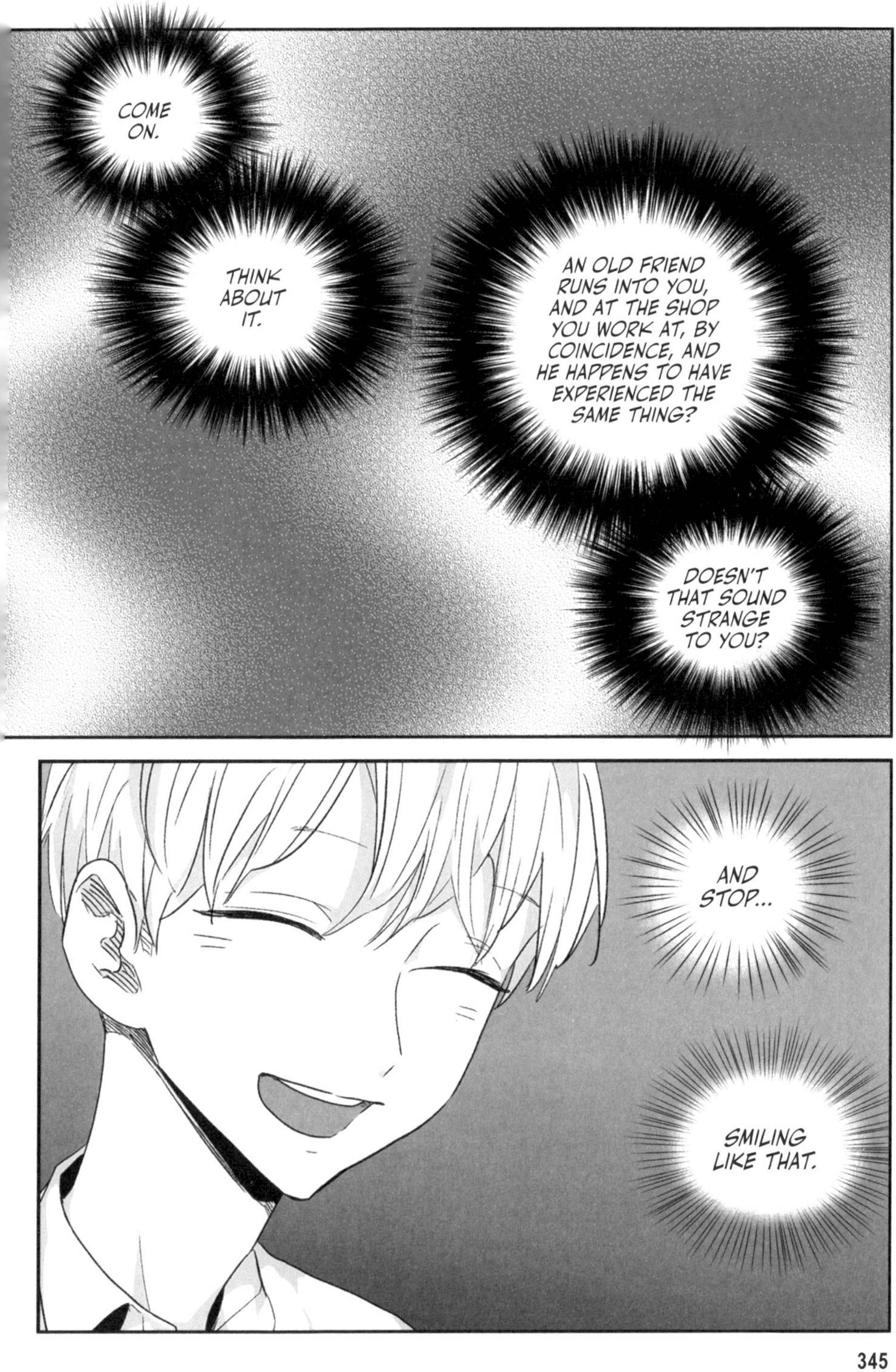
COME ON.
THINK ABOUT IT.
AN OLD FRIEND RUNS INTO YOU, AND AT THE SHOP YOU WORK AT, BY COINCIDENCE, AND HE HAPPENS TO HAVE EXPERIENCED THE SAME THING?
DOESN'T THAT SOUND STRANGE TO YOU?
AND STOP...
SMILING LIKE THAT.

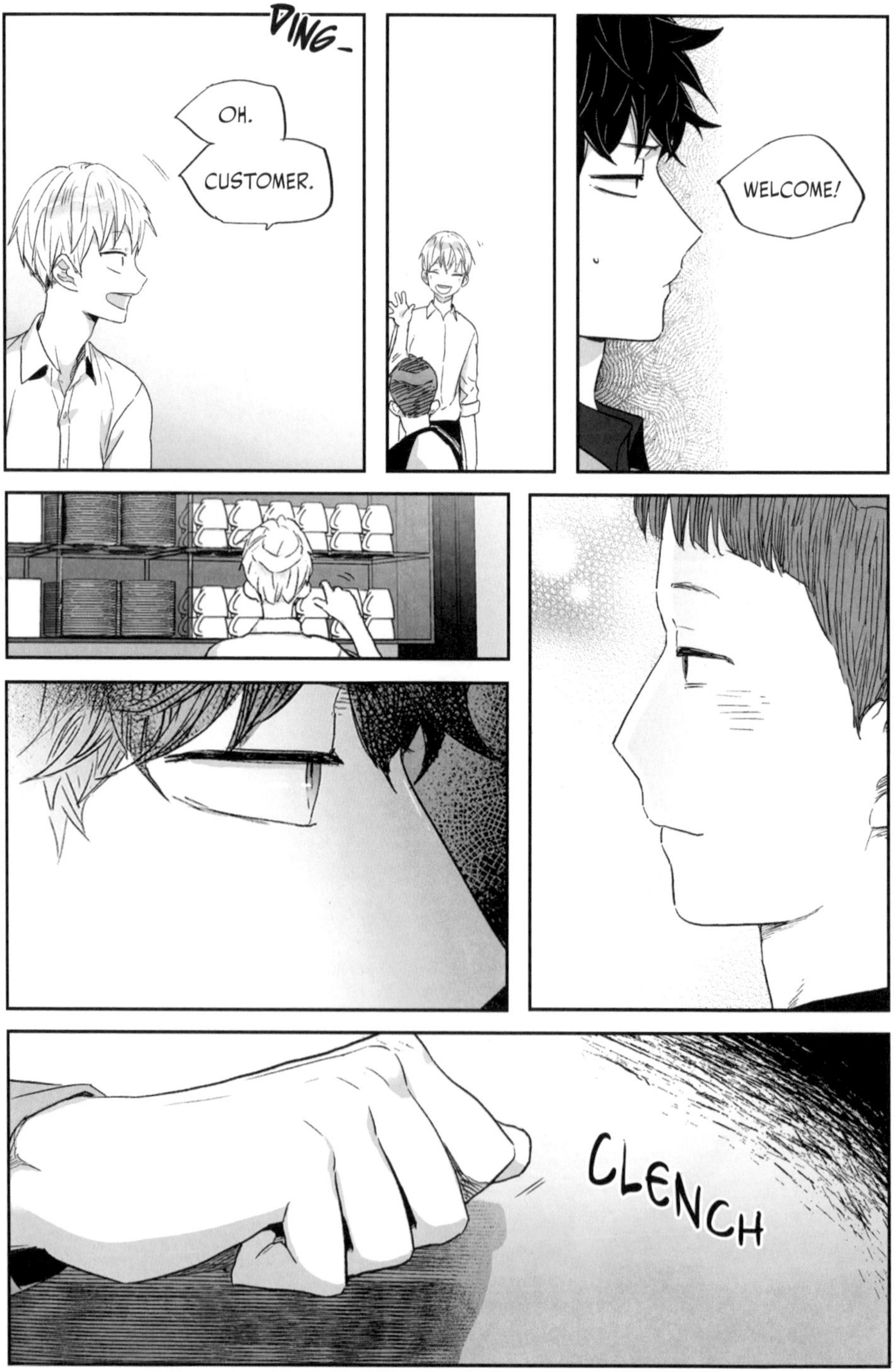
DING-
OH.
CUSTOMER.
WELCOME!
CLENCH

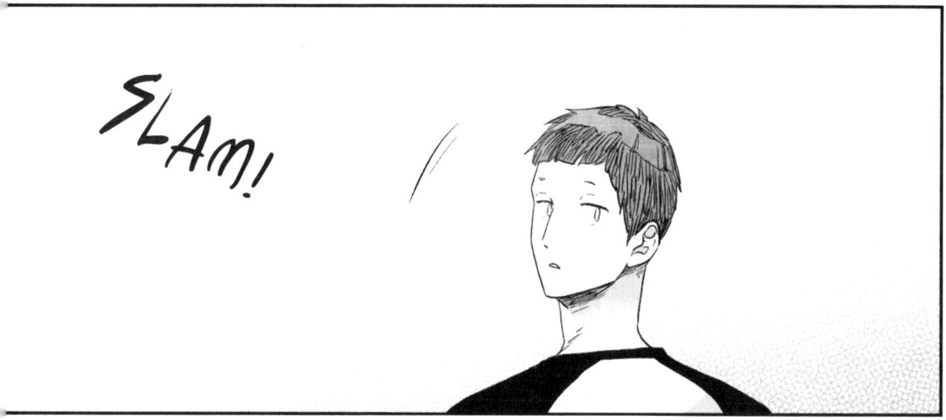
SLAM!

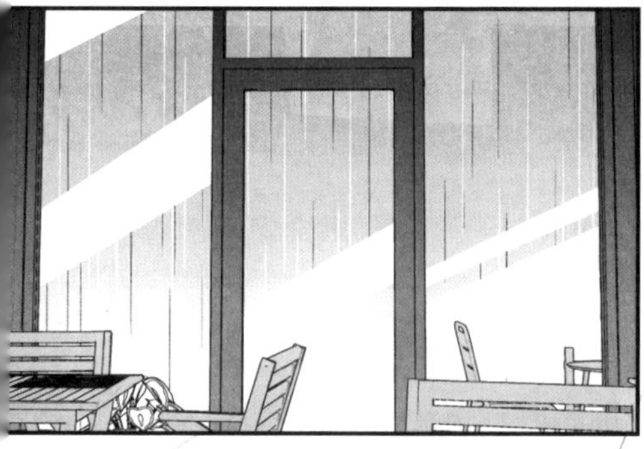

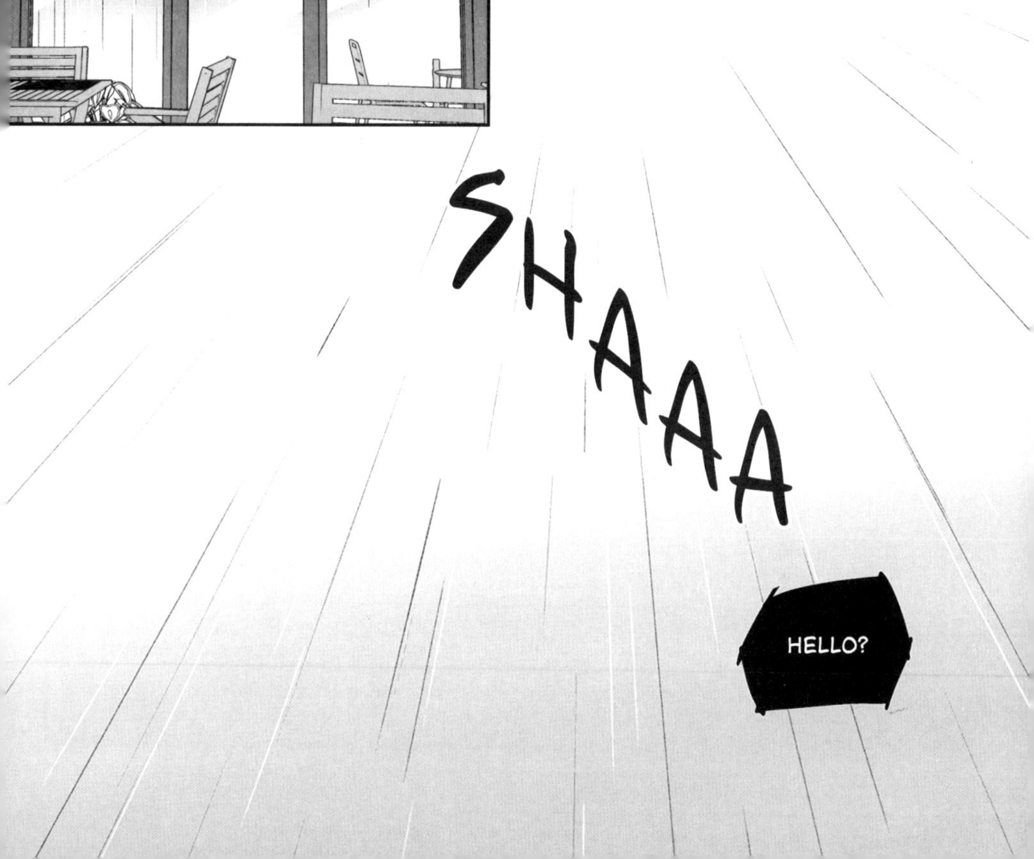
SHAAA
HELLO?

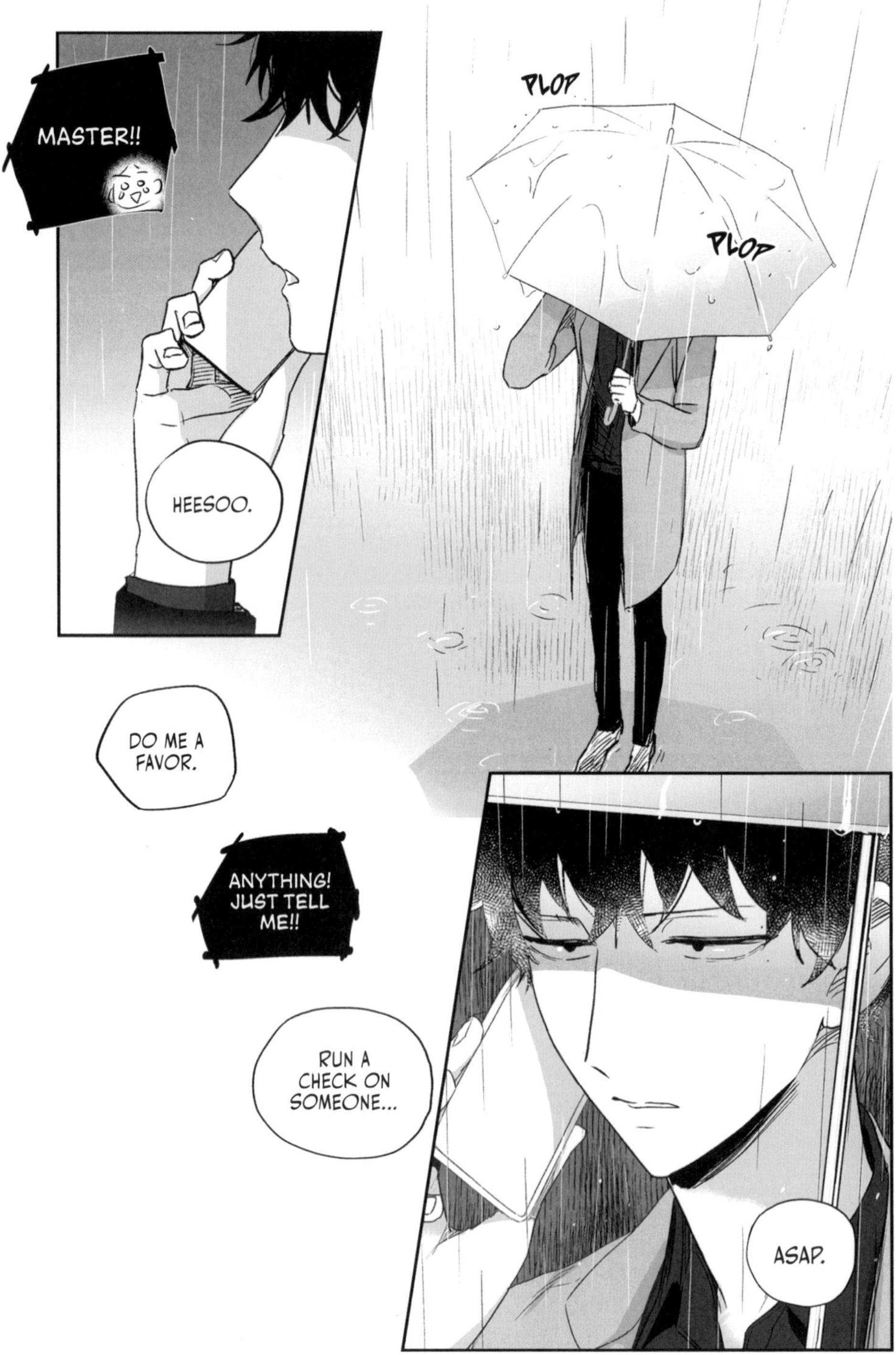
MASTER!!
HEESOO.
PLOP
PLOP
DO ME A FAVOR.
ANYTHING! JUST TELL ME!!
RUN A CHECK ON SOMEONE...
ASAP.

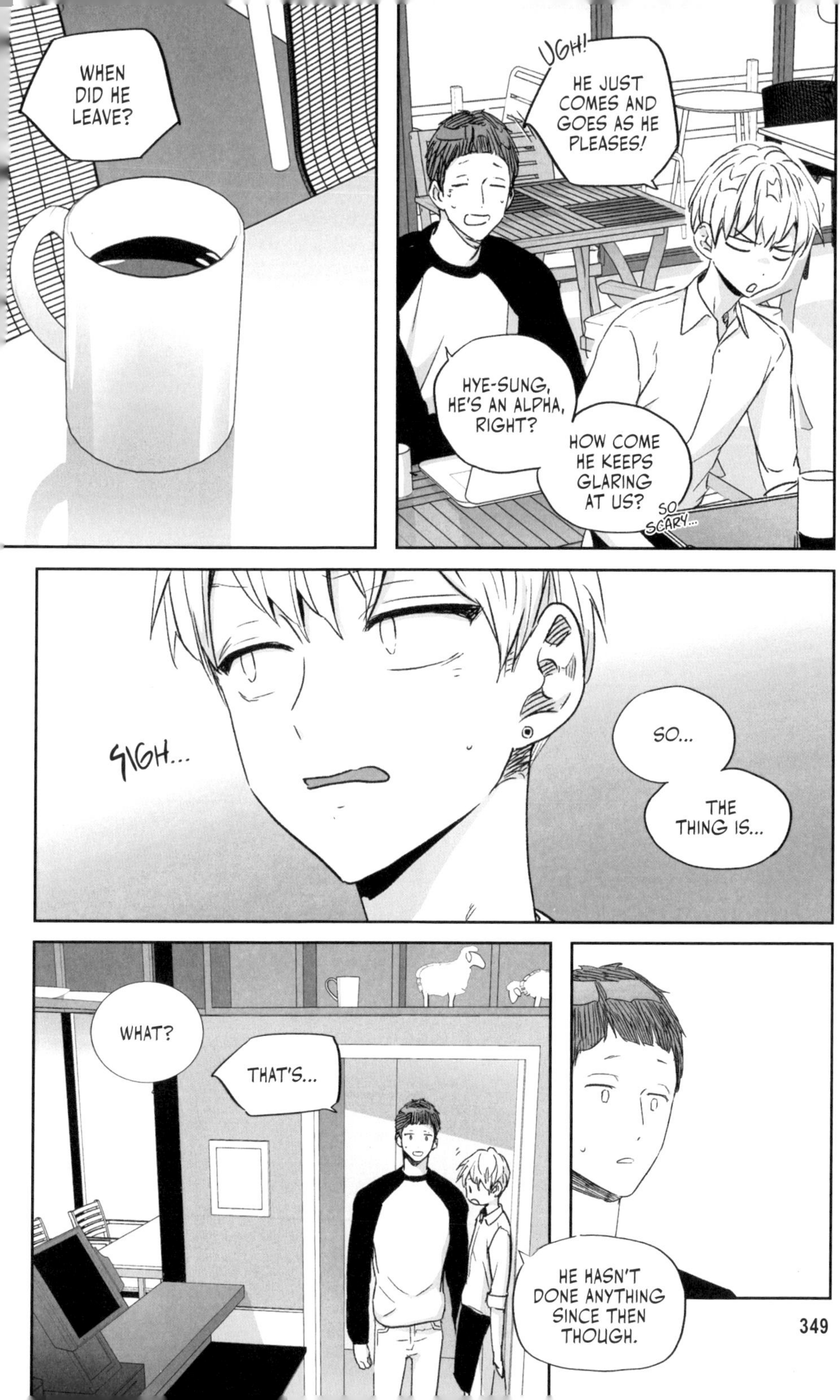
WHEN DID HE LEAVE?
UGH!
HE JUST COMES AND GOES AS HE PLEASES!
HYE-SUNG, HE'S AN ALPHA, RIGHT?
HOW COME HE KEEPS GLARING AT US?
SO SCARY...
SIGH...
SO...
THE THING IS...
WHAT?
THAT'S...
HE HASN'T DONE ANYTHING SINCE THEN THOUGH.

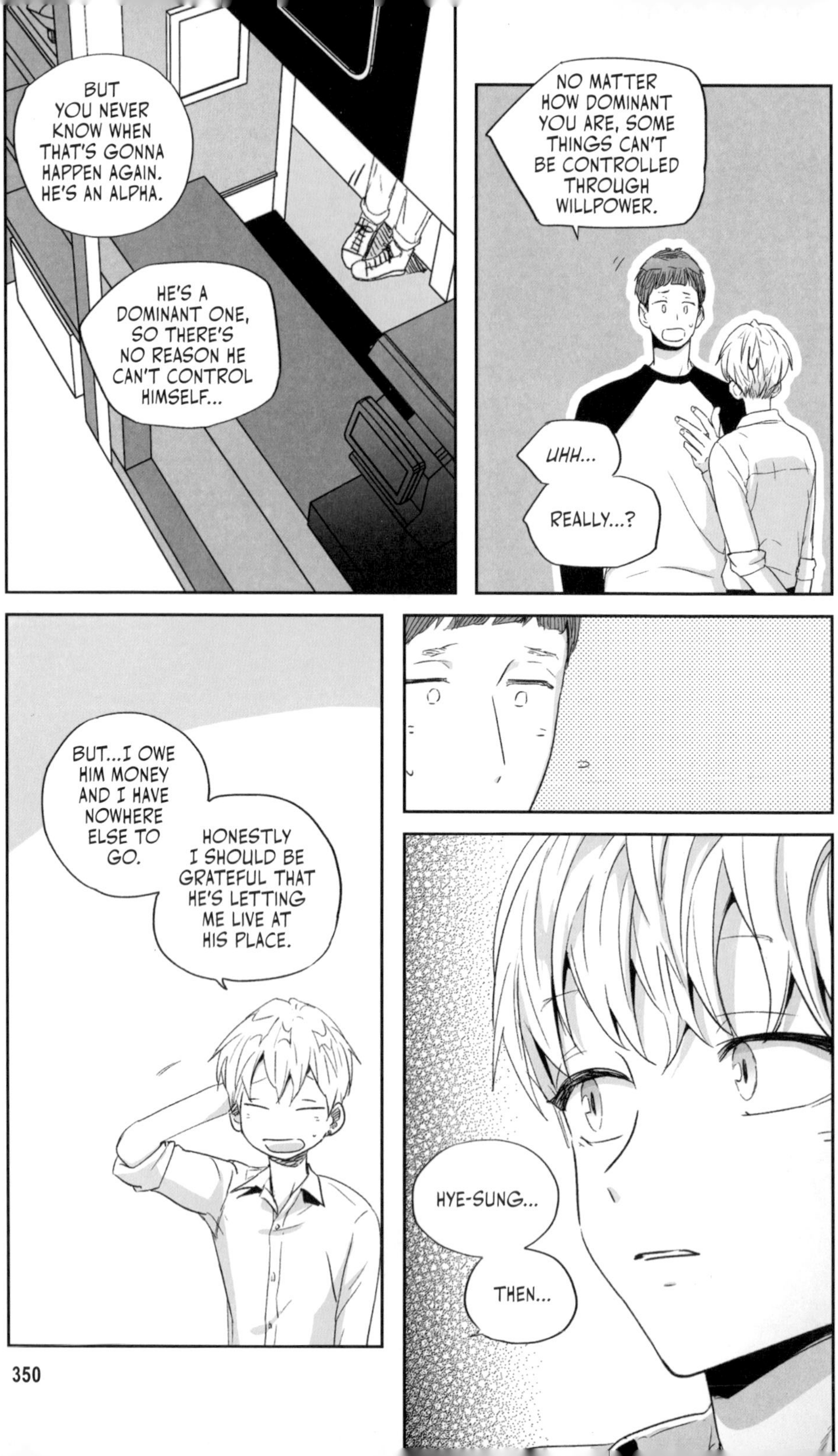
BUT YOU NEVER KNOW WHEN THAT'S GONNA HAPPEN AGAIN. HE'S AN ALPHA.
HE'S A DOMINANT ONE, SO THERE'S NO REASON HE CAN'T CONTROL HIMSELF...
NO MATTER HOW DOMINANT YOU ARE, SOME THINGS CAN'T BE CONTROLLED THROUGH WILLPOWER.
UHH...
REALLY...?
BUT...I OWE HIM MONEY AND I HAVE NOWHERE ELSE TO GO.
HONESTLY I SHOULD BE GRATEFUL THAT HE'S LETTING ME LIVE AT HIS PLACE.
HYE-SUNG...
THEN...

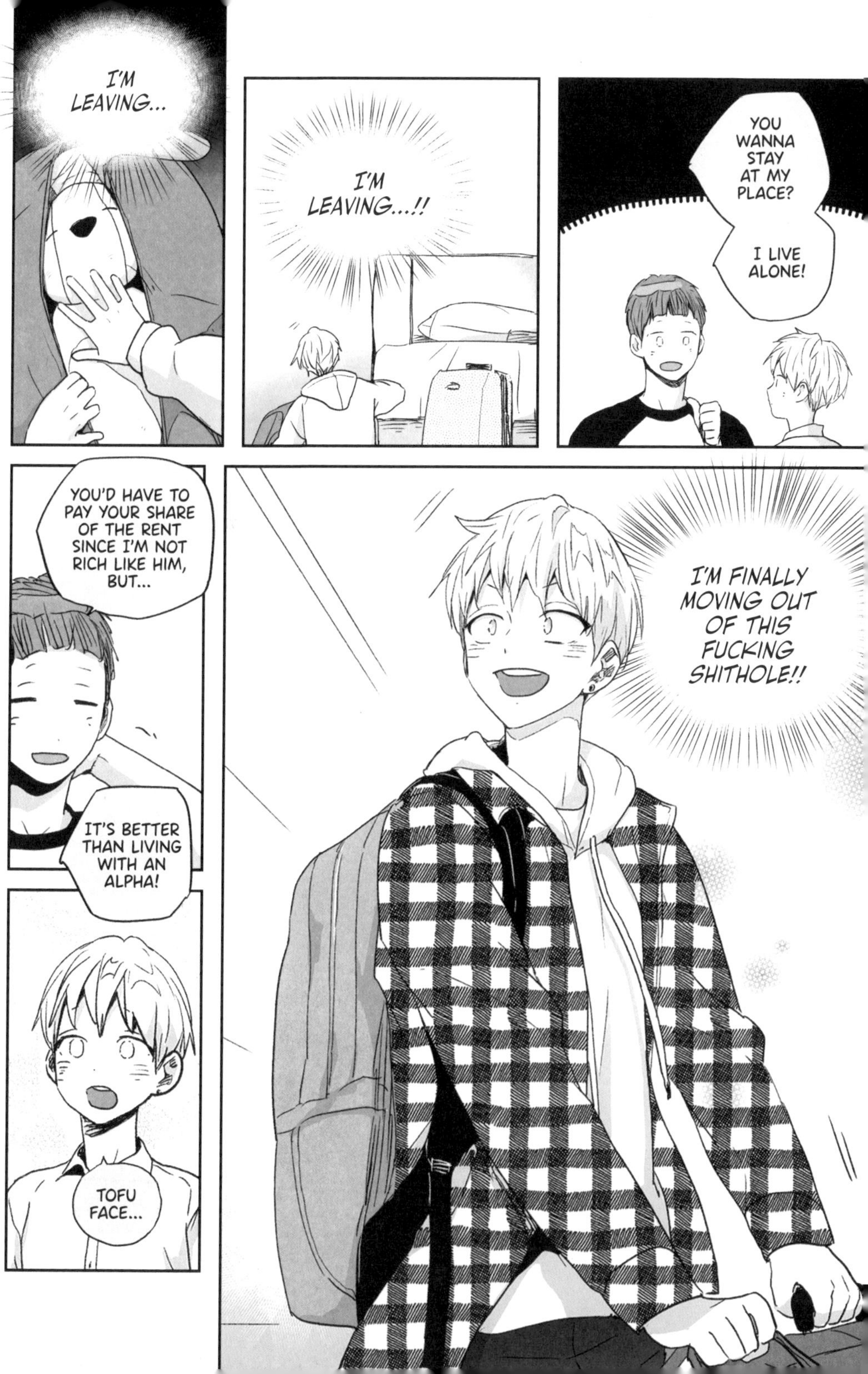
I'M LEAVING...
I'M LEAVING...!!
YOU WANNA STAY AT MY PLACE?
I LIVE ALONE!
YOU'D HAVE TO PAY YOUR SHARE OF THE RENT SINCE I'M NOT RICH LIKE HIM, BUT...
IT'S BETTER THAN LIVING WITH AN ALPHA!
TOFU FACE...
I'M FINALLY MOVING OUT OF THIS FUCKING SHITHOLE!!

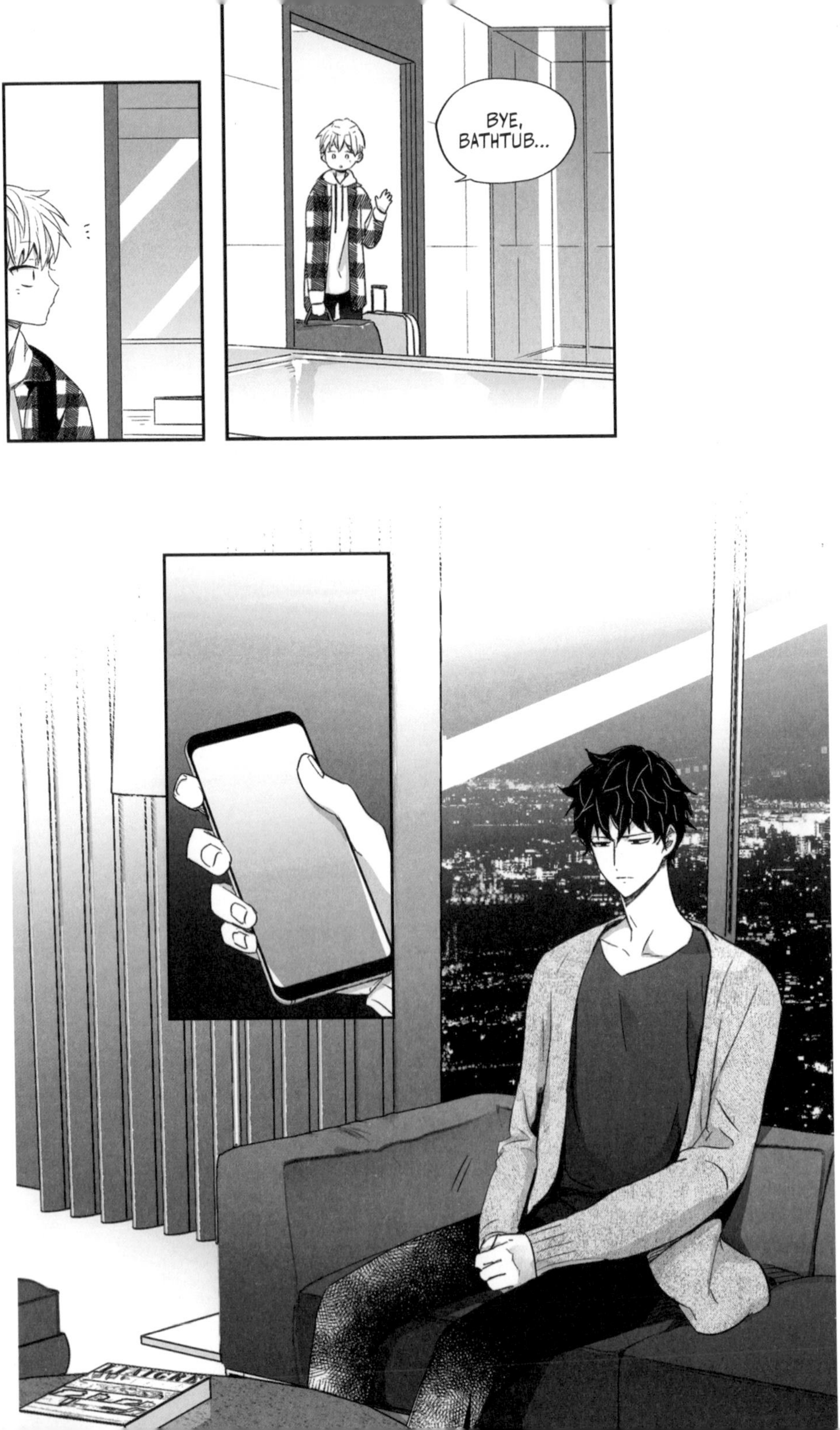
BYE, BATHTUB...

RATTLE

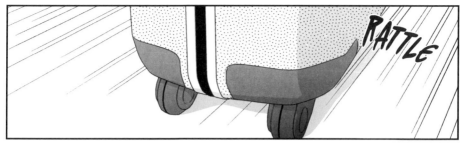

I'M OUTTA HERE!

WHAT? WHERE...

I'M GONNA LIVE WITH SOOYOUNG!

WHAT?

THANKS FOR EVERYTHING!

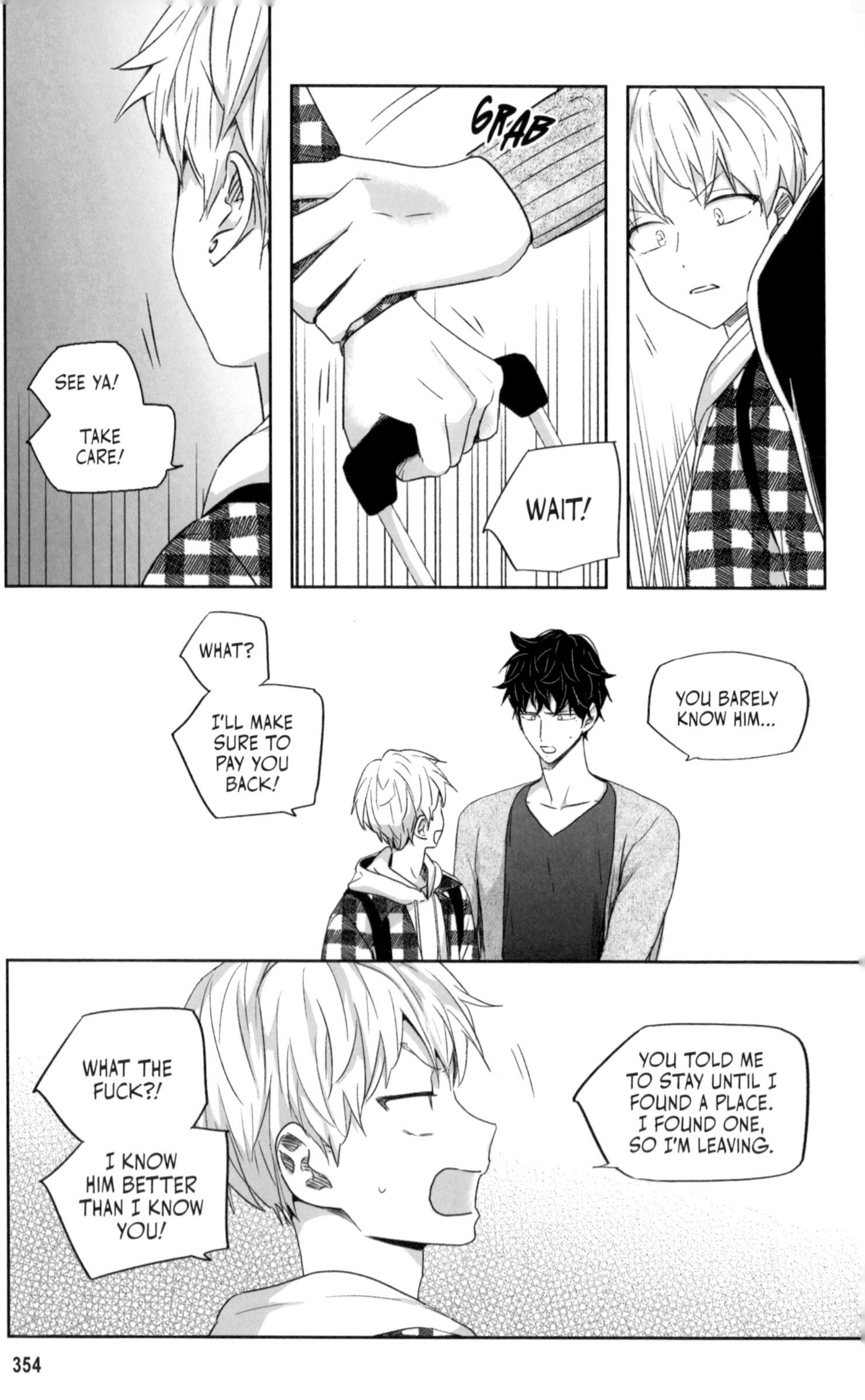
SEE YA!
TAKE CARE!
GRAB
WAIT!
WHAT?
I'LL MAKE SURE TO PAY YOU BACK!
YOU BARELY KNOW HIM...
WHAT THE FUCK?!
I KNOW HIM BETTER THAN I KNOW YOU!
YOU TOLD ME TO STAY UNTIL I FOUND A PLACE. I FOUND ONE, SO I'M LEAVING.

Love is
an Illusion!

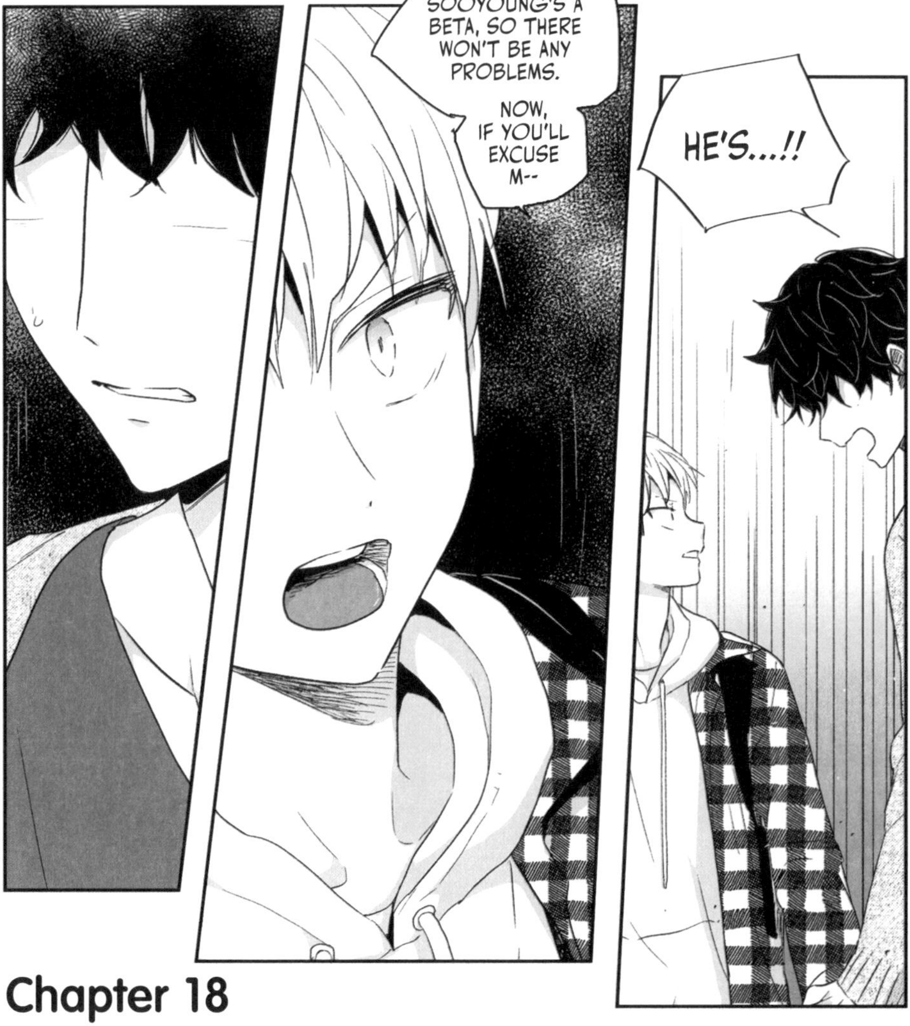
SOOYOUNG'S A BETA, SO THERE WON'T BE ANY PROBLEMS.
NOW, IF YOU'LL EXCUSE M--
HE'S...!!

Chapter 18

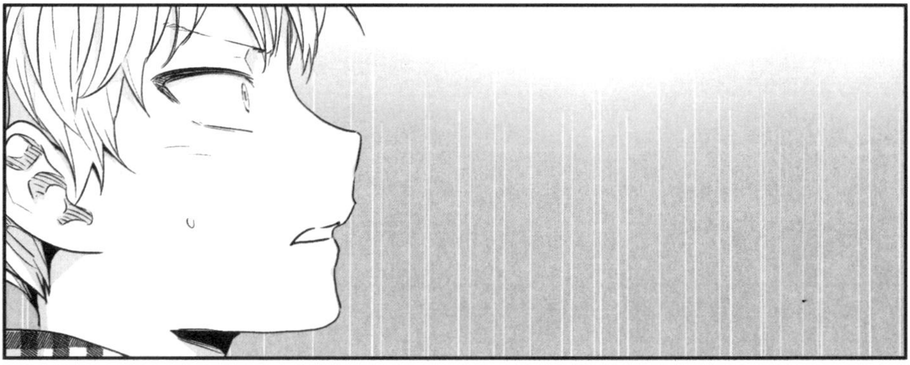

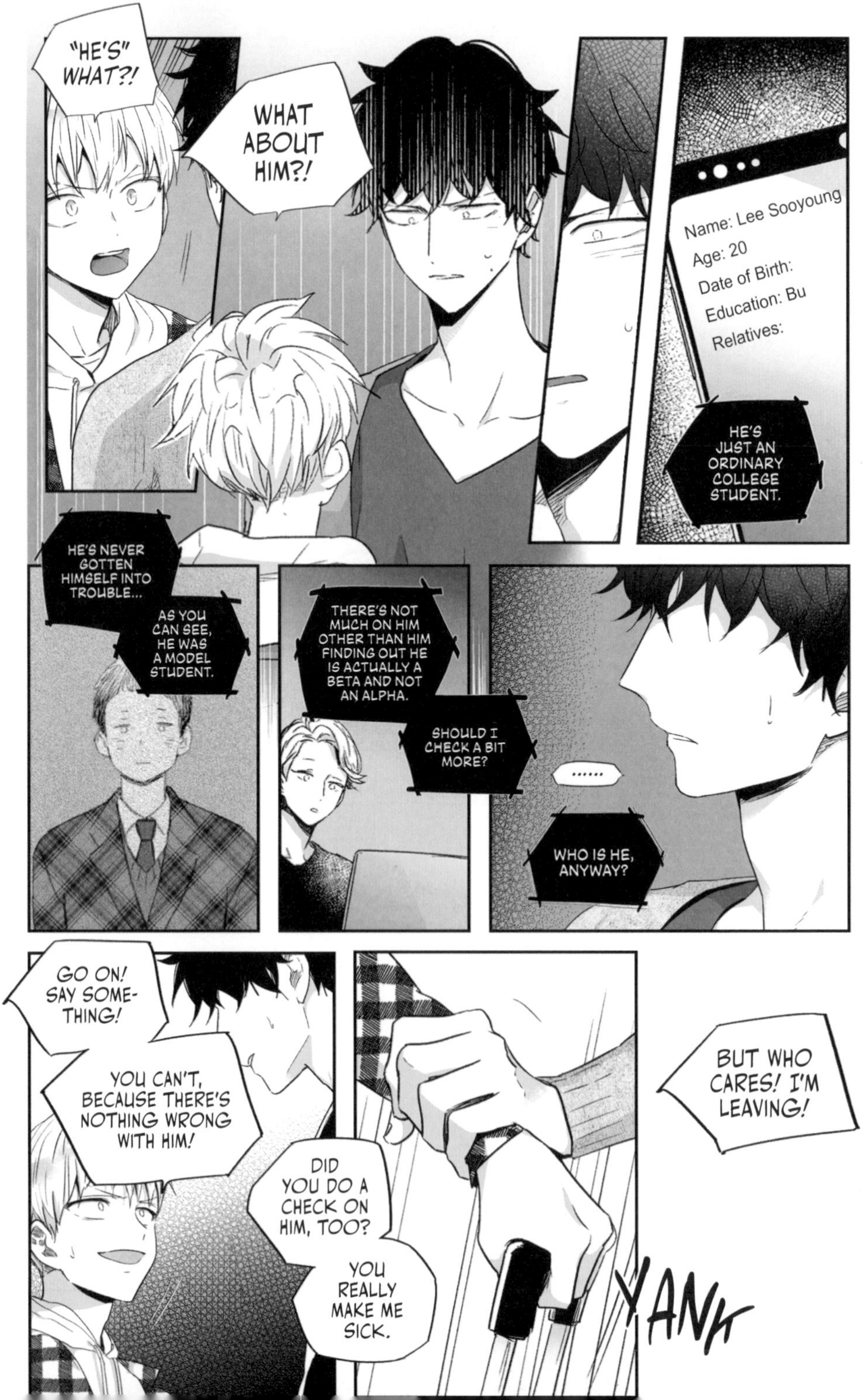
"HE'S" WHAT?!
WHAT ABOUT HIM?!
Name: Lee Sooyoung
Age: 20
Date of Birth:
Education: Bu
Relatives:
HE'S JUST AN ORDINARY COLLEGE STUDENT.
HE'S NEVER GOTTEN HIMSELF INTO TROUBLE...
AS YOU CAN SEE, HE WAS A MODEL STUDENT.
THERE'S NOT MUCH ON HIM OTHER THAN HIM FINDING OUT HE IS ACTUALLY A BETA AND NOT AN ALPHA.
SHOULD I CHECK A BIT MORE?
......
WHO IS HE, ANYWAY?
GO ON! SAY SOME-THING!
YOU CAN'T, BECAUSE THERE'S NOTHING WRONG WITH HIM!
DID YOU DO A CHECK ON HIM, TOO?
YOU REALLY MAKE ME SICK.
BUT WHO CARES! I'M LEAVING!
YANK

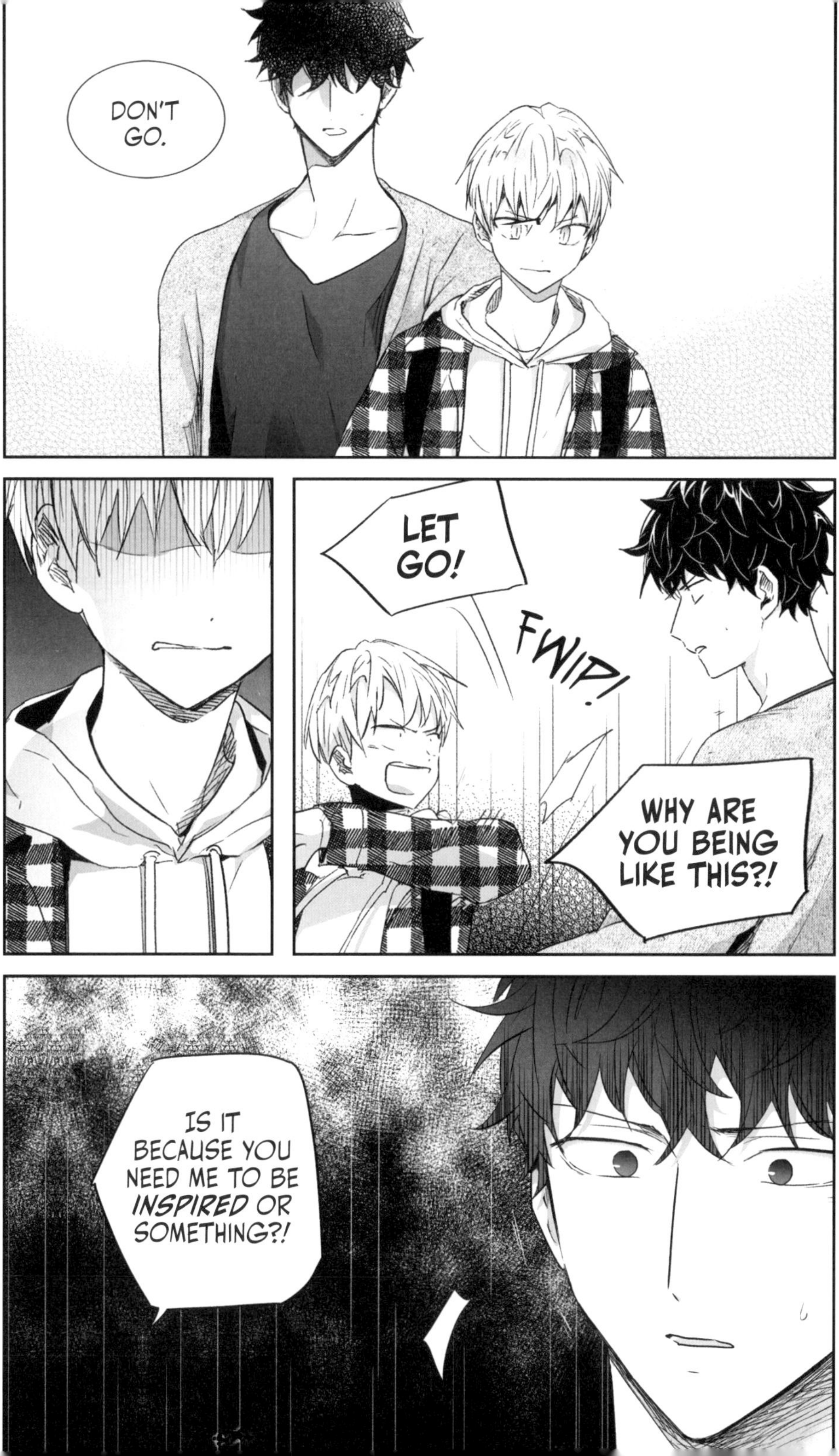
DON'T GO.
LET GO!
FWIP!
WHY ARE YOU BEING LIKE THIS?!
IS IT BECAUSE YOU NEED ME TO BE *INSPIRED* OR SOMETHING?!

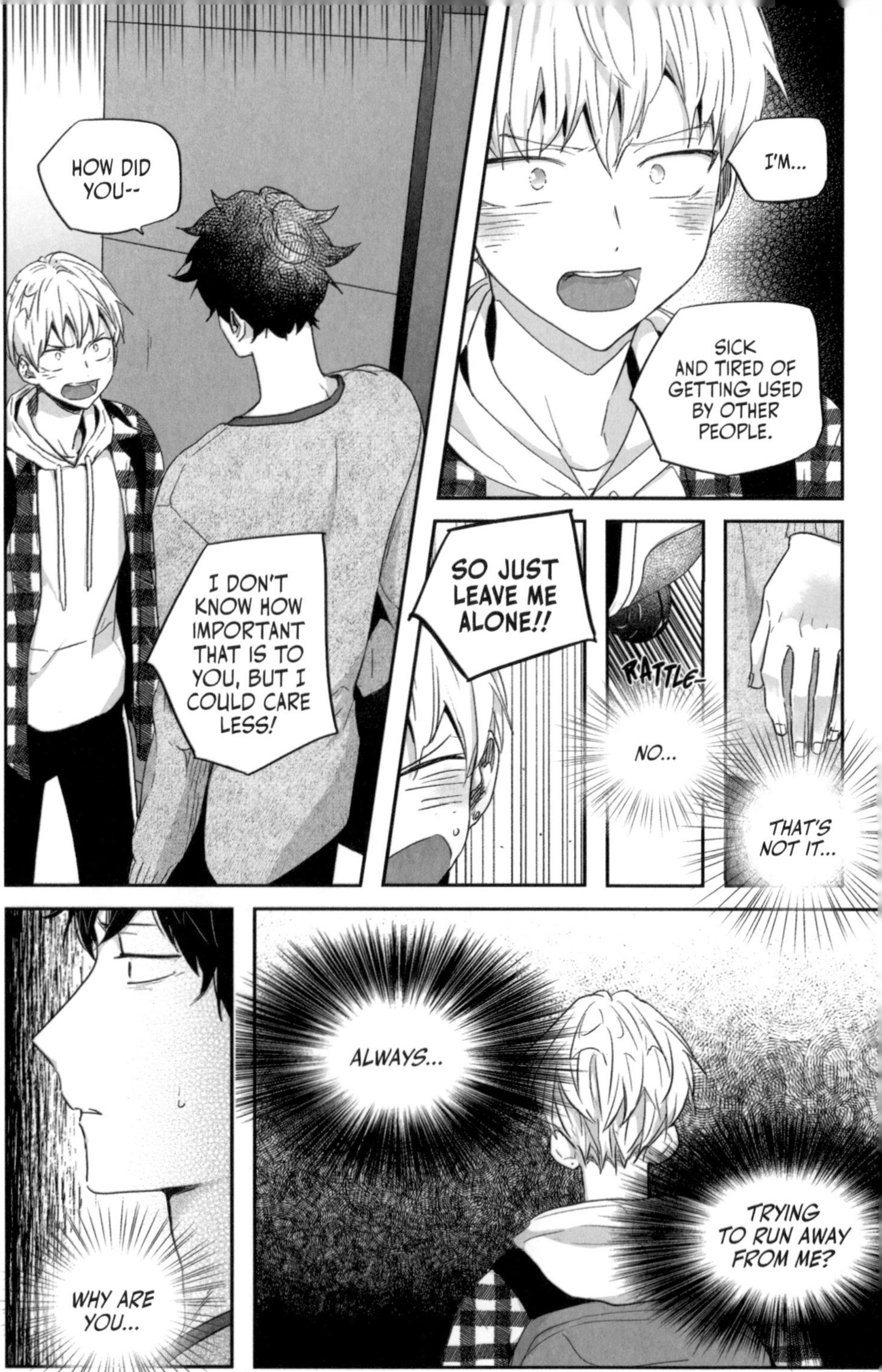
HOW DID YOU--
I DON'T KNOW HOW IMPORTANT THAT IS TO YOU, BUT I COULD CARE LESS!
I'M...
SICK AND TIRED OF GETTING USED BY OTHER PEOPLE.
SO JUST LEAVE ME ALONE!!
RATTLE
NO...
THAT'S NOT IT...
WHY ARE YOU...
ALWAYS...
TRYING TO RUN AWAY FROM ME?

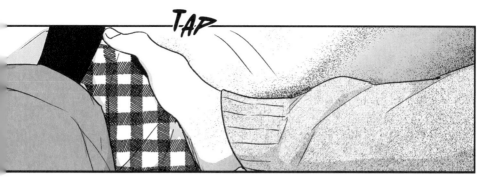

TAP

DON'T GO.

LET'S TALK.

Sssss...

Sssss

FLINCH

HA!

SO YOU'RE THREATENING ME NOW?

YOU DON'T SCARE ME AT ALL!

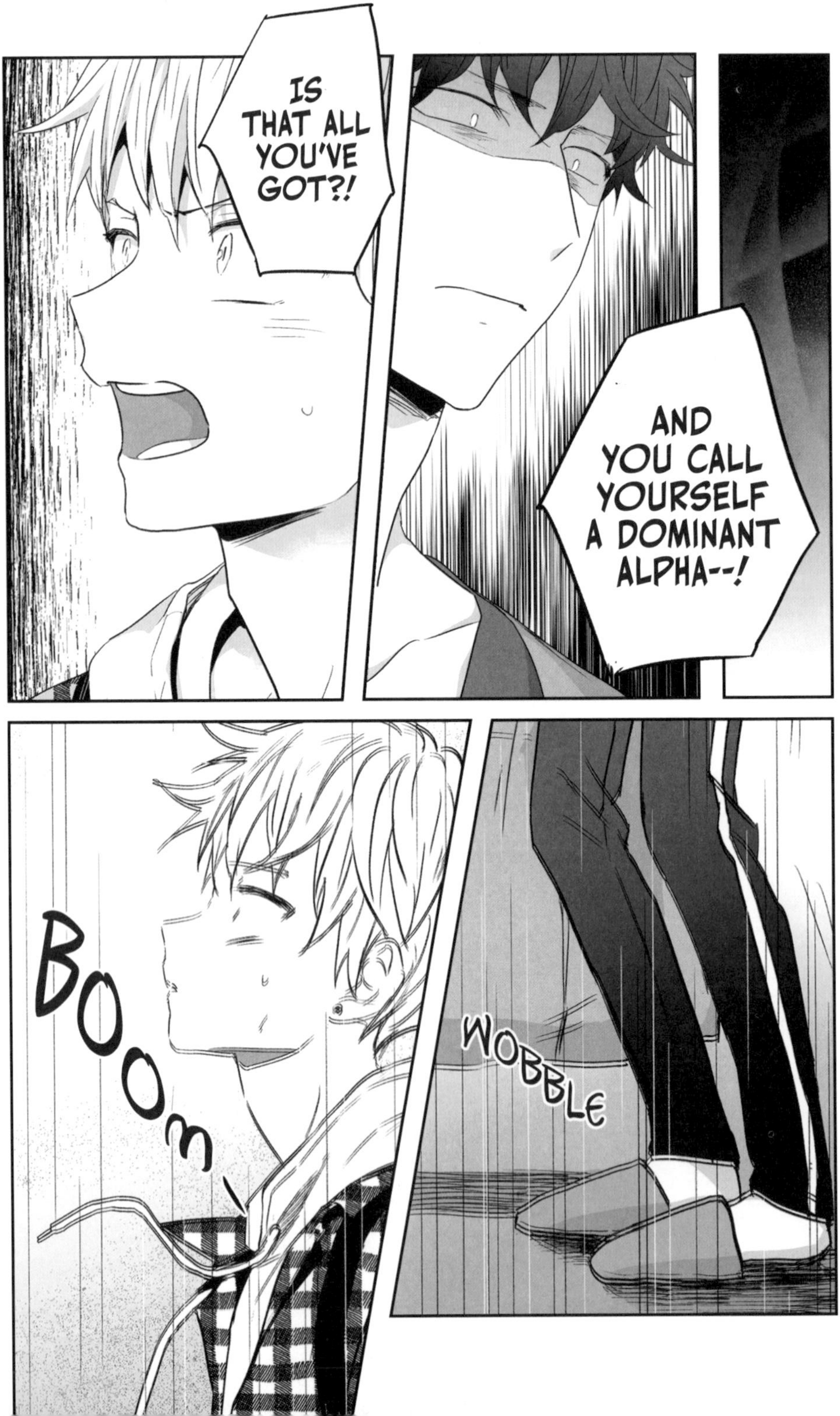
IS THAT ALL YOU'VE GOT?!
AND YOU CALL YOURSELF A DOMINANT ALPHA--!
BOOM
WOBBLE

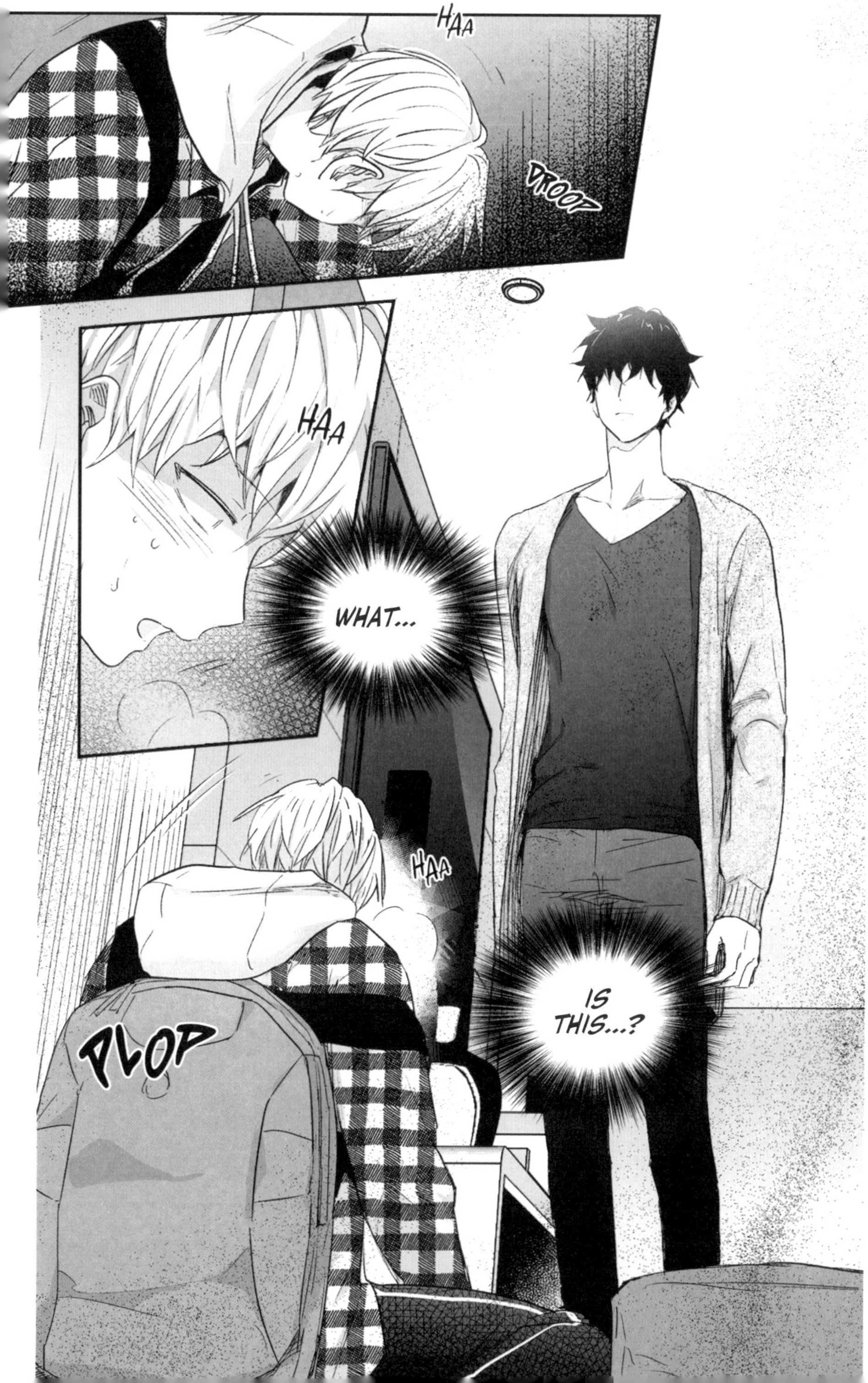
HAA
DROOP
HAA
WHAT...
HAA
IS THIS...?
PLOP

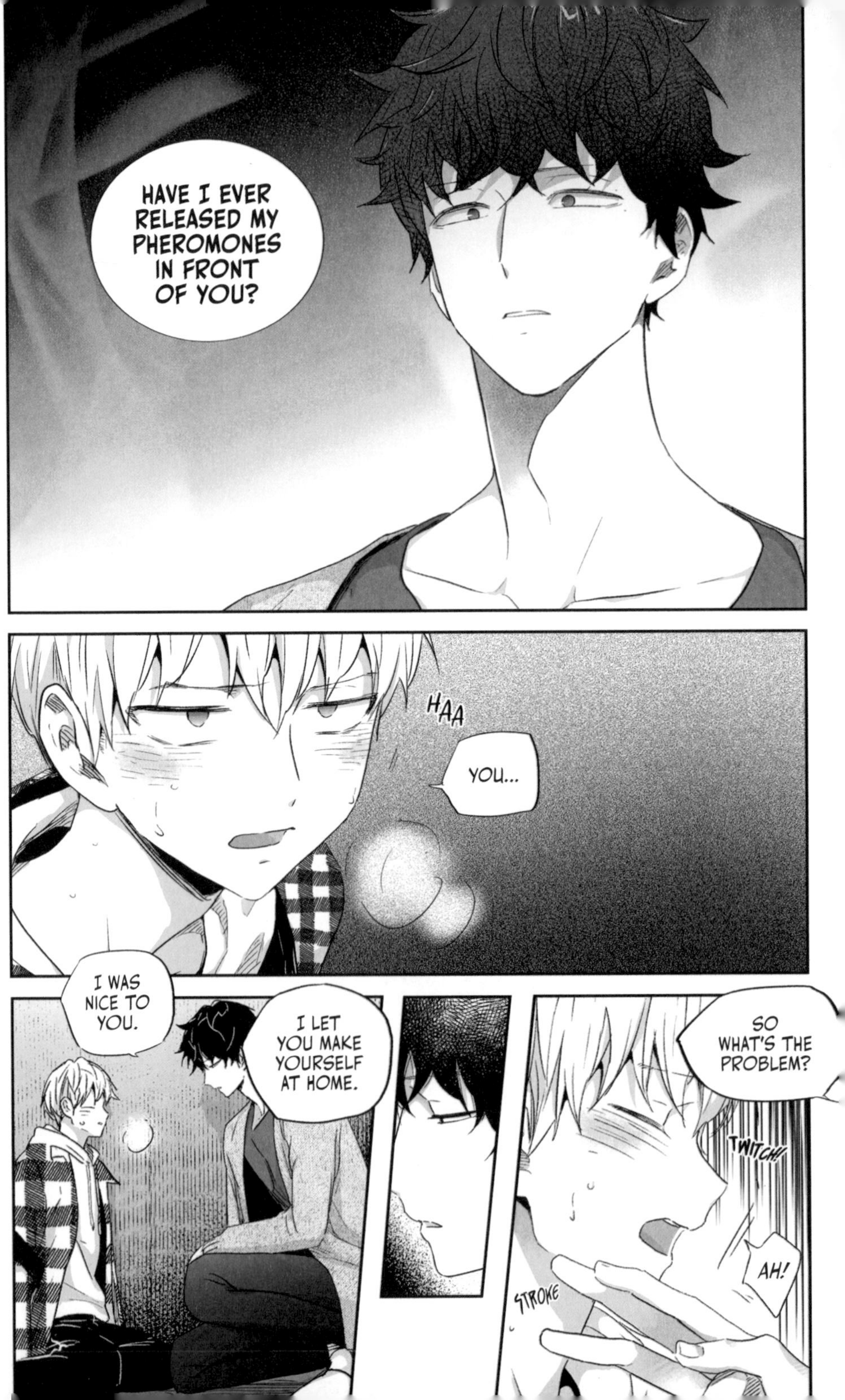
HAVE I EVER RELEASED MY PHEROMONES IN FRONT OF YOU?
HAA
YOU...
I WAS NICE TO YOU.
I LET YOU MAKE YOURSELF AT HOME.
SO WHAT'S THE PROBLEM?
TWITCH!
AH!
STROKE

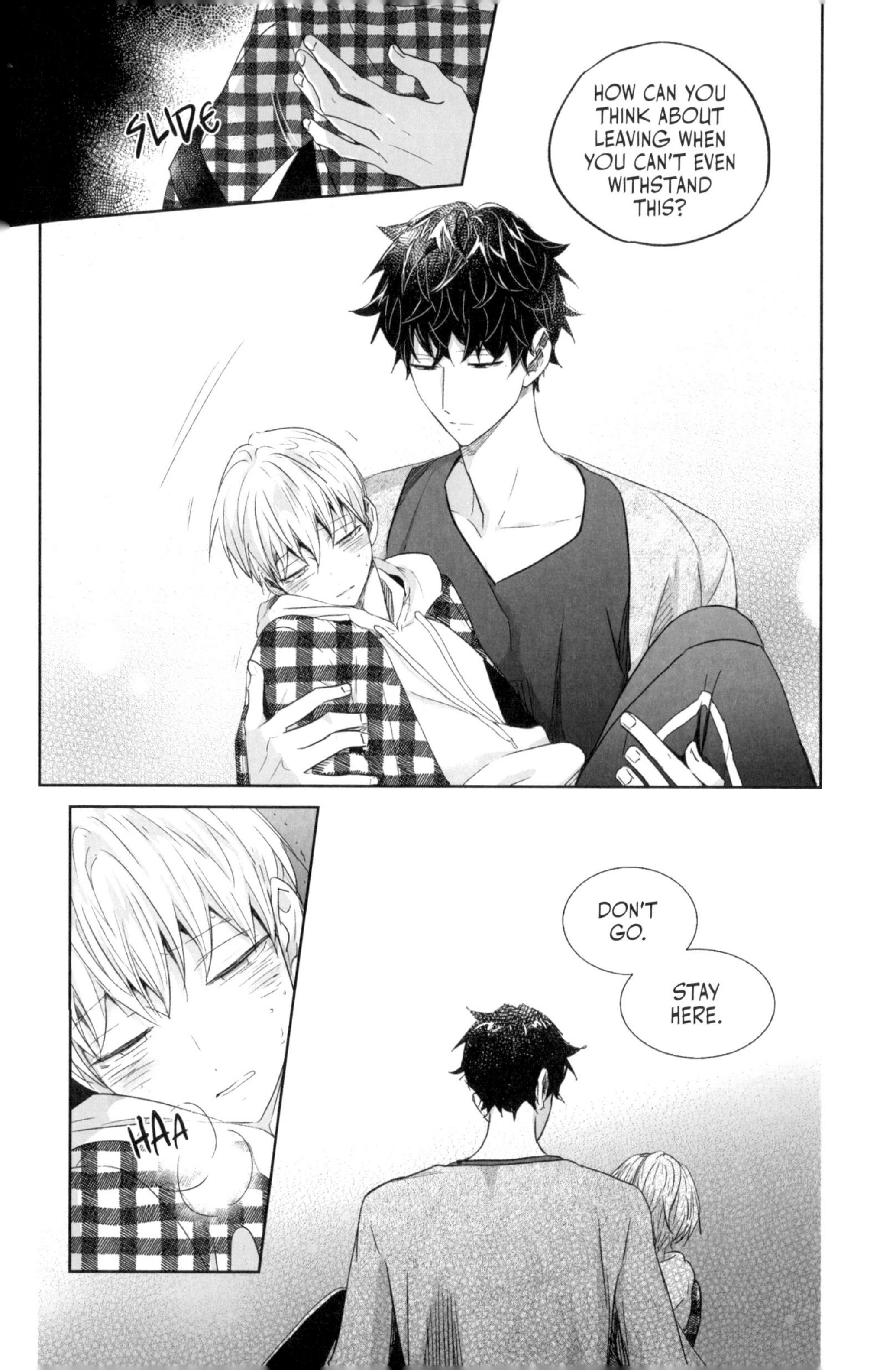
SLIDE
HOW CAN YOU THINK ABOUT LEAVING WHEN YOU CAN'T EVEN WITHSTAND THIS?
HAA
DON'T GO.
STAY HERE.

HAA!
PANT
MMM!
NGH...
AAH.
KISS
TWITCH
SUCK
AGHH...

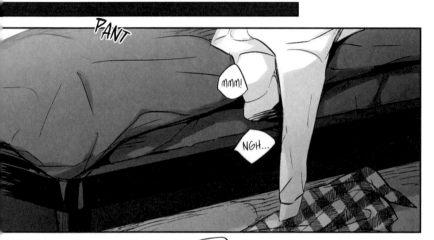

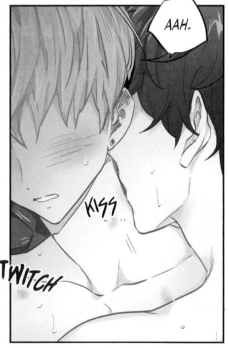

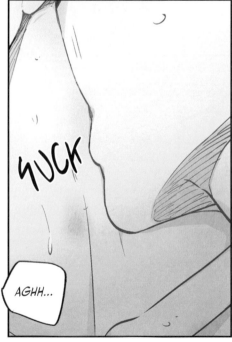

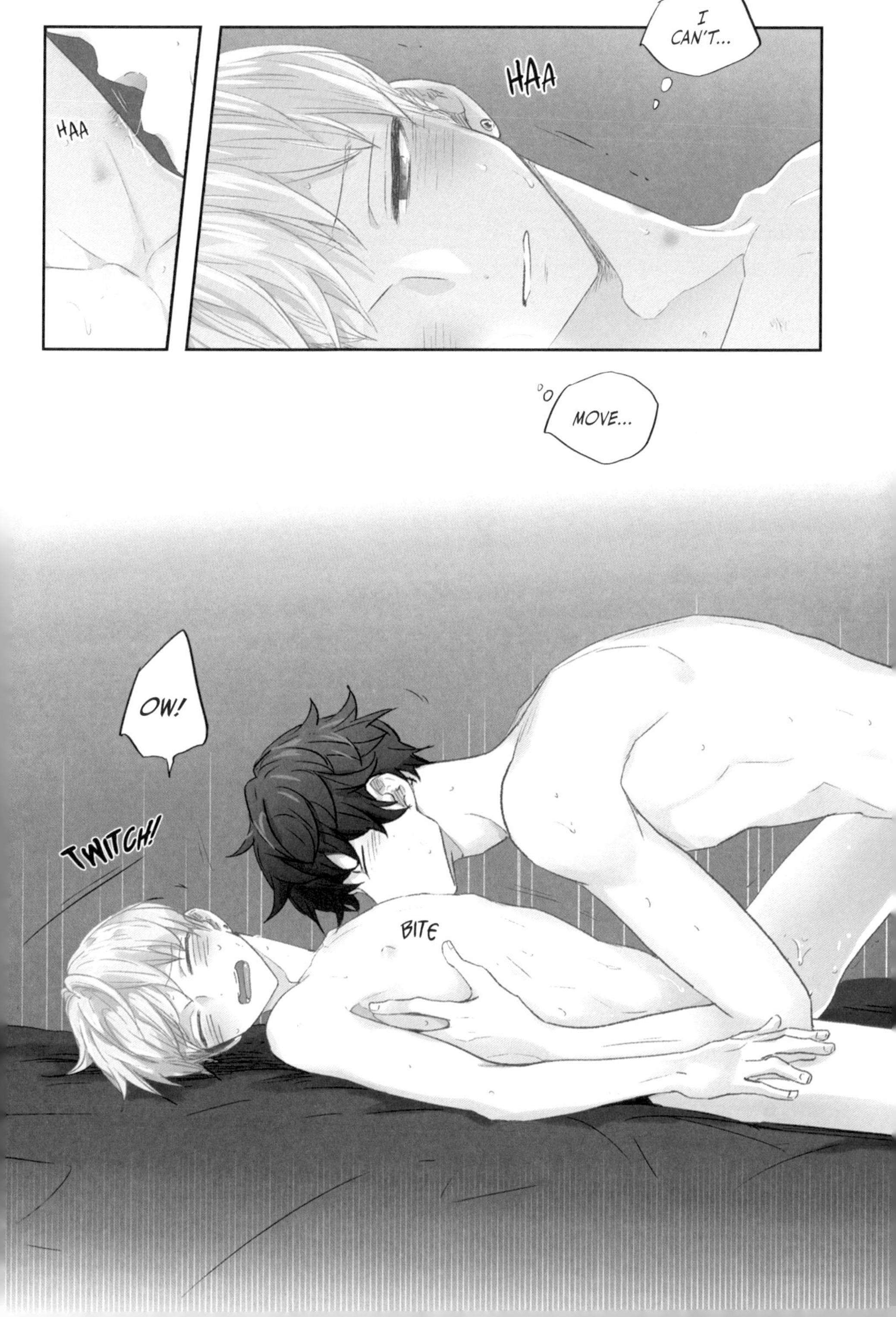
HAA
HAA
I CAN'T...
MOVE...
OW!
TWITCH!
BITE

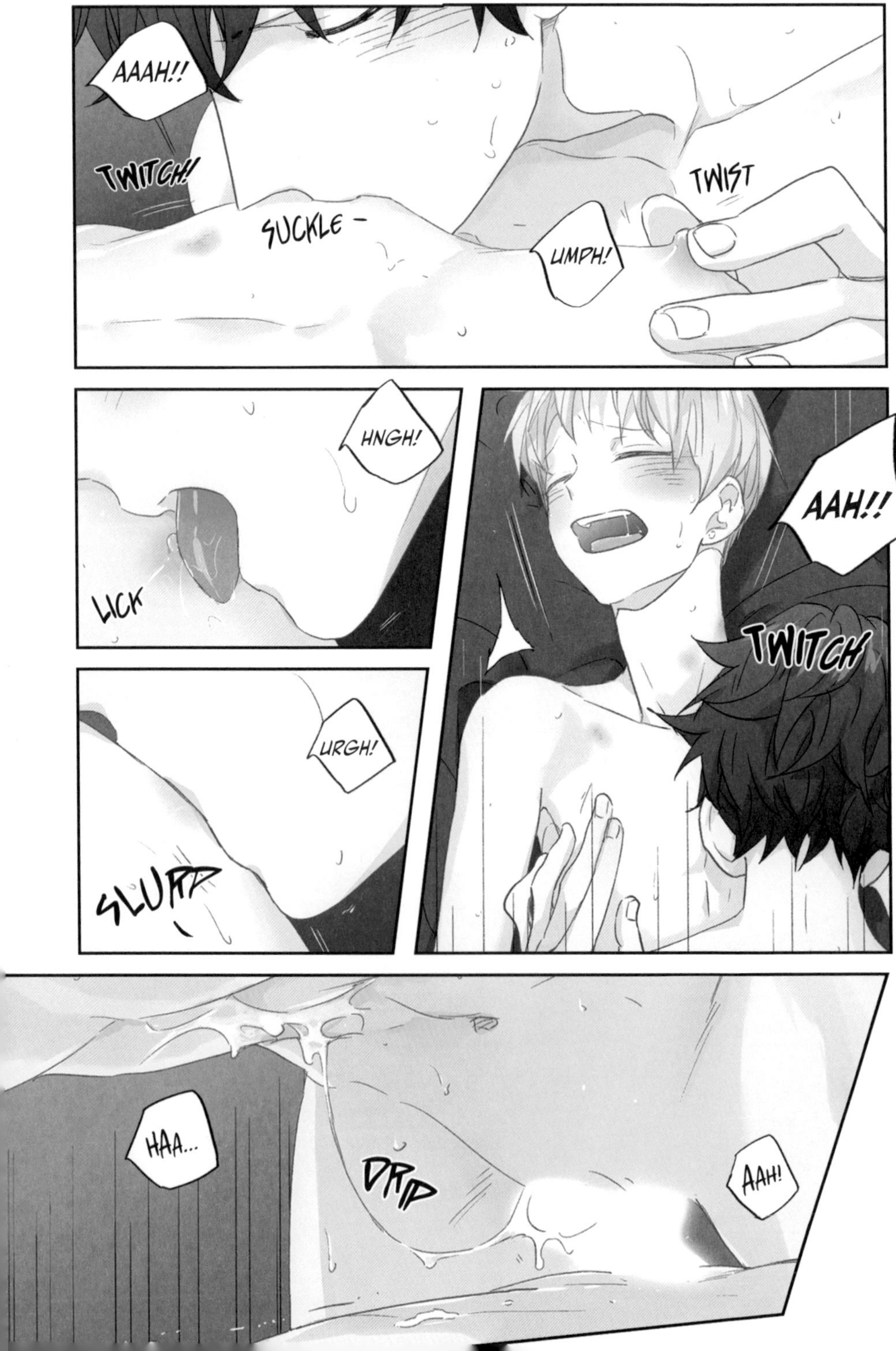
AAAH!!
TWITCH!
SUCKLE –
UMPH!
TWIST
HNGH!
LICK
URGH!
SLURP
AAH!!
TWITCH
HAA...
DRIP
AAH!

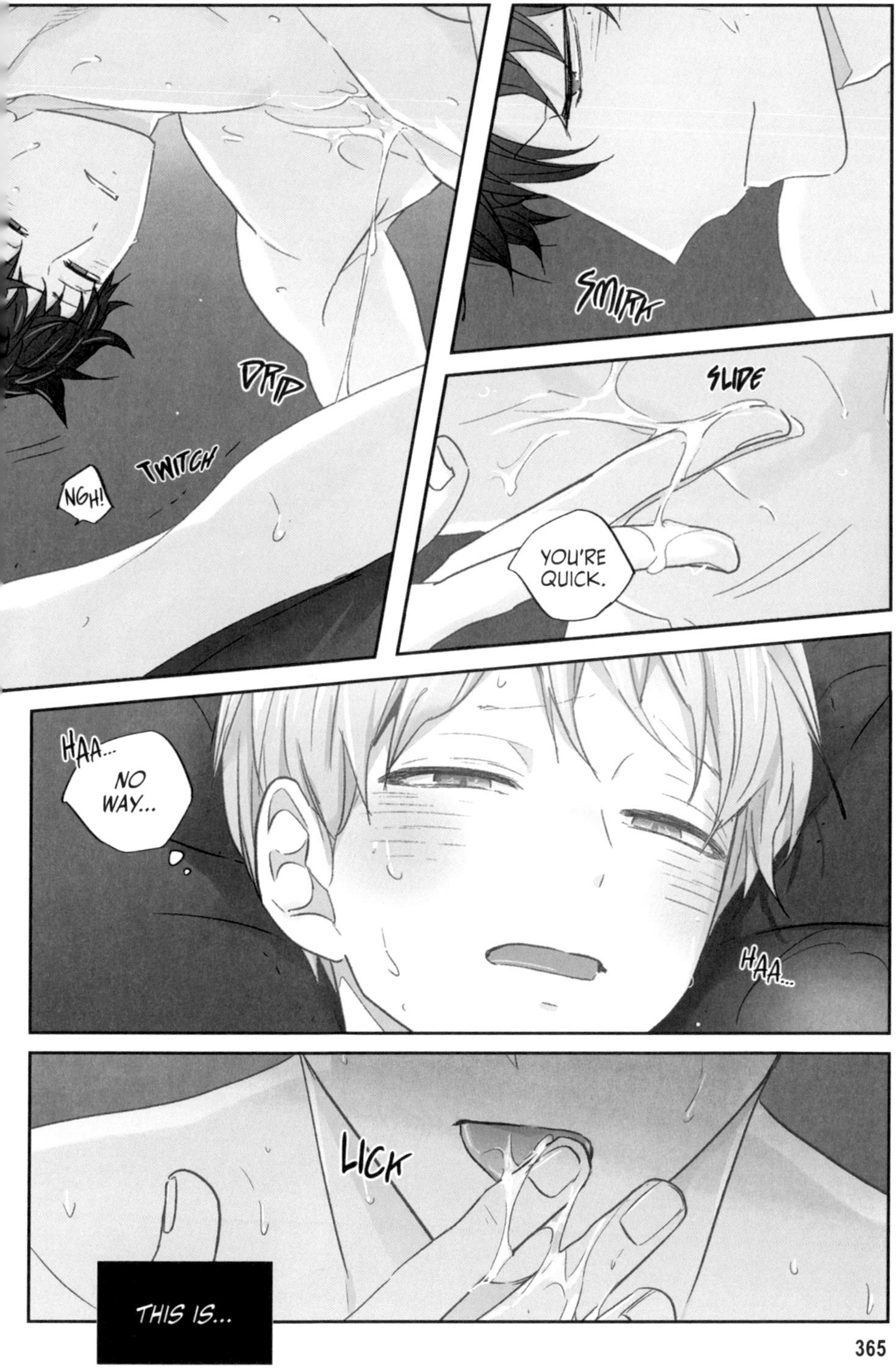
DRIP
TWITCH
NGH!
SMIRK
SLIDE
YOU'RE QUICK.
HAA... NO WAY...
HAA...
LICK
THIS IS...

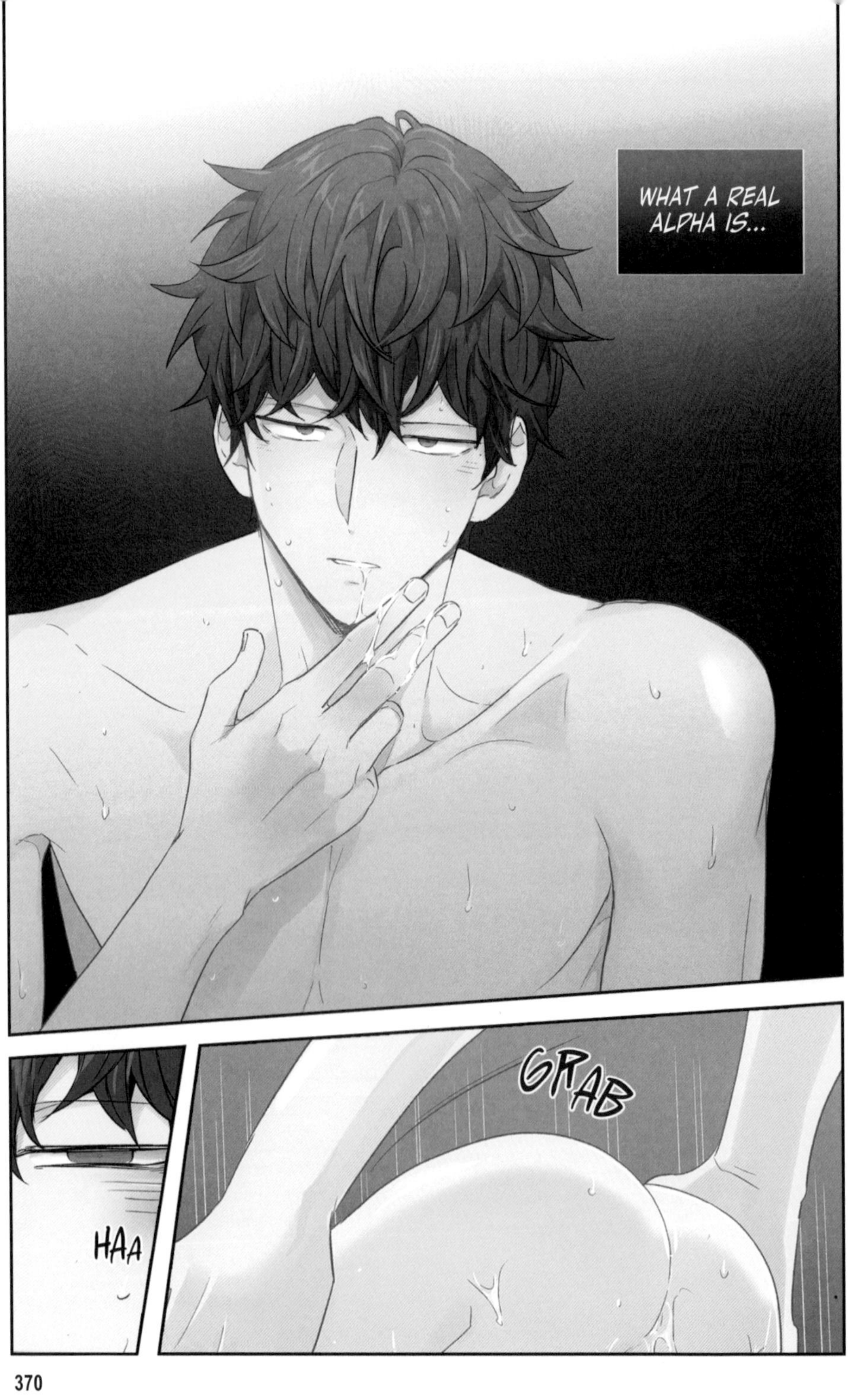
WHAT A REAL ALPHA IS...
HAA
GRAB

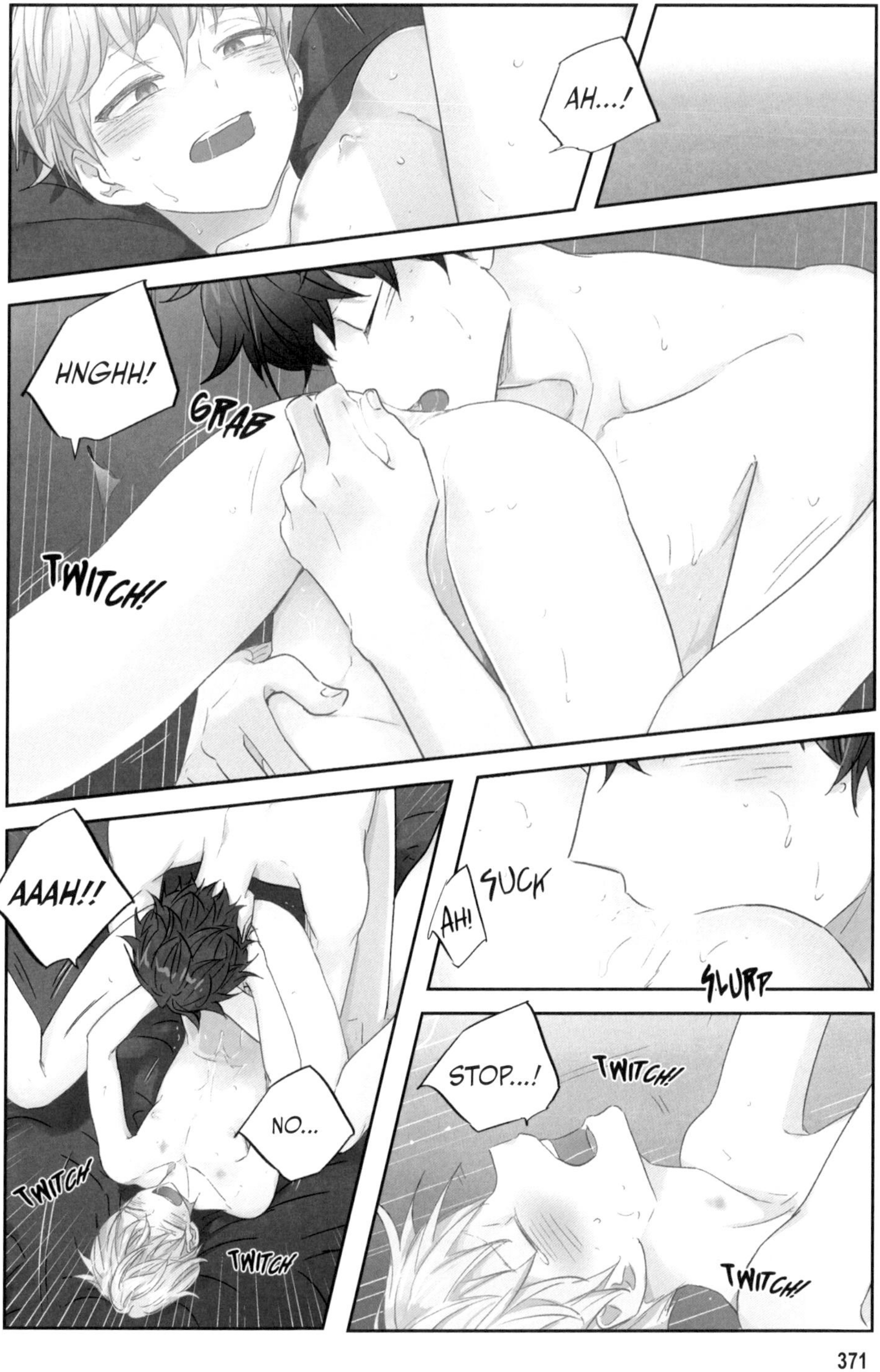
AH...!
HNGHH!
GRAB
TWITCH!
AAAH!!
NO...
TWITCH
TWITCH
SUCK
AH!
SLURP
STOP...!
TWITCH!
TWITCH!

UNNGH...

I WON'T DO ANYTHING IF YOU PROMISE NOT TO LEAVE.

KISS

FUCK OFF...

HAA

YOU BASTARD.

HAA

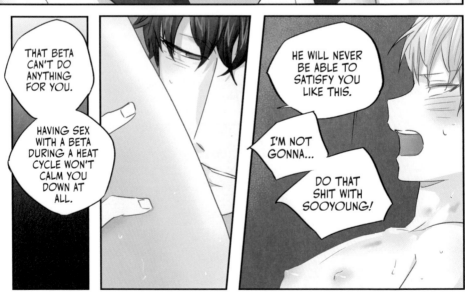

THAT BETA CAN'T DO ANYTHING FOR YOU.

HAVING SEX WITH A BETA DURING A HEAT CYCLE WON'T CALM YOU DOWN AT ALL.

HE WILL NEVER BE ABLE TO SATISFY YOU LIKE THIS.

I'M NOT GONNA...

DO THAT SHIT WITH SOOYOUNG!

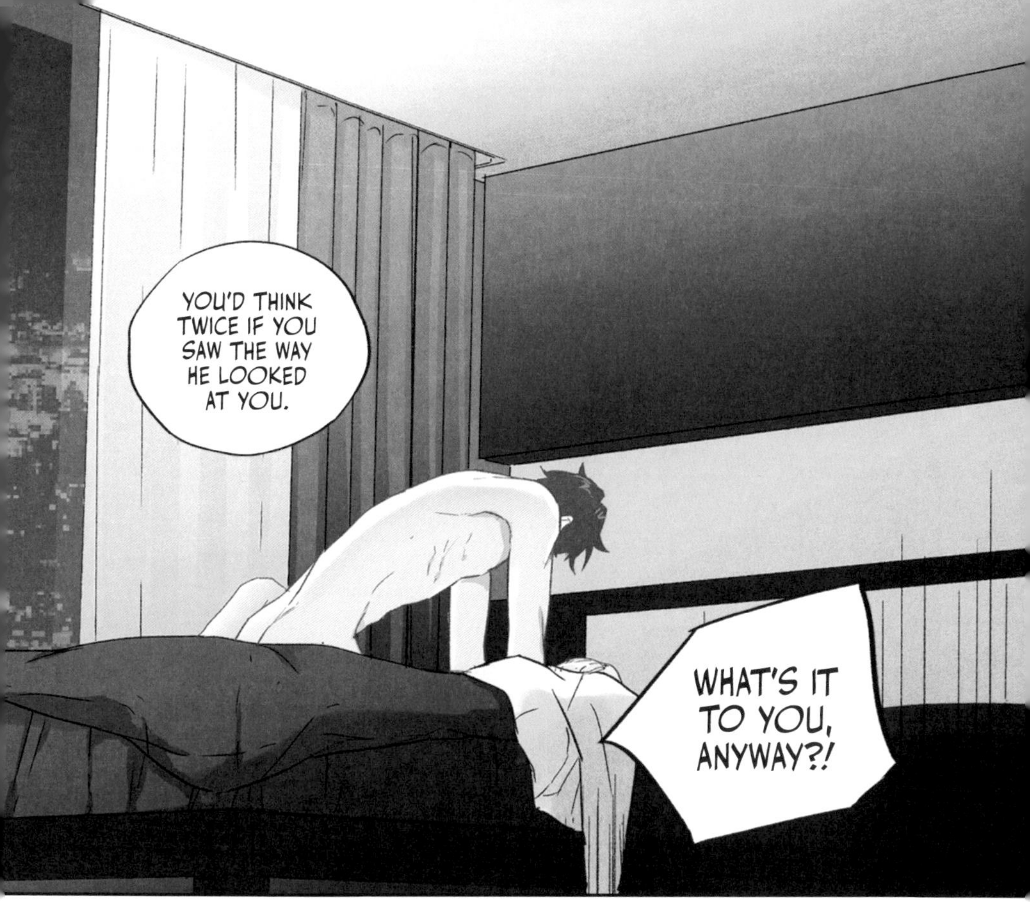
YOU'D THINK TWICE IF YOU SAW THE WAY HE LOOKED AT YOU.
WHAT'S IT TO YOU, ANYWAY?!
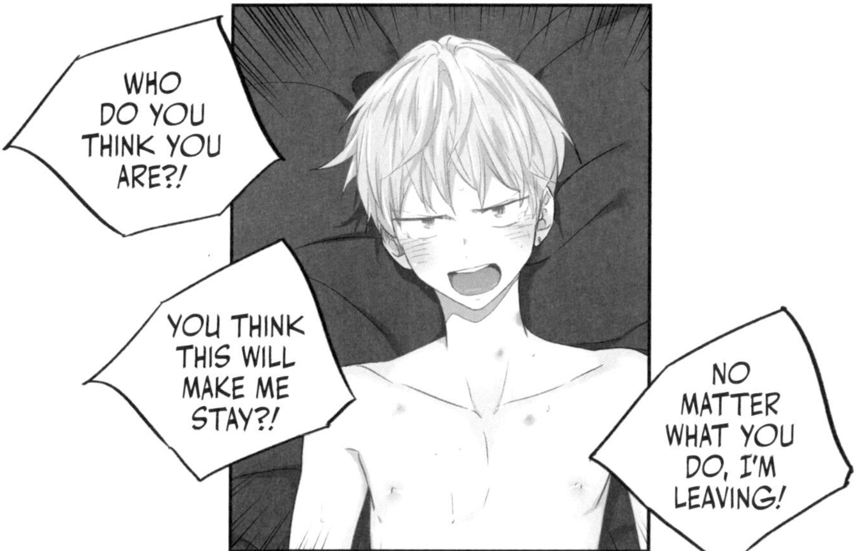
WHO DO YOU THINK YOU ARE?!
YOU THINK THIS WILL MAKE ME STAY?!
NO MATTER WHAT YOU DO, I'M LEAVING!

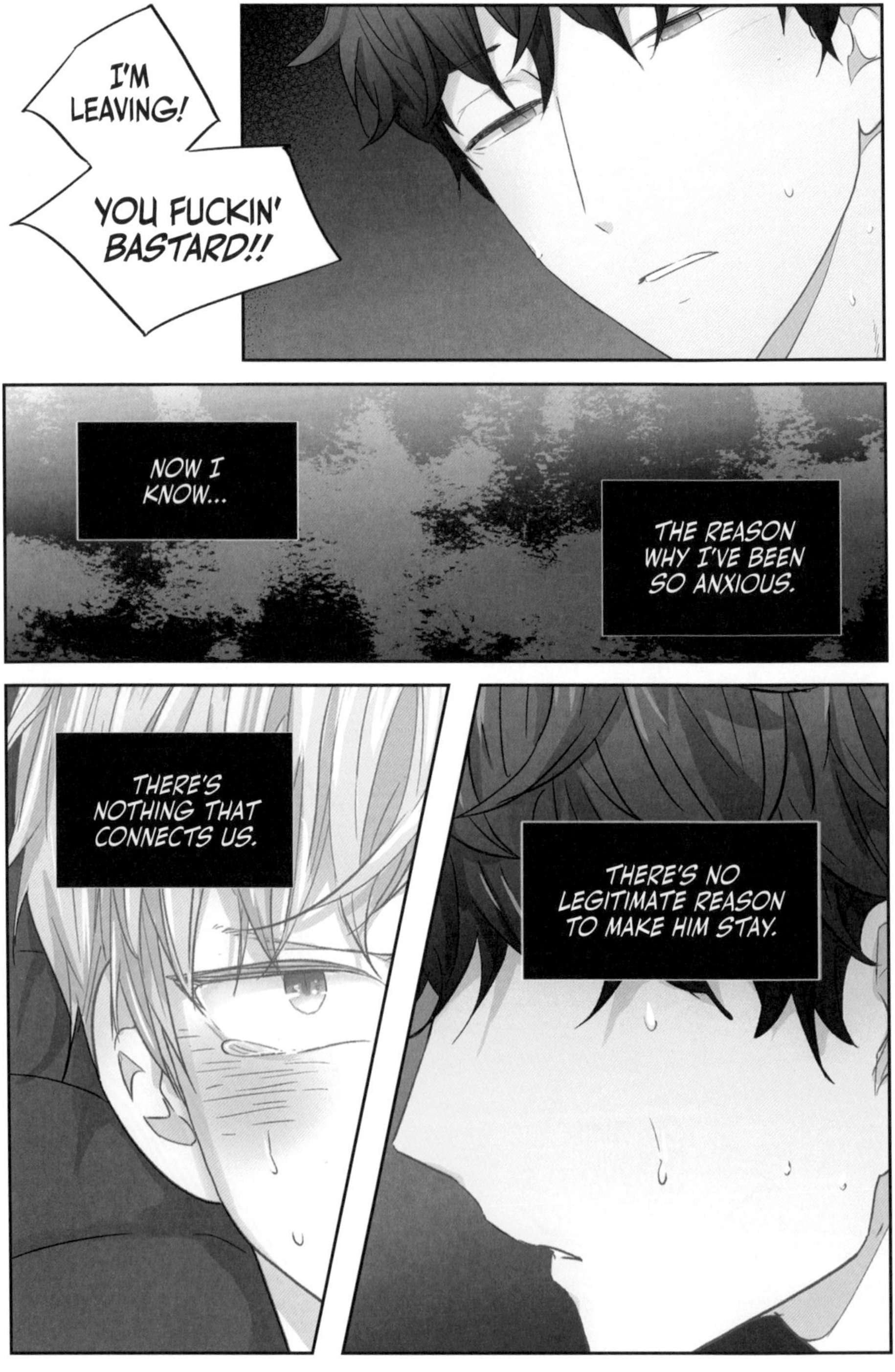
I'M LEAVING!
YOU FUCKIN' BASTARD!!
NOW I KNOW...
THE REASON WHY I'VE BEEN SO ANXIOUS.
THERE'S NOTHING THAT CONNECTS US.
THERE'S NO LEGITIMATE REASON TO MAKE HIM STAY.

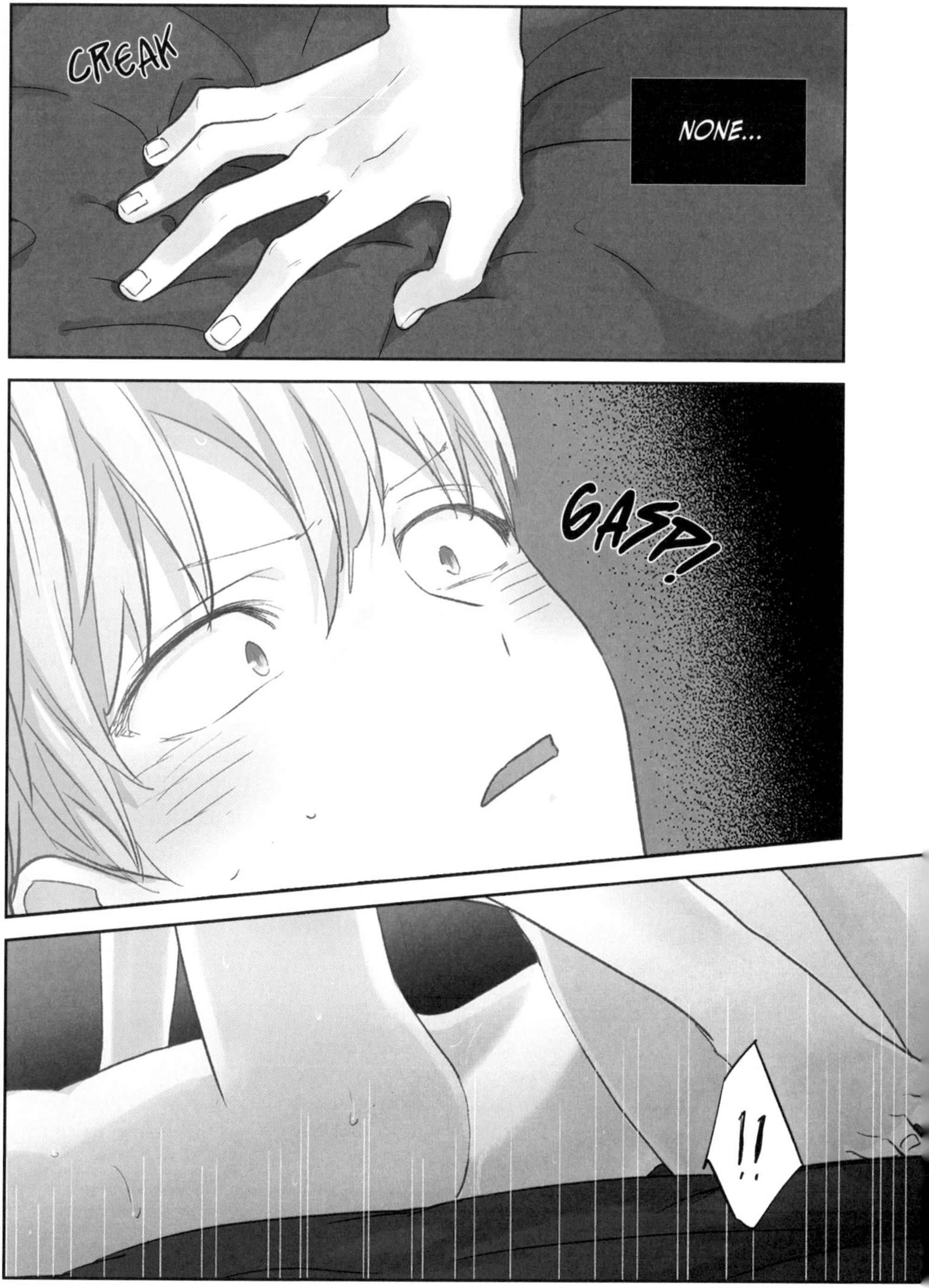

CREAK
NONE...
GASP!
!!

Love is
an Illusion!

Chapter 19
VRRR
VRRRRR
Tofu Face
SHAAAA
WHY ISN'T HE PICKING UP...?
TAP
TAP

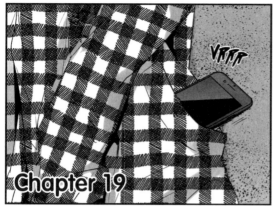

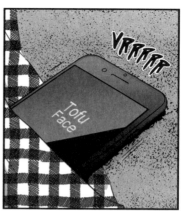

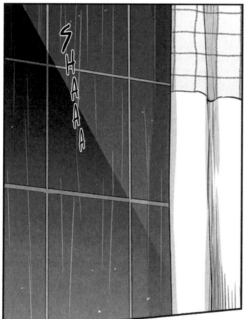

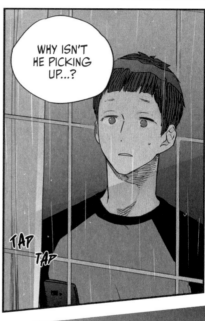

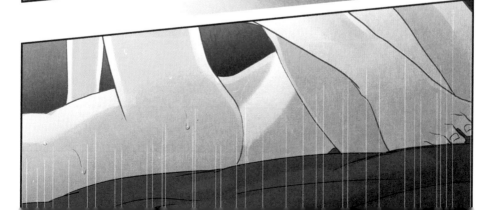

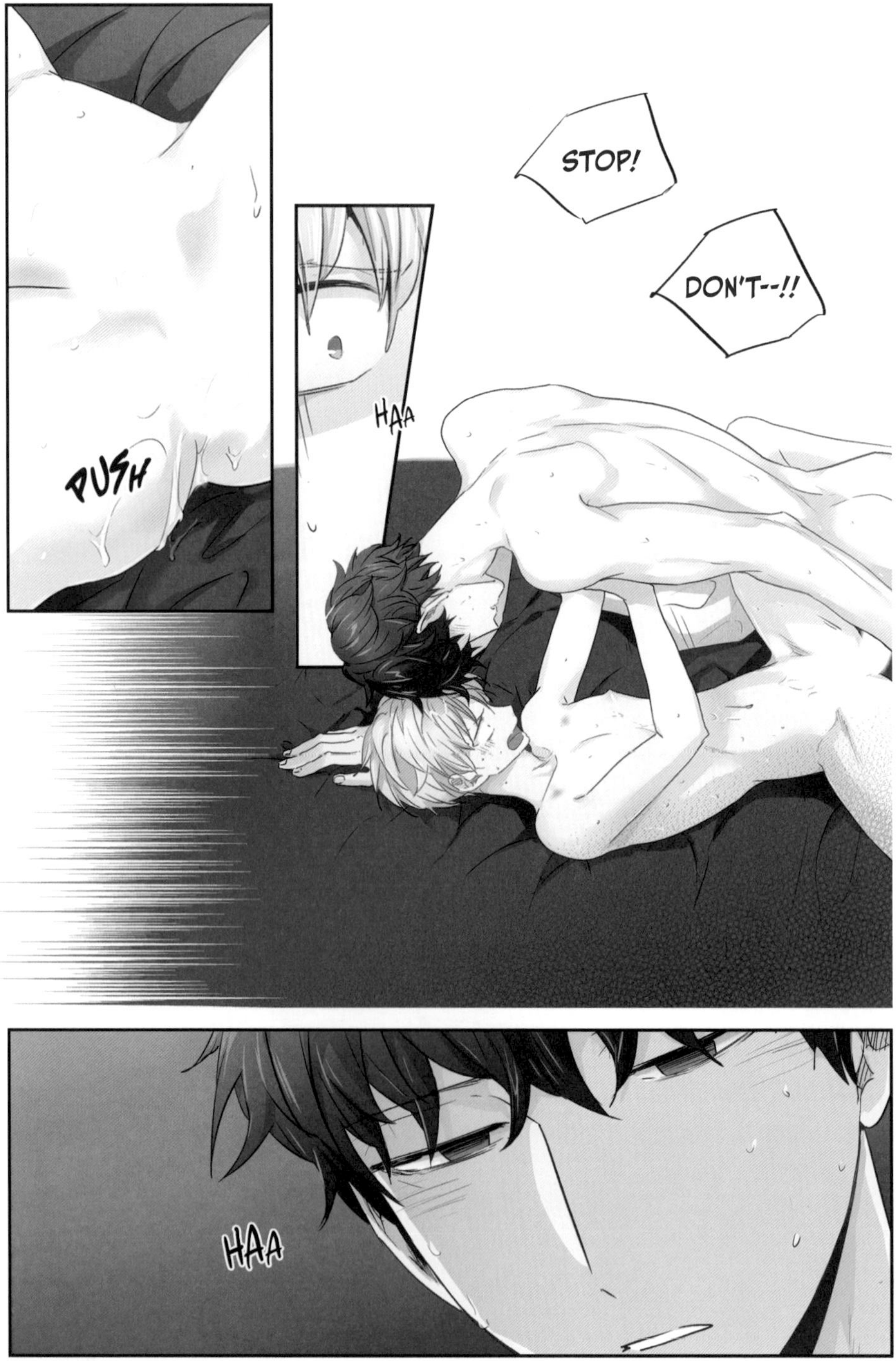
PUSH
HAA
STOP!
DON'T--!!
HAA

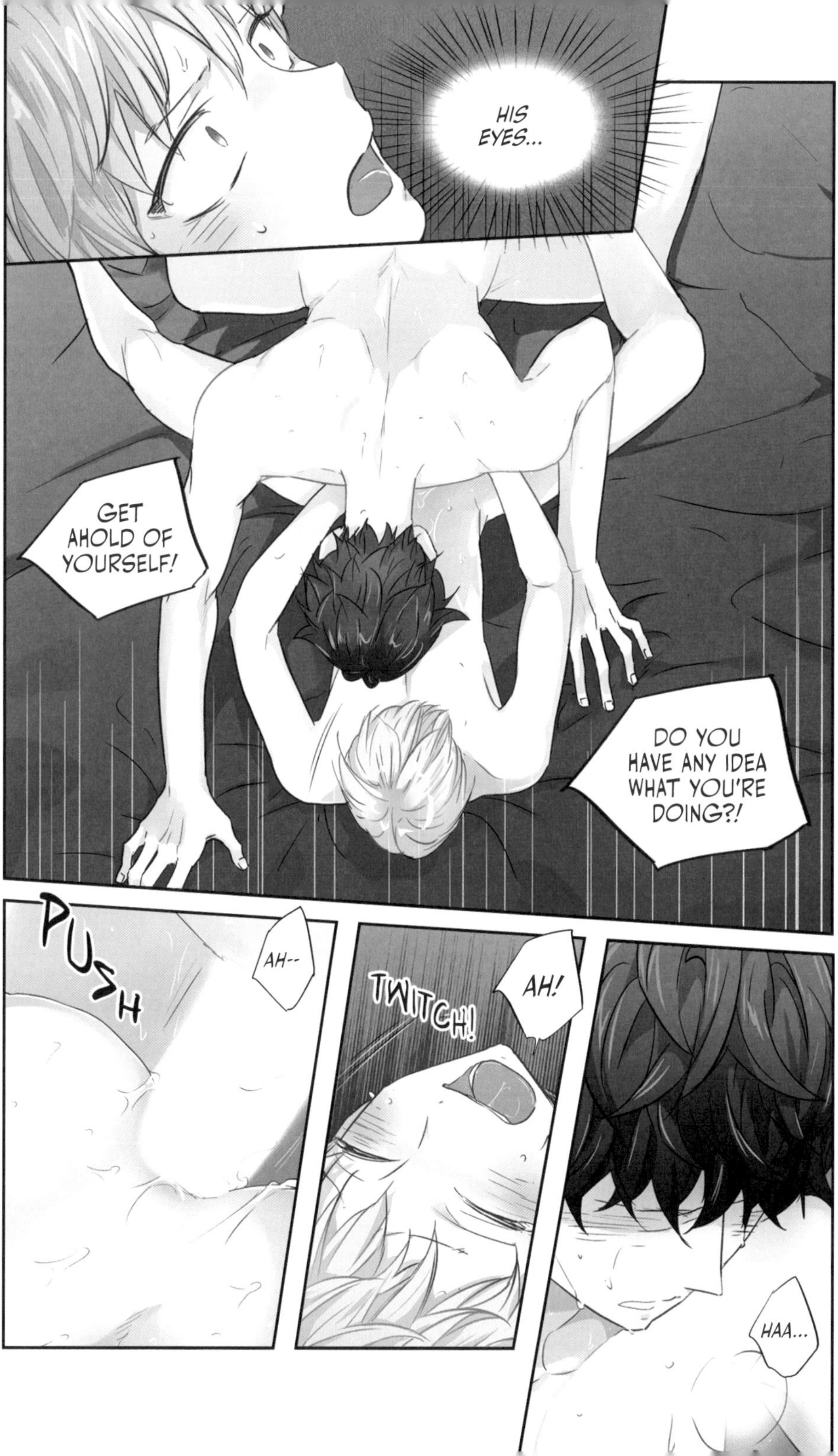
HIS EYES...
GET AHOLD OF YOURSELF!
DO YOU HAVE ANY IDEA WHAT YOU'RE DOING?!
PUSH
AH--
TWITCH!
AH!
HAA...

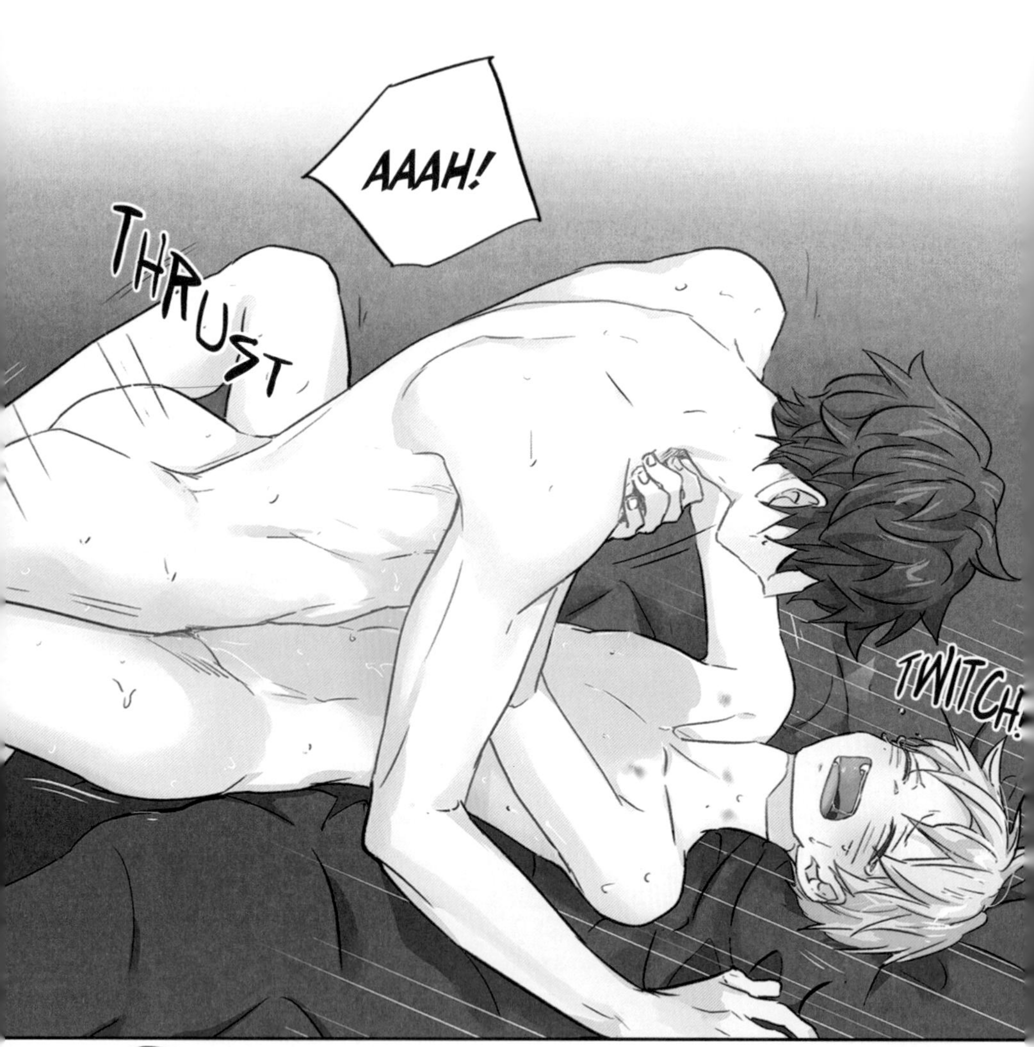
AAAH!
THRUST
TWITCH!

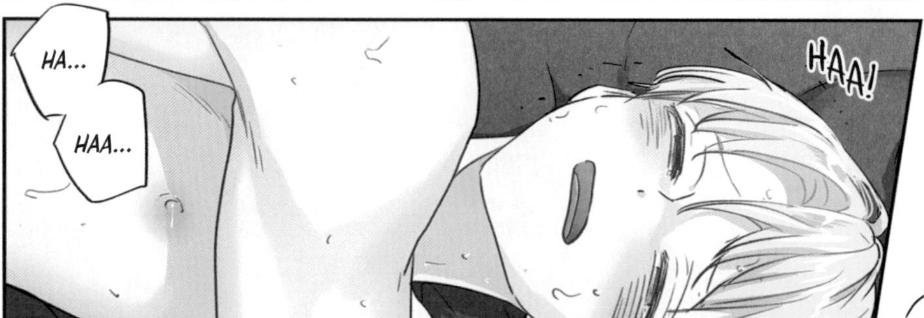
HA...
HAA...
HAA!
HAA!
NO...
AH...

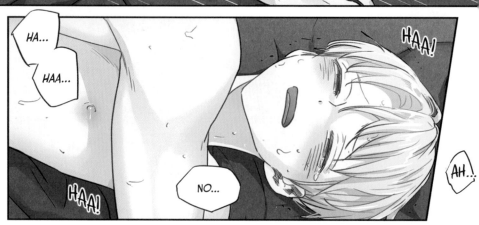

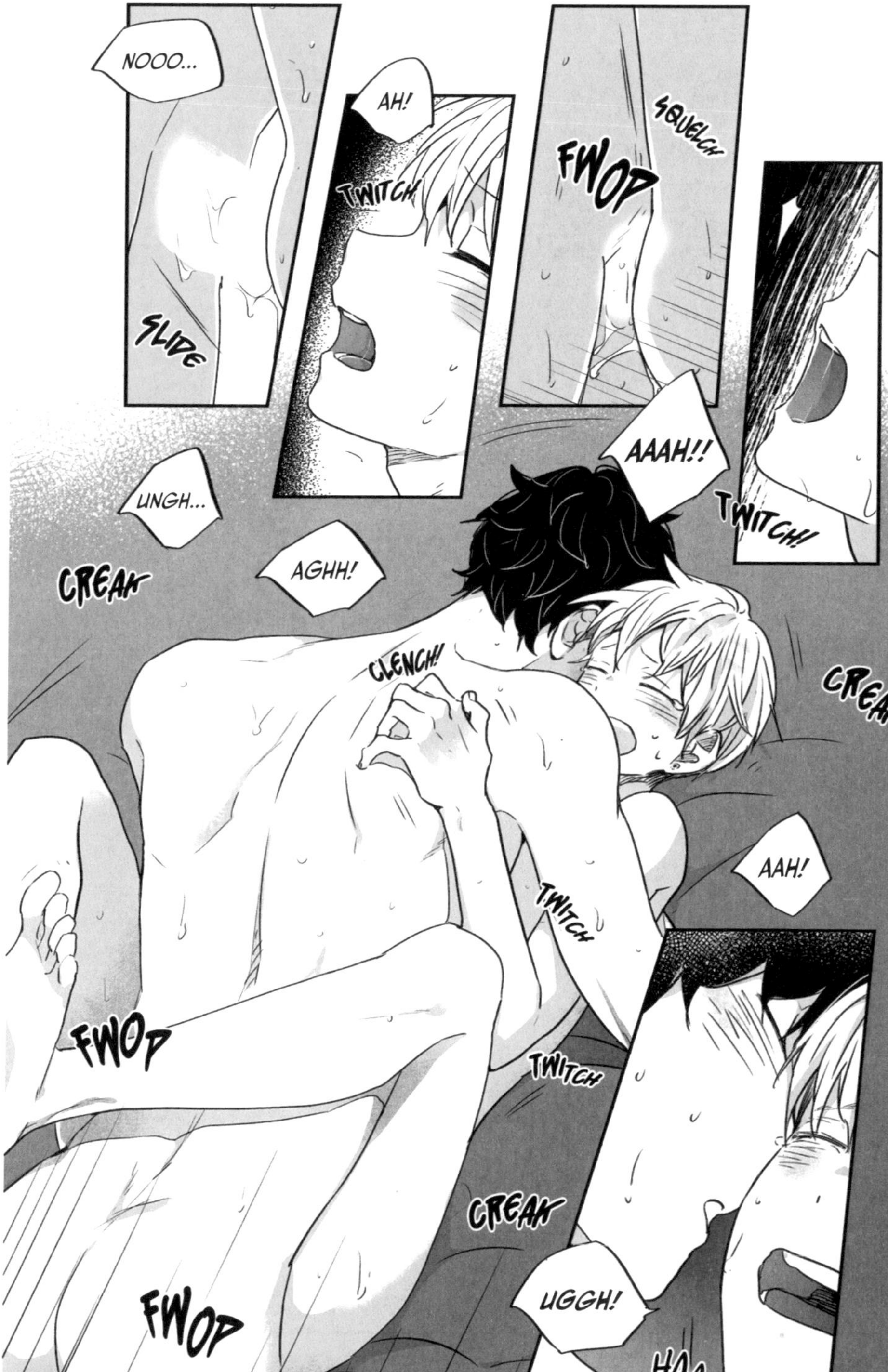
NOOO...
SLIDE
AH!
TWITCH
SQUELCH
FWOP
AAAH!!
TWITCH!
UNGH...
CREAK
AGHH!
CLENCH!
CREAK
AAH!
TWITCH
FWOP
TWITCH
CREAK
FWOP
UGGH!
HAA

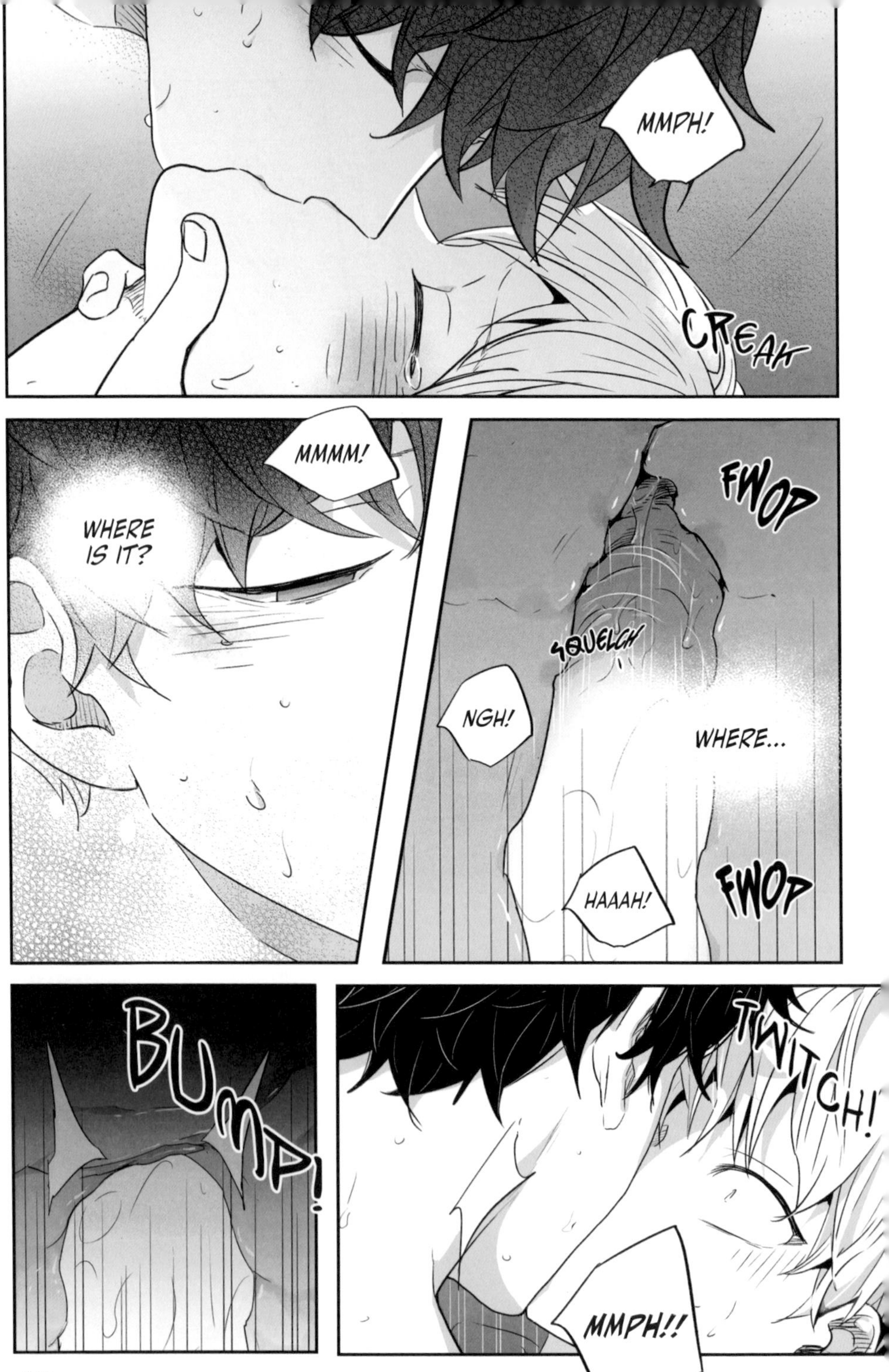
MMPH!
CREAK
MMMM!
WHERE IS IT?
FWOP
SQUELCH
NGH!
WHERE...
HAAAH!
FWOP
BUMP!
TWITCH!
MMPH!!

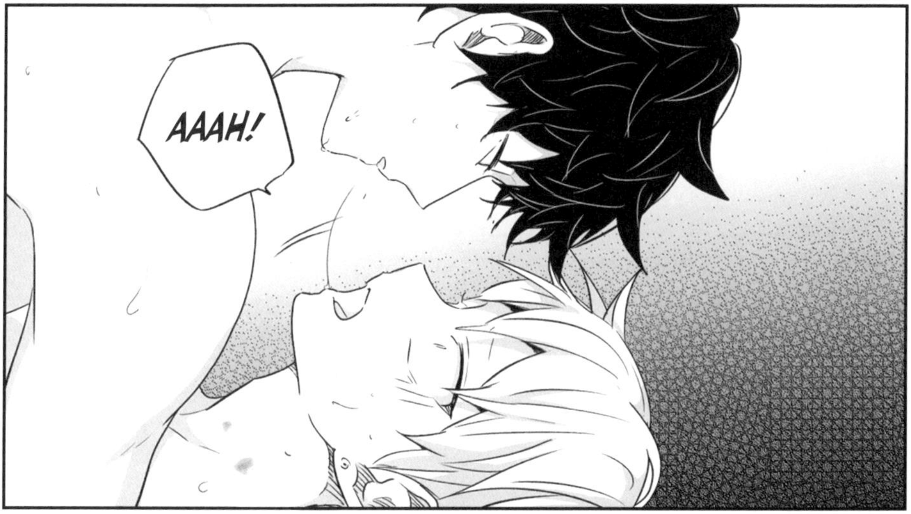
AAAH!

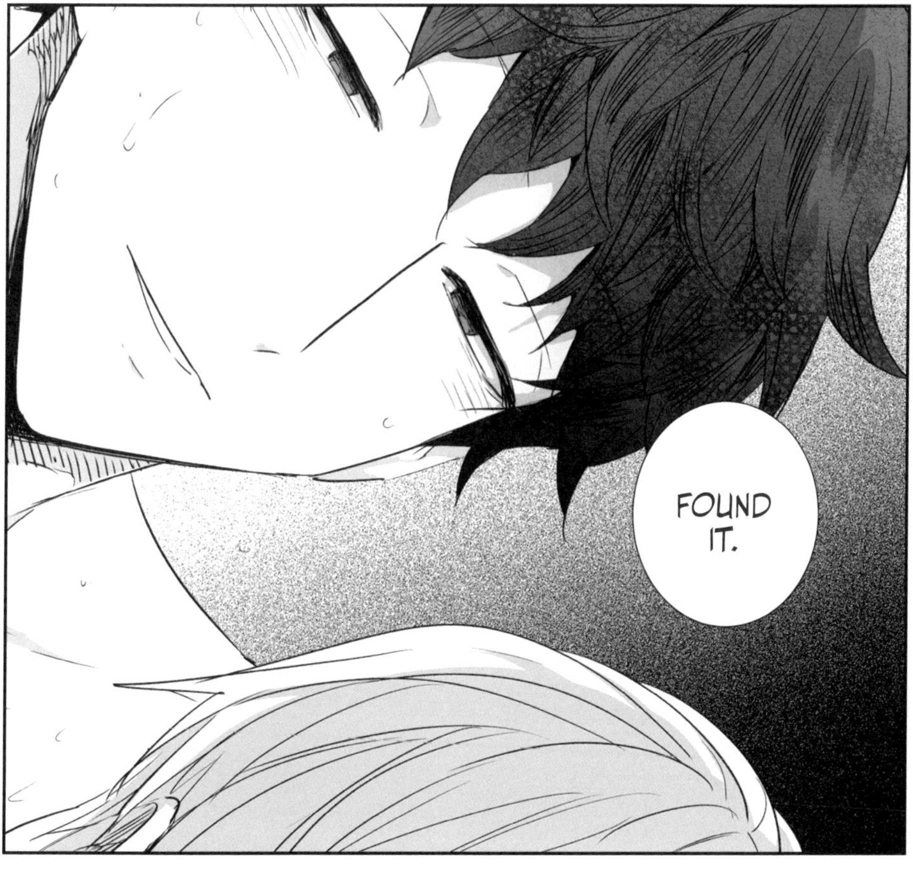
FOUND IT.

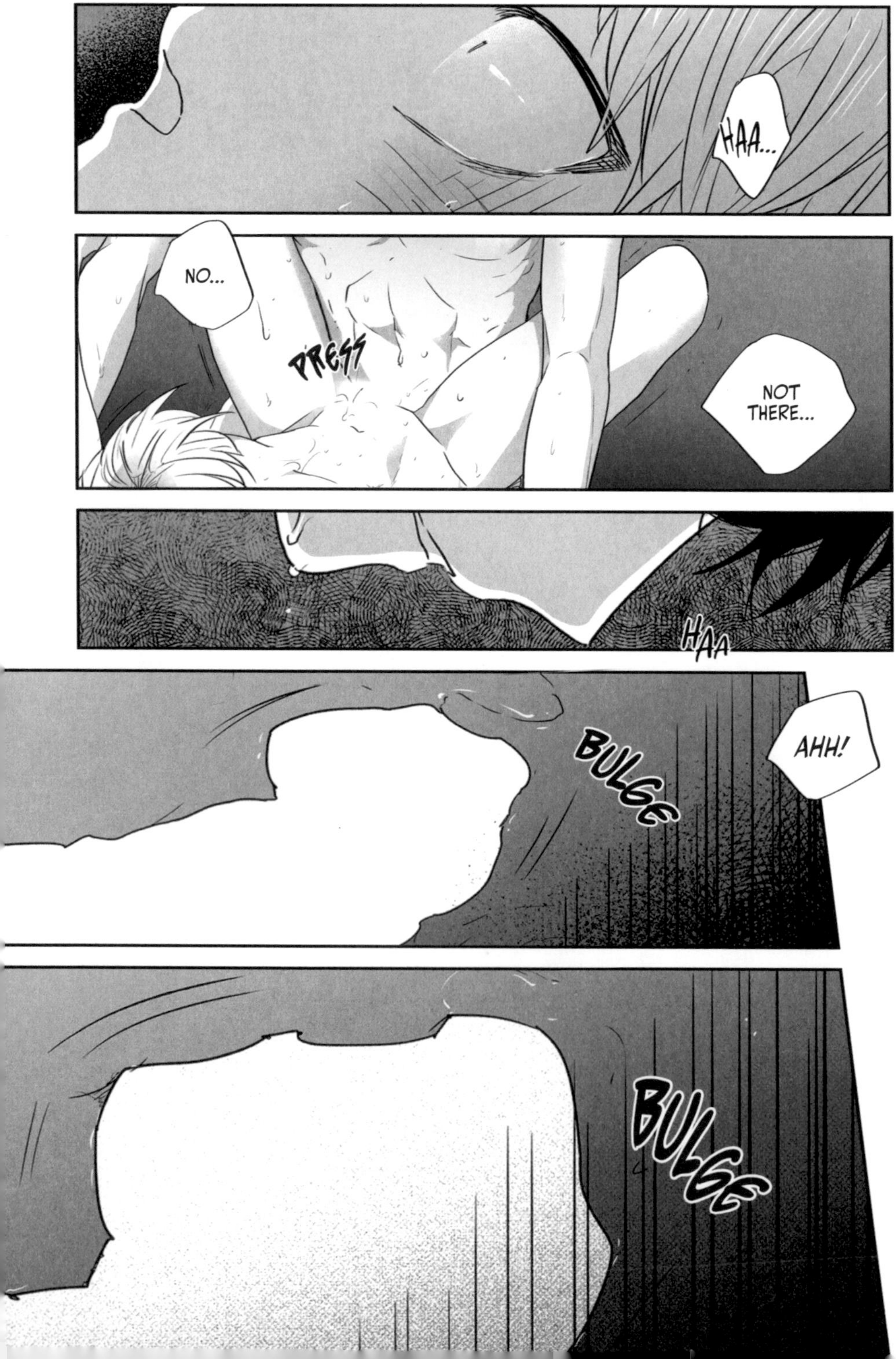
HAA...
NO...
PRESS
NOT THERE...
HAA
BULGE
AHH!
BULGE

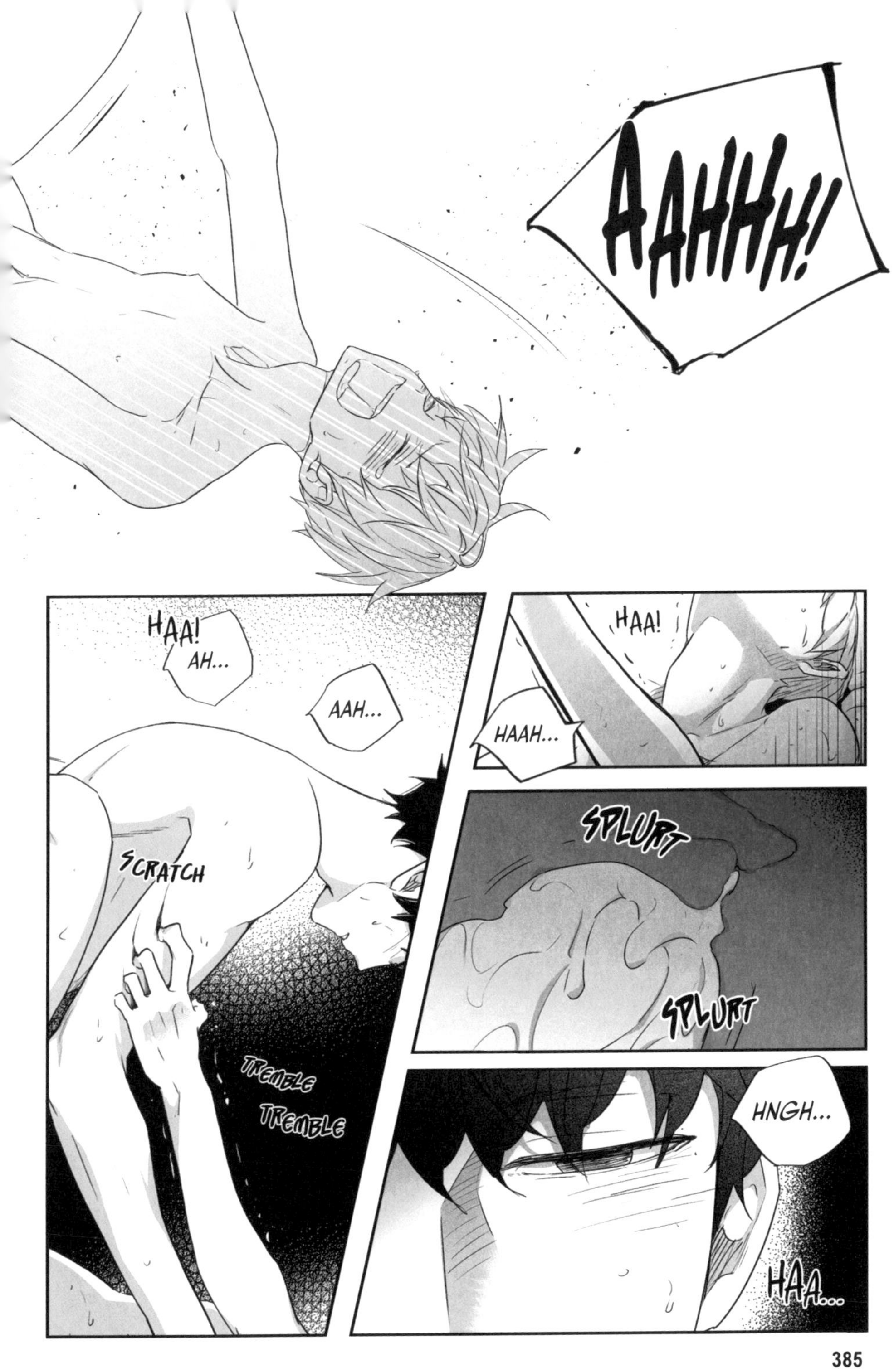
AAHHH!
HAA!
AH...
AAH...
SCRATCH
TREMBLE
TREMBLE
HAA!
HAAH...
SPLURT
SPLURT
HNGH...
HAA...

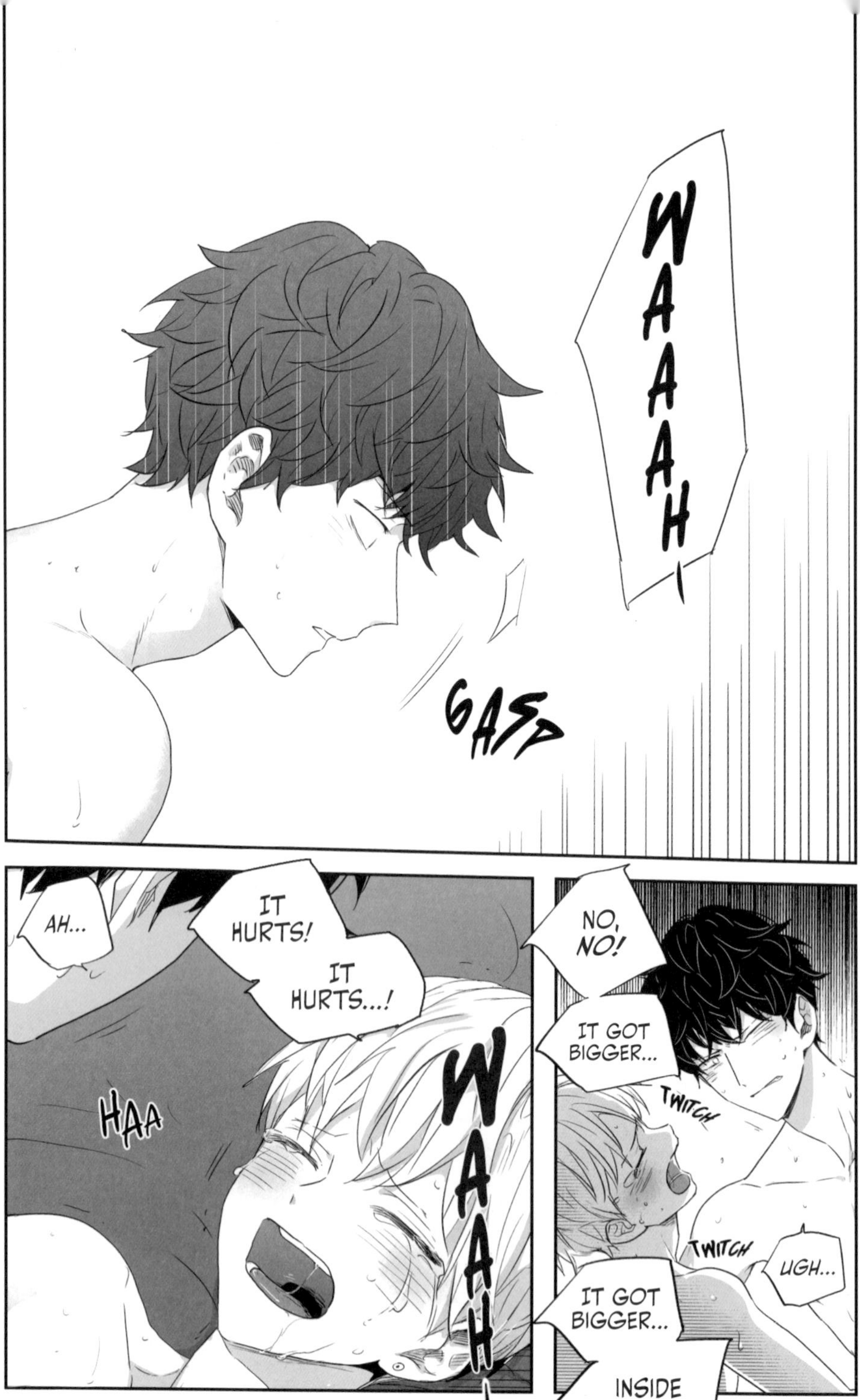
WAAAAH!
GASP
AH...
IT HURTS!
IT HURTS...!
HAA
WAAAH!
NO, NO!
IT GOT BIGGER...
TWITCH
TWITCH
UGH...
IT GOT BIGGER...
INSIDE OF ME!

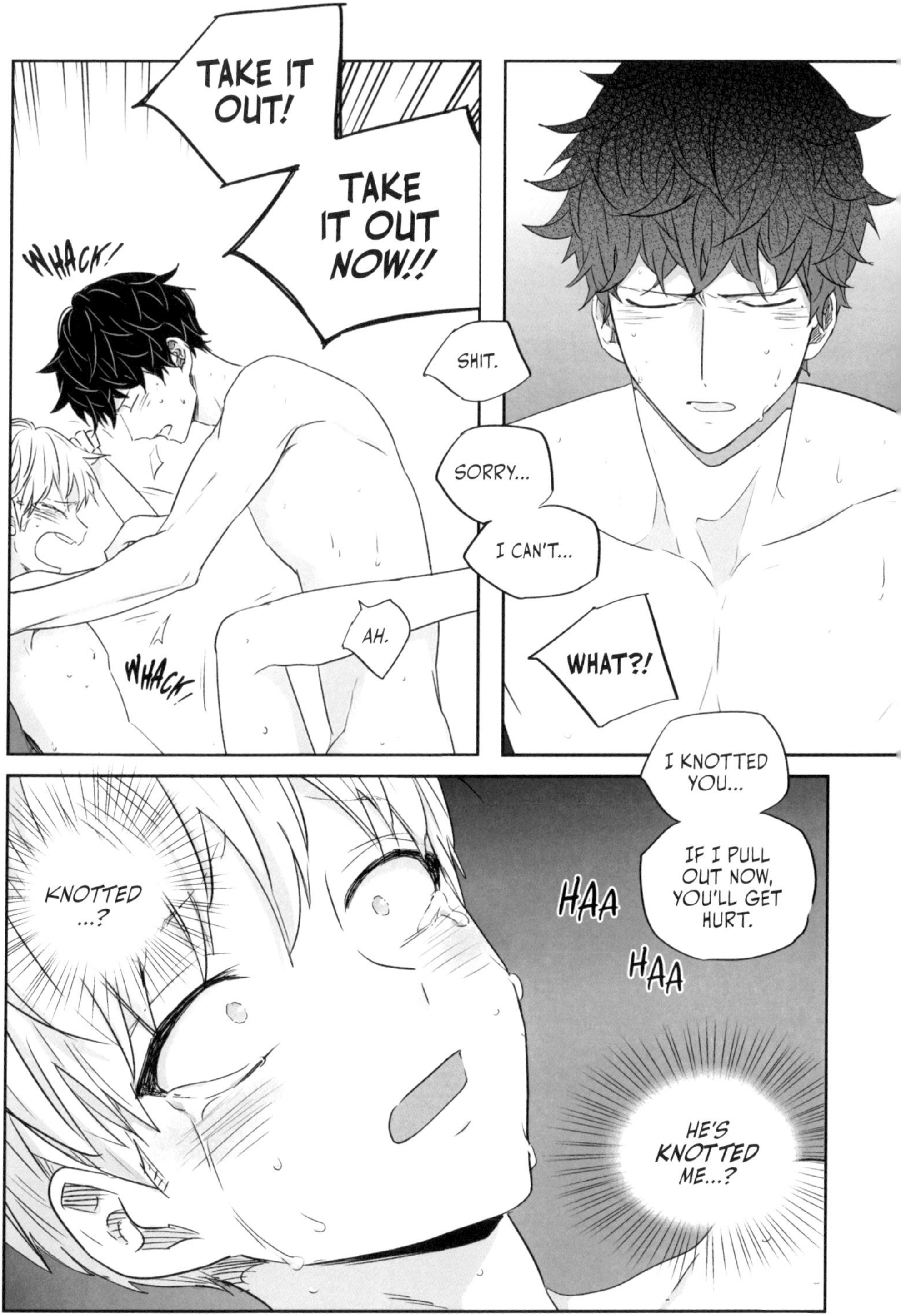
TAKE IT OUT!
TAKE IT OUT NOW!!
WHACK!
WHACK!
AH.
SHIT.
SORRY...
I CAN'T...
WHAT?!
I KNOTTED YOU...
KNOTTED ...?
IF I PULL OUT NOW, YOU'LL GET HURT.
HAA
HAA
HE'S KNOTTED ME...?

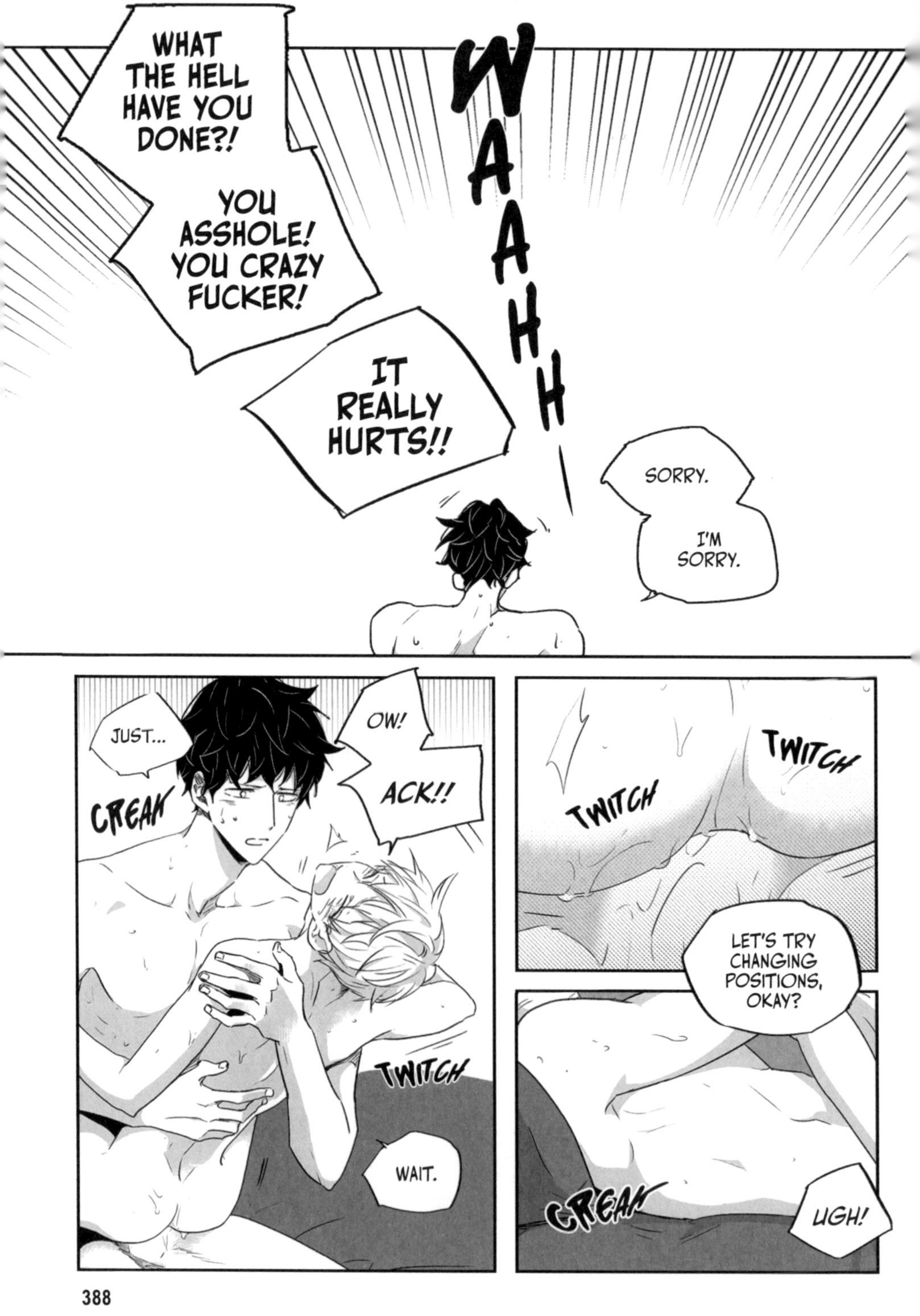
WHAT THE HELL HAVE YOU DONE?!
YOU ASSHOLE! YOU CRAZY FUCKER!
WAAHH
IT REALLY HURTS!!
SORRY.
I'M SORRY.
JUST...
CREAK
OW!
ACK!!
TWITCH
WAIT.
TWITCH
TWITCH
LET'S TRY CHANGING POSITIONS, OKAY?
CREAK
UGH!

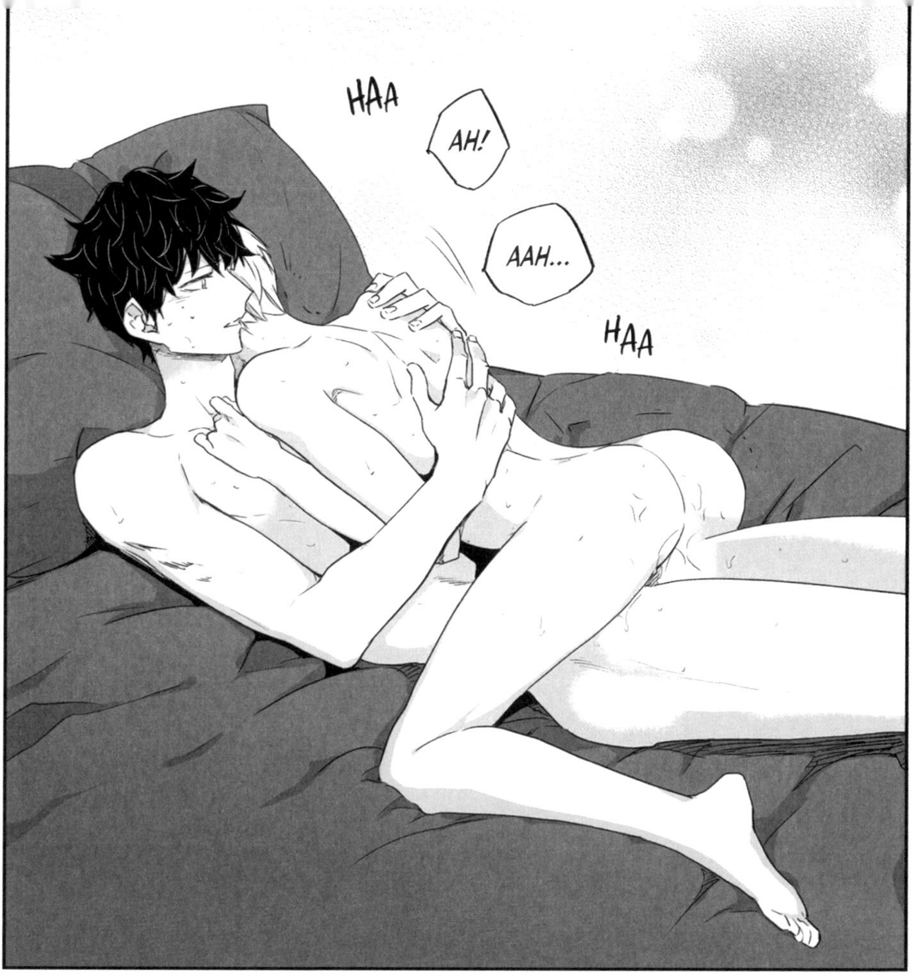
HAA
AH!
AAH...
HAA

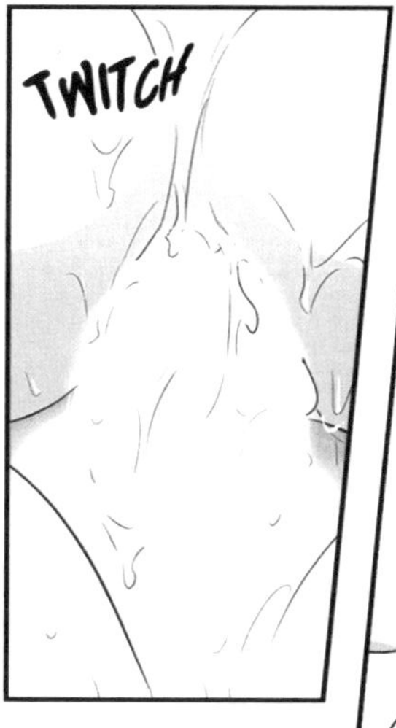
TWITCH

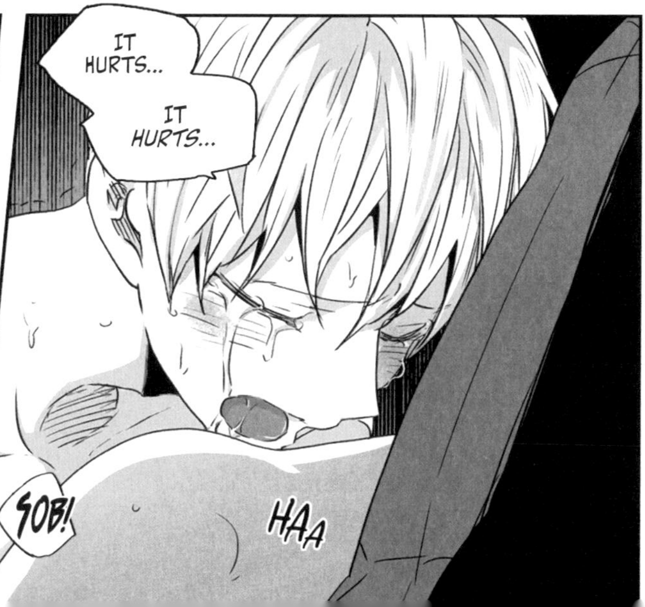
IT HURTS...
IT HURTS...
SOB!
HAA

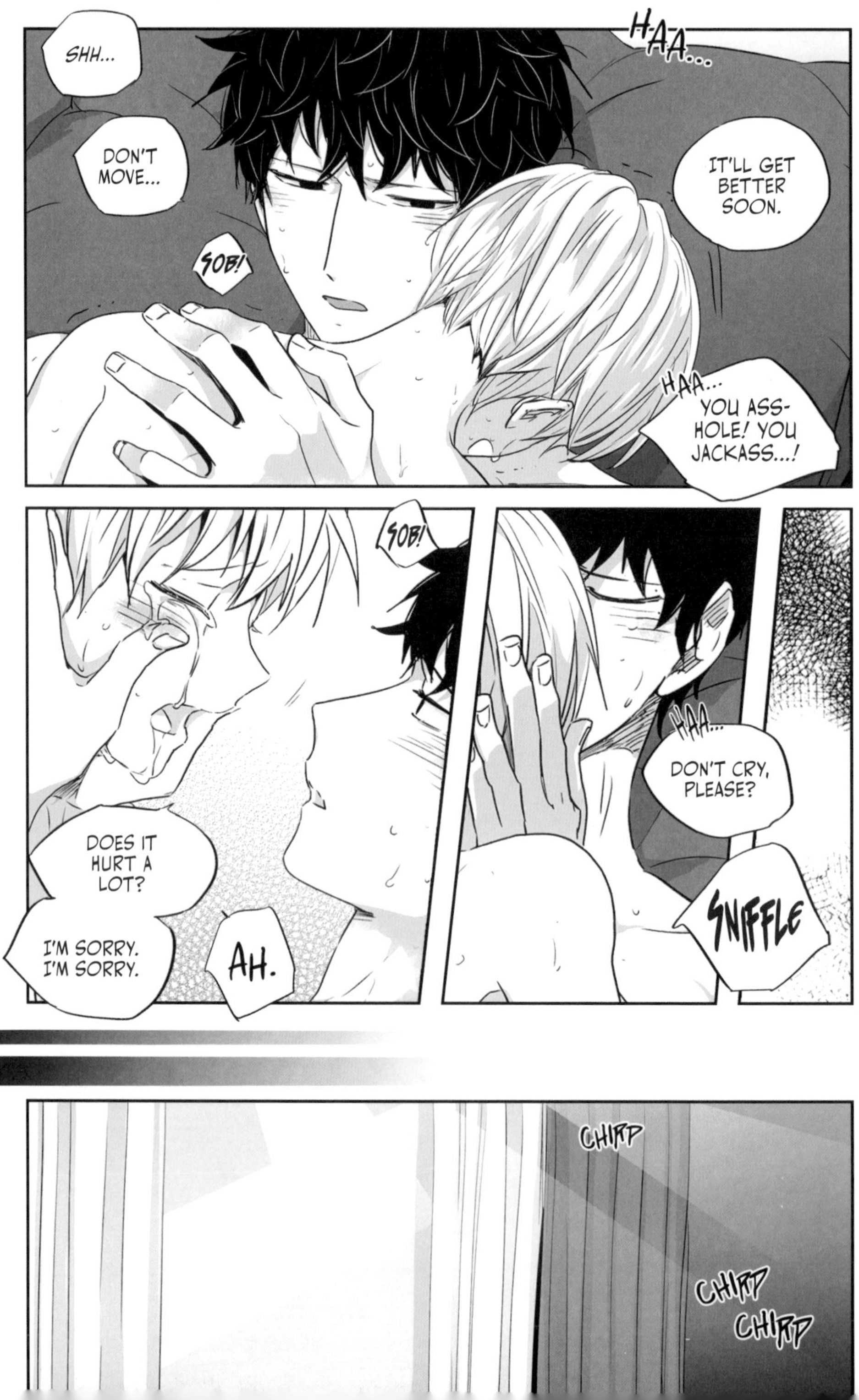
SHH...
DON'T MOVE...
HAA...
SOB!
IT'LL GET BETTER SOON.
HAA... YOU ASS-HOLE! YOU JACKASS...!
SOB!
DOES IT HURT A LOT?
I'M SORRY. I'M SORRY.
AH.
HAA...
DON'T CRY, PLEASE?
SNIFFLE
CHIRP
CHIRP
CHIRP

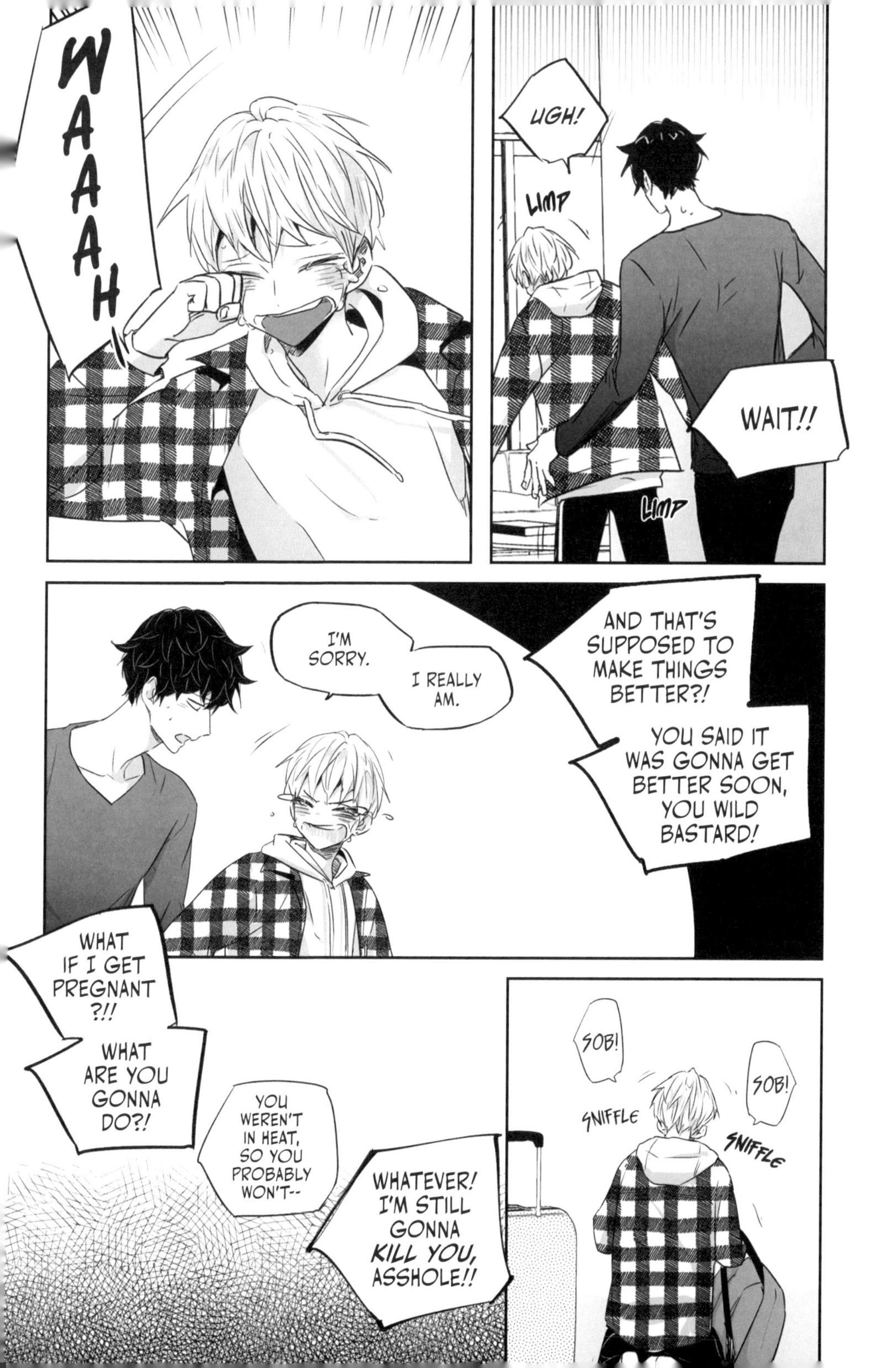
WAAAAH
UGH!
LIMP
WAIT!!
LIMP
I'M SORRY.
I REALLY AM.
AND THAT'S SUPPOSED TO MAKE THINGS BETTER?!
YOU SAID IT WAS GONNA GET BETTER SOON, YOU WILD BASTARD!
WHAT IF I GET PREGNANT?!!
WHAT ARE YOU GONNA DO?!
YOU WEREN'T IN HEAT, SO YOU PROBABLY WON'T--
WHATEVER! I'M STILL GONNA KILL YOU, ASSHOLE!!
SOB!
SNIFFLE
SOB!
SNIFFLE

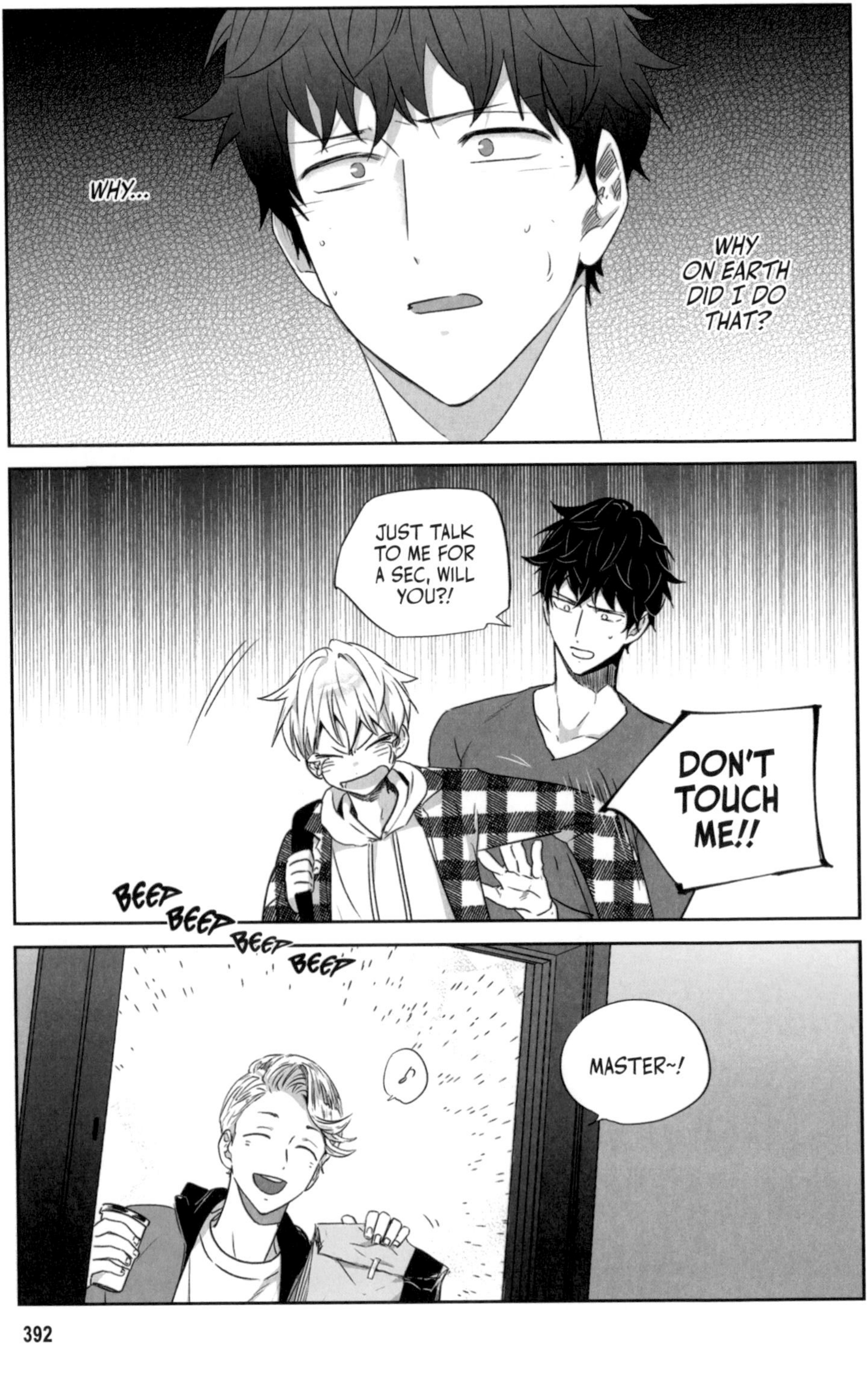
WHY...
WHY ON EARTH DID I DO THAT?
JUST TALK TO ME FOR A SEC, WILL YOU?!
DON'T TOUCH ME!!
BEEP BEEP BEEP BEEP
MASTER~!

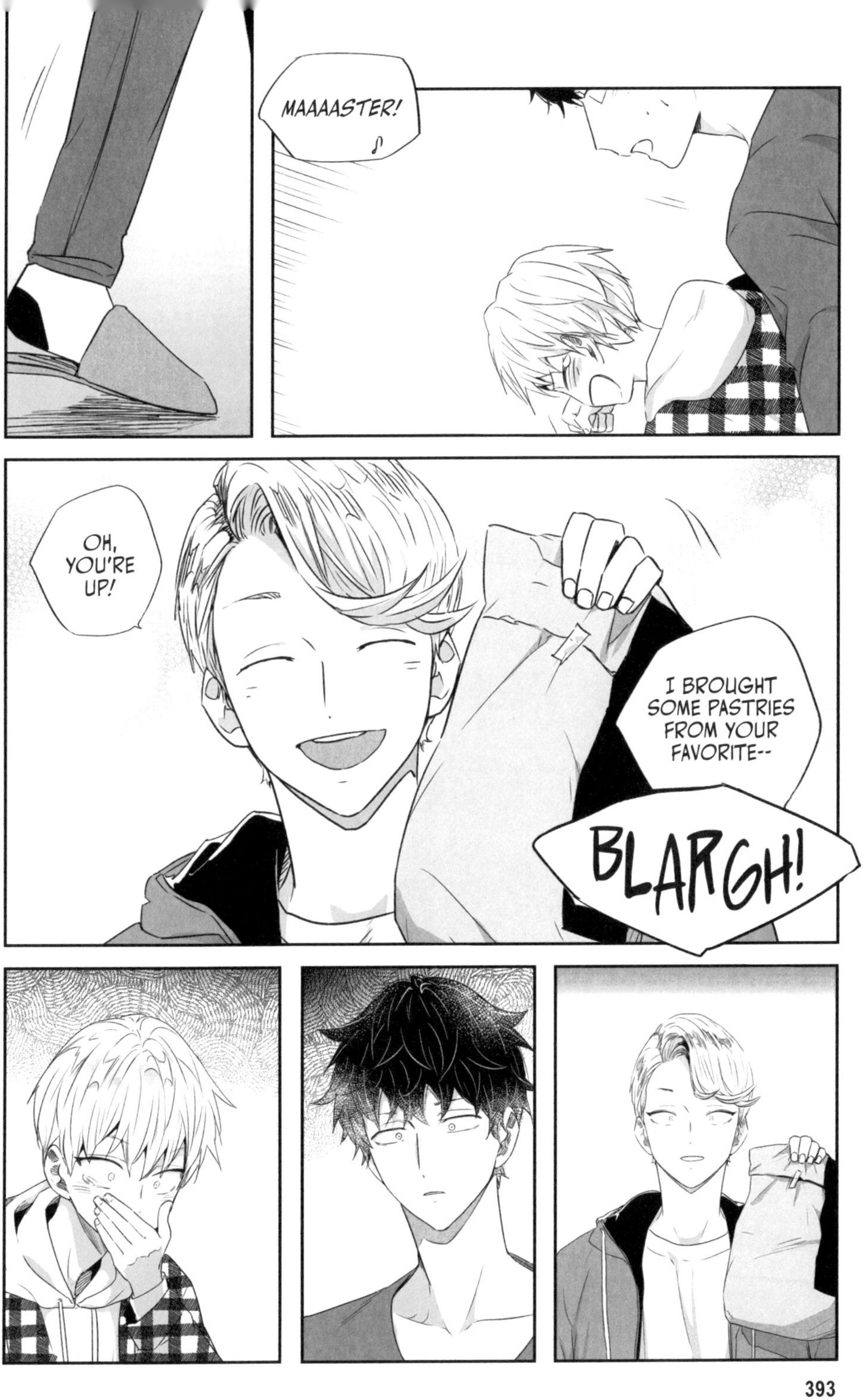
MAAAASTER! ♪
OH, YOU'RE UP!
I BROUGHT SOME PASTRIES FROM YOUR FAVORITE--
BLARGH!

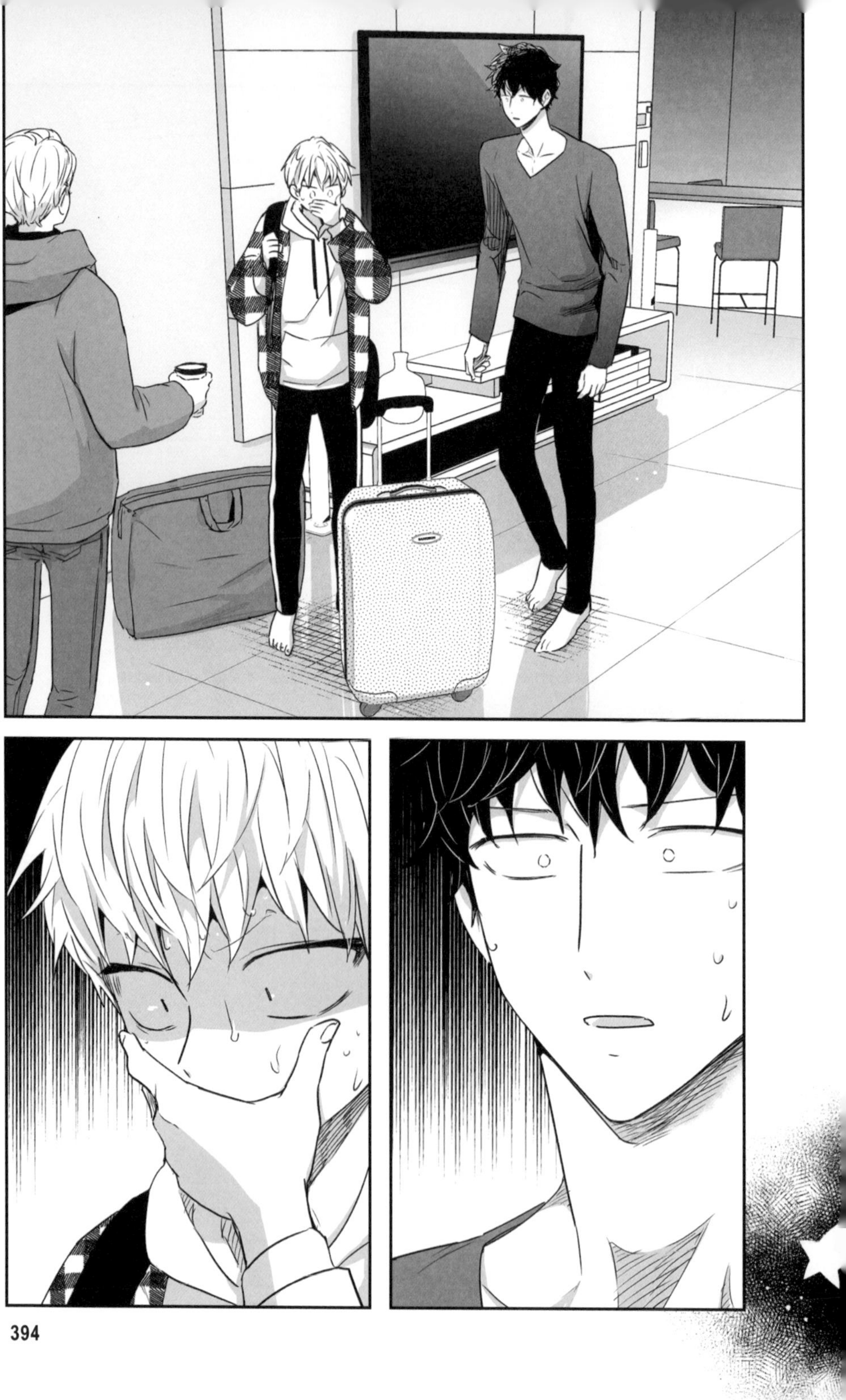

Love is
an Illusion!

Love is an Illusion!

COMING SOON IN VOLUME TWO!

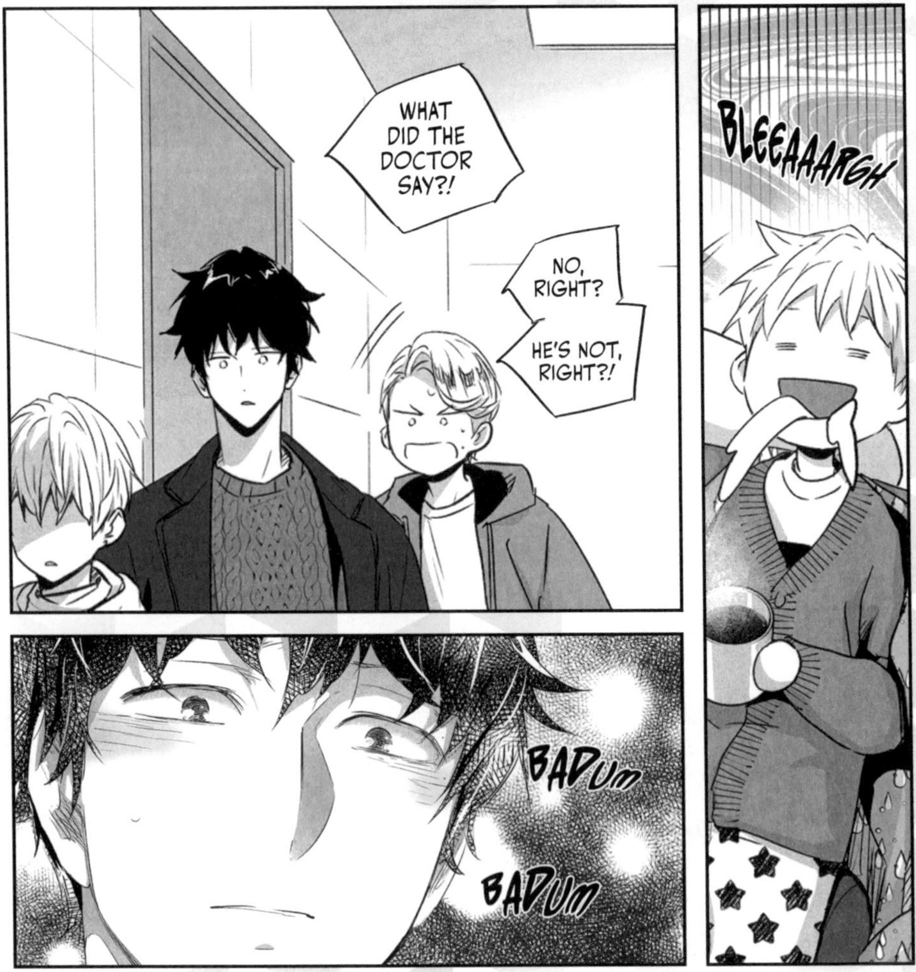
WHAT DID THE DOCTOR SAY?!
NO, RIGHT?
HE'S NOT, RIGHT?!
BADUM
BADUM
BLEEAAARGH

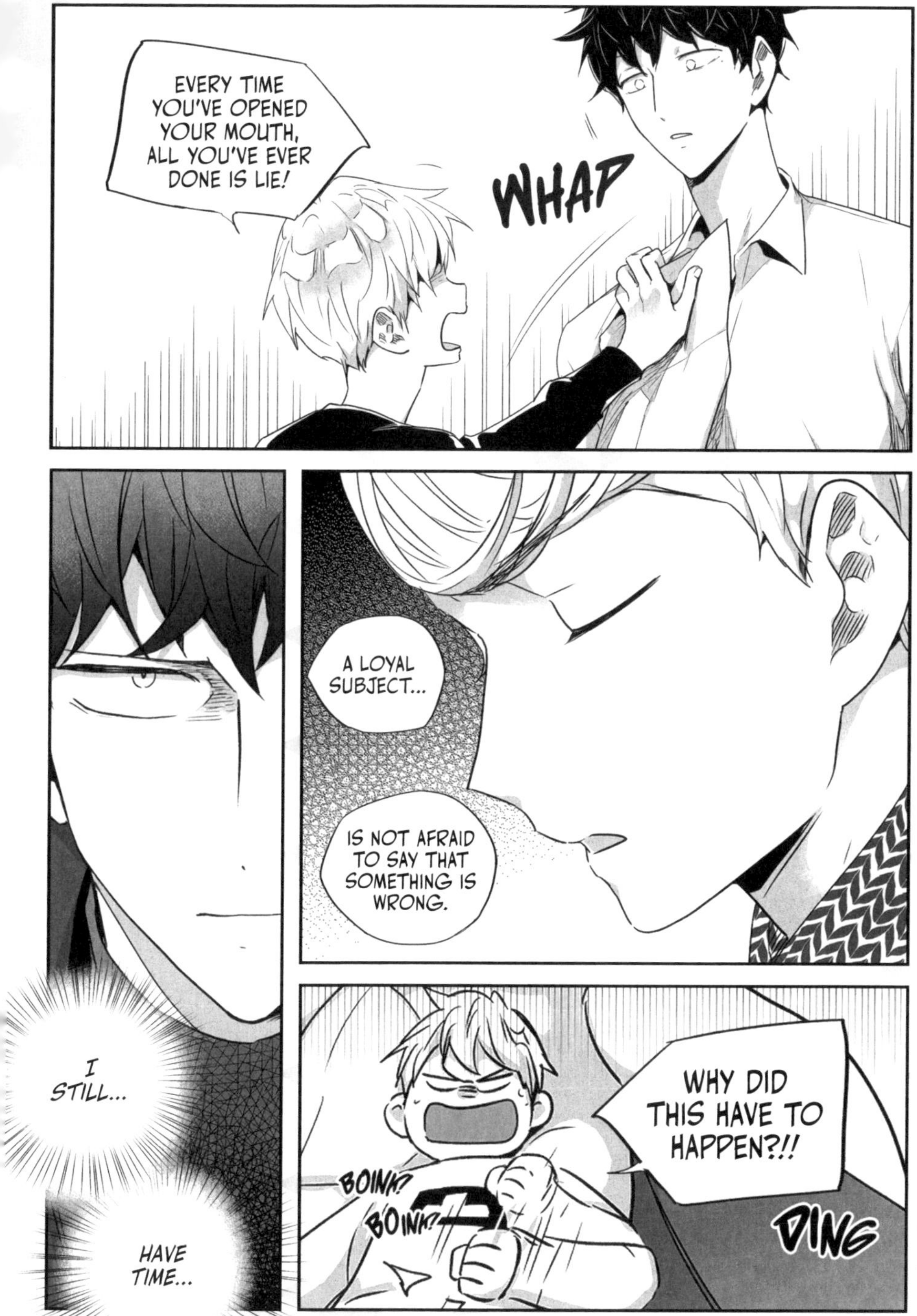
EVERY TIME YOU'VE OPENED YOUR MOUTH, ALL YOU'VE EVER DONE IS LIE!
WHAP
I STILL...
HAVE TIME...
A LOYAL SUBJECT...
IS NOT AFRAID TO SAY THAT SOMETHING IS WRONG.
WHY DID THIS HAVE TO HAPPEN?!!
BOINK!?
BOINK!?
DING

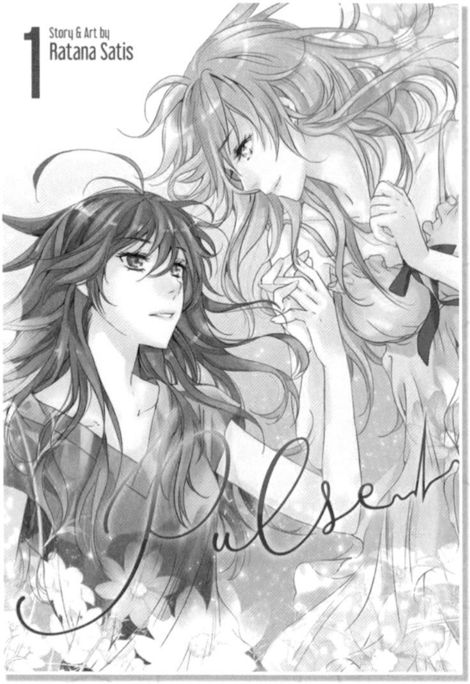
1
Story & Art by
Ratana Satis
Pulse

PULSE

Story & Art by Ratana Satis

A cardiologist with no "heart" and the woman who needs one.

Mel, a renowned heart surgeon, is well-known for being a stoic loner. She views her erotic flings with other women as a tool for pleasure rather than a show of affection. Then she meets Lynn, a beautiful and spirited cardiac patient who needs a new heart, but refuses a transplant. The two women meet with minimal expectations but soon become enthralled in a relationship that changes everything for them both.

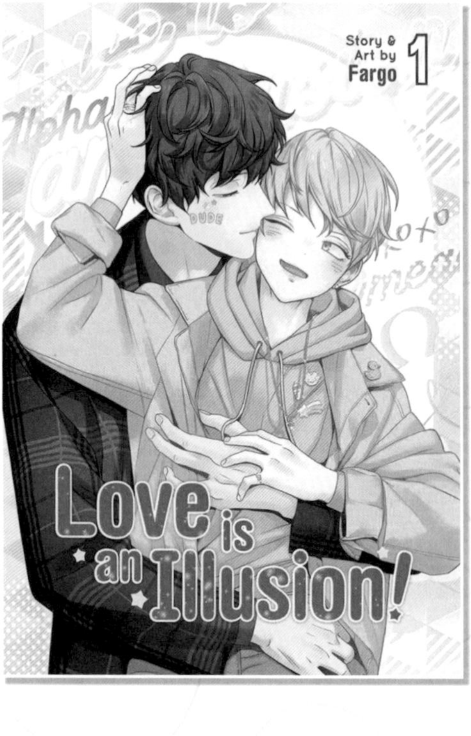
Story &
Art by
Fargo
1
Love is an Illusion!

Love is an Illusion!

Story & Art by Fargo

An Omega with Alpha-tude!

Hye-sung spent his entire life believing he was an alpha, the jackpot of the genetic lottery. His world flips upside down when he learns that he's not a dominating alpha, but a submissive omega instead! His frustration redlines whenever he crosses paths with the handsome Dojin, a true alpha. Dojin can't stand omegas, but sparks fly when he butts heads with Hye-sung, and their explosive arguments set off an unexpectedly spicy relationship. Is their sizzling chemistry truly just pheromones?!

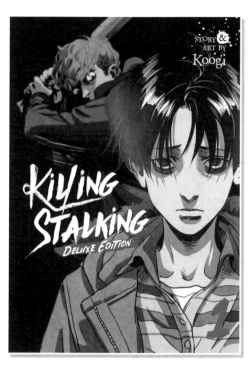

Killing Stalking
Story & Art by Koogi

Crazy For You.

Yoon Bum, a scrawny and quiet man, has a crush on one of the most popular and handsome guys in his college: Sangwoo. After the two cross paths again, Yoon Bum's feelings grow in intensity until they become an obsession—and he breaks into Sangwoo's home. But what he sees inside is not the Sangwoo of his fantasies; his dreams of this alluring man abruptly turn into a nightmare.

Each large-trim volume will contain 400+ full-color pages and a bonus fold-out insert!

POPULAR WEBTOONS BROUGHT TO PRINT BY
SEVEN SEAS ENTERTAINMENT

An all-new imprint launching with this debut trio in conjunction with Lezhin Comics

Seven Seas
Webtoons

sevenseaswebtoons.com